W9-CKJ-893

MASSACHUSETTS
HANDBOOK

MASSACHUSETTS HANDBOOK

FIRST EDITION

JEFF PERK

MOON
TRAVEL
HANDBOOKS

MASSACHUSETTS HANDBOOK
FIRST EDITION

Published by
  Moon Publications, Inc.
  P.O. Box 3040
  Chico, California 95927-3040, USA

Printed by
  Bertelsmann

© Text and photographs copyright Jeff Perk, 1998.
  All rights reserved.

© Illustrations and maps copyright Moon Publications, Inc., 1998.
  All rights reserved.

  Some photos and illustrations are used by permission
  and are the property of the original copyright owners.

ISBN: 1-56691-083-8
ISSN: 1096-9535

Editor: Gregor Johnson Krause
Map Editor: Gina Wilson Birtcil
Copy Editor: Asha Johnson
Editorial Assistance: Emily Kendrick, Diane Wurzel
Production & Design: Carey Wilson
Cartography: Chris Folks and Mike Morgenfeld
Index: Gregor Johnson Krause

Front cover photo: Will McCoy/courtesy Rainbow

All photos by Jeff Perk unless otherwise noted.

Distributed in the United States and Canada by Publishers Group West

Printed in the USA.

All rights reserved. No part of this book may be translated or reproduced in any form, except brief extracts by a reviewer for the purpose of a review, without written permission of the copyright owner.

Although the author and publisher have made every effort to ensure that the information was correct at the time of going to press, the author and publisher do not assume and hereby disclaim any liability to any party for any loss or damage caused by errors, omissions, or any potential travel disruption due to labor or financial difficulty, whether such errors or omissions result from negligence, accident, or any other cause.

Please send all comments,
corrections, additions,
amendments, and critiques to:

**MASSACHUSETTS HANDBOOK
MOON TRAVEL HANDBOOKS
P.O. BOX 3040
CHICO, CA 95927-3040, USA
e-mail: travel@moon.com
www.moon.com**

Printing History
1st edition—May 1998

In memory of my mother

Dream dreams
And then write them
Aye, but live them first.

—SAMUEL ELIOT MORISON,
SAILOR AND HISTORIAN

CONTENTS

ABBREVIATIONS

a/c—air conditioning
AT—Appalachian Trail
B&B—bed and breakfast
CCC—Civilian Conservation
   Corps
d—double

HI—Hosteling International
pp—per person
Rt.—Route
SPNEA—Society for the
   Preservation of New
   England Antiquities

s—single
tel.—telephone
TTOR—The Trustees of
   Reservations

ACCOMMODATION PRICING KEY

Rankings represent the average price charged
for a double. Call specific accommodations for
single, seasonal, and special rates.

Budget: $35 and under
Inexpensive: $35-60
Moderate: $60-85
Expensive: $85-100
Very Expensive: $110-150
Luxury: $150 and up

MAPS

MAP SYMBOLS

◉ State Capital   ═══ Superhighway   ★ Point of Interest

○ City   ══ Primary Road   ▪ Other Location

○ Town   ══ Secondary Road   ▲ Mountain

⬭ U.S. Interstate   - - - - Footpath   ✕ Airport/Airstrip

⬡ U.S. Highway   ·········· Ferry   ▫ Terminal Stops

◯ State Highway   ├──┼── Railroad   ⌁ State Park

    - - - - - Tunnel

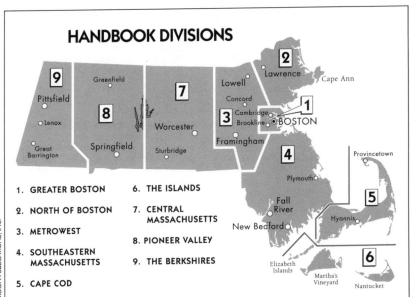

HANDBOOK DIVISIONS

1. GREATER BOSTON
2. NORTH OF BOSTON
3. METROWEST
4. SOUTHEASTERN MASSACHUSETTS
5. CAPE COD
6. THE ISLANDS
7. CENTRAL MASSACHUSETTS
8. PIONEER VALLEY
9. THE BERKSHIRES

© MOON PUBLICATIONS, INC.

ACKNOWLEDGMENTS

To list the names of the small army who helped make this book possible would require a veritable phone book. But a significant number deserve special mention.

Jacqueline Romeo tops the charts for being research goddess, queen of the self-published and out-of-print book search, personal Orpheus to Brahmin World and Boston theater—and especially for being so patient. Doug Berman and his amazing Rolodex is right up there, too—proof positive that nothing beats old school ties and good networking. And heaps of gratitude go to the best manager I ever had, Bob Frankel, for also having friends in all the right places.

Thanks to Chris Rich for early sparks that got the curiosity burning, and for his gleefully Hunter Thompsonesque tour of the state. And to Arthur Krim for illuminating many fine details on everything from Native American toponymy and Norfolk millinery to the history of three-deckers and neon "spectaculars." If there's a juicy historical fact in these pages that local residents never knew before, the odds are that Arthur was its source. Special thanks as well to the other professionals who kindly shared results of their own research, including Lila Parrish, Peter Dunwiddie, and Andy Rubel.

Chris Greene generously gave me buckets of information (to say nothing of his time), while I tried to soak it all up; and Geordie Vining brought clarity to a set of issues otherwise muddied by contradictory uninformed opinions. If every state agency were so lucky as to have people like these two gents, bigger government would be on every citizen's wish list. Danny O'Brien, Cara Seiderman, and Steve Roper were among the many other civil servants who helped take the devil out of the details.

To all those who shared their local or topical expertise, thanks for the contributions that are the very life and color of this book. In chronological order: Nat Herold, Dan Okrent, Pippin Ross, BJ Roche, Al Jangel, Tom Reney, Maureen McManus & Kirsten Gorenson (the Espresso Lovelies), Liam McNamara, Dandy Bro, Richard and Karen Pini, Jim McConnell, Noland Hisey, Floyd Sherman, Richard Babcock, Mike Collins, Vincent Dowling, Ron Meffier, Sheila McElwaine, Carolyn and Arnold Westwood, Bunny Tavares and John Bos, Judy Brownell, Jamelle Tanous, Judith Maloney, Inga and Joe Wennik, Ellen Kenny, June Manning, Tonya Lockyer, Dodi Swope, Bud Gurney, Bill Perry, and Natachaman. I'm also grateful to John Hicks-Courant, Bruce Lessels, Paul Rezendes and Paulette Roy, and Chet and Ann Kulisa for letting me tag along, and for sharing some of their favorite places.

Thanks to all the B&B owners who contributed an abundance of good suggestions to a particularly inquisitive guest. To Dave and Judy Loomis, thanks for lending an ear (and snug berth) to the sailor home from the sea, and the author home from the café. Thanks, Wendy Breiby and Steve Ruzanski, Tom Paulus and Ginny Kolvek, Jon Baxter and Lisa Walker, and Charles and Dot Hopton, for offering friendship along with the food, alcohol, and opinions—all crucial supplements to the writer's craft. Special appreciation goes out to Wendles and Tom for always having a spare sofa for a weary scribbler.

A big three cheers for the patient librarians, registrars, curators, and archivists who lent their hands to this whole affray, including David Proper, Suzanne Flynt, Mary Jean Blasdale, Peter Van Tassel and Jill Bouck, Mark Bograd, BJ Allen, Jim Zimmerman, Hope Morrill, Courtney Peckham, and Aaron Schmidt of the incomparable Boston Public Library Print Dept. A special nod also to Mark Adams of the National Park Service for both sharing his photo research and providing some critical GIS support, and to the Massachusetts Highway Dept. for their invaluable GIS plots of the Commonwealth's roads.

Many thanks to Cindy Cohen for generously allowing me to excerpt her work, and to Norman Leventhal for permission to draw upon his map collection. And to Yvonne Dunton for contributing illustrations before cruising off to bigger and better things. Joe Peidle earns a tribute for dragging me into the zesty world of contras, but he also deserves a medal for patiently putting up with the roommate from hell and *still* sharing his mom's amazing Hungarian pastries. I think I have time to help move that filing cabinet now, Joe.

In addition to the literally hundreds of friendly and efficient museum marketing assistants, park superintendents, supervisory rangers, site directors, and PR staffers everywhere who graciously endeavored to satisfy my scattershot curiosity, I'm grateful to the state's tourism professionals for their support: Milly Spence, Michele Ellicks, Ann Hamilton, Ron Schetzel, Peter Brooks, Randi Vega, and particularly Steve Ziglar. Thank you, all.

I'm especially indebted to Dr. Ian Cox of the International Pie Rating Commission, for both the confidence in my work and the research fellowship that helped support it.

Thank you, Jim Puccio, for that inaugural pizza, and Nancy Gottlieb, for the loan of your canoe. Thanks to fellow Moon author and Allstonian-at-heart Steve Lantos for being a real mensch. (Reader, go this instant and buy the *New Hampshire Handbook*—help Steve stay off the streets.) Thanks as well to Adrian and Cristina Iovita, for providing humor and friendship to outlast any exile. I owe my hiking buddy, Noddy, at least a hogshead of lager for all the times he carried the gin glasses without mishap, but for now this mention will have to do. Hasta Las Vegas siempre, amigo.

It may be all in a day's work, but Pauli Galin, Gregor Krause, Bill Newlin, and untold others at Moon Central, both present and past, have been more accommodating than I could have ever anticipated or hoped for, and certainly more than I deserved. For keeping whatever doubts you had to yourselves—and for the restraint in applying the electrodes there toward the end—my effusive thanks.

Finally, it goes almost without saying that none of this would have been possible without family—not just the social safety net of meals and company, but the unwavering support, indulging my unreason and never, ever, ever even hinting at the obvious (namely, that it would have been more sensible to get a real job). This is the stuff that knows no currency or coin. Dad, David, Henia, and Joel, great big hugs for you all.

WE WELCOME YOUR COMMENTS

Marshaling the facts that make up a travel guide is rather like herding cats. Inevitably, despite every effort to hold a firm line, some will go astray, sneak off, or refuse to come when called. Businesses revamp their menus, tweak their hours of operation, change hands, or go under entirely. Restaurants, museums, and tour outfits are no more able to keep prices constant than nature is able to keep a vacuum empty (so be gentle with those whose prices or hours differ from those printed here—the fault is mine, not theirs). With your help, however, this sort of entropy can at least be kept to a minimum. If you find in your travels details that differ from what's in these pages—or any inconsistencies, ambiguities, or misleading statements—jot them down on the back of a postcard, or make notes in the margins of this handbook and then transcribe them into an e-mail when you get home.

Please don't limit yourself to details—if the opinions expressed about towns, restaurants, commercial development, Pilgrim ideology, or anything else in the book rubbed you the wrong way, go ahead and let rip on those, too.

Of course, don't feel you have to complain to write in or to be heard. It's always great to read a good word from people who've been won over by Massachusetts' charms, or who want to share a discovery with readers of the next edition. Here's how to get in touch:

Moon Travel Handbooks
PO Box 3040
Chico CA 95927-3040

Or e-mail: jperk@moon.com

CAPE COD NATIONAL SEASHORE

INTRODUCTION

Outside of New England, Massachusetts is often thought of as little more than an extension of Boston, a historic but amorphous state of dour Puritans and brave minutemen, pristine village commons overtopped by sharp white church steeples, and quaint seaside towns replete with lobster pots. Since even many Bostonians tend to share this sensibility, much of the state lies truly hidden from all but the most local appreciation—quite a feat for a place that draws and entertains millions of visitors each year.

It's true that where other states may have water towers and grain elevators, Massachusetts' horizon *does* more often offer church steeples. And where courthouse squares in other states' towns may boast surplus artillery from WW II, the town commons in Massachusetts generally showcase statues of Puritan settlers or yeomen of the Revolutionary War.

In fact, the stereotypes about Massachusetts are *all* true, if you want them to be. The state does have an exceptional track record of conservation and preservation (it's hard to throw a stick here without hitting something historic), and it has made a good business out of fulfilling tourists' expectations at least as long as tourists have had dollars in their pockets.

But push yourself through the New England you think you know, and you'll find things you'd never have anticipated. Less than a hundred miles west of bustling Boston, you're in a surprisingly rural commonwealth where you can wander through you-pick apple orchards, spend a night on a llama farm, or tour a selection of wineries (adventurous oenophiles will want to sample Massachusetts' piquant cranberry vintages, from the southeastern portion of the state). As famous as Massachusetts is for its biggest city, it's almost as popular for its small seaside towns, replete with picturesque heaps of lobster traps. Less well known but equally great are the state's college towns, rich in museums and the arts. (Don't let Boston's smorgasbord of offerings in the arts and culture keep you from venturing west to the Berkshires, whose artists, performers, and restaurateurs bring a dollop of Manhattan sophistication to the state's scenic western end.) Think of New England and athletics and what comes to mind? The Patriots, foraging in the snow for fumbles? Hockey? The deceptively sedate and gentlemanly sport of sculling? Then you'll be surprised to find a state offering a wealth of opportunities for whitewater rafting, sea kayaking, hiking, cycling, and cross-country skiing.

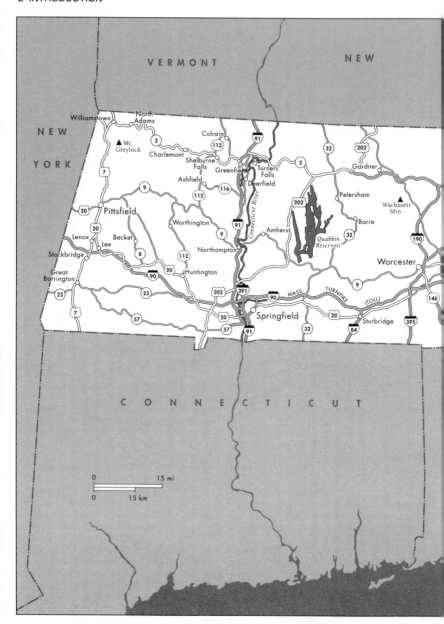

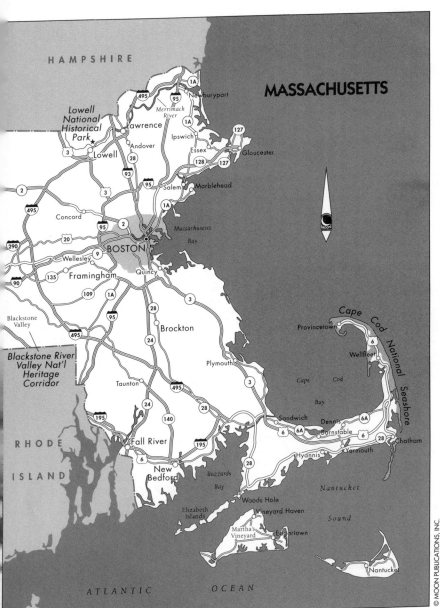

HAMPSHIRE

Lowell
National
Historical
Park ★

MASSACHUSETTS

Newburyport

Merrimack River

Lawrence

Ipswich

Essex

Gloucester

Andover

Salem

Marblehead

Concord

Massachusetts
Bay

BOSTON

Wellesley

Quincy

Framingham

Blackstone
Valley

Brockton

Blackstone River
Valley Nat'l
Heritage
Corridor

Plymouth

Cape Cod National Seashore

Provincetown

Wellfleet

Taunton

Cape   Cod

Bay

RHODE

Sandwich

Dennis

Barnstable

Chatham

Fall River

Yarmouth

New
Bedford

Buzzards
Bay

Hyannis

ISLAND

Nantucket

Woods Hole

Elizabeth
Islands

Vineyard Haven

Sound

Martha's
Vineyard

Edgartown

Nantucket

ATLANTIC   OCEAN

© MOON PUBLICATIONS, INC.

You might look at the dimensions of the state and assume you can pack everything into a single trip. But one of the indescribable joys of Massachusetts is that some of its most flavorsome attractions lie down dead ends and detours and defy the quick trip: the small, unaffected fishing ports and broad sandy beaches along the southeast coast, more Cape Cod than Cape Cod itself these days; the island wildlife refuge off the Cape's southeastern tip; the rugged slopes and frothy mountain streams filled with brook trout in the Hilltowns; the Buddhist sanctuary on a mountain in the Pioneer Valley; or the Trappist monastery whose monks churn out jams and jellies near Worcester.

Slow down and allow yourself time to explore not only what's within these pages, but also what's between the lines and beyond the margins. Leave time and room to get lost. Given the sometimes incomprehensible laout of Massachusetts' cities and the quality of the road signage, you're bound to lose your way anyway, and that just may be the best way to see the real Massachusetts, the state that both celebrates and transcends quaintness and colonialism, baked beans and Ben Franklin.

THE LAND

Before we present you the matters of fact, it is fit to offer to your view the Stage whereon they were acted, for as Geography without History seemeth a carkasse without motion, so History without Geography, wandreth as a Vagrant without a certaine habitation.

—CAPTAIN JOHN SMITH,
THE GENERALL HISTORIE OF VIRGINIA NEW-ENGLAND AND THE SUMMER ISLES,
published in London in 1624

STRADDLING BOUNDARIES

Although its population of just under six million places Massachusetts among the 15 most populous of the United States, in land area the state is sixth *smallest.* With barely more than 8,200 square miles, the state could comfortably fit in any of a number of single *counties* in the western US. But despite its relatively diminutive size and its lack of dramatic topographical extremes (there's no Denali, no Grand Canyon), Massachusetts' landscape is anything but homogenous. In fact, for a place so small, it is disproportionately diverse, from island heaths to post-agricultural rural uplands, rocky granite coasts to steep-sided mountains with old-growth arboreal forests, coastal sand plains to heavily urbanized areas. Massachusetts has actually been divided into 27 distinct subregions—based on climatic variation, population density, types of vegetation, and geological characteristics. Contributing to these differences is the fact that the state happens to straddle several important ecological boundaries or transition zones. In the less than 30 miles from north to south of Boston, for example, the shoreline changes from the exposed bedrock granite ledges of northern New England to the sandy cedar swamps and low-lying piedmont of the Mid-Atlantic. Off Massachusetts' shores, the warm Gulf Stream mixes with cold Labrador currents. And inland, the conifer forests of northern New England yield to the mixed oak and hickory forest of southern New England.

GEOLOGY

The land beneath Massachusetts has suffered a lot of abuse over the last billion years, having been thoroughly folded, spindled, and mutilated by the forces of plate tectonics. Sometime before the beginning of the Paleozoic Era, 570 million years ago, the so-called Laurentia plate—carrying the bulk of the present North American landmass—split apart from its neighbor, forming a shallow ocean called Iapetus. The continental shelves on these rifting plates witnessed the same sort of volcanic activity found today in Hawaii, Iceland, and other mid-ocean hot spots—the semi-solid mantle below the Earth's crust spewed forth molten material, completing the tectonic cycle of subduction along a drifting continent's leading edge, and divergence at its trailing edge. Over the Paleozoic's next couple hundred million years, the convective gears reversed, and North America rammed into its neighboring volcanic island continent, then split apart, and then rammed it again, all with help from Gondwana—the combined forerunner to all of today's southern landmasses. The resulting big squeeze fused these various drifting plates into the supercontinent known as Pangaea. The first of these mountain-building cataclysms occured over 430 million years ago and thrust the mud-covered bottom and reef-covered shores of Iapetus up into the Taconic Mountains. The second, which occurred 350-400 million years ago, tilted the Taconics on their side and pushed up the oldest "basement" rock layers (giving the geology of central and western Massachusetts the appearance of being inverted, with older rock on top). These are the Acadian Mountains, New England's portion of the Appalachians. Along the zone of convergence between the old continental edges, extraordinary heat and pressure metamorphosed rocks and minerals, which bubbled up in dome formations or not-quite-molten intrusions through overlying formations. Compression wasn't the only force at work; after each uplift, the resulting mountains were also subject to massive erosion, shedding a sedimentary blanket of old Iapetus muds and limestone reefs westward to the Great Lakes.

Around the beginning of the Mesozoic Era, some 225 million years ago, convection again shifted gears, and a new rift opened up in Pangaea, which eventually became the Atlantic Ocean. The tension produced great earthquake-rattling faults in what's now the Pioneer Valley as well as New Jersey, steep-walled cracks in the Earth's crust filled from below by rock from the upper mantle just beneath the continental plate—preserved today in rare local formations of serpentinite, or soapstone—and filled from above by eroded sediments, on whose layers are recorded the footsteps of the dinosaurs. The rift also tore apart the formations once comprising that small island continent, in what's now Boston's backyard. Which is why the city's Roxbury puddingstone, a 650-million-year-old conglomerate rock used in lots of local 19th-century building foundations, is also found in both Scotland and Morocco's Atlas Mountains.

Since bidding adieu to Africa and England, Massachusetts has remained on the trailing edge of this big planetary demolition derby. As the Atlantic widens, it's the Pacific coast's turn to subduct. Now mountains are born in Nevada and California; New England simply erodes. In recent geological time—the last couple of million years—a score of ice ages have come and gone, abetting the erosion process by grinding away the peaks of the old Paleozoic mountain ranges. A few, like Wachusett Mountain, in central Massachusetts, are of hard enough material to have successfully resisted the ice. These are known as monadnocks and are easily recognized—they rise above the glacier-leveled peneplains now found on the Worcester uplands and Berkshire Plateau, on either side of the Connecticut River. But the glaciers were only borrowers, not thieves: when they retreated north, they left behind everything they'd taken from these central uplands and then some. Cape Cod and the offshore islands of Nantucket and Martha's Vineyard are partially such remnants, fashioned 14,000-21,000 years ago by the Wisconsinan Ice Age. The melting that accompanied the end of this last period of glaciation also produced Southeastern Massachusetts' outwash plains, and the knobby hills, or drumlins, underlying both Boston and her harbor islands.

CLIMATE

There is a sumptuous variety about the New England weather that compels the stranger's admiration—and regret.

—MARK TWAIN

When the first European explorers wrote of their impressions of Massachusetts, they almost invariably heaped as much praise on its wonderful climate as on its abundance of fruits and fishes. When the first colonists compelled by such tantalizing descriptions ventured to establish permanent residence, they discovered that the explorers had omitted a few things from their reports. Like winter. This actually isn't so surprising: even today, the warmer months of the year somehow so intoxicate most Bostonians that the return of cold weather is greeted with a measure of genuine surprise—Isn't there a finite supply of this stuff? And didn't we use it up last year? Massachusetts weather is famously (and understandably) fickle. It is influenced by both the ocean and a number of high and low pressure systems interacting with some half dozen different air masses over the region. Recent years have produced record-breaking cool summers and snowy winters—and also unusually *mild* winters, dry summers, late springs, and early frosts. In short, prediction is difficult in this state and must always be regarded with a skeptical eye. That said, it is possible to make a few generalizations.

Temperatures in coastal areas are moderated by the proximity of the ocean, whose vast capacity for gradual heat absorption (and discharge) ensures that the mercury on the waterfront doesn't climb as high in summer—or drop as low in winter—as it does in inland areas. However, remember that wind chill can make temperature irrelevant, and that the wind is *always* cooler coming off the ocean. This means that if you go whalewatching on a broiling, 90° F August afternoon, you'll probably regret it if you don't dress for 68° F. In winter, when the pre-

vailing wind shifts around to the northeast, a simple waterfront walk can become downright painful. Unless the Bermuda High pressure system stalls weather over the coast, though, summer's prevailing southwesterly winds blow air masses through the region quickly. This heightens variability, but it also means that bad weather tends not to stick around very long.

There is no dry season in Massachusetts. Precipitation occurs throughout the year—on average, once every three or four days. In spring, consistently warm weather doesn't arrive until well into May, although temperatures may spike up into the short-sleeve zone for a day or three as early as March. Similarly, fall's resurrection of long-sleeve weather and overnight frosts in late September is broken in October by "Indian summer," a modest but unforgettable series of georgeous warm days that rival summer itself. Once fall sets in, the days grow short and the temperatures chilly. Winter's first snow varies by elevation and distance from the ocean but generally hits in December. January and February are Massachusetts' coldest months. Despite thaws in March and April, snowstorms are not at all unheard of right through the end of March.

HISTORY

NATIVE AMERICANS

At the time of first contact with 16th-century Europeans, southern New England's indigenous Native Americans are estimated to have numbered in the thousands in the region now within Massachusetts borders. At least 100 villages have been identified as having belonged to bands of some half-dozen tribes: the Massachusett, Wampanoag, Nipmuck, Pawtucket, Pocumtuck, and Mahican. Each tribe comprised many bands, some more loosely allied than others. All shared the language of the Eastern Algonquian, the linguistic group encompassing most of the tribes on the East Coast between the Carolinas and the Iroquois Confederation. Although effectively a dead language (the last native speaker died in the early 1900s, and, in 1995, a Wampanoag Indian who had spent some 21 years working to revive it passed away,

too), several Algonquian nouns have made their way into English, including "skunk," "chipmunk," and "powwow."

The Europeans brought with them, among other things, several diseases against which the natives had no resistance. These afflictions, particularly smallpox, proved disastrous for New England's Indians. An epidemic in the years just prior to the arrival of the Pilgrims at Plymouth virtually depopulated the entire Boston basin (Squanto, famous for serving as both a friend to and interpreter for the Pilgrims, was kidnapped from his village on Plymouth Bay in 1614, and by the time he returned from his adventures in Spain and England, the Patuxet band to which he belonged had been utterly wiped out by disease). A second major epidemic swept the New England tribes again after the Puritan migration in the 1630s, and smaller scourges took place periodically well into the 1700s. But despite the depredations of disease, loss of tribal identity through acculturation, and two devastating wars with the English, the Native Americans did not entirely vanish. Indeed, they're still here: several bands of the Wampanoag and Nipmuck tribes reside in Massachusetts, and two have even obtained federal recognition.

EARLY EXPLORERS

After the Pilgrims had desecrated a few Native American burial mounds in their explorations of their landing spot on Cape Cod, the Pilgrims decided that it was "odious unto [the Native Americans] to ransack their sepulchres." But one mound was uncommonly large, which made them curious enough to dig into it. What they found was a double grave, containing a child and blond-haired man—who had been buried with belongings including a knife, "a saylers canvas Casacke, and a payre of cloth breeches." The following spring, a solitary Indian strolled into the settlement at Plymouth and greeted the surprised Europeans in clear English. Plainly, the Pilgrims were not the first Europeans to have visited these shores. Exactly how many had come previously isn't known, but the codfish-rich waters off the coast were well known to Portuguese and Basque fishermen in the 1500s, and some of these fishermen had traded with the Indians who lived along the shore. A number of explorers also left records of trips to Massachusetts (some of these written accounts and crude charts were the very guides used by the Pilgrims).

It is often supposed that Vikings were the Bay State's first European visitors, arriving sometime around 1000 A.D. Although more than 30 years have passed since archaeological traces of a Norse settlement were discovered in Newfoundland, there's never been incontrovertible proof of any settlement farther south. This isn't to say that Vikings didn't venture up the Charles River or around Narragansett Bay, but lines from Norse sagas describing days longer than those in Iceland and wood resembling oak aren't enough to support the assertions of most modern theorists. Amateur historians and local mythmakers have been beguiled for generations by the idea that the Vikings' mentions of

"Vinland" refer to what is now Martha's Vineyard (or any other wild-grapevine-covered beach between Maine and New Jersey). But despite gaining a measure of credibility from various less-than-scholarly museum displays, there is no real evidence to distinguish such claims from pure theory (for a start, the Old Norse word *Vÿnlãd* refers to grasslands, not grapevines).

PILGRIMS AND PURITANS

The *Mayflower*

The English claim to North America is based on John Cabot's 1497-98 voyage along the Atlantic coast. It's uncertain whether Cabot ever actually laid eyes on New England, but rivalry with other colonial powers—including the Dutch and the French—inspired Queen Elizabeth to use his voyage as grounds for bestowing the first royal sanction upon a New England colony in 1578. Sir Humphrey Gilbert was the lucky fellow who obtained her permission to try housekeeping on the Maine coast. Unfortunately, Gilbert's ship sank on its first voyage to Gilbert's prize.

In the first decade of the 17th century, Elizabeth's successor, King James I, made new grants and patents—royal permissions—to various wealthy financiers and aristocrats, who invested in settlements from the Kennebec River in present-day Maine to the James River in Virginia. The results were decidedly mixed; most of the settlements fell far short of their founders' aspirations. Ships laden with cod, sassafras, and beaver pelts motivated the deep-pocketed speculators, but domestic problems in England made colonization as important as profit-making. Exploding population, crop failures, and the societal shift from self-sufficient villages to a market society created a large migrant pool of tenant farmers and landless artisans willing to emigrate to wherever they might be able to eke out a living. Thousands had already gone to Europe in the decade before the *Mayflower* set sail. Any risks in the New World—violent clashes with Indians, for a start—were conveniently dismissed by colonial promoters.

Captain John Smith, the founder of Virginia's successful Jamestown, was one author of glowing reports on New England's bountiful re-

A FEW MYTHS ABOUT THE PILGRIMS

Myths about the Pilgrims and the Puritans are rampant, and cottage industries have sprung up to both stoke and debunk them. For example, compare the following to what you learned in high school.

Myth: The Pilgrims were bound for Virginia and made landfall at Cape Cod only because they were lost.

Facts: The Pilgrims had originally been given a grant to settle in Northern Virginia, but the royal grant for "Virginia" initially comprised everything between the Jamestown settlement and the 41st parallel (around present-day New York City). William Bradford, the Pilgrims' most thorough annalist and sometime governor, recorded that their destination was the mouth of the Hudson, but there's plenty of evidence that the Pilgrim leaders never intended to subject themselves to the Old Dominion authorities in Jamestown, and merely took a patent from them as a precaution in the event that their other plans failed to materialize.

Before they left England, it was known that Sir Fernando Gorges, an ambitious colonialist who already had a string of failures to his credit, from Massachusetts to Maine, had requested a new royal patent for his "Council for New England." In fact, royal transfer of the northern territories from the Virginia Company to Gorges became official just days before the Pilgrims landed. As soon as the newly empowered Council had word of the *Mayflower*'s success, the charter the Pilgrims probably hoped to have all along was dispatched without any negotiation, granting the autonomy the Pilgrims desired.

The historical record is sketchy, but it's hard to believe that the Pilgrim leaders had no dealings with Gorges prior to their departure. Bradford even had a copy of a firsthand report from one of Gorges' agents, Thomas Dermer, assessing the colonizing potential of different parts of Cape Cod Bay, including Plymouth.

Myth: The Mayflower Compact is one of the cornerstones of American democracy.

Facts: There is some merit to this statement, in light of the fact that until this century, American "democracy" legally abridged the rights of anyone other than white males. The Mayflower Compact was never signed by most of the indentured servants, or by any of the women. But it really wasn't conceived in a generous democratic spirit: mutiny was afoot, and the compact was the tool used to quash it. The Pilgrims felt threatened by at

the Mayflower II

TED CURTIN/COURTESY OF THE PLIMOTH PLANTATION;

least one of the Strangers. This was probably Stephen Hopkins, a survivor of the Bermuda shipwreck that befell another Virginia-bound company in 1609. Hopkins had encouraged fellow wreckmates to reject their governor's authority on the grounds that his jurisdiction was limited to their original destination, not the site of their accident. Although he escaped execution by begging for mercy on behalf of his family, he may have voiced the same seditious logic 11 years later at Cape Cod. Although it's most remembered now for codifying the principal of majority rule, the compact kept the group from being splintered by what Bradford called "mutterings of dissent." Throughout the Plymouth colony's existence, some 80% of the population was permitted to neither vote nor hold office—so it would seem that the notion of "majority rule" may not have represented to the Pilgrims what we may like to think it did.

Myth: The Pilgrims landed in a howling wilderness with nothing but their wits and industriousness to save them.

Facts: The *Mayflower* contingent chose for their settlement the site of an abandoned Indian village—one not at all unknown to Bradford and others. Champlain had thoroughly charted it 15 years earlier—when it and the surrounding bay was still occupied by some 2,000 Patuxet Indian (before they were wiped out by a European epidemic). Thomas Dermer, whose letter Bradford carried, had been to the village site just five months before the Pilgrims arrived.

"I would that the first plantation might here be seated," Dermer wrote his sponsor (although he did go on to warn that the local Indians were hostile to the English, whom they accused of murder). The *Mayflower* pilot had also been to the place before. And its name appeared on Captain Smith's six-year-old chart of the New England coastline—which the Pilgrims used to guide them to Cape Cod.

The village site included fields cleared for cultivation, overgrown only two or three years. Paths through the woods were well maintained by regional Indian bands engaging in constant social and trading activities. Thanks to the Indian's forest-management practice of setting small fires in order to improve game hunting, much of the forest understory was so clear that all the settlers remarked on how easy it was to ride through the woods.

One hardship they *did* encounter was the weather (their arrival was ill-timed with the start of winter). Probably the greatest obstacle they faced, however, was their own lack of skills appropriate to building a coastal colony. As villagers and artisans, none of the settlers was very proficient at fishing or farming, for example. And they were so incurious about their new surroundings that it took some three months to venture even as far as two miles from their settlement (and then only because one young Pilgrim, having climbed a tree, thought he saw an inland sea—which turned out to be a large pond).

Myth: After difficult beginnings, the Pilgrims celebrated their first harvest with a big Thanksgiving feast, including turkey and all the trimmings.

Facts: Pilgrim theology permitted but three holidays: Sabbath; Fast Day; and Thanksgiving. These last two weren't necessarily regular events tied to a specific day, as the Sabbath was. Instead, church leaders would declare a day of penance or thanks if and when they thought it necessary. In the fall of 1621, the Pilgrims did indeed hold a three-day feast, but they didn't feel they'd acquired enough of God's bounty to declare a proper Thanksgiving until two years later, in 1623.

Thanksgiving proclamations continued to be random events. The warring American colonies joined in the first common Thanksgiving in 1777 to celebrate victory over the British at the Battle of Saratoga. (Two year later, George Washington's proclamation of a national Thanksgiving was ignored as premature.) Various state governors continued the practice up through 1827, when Boston *Ladies' Magazine* editor Sarah Josepha Hale took up the cudgel, inaugurating an editorial campaign on behalf of an annual national Thanksgiving. Abe Lincoln finally made it a holiday after Gettysburg, in 1863.

As for the practice of including turkey in the meal, that most likely derived from the English custom of a turkey *Christmas* dinner, established some 35 years before the Pilgrims departed for the New World. The meal the Pilgrims ate that first fall comprised more venison than wildfowl. While there were wild turkeys in New England, the Pilgrims preferred domesticated European breeds, which are, in fact, the progenitors of the turkeys we eat most commonly today.

sources. Among the audience for his public relations campaign was a group of disaffected Protestants, who had fled to Holland after "Bloody Mary" forcefully reimposed Catholicism on England. These "Saints," as they called themselves, declined Smith's offer to guide them to the new colony, frugally preferring to simply buy his book and sea chart and try their luck on their own. Backed by venture capitalists in London and half-believing that they would be united with the Lost Tribe of Israel when they reached their new home, these emigrants were joined by a cadre of middle-class allies known as the Merchant Adventurers (graciously dubbed "Strangers" by their saintly shipmates). Aboard the tiny *Mayflower,* The 102 passengers and an unknown number of crew succeeded in crossing the stormy Atlantic, where the emigrants established their "plantation" on Cape Cod Bay.

Half of these settlers died their first winter in the new land. But eventually, with infusions of new blood from home and life-saving agricultural lessons from their new Native American neighbors, these Pilgrims (as they came to be called only after 1840) did well enough to both completely repay their investors and attract a slew of new homesteaders to burgeoning outposts from Boston Harbor to Cape Cod.

The *Arbella* Brings the First Bostonians

Eight years after the arrival of the Pilgrims, a small group of "lord brethren," keen on "purifying" the Anglican Church (instead of rejecting it outright, as the Pilgrims had done), arrived in present-day Salem and laid hold of an English fishing community, a remnant of a failed settlement farther up the coast. Within two years, these zealous brethren's simple land grant was converted into a royally chartered trading organization called the Massachusetts Bay Company, setting the stage for John Winthrop, an influential autocrat, to come a-calling in the *Arbella* and a fleet of nine other ships. This huge flock of "Puritans" moved twice before settling on the hilly peninsula they named Boston.

Back home, dissent against the Anglican bishops and economic stagnation from farm shortages proved so widespread that within a generation, 20,000 English—predominantly from East Anglia—joined the Great Migration to the Bay Colony.

Puritans Pull a Fast One

Like the Pilgrims, the Puritans eluded direct English control by design. Winthrop, a well-trained lawyer, recognized an omission in the text of his company's charter: while stockholder meetings to direct the company had to be held where the charter was kept, nothing required the charter to be kept in England. This loophole made it possible to simply pocket the document and bring it along to America—putting the whole wide Atlantic between the colony and oversight by Parliament and the Crown.

Unlike the hereditary or proprietary (i.e., feudal) royal charters given to Maryland's plantation owners or the Duke of York, the Massachusetts Bay political framework of "freemen" (stockholders) assembling in a General Court established the basis for representative government by a company of equals. This may sound democratic, but only shareholders could vote, and out of 1,000 emigrants, exactly four were first enfranchised in the Great & General Court. Only mutinous threats forced revision of the court's composition, creating a bicameral chamber—one part elected by all freemen, the other appointed by Bay Company officers—and expanding voter eligibility to other men of property.

Intolerance

Despite legal documents that seemed to institute a measure of democratic rule, the early Puritan colony, under Governor Winthrop, was as harsh a theocracy as Iran under the Ayatollah Khomenei. Religious and social dissenters faced serious censure, cruel punishment, or even death for disagreeing with or denying the will of church leaders. Since Puritans equated change with sin, the status quo justified the most abominable abridgements of what we now call civil and human rights.

The Pilgrims in the adjacent "Old Colony" were no better. You could get part of your ear sliced off if you were caught eavesdropping. Doze off during the many hours of sermonizing on the Sabbath and your tongue might be impaled on a sharp stick. Notwithstanding such cruelty—and the liberal application of both banishment and the death penalty—the authorities of both colonies left records rich in human transgressions including drinking, incest, adultery, homosexuality, bestiality, and plain old crooked business dealings.

These early English settlers were often a disputatious lot and frequently dragged each other into court. Despite an apparent love of legalisms and litigation, actual justice was in short supply—particularly with regard to relations with various indigenous peoples. After enduring epidemics and the consequent destruction of tribal alliances, native populations around Massachusetts had managed to stabilize. But this increased the potential for cultural misunderstandings over all sort of issues, especially as the English became hungry for more land. Tensions quickly escalated after the 1661 death of the Pokanoket (Wampanoag) chief Massassoit, a steadfast Pilgrim ally, and subsequently of his son and successor, Alexander, who died of an illness after being forcibly detained by the English on suspicions of conspiring against them.

Unfortunately for all concerned, the colonists' fears became self-fulfilling. Alexander's brother, Philip, known to his people as Metacom, strategized with various allies across Massachusetts to boot the Anglos back across the Atlantic.

King Philip's War

Philip came close, but not close enough. His rebellion began prematurely, in 1675—after the colonials had gotten wise to his intent—and without the vital cooperation of a couple of other tribes in central and western New England. So the "Red King" missed his mark, though not without inflicting serious setbacks on both Pilgrim and Puritan colonies: 50 of 90 existing towns were destroyed, many more were abandoned by fearful settlers, and the colonial militia was given a run for its money. Ultimately, however, victory over Metacom's coalition brought uncompromising and indiscriminate revenge and reprisals against Native Americans throughout the region.

The colonists paid a heavy toll in the war besides lost lives and abandoned towns. The cost of arming and operating its military force financially crippled them. Plymouth's share of the debt exceeded the value of all its real estate. A further consequence was that the troubles called into question the colonies' ability to conduct their affairs outside the purview of English authority, and ended the prized independence.

Parliamentary demands for security after the war reinstituted imperial dominion: in 1684, the Restoration monarch, Charles II, officially dissolved the Puritan charter. After seven years of jockeying by various political factions, in 1691 a new charter was finally issued by the Merry Monarch's successors, William and Mary. With that, at long last, Massachusetts became a true royal province.

REVOLUTION

What do we mean by the American Revolution? Do we mean the American war? Revolution was effected before the War commenced. The Revolution was in the minds and hearts of the people.

—JOHN ADAMS

In the century following the crown's imposition of control over its wayward colony, the bond between the English colonists and their king deteriorated as ineluctably as had the earlier generation's relations with the Native Americans. Some scholars point out the influence of mercantile interests, which effectively used propaganda to sway the colonists in what was actually a struggle to practice capitalism unfettered by strictures from abroad. Others suggest that this is a simplistic view, and there is certainly plenty of evidence that antipathy toward the tactics of the crown ran deep among a variety of social and economic classes. The upshot is that before the war, both sides regarded themselves as British; by the end, one side considered itself American. And, of course, that was the side that won.

Shays' Rebellion

The Revolution had been enormously expensive for the colonialists, and in the aftermath America was saddled with debt. The new nation's yeomen farmers perhaps felt the squeeze most sharply. Merchants in Boston, no longer extended credit by their English trading partners, began requiring customers to pay in cash rather than in kind. But the farmers had no cash. Massachusetts' merchant-dominated state government turned a deaf ear to the farmers' pleas for financial reforms or bailouts, so the farmers, led by Daniel Shays (who had fought in the Revolution), rose in armed revolt. They attacked the Springfield arsenal, shut down debtor courts, and prevented enforcement of land foreclosures.

Shocked merchants declared the rebellion treasonous and took their concerns all the way to the provisional Congress, in Philadelphia. There, the 18th-century version of the domino theory—the image of individual states falling, one after another, to the control of the unwashed mob—proved so persuasive an argument against a weak federal executive that the business-minded Congress promptly voted to raise an army—and soon thereafter ratified a Constitution that bound the component states together into a strong federal republic.

In England in March 1787, a writer in the *Bath Chronicle* declared, "America exhibits a curious scene at this time, rebellion growing out of rebellion; particularly in that seedling-bed and hotbed of discontent, sedition, riot and rebellion Massachusetts Bay." And in April, Jonathan Mallet wrote to American Robert Watts, "Strange that the ungrateful multitude should turn upon the illustrious patriots, who led them to seek such happiness."

Shays, who had escaped the state troops' successful dispersal of the rebellious farmers, was pardoned in 1788.

INDUSTRIALIZATION

For Yankees interested in applying their famous ingenuity to the drudgery of turning grindstones or raising forge hammers, New England's fast-flowing rivers presented a ready source of clean, abundant, free power. And as technology advanced, industrial applications of all sorts sprang up along the banks of almost every rill and trickle in the state. Most water-powered mills remained small affairs, however, until the Revolution freed American capitalists to compete with mother England.

Thanks to a keen bit of memorization (or, in another light, industrial espionage), in 1814 some key English textile machinery was successfully copied by Boston's own Francis Cabot Lowell. Fed with cotton from the South and powered by local rivers, Lowell's looms begat Massachusetts' first economic miracle: the mill town.

At their peak, the industrial cities of Lowell, Fall River, and New Bedford churned out thousands of *miles* of cotton and wool each year, while Haverhill, Lynn, and Brockton factories cobbled millions of pairs of shoes. As the nation was clothed and shod, the state was transformed. By the end of WW I, some 60-75% of all industrial workers were employed in the textile or shoe manufacture, and 95% of the state's population lived in urban areas. (Such a lopsided concentration of business made Massachusetts vulnerable to economic fluctuation, however. When mill and factory owners, increasingly beset by efforts to organize labor and by aging physical facilities, took their exploitative wages and working conditions to the non-unionized South, they put the state on the brink of an economic nosedive.)

Massachusetts' mills did give rise to widespread prosperity, but they also contributed to appalling social problems: rampant urban overcrowding; epidemics of tuberculosis, typhoid, cholera, and "brown lung" (the cotton worker's equivalent of asbestosis); and unimaginably high infant mortality (the nation's worst). Work-related accidents and illness claimed the lives of *one in three* textile workers within 10 years of entering the mills. Half of the victims were under 25.

Nostalgia

Compared to England's soot-blackened manufacturing centers, Massachusetts' water-powered industrial capitals began as showpieces. But as competition increased, businesses grew less concerned with social responsibility, and erstwhile model communities of clean, virtuous living became as fit for Charles Dickens' scathing pen as any poverty-stricken Manchester mill town.

As these new industrial cities bred physical and social ills, movements sprang up to improve urban lives through education, temperance, or political activity. But some people—those few able to afford a reflective pause—battled the present by promoting a yearning for the bygone simplicity and rural beauty of the colonial age. Such nostalgia was often implicitly racist (part of the yearning was not just for small, devout towns and neat, well-tended fields but also for an age dominated—in memory, if not in fact—by honest Anglo townsfolk and farmers), but its legacy is one of New England's most enduring icons: the

COURTESY OF LOWELL NATIONAL HISTORICAL PARK

the spinning room at Boott Cotton Mills, Lowell, circa 1910

town common resembling a perfectly green croquet lawn in front of the tall, white, Congregational church steeple.

In fact, prior to the mid-19th century, town commons were usually muddy stockyards, and churches outside Boston were rarely wealthy enough to put up anything remotely resembling Christopher Wren's needle-sharp London spires. After his 1842 visit to the U.S., Charles Dickens wrote of the New England landscape, "The well-trimmed lawns and green meadows of home are not there, and the grass, compared with our ornamental plots and pastures, is rank, and rough, and wild." Cultivating lawns and proud ecclesiastical architecture didn't begin until there were enough rich people to care about them. Interest in the Pilgrim "forefathers" arose around the same time.

With the continued ascendancy of the industrial city and with an influx of immigrants (notably Irish and Italian Catholics, and Russian Jews), a bit of English greensward and a Protestant facade soon came to emblematize the Good Old Days. Even today, some folks count Mayflower bloodlines and Revolutionary War grandfathers as a measure of a true American, and some romanticize the backbreaking toil of colonial farming as a pastoral spring idyll—proving the the Good Old Days are as intoxicating as ever.

FAST FORWARD TO THE PRESENT

National security has always been good business for Massachusetts, beginning with the need for wooden frigates for the U.S. Navy and rifles for the peacetime army under President George Washington. During the Cold War, guidance systems, missiles, jet-aircraft components, and long-range missile detection systems (such as the Distant Early Warning line of defensive radar in place around Alaska and Canada) became the bread and butter of the state's electronics firms and university research labs. During the 1970s, commercial computers overtook defense-related electronics, and by the 1980s, the "Massachusetts Miracle"—a potent entrepreneurial boom in high-technology firms, financial services, and real estate development—pushed the state's economy skyward.

The 1987 "Black Monday" stock market plunge dealt the state's economy a blow, and the damage was worsened overleveraged corporations both in and out of state, retrenchment in an electronics industry blindsided by personal computers, and a saturated commercial real estate market. By the time ripples from Reaganomics' collapse had reached the West Coast, Massachusetts, eager to escape its economic doldrums, had downsized, streamlined, and otherwise all but bitten its own leg off (electing a Republican governor to fill the corner office previously occupied by Michael Dukakis, humiliated by his loss to George Bush in the 1988 presidential election). Since the mid-1990s, tremors of economic vitality have been felt around the state, most keenly in eastern Massachusetts.

GOVERNMENT AND ECONOMY

Political Geography
There are still places in the US where gaps exist between towns, unincorporated territory belonging to county or state jurisdictions. Massachusetts has had a head start of a couple hundred years in filling those gaps, covering the state with townships as tightly packed as floor tiles. Look at a map of these township lines, though, and you can't help noticing their unruliness, as if they've been drawn by a four-year-old. Actually, like growth rings on trees, these boundaries illustrate the evolution of the Bay State from a colonial theocracy, with roots in feudal England, to a more secular body taking cues from Thomas Jefferson.

Early colonial boundaries represented the dreams of commercial enterprise (tinged with religious zeal), encompassing all the good land a few boatloads of settlers thought they would need for their own subsistence and to permit them to make debt payments to investors back home. Towns grew up around the most important civil authority—the church—so political boundaries came to match a minister's influence. As congregations divided over theological disputes, or when rural parishioners began complaining of the distance they had to travel to attend church, new ministries were founded—and with them, new towns. As the towns grew wealthy, a merchant class arose—with distinct, non-theological interests—and began flexing its political muscle. This coincided with an increase in rationalism and scientific inquiry, and town lines came to be drawn by professionals versed in the latest geometry. The differences between these methods of laying out townships—constantly subdividing congregations versus a mathematical survey of the physical geography—is evident in today's map of Massachusetts. Eastern and central Massachusetts are riven with irregular lines, while to the west, in the Berkshires (virtual *terra incognita* nearly until the 19th century), the outlines come much closer to matching the earth's hypothetical girdle of parallels and meridians—that perfect platte any transcontinental airline passenger can see inscribed across the farms of the Midwest.

Town Meetings
Each winter, in meetinghouses and school auditoriums around the state, cities enact the annual rite of the Town Meeting—an open, public discussion of a town's innermost workings. There's a certain confessional aspect to these budgetary wranglings both irresistible and tedious—sort of an alternation between *Twelve Angry Men* and the Worst of C-Span, ranging from the cost of streetlights and whether to repair or replace the town's 40-year-old fire truck to new development projects, with each side presenting nervous but impassioned speeches. It's something like a baseball game: a lot of swinging at empty air, and then, just when you're going to fall asleep, someone acts as if he got hit by the pitcher, the dugouts empty in support of each side, and there's a sudden electricity in the air. Washington may have more pomp, but the civics and democracy lesson is more accessible here in the bush leagues. Watching an hour of debate at one of these affairs, though, may lead you to conclude that Tip O'Neill had it backwards when he said that all politics is local: even if all politics *aren't* local, everything local can certainly be politicized.

MADE IN MASSACHUSETTS

It wasn't too long ago that Massachusetts companies still *made* things—big, tangible things, like Model Ts and Navy warships. But these days, the state's economy depends more on *doing* things for people: hello, service economy. Actually, while manufacturing has declined as a component of the state's overall economy, the sector has enjoyed a huge boom, and the value and diversity of what's still manufactured here is higher than ever before. The machine tools, electric cars, aircraft-interior fabrics, and electronic instruments made here today are all higher-ticket items than the apparel, furniture, and paper products of the 19th and early 20th centuries.

But the new cornerstones of the state's prosperity are the clean-fingernail companies concentrated in electronics, biotechnology, computers and peripherals, and higher service industries. Massachusetts ranks second in the nation in the value of its software products, for example (right after Microsoft's home state of Washington); it's on par with New York in financial services (thanks to Boston-based mutual fund giant Fidelity Investments); and it's a national leader in both business consulting and higher education.

Once a hotbed of unionism, Massachusetts is now just the opposite, with a lower percentage of unionized workers than the national average.

Despite the fact that the Bay State's largest employers are health-care conglomerates and regional supermarket chains (with higher education close behind), the Bay State's biggest moneymakers—Digital Equipment Corp., Polaroid, Raytheon, and Bose, those producers of computer workstations, instant film, Patriot missiles, and Paul Harvey's favorite radios—need little introduction. You've probably also heard of GE Aircraft Engines, and there's a good chance your razor blades come from Gillette's "world shaving headquarters," in South Boston. That game of *Monopoly* you played as a kid? Made in Salem. Besides Harvard and MIT, Cambridge is home to fragrant confectionery plants that produce zillions of Junior Mints and pastel-colored "conversation heart" Necco candies. Outdoor enthusiasts stay warm and dry with Polartec fleece made in Methuen; early risers everywhere dream of their daily dose of Dunkin Donuts, initially a Massachusetts firm; and anyone mixing a Cape Codder probably reaches for a bottle of Ocean Spray, the nation's leading non-citrus fruit juice producer, based in Plymouth.

In addition, plenty of the state's small firms dominate their product niches—even if they aren't household names. You may be adding to the state's bottom line by using EMC disk drives, Interleaf publishing software, Scitex prepress systems, or Avid video editors. Punch a time clock? It's probably made by Simplex Time Recorders, in Gardner. On the smaller scale of true cottage industries, the Bay State is also a strong national contender in stained-glass restoration, pottery, woodworking, specialty bookbinding, and flutes and piccolos.

Dominated in dollar terms by berry growers, agriculture is only a tiny part of the state's economy. Cranberries are the top crop, worth nearly $90 million a year—more than twice the annual intake on the next closest contender, apples. Strawberries, blueberries, and blackberries collectively rank third, totaling about $30 million (a mere 10% of the value of Oregon's berry crop). Once the largest component of the state's farming sector, the dairy industry has lately gone the way of the horse-drawn buggy. New England can't compete with the Midwest in dairy production and has seen a viscious decline over the last 25 years. If yuppies continue their current love affair with fancy cigars, Massachusetts' high-quality shade-grown tobacco (popular for the leaves used for wrapping fine cigars) may soon eclipse its milk.

Leader of the Pack

Massachusetts' economic firsts would fill a book by themselves: from manufacturing machines for making square-bottomed paper bags, gumming and folding envelopes, or weaving patterned carpets, to the first all-electronic computer, self-developing instant film, and oral contraceptive. Massachusetts was home to the invention of I. M. Singer's patented sewing machine; the manufacture of America's first mass-produced bicycles, motorcycles, and cars; and the first minted coins. The player piano, coffee percolator, and golf tee were patented here. The radio tube, microwave radar, and typhus vaccine were pioneered here. America's first chocolate factory (1765); first producer of authentic, prefabricated diners (1887), and first minicomputer manufacturer (1967) all began here. Some communities around the state so dominated the nation's 19th-century production of certain commodities that they earned nicknames like "Toy Town" (Winchendon), "Paper City" (Holyoke), "Chair City" (Gardner), "Queen Shoe City" (Lynn), and "Watch City" (Waltham). The legacy is substantial, but we try not to brag—it's all just business as usual.

One of Massachusetts' hottest commodities today is a college degree. Three and a half centuries after the Puritans established North America's first public school (Boston Latin, still extant) and a private college (Harvard University's precursor), higher education is to Massachusetts what gambling is to Nevada. Besides some of the most recognizable names in the business (from Amherst to Wellesley, Berklee College of Music to the Massachusetts Institute of Technology) the sheer number is so high that college towns in the state are apt to have not just one school, but three or four. And whether historically a result of Puritan-instilled self-reliance or upper-class attempts to protect privilege, Massachusetts is the only state where private colleges and universities outnumber public, awarding four times as many degrees on their graduates.

LESLIE JONES/COURTESY OF THE BOSTON PUBLIC LIBRARY, PRINT DEPARTMENT

ON THE ROAD
SIGHTSEEING HIGHLIGHTS

History Fresh from the Source . . .

From the nation's largest concentration of 17th-century First Period dwellings to whole cityscapes left over from the Industrial Revolution, history has left copious traces across Massachusetts. Scores of towns have residential neighborhoods or downtown civic areas so well preserved that they qualify as nationally significant; many more villages have maintained the integrity of their landscapes and architecture to such an extent that they've been placed on the National Register in their entirety. Not surprisingly, Massachusetts is number one in National Register listings: 4,000 and counting, encompassing over 60,000 buildings.

The National Park Service (NPS) has made attractions out of many compelling historic sites around the state and in general provides the best visitor services and programs at the best price 12 months of the year. (These are your tax dollars at work. Your senators and representatives need to know whether you prefer they spend your taxes on these sorts of parks, or on billion-dollar weapons systems. Help them out with your opinion.) Among the NPS highlights are Boston's Charlestown Navy Yard and African American Meetinghouse, the Revolutionary Battle Road in Concord and Lexington, maritime Salem, industrial Lowell, and the vestiges of the Blackstone River Canal from Worcester to Rhode Island.

The Massachusetts park system also has a historical component, represented by nine **State Heritage Parks.** From Lawrence ("the Immigrant City" and 19th-century textile powerhouse on the banks of the Merrimack River) to North Adams (the Berkshires' railroad gateway to the west), nearly all include museums-cum-visitor centers showcasing the state's industrial past, often with strong focuses on labor and community. The Department of Environmental Management, tel. (617) 727-3180, overseer of the state park and forest system, can furnish you with a complete *Historic State Parks* brochure upon request.

Many unique historic homes are maintained for the public by a pair of nonprofit organizations, the **Society for the Preservation of New England Antiquities (SPNEA),** and **The Trustees of Reservations (TTOR).** SPNEA's dozen treasures in Massachusetts range from the great manorial 17th-century Spencer-Pierce-Little Farm, in Newbury, north of Boston, to the home of Bauhaus founder Walter Gropius, in the MetroWest area of suburban Boston. Send requests for a complete property guide and calendar of seasonal programs to 141 Cambridge St., Boston MA 02114, or tel. (617) 227-3956. Primarily engaged in helping conserve open land in Massachusetts, TTOR also has some half-dozen exceptional houses scattered across the state—mostly west of the Pioneer Valley. Properties include Nathaniel Hawthorne's Old Manse, in Concord; poet William Cullen Bryant's country farm, in the Hilltowns; a pair of 1730s frontier homes in the southern Berkshires; and such magnificent Belle Epoque estates as Castle Hill, on Boston's North Shore, and Naumkeag, outside Stockbridge in the Berkshires. With minor exceptions, visits and special programs at all SPNEA and TTOR properties are offered only May or June through October.

Every region in the state has at least a few museums or collections of thematic or topical interest. Prime examples, open year-round, include Lexington's Museum of Our National Heritage; Lowell's vast American Textile History Museum; New Bedford's Whaling Museum; the Willard Clock Museum, in the rural Central Massachusetts village of North Grafton; the elegant Victorian Wistariahurst Museum, in Holyoke (north of Springfield in the Pioneer Valley); and the Chapin Library of Rare Books, in Williamstown.

More obscure are the exhibits maintained by small volunteer historical societies, usually ensconced in a home or mansion significant only to the immediate community and discreetly signposted on the main street. Nearly every rural town in Massachusetts seems to have one of these—a place bereft of explanation, filled with faded labels and the poignant air of objects whose purposes have been forgotten (although amateur genealogists tracing their local roots will find them—and the local libraries—to be

first-class resources). Most of these places seem to be open only on summer weekends and elementary school holidays. For a marvelous introduction to some of these very collections, Howard Mansfield's *In the Memory House* (Golden, Colorado: Fulcrum Publishing) will whet your appetite for poking about in what amounts to the attics of perfect strangers.

... Or Re-enacted

While many of the NPS properties and some of the more high-profile homes and museums offer costumed or interactive history programs, the stars of the "living history" genre are Massachusetts' interpretive historic villages. If you just want to hit the high points, take a walk through 1627 at the southeastern coast's Plimoth Plantation and the *Mayflower II;* visit the 1830s in Central Massachusetts' Old Sturbridge Village; gather stories of more than a century of colonial life at the Pioneer Valley's Historic Deerfield; and observe the workings of utopian religious community at Hancock Shaker Village in the Berkshires.

Historic and Scenic Byways

Several Massachusetts highways still provide resonant echoes of the traditional Sunday drive—joyrides with with the top down and the rumble seat full of friends. A fair amount of Massachusetts' infrastructure is frozen in the pre-interstate era of WPA bridges and vintage motel cottages built like birdhouses. The Hilltowns' Mohawk and Jacob's Ladder Trails, improved specifically to encourage tourism early in this century, have been bypassed by the Massachusetts Turnpike, whose 135 tree-lined miles manage to avoid every place of human habitation between Boston and the New York state line. Other routes, unchristened by promoters but equally redolent of the pursuit of tourist dollars that characterized the early 1900s, stripe the state's interior—in Central Massachusetts' Blackstone River Valley and along Rt. 32. Routes 68 and 78, by the New Hampshire border, and Rt. 57, along the Connecticut line, pass less through twilight than through the Twilight Zone, with towns such as Royalston, Warwick, New Boston, and Tolland showing little evidence of contact with the 20th century.

THE GREAT OUTDOORS

As one drives the newer, divided highways of Massachusetts, however—especially in summertime—it is quickly evident that despite large urbanized areas and New England's second-highest population density (after Rhode Island), much of the state is still covered with forest. This is particularly true of the central and western parts of the state, where some 85% of the land is wooded (a historic high, since colonial farmers cleared much of the land for crops and grazing). Many of these forests—over 275,000 acres—belong to the **Department of Environmental Management (DEM),** keeper of the state's public lands, which constitute the nation's sixth-largest state park system. These acres comprise little jewels like Concord's Walden Pond (yes, the one made famous by Henry David Thoreau), Purgatory Chasm, and Maudslay State Park, a landscaped riverside estate that once belonged to one of New England's wealthiest families. The DEM land also comprises paved bike paths, such as the 25-mile Cape Cod Rail Trail and the Pioneer Valley's 10-mile Norwottuck Trail, as well as networks of bikeable fire roads in places like Plymouth's Myles Standish State Forest (the state's second-largest park) and Manueal Correllus State Forest, on Martha's Vineyard. DEM's largest holdings lie in the state's western half, where panoramic ridges overlooking the Connecticut, Deerfield, and Hoosac Rivers vie with the beaches at sunset for the state's most eye-catching views. All state parks and forests—particularly those with fishing and camping—are reasonably well signposted from adjacent major roadways.

Private Lands for Public Use

Complementing DEM's parks and forests are a number of sanctuaries and conservation properties owned by private organization, most notably **the Trustees of Reservations**—perhaps the oldest land protection organization in the world. Founded in 1891 (with a charter that became the model for England's National Trust), the Trustees' mission is to acquire for public enjoyment lands of "uncommon beauty and more than usual refreshing power, just as the Public Library holds books and the Art Museum pictures." By any measure, their nearly 80 Massachusetts preserves are among the state's finest open lands, including wildlife refuges on Martha's Vineyard and Nantucket, small islands and large barrier beaches on the coast north of Boston, rocky woodlands bordering the MetroWest reaches of the Charles River, hidden waterfalls in Central Massachusetts and the Hilltowns, and flora-rich Berkshire cobbles (one of which is a National Natural Landmark). Although few TTOR properties charge admission for nonmembers, if you anticipate visiting more than a few of their beaches and historic homes, or you want a good discount on various ancillary services—including summer canoe rentals and natural history tours—you may wish to become a member. Charge is $40 for individuals, $60 for families. Send checks to The Trustees of Reservations, Membership Office, 572 Essex St., Beverly MA 01915-1530. For more information, call (978) 921-1944.

The other major conservator of nature here is the **Massachusetts Audubon Society,** whose nearly two dozen sanctuaries showcase the diversity of the state's habitats, from Wellfleet Bay's saltwater marsh, on Outer Cape Cod, to the beaver ponds and hemlock gorge of the Berkshires' Pleasant Valley, in Lenox. Nearly all the Audubon sanctuaries offer programs throughout the year, from canoe trips and after-hours stargazing to butterfly watching, reptile talks, and nature walks. Most of these are offered on weekends, but frequency increases with warm weather and demand. Advanced reservations are usually required; for current offerings, call the individual properties (listed in the following chapters) or check out the society's Web site: www.massaudubon.org. All Audubon sanctuaries charge a nominal admission to nonmembers, so here, too, you may find membership quickly pays for itself, especially if you go on a shopping binge at any of their gift shops: members get discounts on cash purchases. (Members of the national Audubon Society have no privileges with Mass Audubon. The two are wholly separate entities.) Individual membership is $30, family $35; checks for dues may be sent to Massachusetts Audubon Society, 208 South Great Rd., Lincoln MA 01773.

MASSACHUSETTS BEACH ACCESS: NO TRESPASSING

Only four of the more than twenty coastal states in the U.S. restrict shorefront property ownership to the high-tide line, thereby placing all tidal land in "public trust" (a legal arrangement dating back to the Roman Empire). Most other coastal states don't permit ownership of the *inter*tidal zone—the area between high and low tides—but do permit owners of waterfront property to build wharves and otherwise exercise "franchise rights," so long as beach users aren't impeded from passing over or under whatever structure is built.

Thanks to a 1647 colonial ordinance, enacted to promote maritime industry, only Massachusetts and Maine (which was part of Massachusetts until 1821) allow private ownership of the coast to extend clear down to the mean low water line. With over 70% of the Massachusetts coast in private hands, it should come as no surprise that you'll often encounter No Trespassing signs at both ends of nearly all public beaches.

However, that same 1647 law enshrines use-exceptions to these exclusive property rights. The public, it says, has the right to use the intertidal zone for "free fishing and fowling"; also, the public may not be prevented from freely passing by "boats or other vessels . . . to other men's houses or lands." In general, this means that you can walk across otherwise private beaches (always below the high-tide mark, usually indicated by a wrack line of organic debris) only if you're carrying a surfcasting rod or blunderbuss for bagging blackbirds. Massachusetts courts *have* upheld certain modern activities as natural derivatives of one or another of the allowable uses—sport hunting and windsurfing, for example—but many coastal towns have their own restrictions concerning both guns and sailboards, so don't get your hopes up. On the other hand, courts have been unequivocal about most other beach pastimes: the law in no way allows you to set down a towel or a chair; to stop for a picnic or sunbath; or practice beachcombing or birdwatching.

Back in the 1970s, an attempt was made to amend the colonial statute to include walking as one of legal uses of privately owned beaches, but it took 17 years to finally arrive at wording which wouldn't violate the Massachusetts Constitution. When finally passed, in 1991, the law simply said that since it would be a good idea to give the public access to the state's entire coast, the state's Department of Environmental Management has a mandate to acquire the necessary rights for trespass on the intertidal zone. In other words, the state authorized one of its agencies to dicker with landowners to let the unwashed masses take a walk by the water. Given that shoreline property tends to belong to the wealthier and more influential of the state's citizens, the execution of this mandate is an extremely contentious issue. Meanwhile, the state won't even fund publication of a guide identifying the 27% of the state's coast that's *already* supposedly accessible to everybody.

The bottom line is this: posted restrictions should be taken seriously. Ignoring them doesn't just put you at risk of arrest but also jeopardizes the entire effort to persuade beach owners that people won't abuse the right to trespass, if that right is ever granted. Someday, the amendments found on a few signs—"walkers welcome"—may become more widespread. In the meantime, if you want unfettered beachcombing, go to Virginia.

Biking

When it comes to building bike paths or enhancing existing roadways and bridges to more safely accommodate cyclists, Massachusetts trails nearly the entire nation. Tens of millions of dollars in both federal appropriations and state-authorized bonds are available, and planners across the Commonwealth have a long list of popular proposals in need of funding. Yet for some inexplicable reason, the Massachusetts Highway Department seems determined to keep bike-related projects from ever seeing the light of day—even going so far as taking control of millions of federal dollars that legally may go directly to local planning agencies, and then leaving three-quarters of it unspent. Despite such official neglect, the handful of designated bikeways and converted railroad beds around the state are thoroughly enjoyable, from Cape Cod's "Bicycle Route 1" to the Pioneer Valley's Norwottuck Rail Trail. Moreover, scores of country roads are simply perfect for exploration by cyclists, from 100-kilometer "century" rides through Central Massachusetts to more modest touring loops around the Berkshires. You'll find several suggestions in the following chapters, but there's no substitute for such touring-bike guides as Lewis Cuyler's *Bike Rides in the Berkshire Hills,* Nancy Jane's *Bicycle Touring in the Pioneer Valley,* or the Pioneer Valley Planning Commission's *Touring Jacob's Ladder by Bicycle or Car.*

Mountain bikers will find plenty of parks and other off-roads areas catering to their crazy, fat-tire appetites, but guidebooks such as Paul Angiolillo's *Mountain Biking Southern New England* (part of Falcon Guides' national series) and Robert Morse's *25 Mountain Bike Tours in Massachusetts,* one of many fine guides published by Vermont's Backcountry Press, are still highly recommended additions to your pack. All these titles are available in various spots around the state, or you can consult the Booklist for specific publishing data.

Beaches

Free, public, warm-weather swimming is a rarity in Massachusetts. In summer (June through early September), most bodies of water—either fresh or salt—are restricted to local residents and summer renters or saddled with stiff parking fees. Pedestrians and cyclists are usually exempted from parking fees, but not always: the beaches of the Cape Cod National Seashore, for example, charge everyone who enters during daylight hours all summer. About the only place where public beaches *are* free and unrestricted is offshore: the Boston Harbor Islands, Martha's Vineyard, and Nantucket. Needless to say, while beaches at all three are free, the boats to reach them are not.

ACCOMMODATIONS AND FOOD

LODGING OPTIONS

Not all the superlatives applicable to Massachusetts are favorable. Unfortunately for overnight visitors, the state is the nation's third-most-expensive in terms of restaurants and accommodations, according to AAA's annual survey of American vacation costs. Boston can take a good chunk of the blame for this ranking—its average room rate is second-highest in the nation. Private baths, generous breakfasts, large rooms, fireplaces, and proximity to water are all extras. Any one of them, as a rule, will add about 25% to the rate for your basic four walls and a mattress—and a combination of several can quickly spike the price from $95 to $180. In other words, you face this dilemma: affordable, tasteful, or indulgent—pick *one.* In this book, exceptions—mostly among B&Bs rather than motels—are noted where they exist. It should go without saying that places with reputations for good value have darned low vacancy rates, so, you need to plan ahead a little if you want to try to save a little.

Wheelchair travelers and anyone unable to negotiate stairs should never assume—ever—that anything in Massachusetts called a motel or inn (even in major resort areas) is in compliance with Americans with Disabilities Act guidelines for accessibility. Major national chains all have fully accessible rooms, but the situation is very different in smaller places. It's easy to find out who does comply, though: order a copy of the *Massachusetts Getaway Guide* from the Massachusetts Office of Travel & Tourism, tel. (800) 447-MASS. Its accommodations listings identify accessibility.

Camping

While it's true that you'll routinely pay more for rooms in the state's hotels, inns, and B&Bs than you would for a beachside condo in Kauai, when it comes to state-owned campgrounds Massachusetts can't be beat. Camping options among the 33 parks that offer it range from hike-in wilderness sites in Mount Washington State Forest and wood-stove-equipped rustic lakeside cabins at Savoy Mountain (both in the Berkshires), to RV hookups by the score at Scusset Beach, on the Cape Cod Canal. For $10 or less, these are some of the cheapest moonlit sleeping spots in the nation—and some are darned nice, too. (There are also some real clunkers, of course; we offer warnings where appropriate.) The operating seasons at many state campgrounds limited to mid-May to Columbus Day, although campgrounds in southeastern Massachusetts and on Cape Cod tend to open a month earlier, and a handful of parks allow self-contained vehicles (RVs with septage and gray-water holding tanks) any time of year. Nearly all the wilderness campsites scattered around the state are likewise available year-round (and free). The handful of $8-10 cabins, in each of two forests in the western half of the state, are available year-round but are so popular that they require both advance reservations and minimum stays.

More family-oriented camping is also available at numerous private campgrounds, which are often equipped with recreation and game rooms, playgrounds, convenience stores, RV hookups, and laundry facilities. Send for your free annual statewide directory from the Massachusetts Association of Campground Owners, P.O. Box 548, Scituate MA 02066, tel. (781) 544-3475.

Hostels and Ys

Except for a few rustic cabins in public and private campgrounds, hostels are the only budget accommodations in Massachusetts that don't require sleeping outdoors. Fewer than a dozen exist statewide, including several small home hostels outside of Boston and a handful of seasonal properties on Cape Cod and the Is-

lands. Only three hostels stay open year-round: Boston's two, plus Bunk & Bagel in Plymouth, a modest backpacker's accommodation south of Boston. This last is one of the several hostels independent of any national or international affiliations; the rest are all branches of Hostelling International (formerly known in this country as American Youth Hostels), which means they offer discounts to HI members from around the world. (Membership can be purchased at any HI hostel in Massachusetts.) The organization's new identity should underscore the fact that hostels are not just for kids: besides the stereotypical bunk beds in gender-segregated dorm rooms, many offer private rooms for couples and families. For a complete guide to HI affiliates in Massachusetts and the rest of North America, contact HI's American headquarters: tel. (202) 783-6161, e-mail hiayhserve@hiayh.org, or visit its Web site at www.hiayh.org.

Ys can offer clean, safe, inexpensive alternatives to pricey city motels. Both the YMCA and the YWCA have nationwide strings of "residence" properties with no-frills rooms at low cost; the Massachusetts Ys are in Boston and Springfield. *The Y's Way,* a directory of about 40 YMCAs offering lodging in North America and overseas, is available free by calling (800) USA-YMCA. A similar guide to YWCAs may be obtained by calling (212) 614-2700.

Bed and Breakfasts

There's plenty of charm in Massachusetts' B&Bs, but there are also several factors to keep in mind. For example, caveat emptor about booking service reservation fees, single-night surcharges (in high-traffic areas, expect to encounter a discouraging trend toward minimum-stay requirements in high season), credit card surcharges, and cancellation fees. Deposits are almost always required by both services and individual properties, and you should take those cancellation policies seriously—they aren't just for show. (Thankfully, the practice of adding surcharges to the bill if you don't vacate your room by some ungodly early hour hasn't made it this far east yet—and hopefully never will.)

When comparing prices, keep in mind that places with three rooms or fewer are not required to charge tax, so you save some of what you'd pay at larger establishments.

You won't find many places truly overlooking the waves on Massachusetts' coast, because those places get washed away in storms. If you're looking for a room whose windows get speckled with salt spray, look to places on the firm granite ledges of the North Shore. Oodles of places on Cape Cod and the Islands are, however, within *eyeshot* of water. A few places also have "private beaches"—but on the islands this usually means something about the size of a sandbox, and on the Cape they're usually attached to large Daytona Beach-style motels catering to large families.

If there is a trend as disturbing as the move away from accepting single-night reservations, it's the shift away from full breakfasts toward boxed cereal and Thermos coffee. Purists who want to be sure they're getting both bed *and* breakfast must be sure to ask—nothing in this niche of the hospitality industry can be taken for granted anymore. If it's important to you, inquire closely, too, about what is really meant by such terms as "hearty" or "gourmet continental"; personally, I think a continental breakfast is still skimpy even if I have the whole jar of shredded wheat and basket of mix-and-bake muffins to myself.

Diabetics and other travelers with special needs will find most traditional owner-operated B&Bs willing to handle special breakfast requests if you give them clear guidance. For anyone looking for a kosher B&B, the choice is easy: the Four Seasons B&B, in the Boston suburb of Newton, tel. (617) 928-1128; it's the only one in the state (at $70 d, including a full homemade breakfast, it's also a very good value).

The increasingly common self-styled "B&B inn," which pretends to represent the best of both worlds, may prove less tractable to menu modifications—especially those run by seasonal staff who haven't quite got the hang of the concept of "customer satisfaction."

Nothing substitutes for planning ahead when it comes to landing a room where and when you want it, but don't give up on last-minute luck—there's *always* a cancellation someplace, and with patience and a bit of phone work, you may just find it. (*Affording* it is another matter.)

Motels and Hotels

Most of the major chains are represented in Massachusetts, but you'll also find independent places—particularly in the traditional resort areas, along the coast and Cape, on the islands, and in the Berkshires. Don't use appearance as gauge of price: some of those pocket-sized New Deal-era bungalows and dreary-looking little motel courts straight out of *Key Largo* are anything but cheap (the high prices keep the riffraff away). Some of these places have had the same owners and the same regular customers since Nixon was president. McGovern voters, single-sex couples, and anyone young enough to think nose rings are cool may be met with vague suspicion upon check-in, but don't take it personally—the ice will thaw and downright gracious hospitality blossom forth if you judiciously refrain from trashing your room, playing hip-hop tapes at top volume in the wee hours, or otherwise enacting their worst nightmares.

Splurges

Besides Boston's luxury-priced hotels, Massachusetts' most popular vacation destinations (Cape Cod, the Islands, and the Berkshires) have their share of sumptuous B&B inns and full-scale resorts, too, ready to swaddle you in service and comfort. If you consider a few hundred dollars a night reasonable, you may also want to take a look at the Berkshires' castle-like Blantyre (the state's only member of the prestigious Relais & Chateaux Hotels). Or consider a retreat to Blantyre's neighbor, Canyon Ranch, a full-service, all-inclusive spa consistently voted by readers of *Condé Nast Traveler* as one of the world's best places to stay.

FOOD AND DRINK

Happily for visiting food mavens, Massachusetts cookery over the past couple of decades has embraced salutary influences—of, among others, local resident Julia Child—raising awareness for good food throughout the state and firmly putting to rest comparisons to the infamous cuisine of New England's namesake across the Atlantic. Most recently, an improving economy and a gigantic yuppie demographic have brought a major restaurant revival to Boston and its suburbs, making it a candidate for the same laurels worn by San Francisco, New Orleans, Chicago, Los Angeles, and other great restaurant cities. Good chefs are becoming known by name here, with bulletins about their careers regularly appearing in newspaper food columns and Usenet chat groups.

Neither is the rest of the state entirely immune: on the western end, century-old ties to Manhattan's social and artistic elite ensures that Berkshire restaurateurs must routinely satisfy palates accustomed to New York's finest dining. The same is true of Martha's Vineyard, another playground for Big Apple movers and shakers.

Admittedly, mediocre meals are by no means an endangered species (Cape Cod, Plymouth, and parts of Central Massachusetts swim in them), and nearly all the national fast food chains or their local imitators are invariably only as far away as the next strip mall, interstate rest stop, or family resort. But if you aren't indifferent to what you eat, you won't have to look very far to find stellar food, whether in trendy, chef-owned urban bistros that draw customers from clear across town lines (the true measure of success among parochial Bay Staters), homey neighborhood holes in the wall in which natural-born cooks hold court, or, at its most elemental, in the fields and orchards of you-pick farms.

From Land and Sea

Massachusetts is no California, but the movement epitomized by California cuisine, with its firm emphasis on super-fresh regionally-grown ingredients, is one that's strongly evident among the better restaurants around the state. Enjoying meals prepared from the cornucopia of Massachusetts farms usually (but not always) carries a premium price, since small-scale and organic farmers with short growing seasons can't hope to compete in price with America's agribusiness giants. If getting a taste of New England is important to you, come during the summer or fall and visit local farmstands, or come during spring thaw and visit a sugar shack for a pancake breakfast doused in fresh, 100% maple syrup. Or leave room on a credit card for a small splurge at the kind of restaurant which respectfully pays homage on every plate to those of our neighbors who have chosen to keep farming and dairying alive.

Descriptions of such establishments are sprinkled throughout the pages that follow, particularly in the chapters for Greater Boston, the

Bearskin Neck seafood-in-the-rough menu boasts that everything can be "packed to travel"

Islands, and the Berkshires. An incomplete set of suggestions from the rest of the book would include Cafe Beaujolais and Jan's Encore, north of Boston; La Boniche, in the MetroWest region; Worden's, in Southeastern Massachusetts; Painter's, on Cape Cod; Sienna, in the Pioneer Valley; and the Green Emporium, in the Hilltowns.

Of course, most out-of-state visitors to Massachusetts come looking for seafood. It's one expectation that's easily met, from humble Essex clam shacks (birthplace of the fried clam) and family-friendly Cape Cod chowder houses to the many sushi bars and upscale restaurants highlighting exotic or underutilized fish species in Boston. Besides luscious quahog clams, fresh Massachusetts oysters, mussels, scallops, lobster, monkfish, bluefish, striped bass, shad, yellowtail flounder, bluefin tuna, and, yes, even cod are all worth the tariff on local menus. (Scrod, it should be noted, isn't actually a species of fish—it's a catchall term at the Boston fish auction for baby cod, haddock, and any other flaky white-flesh fish under 2.5 pounds in weight.)

Do not, however, fall into the common trap of assuming that waterfront restaurants are the best places to dine on the bounty of the sea: some of the finest seafood meals to be had in the state are hours from any coastline. Given that Massachusetts is a net *importer* of seafood (overfishing has caused offshore fisheries to collapse, rendering numerous species commercially extinct), you may also be disappointed to learn that even in seaside towns with local fishing fleets, there are restaurants whose scallops are more likely flash-frozen and then shipped from Asia or Iceland than they are to have come out of the water off Martha's Vineyard—and whose delicious-sounding special salmon is probably raised on the same aquaculture farm up in Maine that express-ships its product to Atlanta and Chicago. But don't worry—plenty of places cited in the following chapters *do* serve tonight something caught this morning by that picturesque boat at the end of the working pier.

Besides, in this age of overnight cargo, don't let my caveats obscure the more relevant fact that Massachusetts draws on such a deep *tradition* of seafood preparation that you could give many of our chefs a frozen fish stick and they'd still make something so wonderful and tasty of it that you'd never know or care what it looked like or where it came from before ending up on your fork.

Specialties of the House

Like Southern barbecue, Southwest chili, or the smoked fish of the Pacific Northwest, Massachusetts has its own set of recipes and restaurant specialties which, while not necessarily unique to the state or the region, are definitely idiomatic. Lobster rolls, for example. A basic commodity at beachfront concession stands and other indigenous fast-food stalls, these resemble tuna salad served on a hot dog bun, except that lobster meat is used in place of the tuna. Clam chowder is equally ubiquitous, and though it's never, ever made with tomatoes (that's . . . Manhattan's recipe), diligent chowderheads will find almost no two versions alike. Middlebrow theme restaurants that come in from outside the region, like the Elephant and Castle in downtown Boston,

often mistakenly assume that New England clam chowder should have the texture of wallpaper paste, but don't be fooled: proper "chowda" never requires a spackling knife. Cod cakes have been getting a boost from creative city chefs who dress them with garlicky aiolis, peppery Asian spices, or other multicultural exotica—but at their most traditional, these deep-fried patties of minced white fish are served for breakfast.

Roast beef sandwiches are a staple of eastern Massachusetts. They're all offered with names suggesting that these artery-filling alternatives to your billionth-served burger are a gift of the state's Irish population. Speaking of sandwiches, there isn't a town in the realm that doesn't seem to have a pizza and sub take-out joint within its borders, usually run by Greeks. Though the franchising of Subway sandwich shops has diluted regional differences in food terminology, outside of Boston subs are still usually called "grinders," as they are in New Hampshire and Rhode Island (it's a "hero" to New Yorkers, a "hoagie" to Philadelphians).

Indian pudding (a cornmeal and molasses concoction) and Grape-Nut custard aren't as common as they used to be, but you'll still find them on diner menus here more often than elsewhere in the country. Saltwater taffy and fudge are summertime standards in nearly all the state's coastal resorts, and super-premium ice cream, though found nationwide, achieves perfection at summer dairy stands and college-town ice cream shops around the state. If you want a milkshake from any of these places, order a "frappe" (rhymes with trap) or you'll get nothing more than milk and flavored syrup.

Finally, chocolate lovers will be gratified to learn that Massachusetts has a serious addiction to sinfully rich chocolate desserts. The scarce few who do resist the chocolate hegemony are almost all on Cape Cod. Pie aficionados, on the other hand, had best resign themselves to doing without: despite the wonderful apples and berries grown in the region, the vast majority of the state's pastry chefs leave pie-making to the folks in Maine and the Midwest.

Ethnic

Though red-sauce Italian and Americanized Chinese are Massachusetts' most common ethnic foods, the state's polyglot history of immigration has provided it with a delectable variety of ethnic restaurants. Not surprisingly, Boston leads the pack in terms of its sheer United Nations roll-call of cuisines: Afghan, Armenian, Brazilian, Cajun, Caribbean, Chinese (including Buddhist and glatt kosher), Cuban, Dominican, Eastern European, Ethiopian, French, Greek, Indian (north and south), Irish, Israeli, Italian, Japanese, Jewish, Korean, Lebanese, Malaysian, Mexican, North African, Persian, Peruvian, Portuguese, Russian, Spanish, Thai, Turkish, and Vietnamese are all represented—some more strongly than others. Subsets of this line-up are found in suburbs and college communities throughout Massachusetts—Thai food in particular seems destined for ubiquity—although where newcomers to these shores have settled in large numbers, certain local differences inevitably arise. The Portuguese who dominate the fishing industry, for instance, have made Gloucester, New Bedford, Fall River, and Provincetown the best places to go for a taste of their robust seafood stews, soups, and spicy sausages. Large Latino populations have injected the cities of Springfield and Lawrence with doses of cheap eats Puerto Rican and Dominican style. And one of the nation's largest communities of Southeast Asians has brought Lowell the gift of authentic Cambodian and Laotian food.

Drinking

Massachusetts is enjoying a surge in the popularity of wineries (here specializing in fruit wines) and, along with much of the rest of the country, microbreweries and brewpubs.

Minimum legal drinking age in the state is 21. Happy hours are illegal, and bars close at 2 a.m. or earlier. Hard alcohol, beer, and wine are sold in package liquor ("packy") stores. Supermarkets can't sell liquor, and any given market chain may sell beer and wine in only as many as three of its stores statewide. No package alcohol, beer, or wine is sold on Sundays except at bonded wineries (although the legislature has taken to granting a holiday exemption to this old blue law in the month of December).

TRANSPORTATION

GETTING THERE

By Air

Logan International Airport, in Boston, is the major point of entry into New England for commercial airline passengers. With no single carrier dominating, there is a fair amount of competition. But don't assume that's true for all routes. Budget carrier Southwest Airlines now flies into T.F. Green airport, in neighboring Providence, Rhode Island, so selected fares within markets they serve may be hundreds of dollars cheaper if you choose Providence over Boston (especially if you're looking for flights and don't have the 14 or 21 days usually required to get supersaver fares—since Southwest doesn't require such extended preplanning to take advantage of their low fares). T.F. Green is a $13.50 express bus ride away from Boston via Bonanza Bus Lines, tel. (401) 751-8800. Other regional airports—Albany, New York; Bradley International (Hartford, Connecticut/Springfield); Manchester, New Hampshire; and Worcester, west of Boston—may also be sufficiently close to wherever you're trying to go in Massachusetts (or offer significantly lower rental car rates) that any premium in airfare is more than compensated by ground transportation savings. The bottom line is this: have your travel agent or airline sale representative check across state lines.

Neither should you overlook the potential savings offered by small, cut-rate, no-frills regional carriers you might not have heard of. These include AirTran, with cheap direct flights to Orlando, Atlanta, Washington, Philadelphia, and Allentown; Eastwind, serving secondary airports in New Jersey and the Carolinas; Kiwi International Airlines, providing budget flights to Boston from all along the East Coast, Puerto Rico, Chicago, and even Las Vegas; Midwest Express, connecting to numerous cities west of the Great Lakes via a Milwaukee hub; and Spirit, a low-cost airline connecting Boston with Atlantic City, Myrtle Beach, and Florida. Continental Connection (Colgan Air), Comair, and Business Express are among the commuter air-

AIRLINE TOLL-FREE PHONE NUMBERS

DOMESTIC

AirTran, (800) 247-8726, www.airtran.com

America West, tel. (800) 235-9292, www.americawest.com

American Airlines/American Eagle, tel. (800) 433-7300, www.americanair.com

Business Express/Delta Connection, tel. (800) 345-3400

Cape Air, tel. (800) 352-0714, www.capeair.com

Colgan Air/Continental Connection, tel. (800) 272-5488

Comair, tel. (800) 354-9822, www.fly-comair.com

Continental/Continental Express, tel. (800) 525-0280, www.flycontinental.com

Delta Air Lines/Delta Express/Delta Shuttle (to LaGuardia, NY), tel. (800) 221-1212, www.delta-air.com

Eastwind Airlines, tel. (800) 644-3592, www.eastwindairlines.com

Frontier Airlines, tel. (800) 432-1359, www.frontierairlines.com

Kiwi Air, tel. (800) 538-5494, www.jetkiwi.com

Midway Airlines, tel. (800) 446-4392, www.midwayair.com

Midwest Express, tel. (800) 452-2022, www.midwestexpress.com

National Air, tel. (800) 248-9538

Northwest/NW Airlink, tel. (800) 225-2525, www.nwa.com

PanAm, tel. (800) 359-7262, www.carnivalair.com

Southwest Airlines, tel. (800) 435-9792, www.iflyswa.com

Spirit Airlines, tel. (800) 772-7117

TWA, tel. (800) 221-2000, www.twa.com

United/United Express, tel. (800) 241-6522, www.ual.com

USAirways/USAirways Express/USAirways Shuttle (to LaGuardia, NY), tel. (800) 428-4322, www.usairways.com

INTERNATIONAL

Aer Lingus, tel. (800) 223-6537, www.aerlingus.ie

Air Atlantic/Canada Air, tel. (800) 426-7000, www.airatlantic.com

Air Canada/Air Alliance/Air Nova, tel. (800) 776-3000, www.aircanada.ca

Alitalia, tel. (800) 223-5730, www.alitalia.com/english

American Trans Air, tel. (800) 225-2995

British Airways, tel. (800) 247-9297, www.british-airways.com

Icelandair, tel. (800) 223-5500, www.icelandair.is

KLM, tel. (800) 374-7747, www.klm.nl

Korean Air, tel. (800) 438-5000, www.koreanair.com

Lufthansa, tel. (800) 645-3880, www.lufthansa.com

Olympic, tel. (800) 223-1226, agn.hol.gr/info/olympic1.htm

Sabena, tel. (800) 955-2000, www.sabena.com

SwissAir, tel. (800) 221-4750, www.swissair.com

TAP Air Portugal, tel. (800) 221-7370, www.tap-airportugal.de

Virgin Atlantic Airways, tel. (800) 862-8621, www.fly.virgin.com

---

lines that feed passengers to Boston from small cities and towns throughout the Northeast; all three have code-sharing arrangements with major national carriers. Even Pan Am has been resurrected, its venerable old livery now adorning the fuselages of jets shuttling between Boston and New York.

By Rail

Up until very recently, train travel in the Northeast, as in much of the country, was guaranteed to give migraines to the sort of traveler who asks, "Are we there yet?" minutes after sitting down. But the increasingly sclerotic condition of roads and airports has made railroad time competitive over

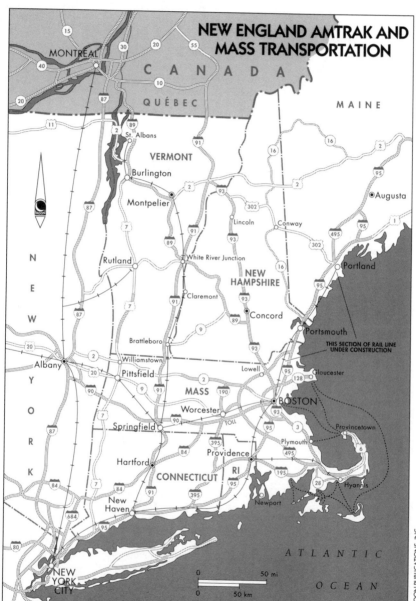

NEW ENGLAND AMTRAK AND MASS TRANSPORTATION

© MOON PUBLICATIONS, INC.

certain routes—even without factoring in the convenience of not worrying about traffic or parking or whether the airport cabbie speaks a language you recognize. Of course, there's no getting around the fact that trains *feel* slow, so if you can't relax and enjoy a book, a nap, the scenery, or the savings, don't call Amtrak.

Boston and southeastern Massachusetts are served from the south by Amtrak's coastal line through Rhode Island, Connecticut, and New York City. From the west, Boston and central and western Massachusetts are connected through Albany to Buffalo and Chicago. There's also a short Amtrak line to Boston from Portland, Maine, and southern New Hampshire. Springfield and the Pioneer Valley are also linked by passenger service from White River Junction, Vermont, and Claremont, New Hampshire, to New Haven, Connecticut, and onward to New York City.

If you *do* choose the train and will be traveling the always-crowded New York-Boston route, consider springing for a seat in the club car—it's roomier and more relaxing than the regular coaches, and handier to a ready flow of libation. And try to avoid the infamous "Roach Coaches," the trains that make the coastal-route

run at either end of prep school vacations (last weeks of August, January, and May, and mid-December), lest your quiet contemplation of the austere Connecticut seashore be shattered by hordes of rambunctious Manhattan adolescents heading to or from prestigious boarding schools.

By Bus
No matter where you're coming from in the U.S. or Canada, you can reach most regions of Massachusetts using a major interstate bus company, such as Trailways, or regional players, such as Vermont Transit or Rhode Island-based Bonanza Bus Lines. Consult the "Getting There" section within each destination chapter to find out who to call for service to that region.

One offbeat option is **Green Tortoise,** an outfit whose rolling stock consists of vintage Greyhound-type buses refitted with futon-covered benches arranged to create a couple of discreen conversation/social interaction areas. By night, the futons unfold to create a communal sleeping area where passengers can lay down sleep sacks (there are also Pullman-style beds suspended from the roof and walls). While most of Green Tortoise's passengers tend to be young, single, and on a budget, anyone who

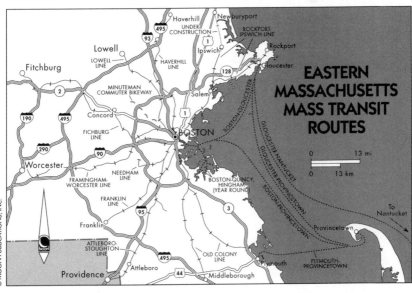

EASTERN MASSACHUSETTS MASS TRANSIT ROUTES

0   13 mi
0   13 km

To Nantucket

can appreciate the communal quarters, spontaneous music jams, and the driver's uncanny skill at ferreting out swimming holes should enjoy these cross-country adventures. Buses bound for Boston depart from San Francisco about a dozen times April–Sept., with stops in Chicago and New York along the way. For reservations (advisable at least a month in advance) call toll-free (800) 227-4766.

A second low-cost seasonal alternative is the **East Coast Explorer,** tel. (800) 610-2680 or (718) 694-9667, shuttling between Boston and New York City twice a week spring through fall, with additional connections from Washington, D.C. via Pennsylvania's Amish country. East Coast's 14-passenger vans are not for anyone in a hurry, though—as the name implies, they meander along back roads, stop at a half-dozen or so interesting places, and generally do their best to deliver you happy and relaxed after a day of sociable traveling. They do all this for a price only a few bucks higher than the regular national bus companies charge for a boring four or five hours on interstates.

GETTING AROUND

Driving—Pros, Cons, and Regulations
Having a car at your disposal is admittedly a great convenience in much of Massachusetts, and it's essential for reaching the state's nooks and crannies. In Boston, quite the opposite holds true: a car is an expensive liability for most tourists, wholly unnecessary for getting around the city and very expensive to park. The Greater Boston chapter explains the ins and outs of city tranportation, and the accommodations listings tell you which establishments

offer free or inexpensive parking—an important consideration for price-sensitive comparison shoppers.

On most interstates and some state highways within Massachusetts, the speed limit is 65 mph; around metropolitan Boston, it's 55 mph. You'll soon see—from traffic in most areas—that these are polite suggestions more than true limits. Still, don't push it—when the selective dragnet finally picks you, the fines will make you wince. Also, don't forget to buckle up (it's the law). And don't even *think* of drinking and driving—driving while intoxicated entails automatic license suspension.

Speeding tickets may be paid by phone with a call to the Registry of Motor Vehicles' **Customer Phone Information Center,** tel. (617) 351-4500; have the citation number and a valid credit card handy. You can also pay over the Internet, at www.state.ma.us/rmv. Treating tickets as souvenirs—i.e., not to be taken seriously once you're safely back home or across the border—is inadvisable, since Massachusetts shares outstanding ticket data with many states and several Canadian provinces.

Transit Alternatives
Massachusetts is fairly well served by a variety of land and sea alternatives to private autos. Options include commuter rail service, commuter ferries, summer day-trip ferries, island ferries, intercity bus lines, public buses, subways, and tourist park-and-ride trolleys. Boston and its suburbs are the most efficiently interconnected, albeit in a predominantly radial pattern that often requires a trip between outlying destinations to connect through downtown. Getting to and around each region is thoroughly detailed within the chapters themselves.

INFORMATION AND SERVICES

Maps
Massachusetts is like one of those suspicious foreign nations in which accurate cartographic information is kept under lock and key—the better to foil the treasonous plots of enemies of the state. For getting to and from major destinations via numbered state and federal highways, the free map available at MassPike information

booths is sufficient. For more detailed coverage of local roads, most existing maps are flawed. If you really intend to explore plenty of side and back roads, you may come across such navigational challenges as washed-out bridges, reconfigured intersections, and renamed streets unaccounted for by commercial cartographers. If you're a stickler for accuracy, consider forearming yourself with the series of combination bicycle and road maps/B&B guides from Rubel BikeMaps. Look for them in Massachusetts at well-stocked bookstores (and many bike shops), have your local bookstore order them through MapLink, or order them for them yourself from P.O. Box 1035, Cambridge MA 02140 (four maps cover Cape Cod, Eastern, Central, and Western Massachusetts; cost is $5.25 each, postpaid).

HEALTH AND SAFETY

No part of Massachusetts is so remote that it isn't within range of emergency medical services, so you can dial 911 with confidence.

Prescriptions
If you use any sort of prescription medication, be sure to bring the *medicine* (not the prescription) when you come to the state. Massachusetts pharmacists are prohibited from refilling any prescription from out of state.

Tick-Borne Diseases
Massachusetts may not boast exotic dangers like tarantulas or green mambas, and even its once-widespread timber rattlers have all but vanished from the state's forests. But the state *is* home to both the bloodsucking wood or dog tick and the more notorious deer tick, *Ixodes dammini,* which, as its Latin name suggests, is a little damn thing—no bigger than the period at the end of this sentence. Though indigenous throughout the state, these ticks are most common in eastern Massachusetts, Cape Cod, and the Islands.

To avoid getting bitten by a tick, wear a hat and light-colored clothes with long sleeves and legs that may be tucked into socks. Commercial tick repellent is also advisable. Avoid favorite tick habitats such as tall grasses and the edges of woods and meadows (they drop out of trees when detecting movement). If you do find a tick on yourself, there's still no reason for panic, but early removal dramatically improves chances for avoiding illness (it usually takes a day or two for any infectious agents to be transmitted to the host). The deer tick's larval stage, which it reaches in July and August, is when it is be-

lieved to be *most* capable of passing on bacteria or parasites, but it is infectious throughout its life.

Above all, use the proper removal technique (described by Dirk Schroeder in Moon's *Staying Healthy in Asia, Africa, and Latin America*): if it isn't visibly walking and can't be lightly brushed away, use tweezers to grasp the tick's head parts as close to your skin as possible and apply slow steady traction. (Don't squeeze—you don't want its saliva in your skin.) Don't attempt to get ticks out of your skin by burning them or coating them with anything like nail polish or petroleum jelly. If you remove a tick before it has been attached for more than 24 hours, you greatly reduce your risk of infection. After you've removed the tick, wash the bite with soap and clean water, and watch for signs of infection over the following days.

Precautions against tick bites are advisable because of the diseases they can transmit to their hosts. Dog ticks carry Rocky Mountain spotted fever, while deer ticks have been identified as carriers of Lyme disease, human babesiosis, and human granulocytic ehrlichiosis (HGE). None of these maladies is serious if treated early and properly, since all are caused by either bacteria or microscopic parasites susceptible to antibiotics.

Lyme disease produces a distinctive concentric-ringed rash—like a tiny bull's-eye—around the point of infection and such flu-like symptoms as fever, chills, aches, fatigue, and headaches. These first-stage indicators may not appear for up to a couple weeks after a bite. As the disease progresses, it affects muscles, joints, the heart, and the nervous system, ultimately attacking the brain and producing Alzheimer-like conditions. Babesiosis is a parasite that attacks the red blood cells much like malaria, with similar symptoms and results: fever, chills, swollen liver and spleen, and dangerously depressed red blood cell count. HGE is the latest addition to the deer tick's arsenal, a potential immune system suppressant with flu-like symptoms.

Personal Safety
Most casual travelers to Massachusetts will never have to worry about making headlines as victims of gang wars, mafia crossfire, or serial killing sprees. Neither should you be unduly

anxious about coming to visit the big, bad city. Boston may be big, but it really isn't all that bad. Although Seattle may be able to boast less violence, Boston does have a lower homicide rate than Kansas City, Missouri; Nashville, Tennessee; Charlotte, North Carolina; Jacksonville, Florida; Oklahoma City, Oklahoma; Denver, Colorado; and half a dozen other U.S. urban areas of comparable size. (New Orleans, with nearly the same population, has about *six times* as many murders annually as Boston. *Laissez les bon temps roulez,* indeed.) For what the statistics are worth, Boston is even safer than parts of Cape Cod.

On the other hand, according to the makers of Kryptonite locks, Boston ranks second—after only Chicago—for number of bicycle thefts. And over 10,000 cars are stolen in an average year here. So if you are looking for something to be worried about, let it be your wheels.

MONEY AND BANKING

Foreign Exchange

Don't take it personally, but if you're traveling from abroad, you'll find Americans tend to prefer US dollars or traveler's checks in dollar denominations. Bring these with you and you'll save yourself the hassle of shopping for the best exchange rates—or even finding a place willing to perform exchanges in the first place. If you have to choose between cash and traveler's checks, the security-conscious tourist will opt for the checks. True to the vendors' claims, almost everyone but taxi drivers will treat them like cash.

Your next-best strategy is to take care of your exchange needs in the financial hub of Boston. Keep in mind that despite competition among the city's banks and brokers, there's enough range in rates and fees to make shopping around worth a few local phone calls. (Phone numbers,

addresses, and fees are listed in the Boston chapter in the Special Topic, Foreign Exchange Brokers) Outside the metro area, the simplicity of the transaction diminishes rapidly. If Boston isn't in your travel plans, learn to recognize the Bank-Boston logo—it's the state's only bank chain whose every office handles on-the-spot foreign exchange of major international currencies at rates identical to their airport or downtown Boston locations. (Strictly speaking, any bank in the state can do exchanges—if you've got two weeks to wait while your drachmas are sent to the Federal Reserve via expensive messenger turtles.) You'll find that only the most luxurious hotels offer immediate foreign exchange—and, even with competition within walking distance, you will pay dearly for the privilege of trading pesos and pounds for portraits of dead American presidents.

Another option is automatic teller machines (ATMs). These are more commonplace and convenient than banks and permit you to make dollar cash advances against your VISA or MasterCard—or to make withdrawals from your home bank account if you carry a Cirrus- or Plus-affiliated debit card.

Be aware that different brands of traveler's checks are *not* treated equal if they're in the denominations of your own national currency. Bank-Boston and the Thomas Cook Foreign Exchange office in Boston will accept all major brands, but American Express representatives will only cash their own. Foreign-denominated checks are cashed for free only by local affiliates of the issuer—and only AmEx has a large number of such offices outside of Greater Boston. (By the way, Thomas Cook Travel and Thomas Cook Foreign Exchange are related but wholly distinct entities: although the distinction is blurred by the fact that in other parts of the country Cook Exchange facilities are inside Cook Travel storefronts, American banking regulations prohibit Cook Travel from taking your foreign currency or checks—although their many offices certainly

Massachusetts Bay coins

can help expedite the paperwork if you need emergency assistance with replacing lost or stolen Thomas Cook travelers checks.)

ATMs

Destination chapters note specific ATM locations where necessary (e.g., if obscure), and any unusual absences of the machines. Otherwise, you may assume some sort of ATM will be self-evident in the vicinity of listed attractions and restaurants. The practice of adding a surcharge for users who don't hold accounts with a given ATM's proprietary bank has cropped up in recent years, notably at machines owned by Compass Bank on Martha's Vineyard and Cape Cod. By the time you read this, it may also have spread—the owner of New England's largest ATM network proprietor, BankBoston, has made unappreciative noises about the volume of cash it dishes out to competitors' customers. Machines that apply these charges carry notices to that effect, so at least you needn't worry about being charged unknowingly.

COMMUNICATIONS AND MEASUREMENTS

Mail

The US Postal Service is not hard to find or use, although in some hinterlands and rural areas you'll find their services at the local general store.

Telecommunications

All public pay phones around the state are not alike. Many belong to third-party service providers, and rates for making collect or direct-dial calling-card calls on these phones are not always comparable or even competitive. If a pay phone doesn't carry a brand name you recognize, use an access code to reach your own trusted long-distance carrier or you'll likely be billed for the equivalent of a conference call to the Moon. As an alternative to collect calling, buy a prepaid long-distance phone card. These are now sold by post offices and convenience stores throughout the state (although most often in urban areas). In the Boston area, you can even find them at some ATMs.

Urban convenience stores and rural general stores are also often able to handle outgoing faxes, although if you want the most experienced and reliable fax capabilities, look for a copy shop. Many of these—again mostly in urban areas—are also entering the on-line world of public e-mail access. (Greater Boston now also boasts a number of cybercafes offering this service.)

Measurements

Except for some beverage containers and nutritional information labels, the metric system is just about nonexistent in Massachusetts. For help when you need it, consult the conversion table at the back of this book.

COURTESY OF BOSTON PUBLIC LIBRARY, PRINT DEPT.

GREATER BOSTON

Tomorrow night I appear before a Boston audience—4,000 critics.
—MARK TWAIN,
in a letter to his sister

Boston has been the setting for so much American history that every block seems layered with people and events straight out of the textbooks: wharves where angry colonists dumped British tea into the harbor, pulpits from which abolitionists lambasted slavery, a plaque denoting Alexander Graham Bell's workshop, the bar that inspired television's most famous watering hole. Steeped in such a heady brew, Boston understandably lapses every so often into tipsy braggadocio. Whether the "Autocrat at the Breakfast Table," Oliver Wendell Holmes, had his tongue in his cheek when he called Boston's State House "the Hub of the solar system," the city promptly adopted the nickname for itself and has worn it without irony ever since. The Hub it is, and shall remain—especially if there's a New Yorker or, worse, Yankees fan within earshot.

The rough side of history's mantle is a mulish aversion to change. This is perhaps a legacy of the founding Puritans, who cherished status quo

with as much ferocity and litigation as any modern NIMBY activist (although the Puritans pilloried their opponents in irons instead of print). Boston's provincialism has been satirized at least since Edgar Allan Poe nicknamed the city "Frogpondium," but unless you try producing experimental theater or applying for a late-night entertainment license, you probably won't even notice.

Far more obvious to casual visitors are the city's students—more than 200,000 of them, attending 60 colleges, universities, and seminaries in the metro area, supposedly a higher concentration than anyplace else on the planet. Collectively, they justify another of Boston's sobriquets—"Athens of America." They also lend a great varsity youthfulness to city shopping, nightlife, and personal ads.

For anyone who doesn't have homework due or a thesis to write, Boston also offers world-class museums, top-notch performing arts, and three major-league sports franchises.

Block after block of neoclassical architecture and the intimacy of historic buildings preserved amid imposing modern office towers give Boston a distinctly European flavor, but the city's famously close-knit neighborhoods are becoming increasingly polyglot (a fact manifest in multilingual signs, brochures, and ATMs). You can literally sample the results of this melting pot all over town: from Vietnamese spring rolls to Sicilian calamari, Brazilian *feijoada* to glatt kosher quiche, there's no shortage of ethnic alternatives to cod and baked beans. (It may be through association with this last dish that Boston has been dubbed "Beantown," but rest assured that Bostonians themselves *never* use the term.)

Because of the city's small size (Houston, Texas, almost has more open water within its limits than Boston has dry land), all these charms are best appreciated at a pedestrian's pace—especially since touring by car is about as convenient as walking around inside your house with a wheelbarrow. So ditch the gas-guzzler and bring comfortable walking shoes. And welcome to the Hub.

HISTORY

We must Consider that we shall be as a City upon a Hill, the eyes of all people are upon us.

—JOHN WINTHROP, 1628

City on a Hill
The fact that much of Boston predates the advent of professional archaeology hasn't made the city's prehistoric record very easy to read, but subway and building excavations have at least been proven that the local fondness for seafood dates back some 4,000 years. While ancient Egyptians stacked big blocks and perfected the art of embalming, their Late Archaic contemporaries in Boston supped on fish caught in the vicinity of Copley Square and clams gathered near present-day Quincy Market. A wooden fish weir (preserved in estuarine mud), shell middens, stone tools, and ashes of the cremated aren't the oldest artifacts of human habitation in the area, but higher sea levels have made traces of the earliest residents—Paleoindians from 8,000 to 9,000 years ago—even scarcer.

When 16th-century European fishermen started coming over to catch some dinner of their own, Boston's future home was a hilly, treeless, 750-acre peninsula called *mushauwomuk* ("tide fishing area") by the area's indigenous Massachusett Indians. Anglo-Saxon tongues shortened

---

"I HAD A TEACHER": BEING BLACK IN BOSTON

I had a teacher at Cambridge High and Latin who I think helped me a great deal. She was head of the department of Office Practice, and she sent me on a job.

One of the papers in Boston wanted some girls to do some typing, and I was a good typist, and she sent me with three or four other girls, and it just so happened that I was the only black one, and I was the only one that wasn't taken, and I couldn't understand. I knew I was a faster typist than any of the others. And she took me in her room, and talked to me.

Her name was Miss Dennis; I'll never forget her. She called them and asked them why they didn't take me and they said, "We only needed so many."

And she said, "But I sent my best." I can hear her now, I was sitting right there. But she took me in her room, and she said, "Henrietta, you are going to see this over and over and over. But remember, I told them and I know, I sent my best." And she said, "You just remember that when you go to do something, if you don't get it, if you're rejected for any other reason than performance, don't let it get to you. Just remember that you are capable."

She gave me such a feeling of worth. I think she had even more influence than my mother, because much of what my mother did was from love, you know, but this woman had no reason to build up my ego other than her belief that I was worth something. And she went out of her way to make opportunities.

I'll always remember that afternoon. I was bitterly disappointed.

—Henrietta Jackson, from *From Hearing My Mother Talk: Stories of Cambridge Women,* collected and edited by Cynthia E. Cohen

---

the typically utilitarian Algonquian name to "Shawmut." Smaller than New York City's Central Park—and virtually an island at high tide—the peninsula was apparently unoccupied by the disease-ravaged tribe when the young Reverend William Blaxton arrived, in the 17th century.

A refugee from a failed 1623 fishing colony on the nearby South Shore, Blaxton was one of a handful of Englishmen who took up residence around the Charles River estuary and harbor islands in the 1620s. The happy hermit lived alone with his orchard and library until the summer of 1630, when some 800 Puritans from Salem showed up in search of well-watered land. Admiring the strategic heights, abundant springs, and easily defended umbilical to the mainland, John Winthrop and his flock accepted Blaxton's invitation to join him, and by fall their new settlement was officially christened "Boston," after the Lincolnshire hometown of some of the Puritan leaders.

But Blaxton soon decided that he hadn't escaped England's lord bishops only to wind up in the laps of Salem's lord brethren. With his cattle and his books, he rode beyond the frontier to the banks of the river that now bears his name, the Blackstone, near the present-day Rhode Island border.

Healthy, Wealthy, and Wise

Spared the "three great annoyances of Woolves, Rattle-snakes and Musketoes" (as William Wood reported in his 1634 chronicle, *New England's Prospect*), Boston quickly became the head and heart of the Puritan Massachusetts Bay colony. As seat of the colonial government and center of seaborne trade, Boston quickly overtook nearby Newtown (now Cambridge), home of the Puritans' first ministerial college (now, of course, Harvard University), and other coastal communities engaged in the lucrative import-export business. Until well into the 18th century, Boston's size and wealth made it the British capital of North America.

Although dried cod was Boston's top export, the city profited mightily from seafaring "triangular trades"—shipping fish, timber, and other local supplies to Caribbean sugar plantations or Southern Europe, for example; exchanging them there for tropical commodities; and taking these to England to trade for manufactured goods. The most nefarious of these triangulations involved trading New England rum in Africa for slaves, who were sold in the West Indies for molasses, which was brought back to Boston to be distilled into more rum. Commerce with non-English ports flagrantly violated England's Trade and Navigation Acts, but duty-evading colonial smugglers made too much money to care about legality.

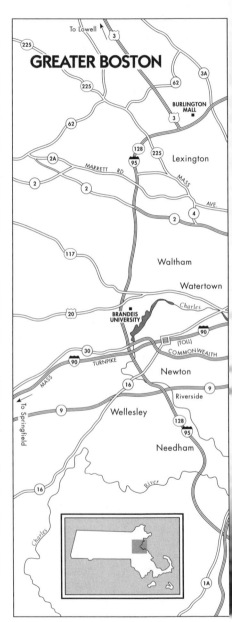

GREATER BOSTON

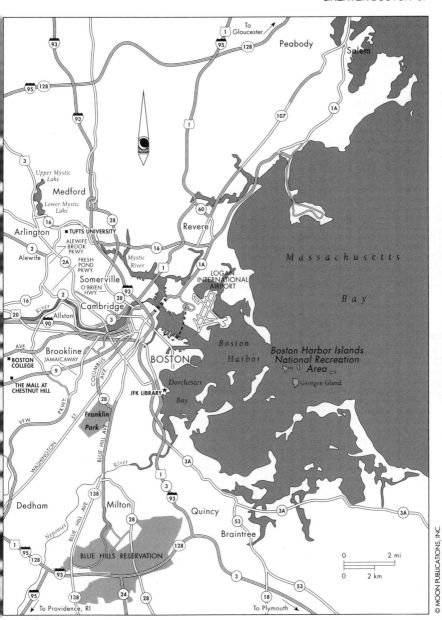

© MOON PUBLICATIONS, INC.

Puritanism alone couldn't protect the new riches of Boston's merchant class, so it embraced politics and trade associations on the one hand and Unitarianism—a religion with a more liberal attitude toward their secular activities—on the other.

Revolutionary Acts

As capital of a veritable empire built on smuggling, Boston soon found its economic interests clashing with Mother England's. Year after year, Parliament tried to close tax loopholes and capture what it perceived to be lost revenue. But these increasingly restrictive measures backfired, alienating the Bay Colony's businessmen; their employees, subcontractors, and lawyers; and pamphleteers. Since subsistence farmers made up the vast majority of the colonial population, the romantic image of an aggrieved American yeoman putting aside his plow to fight a parasitic monarchy in defense of some inalienable rights makes a great statue. But farmers would never have been equipped and encouraged to serve as soldiers had the matter not been in the interests of the colony's moneyed men.

Boston's kettle had been steaming for years before the March 1770 Massacre or December 1773's Tea Party, but it came to a full boil with the closing of Boston's port in 1774—one of Parliament's much-despised Coercive Acts. Revolution finally sprang up in Lexington and Concord in April 1775. It advanced to Boston's threshold with the bloody Battle of Bunker Hill two months later. After enduring an eight-month seige by newly commissioned General Washington and his fledgling Continental Army, Boston's British occupiers finally evacuated under the threat of their own cannon, which had been captured from Fort Ticonderoga and dragged to Dorchester Heights by the indefatigable Henry Knox. Boston remained free for the duration of the war.

Pacific Traders

After the Revolution, Americans were understandably denied access to English markets and credit. Initially, this proved a severe hardship for Boston merchants and mariners, many of whom had profited as privateers during the war. But shipbuilding and exports rebounded to record heights by the start of the 19th century, thanks to

trade with the Pacific Northwest and China. Although pioneered by Salem and New York, the sea otter fur trade between "the Coast" and Canton was so dominated by ships of Boston registry and crew that Native Americans in Oregon initially called all U.S. sailors "Boston men."

En route to the Far East, Boston's vessels inaugurated contact with the Marquesas Islands in the South Pacific and the Spanish missionaries on the California coast. Following Captain Cook to Hawaii, they initiated the sandalwood trade to Asia. The Boston ship *Columbia,* later the namesake of the Northwest's mightiest river, in 1790 brought the first of many colorfully feathered "Owyhee" emissaries back to meet Massachusetts' governor; in return, Boston sent to Hawaii horses, bricks (called *pohaku winihepa,* or "Winship stones," after the family that introduced them), infectious diseases, and Calvinist missionaries. One of those missionaries was Sanford Ballard Dole, who became Hawaii's provisional president after the 1893 overthrow of Queen Liliukolani. (Appropriately, the warship that delivered Marines for the coup was the USS *Boston.*) A slightly more salutary contribution to the Oregon Territory was made by Boston's Colonel Wilder: the first cultivars of d'Anjou pears, planted in 1842. And during the California Gold Rush, Boston's famous clipper ships sped passengers, provisions, and supplies to the Golden Gate—establishing sailing records that would stand unbroken for over 130 years. (The tons of Telegraph Hill stone brought back as ballast gave rise to the modern lament that some of San Francisco's best real estate lies at the bottom of Boston Harbor.)

The Landscapers

Boston is truly a manmade city—not merely the buildings but even the ground beneath them. Making usable land out of tidal mudflats abutting the original peninsula began early in the colonial era, but the most extensive quarrying of the city's drumlins (oval hills of soil and stone) began in the Federal era, following U.S. independence. In various stages throughout the early 19th century, property developers cut down Beacon Hill—once as tall as the State House is now—and its neigboring eminences, and carted their crowns into the adjacent flats to create commercial and residential lots (present-day Charles

Street and much of the North End), sometimes amid lawsuits from owners of homes undermined by removal of so much earth. Most of the peninsula's original hills are now preserved only in the layout and naming of downtown streets, many of which still conform to the long-vanished topography. (Stray cows, despite what some people still believe, are *not* to blame for Boston's crooked thoroughfares.)

Even more ambitious than the project of flattening the peninsula was the late-19th-century filling in of the Back Bay, which nearly doubled the city's size. Once part of the lower Charles River's enormous tidal basin, this 580-acre mudflat between Boston and Brookline had become a noxious cesspool by the 1840s, literally bubbling with fermenting raw sewage trapped behind a failed mill dam and a skein of railroad levees. While Thoreau enjoyed his Walden woods, Boston was stewing in its own effluent; after much debate, the state seized the land by eminent domain and implemented a plan to develop the Back Bay as a high-class residential area–in one stroke burying the health hazard, relieving city overcrowding, and raising money through the sale of the new property. Trainloads of Needham sand and gravel started arriving at the foot of present-day Commonwealth Avenue shortly before the Civil War and continued to arrive every 45 minutes, day and night, for the next 35 years.

The Great Fire

Despite the modern additions to Boston's skyline, much of the streetscape is old enough to suggest that it has always been this way. Not so. Very few buildings actually predate the Civil War, thanks in large part to the city's many early fires—the most devastating of which hit Boston right on the heels of Chicago's encounter with Mrs. O'Leary's cow. On November 9, 1872, sparks in a department store at Summer and Kingston streets raced through the store's hoop skirts and other combustible wares until the building was a fireball; within 24 hours, over 700 of its downtown neighbors had been engulfed. Most of the densely packed structures had flammable wooden roofs two stories higher than the reach of any available fire equipment. Blazing-hot walls of supposedly fireproof granite became explosive stone grenades when doused

with water. Aging mineral-clogged water mains, an equine flu epidemic among fire-department horses, gas lines buried too near the surface, and crowds of rubber-neckers and looters made a bad situation even worse. Numerous regional fire companies responded to the general alarm—some by train, others running 10 miles or more—but suburban hoses didn't fit city hydrants, and fights broke out over the lack of coordination and fuel for steam-powered pumpers. Not that there weren't heroes: firemen from Portsmouth, New Hampshire, used sea water pumped from the harbor to halt the flames at the very doors of the landmark Old South Meeting House. And the postmaster not only rescued the city's mail, but even kept up deliveries.

By the time the conflagration spent itself, some 65 acres of real estate and $75 million worth of commercial stock had become a smoldering ruin. Compassionate citizens from across the country quickly responded with aid, including major contributions from a sympathetic (and resurrected) Chicago. Although reforms were instituted over such matters as building heights and materials, private interests with a stake in the burned blocks opposed any proposed comprehensive change in urban design. Aside from a few street alterations and the creation of Post Office Square, much of the affected area was rebuilt nearly exactly as before. (Harvard, whose operating budget depended upon rental income from its property in the area, actually *expanded* its holdings.) As for the generosity of the nation, with characteristic Bostonian propriety, surplus money not disbursed by relief agencies after one year was returned—with interest.

And this is good old Boston
The home of the bean and the cod,
Where the Lowells talk to the Cabots,
And the Cabots talk only to God.
—DR. JOHN COLLINS BOSSIDY, 1910

Fleeing Yankees

The insularity of the Lowells, Cabots, and their upper-crust Boston Brahmin peers has become a topic of benign humor, best exemplified by Cleveland Amory's unsurpassed anecdotal study of the breed, *The Proper Bostonians.* Teasing stories about their ossified social conventions and limited repertoire of first names

LESLIE JONES/COURTESY OF BOSTON PUBLIC LIBRARY, PRINT DEPT.

Bostonian Charles Ponzi (carrying diamond-headed cane), originator of the Ponzi (or pyramid) scheme, heads to federal court in 1920 after the collapse of his international postal coupon trading scam (he eventually spent five years in federal prison).

aside, the clubbiness of these powerful 19th-century mercantile dynasties shaped the city's design as significantly as landfill and fire. Their wealth supported Boston's banks, backed its real estate, invested in its capital bonds, and endowed many of its institutions, from hospitals and schools to the Athenæum and the symphony. Allied by marriages, education, and church affiliations against Boston's swelling foreign-born population, Boston's Harvard-educated Unitarian and Episcopalian Yankee oligarchy held disproportionate sway over civic affairs through much of the 1800s. (Even a bank founded in 1816 at the behest of a Catholic archbishop and patronized predominately thereafter by Irish immigrants wasn't immune: no Irish Catholic was named to its board of directors until the end of WW II.)

But as these merchant princes improved the downtown streetscape with stately townhouses and museums, they may also unintentionally have changed the appearance of Boston's turn-of-the-century neighborhoods—results of a backlash to their long political dominance.

In 1910, John "Honey Fitz" Fitzgerald, in one of the great political upsets in American history,

won the mayoral election. His victory gave Yankees reason to rue the decades of their bigotry and discrimination. Honey Fitz had been mayor before, but reformers confident of a Yankee victory had since altered the city charter to give the office unprecedented executive powers and double the length of the term in which to exercise them. The richest of Beacon Hill's bluebloods could always count on their fortunes and private social clubs to insulate them from the populist rabble, but middle-class Yankees around the city were given a taste of comeuppance. A generation of mostly Irish Democratic pols used municipal payrolls and city services to build a dedicated constituency among Irish, Italians, Eastern Europeans, and other ethnic groups previously excluded from the city's feedbag. Boston's densely populated poor and working-class wards acquired new roads, schools, playgrounds, and bathhouses, while more affluent Yankee enclaves were all but neglected . As the end of WW I brought a flood of tenement dwellers to the city, districts that only a decade earlier seemed destined to be developed as streetcar neighborhoods of single-family homes for Yankee professionals were instead forested with multi-family three-deckers. Affordable to city workers and their families, anathema to conservative Anglo property owners, three-deckers fueled the Yankee exodus to greener suburban pastures. These days, this indigenous housing style has become as emblematic of Boston as Bulfinch's Federal mansions on Beacon Hill, and remains an important symbol of a constituency essential to any mayor's election.

The Athens of America Atrophies

As the populism of Irish mayors scared away private Yankee capital and low-wage Southern labor siphoned away any manufacturing still intact after the Depression, Boston entered an economic and cultural tailspin, becoming something of a provincial backwater neighbor to New York. The population leveled off during the Roosevelt and Truman years and then declined, a process arrested only briefly by WW II's boosted payrolls. (The city will end the 20th century with nearly the same number of residents it had at the beginning—a full 25% below its peak of 800,000.)

But outfitting the military didn't improve the city skyline any more than Depression had, and

SACCO & VANZETTI: A GOOD SHOEMAKER AND A POOR FISH PEDDLER

During the first half hour of August 23, 1927, as thousands of protesters from around the globe held a vigil outside, three so-called radical conspirators were sent to the electric chair for the murder of two shoe-factory employees during a 1920 payroll robbery south of Boston. Convicted almost entirely on the basis of their "suspicious behavior" (i.e., their anarchist beliefs), the immigrants arrested for the crime—shoemaker Nicola Sacco, fishmonger Bartolomeo Vanzetti, and the often-forgotten Celestino Madeiros—might have been executed in obscurity but for a diligent letter-writing campaign that awakened the world to justice in mid-miscarriage.

Despite State House picketing, reams of newspaper editorials, entreaties from foreign leaders, and a bombing of the American ambassador's house in Paris, Massachusetts' civil authorities stubbornly opposed the mounting international outcry for a retrial. Distinguished law professor and future Supreme Court justice Felix Frankfurter's exposé in the *Atlantic Monthly* of the original trial's flaws was roundly rebutted by the Boston *Evening Transcript*, the newspaper of the city's elite. All-powerful Cardinal William O'Connell (who would later salute Generalissimo Francisco Franco as a fighter for Christian civilization) flatly refused to intercede for clemency. The Dedham trial judge swatted down one appeal after another while boasting to friends what he was doing to those "anarchist bastards."

After several years, a governor-appointed blue-ribbon panel—including the presidents of both Harvard and MIT—reviewed the case to determine whether a retrial was warranted but wound up rubber-stamping the original findings. Public consciences thus salved, the tyranny of xenophobia finally proceeded with the electrocution. At the end, Vanzetti wrote, "Never in our full life could we hope to do such work for tolerance, for justice, for man's understanding of man as now we do by accident." Two hundred thousand people turned out for the funeral procession—to a Jamaica Plain crematorium.

Papers and artifacts from the Sacco-Vanzetti Defense Committee are now kept by the Boston Public Library (artifacts include a model by Gutzon Borglum, sculptor of Mt. Rushmore, for a memorial sculpture, which was rejected by both the city and the state governments). The two men's ashes are there, as well. A shelf of books has been written about the case; among the more interesting are Katherine Ann Porter's *Never-Ending Wrong*, Francis Russell's *Tragedy in Dedham*, and Upton Sinclair's *Boston*, which was banned locally upon its release.

I had a relative, a poet who lived in New York City and in Maine, who came up for the protests about Sacco and Vanzetti. And I can remember, and this was in 1927, when the two men were executed. And there was an enormous outturning of literary people (Katherine Ann Porter and Edna St. Vincent Millay) and lots of people from the arts as well as from politics.

And I remember that night well, although I must say my family didn't think much of Edna Vincent's political and social and other activities.

And I remember going to the vigil outside the prison. And I think I remember, I think I remember . . .

There were always people who believed, and maybe it was a fact, but that when people were executed . . . (It was in Charlestown, just across the river from where the Science Museum is now) . . . that when people were electrocuted, they always said it took so much power (this may have been just a street myth) that the lights blinked. But I think I could say that I remember the lights dimming when they were executed.

—Recollected by PAULINE SWIFT, from
*FROM HEARING MY MOTHER TALK:
STORIES OF CAMBRIDGE WOMEN,*
collected and edited by
CYNTHIA E. COHEN

entertaining the military made some districts even seedier. The blue-blooded Watch and Ward Society, de facto public censors for the city since 1878, had become so active before the war that "Banned in Boston" became a national joke. Civic culture guardians were no more open-minded afterwords: in 1948, Boston's Institute of Modern Art changed the "modern" in its name to "contemporary" in order to disassociate itself from such avant-garde work as Abstract Expressionism (branded by an Institute spokesman as "a cult of bewilderment").

The growth of service industries brought new economic life to the city in the early 1960s—around the same time that urban renewal and the interstate highway system transformed the city's face. Neglected old neighborhoods like Beacon Hill and the South End also got new life from bumper crops of middle-class university graduates, who settled down after obtaining their degrees. While these young constituents of the "new" Boston and the blue-collar workers who grew up here often shared allegiance to the Democratic Party, their views about the city's future diverged widely. The clash between social conservatives and liberals who would remake Boston as a multicultural society finally culmi-nated in the painful and violent battle over school desegregation, an eruption so long and loud that it splashed into headlines across the nation. Repercussions and aftershocks are still felt in the city today.

Hackers, Bankers, Brokers, Students
Despite rents in the the city's social fabric over issues of class and race in the 1960s and '70s, mushrooming skyscrapers attest to Boston's having shed at least *some* of its old strictures. All that's new is no longer anathema. Even Robert Mapplethorpe doesn't threaten Boston's foundations as Isadora Duncan or D. H. Lawrence once did. Business—insurance, money management, high technology—and academia have wrought significant, visible changes over the past two decades. Why, half Boston's current population has been here only since 1980. The core of the city is lively and liveable, and promises to become even more so as the multi-billion-dollar Central Artery/Tunnel project buries the aging elevated interstate dividing downtown from its waterfront and the residential North End. Perhaps the city's millenial energy will even bring baseball's Boston Red Sox the World Series victory they have sought for so long.

BOSTON SIGHTS

Most of Boston's major historical attractions lay within the confines of the city's old seagirt boundaries, which effectively means they're all within a short, walkable radius from Boston Common. Being of more modern vintage, most of the city's cultural institutions are widely scattered about, but don't let that be an excuse to reach for the car keys—any blitz of the city's tourist Top 10 would require a good bankroll for parking fees and a saint's patience for navigating the city's streets. Better to rely on public transportation or the un-limited boarding privileges offered by sightseeing trolleys that loop around the major attractions on both sides of the Charles River. Some of the attractions described below are best reached by public bus; in such instances, the route number and destination will be identified just as they're displayed over the bus windshield. For nitty-gritty details about navigating the city via the subways, trolleys, buses, and ferries of the **Massachusetts Bay Transportation Authori-ty** (the MBTA, or "T," for short), see "Getting Around" under "Transportation," below.

BEACON HILL AND THE WEST END

Beacon Hill is Boston's cornerstone. New, modern sections of the city are fairly generic, but these slopes—on which the city was founded over 350 years ago, decked out with Federal-style mansions and crowned by the gold dome of the State House—are unequivocally and ir-replaceably Old Boston. Beacon and its lower

For latest Boston weather, call the **Bell At-lantic Accu-Weather** forecast, tel. (617) 936-1234.

cobblestones and coachmen's quarters today in Beacon Hill's 19th-century Acorn Street

adjoining hills, Pemberton and Mt. Vernon (known collectively to early colonists as "Trimountain," or, more colloquially, "Tremont"), remained undeveloped boondocks for Boston's first century. Isolated behind a town with its feet in the harbor, the settlement that finally grew up on the backside of the hills in the early 1700s included a red light district so steeped in a "torrent of vice" that Mt. Vernon was all but renamed "Mt. Whoredom" in colonial annals and maps.

When government outgrew the Old State House in the late 1700s, real estate speculators who were aware that the new building was planned for Beacon Hill acquired most of Trimountain's summit acreage, cropped the top of Beacon Hill, altogether erased Mt. Vernon, and developed the area, during the first decades of the 19th century, into a fashionable mansion district. By the Civil War, changing notions of acceptable urban density replaced trees and gar-

BULFINCH—THE BUILDER OF BOSTON

The individual arguably most influential in shaping the look and feel of Boston during the decades following American independence was Charles Bulfinch. Born in 1763 to a Boston doctor, Bulfinch was sufficiently privileged in upbringing and education initially to pursue "no business but giving gratuitous advice in architecture." But a bankrupted residential scheme drove Bulfinch into becoming America's first professional architect.

In practice, his adaptations of English design pioneered what is known as the Federal style of architecture. In Boston, he designed mansions, churches, a theater, entire blocks of townhouses, the grid plan for the whole South End, offices, hospitals, banks, markets (including the expanded Faneuil Hall), schools, halls for Harvard (his alma mater), a courthouse, state and local jails, and the State House—one of three New England capitols in which he had a hand. It's no wonder that he felt

that architects had so little left to do that it would be useless to encourage his children to join the profession. Many of his buildings are long gone, or—like the curve of Franklin St. from his failed Tontine Crescent development—remain in nothing more than the merest outline.

But as an architect, a developer, a town planner, the de facto mayor (Chairman of the Board of Selectmen), and even the police superintendent, Bulfinch built a 30-year career in Boston that has accurately been described as having transformed a small town of wood into a city of brick and granite (much of which *does* remain).

However, while Boston prospered, Bulfinch did not. Perennially poor, in 1818 he accepted a presidential appointment to rebuild Washington's war-ravaged US Capitol. After 12 well-paid years (his happiest), he finally returned to Boston. There, he rested on his laurels until his death, at 81.

dens with townhouses, making even the chic "sunny" side resemble the rowhouse-dominated servants' neighborhood on the shadier north slope. But the resemblance was only superficial: socially and ethnically, the south side of Beacon Hill remained a bastion of Brahmin WASPs until Boston's 20th-century malaise further subdivided many a fine home into small apartments and faded the finery of the rest. Since the 1970s, Beacon Hill has both recovered its appeal as one of the city's most desirable addresses and received recognition (and protection) as a National Historic Landmark.

Strolling the undulating brick sidewalks of the Hill's labyrinthine streets and alleyways is an end in itself. Notice the bootscrapers embedded in granite front steps, the occasional hitching posts, and the abundance of lacy wrought-iron fencing. Among the facades of Beacon Street facing the Common, look for rare purple window panes; these are chemically flawed panels of clear glass turned amethyst by early 19th-century sunlight. Discover William Ralph Emerson's "House of Odd Windows," at 24 Pinckney St., whose design might be called postmodern if Ralph Waldo Emerson's architect nephew had conceived it in 1984 instead of 1884. Hunt for the cul-de-sacs off Revere and Phillips Streets, or for Boston's most photogenic block of cobblestones—Acorn Street. And don't miss Louisburg Square, the epitome of the Hill's classical elegance and proportion, centered upon a tiny private park jointly owned by adjacent residents. Among past holders of a key to the park gate are Louisa May Alcott (who was living at No. 10 when she died) and *Atlantic Monthly* editor William Dean Howells (who introduced Mark Twain to local literary circles); Massachusetts Senator John Kerry is among those who have one now.

Charms of a more commercial nature are found at the foot of Beacon Hill along Charles Street, whose gas lamps and red brick frame cute little boutiques and a thicket of antique shops. Can't afford deacquisitioned museum pieces, $10,000 Asian furniture, Scandinavian long clocks, or turn-of-the-century china dinnerware? Perhaps the always-interesting Beacon Hill Thrift Shop, at No. 15, has something more in your range; the antiques in front are generally priced under four figures. Sustain your

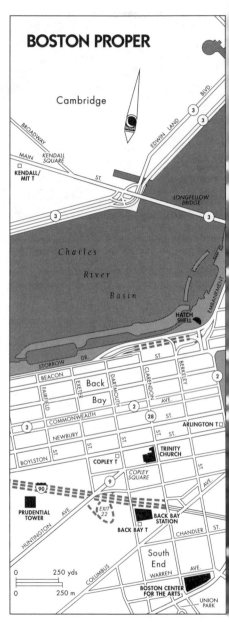

O'BRIEN HWY

Charles River

U.S.S. CONSTITUTION ★

CHARLESTOWN NAVY YARD

Boston National Historical Park

MUSEUM OF SCIENCE

SCIENCE PARK T

CHARLESTOWN BRIDGE

MBTA FERRY

COMMERCIAL ST

MBTA FERRY

The Esplanade

West End

NORTH STATION

LOVEJOY WHARF

WASHINGTON ST

PRINCE ST

HULL ST

OLD NORTH CHURCH ★

Boston Harbor

NORTH STATION T

North End

CENTRAL ARTERY

SALEM ST

HANOVER ST

NORTH ST

SUMNER TUNNEL

CALLAHAN TUNNEL

MASS. GENERAL HOSPITAL

FRIEND ST

CANAL ST

HAYMARKET T

HANOVER ST

COMMERCIAL AVE

ATLANTIC AVE

CHARLES/ MGH T

CAMBRIDGE ST

HARRISON GRAY OTIS HOUSE ★

BOWDOIN T

COURT ST

GOVERNMENT

CHARLES ST

RD

28

Beacon Hill

AFRICAN MEETING HOUSE ★

LOUISBURG SQUARE

NICHOLS HOUSE MUSEUM ★

GOVERNMENT CENTER T

CENTER

FANEUIL HALL MARKETPLACE ★

AQUARIUM T LONG WHARF

MT. VERNON ST

STATE HOUSE

STATE ST

CUSTOM HOUSE ★

NEW ENGLAND AQUARIUM

JOY ST

STATE T

INFO

LIBERTY SQUARE

Freedom Trail

PARK STREET T

Waterfront

AIRPORT WATER SHUTTLE

The Lagoon

CHARLES ST

Frog Pond

INFO

WINTER ST

FILENE'S

FRANKLIN ST

ROWES WHARF

Public Garden

2

28

Boston Common

DOWNTOWN CROSSING T

WINTHROP SQUARE

Post Office Square Park

BOYLSTON T

MACY'S

LAFAYETTE PLACE

93

FEDERAL COURT HOUSE

ARLINGTON ST

CHINATOWN T

ESSEX ST

SOUTHEAST EXPY

SOUTH STATION T

BEACH ST

SOUTH STATION

MUSEUM WHARF

NORTHERN AVE

Theater District

TREMONT ST

WASHINGTON ST

HARRISON ST

China- town

ATLANTIC AVE

BUS STATION

CONGRESS ST

SLEEPER ST

NEW NORTHERN AVE

NORTHERN AVE

To World Trade Center

N.E. MED CENTER T

MASS PIKE

90

POST OFFICE (24 HR)

Fort Point Channel

SUMMER ST

A ST

E. BERKELEY ST

SHAWMUT AVE

93

1

3

UNDER CONSTRUCTION

UNDER CONSTRUCTION

To Airport

© MOON PUBLICATIONS, INC.

buying and strolling with a big muffin from the bakery case of **DeLuca's,** 11 Charles, near Beacon (a vastly better value than the dainty morsels from Starbucks next door), or give your soles a rest over an inexpensive lunch (great focaccia, lousy croissants) and coffee from attractively casual **Panificio,** 144 Charles, tel. (617) 227-4340, open till 10 p.m. On the land-filled flats of Beacon Hill, beneath the stout brick facade of the Hampshire House, on Beacon Street opposite the Public Garden, is one of the city's most popular tourist attractions, the Bull & Finch Pub. Better known as the *Cheers* **bar,** it's a far cry from the quiet neighborhood spot that once caught the television producers' fancy (nor does it bear great similarity to the TV series' set), but don't let that stop you from hoisting a few at the bar with the million other pilgrims who've come to pay their respects.

House and Garden Tours
One of the few Beacon Hill houses open to the public is the 1804 **Nichols House Museum,** 55 Mt. Vernon St., tel. (617) 227-6993. Per the bequest of its last owner, Rose Standish Nichols, the place is a window into heirloom-filled Beacon Hill gentility; tours (noon-4:15 p.m. Monday, Wednesday, and Saturday; $5) highlight Miss Rose's idiosyncrasies as well as her possessions. The house itself was built by wealthy Jonathan Mason, one of the original Mt. Vernon Proprietors—the group whose ringleader, Harrison Gray Otis, used his knowledge of impending State House construction to acquire the adjacent 18-acre farm of expatriate painter John Singleton Copley. A Tory sympathizer who moved to London before the Revolution, Copley made several hundred percent profit on the sale of his hillside pastures. To his everlasting regret, however, even that sum was a pittance compared to the killing Otis, Mason, and their cronies made on the property.

The son of a Declaration of Independence signer and sometimes elected officeholder himself, Harry Otis made his mint developing Boston land while most of his wealthy contemporaries fattened their bank accounts with maritime trade or shipbuilding. The fruits of Otis' Midas touch are preserved on and around Beacon Hill in part through his three private mansions, all built by his friend Charles Bulfinch (whose own ill-

timed property developments were often profitably acquired by the deeper-pocketed Otis). The first of the three homes, the 1796 **Harrison Gray Otis House,** 141 Cambridge St., is the only one open to the public. Compensating for the plain facade, lost gardens, and much-altered neighborhood is the opulence of the interior, restored to the busy patterns, bright colors, and expensive materials with which Otis and his wife surrounded themselves. Tours of the property—now headquarters for SPNEA, the Society for the Preservation of New England Antiquities—are given on the hour, noon-4 p.m. Tues.-Fri. and 10 a.m.-4 p.m. Saturday ($4; tel. (617) 227-3956).

SPNEA also offers guided walks of Beacon Hill starting at 10 a.m. every Saturday, June-Oct. ($10; reservations recommended), commencing with a slide show here at Harry's old digs. For anyone more interested in horticulture than history, the Beacon Hill Garden Club offers a famous **Hidden Garden Tour** ($20; tel. 617-227-4392). Rain or shine, this annual self-guided rite of spring takes place the third Thursday of May; tickets and maps are sold from booths set up on Charles Street for the occasion. The first weekend of June offers another peek behind closed doors and gates—this one free—during the annual **Beacon Hill ArtsWalk,** when local artists hold a grand yard sale of their works in courtyards, backyards, and indoor studios all over the funkier north slope.

Beacon Hill's Other Half
Beacon Hill's shady side was a center for the city's African American community from colonial times through the Great Depression, initially because it was affordable (it was a buffer between town propriety and riverside brothels), then because it was convenient for residents employed in mansions on the other side of Pinckney Street. But it wasn't all laborers' rooming houses and servants' quarters; after Massachusetts abolished slavery, in 1783, Boston's free black community grew to include tradesmen and professionals, from barbers and printers to doctors and lawyers (including the first black lawyer to argue a case in front of the U.S. Supreme Court—*before* the end of the Civil War or ratification of the 13th Amendment, abolishing slavery). The support these residents gave to the

BOSTON ATTRACTION DISCOUNT DAYS AND OTHER DEALS

The following paid attractions around town offer free or discounted admission at certain times of the week, or offer special deals for anyone with a valid MBTA Passport or T Pass.

THURSDAY

The Institute of Contemporary Art: free 5-9 p.m.

FRIDAY

The Children's Museum: $1 admission 5-9 p.m.

SATURDAY

Museum of Fine Arts: free admission until noon

Harvard University museums (all): free admission until noon

Franklin Park Zoo: free admission 10 a.m.-noon, first Saturday of the month only

SUNDAY

The Computer Museum: half price admission 3-5 p.m.

MBTA PASSPORT HOLDERS' DISCOUNTS

The Institute of Contemporary Art: two-for-one admission

Old State House Museum: two-for-one admission

Boston Tea Party Ship & Museum: 20% off adult admission

Museum of Transportation: 50% discount on individual admission

The John F. Kennedy Library and Museum: $2 off adult admission

Boston Duck Tours: $2 off adult ticket

Museum of Science, Museum of Fine Arts, Computer Museum, and the USS *Constitution* Museum: $1 off adult admission.

May-early September, or by appointment Sept.-May). Behind the Smith School—established by the city in the 1830s to avoid desegregating existing public schools—is the **African Meeting House,** 8 Smith Court, the nation's oldest remaining black church and home to the contemporary gallery of the **Museum of Afro American History,** tel. (617) 742-1854, open daily late May-early Sept., otherwise Mon.-Fri. only; free, but $5 donation suggested. Built for black Baptists who faced discrimination in other local churches, the 1806 structure is most famous as the site of the founding of the New England Anti-Slavery Society by the unequivocal abolitionist William Lloyd Garrison, and for being the recruiting center for the Massachusetts 54th Colored Infantry Regiment. As the religious, educational, and civic cornerstone in the African American community for decades, it was also a forum for 19th-century campaigns for integrated schools, women's suffrage, and other nearly forgotten chapters from Boston's history. Take a tour, mentally block out the anachronistic plastic seating (a product of the hall's continued use for public lectures, concerts, and even weddings), and even today you can almost hear echoes of those old debates. Though you won't find it equal in depth or scope to the ranger-led tours, do-it-yourselfers can pick up a free, self-guided **Black Heritage Trail** brochure at either the Meeting House or Smith School, describing 14 well-preserved sights around Beacon Hill's north slope.

The State House

Whatever you do, *don't* call it the Capitol: Charles Bulfinch's 1797 gold-domed masterpiece is properly referred to as the State House, and the elected representatives and senators who gather inside to make the Commonwealth's

abolitionist movement also made the Hill's north slope a major stop on the Underground Railroad, helping fugitive slaves escape to freedom in Canada.

The **Boston African American National Historic Site** pays tribute to this underappreciated community, partly with exhibits at the newly renovated **Abiel Smith School**—46 Joy St. (currently under restoration until early 1999; free), tel. (617) 742-5415—and partly through excellent ranger-led neighborhood walks (thrice daily late laws are collectively known as the Great and General Court. From the pine cone ornament (symbolizing the state's abundant timber—most of which was then in what eventually became the state of Maine) on top of the (originally wood-shingled) dome to the commemorative Dog and Horse tablet in the east wing, there are many stories to this place. Some of them are related on the Mon.-Fri. tours that begin amid the tall Doric columns inside the front entrance. Not all the young guides have their facts straight, unfortunately; some don't correctly explain, for example, that the Sacred Cod hanging over the second-floor House of Representatives chamber was a 1783 gift from a merchant who wished to remind the legislators where the state earned its bread and butter—kind of an 18th-century "it's the fisheries, stupid."

Across the street from the State House is the **Robert Gould Shaw Memorial,** honoring the Civil War commander of the Massachusetts 54th Regiment, who was slain with scores of his men in a suicidal attack on Fort Wagner, South Carolina. Sculptor Augustus Saint-Gaudens, known for his Adams Memorial in Washington, D.C., spent over a decade working on this bas-relief, which the abolitionist Shaw family intended to honor black enlisted men as well as their son. The young colonel is also memorialized at Cambridge's Mount Auburn Cemetery, with a plaque on the family monument.

Around the corner from the State House, the **Appalachian Mountain Club,** 5 Joy St., tel. (617) 523-0636, dispenses books, maps, field guides, and other planning aids for hikers, campers, and paddlers contemplating outdoor excursions anywhere in New England. If you hadn't yet considered taking to the hills, dales, and streams of the region, check out the bookshelves here at headquarters. The AMC is also an excellent resource for Appalachian Trail hikers; besides buying topos and incredibly detailed trail guides to the famous 2,100-mile Georgia-to-Maine footpath, you can find out how to make reservations for the AMC's network of alpine huts and mountain lodges in New Hampshire and western Massachusetts.

The Museum of Science

Behind Beacon Hill and across busy Cambridge Street lies the old West End, birthplace of Leonard Nimoy and one of the nation's first casualties of federally funded urban renewal. Where once were tenement-crowded streets, street-corner social clubs, and laundry on lines now stand massive institutional office complexes and apartment towers. Although the project was initially hailed for eradicating a blighted part of the city, hindsight has brought rueful awareness that outsize modern buildings often subtract more than they add to a city's quality of life.

Atop the Charles River Dam, off the banks of the West End, sits Science Park and its Museum of Science, tel. (617) 723-2500, best approached via a walk along the river (cross Storrow Drive via the footbridge at the end of Charles Street) or by riding the T. Almost always abuzz with crowds of school groups, families, and faithful members returning to explore yet another of its innumerable exhibit halls, this is one museum that doesn't make you keep your hands to yourself or your voice down. Catch a demo of the world's largest Van de Graaff generator, whose whip-cracking bolts of indoor lightning are showcased in the Theater of Electricity. Let interactive exhibits teach you to think like a scientist. Play virtual reality volleyball. Or take an elevator deep under Boston Harbor to learn more about the Big Dig construction project causing so many of downtown's traffic woes. Planetarium shows take you through the solar system and beyond—especially at one of the trippy laser presentations set to music from the Grateful Dead, Jimi Hendrix, or Smashing Pumpkins. There's a giant OmniMax film theater, too. Open daily year-round ($8 adults, $6 kids and seniors, planetarium and Omni shows additional, combination and family discounts available).

DOWNTOWN AND THE WATERFRONT

Ever since the first State House and Market Square sat at the head of the town wharves, Boston's civil, financial, and commercial functions have been close neighbors. Although that original waterfront lies buried beneath hotels and multi-story glass boxes, "downtown" retains its multiple identity in Government Center's bureaucracy, the Financial District's money managers, and Washington Street's department stores. City planners may lump it with Midtown, but Boston Common, too, is "downtown" to most locals (as are Chinatown and the Leather District around South Station—unless you live there).

This is the city's economic heart, nearly 200,000 workers strong. With several thousand apartment dwellers and a mix of luxury and working class residential neighborhoods on nearly all sides, downtown Boston isn't the kind of inner city that rolls up its sidewalks after 5 p.m., either. With the vast majority of the city's 17th- and 18th-century remnants—burying grounds, certain streets, and a handful of buildings—downtown would seem to exemplify Boston's commitment to preservation of the past. But with every megasized skyline addi-

tion, it affirms a stronger desire to face the future. Here the city's urban history is as condensed as a college survey course, from its first page—the purchase of the Common—through pages yet unwritten, awaiting the day the dust clears from burying the now-elevated Central Artery. Maybe those pages, when filled, will explain the paradox of the "Big Dig," whose high-capacity subterranean interstate promises to deliver a lot more vehicles to the one part of Boston most ill-suited to accommodate it.

For those visitors who wisely skip driving, one of the pleasures of strolling downtown is discovering alleys like Spring Lane, off lower Washington Street, or Winthrop Lane between Arch and Otis Streets, whose landmark- and history-in-

THE FREEDOM TRAIL

Y ou may have noticed a red stripe threading all around the downtown area, connecting various high-profile historic attractions that date back to the colonial era. This 2.5-mile stripe and its 16 appurtenant historic sites constitute the Freedom Trail.

While first and foremost a walk among actual places associated with events leading up to the American Revolution, the Trail encompasses or connects to sites relevant to other elements of Boston's political, religious, and cultural history. Taking in much more than just dead patriots and battle monuments, the Trail touches on the contributions of colonial women to the cause of liberty, 19th-century artifacts of African Americans' and immigrants' struggle to share in the Revolution's freedoms, the very visible architectural legacy of the city, and the downtown neighborhoods whose changing ethnicity mirrors the city's evolving identity.

If you walk the trail on your own, of course, you can start where you like. But most Trail brochures and guidebooks begin at the Common. Allow most of a day to cover the whole route—or you can divide it into smaller segments: downtown, the North End, and Charlestown. You can also cut some of the walking mileage by taking the $1 MBTA water shuttle between the downtown waterfront (Long Wharf, next to the Aquarium) and the Charlestown Navy Yard, where the U.S.S. *Constitution* is berthed. Day-trippers coming into the city will find both Commuter Rail stations to be within blocks of the Trail,

but at the Navy Yard you will find abundant parking—at more attractive rates than downtown, including some lots offering four hours free.

Between Patriot's Day, in mid-April, and Thanksgiving weekend, in late November, National Park Service rangers offer free abbreviated Trail tours starting in front of the **Boston National Historical Park Visitor Center,** at 15 State St., tel. (617) 242-5689, opposite the Old State House entrance to the Orange Line's State Street station. These walks cover most of the sites in downtown and the North End but (like most paid tours, too) stop short of crossing into Charlestown. Besides ranger programs, the Visitor Center also has free Trail maps and brochures, scores of great local-interest books for sale (including a good self-guiding booklet to the 46 sites of Boston's scantily recognized Women's Heritage Trail), and, perhaps most important, public bathrooms.

It's worth noting that while the Boston NHP and the Freedom Trail overlap, they are *not* synonymous. (One of the National Historic Park's eight components is far off the Trail, in Dorchester—and nine of the Trail stops have nothing to do with the NHP.) Also note that there are no consistent rules about admission fees—some components of both the Trail and the NHP are free, others aren't. And you can't purchase a single ticket good for admission to all the privately maintained sites. In computers this is known as a sloppy user interface; in Boston, it's business as usual.

spired "City Bricks" beguile the downward-cast eye. Observant strollers will also find numerous plaques affixed to buildings or embedded in pavement, each one designating a pinch of city history. When the weather's nice, do what the locals do: find a sunny spot in a small urban oasis like Winthrop Square, Liberty Square, Post Office Square, or adjacent Angell Memorial Park. A brief respite in any of these art-filled spaces is a great antidote to the weariness that otherwise attends walking on hard pavement all day.

The Common

Misleadingly billed as the nation's oldest public park, Boston Common was originally set aside in 1634 as a military training field and public pasture for grazing cattle. Although greatly altered botanically and topographically—the 17th-century Common had several more hills and ponds, but only one or two trees—the size and boundaries are about the same as when it was first purchased from Rev. William Blaxton. Besides feed-

Peter Banner's 1810 Park Street Church at the entrance to Boston Common

ing the town's early dairy herd and accommodating centuries of soldiers, the Common was home to the Great Elm, from whose stout branches were hanged many petty thieves, adulterers, Quakers, and other criminals back in the days when capital punishment was proper Boston sport. (Executions were often cause for a holiday and could attract boisterous mobs; one triple hanging on the Common in 1789 attracted an estimated 20,000 spectators.) Gallows gave way in the 19th century to healthier recreations: the Oneida Football Club, credited as the first American football team, which played on the Common during the Civil War. A detailed map of nearly all the Common's statuary and monuments, including the plaque to the undefeated Oneidas, is available free at the Visitor Center along the Tremont Street side. The one statue omitted is the troop of gaunt horseback riders on Charles Street near the corner of Beacon; called *The Partisans,* the modern metal casting by Polish-born Andrzei Pitynski wasn't supposed to be permanent, but 20 years later the city is still waiting for the artist to pick it up.

Besides nice public art, pushcarts selling tourist claptrap, and the Frog Pond—where toy boats sail in summer and skaters congregate in winter ($3 skate rental; for winter conditions, call 617-635-2197), one oft-overlooked feature is the 1756 **Central Burying Ground.** Initially this plot was for marginal figures, such as Boston's first Catholics (note the Celtic crosses), Freemasons, paupers (painter Gilbert Stuart among them), and foreigners, such as the British soldiers who occupied Boston during the Revolution, and Chow Manderien, a teenage Chinese sailor who fell from a ship's mast in 1798. Located on the short, Boylston Street side, this historic burying ground is across from the concentration of musical instrument showrooms known as "Piano Row."

The Boston Park Rangers conduct one-hour tours around the Common every Saturday in July and August, and at least once a month April-Oct.; for a precise schedule of these and other Common events, call the Boston Parks & Recreation **Events Line,** tel. (617) 635-3445.

Downtown Crossing

The intersection of Washington, Summer, and Winter Streets and several adjacent blocks form a brick-paved pedestrian shopping mall, anchored by Macy's and Filene's department stores. Major chains like Borders, HMV, the Gap, and General Nutrition Center are well represented, along with a handful of new and used camera shops on Bromfield Street, but the major retail trend in the area is toward off-price clothing stores. Shoppers in search of something unique should hunt out the **Society of Arts and Crafts'** downtown gallery, in the shopping concourse of 34 Summer/101 Arch St., behind Filene's.

Though now an entirely separate company from its above-ground namesake, **Filene's Basement,** tel. (617) 542-2011, remains the city's semi-sacred bargain-hunters' mecca, located in what used to be, prior to the 1872 Great Fire, Trinity Church's catacombs. Don't settle for the suburban or out-of-state satellites— they're pale imitations of Washington Street's 1912 original, connected directly to the Downtown Crossing T station. From coats to lingerie, famous labels to generic store brands, there's no shortage of wearables to choose from. There's no shortage, either, of eagle-eyed Basement veterans who brook no interference with their Holy Grail-quest-like search for that bargain of a lifetime. Some one-day blowout sales on high-end items like furs and wedding dresses unleash such human tsunamis through the aisles that accidental visitors may feel as if they've been swept into a reunion of punk-rock moshers and their elbow-swinging mothers.

Although there is a food court at The Corner, opposite Filene's, and various purveyors of sweets and sandwiches are installed all around the skirts of that venerable department store, peckish walkers should keep eyes aloft to spot **Anais,** a convenience store-cum-Armenian luncheonette on the second floor of the **Jewelry Exchange Building,** at 333 Washington St., across from Woolworth's. Fresh, delicious falafel, hummus, lahmajun, grape leaves, and great honeyed treats baked by owner Arto's wife are complemented by an unsurpassed bird's-eye view of Downtown Crossing's crowds. Anyone in the market for a diamond tiara or gold wedding band will want to shop the building's dozen other tenants, whose combined window displays create a sparkling labyrinth of precious metals and stones.

Pews and Graves

Lower Tremont Street, between the Common and Government Center, is lined with two of Boston's historic graveyards and several equally historic houses of worship. Among the latter is the 1810 **Park Street Church,** opposite the Park Street T station, whose 21-story steeple is as exemplary of New England's Congregational architecture as they come. Gunpowder stored in the basement during the War of 1812 is said to have prompted the name "Brimstone Corner," although Unitarians also used the nickname to mock the church's Bible-thumping Trinitarian preachers. The corner's previous occupant, a storage house, lent its name to the next-door **Granary Burying Ground,** founded in 1660 (wheelchair-accessible entrance is at the end of Tremont Pl. off Beacon St.). Among the illustrious Bostonians interred here are Crispus Attucks and the other victims of the Boston Massacre; patriots James Otis and Paul Revere; signers of the Declaration of Independence Samuel Adams, John Hancock, and Robert Treat Paine; Ben Franklin's parents (whose memorial obelisk bears an epitaph from their famous son); Boston's first mayor; and John Hull, whose 1652 Pine Tree Shilling was the first coin of the English colonies. Elizabeth Foster Goose is believed to be buried in an unmarked grave somewhere near the marked plot of her son-in-law Thomas Fleet, who collected and published the verses "Mother" Goose recited to her kids. (The stone for Mary Goose, despite what some may say, does *not* mark the famous nursery rhymer. For that matter, Elizabeth isn't the first, either: that honor belongs to the unnamed and possibly fictitious Mother Goose, *mére l'oye,* whose stories were published in 17th-century France by Charles Perrault 22 years before Fleet's alleged collection, no copy of which has ever been found by modern scholars.) Occasionally in summer and around Halloween you'll encounter some of these historical figures wandering around in costume giving autobiographical speeches; their resurrection is courtesy of the Boston Park & Recreation Deptartment. As in all Boston's historic burying grounds and cemeteries, grave rubbings are absolutely *verboten,* since the stones can't stand the abuse.

The city's oldest graveyard is just down the block: the 1630 **King's Chapel Burying**

Ground, near the corner of School St. Compare the bare-toothed skulls on the Puritans' slate markers with the plump-cheeked cherubs of a later age to get a rough idea of what the Bay Colony's earliest settlers felt about death and dying. Among the most prominent residents awaiting their maker here are Puritan leaders and Colonial governors John Endicott and John Winthrop, who took turns as top office holder for 28 of the Bay Colony's first 36 years. Other notables include *Mayflower* passenger Mary Chilton, Paul Revere's fellow alarm rider William Dawes, and Elizabeth Pain, who may have been the inspiration for Nathaniel Hawthorne's *The Scarlet Letter.* Despite common usage, the burying ground actually predates its neighboring namesake by more than half a century. Prior to becoming the first Unitarian church in the U.S. after the Revolution, King's Chapel was headquarters for the Church of England. Its location is a deliberate insult: epitomizing the Anglican contempt for those who tried to escape its high bishops, the original structure was unceremoniously built atop the Puritans' graves. If the current squat stone building, erected in the 1750s, looks like it's missing something, it is: a planned tower was never built for lack of funds.

Just minutes' walk away at the other end of short School St. is **Old South Meeting House,** 310 Washington St., tel. (617) 482-6439. Like the slightly older Old North Church, this landmark 1729 building is remembered primarily for the events of a single night during the prelude to the Revolution. On December 16, 1773, an overflowing crowd of 5,000 Bostonians hotly aired their resentments over a tea tax the English Parliament had refused to rescind. The debate—which had been running for days—was prompted by a recently arrived shipment of tea waiting to pass through customs. (To learn more about the outcome of the evening's alcohol-stoked gathering, head down to the waterfront and visit the Boston Tea Party Ship & Museum.) Old South's ecclesiastic history ended in 1872, but its role as a traditional New England meeting house—a forum for public address and debate—has never ceased. Highlighting three centuries of upholding freedom of expression, exhibits chronicle the controversies surrounding speakers from those now enshrined as heroic patriots and noble abolitionists to others, like

Ku Klux Klan leader David Duke, who challenge the notion of unconditional rights. Some cases have contemporary resonance: the eventual success of birth-control advocate and Planned Parenthood founder Margaret Sanger's campaign to give women unfettered access to contraception may be taken for granted by millions of adult Americans today, but if Sanger's ghost could return to Boston and call for distributing condoms in schools, she'd still cause a fuss. Gift shop and exhibits are open daily; "Middays at the Meeting House" public lecture and concert series held Thursdays at noon, year-round (admission charged).

Ben Franklin's baptism at Old South and the years he spent at the nation's first public school—Boston Latin—are among the thin threads by which Boston tries to lay an honest claim to the great Philadelphian's legacy. Tenuous or not, they won Franklin a statue in front of the Old City Hall, midway up School St. (you passed it coming from King's Chapel), and a place on the Freedom Trail. Far more obscure is his memorial on the Milk St. side of Old South, in the middle of the facade at No. 17 across the way—you have to look up or you'll miss it.

Old State House
Opposite the Boston National Historical Park Visitor Center and atop the subway entrance is the 1712 Old State House, one of Boston's few 18th-century buildings. The gilded lion and unicorn roof decorations, once despised symbols of the English crown rule, are an easily identified landmark over one of downtown's busier intersections, but for some inexplicable reason many of the passing pedestrian throng have never visited the **Old State House Museum,** tel. (617) 720-3290, within (open daily; $3). They don't seem to realize they're missing one of the most interesting (and inexpensive) historical museums the city has to offer. Permanent and changing exhibits complement the legacy of a structure that witnessed the Boston Massacre on its doorstep and the reading of the Declaration of Independence from its balcony. Annual re-enactments of these two events (every March 5 evening and July 4 afternoon, respectively) are only the most visible of the museum's programs; as steward of Boston history, the museum also hosts lectures, teacher workshops, and walk-

ing tours (nominal fees apply and reservations are recommended; tel. 617-720-3292), as well as regular gallery talks on a diverse set of topics (free with museum admission).

Faneuil Hall Marketplace

Since its rebirth in the mid-1970s, this renovated set of 19th-century market buildings, built over the original Town Cove docks, has become emblematic of the New Boston. As a high-quality tourist trap its singlehanded success in revitalizing what was then just another dilapidated downtown was so spectacular that nearly every major American city decided it had to have a copy of its own. Many have been developed by the same firm—the Rouse Company—and most follow a now-familiar theme: take a big rundown artifact whose original purpose has become obsolete, fill it with specialty food vendors and gift-oriented retailers, liberally deco-rate with pushcarts and colorful banners, and anchor where necessary with a museum, aquarium, or hotel. Derelict wharves, factories, and golden-age-of-steam railroad stations become an instant magnet for yuppies, suburbanites, tourists, and anyone who appreciates urban renewal à la Disney. But why knock it: hot food, cold drink, and clean bathrooms are in ready supply, and from the Disney Store off in the wings to Waterstone's Booksellers above the food court, you can scratch that shopping itch till your credit card cries uncle. The people-watching possibilities are superb, too, and street performers take to the cobblestone courtyards in summer (for a schedule of events and performers, call 617-446-8364).

Technically, the big shopping spread is Quincy (rhymes with "flimsy") Market, as the gold lettering over the mighty Greek Revival facade attests. Although locals apply its name to the whole modern complex, Faneuil (rhymes with spaniel) Hall, tel. (617) 635-3105, is really just the small rectangular building with the golden grasshopper on top. This structure is the third, designed by Charles Bulfinch in 1805; both name and weathervane were keepsakes from the first, which was donated to the city by wealthy merchant Peter Faneuil (whose tomb records his last name as "Funnel") and eventually destroyed by fire. The anti-royalist gatherings that inspired the "Cradle of Liberty" nickname are revived each summer during mock town meetings staged by the National Park Service, whose costumed interpreters debate political self-determination yards from the tumult of the marketplace just as people did in Sam Adams' day. Such colonial rabblerousing belongs to Faneuil Hall's second incarnation. The present portrait-filled and column-lined second-floor meeting hall has only been in use since Bulfinch's day, hosting everything from declarations of Presidential candidacies and primary debates to school graduations, concerts, and book signings (open daily unless pre-empted by special events; free. Not all the paintings are originals: the famous Gilbert Stuart portrait of America's first president—purposely posed next to his horse's posterior by the underpaid artist—is actually a copy by his daughter.

Occupying the attic is the **Armory of the Ancient and Honorable Artillery Company,** tel.

CELEBRATION OF ICE CREAM— IT'S THE SCOOPER BOWL!

If you've graduated to the expensive super-premium dairy desserts in your grocer's freezer, you won't want to miss the annual **Scooper Bowl,** tel. (617) 632-3300, on City Hall Plaza, across Congress St. from Faneuil Hall and the Haymarket area. Tuesday through Thursday the first full week of every June, tens of thousands of Bostonians reschedule work and suspend their diets in order to head down for their daily recommended dose of dairy products. Over the course of the three days, more than three dozen vendors scoop and serve 11 *tons* of ice cream, sherbet, frozen yogurt, and everything in between for the happy hordes.

Your selfless participation in the all-you-can-eat frenzy also helps two worthy causes: first, all proceeds are donated to the Dana-Farber Cancer Institute's Jimmy Fund, which supports research into childhood cancer; second, if you get hooked by the quality and flavor of what you taste, maybe you'll go out and buy more—and thus help preserve New England's dairy farmers from extinction (given the greater profit in houses than Holsteins, it's probably a losing battle, but every little bit helps—so stop counting calories and eat more ice cream!).

(617) 227-1638, displaying old documents, uniforms, weapons and other mementos of the nation's oldest existing military unit (Mon.-Fri.; free). Commissioned as a Puritan defense force in 1638, its subsequent ceremonial role (and blue-blooded membership) inspired James Michael Curley's irresistible quip: "Invincible in peace. Invisible in war."

Faneuil Hall still serves a commercial function, too, as it has since it was first built. Among its modern retailers is the basement **Boston City Store,** tel. (617) 635-2911, open Mon.-Sat. and selling real Beantown souvenirs—old porcelain enamel street signs, parking meters, traffic lights, and other cast-off pieces of City property. This shop will never stand accused of dealing in stylish contemporary design—city budgeteers paid for utility more than beauty—but you never know what quirky object may strike your fancy.

T riders should note that the nearest stations to Faneuil Hall and Quincy Market are Government Center and State Street; the three Quincy stations on the Red Line are outside Boston entirely, in the South Shore suburb of Quincy.

Haymarket

While Boston's early waterfront was erased by the great market built under mayor Josiah Quincy (whose identically named son and great-grandson also served as mayors), its character is partially preserved in the adjacent Haymarket. In the center of the so-called Blackstone Block, behind the luxury hotel whose stripped awnings face Faneuil Hall Marketplace from across North St., is a neglected remnant of the city's original shoreline. Enter from the wide alley next to the hotel's glass elevator to find informative historical displays hidden in diminutive **Creek Square.** But for the metal restaurant dumpsters and parked cars, the tight little lanes are as authentic a part of Olde Boston as you'll find anywhere in the city—smells and all. The 200-year time warp is reinforced a few yards west at Marshall St., where the 1767 Ebenezer Hancock House and a pair of taverns from the early 1800s face each other across the old cobblestones.

The inscribed Boston Stone by the gift shop door has a story behind it, now often mangled in the retelling. It was originally part of a paint mill's mixing trough, later made a cornerstone of a

potatoes and cabbage in Haymarket

private house built on the mill grounds. Since the mill was such a popular local landmark, the old trough was made into a Boston facsimile of the London Stone, and occasionally used as a surveyor's reference for measurement of distances from Boston—a function now served by the State House dome. In 1835, when the current building was erected, the trough was broken up into four pieces, with only the inscribed portion retained here in the foundation, reunited by mortar with its "mullen," the round stone that ground and mixed the trough's contents.

Imagine what other stories these stones could tell: Ben Franklin and his siblings scampering around here as sprats (their father's ship chandlery sat on the corner, about where the Bell in Hand Tavern now stands); patriots wetting their whistles at the Green Dragon, originally around the corner on Union Street. Isaiah Thomas, publisher of the outspokenly pro-independence *Massachusetts Spy,* probably trod these lanes as he went about his business opposing compromise with George III on the second floor of today's Union Oyster House. Ironically, in 1797 the same digs were rented by the Duc de Chartres, the future King Louis Philippe, in flight from the sharp tongue of Madame Guillotine; although Bostonians initially rallied in support of the French Revolution, by the time the Duke arrived Franco-American diplomatic relations were near breaking point.

Facing the Central Artery on the Blackstone St. side of the block is the Haymarket itself, the raucous, colorful, and almost insufferably crowded Friday and Saturday descendant of the meat and produce mart that once spilled out of Faneuil Hall and Quincy Market. Wooden stalls with pyramids of fruit, bushels of greens, and tables of iced seafood constantly threaten to overflow from either end of the street, particularly on Saturdays, the most hectic and picturesque of the two. Unlike the farmers' markets that sprout up around the city in summer, these gruff whaddaya-want and don't-touch guys are retailers, not growers; their prices kept low mostly by selling straight off the back of the truck. Deals that are too good to be true generally are: whatever it is, half will be spoiled rotten. A worthy reward for anyone wading into the shopping horde is a fast, cheap, tasty slice or two from **Haymarket Pizza,** midway along the block; weekdays, when the open-air stalls are stacked away, it's even easier to sniff out.

In sober counterpoint to such a festive contemporary and colonial brew stand the glass towers of the **Holocaust Memorial,** in Carmen Park on Union St. Each column represents one of the principal Nazi death camps: Majdanek, Chelmno, Sobibor, Treblinka, Belzec, and Auschwitz-Birkenau. Etched on the glass are numbers recalling the victims' identification tattoos, numbers no bigger than your signature covering every inch of every pane on every side, rising by the million up each five-story tower—six million numbers for the six million men, women, and children murdered by the Third Reich because they were Jews. Their memory reaches out through inscriptions by survivors; annotations also remind us that Nazi persecution also touched Gypsies, Jehovah's Witnesses, gays, Communists, and Catholic priests. At the dedication of the towers, Elie Wiesel said they stood so "no one should ever speak again about racial superiority."

Waterfront

In any reasonable weather, one of the best ways to spend an aimless hour or two is taking a prowl along the city's **Harborwalk.** For the full self-guided tour of Boston's waterfront, pick up a brochure from the Boston National Historical Park Visitor Center on State Street. Alternatively, just find your way down to the wharves

and start moseying. Eventually encompassing 43 miles of landscaped promenades, piers, and beaches, Harborwalk is still a work in progress; presently its best sections are between the North End's Christopher Columbus Park (next to the Long Wharf Marriott) and the new Federal courthouse on Northern Avenue's Fan Pier. Fetch some great take-out from **Sultan's Kitchen** or **Al Capone's,** on Broad St. landward of the Central Artery, and sate your hunger while soaking up the rays and listening to halyards smack against masts of gently rocking yachts. Here and there, stone walls, benches, or bollards provide a front-row seat on the marine minuet of small sloops and big motor cruisers, while everywhere greedy seagulls eye unattended snacks, or brazenly excavate discarded pizza crusts from trash receptacles. Jetliners wing in and out of Logan Airport across the harbor, and giant container cargo carriers inch through the dredged shipping channel between the open seas and the Chelsea docks. Although their collective tonnage barely puts Boston among the nation's top 40 ports, these leviathans are the local lifeline for oil, road salt, beer, shoes, raspberry concentrate, porcelain sinks, and olive oil, among other things.

For a look at life below the waterline, head over to the **New England Aquarium,** on Central Wharf, tel. (617) 973-5200 (daily; $10.50 adults, $9.50 seniors, $5 kids). The free outdoor exhibit of harbor seals and sea otters alone can bring a smile to the grumpiest kid or adult; the three-story saltwater tank and its surrounding aquaria— filled with creatures large and small, from sharks to nudibranches, sea turtles to sea anemones— will have you speaking like Jacques Cousteau. Penguins, sea lions, rainforest exhibits, and interactive displays on Boston's own harbor ecology add to the infotainment. The Aquarium's highly recommended whalewatching tours, departing from their doorstep, run weekends in April and late October, daily May through early October; reservations are strongly advised and may be held with a credit card, but payment must be made in cash or traveler's checks ($24 adults, $16.50-19 kids and seniors; tel. 617-973-5281).

The Aquarium is flanked by downtown's two major ferry terminals, Long Wharf and Rowes Wharf. The former is for seasonal Harbor Island ferries and year-round MBTA water shuttles to Charlestown Navy Yard and Lovejoy Wharf at North Station; the latter is for the Logan Airport Water Taxi and commuter boats to the South Shore. Various harbor cruises also depart from both wharves.

Museum Wharf

Narrow Fort Point Channel divides downtown from South Boston, a mostly residential neighborhood whose commercial and industrial end along the Channel is distinguished by block upon block of 19th-century warehouses. Three-score or more of these large brick buildings, decorated with faded old advertisements and wearing metal medallions stamped with their construction date and the logo of their owner, the Boston Wharf Company, sit squarely across the Channel from South Station and shiny modern towers like the Federal Reserve Bank, whose aluminum skin is reminiscent of the St. Louis Gateway Arch. Shunned for years by commercial renters, the huge warehouses, with their magnificent light and unfinished beam-and-brick interiors, became home to scads of artists; then, during the real estate boom of the 1980s, office-hungry professionals suddenly looked across the Channel, liked what they saw, and jump-started Fort Point's transformation into prime commercial space, crowding out the artists. An economic lull has given the arts community the opportunity to buy or take long-term leases on a couple buildings, thus preserving some permanent studio space for working artists, but plans for a nearby convention center and increasing demand for office space are causing the professionals to start licking their chops again over these lovely old industrial buildings. The sad paradox is that the artists whose presence and vitality make derelict industrial neighborhoods trendy and desirable then become victims of their own success. The city's movers and shakers have been slow to recognize the value of protecting artists' habitat; for now, Fort Point is still funky and art-savvy, but it seems inevitable that the cubicles and Dilberts and Starbucks will come. Until then, though, several nifty shops and galleries on the 300 blocks of both Summer and Congress Streets are worth a visit, especially if you enjoy vintage 1950s accessories and furnishings or theatrical masks and costumes. Don't miss the

Fort Point Arts Community's autumn Open Studios Weekend, tel. (617) 423-4299, either, if you're around the weekend after Columbus Day. Who knows? If you help ring the cash registers loudly enough, it may even wake up City Hall.

Permanently anchored in the middle of the Fort Point Channel next to the Congress Street bascule bridge is the *Beaver II,* a reproduction of one of the three brigs boarded that December night in 1773 by groups of colonials who dumped the ships' cargo—nearly 45 tons of Ceylon tea—into Boston Harbor. If it sounds like an event that shouldn't have been missed, step aboard the **Boston Tea Party Ship & Museum,** tel. (617) 338-1773, and take part in a reenactment, complete with bales of "tea" that you may heave into the drink (daily March-Nov.; $7 adult, $3.50-5.50 kids and seniors). Sailors aboard the vessel acquaint you with life on an 18th-century merchant ship; dockside exhibits explain what motivated the colonials' actions. The nominal tax imposed by the English Parliament's April 1773 Tea Act is the most frequently cited spark, but equally offensive to many of Boston's most influential patriots was the monopoly that legislation gave to the financially troubled East India Company, at the expense of local importers. Winter visitors in town on the Sunday closest to December 16th can catch the Tea Party's anniversary, a spectator event celebrated with the aid of the costumed Middlesex County Volunteers, who swarm the ship and apply their axes to tea chests in a rousing demonstration of patriotic fervor.

On the South Boston side of the Channel a stone's throw from the *Beaver II* stands the three-story Milk Bottle, a home-grown example of "googie" fast-food architecture. One of a handful built around the state in the 1930s to advertise and sell milk products for locally based J. P. Hood Dairy, this particular bottle was destined to be scrapped but was revived as a summertime dairy bar and snack shop. It's also become the emblem for Museum Wharf, whose giant brick warehouse holds two outstanding places to while away an afternoon or two. **The Computer Museum,** tel. (617) 423-6758, the world's only museum wholly devoted to computers, from their history to relics of their evolution, from R2-D2 to a walk-through PC (the mouse is half as big as a Honda Civic). If it pertains to computational machinery, it's here. The extensive interactive exhibits are, of course, where visitors spend most of their time, discovering the computer's power to teach and amuse (and often do both at once). Open daily mid-June through early September, Tues.-Sun. and Monday holidays the rest of the year ($7, half price Sunday 3-5 p.m.).

Sharing the warehouse with the high-tech stuff is **The Children's Museum,** tel. (617) 426-8855, one of the leading museums for kids in the country, with hours of activities and plenty of encouraging staff. Here, too, emphasis is on interaction: karaoke in a soundproof booth, an ingenious climbing cage, giant Legos. Mock-ups of such places as grandma's house (frozen in 1959, from toys to TV commercials), a Japanese home, and a Hispanic supermarket are full of things to play with. Exhibits such as "Teen Tokyo" engage older children, too. A popular place for kids' birthday parties, adult office parties, and even weddings, the museum is open daily June-Sept., Tues.-Sun. and Monday holidays the rest of the year ($7 adults, $6 kids 2-15, $2 for one-year olds, infants free; Friday after 5 p.m. all admissions are $1).

Appetites piqued by perambulating around Fort Point can be sated inside the grand concourse of magesterial old South Station, on the downtown side of the channel, where everything from pizza and salads to croissants and yogurt are on offer in the food court. (Dessert mavens and devotees of Judy Rosenberg's *All-Butter Fresh Cream Sugar-Packed No Holds Barred Baking Book* will be thrilled to know there's an outpost of the author's famed **Rosie's Bakery** here, too.) Of course, if you're like Julia Child you may prefer to stick with the french fries from McDonald's, located on the ground floor of the Children's Museum.

Chinatown

Though geographically quite tiny, Chinatown's outsized appeal is based on its food and unruly urban atmosphere. It's also the natural destination for shoppers seeking the chunky porcelain table settings or industrial aluminum cookware found in your average Chinese restaurant. For a traditional Chinese remedy to restore balance to your *ch'i,* consult the friendly and helpful herbalists in the dispensaries on

Harrison or Washington Streets; just look for the aromatic storefronts whose walls are covered with wooden apothecary cabinets. Or, for some simple attitude adjustment, check out **Jack's Joke Shop,** 38 Boylston, near Tremont, a unique assemblage of silly, sophomoric, and playful gifts, gags, and disguises.

Beneath the gift shops and culinary attractions, Chinatown has a rich and variegated history as deep as any section of Boston. The yards-wide Roxbury Neck that joined the peninsular town to the mainland lay under present-day Washington St. (which by a commemorative legislative fiat runs all the way to the Rhode Island line). In the early 1800s, the rural isthmus was widened with landfill for new middle-class housing; a generation later, these tradesmen's houses were subdivided into tenements for the new influx Chinese, Irish, Europeans, and Syrians. Like every other Chinatown on the East Coast, Boston's carries a legacy of labor disputes and the 1869 completion of the transcontinental railroad, which made low-wage workers from California viable strike-breaking alternatives to those from Europe. Boston's community can be traced specifically to North Adams, in western Massachusetts: after strike-breaking Chinese shoemakers imported from San Francisco had served their purpose, many were drawn to the state's capital port. Some stayed, employed by local garment manufacturers. Tyler Street's restaurants are one result; the oldest has been serving Chinese cuisine since 1879.

Since the arrival of the railroad at South Station in the late 1800s, the neighborhood has been continually eroded at the edges: first by the industry that lent its name to the Leather District next to South Station, then by highways and street widenings on two sides, and finally by burgeoning growth in the hospitals and medical schools at its southwestern corner. For 20 years, it was also hemmed in by the "Combat Zone," a city-sanctioned strip of porn shops and triple-X cinemas that once inhabited three blocks of Washington Street. Made nationally famous by Arkansas congressman Wilbur Mills and his swimming partner Fanne Fox (the "Argentine Firecracker" whose companionship sank Mills' career in the mid-1970s), the Zone has all but vanished under a blanket of asphalt parking lots. But lack of residential character doesn't mean lack of residents; since the post-WW II adoption of its modern sweatshop-free identity, the replacement of tenement rowhouses with huge apartment blocks has made the neighborhood far and away the city's most crowded.

The human throng and overlapping layers of multilingual signage give the area an exciting high-octane, gotta-hurry feel well into the late-night hours, but if you slow down you might notice minor details, such as the Liberty Tree embellishment in the brick facade of one ancient Washington Street building, or the soot-blackened bust of Shakespeare next to a Beach Street doorway. For some historical guidance, purchase a Women's Heritage Trail booklet from the Boston National Historic Park Visitor Center on State Street—Chinatown is one of its four discreet tours.

The Theater District

Although Boston's Puritan taboos on public music, art, and even Christmas lingered well into the 19th century, by the end of the Civil War the city had begun sharing in widely popular entertainments such as burlesque and vaudeville. (It was a pair of Hub business partners, B. F. Keith and Edward Albee, who first packaged formerly risqué vaudeville as wholesome family fare in 1885; their "Sunday school circuit" of tightly orchestrated variety shows in lavishly decorated theaters launched the careers of many famous American hoofers and comedians, and shaped popular entertainment for almost a century.) So many Broadway-bound productions were whipped into shape here that Boston was typecast as Times Square's testing ground, but by the 1920s celluloid was eclipsing all but the bawdiest live acts. During the Depression, many of the city's 55 theaters became cinemas, but time, TV, and the lure of the suburbs have wiped out numerous once-proud landmarks. Along with the demolition of legitimate theaters, urban renewal and fewer Navy Yard battleship visits forced the retirement of less virtuous Boston icons like Zorita the Snake Girl, whose act at Scollay Square's Old Howard was the talk of swabbies around the world.

After a long dry spell, a series of multimillion-dollar renovations has brought some of the original luster back to a smaller, less cohesive Theater District around the intersection of Tremont and Stuart Streets, between the Orange and Green lines. None of the theaters currently offers public tours, but you can usually peek inside with a simple box office visit. From the outside, **The Wang Center for the Performing Arts** looks like it could be an old department store in downtown Chicago or Philadelphia, but the interior is possibly the district's most breathtaking, with its bedazzling multi-story marble and gold-leaf lobby modeled after Versailles, and a cavernous auditorium copied from the Paris Opera. Originally built as a movie palace in 1925—then as now one of the world's largest stages—the Wang is one of three opulent Theater District confections by Clarence Blackall, Boston's preeminent theater architect. The more staid 1914 **Wilbur Theatre,** next door; the beautiful *fin de siècle* **Colonial Theatre,** on Boylston St.; and two others a few blocks away (no longer used as theaters) are the last remaining of the 14 he designed.

THE NORTH END

The North End is Boston's Italian neighborhood. It hasn't always been; a century ago, it was still a strong Irish and Jewish quarter, along with the neighboring West End. As both groups moved up socially and migrated toward more spacious neighborhoods—Jews to Roxbury, Irish to South Boston and Jamaica Plain—the new Italian and Sicilian immigrants took their places. The old-world feel remains stronger here than in many parts of the city despite the conversion of waterfront apartment buildings and warehouses into high-priced yuppie condos.

Overlooking the picturesque granite cobblestones of handkerchief-sized North Square—where Sun Court meets Moon Street—is the home of America's most famous messenger and silversmith, and Boston's only 17th-century building open to the public. The **Paul Revere House** was modified in both the century before Revere lived in it and in the centuries since, but it remains a fine example of what much of early Boston looked like. Besides interpreting Revere's life and times, this and the associated 1711 Pierce-Hichborn House, next door (Nathaniel Hichborn was one of Paul's cousins), are a museum of Boston's pre- and post-Revolutionary history (daily except winter Mondays; $2.50; tel. 617-523-2338).

CEMETERIES AND BURYING GROUNDS

A cemetery (from the Greek word for "a sleeping place") was conceived in the mid-19th century as landscaped gardens in which the dead reposed peacefully. The first (and perhaps still this country's most outstanding) was Mount Auburn Cemetery, across the river in Cambridge.

By contrast, burying grounds were unkempt plots of land to which the dead were rudely consigned to molder in their graves until Judgment Day. The idea that decent burial and the maintenance of the grave of the dearly departed might make one whit of difference to the disposition of his or her soul was foreign to the Puritans, who set aside and named Boston's burying grounds. The Puritans believed in predestination: if you were of the Elect, you'd make it to Heaven, and if you, like most people, shared in the sins of Adam and Eve, you didn't. In either case, there was no point in wasting effort prettying up your grave.

The fact that the city's 17th- and 18th-century burying grounds today bear a strong, manicured resemblance to 19th-century cemeteries is the result of modern-day tidying up. What you see on the surface is wholly unlike the true state of affairs underground—where the residents are actually strewn about haphazardly, often unmarked; piled in on top of previous burials; or evicted by later interments.

The fame and attention accorded the **Old North Church** (Christ Church), tel. (617) 523-6676, on Salem St. derives almost entirely from its role on April 18, 1775. That night, two men hung lanterns in its steeple as part of Paul Revere's contingency plan to convey a message he himself might be detained from delivering—namely, that British troops were on the march to Lexington and Concord, and someone in Charlestown needed to raise the alarm. As it turned out, Revere succeeded in evading the cordon of British security thrown up around the city and was able to carry the message in person. At the same time, the anonymous express rider who *did* set off to raise the alarm after seeing the signal lights was apparently intercepted by a British patrol. An 18th-century meetinghouse across from Paul Revere's home had a nickname so similar—"Old North Meeting"—that it raised modern questions about which structure actually deserved the credit for being the scene of all this nocturnal intrigue. The people involved (Christ Church's sexton and vestryman lit the lanterns), the less suitable nature of North Meeting's lower steeple (nowhere near as visible from Charlestown), and unconvincing suggestions that Revere confused an Anglican church with a Puritan meetinghouse in his subsequent testimony on the affair all argue against the meetinghouse, which was dismantled by the British in 1776.

As for the remaining Old North, it's a beauty, built in 1723 after the inspiring designs of London church architect Sir Christopher Wren (open daily; free; special events scheduled the Sunday and Monday closest to April 19). The present 175-foot steeple is the third—and less than 50 years old; its predecessors both fell victim to strong winds. Housed in the tower are the nation's oldest church bells, cast in 1744. (Paul Revere served as one of the ringers as a teenager.) In the rear of the next-door gift shop are an assortment of curios, from a misprinted Bible to tea leaves from the Boston Tea Party. Behind the church, a narrow walkway between apartment gardens descends into the **Paul Revere Mall** ("the Prado" to neighborhood residents), a popular tree-lined plaza adorned with bronze tablets commemorating local people and events. The former 1802 New North Church (now St. Stephen's), across from the Hanover Street end, is the only remaining of five Boston churches by noted Federal-style architect Charles Bulfinch.

Up Hull Street from the front of Old North is 17th-century **Copp's Hill Burying Ground.** Fine views and interesting stories attend the stones here, atop what was originally known as Windmill Hill, where the Puritan ministerial Mather dynasty shares the dust with a state governor, Revolutionary War patriots, sexton Robert Newman of Old North, and some thousand mostly unidentified colonial African-Americans. From here, British cannon shelled Charlestown during the Battle of Bunker Hill; during their occupation of Boston, the Redcoats also took potshots at Copp's Hill grave markers, as you can still see.

What today is the playground on Commercial Street below Copp's Hill was the epicenter of Boston's most improbable disaster: the Molasses Flood. On January 15, 1919, a ruptured metal storage tank unleashed a tidal wave of 2.5 million gallon of molasses onto North End streets. The 14,000-ton surge swept dozens of buildings off their foundations, bent the iron stanchions of the elevated street railway like paper clips, and injured 150 people and gruesomely drowned or asphyxiated over a score more in the viscous brown syrup. The cleanup took weeks, and the smell lingered for years.

Boston may yet be the home of the bean and the cod, but a modern rhymer might be moved to add lobster to that list. If you want some of these crustaceans of your own—live, cooked, prepared as a salad or packed to ship anywhere in the U.S.—stop by **Bay State Lobster Company,** 379 Commercial St., the region's largest wholesale and retail seafood market, open daily except Christmas, tel. (617) 523-7960.

CHARLESTOWN

Like Boston, Charlestown was once a bulbous, hilly peninsula whose original outline has been obscured by extensive landfill. Unlike Boston, Charlestown had a resident population of Native Americans when the first English settler, Thomas Walford, arrived, in 1628. Inhabitants of one of several Pawtucket villages on the north side of the Charles River, Walford's hosts endured a humiliating encounter with Plymouth soldiers in 1621 (who insisted on buying the Native American women's clothing until they were stripped naked), the 1629 arrival of John Winthrop and his Salem crowd, and a 1633 smallpox epidemic before finally being forced to move off the peninsula by its steadily expanding Puritan settlement.

Founded a year before Boston, Charlestown was a separate community until 1874, when it was annexed by the growing metropolis next door. Traces of the colonial past were all but erased when the town was destroyed by British incendiary shells during the Battle of Bunker Hill; one exception is the 1630 Phipps Street Burying Ground, a block south of Main, noted for especially fine carvings and its monument to

university namesake John Harvard. After the Revolution, the town was rapidly rebuilt, producing the maze of narrow streets that confuse and frustrate all but resident "Townies." The late-18th- and early-19th century architecture abounding between City Square and the Bunker Hill Monument is by itself excellent reason to make the decidedly unattractive hike across the bridge from the North End, but if you need further inspiration, simply take a deep breath inside the **Sorelle Bakery,** 1 Monument Ave., or **Figs,** a wood-fired brick-oven pizzeria around the corner at 67 Main St.

Charlestown Navy Yard
Until it was given to the Boston National Historical Park, after the Vietnam War, this 17-acre chunk of the Charlestown waterfront was one of the nation's half-dozen naval shipyards. Numerous reminders of its 174-year history of building and repairing warships remain: drydocks (still in use), a quarter-mile-long ropewalk (a long shed in which rope was once made—this one the work of the same architect who designed Quincy Market), the WW II destroyer USS *Cassin Young,* and the crown jewel, the **USS *Constitution,*** "Old Ironsides"(tour schedule tel. 617-242-5601). Nicknamed for its resistance to British cannonballs in the War of 1812, the *Constitution* is the world's oldest commissioned naval vessel, launched in 1797. Free tours of this grand frigate are given by active-duty Navy personnel, who explain the inner workings of the ship with characteristic by-the-book precision and not a little dry humor—as one would expect from those familiar with captains' whims, sailors' gripes, and the toil of preparing a warship for all contingencies. While tour hours and off-season availability are entirely in the hands of the Navy commander, rather than the Park Service, you can always count on the daily morning raising and sunset lowering of the flag, accompanied by a booming broadside volley from the ship's cannon.

The adjacent **USS *Constitution* Museum,** tel. (617) 426-1812, supplements the actual vessel with exhibits tracing its history. Thumb through nifty "cruise journals" accompanying maps of the ship's globe-straddling missions, compare your crisis management instincts with those of the captains, see what Boston was like when the *Constitution* was launched, and examine the craftsmanship that has gone into its restoration. Interactive videos put you aboard the ship during its maiden voyage or at the helm in battle (daily; $4).

Located in the fairly modern brick pavilion on Constitution St. outside the Navy Yard's main gates, the National Park Service Visitor Center, tel. (617) 242-5601, has free information about both the Yard and the Boston National Historical Park as a whole. Ranger-led activities vary with the season, from year-round *Cassin Young* tours to summer programs focusing on lesser known parts of the yard. The center also has a small bookstore and some all-too-rare public bathrooms.

Bunker Hill Monument

As every student of American history must know by now, the Bunker Hill Monument and the battle that it commemorates are misnamed. The bloody June 1775 confrontation between British regulars and colonial militia from Connecticut, Massachusetts, and New Hampshire actually took place on Breed's Hill, east of taller Bunker Hill. Colonial commander Colonel Prescott had been ordered to fortify Bunker Hill; while at least one map in circulation at the time mislabeled the terrain, the modern consensus is that Prescott chose Breed's deliberately (possibly because it was closer to Boston). Though the British won the day, it was a Pyrrhic victory; their nearly 50% casualty rate was a great morale boost to the

colonists. It also proved that the militia's success against the Redcoats in Concord two months earlier had been no fluke—a fact not lost on either the French, who eventually sided with the Americans, or British General Burgoyne, whose prediction after the battle—that the Crown had as good as lost its colonies—was never brought to the attention of King George.

The 19th-century memorial obelisk marking the battlefield attracted great fanfare, with such celebrities as the Marquis de Lafayette laying its cornerstone and Daniel Webster giving the dedication speech, but insufficient financing prolonged construction over 17 years. The surrounding townhouses are a direct result: residential lots on the battlefield were sold off to raise much-needed cash. Though the windows at the top are small, their views are grand, well worth huffing and puffing up the 295-step spiral staircase. The base lodge explains the battle with artifacts, a large diorama, and quotes from participants on both sides; the attendant park ranger also gives talks and answers questions (daily; free; tel. 617-242-5669).

BACK BAY

The Esplanade

When the Back Bay was first enclosed, in the early 1800s, by a 1.5-mile mill dam, the thoroughfare on top attracted promenading couples fleeing the curiosity of their in-town neighbors.

The Boston skyline backdrops the Esplanade.

Romantic saunters are still possible along the **Charles River Embankment** (better known as the Esplanade), especially on warm evenings accompanied by the floodlit plume of the lagoon fountain and the city skyline painted in lights. Just don't expect much privacy: from sunrise until well after sunset, joggers, skaters, and cyclists fill the landscaped paths of this early-20th century addition to Back Bay (notice the old 1821 seawall, still visible along Storrow Drive), while sunbathers insouciantly sprawl over the grassy open spaces whenever weather permits. Between spring and fall, the lower river basin is sprinkled with a confetti of sails, attended by an audience of ducks. On July 4, a zillion happy celebrants on beach blankets and boat decks listen to the Boston Pops perform at the Hatch Shell—one of many free concerts by the Pops and others, from jazz to alternative rock, offered at the Shell throughout July and August.

Four footbridges connect the Esplanade to Back Bay, from the coral pink Arthur Fiedler footbridge at Arlington St. to the ramp at the Boston side of the Harvard Bridge. The Harvard Bridge—on which Massachusetts Ave. crosses into Cambridge—is easily remembered as the bridge with absolutely no connection whatsoever to Harvard University; the bridge that *does* go to the university is the Anderson Bridge, in Allston. Harvard Bridge instead links Back Bay to the Massachusetts Institute of Technology, which is why the span's sidewalks are calibrated in "smoots"—a length of measure based on the height of an MIT fraternity pledge, Oliver R. Smoot, Jr., who was rolled across the bridge in the late 1950s. Collectors of old Boston band trivia may also recognize the bridge and its terrific backdrops as the location of a mid-1980s music video by the Del Fuegos.

The Public Garden

Although considered part of his city-wide "Emerald Necklace," Frederick Law Olmsted did not design this formal English floral park (whose name is always pronounced as singular, not plural). Occupying a shallow Back Bay marsh originally filled for the benefit of Boston's fire-prone ropewalks, the garden was nearly nipped in the bud by a block of houses, but a sensible 1859 legislative act, backed by public referendum, forever set aside this horticultural jewel for the city

and its people. Each year, 10,000 new tulip bulbs (old ones are recycled in other city parks) and an equal or greater number of annuals dispel all memory of gray December or ice-bound February so effectively that Bostonians are always genuinely perplexed by the following winter's first snowfall. In addition to the hothouse miracles performed by the dedicated park department gardeners, visitors may enjoy the summer shade or autumnal colors of over 400 trees representing 74 species, from oaks, beeches, maples, and elms to a giant sequoia, Amur cork tree, and three species of Japanese scholar tree. Among the garden's tallest trees are the three dawn redwoods, an ancient relic species thought extinct until a living grove was found in Japanese-occupied Manchuria in 1941 by Harvard botanists. When war broke out between the U.S. and Japan soon after, smuggling out seedlings became a major covert operation; therein surely lies a curious tale waiting to be told. To help ensure the species' survival, the specimens were propagated extensively at the university's Arnold Arboretum. If you notice the tree shedding its needles in the fall, don't be concerned—*Metasequoia glyptostroboides* is the only known redwood species that's deciduous.

The Public Garden is also a veritable outdoor art museum. Among its diverse collection of statuary and memorials is the Ether Monument, Lillian Swann Saarinen's *Jungle Book*-inspired "Bagheera" fountain, a 14th-century feudal Japanese warlord's lantern, and the city's most beloved public artwork, the *Make Way for Ducklings* group by Nancy Schön, from Robert McCloskey's children's book. The **Swan Boats** that ply the lagoon are nearly museum pieces, too: inspired by Wagner's *Lohengrin,* the two-ton pedal-powered boat concession has belonged to the same family since 1877, when Robert Paget built the first one out of copper, wood, and bicycle parts. Rides are offered daily mid-April through September ($1.75 adults, 95¢ kids).

A block from the Garden's western corner is the **Gibson House Museum,** 137 Beacon St., tel. (617) 267-6338, dedicated to the Victorian Age. Built the same year as its flowery neighbor, the Italian Renaissance Revival mansion wears its finery on the inside, behind thick drapes and stout double doors. With its low light and lush furnishings—all original, right down to the upholstery—the house and its tchotchkes are such a perfectly preserved time capsule that it needed no retouching before being used as a set for *The Bostonians,* the 1984 Merchant-Ivory film of Henry James' satirical Victorian novel. In addition to house tours, the museum presents a variety of seasonal programs illustrating life in the late 19th century, from period games and kids' parties to afternoon high tea and holiday decorating. Open Wed.-Sun. May-Oct., weekends only Nov.-March (tours hourly 1-3 p.m.; $4).

Commonwealth Avenue Mall

The massive project to fill in the tidal mudflats of Back Bay was built around the idea of a grand landscaped boulevard intended to rival the Champs-Elysées. That boulevard became Commonwealth Avenue ("Comm Ave." to locals), and the fancy townhouses overlooking its center greenway went up about as fast as the gravel fill was put down. Of course, fashions changed over the 35 years it took to fill the flats from the edge of the Public Garden westward to what's now the Boston University campus, so Comm Ave. essentially became a life-size style guide spanning a third of a century. To anyone remotely interested in architectural ornament, a stroll past the alphabetical grid of cross-streets—Arlington, Berkeley, Clarendon, and so forth—is like a bird-watcher's trip to Costa Rica: so many species in so small a space that it makes your head spin. Gothic dormers, corbeled and stacked chimneys, oriel windows, mansard roofs, rusticated arches, polychrome tiles, bow fronts, and conical turrets are among the features adorning the residences and private clubs along the Mall, each block containing some attempt to one-up the competition. The *pièce de résistance* is on the corner of Hereford St. a block from the end of Back Bay: the chateau-like Burrage Mansion is the limestone epitome of exuberance—gargoyles, griffins, and all. Among the avenue's registered historic landmarks is H. H. Richardson's first major work, the 1871 Church of the Holy Bean Blowers. Located on the corner of Clarendon, it's known to its congregation as the First Baptist Church. The nickname comes from the angels at the corner of the campanile's decorative stone frieze, carved by Italian artisans after a design by Frédéric Auguste Bartholdi, better known as the sculptor of the Statue of Liberty.

The Mall itself has plenty of fine statuary. Witness the likeness of historian and sailor Samuel Eliot Morison atop one of his beloved Gloucester boulders, gazing seaward over the tidal litter of bronzed shells, weeds, and scuttling crabs. Several of the pieces here are intriguing anachronisms; famous Yankees and war heroes are not so surprising, but why, you may reasonably wonder, is a statue of Argentine president Sarmiento here? (He copied Boston educator Horace Mann's K-12 grade school model when restructuring Argentina's educational system.) Another incongruity is Leif Eriksson; 19th-century Harvard chemistry professor Eben Horsford, inventor of Rumford Baking Powder, practiced some alchemy over Leif's legend in a vain attempt at proving the mighty Viking explorer lunched here in the Back Bay. While historically unsound, his speculations *were* transmuted into a statue of the Norseman, now standing sentinel at the forgotten far end of the Mall.

Newbury Street

After spending days walking in the footsteps of dead patriots or studying the stone-cold legacy of dead architects, you are to be forgiven if you question whether Boston has a pulse. Come for a stroll down Newbury St. and such doubts will be quickly dispelled. If you wake up on the wrong side of an overpriced bed or get frazzled by the rush-hour crush on the T, come for a stroll down Newbury and feel the warm fuzzies take hold with each step. Rain or shine, day or night, summer or winter, Newbury puts Boston in its best light.

What's the secret? The continuity and elegance of the bowfront rowhouses helps set a good stage. So does that comfortable scale: there are no overpowering buildings here. But the key is probably the simple fact that in addition to being a busy, chic commercial street, people still live here, above the shops, still do their laundry in the coin-op down the block, still buy their aspirin at the CVS and their hardware at the True Value. And while there's no shortage of classy apparel and pricey restaurants, second-hand stores and a smattering of genuinely low-priced eateries help keep the street from becoming exclusively devoted to affluence and conspicuous consumption.

Initial appearances to the contrary, Newbury actually changes quite a bit between Arlington Street and Mass. Ave. The Public Garden end belongs to the Ritz-Carlton crowd, Burberry, Cartier, Versace, and art collectors. The first block alone accounts for about half the street's dozen contemporary art galleries (for a guide to all the street's galleries, stop in at Gallery NAGA, in the Church of the Covenant on the corner of Berkeley, and ask for a copy of the latest Artmap). Approaching the mammoth Tower Records overlooking the Turnpike at Mass. Ave., piercing and tattooing boutiques multiply, and Doc Marten boots outnumber Kenneth Cole loafers. But some constants *do* abide: expensive hair salons (about 80 in eight blocks) and Starbucks, at both ends and in the middle.

Many of the boutiques come and go like spring fashions, but the longevity of Newbury's bookstores happily suggests residents are as devoted to reading as to perfect coiffures and cappuccino. Up the street from DuBarry Restaurant's four-story mural of celebrity Bostonians is the flagship store of **Waterstone's Booksellers,** an Irish-English chain, the best in the Back Bay for just about everything new, from the latest popular fiction to foreign language literature, kids' books to cookbooks and architecture texts. Open until 10 p.m. most nights, it's located in the grand Romanesque rock pile at Exeter St., a can't-miss-it landmark still known to most as the Exeter Street Theater building. Up the next block, at No. 223, **Spenser's Mystery Books** specializes in used and newly published volumes. Be sure to let the owner know what you're looking for; not only will he point you to its precise location, he'll come up with a handful of additional suggestions to match your tastes. (For champagne truffles to die for, cross the street to **Teuscher of Switzerland,** at No. 230, makers of the best chocolate in the world—priced accordingly, of course.) Last but not least, the funkier block between Hereford and Mass. Ave. features not one but two purveyors of the printed word. **Trident Bookseller Cafe** is your source for pop psychology, Eastern religion, some poetry and nonfiction, and a terrific magazine selection; and **Avenue Victor Hugo Books,** across the street, is the second-hand book lover's dream come true.

Boston is also a great place to shop for music, too—either recorded or in raw sheet form. For the widest possible range under one roof, the six-story, Frank Gehry-designed **Tower Records** casting its shadow over this last block is a good place for most CD and cassette shoppers to start. Don't think that just because you've seen one Tower, you've seen 'em all: unlike giant record stores elsewhere in America, Boston's retail music heavyweights stock a few copies of lots of titles, rather than whole bins full of a handful of titles. If your interest is radio-friendly alternative rock, or anything that makes parents and roommates slam doors in disgust, follow the pierced tribe into the **Newbury Comics** store at No. 332, above basement-level **Condom World.** Or, for a true sonic souvenir of Boston, check out **Mystery Train II,** back at 306 Newbury, tel. (617) 536-0216, which carries one of the city's best selections of consignment tapes and CDs featuring local artists. Solicit the expertise of the staff—almost all of whom are band members themselves—and you could save yourself months of clubhopping.

Copley Square

Architecture is, like history, one of Boston's strong suits, and numerous parts of the city have drawn an ace or two. A couple of spots, like Faneuil Hall, have even come up with a full house. But only Copley Square has been dealt a royal flush. Four superb 19th-century buildings in and around the square—a hotel, a library, and two churches—are juxtaposed with a dramatic 20th-century office tower (New England's tallest building). The prevailing ideologies of two centuries are played out in masonry and tempered glass: here the romantic medieval fascination of Ruskinian Gothic and Richardsonian Romanesque, there the classical poise of a pair of Italian Renaissance revivals, all under the reflective gaze of 1970s modernism. Arguably, it's a collection unrivaled in Boston.

Designed by Henry Hobson Richardson a year after his nearby First Baptist commission on Comm. Ave., **Trinity Church,** tel. (617) 536-0944, is recognized as a national architectural landmark. A definitive example of the Romanesque revival that became synonymous with Richardson, this early Victorian fixture in the heart of Copley Square also contains interior decoration by sculptor Augustus Saint-Gaudens and stained glass artist John LaFarge (daily; free). Fridays during the academic year, free organ recitals are presented just past noon. Outside, the square itself is host to special events throughout the year: New Year's ice sculptures, mid-April's Marathon, summer after-work concerts and twice-weekly farmers markets. Skateboarders practice their moves on the upper level of the fountain, kids of all ages cool their heels in the lower level, and the real little tykes pose for snapshots on the Tortoise and Hare sculpture. Those for whom its verses are still fresh pause and recollect *The Prophet* at the Kahlil Gibran memorial near the Bostix discount ticket kiosk. A good time is generally had by all.

From the 60th floor of that mirror in which Trinity is forever admiring herself, the **John Hancock Observatory,** tel. (617) 247-1977, offers New England's highest indoor view over the region's largest city (daily; $4.25). Plagued after construction by problems with falling windows and unanticipated wind stress, the cloud-catching, sharp-edged Hancock Tower has earned local appreciation as one of Boston's most distinctive landmarks.

Also fronting Copley Square is the 1895 Renaissance Revival **Boston Public Library,** identifiable by its thorny Dr. Seuss-like cast iron lamps and the directory of the Western cultural canon inscribed around the frieze. Behind the big bronze doors' allegorical figures of Knowledge and Wisdom, Truth and Romance, and Music and Poetry is a beautifully rosy marble lobby with majestic lions guarding stairs up to the ornate vaulted-ceiling reading rooms. The library's architecture, history, and art are all thoroughly reviewed during the engaging free tours that start inside the Trinity-facing Dartmouth St. entrance (year-round Monday 2:30 p.m., Tuesday and Thursday 6 p.m., Fri.-Sat. 11 a.m., and, October through mid-May, Sunday 2 p.m.). Free copies of the artists' own explanatory essays are also available for several of the library's enormous murals, including *The Muses of Inspiration,* by Puvis de Chavannes, and John Singer Sargent's *Judaism and Christianity.* In warm weather, wet or dry, the quiet Italian courtyard is one of the best reading or postcard-writing spaces in the city.

On the corner of Boylston and Dartmouth opposite the library is the **New Old South Church,** built to house the congregation that outgrew downtown's historic Old South Meeting House. Boston being Boston, even this "new" church is older than the telephone (except for the bell tower—the 246-foot original started to lean so much it had to be dismantled; the shorter replacement was built in 1940). Like Trinity, New Old South is a national historic landmark, an ode to the European Gothicism popularized by the Victorian English art critic John Ruskin.

The Prudential Center and Vicinity

Up Boylston Street from Copley Square is the Hancock Tower's slightly older rival, the Prudential Center Tower, or "Pru," tel. (617) 236-3318. Some might consider the vista from its 50th-floor **Skywalk** better than the one from the Hancock's because . . . it includes the Hancock (daily; $4).

Between Saks Fifth Avenue at the base of the Pru and Neiman-Marcus, opposite Back Bay Station, dozens of shops constitute what amounts to a totally enclosed linear mall, the Shops at Prudential Center. You'll find such typical urban retailers as Warner Bros. Studio, Body Shop, Speedo, Ann Taylor, and Claiborne Men. Larger and more upscale Copley Place, anchored by Neiman-Marcus and a Marriott hotel, includes Tiffany & Co., Crabtree & Evelyn, Williams-Sonoma, Sharper Image, Gucci, Louis Vuitton, Rizzoli Books, and a branch of the Museum of Fine Arts' gift shop, among others. For the kind of shopping experience you won't find at your local mall, check out the natural fiber clothing and accessories at **The Hempest,** behind the Pru on Huntington Ave. at the Greenhouse Apartments, or the snazzy kinte cloth and Ivory Coast prints incorporated into the haute couture Africain at **Meh International,** tel. (617) 262-0099, in the street-level Dartmouth Shops off the park behind Copley Place.

Also worth a visit, back by the Public Garden: the **Women's Educational & Industrial Union,** 356 Boylston St., across from the Arlington St. Church, founded over a century ago to leverage employment and educational opportunities for women (Amelia Earhart got job placement assistance here). The WEIU is supported in part through the sale of crafts, gifts, clothes, housewares, and antiques from its attractive quarters.

If you're in Boston attending a big trade show, there's a good chance you'll spend your days inside the **Hynes Convention Center,** on Boylston next to the Pru. If so, get one of your colleagues to cover for you and go check out the **Institute for Contemporary Art,** tel. (617) 266-5152, next to the Romanesque fire station across the street. Though small and underfunded, the ICA still mounts interesting and provocative shows and regularly showcases new film and video works in its comfortable little theater. Galleries open starting at noon Wed.-Sun. ($5.25), while their bookstore is open daily, noon-5 p.m.

The Mother Church
Properly known as **The First Church of Christ, Scientist,** the World Headquarters of the Christian Science Church has been a Boston landmark for most of the 20th century. The oldest part of the complex is the 1894 Romanesque building of gray New Hampshire granite, erected less than 30 years after the episode that led to founder Mary Baker "Mother" Eddy's discovery of Christian Science. When the huge Byzantine and Italian Renaissance basilica was added in 1906—atop 4,000 wooden piles driven into the Back Bay mud—it was (as it still is) the city's largest house of worship. Appropriately enough, it houses the world's seventh-largest working organ, an Æolian-Skinner "American Classic" with 13,595 pipes and 172 stops. A trio of huge poured-concrete additions designed by I. M. Pei and Araldo Cossutta has kept the Mother Church at the forefront of Boston architecture, punctuating the edge of Back Bay with a 15-acre plaza anchored by a dramatic 670-foot long reflecting pool and framed by neatly pruned linden trees. In winter, the downdrafts from the 28-story Administration Building seem to come straight from the Arctic, but come summer those strong crosswinds keep muggy weather delightfully at bay. (To cool off on *really* sweltering days, take a cue from the kids and skip through the fountain at the Prudential side of the plaza.) For a study in how much the world's political boundaries have changed since 1932, visit the **Mapparium,** a 30-foot diameter walk-through stained glass globe inside The Christian Science Publishing Society's neoclassical headquarters on Mass. Ave., beside the domed church. Up in the Administration Building, over a dozen rare and unusual Bibles—the oldest a 1546 Hebrew-Latin edition from Switzerland, the most recent a 1957 translation of the Eastern Orthodox *Peshitta,* the English interleaved with facsimiles of the ancient Aramaic script—are displayed in the tower's 22nd-floor library, where you may research the history of the thrice-married Mrs. Eddy and her church (visitors' passes are available in the lobby). For the schedule of free guided tours and the occasional organ concerts, call the church's recorded tour and event line, (617) 450-3790.

THE SOUTH END

The South End was originally intended, like Back Bay, to be an affluent residential neighborhood built on landfill, but it ended up nearly becoming a ghetto. State-financed Back Bay, with its minimum required housing values and proximity to upper-crust Beacon Hill, proved more appealing to wealthy prospective residents than the city-financed South End, which tarnished its potential exclusivity in the 1850s by promoting affordable housing. Poor Irish immigrants displaced to the South End by waterfront redevelopment further diminished the area's attractiveness to class-conscious Yankees. By the Depression, the blocks of attached brownstones and London-style squares had devolved into a district of densely packed rooming houses and apartments, separated from genteel Back Bay by large railyards. Southern black sharecroppers displaced by mechanized cotton harvesting settled in the neighborhood, many finding work as Pullman car porters or in other railroad jobs. As the South End stretch of Mass. Ave. became a hotspot for jazz, the Savoy, Hi Hat, Roseland Ballroom (where Malcolm "Red" Little worked back before he replaced his last name with "X"), and other legendary hot spots along "the Avenue" attracted a jazz pantheon, from Pops Foster and Sidney Bechet to Duke Ellington and Lester Young.

Three decades of gentrification have brought the neighborhood back onto the radar screen for the rest of Boston, and though many lower-income residents suffered the usual fate of displacement, some affordable housing has been preserved amid the townhome renovations and condo conversions. A center for Boston's gay and lesbian community, working artists, and professional couples who find the suburbs too sterile and boring, the new South End has become a leading neighborhood for innovative food and theater, lively bars, and aimless urban walking through the nation's largest Victorian brick rowhouse district. Here's a sample figure-eight stroll beginning from the Back Bay: take Berkeley St. over the Turnpike to the **Boston Center for the Arts** on Tremont St., passing the insanely overrated Hard Rock Cafe, attractive B&B-filled side streets like Chandler and Appleton, and artsy shops like **F. Kia,** 558 Tremont. From the BCA, walk away from downtown just a couple blocks, to Union Park Street, whose ellipse—one of several in the vicinity—is a throwback to the English elegance sought by the neighborhood's planners. At the east end of the park, turn left on Shawmut Avenue and enter a pocket of the neighborhood's Lebanese past—note the grocery, and the Cedars Middle Eastern restaurant on the corner ahead. Return to Tremont by any of the next two or three streets that strikes your fancy, turn left and pass the funky shops, gay bookstore, and cafes around the BCA again, this time making a right at Rutland, about six blocks away. After enjoying another oval park, turn right on Columbus and walk back toward the downtown skyline. Return to where you began by taking any street on the left to the **Southwest Corridor Park,** running parallel to Columbus atop the underground Orange Line. (Or stay on Columbus at least as far as the timeless **Charlie's Sandwich Shoppe,** at No. 429, dishing up the South End's best omelets, muffins, sandwiches, and turkey hash since 1927.) Follow the skinny, well-landscaped park to Dartmouth Street and Copley Square, keeping an eye out for art installations like the poetry and prose engraved on the stele outside the Copley Place entrance, or the Back Bay Station lobby statue of A. Philip Randolph, civil rights activist and champion of black trade unionism.

FENWAY

Fenway is the schizophrenic neighborhood on the "other" side of Mass. Ave., a filled-in portion of Back Bay that's generally denied any modern right to share in the snob appeal that name now gives. The alphabetic ordering of street names persists here—Ipswich, Jersey, Kilmarnock—but Back Bay's orderly grid essentially evaporates west of Mass. Ave., riven in part by the meandering course of the Back Bay Fens, whose creation initiated Frederick Law Olmsted's seven-year relationship with the Boston Park System. The system of scenic carriageways Olmsted designed to accompany his parks begins here with The Fenway, whose pastoral curves proved irresistible in the late 19th century to a variety of educational and cultural institutions. Besides music conservatories, colleges, teaching hospitals, and art museums, Fenway also encompasses the exceptional acoustics of Symphony Hall, the rockin' nightlife of clubby Kenmore Square, and the delightfully old-fashioned Fenway Park, where the Red Sox toy with the affections of their long-suffering fans.

Back Bay Fens

The first of Olmsted's six contributions to what today is known as the Emerald Necklace, the Fens was conceived as the wild and picturesque introduction to nature, whose pastoral side would come later, at the end of the chain of parks. Subsequent alterations, total replacement of the original salt-tolerant plantings after the Charles was dammed in the 1900s, and the Back Bay skyline's encroachment over the background trees keep the Fens from sparking the same thrill as when it belonged to the nation's first generation of urban parks, but Olmsted's spirit is preserved here and there along the Muddy River's sinuous banks. Some visitors may in fact find the Pru a welcome addition to willow-framed views of rusticated stone arch bridges, and it's hard to be dismayed by the charming little **Rose Garden,** sheltered by a tall hedge. Olmsted could hardly have anticipated the impact of foreign affairs on his intended oasis: WW II's original "Victory gardens"—still in use—were planted here, and memorials to Bostonians killed in WW II, Korea, and Vietnam are here, as well. Though no longer a great destination in its own right, the Fens certainly enlivens the stroll between Boylston Street and the art museums on The Fenway, and the pocket of casual neighborhood eateries cupped in the D-shaped bend of the park—the excellent and inexpensive Thai cuisine at the handsome **Brown Sugar Cafe** on Jersey St., for example, or the hearty Brazilian fare at **Buteco,** across the street—are generally less-expensive alternatives to the museum cafes.

Whether you arrive on foot via the Fens or aboard the Green "E" Line on Huntington Ave., you certainly couldn't miss the **Museum of Fine Arts,** tel. (617) 267-9300, even in the dark. Sprawling over an entire block, the MFA contains far too much to see in just one visit, so don't wear yourself out trying. Current temporary exhibitions, usually well touted around town, are always found in the modern West Wing, another of I. M. Pei's numerous contributions to the city. The strengths of the permanent collections are legion: 19th- and early-20th-century American painting, including scores of works by regional artists from John Singleton Copley to Edward Hopper; European painting from the Renaissance through the Impressionists; and extensive collections of decorative arts, including English silver, colonial American furniture, and European antique musical instruments.

If you like mummies, you'll love this place: by virtue of having co-sponsored numerous Egyptian archaeological digs, some of the museum's collections of ancient Near Eastern artifacts are unrivaled outside of Cairo.

Interested in textiles from Islamic Central Asia, early Chinese old master paintings, or swords and armor from feudal Japan? From its inception, the MFA has also maintained a strong interest in the Far East, as a result of which its Asiatic collections are among the finest to be found anywhere. Don't miss the room of Buddhas—meditatively dark, quiet, and furnished with benches—or the equally contemplative Japanese *Tenshin-En* (Garden in the Heart of Heaven), outside on the Fens side of the West Wing. And this isn't even to mention the classical Greek vases, gallery of ship models, costumes and textiles, prints and photographs. Guided walks and gallery talks are offered most days, and an exceptionally good film series runs Wed.-Sun. evenings (admission extra). Open daily, sometimes till nearly 10 p.m. ($10 adults, $8 seniors and students, kids 17 and under free).

By comparison, the **Isabella Stewart Gardner Museum,** 280 The Fenway, tel. (617) 566-1401 (Tues.-Sun. and Monday holidays; $9),

doesn't look very impressive from the outside. Like the Venetian-style palazzos it was designed to resemble, its most lavish decorative features are turned inward, reserved for its occupants and their circle of friends. Fortunately, in this instance the public has always been part of that circle: "Mrs. Jack" Gardner, a famous and outspoken socialite, built this palace a century ago to house her exceptional collection of European, Asian, Islamic, and American art, and then threw open her doors to the public while she lived upstairs. Much of the charm comes from her idiosyncratic arrangements, which her will stipulated must remain exactly as she left them. The interior courtyard is one of the city's best public spaces, bar none—and, like the excellent cafe or gift shop, charges no admission (the best view, however, is from above—for which you will have to pay). On weekend afternoons Sept.-April, chamber and jazz music graces the upstairs ballroom ($15, including museum admission).

Kenmore Square

Ground Zero for Boston's biggest bunch of nightclubs and home of Red Sox Nation, Kenmore Square sits beneath the giant Citgo sign, whose prominent flashing red neon triangle is visible after sunset from points all along both banks of the Charles River. Erected in 1965 as a replacement for the City Oil Company's original four-leaf clover logo, the sign was too young to earn protection on the National Register of Historic Places when it was almost junked (in the early 1980s), but a grassroots petition drive to save it prompted the Oklahoma-based owner to restore and relight the vivid 60-foot beacon. The "Giant Delta" is only the most recent left-field target for Fenway Park batters to aim at: big billboards have occupied the roof of the building (now home to a Barnes & Noble superstore) almost since it was built in 1914, the same year Babe Ruth first wore a Red Sox jersey.

Kenmore Square also marks the eastern edge of the lengthy urban campus of **Boston University,** which stretches along Comm. Ave. and is served by seven stops on the Green B Line trolley. The trolley's first aboveground stop, Blandford Street, drops you virtually at the door of the **Photographic Resource Center,** 602 Comm. Ave., tel. (617) 353-0700, under BU's Morse Auditorium. Though small, the PRC's galleries are one of the few places around town to really get a well-curated taste of contemporary photography—high-quality non-commercial work way too fresh for most museums (Tues.-Sun.; $3).

ROXBURY, JAMAICA PLAIN, AND DORCHESTER

These are not glamorous neighborhoods, outlined in brick sidewalks and wrought iron filigree. You'll find no shops selling tourist postcards and Boston-themed T-shirts. Corner storefronts sell cigarettes and soft drinks, not lattes and biscotti. Wandering these predominately residential areas with no destination in mind will not make good copy for letters home ("Wish you were here—today I saw lots of vinyl siding, cracked sidewalks, and apartment blocks with no yards!"). And downtown hotel concierges will ask where you think you're going if you request directions to the area. But despair not! The treasures here are worth searching out, if you have the patience.

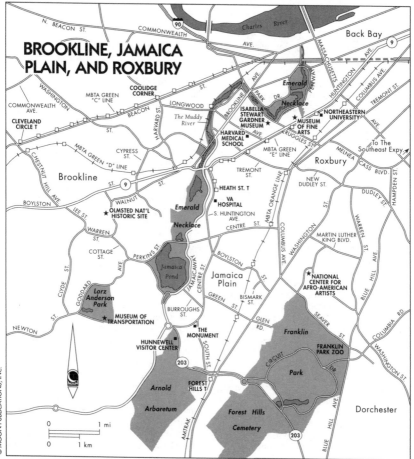

BROOKLINE, JAMAICA PLAIN, AND ROXBURY

Franklin Park and Vicinity

Frederick Law Olmsted's last major public park project was this 527-acre pendant at the end of his seven-mile Emerald Necklace of urban parkways. Intended as a "complete escape from the town," it was originally designed as a pastoral landscape, "a broad expanse of unbroken turf, lost in the distance under scattered trees." Financing came in part from a bequest made in Ben Franklin's will to an unnamed worthy cause to be chosen a century after his death. Boston convinced the executors of Franklin's estate that this park fit the bill—hence the name. Demands for active recreational facilities have wrought dramatic alterations to Olmsted's Arcadia: where sheep once grazed over rolling meadows, the public now comes to play golf, and other quarters have been pressed into service as playgrounds, a stadium, cross-country course, and the **Franklin Park Zoo** (tel. 617-442-2002; in the process of a major long-term metamorphosis, the zoo's huge indoor African Tropical Forest and state-of-the-art Lions of the Serengeti habitats are well worth a visit; open daily; $6 ages over 16, $3-5 kids and seniors). Yet many thickly wooded areas remain, threaded with paths that take advantage of the naturally picturesque outcroppings of Roxbury puddingstone—an ancient conglomerate rock resembling petrified Silly Putty studded with gravel and chipped stone. Look for such other typical Olmsted touches as the 99 stone steps to nowhere emerging from fallen leaves like a vestige of the Appian Way, and the rusticated stonework of footbridges and hilltop promenades.

Unfortunately, the park's scenic beauty has been threatened less by expanding soccer fields and fairways than by the city's neglect. Despite the fact that Franklin Park is as benign as Boston Common (and a lot safer than New Orleans' French Quarter), vast numbers of white Bostonians and suburbanites would sooner vote Republican than set foot in surrounding Roxbury—whose population is over 80% African-American, West Indian, and Hispanic, and disproportionately poorer than other city neighborhoods, not exactly a constituency with lots of friends in high places. Hidebound Boston's loss is your gain: the kite-flying, birdwatching, rockhounding, jogging, barbecuing, and Frisbee-throwing opportunities out here are unmatched by anything downtown—and free of the in-line skater congestion found along the Charles River Esplanade. And while Back Bay menus have only just started picking up on Caribbean flavors, this neighborhood has the real thing—visit on the second Sunday in July for the most concentrated dose, during the **West Indian Jamboree**, a pre-Carnival celebration featuring dance, costumes, arts, music, and all the goat curry, jerk barbecue, deep-fried patties, and sweet sorrel drinks one could ask for.

Franklin Park is one of those rare Boston places where parking supply exceeds demand, but it's also accessible by several subway-bus combinations. From the end of the Orange Line in Forest Hills, take either the free weekend and holiday shuttle to the Zoo, or hop aboard the daily #16 JFK/UMass bus, which passes by the Zoo entrance. More circuitous (but more frequent), the #45 Franklin Park Zoo bus runs daily from the bus platform of the Ruggles Orange Line station. It's also easy to get to Franklin Park by foot: take the Orange Line to Green St., turn right upon exiting the station, walk uphill four blocks, and you'll enter via a grassy old carriage road in the wooded northwest quarter. The path soon splits; both left forks end up at the Zoo's driveway.

A short distance from the foot of Seaver St., on Franklin Park's north tip, is the **Museum of the National Center for Afro-American Artists**, 300 Walnut St., tel. (617) 442-8614. It's housed in a 19th-century Ruskinian Gothic mansion on a stone ledge with a V-shaped lot flanked by a low puddingstone wall; parking and entrance are from the Crawford St. side. Sculptures, including the aptly named *Eternal Presence*, an immense bronze head by John Wilson, dot the grounds. Inside the museum, three spacious galleries host a wide variety of excellent traveling exhibits, mostly by contemporary artists. There's also a permanent full-scale reconstruction of the 25-century-old burial chamber from the Nubian pyramid of King Aspelta, complete with golden sarcophagus. Besides the gallery openings that attend each new installation, occasional performances and other special events are held throughout the year (Tues.-Sun.; $4 adults, kids under 12 free).

Also near the park's north tip is the Boston Beer Company, better known as the **Samuel**

Adams brewery, 30 Germania St., tel. (617) 368-5000, in Jamaica Plain, two blocks from the Stony Brook Orange Line station (turn left upon exiting, follow signs). Here on the premises of the former Haffenreffer Brewery (one of 17 long-vanished beer makers attracted to the now-buried Stony Brook), Boston Beer brews its lagers, ales, and seasonal specials for local draft accounts. Short but interesting tours and tastings ($1) are offered Thurs.-Fri. at 2 p.m. and Saturday at noon, 1, and 2 p.m.

Across from Franklin Park's southern entrance off Rt. 203 is the **Forest Hills Cemetery,** tel. (617) 524-0703, modeled after the better-known Mount Auburn in Cambridge. On its slopes are the final resting places of playwright Eugene O'Neill, poets Anne Sexton and e. e. cummings (whose headstone is engraved in capital letters), author and chaplain Edward Everett Hale, and suffragette Lucy Stone. The classical statuary includes the exceptional *Death Staying the Hand of the Sculptor,* by Daniel Chester French. His Lincoln Memorial has earned more permanent fame, but this piece—just inside the cemetery gates—was considered by contemporaries to be one of his best; the work of the sculptor it memorializes, Martin Milmore, is visible in the Civil War memorial located south of the lake, nearly opposite the fireman statue. A map identifying famous permanent residents is available from the office at the entrance, along with information about regular programs like birdwatching and historical walking tours. The cemetery's pedestrian entrance is at the end of block-long Tower St., opposite the Forest Hills Orange Line station.

A few blocks north of Franklin Park's Blue Hill Ave. entrance (outside the east gates of the zoo) is **Muhammad's Mosque of Islam #11,** 10 Washington St. at the corner of Blue Hill Ave., tel. (617) 442-6082. In 1954, Malcolm X founded Boston's Nation of Islam headquarters here, and served briefly as minister. His house at 72 Dale St. a mile away, is still boarded up and ignored, despite the attention Spike Lee's biographical movie brought to the man.

Arnold Arboretum

While the 7,000 different shrubs, vines, and trees in its collection places this facility in the top rank of North American arboreta, it doesn't take an

Malcolm X in an on-air debate at the WBZ-AM radio station, in 1964

COURTESY OF BOSTON PUBLIC LIBRARY, PRINT DEPT.

academic interest to appreciate Jamaica Plain's botanical jewel, administered by Harvard University under a 1,000-year lease from the city. As with the rest of the Emerald Necklace, Nature is but a handmaiden to Olmsted's vision, which is preserved here more faithfully than in any of his other contributions to the Boston Park System. The great hilltop views to city and sea are best from Peters Hill, in the Arboretum's southern section. On this summit used to stand Roxbury's 18th-century Second Church of Christ. Remains of the church's burying ground—a smattering of markers from 1722 onward, including an unmarked stone for a group of Revolutionary War soldiers—is found among the tulip trees on the hill's steep west flank. Horticultural highlights include the continent's second-largest collection of lilacs; exceptional crabapple, maple, and conifer collections; and the small gazebo-size Bonsai House, near the maintenance offices. As harbingers of spring, nothing quite matches those lilacs (celebrated with Lilac Sunday, the third weekend in May), but the rhododendrons and azaleas are nothing to sneer at, either. It used to have the only tree in the entire Boston Park system on which climbing was permitted—an Amur cork tree—but, sadly, a group posing on it for a photo snapped the trunk in 1995; the remains—and a dedication plaque for its eventual replacement (now just a sapling)—are easily found along the lane not far beyond the Hunnewell Visitor Center.

The quickest way to get into the Arboretum is by walking up South Street from the Forest Hills

Orange Line station, but the Visitor Center is actually closer to the route of the #39 Forest Hills bus (which departs from in front of the Copley Plaza Hotel). Ask to be let off in front of Arborway Natural Foods, at Custer St., just past "the Monument." Walk to the end of Custer and cross the busy Arborway at the pedestrian signal. The Arboretum entrance is on the right.

Kennedy Library and Museum

His name and legacy are routinely used as a lucky talisman by modern politicians, but what do you actually know of his presidency? Relive the 1960 campaign for the Oval Office and get an inside view on JFK's White House years at the museum attached to the National Archives presidential library. As media-savvy as Kennedy himself, the museum makes extensive use of videos to replay both key events—Jack standing up to anti-Catholic paranoia stoked by opponents Nixon and Lodge, his famous "Ich bin ein Berliner" speech—and forgotten sidelights: Frank Sinatra's pro-Kennedy campaign jingle, Jackie's tour of the White House, Walter Cronkite's faltering composure as he reads the news of the Dallas assassination. Jutting into Dorchester Bay on windy Columbia Point (free shuttle bus from the Red Line's JFK/UMass station nearby), the dramatic I. M. Pei-designed building also affords great views of the downtown skyline from both inside and out. Open daily ($6; tel. (617) 929-4523).

The eight-story library isn't solely the province of Kennedy researchers: Ernest Hemingway's papers are deposited here, too. Papa Hemingway is no stranger to Boston; his *Farewell to Arms* was one of the many books censored by bluenose moralists early this century.

BROOKLINE

Surrounded by Boston on three sides, Brookline (pop. 53,000) is nearly an island within the bigger city. Known for large Jewish and Russian populations, excellent public schools, and the only metro area ban on smoking in restaurants *and* bars, Brookline racks up points for being a desirable place to live (if you can afford it) but keeps a relatively low profile among tourists. The few attractions it *does* offer out-of-towners

(besides kosher restaurants and bookstores carrying more than one kind of Haggadah—both most plentiful on Harvard Street) are rather scattered, and only the JFK Birthplace is less than a half-mile from the T. All sights and attractions are good destinations for cyclists, however.

Birthplace of Camelot

At 83 Beals Street, a block from Harvard St. and about 10 minutes' walk from the Green "C" Line, stands the natal home of the nation's 35th president, the **John Fitzgerald Kennedy Birthplace National Historic Site,** tel. (617) 566-7937. The simple three-story house and its furnishings reflect the family's improving middle-class circumstances circa 1917, the year JFK was born. Though they moved four years later, the house was meticulously refurbished under the supervision of Rose Kennedy herself. Guided tours ($2) Wed.-Sun., 10:45 a.m.-4 p.m.

Home With a View

While by no means as famous as the slain President, Frederick Law Olmsted, the mastermind behind major urban parks in dozens of cities from New York to Los Angeles and San Francisco also resided in Brookline, and the house in which he lived and worked for nearly the last 15 years of his life is also preserved by the National Park Service. The **Frederick Law Olmsted National Historic Site,** tel. (617) 566-1689, a small estate named Fairsted, sits on exactly the sort of beautiful lot in exactly the sort of beautiful neighborhood you would expect of the grandfather of landscape architecture. Inside are displays that try to convey the magnitude of Olmsted's contribution to the look of the American built environment, from cemeteries to zoos, college campuses to city suburbs. Simply put, his legacy daily enriches the lives of city joggers, Frisbee players, dog-walkers, bench sitters, and millions of other residents and institutional employees in 45 states, Canada, Cuba, Bermuda, Puerto Rico, and the Philippines. To see if you're among those unwittingly touched by his landscapes, check the master reference list in the bookshop. The Brookline Hills station on the Green "D" Line is the closest trolley stop—about seven tenths of a mile through mostly residential streets. (Take a right on Cypress, another right on Walnut—the second light—and head up the hill past the burying ground and church, curving left onto Warren St.; Fairsted is a block ahead on the right, at No. 99.) Open (free) Fri.-Sun. only, but also, for researchers, by appointment.

Wheels of Fortune
Located even farther from public transit, in the even more affluent, country-club quarter of Brook-line, on the historic Larz Anderson estate, the **Museum of Transportation,** 15 Newton St., tel. (617) 522-6547, documents America's favorite obsession in videos, photos, and cars, cars, cars. In summer, the 1889 Gothic carriage house hosts special celebrations sponsored by various car clubs, but in any season you will find plenty of hands-on displays and vehicles to climb around on (Wed.-Sun.; $5 adults, $3 kids).

CAMBRIDGE SIGHTS

Boston and its neighbor across the Charles River may seem inseparable to the visitor, but residents know better. Boston, often truculent about social and political change, tends to regard the other city as "the People's Republic of Cambridge." Boston would sooner elect Dumbo than vote for a Republican for mayor, but it is equally unlikely to take a gay black candidate to the same office (as Cambridge already has). Before WW II, Cambridge was still a big manufacturing town, but most of the assembly-line workers have been replaced by software and soft money; while conservative Cantabrigians aren't unheard of, they're usually heavily outpolled by more liberal fellow residents. (How many other cities in the nation have a Peace Commissioner?) As dizzying rental rates force marginal residential and commercial tenants out of business or out of town, Cambridge finds itself in the process of discovering whether too much gentrification is a bad thing.

The principal axis of interest for out-of-towners lies between Harvard University and the Massachusetts Institute of Technology, although the Half Crown, Avon Hill, and Mid-Cambridge Conservation Districts are all worth a visit if you have a keen interest in residential architecture (or a desire to see the neighborhoods in which Julia Child and John Kenneth Galbraith live). Like competing superpowers, the two Ivy League schools carve up much of the city's riverside real estate into distinct spheres of influence; in practical terms, attractions may be spoken of as near one or the other, or in the buffer zone in between.

HARVARD SQUARE

Harvard Square has become a major tourist destination in its own right, much to the chagrin of locals who cherish its past. Popularity has brought skyrocketing property values, replacing mom-and-pop stores with national chains (Gap, Barnes & Noble, Tower Records, Structure, Sunglass Hut). Every year, returning students discover that another favorite grease pit has metamorphosed into a gleaming Starbucks. It isn't quite the Mall at Harvard yet—the pierced and punkish local teens still hang out in "The Pit" (the entrance around the subway), musicians and the homeless still play or plead for spare change, and chessmasters still concentrate on their games in front of Holyoke Center. But developers seem intent upon stamping out all uniqueness, so don't be surprised if you arrive to find a Planet Hollywood or Nike Town in place of any of the landmarks mentioned below.

The kingpin of the Square is of course none other than **Harvard University.** With an endowment larger than Colombia's annual cocaine economy and an annual budget comparable to

---

WHAT'S WITH THOSE ADDRESSES?

For some reason, the area around Harvard Square abounds in addresses that begin with (or are) zero. Where else but Cambridge would the postal service respect a cipher, so to speak, as a valid address? Among the most notable zeroes are the Christ Church of Cambridge (0 Garden St.); Tealuxe (0 Brattle St.); and Out of Town News (0 Harvard Square).

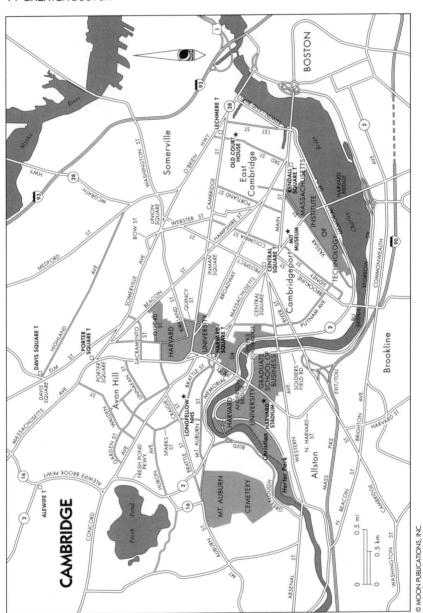

CAMBRIDGE

BOSTON

Somerville

East Cambridge

OLD COURT HOUSE ★

LECHMERE T

MASSACHUSETTS INSTITUTE OF TECHNOLOGY

KENDALL SQUARE T

MIT MUSEUM ★

CENTRAL SQUARE T

Cambridgeport

DAVIS SQUARE T

PORTER SQUARE T

Avon Hill

HARVARD SQUARE T

UNIVERSITY

ALEWIFE T

Fresh Pond

MT. AUBURN CEMETERY

LONGFELLOW NHS ★

HARVARD UNIVERSITY

GRADUATE SCHOOL OF BUSINESS

Christian ★ HARVARD STADIUM

Herter Park

Allston

Brookline

Mystic River

Charles River

© MOON PUBLICATIONS, INC.

0   0.5 mi

0   0.5 km

Old Burying Ground headstones under winter snow

the city of Boston's, Harvard looks and feels about as you would expect: big and powerful. Beginning in the 17th century with a dozen students—mostly candidates for the Puritan ministry—the university has grown to incorporate Harvard and Radcliffe Colleges and 10 other degree-granting graduate schools. Enrollment, drawing candidates from every state and half the world, comes to more than 18,000 students—with another 13,000 taking evening courses through the university's open-enrollment Extension School. Although it has eagerly joined the diversity bandwagon touted by every American college and university these days, this alma mater of six U.S. presidents, 11 Supreme Court justices, 30 Nobel laureates, and the Unabomber also has a well-earned reputation for being a handmaiden to wealth and privilege. Contrary to the pervervid declarations of Republican candidates, Harvard historically hasn't exactly been a den of card-carrying ACLU members and Kennedy liberals—even if having John Reed, William S. Burroughs, and FDR as fellow alumni probably makes a graduate like Antonin Scalia flinch. The school's intellectual trove of prize-winning faculty and their seemingly endless research triumphs is unimpeachable. But so is its steadfast resistance to organized labor (from busting up turn-of-the-century textile factory strikes with militia composed of the freshman class to an underhanded late-1980s campaign against its own clerical workers' efforts to unionize). Neither, mirroring the elite Boston society it

served, did Harvard blaze any trails in admitting Catholics, Jews, minorities, or women—as either students or faculty. Barriers to all these groups have only been seriously discarded within the last generation or two.

Harvard Yard

Befitting its aristocratic English roots and the Oxford ties of its namesake and benefactor, Charlestown minister John Harvard, the campus is dominated by the tree-shaded quadrangles of Harvard Yard, beyond whose tall brick and wrought iron boundary swirl the buses and cars of Mass. Ave. Enter through one of the many ornate gates, named after their donors, and almost instantly the urban tumult fades, overpowered by the tranquillity of the Old Yard. Lending composure to the peaceful academy are many of the university's earliest buildings, including five that predate the American Revolution. Oldest is Massachusetts Hall, just inside the Johnston Gate, across from the First Parish Church; while occupied in part by administrative offices (including the president's), it's also been a dormitory since it opened in 1720. Facing it is the 1764 Harvard Hall, built after a fire claimed its predecessor. Guides always tell an apocryphal story about this blaze destroying the entire library left by John Harvard—all, that is, except one book that had secretly been taken out by a student. Upon returning the volume to the college president, this student was first thanked most gratefully—and then expelled for unauthorized removal of the

SUBWAY BUSKERS
AND SIDEWALK VAUDEVILLE

Besides bringing budding trees, courting songbirds, and final exams, spring also marks the return of outdoor street performers to their usual roosts in and around Harvard Square. Friday and Saturday nights are busiest—a dozen or more musicians, acrobats, and magicians perform in doorways and on corner plazas—but almost any evening warm and dry enough for postprandial strolling is bound to attract at least a busker or two. (Inside the Harvard Square T Station, musicians perform year-round.)

The most famous alumna of the Square's streets and subway is Tracy Chapman, but she's not the only busker to have ultimately landed a record contract—and it isn't uncommon to find many of these performers showing up on club stages around town. Among the current crop of regulars worth looking for are Jim the Juggler (whose finale involves balancing a shopping cart on his chin), unicyclist Peter Panic, tightrope-walking knife juggler Mark Farneth, and Ecuadoran musicians performing Andean folksongs.

Behind University Hall and book-ended by the heavenly reach of Memorial Chapel's white spire and the bedrock mass of monumental Widener Library, is the Tercentenary Theatre—or "New Yard"—where commencement exercises are held, rain or shine, the first Thursday of June. Widener's broad granite steps lead only to the tip of the iceberg, for that is but one of 90 separate units constituting the complete Harvard Library, whose collective holdings outrank every other academic library on the planet and are second in the U.S. only to the Library of Congress. Although the five miles of stacks are off limits to anyone outside the Harvard-Radcliffe community, you may take a look around inside, vicariously absorbing a little of the studious air and if nothing else examining the fascinating dioramas on either side of the inside stair. Depicting the evolution of Harvard Yard and Cambridge from 1667 through 1936, the models also illustrate the waterways whose vanished courses are still outlined by modern streets.

Guided tours of the Yard are offered by student volunteers, beginning at the Harvard Information Center in the concourse of Holyoke Center. During the school year, tours run Mon.-Sat., while during summer they run daily (four times Mon.-Sat., twice on Sunday). The info center also sells self-guided tour brochures in several languages, and a detailed map of the entire campus and the surrounding streets of Cambridge.

Beyond the Yard

Harvard Yard isn't the only oasis from the cascade of walkers and drivers streaming in and out of the Square's T station, ice cream shops, and ATM lobbies. Small greenspaces are scattered about just waiting to revive tired walkers on warm afternoons, or readers impatient to review their purchases from one of the many local bookstores, or anyone wanting to relax over an ice cream frappe or steaming cappuccino. Radcliffe Yard, off Brattle St. northwest of the T station, is one such spot: quiet, attractive, with perfectly even lawns that invite cartwheel practice

book. Whether such a hapless young man existed or whether he actually got off with just an overdue fine, *Christian Warfare* was indeed the sole survivor from the original Harvard bequest (although 403 other books, acquired after the bequest, also survived the fire).

Nearby stand two Federal-style contributions Charles Bulfinch (Class of 1781) made to the Yard. University Hall is the easiest to spot, behind the famous "statue of the three lies," around which tour groups often gather for photos. The irreverent nickname derives from the seated figure's wholly false inscription, "John Harvard, Founder, 1638." Conceived by an act of the Bay Colony legislature in 1636, the college officially existed before John Harvard had even left England, although it took two years to build a classroom and organize a curriculum. Shortly after classes commenced, the newly settled Puritan clergyman died in neighboring Charlestown, leaving his whole library and half his estate to the fledgling college; 1638 is the date the institution changed its name in gratitude for his gift. As for the young scholar in the buckle shoes, it's really the likeness of Sherman Hoar, a popular senior from the class of 1882, since sculptor Daniel Chester French could find no reliable likeness of Harvard himself.

and squirrel watching. Stop by Brattle Street's old-fashioned **Billings & Stover** drugstore soda fountain for some refreshment on the way, and discover why New Orleans has no monopoly on living easy. If you return to the heart of the Square by Garden Street, you'll pass the Old Burying Ground and, just inside the iron fence at the corner, its colonial milestone. Bridges and landfill have more than halved the distance cited to Boston, but back then the only option from here was via the Great Bridge, through Brighton, and across narrow Roxbury Neck—currently a crosstown route you could roughly duplicate by hopping the #66 bus across the street and transferring to the inbound Orange Line at Ruggles, in Roxbury. It was to avoid that eight-mile semicircle that motivated the British Redcoats to take boats across the Charles that night in 1775 when they marched for Lexington and Concord. Alarm rider and Revere sidekick William Dawes made no such shortcut when he took the land route by this stone—in memory of which, brass horseshoes are set in the sidewalk of that traffic island-cum-bus stop.

On the north side of the Old Yard is the **Science Center,** one of several International Style buildings designed for Harvard by Spanish modernist José Luis Sert, dean of the Graduate School of Design during the 1950s and '60s. Its plaza includes the attractive Tanner Fountain, whose dry outer stones are as fine a spot for peoplewatching or cloud-gazing as any in the area. Grab a cup of joe from the Seattle's Best Coffee cart inside the Science Center lobby, or a student-priced polystyrene box of Chinese takeout from the lunch truck usually parked weekdays around the side on Oxford Street. For further diversion, check out the **Collection of Historical Scientific Instruments,** tel. (617) 495-2779, in the Science Center basement. Though small and open only Tues.-Fri. during the academic year (including summer school), the display cases present an imaginative jumble of polished brass, calibrated dials, intricate working models, and other oddities from as far back as 1450.

South of Harvard Yard lie the undergraduate dorms and dining halls of the residential "houses," the Oxford-style colleges-within-the-college built along the Charles during Harvard's major prewar expansion into a full-fledged university. From the Business School, across the

river in Allston, the orderly Georgian brick and white-capped cupolas provide the most cinematic backdrop for the spectacle of crew rowers coordinating their swift daddy-longleg strokes. The elegant dorms also partly frame Kennedy Park, at the foot of JFK Street, whose broad lawn is regularly enjoyed by Frisbee players, sunbathers, and newspaper readers. Pick up a bargain pocket sandwich from **Stuff-It,** on Eliot St. opposite the Harvard Square Hotel, and join the office workers stretching out their lunch hours on the park's sunny benches. On Sunday afternoons during the academic year—or anytime Harvard beats Yale at anything—you may hear the pealing of the Lowell House carillon, a set of 17 bells acquired by an alumnus from a monastery in Stalin-era Moscow. Inscribed in Old Church Slavonic with such names as "The Sacred Oil," and "Pestilence, Famine, and Despair," the bells may sound slightly out of tune, unless your ear is accustomed to the Eastern scale. The 18th member of the 26-ton bunch, "Hope, Felicity, and Joy," tolls by itself in the B-School belfry across the river.

Harvard Museum of Cultural and Natural History

The Harvard Museum of Cultural and Natural History, tel. (617) 495-3045 (daily; $5), comprises four distinct institutions, all physically linked by interconnected galleries in buildings between 26 Oxford St. and 11 Divinity Ave. behind the Harvard Science Center. The first three are such pure examples of the Victorian zeal for taxonomy that they invite reflection on the history and purpose of museums in general. **The Botanical Museum** is perhaps most popular of the four, thanks to its unique collection of **"Glass Flowers."** Properly known as the Ware Collection of Glass Models of Plants, the 3,000-odd specimens illustrating over 840 flower species represent nearly half a century of handiwork by Leopold and Rudolf Blaschka, brother artisans whose techniques went with them to their graves. Exactingly detailed—down to fuzzy stem hairs and pollen-covered stamen—the painted models actually look more like plastic than glass, but sonic booms and other accidents have amply proven that the fragile things are glass in all but appearance. Adjacent halls feature the vast rock, ore, gemstone, and meteorite collections of **The Mineralogical and Geological Museum,** and the great menagerie of fossils, dinosaur bones, preserved fish, insects, and 19th-century stuffed mammals belonging to the **Museum of Comparative Zoology.** Some of the formaldehyde-fragrant zoological specimens are historic in their own right: birds gathered by Lewis and Clark while Thomas Jefferson was in the White House, for example, or spiders collected by Louis Agassiz before the Pony Express. Beyond the fantastical colors and crystalline geometry of the mineralogical collections is the **Peabody Museum of Archaeology and Ethnology,** whose displays draw upon the millions of artifacts the world-renowned Peabody has in its care. From Pacific Northwest totem poles to Andean gold and textiles, Easter Island effigies to Angolan figurines, four floors of exhibits represent indigenous cultures from every continent but Antarctica. In addition to occasional lectures, the combined Museum of Cultural and Natural History maintains modest gift shops at both the Oxford St. and Divinity Ave. entrances.

Across from the Peabody at 6 Divinity Ave. is the **Harvard Semitic Museum,** tel. (617) 495-4631, sponsor of archaeological excavations throughout the Middle East and Mediterranean since the late 19th century. Cuneiform tablets, pottery, coins, and other objects from the museum's field work are on display, along with a significant collection of 19th-century photographs of the Holy Land. Open 10 a.m.-4 p.m. Mon.-Fri. and 1-4 p.m. Sunday (free).

Harvard Art Museums

Harvard's artistic side is a couple blocks from its science; to find it, just locate the only North American building by the Swiss urban planner, architect, and Cubist painter Le Corbusier. (If you spot Henry Moore's appealingly organic sculptures on the eastern perimeter of Harvard Yard, you're close.) Fortunately for Cambridge, the man whose guiding dictum was "buildings are machines to live in" wasn't being asked to design one of his monumental cities-within-a-city; as it is, Corbu's raw concrete **Carpenter Center for the Visual Arts** seems an odd bedfellow among Quincy Street's staid red brick. Provocative installations of contemporary art usually occupy the ground floor, above the ap-

propriately underground **Harvard Film Archive,** tel. (617) 495-4700 (schedule posted outside). The graceful ramp bisecting the building's angled mass allows passersby to peek into studio art classrooms within, too.

Spread along Quincy St. next to the Carpenter Center is the troika of **Harvard University Art Museums,** tel. (617) 495-9400 (daily; $5 for all three). The venerable **Fogg Art Museum,** at 32 Quincy, is oldest, its flamboyant swan's neck pediment over the entrance a foretaste of the treasures within. The Italian Renaissance, British Pre-Raphaelites, French Impressionists, and American landscapes are among the collection's highlights, arranged in galleries encircling the skylit replica of an Italian loggia. Stylishly modern Otto Werner Hall, grafted onto the back of the Fogg and sharing the same entrance, houses the **Busch-Reisinger Museum** collection of 20th-century art from Germany and its linguistic and cultural relatives. The legacy of the Bauhaus art and design school is strong: some of the museum's most significant works are by modernists who taught at this pioneering Weimar Republic school before it ran afoul of the Nazis in the 1930s, and the accumulated Bauhaus memorabilia and design materials—portions of which are routinely displayed—are unparalleled outside Germany. The archives of Bauhaus founder Walter Gropius, who, as Dean of the School of Architecture, spearheaded Harvard's immersion into the International Style, are also here.

Harvard alumnus Arthur M. Sackler must set some sort of high-water mark for art collectors: his hoard of Asian and Islamic art was vast enough to fill *two* museums. One is the Smithsonian's Sackler Gallery, in Washington, D.C. The other is Harvard's **Sackler Museum,** in an unusual postmodern edifice at the corner of Quincy and Broadway. Sackler's extensive bequest has been supplemented by additional collections of Korean ceramics, Japanese prints, Oriental textiles, Persian calligraphy, Indian paintings, and archaic Chinese Buddhist sculptures. The Sackler also houses the university's ancient Greek and Roman artworks.

As with the science museums, a gift shop may be found in the Fogg, but for a quick bite your best bet is to step around the corner to the Broadway Market, a block past the Sackler. There you'll find several deli counters and pay-by-the-pound salad bars, food court style, with indoor seating and a ubiquitous Starbucks on the side.

Tory Row

Beyond the "Washington slept here" parts of Harvard Yard and evocative slate markers of the Old Burying Ground, local history is perhaps most concentrated along Brattle Street. Shops and academic offices have crowded out most of the 18th-century houses on the low-numbered blocks by the T station, but past the busy orbit of the Square, and past the historical marker to the village blacksmith, residential Brattle Street affords postcard views of Ye Olde Cambridge. While there are numerous contemporary homes between the 1882 Stoughton House at Brattle and Ash and the corner of Fayerwether Street, 10 blocks away, the overriding impression is of elegant historic houses. Some of the genuinely old mansions belonged to prominent Loyalists until the Revolution sent them packing to New Brunswick and Nova Scotia; it is on their account that this stretch of Brattle St. is nicknamed "Tory Row." On cloudless summer days, sandwiched between the cropped green lawn and majolica blue sky, the daisy yellow facade of No. 105 is especially photogenic. Its Tory owner was Major John Vassall, but the handsome 1759 Georgian mansion's most famous resident was America's first career poet, Henry Wadsworth Longfellow. Preserved as a museum to the man who penned the memorable lines, "Listen my children, and you shall hear/Of the midnight ride of Paul Revere," the **Longfellow National Historic Site,** tel. (617) 876-4491, is open Wed.-Sun. from mid-March to mid-Dec. ($2). Besides house and grounds tours, the staff conducts an annual "Troupe of Shadows" walk the first Saturday in July through nearby Mount Auburn Cemetery (final resting place of Longfellow and many of his contemporaries). Or sample Cambridge's bountiful literary history with the aid of *Footprints on the Sands of Time,* a 24-page walking-tour guide sold in the Longfellow House gift shop. And as a reminder that this is no mere mausoleum, the National Park Service sponsors an annual "Longfellow Summer Festival" of poetry and music each Sunday afternoon from June through early September. As for those who happen by on a Monday or Tuesday, when the house is closed, you should still visit the formal little garden at the back, where, seated at the bench with eyes closed, you can almost imagine the singing anvil of that blacksmith down the street, "Like a sexton ringing the village bell,/ When the evening sun is low."

One of the oldest houses in Cambridge (only a few years younger than the Revere House in Boston's North End) is up the street at No. 159. Now headquarters to the Cambridge Historical Society, the **Hooper-Lee-Nichols House,** tel. (617) 547-4252 has been greatly altered since its 1680s construction as a two-story farmhouse, but original structural elements have been exposed for viewing, along with the 18th-century Georgian decorations, early 19th-century scenic wallpaper, early 20th-century Delft tiles, and other artifacts from the building's long and lively history (2-5 p.m. Tuesday and Thursday year-round; $5). Judge Joseph Lee, one of the Anglican founders of Christ Church, next to the Old Burying Ground, was a member of the colony's governing council appointed by the Crown as part of England's 1774 Coercive Acts, but an angry mob of fellow colonists persuaded him that resignation would be better for his health. Although forced to flee during the Revolution, Lee was the only Brattle Street Tory allowed to return home when the war ended.

Riverbend Park

On Sundays during summer and fall, the stretch of Memorial Drive between the start of the Alewife/Fresh Pond Parkway and Western Ave. is closed to traffic, making it ideal for skaters, strollers, and joggers. Throughout the summer, Riverbend Park itself, beside a pair of meanders in the Charles, is a favorite place for buff students to catch some Vitamin D and nap over their notebooks. Until the weather turns too cold, it's also an excellent vantage point for watching local crews skimming over the water in their fragile-looking, fly-weight shells. A Hong Kong Dragon Boat Festival adds a dash of the exotic on the fifth day of the fifth moon of the Chinese year (usually sometime in June), as the Charles hosts one of the international qualifying races for teams hoping to compete in Hong Kong (tel. 617-426-6500 x778 for exact date). And in late October a sea of spectators lines the banks for the world's largest rowing competition, the Head of the Charles Regatta, but with a three-mile race course there's always space for everyone to comfortably relax and watch.

"Sweet Auburn"

Located west of Harvard Square on Mt. Auburn St. is one of the more attractive greenspaces on either side of the river: **Mount Auburn Cemetery,** named after the opening line of a poem by author and playwright Oliver Goldsmith. Many illustrious New Englanders rest in its privately owned, 174 landscaped acres, from the founder of Christian Science to the inventor of the geodesic dome. The nation's oldest garden cemetery, Mount Auburn's arboretum landscape was widely acclaimed and imitated, igniting a great movement to bring "rural" spaces to the nation's teeming cities. Boston Common may get top billing as the nation's oldest public park, but it's more fair to say this cemetery is the forerunner and inspiration for America's greatest urban parks as we know them today. As popular today as ever, Mount Auburn still attracts the living with its sculpture, history, horticulture, and birdwatching—all just minutes from the underground busway in Harvard Square Station via the #71 Watertown or #73 Waverly trolley bus.

Every stone has a story, of course, and while you could comb local bookstores for the biographies that cover the more famous few, most are more obscure. Take the grave of Swiss-born zoologist and Harvard professor Louis Agassiz, marked by a chunk of rock. Agassiz' landmark 1840 book on European glaciers, *Etude sur les glaciers,* fundamentally altered our understanding of glaciation, eventually overturning the prevailing scientific view that glaciers existed solely in the Swiss Alps. That tombstone is an erratic from the moraine of the Aar glacier—one of the keys that helped Agassiz unlock the true continental reach of ancient ice sheets, from the very place he'd conducted his research. You'll find a handful of similar tales in the walking-tour pamphlet available at the gatehouse, along with a map keyed to famous graves, tree and bird guides, translations of Latin epitaphs, and postings of what's currently in bloom. If all this literature whets your appetite for more, you may wish to join one of the special programs offered by the **Friends of Mount Auburn,** tel. (617) 547-7105; call ahead for current schedule (nominal fee).

CENTRAL CAMBRIDGE

Cambridge has no "downtown," but **Central Square** is the seat of city government, the halfway mark between its largest universities, and the focal point for nearly every bridge from Boston. Possibly the most racially and ethnically diverse neighborhood in Cambridge, it's the city at its most funky and affordable, rich in ethnic eateries, colorful street murals, cool nightclubs, and unique mostly second-hand shopping opportunities. Got an invitation to a black-tie event on your social calendar? Drop by **Keezer's,** 140 River St., the king of bargain-priced tuxedos and other high-quality, low-price used clothing (mostly for men). Or, for less formal pre-owned apparel and costume jewelry, browse through the **Great Eastern Trading Co.,** 49 River Street. If you collect vintage 45s and other pre-CD music media, **Cheapo Records,** 645 Mass. Ave., next to the T station, has tens of thousands of old vinyl platters in every conceivable rock, pop, and R&B category. It carries tapes, too, and used CDs. Down the street, opposite Blockbuster Video, is the equally remarkable **Skippy White's Records,** 538 Mass. Ave., whose half-million vintage 45s should keep serious soul and R&B enthusiasts busy for a while. Skippy's is *the* place to go for gospel, funk, reggae, and rap—new or used, on record or hard-to-find CD. Folk music fans should mosey up a block past the YMCA to **Sandy's Music,** 896 Mass. Ave. Sandy's specializes in new and used folk and Celtic recordings and should also top the list of anyone shopping for an acoustic string instrument, be it a guitar, ukulele, banjo, or fiddle.

For slick arts and crafts boutiques, make tracks for Harvard Square, but if you share the opinion that art is best bought when fresh, check out the **Zeitgeist Gallery,** tel. (617) 623-1065, open Tues.-Sun., at the corner of Norfolk and Broadway, on Central Square's north side, halfway to Inman Square. There's no telling what you might find here: sculptures, drawings, or mixed media, by turns humorous, inscrutable, or, well, an acquired taste.

Like every self-respecting neighborhood in Cambridge, Central and adjacent Inman Squares also have a pair of bookstores. The **Lucy Parsons Center** is the easiest to find, right above the T station on Mass. Ave.; its specialty is the "literature of liberation." Searching for children's books that don't assume the world is white, or straight? Look no further. The local bookstore back home doesn't carry critiques of society, media, corporations, or foreign policy? Lucy Parsons does. From anarchism to *Z Magazine*, environmentalism to the African-American parenting, if it makes Rush Limbaugh foam at the mouth, you'll probably find it here. Farther afield, at the edge of Inman Square, is the incomparable **New Words Bookstore,** 186 Hampshire St. at Prospect, opposite the Merit gas station. For over 20 years New Words has been the region's leading resource for books and journals by and about women, in all the standard categories: fiction, biography, politics, health, art, and auto repair. Great posters, postcards, and bumper stickers, too, ideal for inspiring or awakening consciousness dulled by the mainstream.

Central Square is easy to find: exit the eponymous Red Line T station and you're smack dab in the center of it. From Back Bay and Fenway, it's also accessible via a brief ride on the #1 Harvard Square bus, which runs the length of Mass. Ave. Subway riders shouldn't rush up from underground before taking a good look around at the ceramic art in the walls—not just the eye-grabbing enameled tiles, but the often humorous medallions atop the wall columns.

AROUND MIT

Occupying over a mile of riverfront real estate along the lower Charles River basin, the **Massachusetts Institute of Technology** may not be as universally recognized—or as lavishly endowed—as the school up the street, but within some circles it stands alone. In entrepreneurship, for instance: corporate America's roster of CEOs may be top-heavy with Harvard grads, but a growing slice of corporate America (about 150 new companies every year, to be precise) is founded by graduates of MIT. We're not talking about lemonade stands on the corner, ei-

ther: 80% of the jobs created by these businesses are in manufacturing, and most involve cutting-edge technologies—no surprise, given that MIT is the nation's leading academic generator of new patents. In fact, unless you live on Neptune it's a safe bet someone with an MIT degree created something that's affected your daily life (consider Campbell soups, Gillette razors, aviation radar, and the World Wide Web, to name just a few). Harvard actually came within a hair's breadth of acquiring this prodigious fount of ingenuity back in 1904, when the presidents and trustees of the two schools voted to merge. Only a state Supreme Court veto of the sale of MIT's Back Bay land grant (and a student riot that injured 50) scotched the deal.

MIT also has a mischievous side, as evidenced by its rich culture of sophisticated pranks, or hacks. The hackers who make headlines for cracking into the Pentagon's computers or tying international databanks in knots are direct descendants of MIT's practitioners of collegiate cleverness, although in its purest form a true hack doesn't damage property and is always motivated by fun, not profit. The most spectacular hacks involve putting something outlandish atop the Great Dome, the campus centerpiece plainly visible from all over the lower Charles basin. A life-size plastic steer, a mockup of a dorm room and another of a campus police car (complete with flashing lights and box of donuts), and a working telephone booth are a few of the more memorable dome decorations, many of which are profiled in the Hall of Hacks at the **MIT Museum,** 265 Mass. Ave., tel. (617) 253-4444, about five blocks from either Central Square or the Charles River (Tues.-Sun.; $3). This main exhibition center is also home to selections drawn from the world's largest collection of holography, an installation of rather hallucinogenic touch-sensitive plasma globes, and a great gift shop for gizmo- and puzzle-happy shoppers. It's also strategically located between the fragrant New England Confectionery Company and one of Greater Boston's best ice cream shops, **Toscanini's,** on nearby Main St. opposite the Shell station. Though Cambridge is no longer the heart of the nation's confection industry, Necco still churns out its signature sugar wafers, conversation hearts, and varied other sweets in the massive 1927 plant across the street from the museum; to buy something fresh off the production line, simply follow your nose to the **Necco factory store** (Wed.-Fri., 11 a.m.-2 p.m.).

Several other museum collections lay scattered around campus; all are free. Along the ground floor corridor of Building 5 are the **Hart Nautical Galleries,** with 40 ship models illustrating nearly a millennium of maritime design. (With some exceptions, campus buildings are numbered rather than named, in chronological rather than geographical order. Most are physically connected to one another, too. Building 5 is adjacent to MIT's main entrance, at 77 Mass. Ave.; the Hart Galleries are down the hall to the right off the domed lobby, past the Information Office.) Changing exhibits devoted to the interplay between art and science are found in **The Compton Gallery,** in Building 10 (enter at 77 Mass. Ave. and proceed straight down "the Infinite Corridor" to the lobby beneath the Great Dome; closed weekends). On the east side of campus, near Kendall Square, is the **List Visual Arts Center,** in the Weisner Building at 20 Ames St., tel. (617) 253-4680, a set of galleries devoted to new works by contemporary artists from around the world (Tues.-Sun.). The I. M. Pei-designed Weisner—whose gleaming white, aluminum-covered facade is integrated with the enameled Minimalist tilework of Kenneth Noland—is famous among Internet digerati as the place where *Wired* pundit Nicholas Negroponte and his cohorts come to grips with the future in the legendary Media Lab. The List Center is also where you may purchase a copy of the campus walking-tour guide, an invaluable aid in locating MIT's excellent collection of outsized outdoor artworks by the likes of Henry Moore, Alexander Calder, and Pablo Picasso, as well as notable architectural contributions like Eero Saarinen's elegantly spare MIT Chapel, facing the concave-roofed Kresge Auditorium. Or for a more personal perspective, join one of the student-led tours of campus that depart from the Information Office inside the main lobby at 77 Mass. Ave. (Mon.-Fri. at 10 a.m. and 2 p.m.).

Like Harvard and Central Squares, MIT is served by the #1 bus along its Mass. Ave. front and the Red Line subway at its Kendall Square back. Subway riders should be sure to stop in the Kendall Square station and play "The Kendall Band," a set of three user-activated sound sculptures by Paul Matisse, grandson of the famous French Impressionist: *Galileo, Pythagoras,* and *Johann Kepler* (thunder-making sheet metal, tubular chimes, and resonating hammer-struck steel ring, respectively).

FUN IN THE HUB

THE URBAN OUTDOORS

It's obviously no match for the open spaces of the West—or even western Massachusetts—but Boston is not wholly devoid of fresh-air activities. The finest involve the city's river and harbor: sailing, kayaking, and hiking around offshore islands. Fans of wooded walks and summit views should head out to the Holyoke Range in the Pioneer Valley or Wachusett Mountain, in Central Massachusetts, but if leaving the metro area isn't an option, there's always suburban Milton's **Blue Hills Reservation,** the largest open space within 35 miles of the city and the highest coastal vantage point between Maine and Staten Island. The Blue Hills Trailside Museum and west entrance is on Rt. 138 at I-93 Exit 2; central and eastern trailheads are off I-93's Exits 3, 5, and 6. The center of the reservation is served by the #240 Avon Line and #240A Crawford Square buses, both of which depart from the Red Line's Ashmont station.

Boston Harbor Islands

Among the many features left behind in the Boston Basin by the last retreating Ice Age glaciers are drumlins. About 30 of these 10,000-year-old Pleistocene souvenirs, marooned by rising ocean levels, now make up the **Boston Harbor Islands National Recreation Area,** a partnership of a dozen public and private property owners and the National Park Service. Explore the ruins of a 19th-century farmhouse or the Civil War fort where Union soldiers composed the song "John Brown's Body." Hunt for wild berries and rose hips overlooked by the abundant bird population or for treasure washed up on shore; pirates are alleged to have used the islands, and a few old ships are known to have run aground on them, scattering 18th- and 19th-century military paraphernalia in the tide-shifted sands. Enjoy wildflowers, salt marshes, wooded trails, and fine views of the city skyline or Boston Light, the oldest lighthouse still in use in the U.S. Maybe you'll catch a glimpse of a shy muskrat, or hear rabbits rustling in the underbrush; in autumn you may spot an early arriving harbor seal spying on you from just offshore. Of the six islands accessible to the public, two have great sandy swimming beaches, and four allow camping (free, but permit required: call 617-727-7676 for details and reservations, and be sure to book ahead—the few dozen sites go fast). The park's gateway island has a snack bar, but neither it nor any of the others have fresh water; come equipped with a proper picnic from the mainland and you'll save yourself a lot of grief. (All six do, however, have composting toilets.) Campers, besides bringing plenty of water, should be sure to pack their food in sturdy animal-proof containers, or be prepared to suspend it from a tree—many critters have come to appreciate the convenience of humans delivering groceries directly to their door.

The park is open between May and mid-October, and access is by boat only. Daily scheduled ferry service is provided every hour 10 a.m.-5 p.m. by Boston Harbor Cruises, tel. (617) 227-4321, from Long Wharf to Georges Island (May-Oct; $7.50). From Georges, a pair of free water taxis loop around the other islands—Gallops, Lovells, Peddocks, Bumpkin, and Grape—but note that at the begining and end of the season (before late June and after Labor Day) this service operates on weekends only. As an alternative to departing from downtown Boston, South Shore visitors can catch a ferry to the islands from the commuter boat dock at Hingham Bay, where there's plenty of free parking (weekends May-June, daily late June-Labor Day, weekends until mid-October; $7.50). If you have your own boat, Georges Island has 12 slips available on a first-come, first-served basis; the other islands have moorings and even provide ship-to-shore skiffs. Off season, the islands are accessible only by such special excursions

as February's seal-watching tour of the outer islands ($10 adults, $8 kids and seniors; tel. 617-727-7676). The Friends of the Boston Harbor Islands, an independent advocacy group, sponsors a half dozen annual sunset tours, each concentrating on a different island (bring picnic for dining ashore). The visits to Boston Light are the most highly recommended, as no other organization has permission to land on the otherwise unapproachable Coast Guard-owned island of Little Brewster. (Be prepared to climb 92 steep steps from the landing dock to the base of the light.) For information and schedule, call (617) 740-4290, or check out the Friends' Web page: www.tiac.net/users/fbhi.

The Charles River
Sailors and scullers aren't the only ones who get to enjoy the beauty of an afternoon among the mallards on the Charles. With the aid of the **Charles River Canoe and Kayak Center,** with locations in Brighton and Newton, you can take up a paddle and hit the water yourself. The Brighton location—in Christian Herter Park off Soldier's Field Rd. a short walk west of Harvard Square—offers access to the river's lower basin; drift downstream toward the busy bustle of those athletic rowing teams and regatta racers to get an eyeful of Back Bay and Beacon Hill, or paddle upstream past yacht clubs and old industrial buildings toward the Watertown dam (weekends and holidays only, May-mid-Oct.). A short drive upriver at I-95's Commonwealth Ave./Rt. 30 exit is their headquarters, opposite the Newton Marriott on the edge of the river's more placid Norumbega Lake district (daily April through the end of October). The peninsula occupied by the hotel used to be the site of Norumbega Park, an 1897 amusement complex replete with bandstand, boating, and zoo. Its swan song was the Totem Pole dance hall, a once-famous destination for young fans of big bands, back before Elvis demonstrated what a pair of hips is really good for; canoeists will notice the old park's memory lingers on in the landscaping around the point. Rental rates at both locations are the same, and include everything but the sunblock: $9 per hour and $36 per day for canoes, $10-12 per hour or $40-48 per day for kayaks. Lessons and courses are also available; call (617) 965-5110 to inquire about details.

The Minuteman Bikeway

Along with the Esplanade and Riverbend Park, leisure cyclists and skaters would do well to consider the 11-mile Minuteman Bikeway heading westward out of Cambridge. Starting at the Alewife T station at the end of the Red Line, the paved rail trail follows the former route of the Boston & Lowell Railroad through the western suburbs of Arlington, Lexington, and Bedford, ending just a couple miles short of historic Concord. The scenery isn't all urban backyards: riders pass ponds, wetlands, wood-fringed meadows, and fields with rusting old farm implements, while Canada geese, chickens, and even a couple of horses enliven the view. The first daubs of color come with spring wildflowers; by summer, large patches of showy purple loosestrife emblazon weedy banks along bridge abutments and backyard fences. Another riot of color comes with autumn's turning leaves. Strewn in desiccated piles across the path, these also add a papery crunch under speeding bike tires. Arlington's **Old Schwamb Mill** museum and Lexington's **Battle Green** are among the historic sights just steps away from the Minuteman's route, and it passes straight through the Boston area's oldest railroad depot (now a bank), an unusual shed-sided 1846 structure later given the Colonial Revival makeover it still wears today. Given the bikeway's immense popularity and the fact that it passes within a block of two downtown commercial districts, quick refreshment is never far. Nor are bike rentals: shops are found at both ends and in the middle. To begin in Cambridge, head up to Porter Square's **Bicycle Exchange,** 2067 Mass. Ave., tel. (617) 864-1300 (closed Monday; rents bikes but no skates; locks aren't included). In Lexington, try **Bikeway Cycle and Sport Center,** 3 Bow St., tel. (781) 861-1199, visible from Mass. Ave/Rt. 4. Contrarians and others who read the last page first—or cross-country skiers looking for a good day's workout close to Boston—should consider renting skates, bikes, or XC skis from **The Bikeway Source,** tel. (781) 275-7799, 111 South Rd., at the very end of the bikeway in Bedford.

Bike and Skate Rentals

Rental rates are roughly comparable around town, with all-day rentals running about $20 for bikes, $15 for in-line skates. With one notable exception, all safety gear is included free. Expect to plunk down a credit card or huge wad of cash for a security deposit. In general, rentals are made on a first-come, first-served basis, so be sure to show up early on any dry, warm weekend day between April and September. The shops listed are open daily in summer unless otherwise noted, and prices are for full-day rentals.

Downtown, Back Bay, and the South End are served by five shops, three with bikes, four with skates. The one with the largest and most varied bike fleet—including road, hybrid, mountain, and exclusive tandem bikes—is **Earth Bikes N' Blade Rentals,** 35 Huntington Ave., tel. (617) 267-4733, next to the Copley Square Hotel. Their rates are also a smidgen lower than anyone else's. **Back Bay Bikes & Boards,** 333 Newbury, tel. (617) 247-2336, is a good choice for skate rentals, with a two-hour minimum, while its bike fleet depends on what used bikes are in stock. Farther up the street is an all-skate shop, **Eric Flaim's Motion Sports,** 349 Newbury, tel. (617) 247-3284; a second is a block from the Common: **Beacon Hill Skate Shop,** 135 Charles St. South, tel. (617) 482-7400, which also has hourly rates and ice skates in winter. The South End's **Community Bicycle Supply,** 496 Tremont at Berkeley St., tel. (617) 542-6177, rents hybrid mountain bikes only, no skates, and charges $5 extra for helmets. While there are no bike rentals around Harvard Square, skates are available on summer Sundays, when Cambridge's Memorial Drive is closed to all but human locomotion; look for the itinerant skate shop vans parked along Riverbend Park by De Wolfe or Flagg Streets.

SPECTATOR SPORTS

Many, many words have been written lamenting Boston's perenially unlucky home team, the **Boston Red Sox.** Come to a home game April-Oct. and decide for yourself whether Babe Ruth's being traded to the New York Yankees in 1920 permanently jinxed the Sox (the "Curse of the Bambino") as you watch another big lead evaporate in the final inning, or another pennant race fizzle in the final stretch. (The Sox won four World Series titles in the early 1900s, the last two with the aid of "the Babe." Those

COURTESY OF BOSTON PUBLIC LIBRARY, PRINT DEPT.

were the last Series victories the Sox have seen.) If nothing else, come for the pleasure of baseball in **Fenway Park,** outside Kenmore Square, a small, odd-angled 1912 ballpark irresistibly unimproved by a retracting dome top, sushi vendors, Astro-Turf, or Sunbelt weather ($9-18; ticket charge tel. 617-267-1700).

If the prayers of the Red Sox front office come true, old Fenway and its infamous left-field wall (the intimidating "Green Monster") will be replaced soon—and, no doubt, eulogized, just as the humid old 1920s Boston Garden arena is reminisced about from the upholstered, climate-controlled comfort of its replacement, the 1995 **FleetCenter.** Built over the Commuter Rail's North Station, on Causeway Street at the foot of the North End, the 19,000-seat Fleet is palatial home to basketball's storied **Boston Celtics** and ice hockey's **Boston Bruins,** as well as host to annual visits from the Ringling Brothers and Barnum & Bailey Circus, Disney World on Ice, the Harlem Globetrotters, champion figure-skating revues, and major rock concerts. The Celtics season runs Nov.-April ($10-18 and up; tel. 617-523-3030), the Bruins Oct.-April ($29-65; tel. 617-624-1000). Fans of pro football have to head south, to Foxboro, to catch the action of the New England Patriots (and pro soccer's New England Revolution), although you can see the legendary Ivy League rivalry of the Harvard-Yale game right at Harvard Stadium,

across the river from Harvard Square, in November on even-numbered years (ticket office tel. 617-495-2211).

The Sox may draw crowds of 34,000 when they get on a roll, but that's peanuts compared to the crowds that turn up for the world-renowned **Boston Marathon,** tel. (617) 236-1652, whose finish line is in Copley Square. Over a million spectators typically turn out each April to cheer on the thousands of runners competing in America's oldest marathon, first run in 1897. The 26.2-mile event coincides with a state holiday, Patriot's Day, celebrated on the Monday closest to the April 19 anniversary of the American Revolution's opening salvos. (April was originally the month of Massachusetts' Fast Day, one of three holidays permitted by 17th-century Puritans—the other two were the Sabbath and Thanksgiving—but patriotism replaced penance three years before the first Marathon.) VIP reviewing stands and media towers make it hard to get a front-row glimpse of the finish unless you have influential friends among the race sponsors, but Boylston Street in front of the Pru, Comm. Ave. between Mass. Ave. and Kenmore Square, and the entire above-ground route of the Green "C" Line all afford good sideline views of the final few miles.

A big turnout is always assured the third weekend in October, too, for the **Head of the Charles Regatta,** tel. (617) 864-8415, the world's largest rowing competition, which attracts thousands of athletes from around the world. Six bridges and miles of riverbank afford plenty of good vantage points from the Boston University starting line to the finish three miles upstream, beside Christian Herter Park in Brighton. Since Cambridge closes several major streets to traffic on the busier second day of the weekend event, you'll usually find Party Central along the riverfront by Harvard University—and anyone who gets claustrophobic in happy throngs of 300,000 should steer clear of Harvard Square then.

Followers of men's tennis may want to catch the **U.S. Pro Tennis Championship** tournament, tel. (617) 731-4500, held each August at the Longwood Cricket Club, 564 Hammond St. in Brookline, immediately adjacent to the Chestnut Hill stop on the Green "D" Line (third or fourth week of the month).

If racket sports are too refined for your tastes since John McEnroe retired, hop on the Blue Line to **Wonderland Greyhound Park,** tel. (781) 284-1300. There, you can cheer on the l'il doggies chasing Swifty around the track (daily year-round). It's the last stop on the line, on the V.F.W. Parkway in Revere. Gamblers who won't bet on anything smaller than a horse need only get off the Blue Line a stop earlier to find themselves at **Suffolk Downs,** Waldemar Ave., recorded info and race results tel. (617) 568-3216, home to thoroughbred racing from the end of September through the first week of June.

TOURS

On Foot

There are scores of guided walking tours of the city, and they aren't confined to just the summer months. The **Boston Park Rangers** sponsor a broad and varying menu of weekly, monthly, seasonal, and annual walks (and rides) throughout the city park system, all free. Call the recorded Events Line (617-635-3445) to find out what's up, when, and where, or pick up a brochure from the Boston Common Information Center on Tremont Street. Among their regular offerings: one-hour walks around the Common and the Public Garden; a stroll along the Commonwealth Avenue Mall; hiking and biking tours of the entire Emerald Necklace, from the Common to Franklin Park; and several flora and fauna tours in Jamaica Plain's portion of the Necklace, from Olmsted Park's ponds to the Arnold Arboretum's trees. The Rangers also celebrate Black History Month (February) and Women's History Month (March) with appropriately thematic tours around downtown. Selected park tours are even conducted in winter—on cross-country skis.

A top contender among paid tours is the nonprofit **Boston by Foot,** tel. (617) 367-3766 (24-hour recorded schedule), whose large repertoire includes separate architectural/historical walks for over half a dozen different downtown neighborhoods, plus an ever-popular "Underground Boston" tour, walks aimed at kids 6-12 years old, and an annual five-hour "Big Foot" Labor Day romp for serious urban hikers. The frequency of the walks ranges from daily to weekly, May 1-Oct. 31. Reservations are never necessary; just show up at the appointed time and place and off you go ($5-8). Promoting awareness of the city's heritage is also the mission of **The Historic Neighborhoods Foundation,** tel. (617) 426-1885, another nonprofit, which funds its extensive school programs with June-Sept. walks around Beacon Hill and the Public Garden/Back Bay ($5). They also do kids' walks around Chinatown, the Waterfront, and other downtown neighborhoods, and a couple of annual "neighborhood discovery" tours—no two are alike, and not all are on foot. (Past examples: a tour of Boston churches with Tiffany stained-glass windows, an Irish pub crawl, and a visit to the Boston Harbor Islands.) Call for prices and schedules.

For architecture and urban history specific to the mid- to late-19th century, join the walks conducted by **The Victorian Society in America,** at the Gibson House Museum, 137 Beacon St., tel. (617) 267-6338. Call or visit to obtain a calendar of upcoming tours, which range all over the metropolitan map, or to reserve a space on the next one (nearly year-round; $7).

If you have a group interested in Boston's social history, call **Discovering Boston Walking Tours,** tel. (617) 323-2554, for an insightful walk with Will Holton, a Northeastern University sociology professor. Holton weaves historical fact and contemporary observation to expose continuity here and evolution there, revealing Boston through a single church building's changing congregations, for example, rather than a who's who of prominent dead men. In addition to walks along the Freedom Trail, Holton conducts tours with such varied themes as Boston's ethnic diversity, sports history, and tabloid tales of infamous crimes and felons.

Across the Charles River, the **Cambridge Historical Society,** tel. (617) 547-4252, holds an appropriately eclectic series of walking tours over four spring weekends, beginning the last Sunday of April. Each is unique and concentrates thoroughly on the layers of social and architectural history within a relatively small section of the city. Call ahead to find out where to rendezvous with the tour leader ($10).

Other special walking tours on both sides of the river are sometimes highlighted in the "Cheap Thrills" and "Events" listings of the "Calendar" section in each Thursday's *Boston Globe*.

TOUR DE GRAVES

One of Boston's unique ways of welcoming fall is with the annual **Tour de Graves,** an all-day 25-mile bike ride around Boston's historic graveyards on a weekend in October. A fundraiser for the city's Historic Burying Grounds Initiative (coordinator of conservation and restoration work in 16 graveyards), each year's tour is slightly different. All include downtown burying grounds you could visit on your own, but most of the other stops are truly obscure—often hidden in residential neighborhoods behind brick walls or locked gates. At each site, local historians discuss gravestone art and its symbolism, trends in landscaping and urban settlement, and famous residents. The ride is such a popular way to visit neighborhoods otherwise far removed from the usual

tourist path that it's routinely booked to capacity, and advance registration is absolutely required (fee includes a picnic lunch). Call (617) 635-4505 x6516 for entry forms (or to contribute to beautification and restoration efforts, or for information about the Initiative), or write to the Historic Burying Grounds Initiative, Boston Parks & Recreation Dept., 1010 Massachusetts Ave., 3rd floor, Boston MA 02118.

For **bike rentals** near the tour's Boston Common starting point try Earth Bikes, 35 Huntington Ave., at Copley Square; tel. (617) 267-4733, Back Bay Bikes & Boards, 333 Newbury, in Back Bay; tel. (617) 247-2336; or Community Bicycle Supply, 496 Tremont at Berkeley St., in the South End, tel. (617) 542-6177.

By Bicycle

An alternative way to see the major sights is by pushing some pedals with **Bike Tour Boston,** based in Copley Square at Earth Bikes N' Blade Rentals, 35 Huntington Ave., tel. (617) 267-4733 (June-Sept. weekends). The two-and-a-half-hour narrated ride is geared for cyclists of all abilities, with frequent stops and a preference for Esplanade bike paths and lightly trafficked side streets. Biking among those crazy Boston drivers is certainly no Sunday cruise in the country, but it isn't as much of a suicide gamble as you may think, either; downtown traffic is generally congested enough to make you the fastest thing on wheels—and you have a lot more maneuvering room and escape routes than the average car. The $25 tour price includes bike rental and all safety gear—a great value.

Chauffeured

Whether you're tired, in a hurry, or looking for a new perspective, several outfits stand ready to provide a Boston-in-a-day whirlwind tour without you having to either lift a toe or carry change for parking meters. The one with the best gimmick by far is **Boston Duck Tours,** tel. (617)

723-DUCK, whose vintage-WW II amphibious vehicles cut a distinctive and colorful swath through city traffic April-November. Departing from the Huntington Ave. side of the Pru, these streetwise steel tubs make a circle through Back Bay and downtown, plus a much-anticipated drive straight into the Charles River for a little cruise around the Esplanade. The quack-filled commentary is several notches above the rest, but sheer novelty is the big draw: nobody else can touch the Duck's-eye view of the city from out among the gulls and cormorants—neither do any other tours let kids take a turn at the tiller. Not surprisingly, it's the one tour guaranteed to sell out hours ahead of time, so plan accordingly. Tickets are all sold inside the Pru's main shopping concourse, with a limited number available up to two days in advance; departures are every half-hour from 9 a.m. to an hour before sunset, rain or shine ($19, discounts for kids, seniors, and military).

More conventional, bus-style excursions are available year-round from **Boston Trolleys,** tel. (617) TROLLEY; **Old Town Trolley Tours,** tel. (617) 269-7010; and Gray Line's **Beantown Trolleys,** tel. (617) 236-2148. All three are narrated by drivers whose ability to keep cool and

BOSTON WHALERS

Both Gloucester and Provincetown are closer than Boston to the great whale feeding grounds of Stellwagen Bank, but if those towns aren't in your travel plans, you can hop a boat from Boston's waterfront and enjoy a brisk afternoon on the high seas and a powwow with whales. Unless otherwise noted, all boats accept credit cards and depart from within two blocks of the Aquarium T station.

New England Aquarium, Central Wharf. You'll pay more, but there's good reason. Passengers have access not only to color commentary from naturalists privy to the Aquarium's latest cetacean research, but also to a fish finder, navigation radar, and weather instruments; a "wet lab" touch pool filled with tidal critters; and a CD-ROM terminal with a database of New England's known whales, identified by markings. Tours run weekends only in April and the latter half of October, daily May through Columbus Day ($24 adults, $16.50-19 kids

and seniors); recorded schedule and sightings tel. (617) 973-5277, reservations 973-5281. Final payment must be in cash or traveler's checks.

A.C. Cruise Line, 290 Northern Ave., in South Boston, past the World Trade Center, tel. (800) 422-8419. Tours run weekends only May-June, Tues.-Sun. from late June through early September ($19 adults, $14 kids and seniors). Pier is a 20-minute walk from South Station or the Aquarium T station, or a short bus ride on the #6 Boston Marine Industrial Park or #7 City Point from South Station (no Sunday service). A.C. also has free parking on its pier.

Boston Harbor Cruises, tel. (617) 227-4321, Long Wharf. Weekends only in May, daily June-Sept. ($22 adults, $16-19 kids and seniors).

Boston Harbor Whale Watch, tel. (617) 345-9866, Rowes Wharf. Tours run weekends only the last two weeks of June, then daily July through early September ($20 adults, $18 kids and seniors).

chatty in Boston traffic deserves more admiration than the depth and accuracy of their scripts ($18 adults, $14 seniors, $5-7 kids). If it's door-to-door convenience you're after more than the color commentary, it's probably cheaper and faster to use taxicabs, since the trolleys are confined to wide and heavily trafficked arterial streets as far from specific attractions as any T station. Tickets are available from most major hotels, the "Trolley Stop" storefront at the corner of Charles and Boylston, and booths set up on Boston Common near Park Street Station; or just step aboard and the driver will help you.

Harbor Cruises

The cheapest way to see the city from the water is to simply take **MBTA ferries** around the inner harbor. They're noisier up on deck than the tourist boats (they're smaller, so passengers are closer to the engines), and they don't make lazy detours to maximize photo ops, but the scenery is the same and the price can't be beat: all are just $1. The only one that operates daily—and late enough in summer to catch sunsets—is the one that shuttles between the base of Long Wharf, next to the New England Aquarium, and the Charlestown Navy Yard. Weekdays,

you have a couple more options: at the Navy Yard you can connect to a second ferry to Lovejoy Wharf, behind North Station and the Fleet-Center; from Lovejoy, continue to the World Trade Center in South Boston, a wonderful 20-minute journey down the length of the inner harbor. Service is most frequent during morning and evening rush hours; middays, the South Boston boat operates only once an hour. Schedules for all these ferries are available at the Long Wharf gangway, or simply ask the crew.

For a more typically tourist-oriented ride, Long Wharf's **Boston Harbor Cruises,** tel. (617) 227-4321, and nearby Rowes Wharf's **Mass Bay Lines,** tel. (617) 542-8000, each offer basic 45- to 55-minute narrated trips around the inner harbor, ideal for a brown-bag picnic lunch on a hot day (it's always much cooler on the water). Both have multiple daily departures late May through early October; fares are $6 BHC, $8 Mass Bay. BHC also offers sunset cruises, 90-minute outer harbor loops, and trips to the Boston Harbor Islands ($7.50-10). Mass Bay Lines runs evening party cruises with a live blues band (every Wednesday June-Sept.; $12). For classy (if expensive) on-board dining and dancing, consider the sleek *Spirit of Boston,* tel. (617) 457-1450, or the sleeker *Odyssey,* tel. (888) 741-0275, for lunch and dinner cruises, sunset cocktails *(Spirit)* or jazz brunch *(Odyssey).* The *Spirit* departs daily year-round from Commonwealth Pier, next to the World Trade Center out on Northern Ave. in South Boston. The *Odyssey,* which looks like it belongs in a James Bond movie, has the more demanding dress code of the two (as well as the more contemporary food and music); it departs daily from Rowes Wharf, behind the Boston Harbor Hotel.

Perhaps more befitting Boston's maritime history are the S/V *Liberty* and its sister, the S/V *Liberty Clipper,* the only regularly scheduled cruise ships with masts. For atmosphere, it's hard to beat running under sail aboard an 80- or 125-foot schooner, especially at sunset. When the winds howl and small motorized craft head for shelter, join the "30-knot club" and find out what it means for a boat to have a "bone in her teeth." Besides weighing anchor ($25) several times a day from mid-May through early October at Long Wharf's Waterboat Marina, tel. (617) 742-0333, the *Liberty* sisters also play host to "Tall Ship Theatre" on weekends ($35), telling tales of Boston's shipwrecks and pirates with song, dance, rattling chains, and other swashbuckling mischief suitable for all ages—be prepared to salute the Jolly Roger and share your grog.

PERFORMING ARTS

For a general roundup of what's on stages and in clubs around town, pick up a copy of *The Boston Globe* (whose club listings are limited to Thursday's "Calendar" and Sunday's "City" sections), the overpriced weekly *Phoenix,* or the free weekly *Tab,* in the red plastic newsboxes on streetcorners around town. If you know what you want to see, call **TicketMaster,** tel. (617) 931-2000, and charge by phone, or go directly to the box office if it's vital that you see what seats are available. If you want to scope out the menu of what's on stage around town tonight and at what price, visit a ticket agency. Best is **BosTix,** tel. (617) 723-5181 (10-6 Mon.-Sat., 11-4 Sunday), a cash-only discounter and TicketMaster outlet in the little round kiosks next to Faneuil Hall (closed Monday) and in front of

Trinity Church in Copley Square, as well as on the ground floor of Harvard's Holyoke Center, among the Shops at Harvard Square. Their specialty is half-price same-day tickets to nearly everything from baseball to ballet, but they also sell full-price advance tickets. You can't beat the 50% discount by going in person to theater box offices—most day-of-sale rush tickets are reserved for students with valid IDs (the Boston Symphony Orchestra is an exception). While it doesn't do discounts, the **Hub Ticket Agency,** tel. (617) 426-8340 (9-5 Mon.-Fri., to noon Saturday), in the trailer at the corner of Tremont and Stuart in the heart of the Theater District, does do credit cards—and covers the full panoply of concert, theater, comedy club, and sports events. If you're near Copley Square, try Back Bay Station's **Out-of-Town Ticket and Sport Charge,** tel. (617) 492-1900 or (800) 442-1854 (9-5:30 Mon.-Fri.), on Dartmouth St., across from Neiman-Marcus. They accept plastic and phone orders, and have the standard selection of tickets at their fingertips. All agencies charge fees for their services.

As for those occasional hot bands whose local appearances are guaranteed sell-outs, your best bet is to either call TicketMaster, tel. (617) 931-2000 (unless, of course, it's a Pearl Jam show or you're ethically opposed to the T-meister's monopolistic behavior), or visit the cash-only **Ticketron** counter at any Tower Records or Strawberries music store.

Theater and Opera

Most of Boston's major stages continue to maintain their historic attachment to Broadway, now as the first stop for blockbuster touring companies rather than as the tryout capital for new plays. As an alternative to hopping an express to Manhattan, the gilded palaces at Chinatown's perimeter do very nicely, although sometimes their meticulously restored Beaux Art interiors outshine the action on stage. **The Wang Center for the Performing Arts,** tel. (617) 482-9393, at 270 Tremont, is the city's pride, its 3,700 seats and marbled decor ideally suited for Broadway's biggest musical extravaganzas. The smaller **Wilbur Theatre,** next door, tel. (617) 426-7491 x13, and the Wang-affiliated **Shubert Theatre,** across the street, also book New York's boxoffice hits, while the dashing, gold-clad **Colonial**

KEN FRIEDMAN

playwright and performer Anna Deavere Smith, as Stanley K. Sheinbaum in her Twilight: Los Angeles, 1992

Theatre, tel. (617) 426-9366, two blocks away at 106 Boylston St., opposite the Common, occasionally tempers its Broadway and off-Broadway mix with such postmodern fare as Anna Deavere Smith's *Twilight: Los Angeles, 1992.*

At the nether end of alley-like Warrenton St., behind the Shubert, is the intimate twin-stage **Charles Playhouse,** occupying an 1839 Asher Benjamin-designed church hemmed in by the broad brick backsides of its neighbors. It's best known as the 1980 birthplace of *Shear Madness,* tel. (617) 426-5225, an ongoing interactive comic whodunit that's been franchised to six other American cities and nearly a dozen international ones. Whether or not the Chicago, Budapest, or Buenos Aires versions are popular favorites, none quite compares to the original, whose thousands of consecutive performances have earned it a place in the *Guinness Book of World Records* as the nation's longest-running nonmusical show. The larger stage upstairs, tel. (617) 426-6912, hasn't quite found a keeper yet, although recent productions by the likes of the irrepressible Blue Man Group have proven popular.

The district's second-oldest survivor, the 1903 **Emerson Majestic Theatre,** tel. (617) 824-8000, at 219 Tremont St., eschews Andrew Lloyd Webber and murder mysteries in favor of an eclectic mix by a variety of troupes. Originally built for opera, the crown jewel of adjacent Emerson College's Division of Performing Arts is known as an "empty house" in the trade—it's not home to any particular performing group. Any given season is guaranteed to include professionally assisted Emerson student productions, full-scale operatic works by the **New England Conservatory Opera Theater** (Feb.-Apr.) and **Boston Lyric Opera** (Oct.-Mar.), and an annual Thanksgiving season Gilbert and Sullivan production by the **Boston Academy of Music.** Dance and music groups are also among its regular tenants.

Since crowd pleasers and good theater aren't always synonymous, there are a couple regional stages that take up where the pop musicals leave off. The **Huntington Theatre Company,** tel. (617) 266-0800, professionals in residence at Boston University, presents one of the best theatrical seasons in town at their well-appointed namesake on Huntington Ave. diagonally across from Symphony Hall. Besides American classics and recent works by top English-language playwrights, it's the only major Boston stage that consistently gives African-American playwrights their due (Sept.-May). The Huntington sticks to mostly traditional stagings, but Cambridge's **American Repertory Theatre,** tel. (617) 547-8300, goes for more spectacle, contemporizing classic dramas (with mixed results), reprising past winners (Andrei Serban's version of Carlo Gozzi's *King Stag* is a perennial delight), and premiering new works by the likes of David Mamet, Derek Walcott, Dario Fo, Phillip Glass, and Robert Wilson. It's also a regular venue for performance artists like Eric Bogosian, Karen Finley, and Paul Zaloom. Established by Robert Brustein, founder of the Yale Repertory Theatre, the A.R.T. makes its home at the Loeb Drama Center, 64 Brattle St. outside Harvard Square, with occasional performances at other stages in the area (Oct.-June). Be advised that on-street parking for nonresidents is virtually nonexistent in these parts.

Among the ranks of that rank of theater in which the lower cost of the tickets is offset by an increased risk of winding up at a dud—are **The Lyric Stage,** tel. (617) 437-7172, opposite the Hard Rock Cafe in the YWCA at Clarendon and Stuart (Sept.-May), and the **Nora Theatre Company,** tel. (617) 495-4530, performing at various locations around town. Equally risky, but often buoyed by more artistic passion, are the various small troupes sharing Tremont Street's **Boston Center for the Arts,** tel. (617) 426-0320, in the South End between Berkeley and Clarendon. **The Coyote Theatre** and **Threshold Theatre** are two residents on the BCA's roster whose sharp-edged productions tend to be worth the walk across the MassPike from the Theater District or Back Bay. Finally, if you notice a current production by the **Beau Jest Moving Theatre,** tel. (617) 437-0657, buried in the small print of the theater listings, run, don't walk, to catch it. Though infrequent and often wacky, Beau Jest gives audiences some of Boston's best live entertainment for the money, usually in a small "black box" space at the South End's Piano Factory, 791 Tremont, four blocks from the Mass. Ave. Orange Line station.

Dance

Several top-ranked academic dance programs call Massachusetts home, making the state a hotbed of kinetic research, particularly in the Five College area of the Pioneer Valley. Although Boston's dance community is imperiled—as are all the city's artists—by a chronic lack of affordable studio space, for the time being Boston still benefits from many formally trained dance students sticking around after graduation, supplemented by professionals escaping New York's even higher cost of living and others drawn in from outside academia. With so many modern improvisers here—many of whom contribute choreography to nationally known dance companies—there's no reason why you should go home without a dose of good dance. Scan the listings in Thursday's *Globe* or the *Phoenix* for such sure-bet performers as the intergenerational, all-women Back Porch Dance Company, Caitlin Corbett Dance, the jazz-inspired Impulse Dance Company, or Paula Josa-Jones & Company. You'll also be fairly certain to get your money's worth at any performance at the **Dance Complex,** 536 Mass. Ave., tel. (617) 547-9363, or nearby **Green Street Studios,** 185 Green St., tel. (617) 864-3191, both in Cambridge's Central Square. (The Dance Complex sponsors an open movement improv jam every other Monday night at 8 p.m. for $6, if you're inspired to do more than just spectate. All ages and abilities are welcome.) For a preview of modern dance's next generation of aspiring professionals, check out the **Boston Conservatory Dance Theater,** tel. (617) 536-3063, whose three faculty recitals and student productions take place between late October and early March at the Conservatory's own theater, 31 Hemenway St. near the Green Line Hynes/ICA station.

If you're leary of spending $12 on works-in-progress in church assembly rooms, or if you just don't want to be so close to the raw edge of alternative movement techniques, there's **Dance Umbrella,** tel. (617) 492-7578, presenting contemporary and multicultural dance. The company has done the hard work of sifting for the gold amid the gravel, not just locally but all over the world, so an Umbrella-sponsored performance is just about guaranteed to blow away your preconceptions about dance. The company's Oct.-June season is staged at well-appointed venues around Boston, from the Theater District's Wang Center and Emerson Majestic to the Tsai Performance Center at Boston University, 685 Comm. Ave. on the Green "B" Line.

Traditionalists will be relieved to know that Boston is also graced with not one but two ballet companies, including the critically acclaimed **Boston Ballet,** in residence at the Wang Center, tel. (617) 695-6955 box office, 482-9393 recorded info. Intenationally respected for its sheer virtuosity and grand stagings, the company performs a half-dozen classic works Oct.-May, punctuating their season in December with that perennial holiday favorite, *The Nutcracker.* José Mateo's **Ballet Theatre of Boston,** tel. (617) 824-8000, also bends to the popularity of Tchaikovsky's old chestnut in December, which launches the company's short Dec.-April season. Dedicated exclusively to its founder's choreography, the Ballet Theatre's singular magic may be enjoyed at the Emerson Majestic Theatre on Tremont St., a block from the Green Line's Boylston station.

Concerts and Recitals

When it comes to classical, early, and even avant-garde music, Boston boasts an embarrassment of riches. Devotees of PBS's "Evening at Symphony" broadcasts will recognize the city's preeminent musical institution, the **Boston Symphony Orchestra,** whose turn-of-the-century home, Symphony Hall, is considered one of the most acoustically perfect concert halls ever built in the U.S. The BSO's regular season runs from late September through early May; come summer, music director Seiji Ozawa and crew take up residence at Tanglewood in the Berkshires. Wednesday evening and Thursday morning open rehearsals are about half the price ($12.50) of the cheapest regular performance ticket, but even better (if you can get them) are the $7.50 rush tickets to Tuesday and Thursday evening and Friday afternoon performances. Also sharing Symphony Hall is the famous **Boston Pops,** which became America's most recognizable orchestra under the late, great Arthur Fiedler. Keith Lockhart, the latest Pops conductor, has brought them back to their old winning ways with sold-out world tours and chart-topping CDs. Catch the Pops in person May-July or al fresco at their Hatch Shell performances on the Charles River Esplanade from the end of June through July 4. For recorded info on BSO and Pops concerts and ticket prices call (617) 266-1492; to charge tickets by phone call SymphonyCharge, tel. (617) 266-1200 or, outside Boston, (800) 274-8499.

Boston is also home to the nation's oldest active performing arts group: the **Handel & Haydn Society,** tel. (617) 266-3605, founded in 1815—back when a Harvard education cost about $300 and there were only 19 states in the Union. Specializing in period performances—played on instruments and in styles appropriate to the selections—H&H presents chamber, symphonic, and choral works between October and early June, usually on a single Friday and Sunday each month. Handel's *Messiah,* which seems to have become the *It's a Wonderful Life* of choral groups, is a December sta-

ORGAN MUSIC

Boston is blessed with a number of fine pipe organs, and, since several downtown churches sponsor regular music programs, you don't have to sit through a sermon or a service to catch an earful of them.

On Fridays September through mid-June, **Trinity Church,** on Copley Square, tel. (617) 536-0944, holds half-hour noontime recitals (donations). Friend, if the voices of those 6,898 pipes don't get your mojo working, at least you came to the right place to ask for help.

On Thursdays Oct.-May, the **Cathedral Church of St. Paul,** 138 Tremont St., opposite Park Street Station, tel. (617) 482-4826 x103, sponsors a more general weekly series of vocal and instrumental works, many of which showcase the church's huge 135-rank organs. Recitals start at 12:45 p.m. (donations accepted).

A couple of blocks away, at **King's Chapel,** on the corner of Tremont and School Sts., tel. (617) 227-2155, the baroque sounds of the C. B. Fisk organ are frequently featured either solo or as part of the chapel's eclectic series of classical, jazz, and pop music, offered every Tuesday at 12:15 p.m. year-round (donations).

On Tuesday evenings June-Aug., Boston's **Old West Church,** 131 Cambridge St., tel. (617) 266-2957, near the MBTA Bowdoin Station, hosts solo organ recitals on another excellent Fisk organ, starting at 8 p.m. (donations).

Across the river in Cambridge, the **Organ Recitals at Harvard,** tel. (617) 496-3192, showcase acclaimed national and international guest artists performing on the Adolphus Busch Hall's Flentrop organ, at 29 Kirkland St. behind Harvard Yard. Recitals begin at 3 p.m. every third or fourth Sunday Oct.-Nov. and Jan.-April ($5). The popular March event is always a tribute to E. Power Biggs, who commissioned the Busch Hall instrument (the organ donor, as it were). For a special gothic treat, there's also a free midnight concert every Halloween.

For a calendar of hundreds of organ concerts and recitals all over New York and New England, point your Web browser to http://www.cybercom.net/~tneorg, the homepage of *The Northeast Organist.* For a regular, printed subscription to the magazine, call tel. (800) 841-4030.

ple, but the society is no newcomer on this fabulous oratorio's bandwagon: they've performed it annually since 1854. Concerts are usually held in Symphony Hall, across the street in the New England Conservatory's Jordan Hall, or occasionally at Sanders Theatre, in Harvard University's Memorial Hall, next to the Science Center. All are within a block of a T station. Jordan and Sanders are also home to the period instruments of the popular **Boston Baroque,** tel. (617) 641-1310, whose Nov.-April season of vocal and orchestral performances always includes a delightful "First Day" New Year's matinee concert—and, yes, the *Messiah,* too. Baroque is as *modern* as you'll get in the **Boston Early Music Festival Concerts,** tel. (617) 661-1812 or 262-0650, whose programs are as likely to feature medieval harps, Renaissance lutes, and a cappella court music as often as Bach and Vivaldi. Performances are held in chapels and churches when appropriate, as well as Jordan Hall and Faneuil Hall.

The **Emmanuel Music** chamber ensemble, tel. (617) 536-3356, is in the midst of a multi-year exploration (set to end in 2003) of Franz Schubert's major vocal, piano, and chamber works. Concerts are held late Oct.-early May at Suffolk University's C. Walsh Theatre, 55 Temple St., behind the State House. Musical appetites that enjoy blending 18th-century monody with 19th- and early 20th-century Romanticism should consider a date with the exceptional **Boston Chamber Music Society,** tel. (617) 422-0086 (Oct.-May in Jordan and Sanders), or **The Cantata Singers & Ensemble,** tel. (617) 267-6502 (Nov.-May in Jordan Hall exclusively).

Fans of the truly modern will be pleased to find the Boston area is also a hotbed for 20th-century music, from Stravinsky, Webern, and Varèse to the latest microtonal, minimalist, and electronic compositions—including frequent premieres and commissioned works. Several of the area's half dozen professional new music ensembles have been pushing the envelope for decades, including **Collage New Music,** tel. (617) 325-5200, in residence at Beacon Hill's C. Walsh Theatre (three concerts fall-spring); **Dinosaur Annex,** tel. (617) 482-3852, online http://www.dinosaurannex.org, usually performing in Back Bay's First and Second Church, 66 Marlborough St. (October, February, and

May); and **Boston Musica Viva,** tel. (617) 353-0556, http://www.camellia.org/bmv, in concert at Boston University's Tsai Performance Center and Longy School of Music outside of Harvard Square (five concerts Oct.-May). Look for these and other modern performance groups in the newspaper listings at the head of the classical music page.

Several of the area's music schools present student and faculty recitals and concerts free of charge—truly the most underappreciated entertainment deal in the state. Don't for a minute think "student" and "free" adds up to an evening of dubious quality, either—many of these emerging talents are well on their way to professional careers; next time you want to see them perform, it's likely to cost you big bucks. **New England Conservatory** tel. (617) 262-1120 x700, is by far the most generous, with *hundreds* of free concerts each year, largely classical works with lashings of jazz and new music. Most take place in NEC's resplendent Jordan Hall, 30 Gainsborough St. diagonally across Huntington Ave. from Symphony Hall. Jazz, rock, and country are among the specialties of nearby **Berklee College of Music,** tel. (617) 747-8820)—named after the founder's son, Lee Berk—whose free student and faculty concerts are usually held in a pair of recital halls at 1140 Boylston St. on the edge of the Back Bay Fens. And in Cambridge, classical, operatic, and early music are among the freebies at **Longy School of Music,** tel. (617) 868-0956 x120, presented several times a week during the academic year. All concerts are at Edward Pickman Concert Hall, on Garden St. a block past the Sheraton Commander Hotel.

When Art Comes to Town

If there's a famous diva, instrumentalist, symphony orchestra, or dance troupe on tour in the U.S., he/she/they will likely appear in Boston as part of the **BankBoston Celebrity Series,** a local institution since before WW II. Information and tickets to the Oct.-May. performances (typically held at the Wang Center, Symphony Hall, and other major auditoriums) are available through CelebrityCharge, tel. (617) 482-6661. To get on the mailing list for the season brochure, call (617) 482-2595. A more rootsy potpourri of music and dance is imported by **World Music,**

SELECTED ANNUAL MUSICAL EVENTS

A **Joyful Noise,** tel. (617) 495-4968, Saturday nearest January 15; gospel concert in honor of Dr. Martin Luther King; Sanders Theatre, in Harvard University's Memorial Hall, on the Red Line; admission.

Burns Night, tel. (617) 495-4968, Saturday nearest January 25; celebrates the birthday of Scottish poet Robert Burns. Sanders Theatre; admission.

Scottish Fiddle Rally, tel. (617) 271-0958, April or early May; Boston's large Cape Breton community (second in the US only to Detroit) ensures a strong Nova Scotian showing among the guest artists; at the Somerville Theater, in Davis Square, on the Red Line; admission.

Blacksmith House Dulcimer Festival, tel. (617) 547-6789, in May; at the Cambridge Center for Adult Education, 56 Brattle St., in Harvard Square; admission.

Boston Globe Jazz & Blues Festival, tel. (617) 929-2649, July; at venues all around downtown, including lots of free outdoor performances at the Charles River Esplanade's Hatch Shell.

Celtic Festival, tel. (617) 271-0958, Saturday of Labor Day weekend; at the Hatch Shell on the Esplanade; free.

ern end of the Boston University campus, on the Green "B" Line.

NIGHT CLUBS AND ACOUSTIC COFFEEHOUSES

Dance joints and live music stages are scattered all around both sides of the river, but clubland's major node is Boston's Lansdowne Street, in the shadow of Fenway Park outside Kenmore Square. With a solid block of neon-bedecked entertainment, club-hopping is as easy as walking next door (there are even occasional block parties, with multi-club admission). Other after-hours hot spots include downtown's Theater District, Central Square in Cambridge, and undergraduate-infested Allston, perhaps the most prolific breeding ground for Boston's independent music scene. Don't wait till midnight to start tearing up the town, as most clubs close early—Boston's by 2 a.m., Cambridge ones an hour earlier.

tel. (617) 876-4275, a local promoter that can be counted on for great shows nearly every week of the year (you can scope out the upcoming schedule at http://www.worldmusic.org). Among the many venues booked by World Music is the **Somerville Theater,** in Davis Square on the Red Line, a former vaudeville stage whose year-round musical offerings also include folk, bluegrass, and Celtic music, plus annual extravaganzas like a Women in Folk-Rock Festival, Silly Songwriters' Festival, and Either/Orchestra's annual gig, tel. (617) 625-5700.

To find out if your favorite rock or pop bands are somewhere in town, consult the newspapers or ticket-selling music stores like Tower Records, or call the recorded info lines of the **Orpheum Theatre,** tel. (617) 679-0810, on Hamilton Place (the dead-end lane opposite Park Street Church downtown), the **Berklee Performance Center** on Mass. Ave. at Boylston St., tel. (617) 266-7455, or The Paradise, at 969 Comm. Ave., tel. (617) 562-8800, near the west-

Everybody Dance Now

Kenmore Square's triple crown for the 20-something dance fiend includes **Avalon,** 15 Lansdowne, tel. (617) 262-2424, which doubles as a live stage for major-label bands a step shy of the stadium tour, or big-name musicians taking time out from giant concert-hall crowds; next-door, **Axis,** tel. (617) 262-2437, with its nightly segues among different themes, from techno-house and ultra-lounge to classic old soul; and **Karma Club,** 9 Lansdowne, tel. (617) 421-9595, with the best decor and (mostly because of its high cover charge) the largest post-graduate clientele. Downtown dancers looking for a classier milieu than pierced college kids should check out **The Roxy,** tel. (617) 338-7699, on Tremont St. opposite the Wang Center. It's a large, rather elegant club popular with the Euro crowd and black urban professionals. The DJ-spun house, hiphop, and R&B is regularly supplemented by out-of-town headliners ranging from Brazilian samba queens to the artist formerly known as Prince. Pierced body parts and backwards baseball caps are also notably absent from nearby **Europa,** 51 Stuart St., tel. (617) 482-3939, whose high-energy Asian and Latin nights are leavened with smokey jazz during Cigar Bar Wednesdays. On the Piano Row edge of the Common is Boylston Place, a pedestrian alley off Boylston St. that's filled with clubs, including such dance joints as **The Big Easy,** the more barbecue-party casual **Alley Cat Lounge,** and chic **Club Mercury,** whose young limo-renting patrons seem to drink champagne as hard as they dance. Glamorous and free-spending night owls also consistently flock to **M-80,** 969 Comm. Ave., tel. (617) 562-8820, in Allston next to the Paradise rock club; to get there, take the Green "B" Line trolley to Pleasant St., the sixth surface stop outbound from Kenmore Sq., and walk up the block toward the clot of double-parked cars.

If you're the hardcore kind who prefers deep techno grooves and black leather to cellphones and Italian silk, head to Cambridge and drop in on **Man Ray,** 21 Brookline St. in Central Square, tel. (617) 864-0400. Friday nights feature bondage and fetish themes; the midweek crowd is more relaxed, but the alterna-underground

dance tunes are just as hot. For more of a mixed bill of fare—leaning toward reggae, hip-hop jazz, and good dance-able funk, take a 15- or 20-minute walk toward the river from the Central Square Red Line station and check out the **Western Front,** 343 Western Ave. in Cambridge, tel. (617) 492-7772. And if it's a Monday night and you're in the mood for some great kick-up-your-heels swing dancing to live music, head to Somerville's **Johnny D's Uptown Music Club,** 17 Holland St. in Davis Square, right on the Red Line. Preliminary dance lessons, if needed, start at 8 p.m.

Live (Mostly) Local Bands

Fueled by its vast student population, Boston is fertile ground for new bands, with what seems like millions of groups busy chasing musical immortality in bars, clubs, and mattress-padded basement practice rooms around town in any given week. If you want (or need) a preview before you actually immerse yourself in the sonic pleasures of clubland, call (617) 232-CITY for an automated excursion through sample tracks from some 300 local players. Keep a pen handy: band and club specifics are recited lickety-split.

Two of the best venues for local music are both in Cambridge's Central Square, within a couple blocks of the Red Line. **The Middle East,** 480 Mass. Ave., tel. (617) 497-0576 (press 1 for concert info and box office), earns the biggest raves for its exceptional, independent bookings on three stages—Upstairs, Downstairs, and The Corner—across a broad musical spectrum, from thrash guitar to African *soukous* so infectious it'd make Al Gore get down and boogie. Unplugged acoustic jams, belly-dancing lessons, poetry readings, no service fees on ticket-by-phone charges, and frequent benefit concerts for local organizations add to the club's distinction. It also serves good Middle Eastern food, as the name suggests. Next door on the Brookline St. side—adjacent to that great mural celebrating Cen-

DANCING FOR GROWNUPS

If you want to kick up your heels but feel too old for the barely legal college crowds hip-hopping around the floors of the major clubs, consider dropping in on one of the city's many traditional folk dances. Scottish, English, and Scandinavian country dances, lively Israeli, contra and square dancing, and catch-all international combinations are among the hidden pleasures found in alcohol- and smoke-free auditoriums, churches, VFW halls, YWCAs, and community centers throughout the metro area.

If you don't know a schottisch from a hey-for-four, have no fear: all welcome beginners and stress informality over competition (though dedicated regulars are numerous enough to satisfy experienced visitors, too). No partners are necessary, either (or big bankrolls—cover charges are typically $3-5 for hours of invigorating fun). Cambridge-based **Folk Arts Center of New England** has the most comprehensive recorded forecast of what's on and where, updated twice a week, tel. (617) 491-6084. Or consult the dance listings in the "Calendar" section of any Thursday *Boston Globe.* If you've already mastered English folk dancing, call the Country Dance Society's recorded calendar, (617) 354-1340, for a more select list of events catering primarily or exclusively to experienced dancers.

tral Square's cultural diversity—is **T.T. the Bear's Place,** tel. (617) 492-0082, an equally independent-minded place whose bookings principally mine the rich vein of local hard rock, although plenty of pop-minded songwriters and the occasional world-beat dance band roll through, too.

Another top spot for every flavor of rock, from radio-ready alternapop to heavy-grooving ska, is Boston's **Mama Kin,** on Lansdowne St. across from the mighty left-field wall of Fenway Park. Co-owned by Aerosmith (hence the band logo on the front stoop and framed concert photos above the bar), this intimate two-stage club has one of most reasonable cover charges in town— $5 weeknights, for example. Bookings lean toward the cream of the local crop. Every so often, one of the celebrity owners may drop by, but the staff has no more clue than you do as to when this will happen next. Besides such nice touches as stage curtains, and good draft microbrews (Anchor Steam, Red Hook ESB), this place has some of the best maintained bathrooms in clubland.

For harder-edged stuff—heavy rock, metal, grunge, and the like—check out nearby Kenmore Square's **Rathskeller,** on Comm. Ave. facing the MBTA bus depot and Green Line station, tel. (617) 536-2750. Also known as "the Rat," this indestructible dark and dingy place has seen more headbanging, body-slamming, jump-booted, leather-clad, spike-haired, brain-frying, torn-flannel, beer-pissing good times than a trainload of Lollapalooza fans have known in their collective lifetimes. Careful where you lean: so much punk history oozes from its cinderblocks that your clothes might get permanently stained. Everybody who was anybody on the Boston rock scene—natives and visitors alike—played here on the way up or down or on the rebound. Come check this place out.

For solid roots music, from rockabilly, Cajun swing, and Afropop to Scottish fiddlers and surf guitarists, take the Red Line to **Johnny D's Uptown Music Club,** on Holland Ave. just steps from the Davis Square T station, tel. (617) 776-9667. With good food and draft beer to boot, this is an A-1 hangout. Before they land at Johnny D's, you can often find local singer-songwriters working out new or polishing their materials a subway stop away, in a pair of Cam-

bridge clubs on Mass. Ave. Cover-free **Toad,** next to the Wok 'N' Roll restaurant opposite the Porter Square T station, tel. (617) 497-4950, is so small that most of its acts perform unplugged—and the audience often comprises fellow musicians taking a night off. **The Lizard Lounge,** tel. (617) 547-0759, in the basement of the Cambridge Common restaurant at 1667 Mass. Ave., between Porter and Harvard Square, is larger but equally intimate, its typically diverse audience drawn by great tunes, good vibes, and an atmosphere free of raging collegiate hormones.

Folk and Acoustic

Garage bands aren't the only scene happening in Boston. Folk music thrives in Cambridge. While rock fans gather in smoke-filled clubs and swill beer, folkies sip tea and cappuccino and nibble cookies at events called "coffeehouses"—typically held in church basements throughout the region. Most are weekly or monthly affairs, and many are partially or wholly open-mike—a true grab-bag experience in which anyone may sign up for three songs' worth of stage time. The grandfather of them all is the **Nameless Coffeehouse,** tel. (617) 864-1630, a Friday-night staple of the First Parish of Cambridge, the wooden 1833 Unitarian church facing Harvard Yard from the foot of Church Street. The Nameless (free) has been a home to up-and-coming acoustic musicians since the late 1960s. Thursday nights, the **Naked City Coffeehouse,** tel. (617) 731-6468, brings an open mike for music and poetry to the Old Cambridge Baptist Church on Mass. Ave. next to the Inn at Harvard. At the **Cantab Lounge,** 738 Mass. Ave. in Central Square, tel. (617) 354-2685, Monday features an open mike for folk, Tuesday for country and bluegrass. Not in the mood to gamble on untried talent? Head for the local kingpin of folk, Harvard Square's alcohol- and smoke-free **Club Passim,** under The Globe Corner Bookstore on Palmer St., tel. (617) 492-7679. Monday is for spoken word and Tuesday is open mike night, but the rest of the week Passim offers top-drawer folk and acoustic music from all over. Serious folk enthusiasts looking for a comprehensive listing of where and when to catch your next fix of acoustic music in Boston and around the state should visit the Folk Song

Society of Greater Boston's Web page, www.world.std.com/~fssgb, and follow "other links" to "concerts in Massachusetts."

Jazz

Boston is no Manhattan (or even Hartford), and it was in the city's Symphony Hall that Benny Goodman's first appearance was dismissed by a newspaper critic as more fitting fodder for the baseball reporter. However, there *is* good jazz to be found around town, particularly at Harvard Square's nationally known **Regattabar**, in the Charles Hotel on Bennett St. (tel. 617-661-5000 recorded schedule, 617-876-7777 Concertix number for charge-by-phone tickets). Jan.-May, the annual **Regattabar Jazz Festival** brings a who's who of celebrity jazz artists to the hotel's main ballroom. Other nearby spots to check out include **Ryles,** 212 Hampshire St. in the heart of Inman Square, tel. (617) 876-9330, dishing out jazz most nights, and **Scullers Jazz Club,** in the DoubleTree Guest Suites Hotel on the Allston side of the Charles River, a short cab ride or half-hour walk from the Red Line's Central Square station, tel. (617) 562-4111. Also in Allston is the **Wonder Bar,** tel. (617) 351-COOL, a young hipster jazz bar at 186 Harvard Ave., a block from the Green "B" Line. Be warned that while you may feel out of place wearing sneakers at the two luxury hotel jazz spots, you won't even make it past the Wonder Bar's doorkeep without proper attire.

Wally's Cafe, a local jazz institution dating back to the 1940s, stands in a class by itself. Passed without a second glance by the unsuspecting, this tiny South End hole in the wall truly embodies the roots of jazz. Needless to say, there's no dress code or stuffy attitude here, just cheap beer and damn good music from mostly homegrown groups, including plenty of students from nearby Berklee College of Music. Look for the telltale Bud sign among the brick rowhouses at 427 Mass. Ave. a few dozen yards from the Orange Line and only two blocks from Symphony Hall.

Blues

True blues hounds should make a beeline for Allston's **Harper's Ferry,** 158 Brighton Ave., tel. (617) 254-9743, Boston's preeminent spot for catching both local and national acts. Besides being right on the route of the #66 bus from Harvard Square or a short walk from the Green "B" Line's Harvard Avenue surface stop, Harper's lies within five minutes' walk of eight Vietnamese restaurants. Big-name bluesmen and -women also often headline at the **House of Blues,** on Winthrop St. in Harvard Square, tel. (617) 491-BLUE, the original flagship of this ever-expanding night club chain. Despite the great music lineup, the place is more of a marketing concept than anything else, and most of the audience could probably care less about who's on stage so long as they think it shows good taste to be there. Despite door staff with Secret Service-style earphones and attitudes, wait staff that's been known to tell diners to hurry up because people want their table, and Sunday gospel brunches scheduled in such rapid succession you barely have time to eat, this place never lacks a crowd (proving, perhaps, that if you're cool, you can do anything and people will still love you). It's no surprise that the founder of this Gap-like merchandiser of blues music, soul food, and logo-stamped blueswear was also responsible for giving the world the Hard Rock Cafe; more unusual may be the fact that in addition to celebrities like Blues Brother Dan Aykroyd, financial investors include that rockin' local cat Big Crimson (a.k.a. Harvard University). For a Sunday **gospel brunch** that *doesn't* feel like a cattle call, check out **Dick's Last Resort,** a Texas chain of party-hearty restaurants with a local outpost on the Huntington Avenue side of the Pru. Or, for some serious raise-the-roof gospel singing, try and squeeze in the doors of the always-overflowing Sunday morning services at the **New Covenant Christian Church,** 340 Blue Hill Ave., in Dorchester, tel. (617) 445-0636.

To check out the local blues haps thoroughly, arm yourself beforehand with the blues concert calendar assembled by WGBH-FM "Blues After Hours" diva Mai Cramer. Send your e-mail request to mai_cramer@wgbh.org, or send a stamped, self-addressed envelope to Blues After Hours, WGBH Radio, 125 Western Ave., Allston MA 02134. *BluesWire,* a well-crafted broadsheet on the regional blues scene, also publishes an excellent listing of blues and R&B concerts around New England; order a copy from P.O. Box 657, Bedford MA 01730.

Gay Nights

A number of otherwise straight clubs feature at least one night a week on which they cater to gays, lesbians, or both. Among these, Sunday at Avalon, on Lansdowne St., reigns supreme. Lansdowne's Karma Club, Cambridge's Man Ray and Ryles, and Fenway's Quest (1270 Boylston St., across from the Howard Johnson Inn) also merit mention.

Boston's tiny Bay Village neighborhood, wedged between Park Square and the South End, boasts a range of gay nightlife, from the full-out drag queen and transvestite dance bar **Jacques,** at Broadway and Piedmont behind the Radisson Hotel on Stuart St., to the **Napoleon Club,** 52 Piedmont St., a gay piano bar (allegedly a favorite of Liberace) dating back to 1952. To get the full scoop on gay nightlife, pick up a free copy of *Bay Windows,* the newspaper for Boston's gay community.

MORE TREATS FOR EYES AND EARS

Poetry

While poetry readings have become a fixture at hip coffee shops and cafes around Boston and the nation over the past few years, the local poetry scene actually has deep roots. The **New England Poetry Club** has presented regular readings for longer than most of today's barstool poets have even been alive. Founded in 1915 by Amy Lowell, Robert Frost, and Conrad Aiken, the NEPC presents free Monday-evening poetry readings Oct.-May at Harvard's Yenching Library, on Divinity Ave. off Kirkland St., a block from the university's Science Center, tel. (617) 643-0029. For over 15 years, the club has also co-sponsored a summer series at the Longfellow National Historic Site, 105 Brattle St. outside of Harvard Square, tel. (617) 876-4491 (free). So long as friend-of-the-Beats and general poetical torch-bearer Jack Powers draws a breath, **Stone Soup Poets,** tel. (617) 227-0845, www.stonepoet1.org, will also give audiences a taste of verse—as it has each and every week for over a quarter century. Get a serving of this iconoclastic stew of raw and established voices every Monday night at T.T. the Bear's Place, 10 Brookline St., in Central Square, Cambridge, next to the Middle East Restaurant and Nightclub ($3).

The Monday night poetry readings at the Cambridge Center for Adult Education's **Blacksmith House,** 56 Brattle St. in Harvard Square, tel. (617) 354-3036, have also been steadfastly reveling in the power of language for over 20 years ($3), with local and visiting poets in regular attendance.

The more recent phenomenon of **poetry slams** involves poets competing head to head and being judged, Olympic-style, by a panel of volunteers from the audience. Catch the leading local example of these highly topical performance events ($3) every Wednesday night at the "Third Rail"—the downstairs room of the **Cantab Lounge,** 738 Mass. Ave. in Central Square, tel. (617) 354-2685. If you're fortunate enough to drop in during the spring championships, which determine who represents Boston and Cambridge at the U.S. Grand National poetry slams, you'll hear some of the country's top-ranked slammers.

Check the bulletin board of the **Grolier Poetry Book Shop,** 6 Plympton St. behind the Harvard Book Store, tel. (617) 547-4648, for other poetry-related events, including the shop's own reading series.

Film

Showtimes for the latest commercial releases may be found in any of the local daily and weekly newspapers, or with a touch-tone call to Boston's Moviephone, (617) 333-FILM—an automated menu-driven service that will even give you directions to particular theaters if you navigate through the prompts correctly. But Boston also abounds in films that will never make it to any mall multiplex. Harvard Square's **Brattle Theatre,** on Brattle St. next to the HMV music store, tel. (617) 876-6837, and Brookline's nonprofit **Coolidge Corner Theatre,** on Harvard and Beacon Streets at the Green "C" Line, tel. (617) 734-2500, are stalwarts of the

national art-house circuit. The Brattle—one of the first repertory cinemas in the U.S., whose '50s revivals of Humphrey Bogart films are credited with making Bogie an American classic—also sponsors the annual Boston International Festival of Women's Cinema, while the Coolidge carves a unique niche with plenty of local premieres, animation festivals, occasional silent films shown to live orchestral accompaniment, and autumn's annual Jewish Film Festival, co-hosted with the Museum of fine Arts. The **Harvard Film Archive,** in the Carpenter Center for Visual Arts on Quincy St., tel. (617) 495-4700, has even more freedom to explore non-commercial filmmaking;

its schedule regularly includes obscure, neglected, and experimental cinema, film classics reprised for curricular purposes, and perennial showings of Dusan Makavejev's work. It's easy to be lulled into thinking Hollywood and western Europe have a monopoly on producing compelling films, but a sampling of the films shown at the **Museum of Fine Arts,** tel. (617) 267-9300, then press 800, will open your eyes to the rich and varied storytelling found outside the mainstream, from Iceland to Iran to documentary filmmakers here in our own backyard. The MFA screens its winning picks from contemporary world cinema mostly Wed.-Sun. in the West Wing.

ACCOMMODATIONS

If you won't settle for anything less than the sort of place that routinely earns a fistful of diamonds and stars from Mobil and AAA, know that local hotel rates are entirely out of proportion to the city's size. It's a case study in low-supply-high-demand economics: there are more rooms in Las Vegas's three largest hotels than in all of Boston and Cambridge combined, and the year-round occupancy rate here is close to 80%; consequently, the Hub's average room rate is exceeded only (in this country) by New York City's. Well-appointed downtown rooms—with double beds and private baths, enough room to permit morning calisthenics without moving furniture into the hall, and with views of something other than utility shafts—will almost without exception cost you well over $200. Per night. Parking, 12.45% tax, tips, and breakfast are additional. Sound like highway robbery? Wait till you see what $100 gets you.

Savvy high-end travelers will use corporate discounts, weekend packages, or a discounter like **Quikbook,** tel. (800) 221-3531, to take the edge off the high priced business-oriented hotels, but for anyone on a more modest budget there's precious little relief during a high season that stretches from early spring through November. Unless your child is valedictorian, for Heaven's sake avoid visiting during Harvard Commencement (the Thursday after Memorial Day)—any Boston or Cambridge room that won't make mom squeamish will have been booked years

in advance, and room rates—with a few praiseworthy exceptions—will look uncomfortably similar to the tuition bill. Indicating that somebody's community relations must be falling short of the mark, most local innkeepers target only Harvard and MIT parents, while ignoring the other graduation dates on the spring calendar. As a general rule, lodgings throughout Greater Boston start high and are priced in direct proportion to their distance from either Harvard Yard or the downtown waterfront. If you seek a standard motel room for under $60, you should head for something like the **Tage Inn-Andover,** 30 miles north of Boston right on I-93 at Exit 45, tel. (800) 322-TAGE. With indoor pool, tennis court, exercise facilities, modem ports, guest-room voicemail, and prices $80-120 lower than comparable Boston hotels ($58 d to be exact), the savings may more than compensate for the half-hour drive into the MBTA commuter parking at Lechmere (get off I-93 Exit 30 and follow Rts. 38 and 28 till you see the trolley terminal). To find the scant handful of other inexpensive motels within 50 miles, see the "Southeastern Massachusetts" or "Central Massachusetts" chapters of this book.

Almost the only oasis of even moderate prices ($60-85) is Brookline, which is also nearly immune from price gouging aimed at college parents. B&Bs around the city mostly occupy the middle ground between plain guest houses and fancy hotels, but, while some offer exceptional hospitality and spacious, comfortable quarters at

ADDITIONAL GREATER BOSTON ACCOMMODATIONS

DOWNTOWN AND WATERFRONT

Boston Harbor Hotel, on Rowes Wharf off Atlantic Ave., tel. (800) 752-7077. Pool, fitness center, spa; framing the waterfront with its stunning 80-foot arch, the hotel's rooms all offer impressive city or harbor views; airport water taxi at the door, short walk to T station. Luxury.

Holiday Inn Boston/Government Center, Cambridge and Blossom Sts., tel. (800) HOLIDAY. Outdoor pool; near Massachusetts General Hospital, a couple of blocks from the T. Very expensive-luxury.

Le Meridien Boston, 250 Franklin St., tel. (800) 543-4300. Extra-large rooms in the heart of the Financial District, superb service, 40-foot lap pool; within a few blocks of Amtrak, airport water shuttle, and the T. Luxury.

Radisson Hotel Boston, 200 Stuart St., tel. (800) 333-3333. Luxury. Indoor rooftop pool, weight room, large rooms; a couple of blocks from the T.

Seaport Hotel & Conference Center, on Northern Ave. in South Boston, tel. (800) WTC-HOTEL.

The most convenient hotel to the World Trade Center, just across the street; shuttle to South Station. Luxury.

Tremont House, 275 Tremont St., tel. (800) 331-9998. Across from the Wang Center for the Performing Arts and Tufts/New England Medical Center; a block from the T. Very expensive.

BACK BAY

Back Bay Hilton, 40 Dalton St., across from the Hynes Convention Center, tel. (800) 874-0663. Indoor pool, fitness center; a couple blocks from the T. Very expensive-luxury.

The MidTown Hotel, 220 Huntington Ave., opposite the Christian Science Center, tel. (800) 343-1177. Outdoor pool, free parking; half a block from subway. Very expensive.

The Westin Hotel, Copley Place, 10 Huntington Ave., tel. (800) 228-3000. Fitness room, sauna, 34-ft. indoor lap pool, great views from upper-story rooms; one block from Amtrak Back Bay Station and subway. Luxury.

---

rates reasonable enough to more than offset their extra distance from high-profile attractions, others seem to assume their prime locations will blind you to claustrophobic rooms, threadbare decor, and outrageous four-day minimum stays.

Boston first-timers should remember that most small inns and guest houses, particularly in historic neighborhoods, sport signs not much larger (or better lit) than your average phone book—if they have signs at all. In fact, gas stations are about the only businesses in the metro area that advertise with neon.

BUDGET: UNDER $35

Currently Boston's only budget options are hostels. Anyone who thinks such places are untidy hives of chain-smoking slackers barely out of high school has obviously never been to the immaculate and friendly **Irish Embassy Back-packers Hostel,** 232 Friend St. one block from North Station, tel. (617) 973-4841. Designed by experienced budget travelers to be the best of all possible hostels, the Irish Embassy delights the most jaded backpackers with its bounty of free-bies, including full linen service (no smelly sleeping bags, no regulation sleep sacks), pack storage, earplugs (dormitory rooms are shared, after all), free thrice-weekly barbecues at nearby pubs under the same ownership (including a vegetarian one), and access to live Celtic entertainment in the ground-floor club. All this and no membership requirements! All beds are $15 all the time, including those in the one private double room. This is the best hostel deal in all of New England. Advance reservations strongly advised.

If you can't land a space at Friend St., there's always **Hostelling International Boston,** 16 Hemenway, a few minute's stroll from Mass. Ave. and the Green Line's Hynes/ICA station, tel. (617) 536-1027. Besides the standard hos-

FENWAY, BROOKLINE, AND ALLSTON/BRIGHTON

Best Western Terrace Motor Lodge, 1650 Commonwealth Ave. in Brighton, tel. (800) 528-1234. Free parking; Green Line trolley stops just out front. Expensive-very expensive.

The Buckminster Hotel, 645 Beacon St. in Kenmore Square, tel. (800) 727-2825. Some rooms have kitchenettes; right on subway line. Expensive-luxury.

Days Inn, 1234 Soldiers Field Rd., in Allston, tel. (800) 325-2525. Outdoor pool, free parking; adjacent to city transportation department sand lot; about a 20-minute riverside walk to Harvard Square and the T. Expensive-luxury.

Howard Johnson Inn—Boston/Fenway, 1271 Boylston St., behind Fenway Park, (800) I-GO-HOJO. Outdoor pool, free parking, shuttle to Longwood Medical area; within several blocks of the T. Expensive-luxury.

CAMBRIDGE

Best Western Homestead Inn, 220 Alewife Brook Pkwy., tel. (800) 528-1234. Free parking, indoor pool, less than 10 minutes' walk from west end of MBTA Red Line. Expensive-luxury.

Cambridge Inn Ramada, 250 Monsignor O'Brien Hwy., tel. (800) 2-RAMADA. Two blocks from the MBTA's Lechmere terminal. Very expensive.

Hyatt Regency Cambridge, 575 Memorial Dr. near MassPike Exit 16, tel. (800) 233-1234. Indoor pool, fitness room, revolving rooftop restaurant and lounge; not convenient to public transit. Very expensive-luxury.

Susse Chalet Inn—Cambridge, 211 Concord Trpk. (Rt. 2), tel. (800) 258-1980. Free parking; a short drive past the west end of MBTA Red Line. Moderate-expensive.

AIRPORT VICINITY

Harborside Hyatt Conference Center & Hotel, 101 Harborside Dr. on fringe of the airport, tel. (800) 233-1234. Free parking, indoor pool, fitness center; water shuttle to downtown. Luxury.

Holiday Inn Boston—Logan Airport, 225 McClellan Hwy. (Rt. 1A), tel. (800) HOLIDAY. Free parking, outdoor pool; adjacent to Blue Line subway. Very expensive-luxury.

Ramada Inn Logan Airport, on the airport grounds, tel. (800) 228-3344. Free parking, outdoor pool, fitness room; within shuttle ride of MBTA. Very expensive-luxury.

---

tel self-service kitchen, HI-Boston has some private rooms for couples and families, sponsors a range of special programs, and is open around the clock. Note that during the May-Oct. busy season, its nearly 200 beds (never more than five to a room) are reserved exclusively for HI members—but you *may* join upon arrival if necessary. Rates are $17 members, $20 nonmembers, plus $2 for linens if you don't have the regulation sleep sack. Given the dearth of other cheap accommodations around town, advance reservations are encouraged.

INEXPENSIVE: $35-60

While singletons and winter visitors will find inexpensive rates at many of the places mentioned under the "Moderate" category below, couples traveling in summer aren't nearly so lucky. Other than the hostels, only two *rooms* in the whole metro area—out of some 12,000 in over 140 guest houses, motels, hotels, and B&Bs of all shapes and sizes—cost less than $60 for two people in high season, after taxes (and those rooms, in a South End B&B, are booked so solid that the owner asked not to be identified, so she won't have to turn people away). The only runner-up is the YMCA, with two locations in the city: the **Boston YMCA,** at 316 Huntington Ave. near Symphony Hall and Northeastern University, tel. (617) 536-7800, whose rooms are only available late June to September ($56 d, $38 s, almost all with shared baths); and the year-round **Constitution Inn at the Armed Forces YMCA,** 150 Second Ave., in the Charlestown Navy Yard, tel. (800) 495-9622. If it weren't equipped solely with twin beds, its rooms would be superior to the Harvard Square Hotel's in size and amenities, for about one-third the price ($59 d, $69-79 with kitchenettes, discounts for military personnel or veterans). Being a full-service Y, the modern, flag-draped granite edifice comes with Olympic-sized pool and fitness center (free to guests), and is just a few minutes' walk from the $1 MBTA water shuttle to Long Wharf and downtown. Several good restaurants within walking distance cater to the waterfront condo dwellers and office workers who now inhabit the Navy Yard's renovated brick and granite buildings, including an excellent Italian bistro, Gabriele's, only a block away (closed Sunday), and Biga Breads, a delectable breakfast-lunch bakery-cafe, on Eighth St. in the Navy Yard (open daily).

MODERATE: $60-85

Several establishments have "Beacon" in their names. All are closely related in price, and several in location, but the one to burn into your memory is the **Beacon Street Guest House,** 1047 Beacon St. in Brookline, tel. (800) 872-7211 or (617) 232-0292. The large, simply furnished rooms in this graceful, elevator-less brick townhouse have enough oak trim, paneling, and now-disused hearths to lend it the air of a vintage Ivy League alumni club. Rates are $55-69 d for rooms with private baths (subtract $10 for shared baths, another $10 if you're alone). The front rooms' big bowfront windows overlook one of the city's early Victorian-era boulevards near Boston University, a tree-lined design after the French manner then in vogue. With the convenience of both fine restaurants and the Green "C" Line trolley stop at Audubon Circle just a stone's throw down the block (on the Boston city line), this place is arguably one of Greater Boston's best lodging values.

But for the lack of private baths, almost as good a bargain stands just up the street at **Anthony's Town House,** 1085 Beacon, tel. (617) 566-3972: $55-75 d or $35-60 s, *including* tax (cash only). The ample rooms are quite comfortable and display a quirky charm with their glazed-tile hearths (purely decorative now), painted furniture, lime green carpet, and well-preserved oak woodwork. Reserve parking ahead if you'll need it.

If you enjoy B&Bs, there are two in Cambridge offering exceptional value: **The Missing Bell B&B at the Shaw House,** a few blocks north of Harvard Square, tel. (617) 876-0987 ($70-85 s or d), and Central Square's **Prospect Place,** tel. (800) 769-5303, a few minutes' walk from the Red Line ($75-95 s or d). Each has been carefully restored to exhibit the Victorian craftsmanship that went into their original construction: the Queen Anne-style Shaw boasts gorgeous spindled stairways and elaborately carved woodwork, while the Italianate Prospect Place features delicately rippled cylinder glass and marble fireplaces. Both are appropriately furnished with antiques, too, but genial hosts and genuine lived-in warmth dispel any sense of being in a museum.

If proximity to beautiful Arnold Arboretum or the pleasant jogging path around Jamaica Pond is more appealing than being in the heart of Cambridge—or if you're traveling with a dog, or need a dedicated modem line for your laptop—try the beautifully restored 1855 **Taylor House B&B,** in Jamaica Plain, tel. (888) 228-2956, e-mail taylorbb@ziplink.net, near the Emerald Necklace and within a block of the #39 bus to Copley Square ($85-95 d). Additional moderately priced B&Bs may be found by using one of the area's reservation services: **Bed & Breakfast Agency of Boston,** tel. (800) CITY-BNB or, from the UK, (0800) 895-128; **Host Homes of Boston,** tel. (617) 244-1308; or **Bed and Breakfast Associates/Bay Colony, Ltd.,** tel. (781) 449-5302.

Single travelers unable to land a spot at any of the above, or who are looking for a kitchen-equipped alternative to the hostels, might consider sharing modestly renovated, fully furnished apartment units with three or four other strangers at the **Farrington Inn,** 23 Farrington St. in Allston, tel. (800) 76-SLEEP or, from the UK, (0800) 896-040, for $40-60 (note, though, that if you don't like nicotine dreams, you may be out of luck, given how much the European clientele would rather smoke than breathe). The Farrington—actually a series of rooming and apartment houses in a small residential pocket a block off Allston's commercial Harvard Avenue, 10 minutes by bus to Harvard Square—has tiny, closet-size singles sharing a bath on a hall, too, for the same rates, but Brookline's Beacon St. lodgings are a much better value, and more convenient to most of Boston. (There are also double rooms with private baths and small kitchenettes, vastly overpriced at $90-105, unless you have a weakness for acoustic tile, mismatched dorm-quality furniture, and old cast-iron radiators.)

EXPENSIVE: $85-110

Few Beacon Hill addresses boast the views of **The Eliot & Pickett Houses,** 6 Mt. Vernon Pl., tel. (617) 248-8707, e-mail P&E@uua.org, 19th-century brick townhouses sitting so close to the State House and the Common that their roof deck overlooks both. (Mt. Vernon Pl. is a three-car-length dead-end lane off Joy St. between Mt. Vernon St. and Beacon.) More a modest inn than fancy B&B—there are no in-room TVs or daily maid service, and guests prepare their own breakfasts from the eggs, bread, cereal and other fixings left for them in the fridge—these residences are owned by the Unitarian Universalist Association, whose headquarters are a few doors away. Rooms not booked for church business are available to the public for very attractive rates, given the location: from $80 for small, under-the-gables queen rooms with shared baths to $105 for the more standard twin doubles with private baths. Parking is available in the Boston Common Garage for $19 on weekdays, $6 on Saturday or Sunday.

Once privately run for the benefit of families visiting patients at nearby hospitals, the friendly **John Jeffries House,** 14 Embankment Rd., tel. (617) 367-1866, now also welcomes the world at large. Though standard doubles are minuscule, each room comes with a kitchenette that gives it the feel of a tiny city *pied-a-terre.* The exceptional location faces the Charles Street Red Line station at the foot of Beacon Hill, within easy strolling distance of fine shops, restaurants, the Museum of Science, and the riverfront Esplanade, almost within earshot of the Boston Pops' outdoor concerts if the brick walls weren't virtually soundproof. Rates begin at $97 d; oversized rooms and suites run $110-135; and validated parking is $15 at an adjacent garage.

Rooms come in all shapes and sizes at the **Shawmut Inn,** 280 Friend St., nearly opposite North Station, tel. (800) 350-7784 reservations, (617) 720-5544 information, but most are more spacious than rooms twice their price only 15 minutes' walk away in the financial district. While

furnished as cleanly and simply as a modern hospital, each room at least has a mini-refrigerator and microwave, and hacker tourists can request a room with a modem-compatible phone. There's also a health club across the street available to guests for just $5 per visit. Rates start at $106 d May-Nov., $89 off-season.

If you need to be closer to the Longwood Medical Area—where many of the city's hospitals are clustered—or Boston University; are traveling with a small pet; want a base convenient to both city transit and out-of-town drives (without fighting downtown traffic or paying downtown hotel parking rates), or simply want more than a plain carpeted box for $100, **The Bertram Inn,** in Brookline, tel. (800) 295-3822, is a sure bet. Named after a hostelry in an Agatha Christie novel, the Tudor-style Victorian at 92 Sewall Ave. (one block from the St. Paul St. surface stop on the Green "C" Line) combines well-appointed, "casually elegant," antique-filled rooms with modern amenities and service-oriented staff. Two of the rooms in this former private mansion have working fireplaces, too. Summer rates: $84-174 d, with free parking and continental breakfast.

Unless you value room service, handicap access, or multi-story atriums, the best deal going next door to Harvard University is **A Friendly Inn at Harvard Square,** 1673 Cambridge St., tel. (617) 547-7851. Though neither large nor oriented to receive much natural light, all rooms have private baths and phones, most have small TVs; light continental breakfast is included, and parking is free. Rates run $87-107 d ($10 less for a single). If you aren't picky about price or quality as long as you're next to Harvard, refer to A Friendly Inn's next-door neighbor, the Irving House, under "Very Expensive," below.

VERY EXPENSIVE: $110-150

Some of the city's most comfortable rooms at any price are found in the incomparable **Mary Prentiss Inn,** 6 Prentiss St. in Cambridge, tel. (617) 661-2929. May through mid-November, $119-199 d, depending on size of room (Jan.-Feb., rates drop as low as $89-119), including full or continental breakfast and free parking (limited, so reserve ahead). Like a Chopin etude, the beautifully restored 1843 Greek Revival building exudes the artist-owner's strong command of style and obvious appreciation for grace and comfort, from freshly baked afternoon cookies and personable staff to good-sized rooms with wet bars discreetly built into cabinets—even a couple in-room fireplaces. As for convenient location, the Porter Square Commuter Rail and Red Line station is a few minutes' walk away, Harvard is seven blocks, and plenty of good restaurants are around the corner along Mass. Ave.

Right at the periphery of Harvard is the **Irving House,** 24 Irving St., four blocks from the Science Center and Graduate School of Design, tel. (800) 854-8249 out of state, (617) 547-4600 locally. Rooms vary dramatically in size, condition, and comfort, but in a vivid example of what I dub the Harvard Effect, most are priced $140 d and up (with private bath and modest continental breakfast) in the high Sept.-Nov. season. (Dec.-Feb., doubles with private bath are as low as $100.) Single rooms with shared baths run $75-95. For Commencement Week, the rates jump to $185 d. Despite the steep Ivy League prices, it's still cheaper than the full-service hotels around Harvard; this fact and its European *pension* atmosphere keep it chock full most of the year. For newly constructed, more uniform (and more expensive) rooms in a similarly large and graceful clapboard house, inquire about the Irving's sister B&B inn outside Central Square: the **Isaac Harding House,** 288 Harvard St., tel. (617) 876-2888. Both properties have free but limited parking, available on a first-come, first-served basis.

One of the best deals in Boston proper is the **Newbury Guest House,** 261 Newbury St., tel. (800) 437-7668. More a small hotel than guesthouse, the Newbury allows you to be in the absolute thick of fashionable Back Bay, swaddled in faux Victorian trimmings from hardwood floors and Oriental runners to four-poster beds and ornamental fireplaces in the larger front rooms. (If you're a light sleeper who turns in early, you'll prefer the smaller but quieter back rooms.) For "only" $110-150 d, the comfort and value of even the smallest compares favorably to nearby chains. The tradeoff is space and room service: if you need more of either, in this area you're going to need a luxury-priced hotel.

If you enjoy hospitality with a more personal touch, try the **Clarendon Square B&B,** tel. (617) 536-2229, e-mail ClarSqrBnB@aol.com ($95-160, generally a two night minimum), a South End gem located near the Boston Center for the Arts and Tremont Street's vibrant restaurant row. The lavish continental breakfast buffet serves equally well for early risers and late sleepers, and with an entire sunny floor of common space at their disposal guests are encouraged—rather than forced—to be social. Annotated city maps, suggested itineraries for short stays or rainy days, and informed opinions about neighborhood dining are among the extra touches, although if it's utter privacy you want this place can give you that, too (one room even has kitchen and private entrance). Independent-minded medium- to long-term visitors who'd happily trade room service for a place in which to do their own cooking will find that the South End's historic Victorian rowhouses offer Boston's best selection of fully furnished studio apartments and guesthouse efficiency suites. **Copley House,** 239 West Newton St., two blocks from the Prudential Center, tel. (800) 331-1318, maintains apartments in three buildings around the Symphony Hall edge of the South End and Fenway neighborhoods. Imagine—all the modern conveniences and a generic hotel-Victorian look for only $85-120 per night (three-night minimum; parking $8 extra per night).

LUXURY: $150+

If you prefer, you don't have to settle for anything less than either the townhouse-styled **Ritz Carlton,** tel. (800) 241-3333, or the more modern **Four Seasons,** tel. (800) 332-3442. Overlooking the Public Garden a block apart, these are routinely ranked as Boston's finest hotels, earning their garlands with such niceties as a room-service kitchen on every floor, so you don't have to wait to sate any sudden cravings for caviar and toast (the Ritz), or a ready supply of duck food for your young children to disburse among the Lagoon residents across the street (the Four Seasons). An evening at the Four Seasons' outstanding restaurant, **Aujour'dui,** is a way to sample that hotel's attentiveness for only about a third of the room rate. Afternoon tea at the

Ritz (jackets no longer required for men) offers a similarly luxurious foray into high society at a fraction of the regular admission price.

If these two are the rival princes of Boston's hotels, the undisputed queen mum is **The Fairmont Copley Plaza**, on St. James St. next to the John Hancock Company's 65-story headquarters in Back Bay, tel. (800) 527-4727. Appropriately lavish in its marbled, coffered, and antique-filled interior, the Copley is a grande dame indeed—the sort of place where, if you spend the afternoon in your large, high-ceilinged room, you'll be fussed over to distraction by gracious housekeepers bringing you another pile of fluffy towels, mints to stash by your bedside, fresh flowers, an extra dusting here, a plumping of the pillows there; but what do you expect from a place that stamps its crest into the sand in its lobby ashtrays? Be sure to inquire about package deals ($179-299 d, plus $24 parking).

For one of the best values in its class, look no further than **The Eliot Hotel**, 370 Comm. Ave. on the edge of Back Bay, a block from the Green Line, tel. (800) 44-ELIOT ($165-265 d, $18 parking). Often characterized as European—meaning it doesn't have thousands of rooms, or a giant lobby to park your kids in—the Eliot provides exceptional comfort in all 90 of its two- and three-room suites, from refrigerators and modem-compatible dual-line phones to the tasteful furnishings, house plants, and large marble-appointed baths. For corner views overlooking both Massachusetts and Commonwealth Avenues ask for an "04" room.

The Lenox Hotel, at the corner of Boylston and Exeter streets, tel. (800) 225-7676, is a great little oasis of civility. Classical music wafts gently across the spacious lobby with its chandeliers, cathedral ceiling, and French Provincial decor. Attentive staff prompt you with Sirs and Ma'ams from registration up to your room ($190-245 d depending on size), which, if you've planned far enough in advance, could be one of the nearly two dozen with working fireplaces ($275 d). Be sure to inquire about package deals. The Sam Adams Brewhouse is conveniently located at street level, and the Green Line's Copley station is a block away; hotel parking starts at $22 per day.

Besides having enough gilded lobby decorations to rival Versailles and being the annual sponsor of the quartet of live swans at the Public Garden a block away (hence the swan logo on the brass door pulls), the **Boston Park Plaza Hotel**, 64 Arlington St., tel. (800) 225-2008, is also known as one of the most ecologically concerned hotels anywhere. Its aggressive recycling, waste reduction, and energy conservation program has pioneered the "green" hospitality industry. Package rates as low as $159-179 for cozy, agreeably furnished rooms prove guests can share the savings without sacrificing an ounce of comfort (regular rack rates top off at $245 d). Though the place is enormous, the staff keeps it from feeling impersonal, while a bunch of fine restaurants and dessert shops on the ground floor ensure that you need not walk out of doors to obtain some of the city's finest comestibles.

Cambridge seems to regard luxury as a perquisite of the executive rather than leisure class, given that its finest hospitality is found in modern, efficient, business-oriented establishments such as the **Charles Hotel**, just outside of Harvard Square, tel. (800) 882-1818 ($229-295, with rare super-saver rates as low as $179), or the **Royal Sonesta Hotel** overlooking the mouth of the Charles River and the Museum of Science, tel. (800) SONESTA ($210-270 in high season, $139-179 in low). Both are vastly superior to the **Inn at Harvard**, whose charming four-story atrium masks undersized, underwhelming rooms at prices that betray a uniquely Harvard interpretation of Ludwig Mies van der Rohe's dictum, "less is more." The Sonesta chain is known for its exceptional patronage of 20th-century art, some 70 pieces of which are on display in the public spaces of this flagship hotel, including a Jonathan Borofsky figure suspended over the entrance, a Frank Stella opposite the registration desk, a series of Andy Warhol flowers facing the West Tower elevators, a Sol LeWitt across from the lobby shop, signed Buckminster Fuller "blueprints" along the connecting corridor to the next-door headquarters of Lotus Development Corp., and numerous works by local and regional artists. Pick up a free guide to the whole collection at the lobby Guest Services counter and take a walk through the mini-museum.

FOOD

If you think Boston dining consists of clam chowder, baked beans, broiled cod, and boiled beef, you'll either be surprised or disappointed at the truth.

Sure, seafood is a staple, and two local chains—**Skipjack's** and **Legal Seafoods**—will handily slake your need for chowder, but things with fins and shells are so common that you don't have to confine yourself to these or the big-ticket waterfront places in order to enjoy a good fishy meal.

Traditional New England boiled dinners are a little more rare, but they, too, can be had if you're really, really adventurous: **Amrhein's,** on W. Broadway in South Boston, tel. (617) 268-6189, is the undisputed winner in this category—and it's only a block from the Broadway T stop. Baked beans, too, are something of a novelty outside of the Maxwell House-and-white-bread circuit, but Faneuil Hall's **Durgin Park** does serve a toothsome traditional pork- and molasses-flavored version of the dish.

But most Boston meals worth your dollar reflect a far more varied set of idioms: the 1980s influence of California seen in local bistro menus, for example, or the decade-old Pan-Asian invasion—Thai, Vietnamese, Korean, Japanese—which provides an alternative to their Chinese forerunners all over town. Sicilian pizzerias and Greek-American homestyle eateries are fixtures predating JFK, and the latest restaurant revival has returned Boston to the Mediterranean, this time to Tuscany, Provençe, Perpignan, Spain, Portugal, North Africa, and the Levant. India, Brazil, the Caribbean, and continental Europe are never far away, and both inexpensive burrito bars and upscale brewpubs are common. Irish pubs, roast beef, sinfully rich chocolate desserts, ice cream parlors, and leisurely Sunday brunches are all local institutions. Many places cater to vegetarians and healthful eaters with one or two meatless, but macrobiotic cooking is far more difficult to come by; **Masao's Kitchen,** in the Porter Square Exchange, Cambridge, tel. (617) 497-7348, and **Five Seasons,** on Centre St. in Jamaica Plain, tel. (617) 524-9016, are your best bets for this specialty.

Kosher restaurants, both the meat- and milk-free varieties, are found primarily on Harvard St. in Brookline (home to the only American Hasidic community outside of New York), but downtown's **Milk Street Cafe,** in the Financial District is an excellent fish-and-dairy kosher spot. Since this *is* a student capital, you won't have to dress up for dinner except at the trendy spots frequented by the Armani-wearing Euro-crowd and their local imitators. Even the Ritz has dropped its jacket requirement (in its cafe, anyway).

Many of the best eats are in residential neighborhoods, not downtown near the major hotels, so don't be shy: go where real Bostonians go when their employers aren't picking up the tab. Nearly all the restaurants cited below are within easy walking distance of both public transit and other restaurants, so no venture off the tourist track need be in vain if your first choice has taken the day off. Mind the time, though: due to the political clout of resident associations vigilant about their nightly peace and quiet, extraordinarily few restaurants serve later than 9:30-10 p.m. Exceptions are primarily in the South End and Jamaica Plain, where a few kitchens remain open till 11 p.m. or midnight, and Chinatown, where a handful of places stay open till 3 or 4 a.m.

BEACON HILL AND DOWNTOWN

Charles Street

Just steps away from the civilized bustle of Beacon Hill's main drag is the cozy basement home of **Lala Rokh,** 97 Mt. Vernon St., tel. (617) 720-5511. It's intimate enough to make diners speak in library whispers, but the Persian cuisine is worth shouting about ($12-16). Try leg of lamb stewed in a sauce of fenugreek, scallions, cilantro, chives, and dried lime—or chicken, tomato, and saffron with fragrant basmati rice seasoned with cumin, cinnamon, rose petals, and tart barberries. Even the simple-sounding grilled sirloin kebabs are richly marinated to bring out flavors you might never have thought beef capable of. Add a couple vegetable side

the Old State House (1712-1830), site of the Boston Massacre

the pasta dishes, either ($10.50-16.95). If diner fare suits your taste more than all that gourmet stuff, check out **The Paramount,** next door at 44, whose broiled chops, burgers, and egg breakfasts have been lubricating Beacon Hill digestive tracts since the Great Depression. Feeling sheepish? Order the spinach-feta omelet and you'll get a slab of cheese large enough to satisfy your feta cravings for the rest of the week. Another mostly yuppie-free dining option is **Buzzy's Roast Beef,** a very modern takeout shack nestled in the shadow of the old Charles St. jail's impenetrable stone walls, beside the busy rotary under the Charles St. T station. Heart-stopping sandwiches of blushing beef top the menu here, but there's a mean roast turkey with Dijon mustard, too, and even a half-decent vegetarian hummus wrap. The hand-cut french fries are among Boston's best. Always open, it's a favorite of both cabbies and insomniac residents from nearby hospitals, but the juicy bargains draw a good lunch crowd, too; sit at the picnic tables inside or out and you get free entertainment from drivers playing roller derby a few yards away.

Faneuil Hall and the Financial District

The Faneuil Hall Marketplace is nothing for diners to seek out; in general better value can be had elsewhere in the vicinity without having to contend with either the dizzying crowds or food that's been congealing under heat lamps. For a start, try the Haymarket area across North Street. **Marshall's,** 15 Union St., tel. (617) 523-9396, next door to the Union Oyster House, is a great spot for fresh shellfish. Order a plate of oysters on the half shell and the bartender shucks them for you then and there, instead of plucking them out of a pan of ye olde crushed. The place's barstools may not have been polished by Revolutionary breeches, but are you looking for history or a meal? If you want a little of both, nip into the **Green Dragon Tavern,** around the corner on cobblestone Marshall St., tel. (617) 367-0055, a cozy watering hole named for the spot where Paul Revere, Dr. Joseph Warren, and other thirsty Freemasons active in the American Revolution plotted against King George. Wash down the simple fare with what some say is the best Guinness in town—a fiercely competitive honor, given the city's le-

dishes and pickles and you'll have the makings of a shah's feast. Everything's as good as it sounds, and the wait staff expertly advises anyone reduced to indecision by the exotic-sounding choices. Literally translated as "tulip face" (meaning rosy cheeks), this gem of a restaurant takes its name from a romantic 1817 bestseller by poet Thomas Moore, a copy of which is on display (despite not even knowing the difference between Egypt, Persia, and India, the book was such a success that it made Moore a Persian expert in the West).

Given that Charles Street's best market, **Savenor's,** carries lobster-gorgonzola ravioli, wild boar sausage, and farm-raised zebra steaks, it comes as no surprise that the local pizza chain is also anything but ordinary. So when you're in the mood for the paper-thin Roman variety, wood-fired with toppings like fresh-shucked clams, caramelized leeks, or fig and balsamic jam, get thee to **Figs,** 42 Charles, tel. (617) 742-FIGS. They're no slouches with

SHOPPING HIGHLIGHT: RAGS BY THE POUND!

Surrounded by empty lots, unassuming residential streets, and a car-tire dealership, the nondescript building at 200 Broadway in Cambridge seems an unlikely major shopping destination. But observe for even a short while on weekend mornings and you'll witness a pilgrimage. New immigrants, students, urban survivalists, and others arrive and depart like leaf-cutter ants. The latter-day pilgrims come on bicycles, in cars, on foot, some pushing grocery carts, and all leave bearing bulging black trash bags. It's as if a ritual of yard-waste disposal is occurring within, and these people are acolytes of composting, dutifully carting away a mountain of dead leaves.

The building's most visible mark of identification is a sign (styled like the old Superman logo) reading The Garment District. That refers to the way-cool vendor of vintage clothing, ripped Levis, mod accessories, and Elvisiana—worth a gander, if not a pilgrimage, if only to get an eyeful of the decor (open daily; tel. 617-876-5230)—on the *second* floor inside.

But the trash-bag contingent operates *downstairs*, in the home of an outfit called Harbor Waste Textiles—makers of fine baled rags. What in Boston could make people line up for mere rags?

The pilgrims come not for rags in their finished form, but for rags in the raw—i.e., rags that haven't yet been shredded and bundled, rags that are, in fact, still perfectly ordinary used clothes. Okay, maybe not *so* ordinary—in fact, often so outlandishly out of fashion as to be back in vogue .

Half the pleasure of this place is that you might actually find something that (a) fits, (b) is in excellent condition, (c) is in a color you can live with, and (d) may even bear a designer label that still carries a cachet—a garment, in short, worth wading through a mountain of wide polyester ties, mawkish baby outfits, and unmatched vinyl-textured drapes. That wading is the other half of the fun. And wade you must, for the merchandise is literally (and liberally) strewn across the warehouse floor.

The name of this 9 a.m.-1 p.m. weekend textile circus is **Dollar-A-Pound** (the price is actually $1.50 per pound—with occasional items at 50¢ per pound—but the name predates a wave or two of inflation), which explains those Hefty bags handed out as you enter—and the big industrial scale used to tally your bill as you exit. It also explains the popularity of the place, since if you hit it lucky you can buy a fine wool vest or pure linen dress for less than it would (or will) cost you to dry-clean it.

---

gion of Irish pubs. Additional doses of fish and chips or lamb stew can be had on the downtown side of Quincy Market, in **The Black Rose,** on State St., or the intimate and less-touristed **Mr. Dooley's Boston Tavern,** at the corner of Broad and Batterymarch, deeper in the Financial District. Stalwart **Al Capone's,** 102 Broad, dishes up cheap and tasty thin-crust pizza slices so big they get cut in two just to make them manageable; enjoy them standing at one of the busy counters in the window or al fresco by the waterfront a couple of blocks away on the far side of the massive highway construction zone (open for lunch only).

Around the corner, at 200 High St., is the city's best buffet, **Country Life,** tel. (617) 951-2462 (lunch Sun.-Fri., dinner Tues.-Thurs. and Sunday). Faced with fresh, delicious, and abundant selections from the entrees to the breadboard, it is a rare individual who resists sampling darned near everything. Don't look for cold

cuts, though: in adherence to the precepts of its Seventh Day Adventist owners, it's all 100% vegetarian. Also meatless—except for the fish—is the **Milk Street Cafe,** 50 Milk St., near Devonshire, tel. (617) 542-2433 (you can call for the daily menu; open 7 a.m.-3 p.m.), whose quiches, salads, soups, pizzas and other strictly kosher goodies draw such a big following from surrounding office workers that they discount lunches before noon and after 2 p.m. to try to thin out the midday crush. In warm weather, their second cafe, down the street in Post Office Square, is an ideal place to enjoy Boston's best pocket-sized urban park.

Palates that shudder at the mere mention of pizza and fried food may prefer the classic French cuisine of the unflappable **Maison Robert,** in the grandiose Second Empire-style Old City Hall on School St., tel. (617) 227-3370. If your per diem doesn't cover such splurges—or if you left your dinner jacket at the dry cleaners—**Ben's**

Cafe, downstairs, offers less expensive renditions of similar fare in more casual surroundings.

Chinatown

Chinatown's narrow sidewalks and congested one-way streets never quite seem to sleep. From morning until long after sensible people have gone to bed, visitors to the short stretch of Beach Street between the Leather and Theater Districts are never more than a few steps from a good meal. Two of the best on this main line are **Grand Chau Chow Seafood,** 41-45 Beach, and **East Ocean City** at 25-29, in one of whose fish tanks perhaps swims your next meal. Both offer a zillion inexpensive choices and stay open until at least 2 a.m. weekdays, 4 a.m. weekends. While every menu in the neighborhood has vegetarian choices, **Buddha's Delight,** 5 Beach St., tel. (617) 351-2395, is *entirely* vegetarian. In keeping with traditional Chinese Buddhist cookery, many dishes are named as if they had meat, even though seitan (wheat gluten), braised tofu, and other substitutes are used instead.

Harder to find (but worth the effort) is the **Chinatown Eatery,** on the second floor of 44-46 Beach St., at the corner of Harrison. With their menus crowding the walls above each small counter, half a dozen hole-in-the-wall vendors representing several Asian cuisines ring a large room filled with communal school-cafeteria-style tables. Sample from one or all, claim a seat amid the crowd, and enjoy the busy stew of foreign accents and fragrances as you sip spicy hot-and-sour soup from one or dine on the pad Thai from another. Dirt-cheap prices complement the minimal decor but belie how good the food usually is. Open until 2 a.m. Several blocks away from Beach Street's beaten path is the equally fast-food-simple **Chinatown Cafe,** 262 Harrison, at the base of the Tai Tung Village highrises overlooking the MassPike. It isn't the finest Chinatown has to offer, but it's an unsurpassed value given that most menu items handily feed two people—for under $6. The only catch: no late dining (closing time is 8:30 p.m.).

Fans of that Chinese point-and-eat cuisine, dim sum, should join the weekend lines at either the **Golden Dragon** or **China Pearl,** on Tyler St. between Beach and Kneeland, two places with reasonably priced, above-average

brunches. If you're just looking for something sweet, **Hing Shing Bakery,** at Beach and Hudson, is a good first choice for sweet bean cakes and melon buns, while animal-cracker lovers shouldn't miss the giant zoological figures at **Kam Lung Bakery,** two blocks away on Harrison, which has also added a Chinese touch to many standard American treats, too—in case you have a taste for cross-cultural chocolate chip cookies and the like.

Chinatown is also host to a half dozen Vietnamese *pho* kitchens, fluorescent-and-Formica specialists in bargain-priced soups, as well as one of the best (and busiest) Japanese restaurants in the city, **Ginza,** on Hudson St. near the Chinatown Gate, tel. (617) 338-2261 (open Sun.-Mon. till 2 a.m., Tues.-Sat. till 4 a.m.). Although the unfiltered cigarettes preferred by its Asian customers often overwhelm the ventilation, few other places offer handrolls quite as big, sushi quite as fresh, or maki quite as inventive. Cooked entrees ($9.25-25) provide an alternative to the sushi menu without any sacrifice in quality or presentation. (Nonsmokers should try their sister restaurant in Brookline, listed below under "Fenway and Kenmore.") Even trendy Malaysian cuisine is represented at **Penang,** 685-691 Washington St., the local outpost of a New York-based chain ($4.50-16.95; tel. (617) 451-6373). If the varnished *Gilligan's Island* decor—tree trunks with mesh roof, corrugated metal over the kitchen, rope room dividers—doesn't tempt you to leap straight for fish in *belachan* sauce (a salty minced-shrimp paste) or chicken in a yam pot (a retaining ring of cooked yam, flash-fried crisp on the outside, soft as minced crab inside), the prompt servers will happily guide you to the menu's more familiar Chinese, Thai, and Muslim Indian dishes.

Theater District and Park Square

West of Chinatown's bargains, a number of restaurants showcase ambiance and prices skewed more to theater-goers and luxury hotel guests—although the eateries in the Transportation Building on Stuart St. offer a relatively inexpensive oasis, particularly if you're hankering for a thick juicy burger from the likes of **Fuddrucker's.** More typical of what this area aims for, though, are the sourdough crostini, smoked duck, and garlic mashed potato sprinkled around the menu at **Brew Moon,** on the corner of Tremont and Stuart Streets, one of a high-concept brewpub chain whose flashy grub, slick decor, and shiny, happy clientele almost—but don't quite—obscure the mediocrity of the beers.

Several of the city's most highly regarded chefs ply their trade in the surrounding blocks—to enough acclaim that reservations are necessary for dinner most nights. One such hot spot is tiny little **Galleria Italiana,** 177 Tremont St. on the Common, tel. (617) 423-2092 ($16.50-26), whose menu varies continually with the seasons and never disappoints (until you order tea, that is: maybe the owners are Don Meredith fans, but it's still a rude shock to find a dining room of this caliber serving Lipton!). Serves dinner nightly, buffet lunch Tues.-Sat. Two long blocks away, on the Public Garden, is one of Boston's gastronomic landmarks, **Biba,** whose chef-owner, Lydia Shire, has trained what seems like half the city's culinary vanguard. An evening at the fount of such creative gourmandizing easily tops $100 for two with wine and dessert. If smoke and crowds don't bother you, though, you can graze on appetizers at the bar for about half the tab of a full dinner. Dress as if you own a Porsche or Jaguar and you'll fit in.

Behind Biba, in the Park Plaza Hotel, is that Boston warhorse, **Legal Seafoods,** tel. (617) 426-4444, whose quality and popularity are reflected in the menu prices ($11.95-28.95, lobsters up to over $50). If you'll pay whatever it takes to get your socks knocked off by New England seafood, try Legal's catch of the day or lobster casserole; otherwise check out the North End and Cambridge for less expensive seafood options. The adjoining **Legal C Bar,** tel. (617) 426-5566, puts a Caribbean spin on whatever's fresh from Neptune's realm at a slightly more palatable price ($10.95-19.95).

THE NORTH END

Some unwritten book governing North End restaurants seems to stipulate that portions must be inversely proportional to the size of the establishment. Or maybe North End restaurateurs all believe in giving you your money's worth; at any rate, more often than not, when you order for dinner you get the next day's lunch,

too. The principal streets for restaurants are Hanover and Salem, but hardly a block seems bereft of something good to eat, be it a bakery, salumeria (Italian market), cafe, or restaurant.

Just across from the can't-miss Mike's Pastry marquee on Hanover Street is **The Daily Catch,** tel. (617) 523-8567, where calamari is king. This tiny joint is so warm and inviting that a meal here is like eating in the kitchen: the cook could shake hands with half his customers without leaving his stove, and the menu's mainstay, seafood over linguine, is served in frying pans instead of on plates. Reasonable prices and robust house vino round out the pleasant atmosphere. Since the place only seats 20, bring something to read or someone to talk to if you arrive after 6 p.m. (Cash only, no reservations.) Taking a page out of the same book, next-door **Pomodoro,** 319 Hanover, tel. (617) 367-4348, is also so tiny that the warmth and fragrance of the open kitchen contributes to the ambiance of the room as much as the sponge-painted caramel-toned walls and back-to-back intimacy of the tables. The bathroom, meanwhile, is in a cafe two doors down. Of course, in a room this small, the chef acts only on a grand scale—evident in the Mt. Etna of littlenecks over linguine, the slab of beef tenderloin, the plump chicken with artichokes and capers—so if you can't make good use of leftovers, seriously consider choosing an appetizer and splitting an entree, rather than vice versa. Since big portions are so common in this part of town, and so many of the menus sound so similar, you may wonder why the prices are a tad high. Taste the food and you'll quickly appreciate that you pay on a merit system here—and by almost any measure you're getting a great value. The seafood fra diavolo alone will wipe out any memory of having waited for a table. (Cash only, and it serves no desserts or coffee—if you want to linger over cannoli, head down the street to the excellent **Modern Pastry Shop,** 257 Hanover). Just around the corner from these two restaurants is **Artú,** 6 Prince St., tel. (617) 742-4336, whose extensive trattoria menu offers dozens of robust selections, all served in outsized portions at remarkably low prices ($6.95-15.95). (Cash only, as usual around here.) You can step into **Ristorante Saraceno,** 286 Hanover, tel. (617) 227-5888, and go to town over the excellent spectrum of traditional Neapolitan dishes ($10.95-25.95) safe in the knowledge that your credit card will be welcome when the bill comes. Reservations are also accepted—and downright advisable on weekends if you have no patience for waiting.

Parallel Salem St. is more intimate—effectively just a narrow, one-way back street leading up to the famous Old North Church on Copp's Hill. Dining options here run the gamut from the cozy and reliable—and very pink—**Nicole** at No. 54, tel. (617) 742-6999, to the contemporary exposed brick of **Marcuccio's** at No. 125, tel. (617) 723-1807, whose nouveau greens, garnishes, and plate presentation are as stylish as anything in the city (cash only). In between is a pair of jointly owned restaurants whose chefs cloak great food in what feel like relaxed neighborhood spots: the light and airy **Terramia,** tel. (617) 523-3112, whose menu ($9.50-25) sounds more upscale notes with truffles, wild mushrooms, foie gras, and 25-year-old balsamic vinegar; and the intimate **Antico Forno,** across the street at No. 93, tel. (617) 723-6733, whose menu is weighted toward the rustic delights of wood-fired dishes from southern Italy ($7-16.50). Neither takes credit cards. For a take-home dessert, step into the **Biscotti Pasticceria,** next door, or head up the street to **Bova's Bakery,** at the corner of Salem and Prince, which conveniently remains open to 1 a.m.

Think I've forgotten something? For the obligatory pizza, try the place that's been making them longer than anybody else in town: **Pizzeria Regina,** 11^{1}/2 Thatcher St. between N. Washington and N. Margin. There are others in this local chain—in Faneuil Hall Marketplace, for instance—but none can touch the first for either atmosphere or food.

BACK BAY AND THE SOUTH END

Back Bay is good grazing territory for fans of fusion cuisine, that interesting and funky *mesclado* of colorful, fresh ingredients with south-of-the-border or Pacific Rim flavorings, served in casual but design-coordinated surroundings and often accompanied by microbrews. Places prized for their social cachet more than their food tend to be found along fashionable New-

bury Street, itself a fusion of bowfront townhouses and high-end boutiques; you might find decent things to eat at **Sonsie** or **Armani Cafe,** but that's not the point of going there. When it's finally time to give your gold card a rest, Back Bay's boundary with the lower-rent Fenway neighborhood comprises a string of inexpensive ethnic restaurants dishing up great Asian, Middle Eastern, Indian, and even Cajun food.

The South End, full of food-savvy single men and women, has become one of the city's best dining areas. Many of the chef-owned neighborhood joints spearheading the Boston restaurant revival are found here, either on Tremont Street near the Theater District or spread out on Columbus Avenue parallel to the Orange Line. Fusion happens less in individual dishes than on menus as a whole—chefs demonstrate their skill in preparing creative but authentic dishes combining elements from two or more continents. It comes to exceptional food in cozier quarters with less glitzy veneer and more personality than Back Bay, all for about the same prices—which is to say, not cheap, though exceptions do exist.

Both neighborhoods are within walking distance of subway lines, although nether parts of the South End may be more suited to a short cab ride if you don't like wandering quiet residential streets at night. The restaurants below are listed roughly as one would find them while strolling—or sometimes zigzagging—outward from downtown, despite evidence of street numbers to the contrary; keep in mind that parallel streets in Boston rarely have corresponding numbers from one block to the next, since they rarely begin at the same place.

Back Bay

To share in the kind of sandwich Boston's top chefs put together when set loose in the kitchen after hours, step over to the **Parish Cafe,** 361 Boylston near the corner of the Public Garden, tel. (617) 247-4777. A sandwich and scoop of salad costs $8-10—and service during the late-night see-and-be-seen parade can border on rude—but the food is an inspiration (grilled steak with blue cheese bread and pickled onions, or tortilla-wrapped smoked turkey with cranberry chipotle sauce), perfect for tired city walkers or finicky midnight snackers (yes, the kitchen

Centuries meet as Trinity Church (built 1872-1877) is reflected in the Hancock Tower (built 1972-1975).

serves until 1 a.m.). If you didn't come to coastal New England to eat yuppie designer food, you should try **Skipjack's,** tel. (617) 536-3500, one of the city's seafood kings. Reigning over the corner of Clarendon and Stuart Streets, behind Trinity Church, this local chain isn't content until they can offer a couple dozen choices of the freshest seafood anywhere, even if it means flying orange roughy in on the red-eye from Auckland. (If importing fish to Boston seems like shipping coals to Newcastle, stick to the steamers and cod.) The flash of creativity in sauces is matched by the dash of neon amid the Art Deco interior of this popular establishment, which also features live jazz during Sunday brunch.

Copley Square's **Small Planet Bar and Grill,** 565 Boylston St., tel. (617) 536-4477, is one of the neighborhood's better culture blenders ($5.95-15.95). Designed for maximum aesthetic stimulation, it's good for internationally influenced appetizers, vegetarian dishes, cheap gourmet pizzas, rich desserts, microbrews and eclectic wines, and speedy service—all at moderate prices. The fancier dishes aren't such good value, though; jazzy presentation alone doesn't merit the higher price, and the chefs aren't *that* ready to go head-to-head with San Francisco. Open until midnight most nights.

If you like Middle Eastern, make a beeline for **Cafe Jaffa,** 48 Gloucester, near the Hynes Convention Center, tel. (617) 536-0230 ($3.95-9.25). Exposed brick, a high black ceiling, copper sconces, and lots of gleaming wood fit the off-Newbury address, but prices fit the budgets of Fenway's numerous music school students a few blocks away. As for quality, you won't find a better falafel and hummus plate in town. Israeli and Lebanese beer and wine are available, too. Marching to the Zydeco beat of a completely different drummer is the tasty and affordable **Dixie Kitchen,** 182 Mass. Ave., tel. (617) 536-3068 ($5.95-9.95), next door to the Berklee College of Music. It's one of New England's rare outposts of New Orleans cookery—although lacking the kind of sophistication found in the NOLA kitchens of Emeril Lagasse or Susan Spicer. Come here instead for the timeless simplicity of po' boys, catfish fry, shrimp etouffeé, sausage gumbo, even a passable version of that Big Easy cornucopia of meat, the muffaletta. Cajun tunes, red-checkered tablecloths, and tattooed young wait staff add to the authentically insouciant atmosphere.

Dixie Kitchen's neighbors along the stretch of Mass. Ave. between Berklee College of Music and Symphony Hall are predominately Asian: the all-you-can-eat Korean steam-table buffet at **Arirang,** 162 Mass. Ave. ($5.99 lunch, $7.50 dinner; tel. (617) 536-1277), and the first-in-New-England **Bangkok Cuisine** across the street, whose quality has never rested on its laurels ($7.95-13.50; tel. (617) 262-5377). If you're closer to Copley Square when the craving for good inexpensive Thai strikes, the **House of Siam,** opposite the Westin Hotel on Huntington Ave., will spare you a dash up to Mass. Ave.

Also in the heart of Berklee territory, at 1124 Boylston St. a few doors past Jack's Drum Shop, is the irresistibly kitschy **Mucho Gusto Cafe & Collectibles,** dishing up meaty Cuban comfort food for breakfast, lunch, and dinner amid endearingly overdone Lucy 'n' Ricky decor. The food is good, but it's those collectibles that shouldn't be missed, an amalgam of '50s and '60s home furnishings and cha-cha-tchotchkes recalling an eight-cylinder streamlined era of limbo dancing and hi-fi leisure.

South End

Immensely popular with young South Enders, **Blue Wave,** 142 Berkeley St. at the corner of Columbus Ave., tel. (617) 424-6664 ($6.95-14.95), typifies the neighborhood's embrace of the eclectic American menu. The wait staff all wear "California Dreaming" T-shirts in case the burgers with guacamole or the surfboard over the wine rack are too subtle. Enormous salads, super-rich desserts, and cheese-laden "pizza bread" creations are the safe bets, although if you're caught up in the excitement of the menu go ahead and give the over-orchestrated fish or pasta entrees a whirl. Within a few blocks are two more riffs on the West Coast theme: **Moka,** at 130 Dartmouth facing the back corner entrance to the Copley Place Mall, tel. (617) 424-7768 ($4.00-6.75), and vending fruit smoothies and flavored tortillas; and **Baja Mexican Cantina,** diagonally down the street, tel. (617) 262-7575 ($6.95-12.95). Cultivating more of a restaurant than coffee house atmosphere, the Baja, like the Blue Wave, consistently does best with dishes you'd wash down with beer rather than wine (although the spicy duck fajitas or mussels in parchment cooked in Corona beer go down well with either beverage).

If money is no object, a rich vein of fine but expensive restaurants is found around on what's known as Tremont Street's restaurant row, anchored by the Boston Center for the Arts and **Hamersley's Bistro,** on the BCA's Clarendon St. corner, tel. (617) 423-2700. It's consistently judged one of the city's top dining spots, a "destination" featuring bold, French-influenced cuisine. Reservations are strongly recommended (entrees $21-30). Another cook who knows his sauces and uses eye-catching presentation to complement rather than conceal holds forth a couple of blocks up the street at **Tremont 647,** tel. (617) 266-4600. Hints of Asia, the American South, and the South American weave harmoniously through the menu, along with a missionary's dedication to reviving underutilized

legumes like the monk pea and appaloosa bean. The results—a sirloin appetizer with monk pea hummus, steamed mussels in a lemongrass broth, succulently grilled and glazed duck breast over hand-cut pappardelle with cob-smoked bacon and broccoli rabe—are distinctive, assertive, and wholly satisfying ($14.50-18.50). Excellent desserts include a signature banana cream pie that redefines the genre.

If it's lunchtime and you're in the mood for something unfancy (but appetizing), make a beeline for **Charlie's Sandwich Shoppe,** 429 Columbus Ave., tel. (617) 536-7669, about five blocks from Copley Square, and admire photos gallery of celebrity customers—from the pincushion star of *Hellraiser* to local pols—while chowing down on good burgers, cutlets, fish and chips, chili dogs, and the like (Mon.-Fri. till 2:30 p.m., Saturday to 1 p.m.). Two doors up the block, under the faded purple awning, is **Anchovies,** tel. (617) 266-5088, a seemingly generic bar which actually dishes up belt-stretching portions of delicious Italian comfort food (even the nachos are made with mozzarella) in a small dining area in back ($5.95-8.95). It's one of the South End's hippest hangouts, though, so you'll escape the heavy smoke and loud din only if you come early. A lively, less smoky, kick-back-with-your-buddies atmosphere reigns at nearby **Jae's Cafe & Grill,** 520 Columbus a few blocks from the Mass. Ave. Orange Line or Symphony Hall Green Line stations, tel. (617) 421-9405 ($7.50-24.00). Its across-the-menu excellence, friendly service, and prime summer sidewalk seating make this a top dog—best for sushi lovers and Korean hotpot fans. It carries fine Belgian ale, too. Outdoor tables sprout up in front of neighborhood cafes all over the South End as soon as warm evenings become the rule rather than the exception, but few make as pleasing a destination as the **Claremont Cafe,** 535 Columbus, opposite the Cha Cha Cha! hair salon, tel. (617) 247-9001. In addition to its upscale New American entrees and tapas, the seasonally fresh menu always includes a few specials from the chef-owner's native Peru (no credit cards).

Iceberg salads and meatball subs fit the plastic table and paper napkin style of the **Mass Cafe,** 605 Mass. Ave., tel. (617) 262-7704, a few blocks from both the Claremont and Symphony Hall, but try one of the hearty Eritrean-Ethiopian dishes on the other half of the menu instead and you'll be blissfully transported into the world of the travel posters on the wall. Big portions and low prices make this a steal; open daily ($4.95-7.65). If your palate would be happier with something a little closer to home (but not as close as those meatball subs), check out **Bob the Chef,** 604 Columbus Ave. a block west of Mass. Ave., tel. (617) 536-6204. This is soul food territory, and if you don't know chitterlings from chicken livers, here's where to learn. All the quintessential dishes of the Deep South are here ($5.95-14.95), from "glorifried" chicken to collard greens, but even vegetarians or abstainers denying themselves any truck with fried food will find a few menu items to savor. If these prospects inspire expectations of greasy Formica and shiny metal napkin dispensers on the middle of each table, guess again: Bob's is casual, but the warm, kinte-cloth colors, lofty black ceiling, and original art put it closer to some trendy Chicago or LA bistro than to any Mississippi lunch counter or Tennessee "meat 'n' three" family restaurant. Live jazz combos take over a corner of the restaurant on Sat.-Sun. evenings and during Sunday brunch ($2 cover).

FENWAY AND KENMORE

From the Back Bay Fens residential pocket across the park from the Museum of Fine Art to nightclub-rich Kenmore Square, these large and amorphous neighborhoods are endowed with cozy little local favorites offering good, inexpensive meals in mostly simple settings. A prime candidate: the **India Quality Restaurant,** 536 Comm. Ave., in the heart of Kenmore Square, tel. (617) 267-4499, an aptly named eatery tucked into a tiny nook across the hall from a used record shop and next to a convenience store. For dining worth a ride in from elsewhere in the city, look to the higher-priced cluster of ethnic restaurants at Audubon Circle, where the Green "C" Line comes up from underground, just across the MassPike from Kenmore Square. Although not entirely unique—it's a clone of a restaurant across the river in Somerville—the French-Cambodian **Elephant Walk,** 900 Beacon St. at Park Dr., tel. (617)

247-1500, is unquestionably unusual. Exotic Asian and classic continental are separate on the menu, but judicious border-crossing keeps even the most familiar-sounding dishes deliciously out of the ordinary ($9.50-14.95). The desserts can be quite stunning, although if it's lunchtime or early in the evening you might prefer to take out a magnificent little *gateau* from **Japonaise,** a French-Japanese bakery a block up the street at 1020 Beacon, across from the T stop. (The Boston city line lies beside Elephant Walk, so both Japonaise and its neighbors are technically in the town of Brookline.) If you're more in the mood for straight Japanese or Chinese cuisine, look to either the sushi and seafood of **Ginza,** tel. (617) 566-9688, or the Sichuan and Mandarin fare at **Chef Chang's House,** tel. (617) 277-4226, both within the 100 yards separating Elephant Walk and Japonaise.

CHOW DOWN N THE HOOD: ALLSTON AND JP

Several of Boston's residential neighborhoods have become dining destinations in their own right. Allston and Jamaica Plain ("JP" to locals) are two of the most accessible, with direct trolley or subway service to downtown and several bus connections to Back Bay, Cambridge, Brookline, and each other. Few tourists venture here—the land of ten-year-old Hondas, where chain link is more common than prim white pickets—though a few B&Bs cater to the intrepid travelers who do. Try it yourself and you'll discover a more honest depiction of where citizens live, shop, and eat than at either Faneuil Hall or the gaslit, cobblestoned cloister of Beacon Hill.

Cheap Eats Mecca: Allston
Within a handful of blocks around "downtown" Allston—the large, ever-congested "H" formed by the intersection of Commonwealth, Harvard, and Brighton Avenues, bounded on one side by the Green "B" Line trolley—lay more than a dozen inexpensive restaurants. Several are worth a trip in from outside the neighborhood. Reflecting Allston's diverse demographics, the cuisines in this densely populated area include Chinese, Brazilian, Indian, Middle Eastern, Thai, Vietnamese, Italian, Greek, Tex-Mex, buffalo

(wings), Chicago (pizza), Seattle (espresso), jazz bar, and yuppie brewpub, all within a ten-minute walk of the Harvard Ave. T stop. A high concentration of nightclubs keeps parking scarce, but the neighborhood is less than 30 minutes from downtown via the Boston College-bound trolley, or barely an eight-minute bus ride from Harvard Square in Cambridge (via the #66 Dudley) or Coolidge Corner in Brookline (via the #66 Harvard).

For Indian food, **Rangoli,** 129 Brighton Ave., tel. (617) 562-0200, should be a top candidate. Presentation earns as much thought as preparation, and the menu features a number of specialties from southern India—crepe-like dosas, broth-like sambhar—not often found in the northern-dominated Indian restaurant trade. Though priced about the same as its brethren around the city, Rangoli is a bargain given the quality and attractiveness of its meals ($4.95-9.95).

Vietnamese may be the neighborhood's best-represented food group. **Pho Pasteur,** on Brighton Ave. next to Rangoli, specializes in the giant bowls of soup, or *pho.* **V. Majestik,** a block up Brighton, next to Harper's Ferry blues bar, is best for its cheap "special noodle" dishes, its rolling beef, and anything in caramel sauce. **Viet Hông,** farther up at 182 Brighton Ave. opposite the Osco Drugs plaza, tel. (617) 254-3600, is known all over town for the mountain of piping hot vegetables piled atop most of its entrees, for its pungent seafood soups, and for its generous fresh spring rolls (closed Monday). Behind the Osco plaza, next to the delicious and inexpensive **Café Brazil** on Cambridge St., **Sài Gòn,** tel. (617) 254-3373 carves a niche with its ground shrimp with fresh sugar cane, salmon served sizzling in clay pots, and omelet-like *bánh xèo* (daily to 10 or 11 p.m.). Sài Gòn also has the most attractive decor, ideal for lingering over chicory-laced Vietnamese coffee sweetened with condensed milk. The others have as much charm as any Chinese take-out joint, but who's complaining: at any of these places, $15 will get you a good dinner, possibly a carton of leftovers, and probably more than enough change to catch the trolley or bus back to your lodgings.

None of its regulars was surprised to see **Carlo's Cucina Italiana,** 131 Brighton Ave., tel. (617) 254-9759, end up on the top of Zagat's list of best Southern Italian spots in the city. A favorite hangout of young city chefs on their nights off, Carlo's demonstrates that sometimes traditional comfort food can beat the pants off fancier fare. The professionals know honest talent when they see it, and their patronage is a mark of respect. Try the home-made tortellini, any seafood dishes, or the veal. Despite upscale appearances—the dark wood wainscoting, linen napkins, trompe l'oeil paintings on the walls—the prices recall the room's former life as a take-out pizzeria, so expect to wait for a table most nights ($7.95-11.95).

In a category by itself, there's the **Sunset Grill & Tap,** 130 Brighton Ave., tel. (617) 254-1331, next to Fern Cleaners. The food leans toward nachos, BBQ ribs, and the like; if you want something ritzier than fish and chips—pan-seared cod with shaved fennel, for example, washed down with fresh beer made on the spot—try the **North East Brewing Company,** tel. (617) 566-6699, a few blocks away at 1314 Comm. Ave. But for a global perspective on the brewer's art, don't miss the Sunset. With nearly 80 beers on tap and another 400 or more in bottles—lagers, bocks, Belgians, Lambics, ESBs, wheats, porters, stouts, Irish reds, ambers, IPAs, Scotch ales, potato ales, cream ales, barley wines, seasonal brews, and many, many more, plus mead, sake, hard ciders, nonalcoholic beers, and root beers—no other bar in New England comes close to providing so many hours of enjoyable globe-trotting in a glass.

Jamaica Plain

Centre Street is this neighborhood's main thoroughfare. From the Orange Line T station at Jackson Square through the Hyde Square rotary at Perkins Street to "the Monument," south of the fire station, Centre reflects JP's diversity: most of Boston's Cubans and Dominicans, many of its gays and lesbians, and a rising class of young homeowning families reside along its length. JP's eateries span an equally broad range, from American diner to Korean-Japanese sushi shop, Mexican roadhouse to Lebanese cybercafe. Unless noted otherwise, the best access is via the #39 Forest Hills bus from in front of the Copley Plaza Hotel, a 20-35 minute ride, depending on which end of the neighborhood you want and what hour of the day you travel.

Transport yourself to the *criolla* village of San Luis, south of Santiago de Cuba, with *bistec encebollado* (steak and onions) and *mofongo* (plantain mashed with pork rinds and garlic) from **El Oriental de Cuba,** tel. (617) 524-6464, Formica-booth and fluorescent-light casual at 416 Centre St., opposite the Hi-Lo supermarket. Meaty simmer-all-day seafood, chicken, and tripe soups and rich fruit *batidos* (smoothies) are among the many other specialties ($4-10.50). If cheery tropical decor is key to your food enjoyment, cross the street to the Chilean-owned **Bella Luna,** 405 Centre, tel. (617) 524-6060, a gourmet thick-crust pizzeria with low prices, big portions, uniquely painted dinnerware, service to at least 10 p.m., and seductive live jazz or flamenco many nights and weekends (closed Monday; $6-12).

Stroll around the curving facade of small shops to the **Black Crow Caffé,** at 2 Perkins, tel. (617) 983-2747, a cozy, colorful cafe whose short, ever-changing menu might include such tempting dishes as peppery collard greens soup, hoisin-glazed grilled salmon, or turkey lasagna with eggplant. Beer, wine, good brunches, and pricy but superb desserts are also available ($10-14). Solid, Mexican-style blue-plate specials are the order of the day a couple blocks away at **Tacos el Charro,** 349 Centre, tel. (617) 522-2578, a popular plastic-chairs-and-big-mirrors hole in the wall whose chili rellenos and mole poblano will dance off your plate when the live mariachi band rocks the joint on weekend evenings. Open Fri.-Sat. till midnight, too, and to 11 p.m. Sun.-Thurs. (closed Tuesday); $4.95-16.95.

Half a world and half a mile away in "downtown" JP, the **Barefoot Café,** 697 Centre, tel. (617) 983-CAFE, dishes up such Lebanese specialties as red-bean *fassoulya,* diced potato *yakné,* and a vegetarian version of Lebanon's national dish, *kibbe,* made with pumpkin instead of ground beef. Meat kebabs, falafel, stuffed grape leaves, and other Middle Eastern standards are available, too, all at such rock-bottom prices ($3.25-6.49) that it doesn't matter that the place feels like a Domino's. Leave room to sample the incredible phyllo pastries (open to 11 p.m. daily). Comforting Korean food beckons from across the street at the modest storefront **JP Seafood Cafe,** 730 Centre, tel. (617)

983-5177, open to 10:30-11 p.m. nightly. The mean chili-laced beef-and-rice *bibimbop* has caught the palates of local reviewers, but from grilled salmon to vegetarian pan-fried noodles, it's all tasty, sparklingly fresh, and reasonably priced ($7.95-14.95). Dozens of great sushi choices, too.

If weekend brunch is the meal you savor most, check out **Sorella's,** 388 Centre, at the Hyde Square rotary, for more omelet choices than Baskin-Robbins has flavors. The **Centre St. Cafe,** 597 Centre, just past the Sunoco and Global gas stations, serves up a little more sophistication, although the setting is equally intimate. Folks who love flea-market Americana mustn't miss the collection of salt and pepper shakers on the tables. These spots are among Boston's best, so arrive early to beat the line of loyal patrons who turn out in force. While both still count as a bit of a neighborhood secret, weekend brunch at **Doyle's,** a mile away, at 3484 Washington, tel. (617) 524-2345, is a bona fide city-wide institution. (Upon exiting the Orange Line's Green St. station, turn right and walk uphill to the traffic light at Washington. Turn right again; two blocks ahead, at the corner of Williams St., you'll see Doyle's on the left, behind a brick facade misleadingly labeled Braddock Restaurant.) From huge omelets and gravy-soaked turkey to pumpernickel bagels and veggie quiche, you'll get good food at a good price, accompanied by one of the best beer menus in town, in a setting redolent of cigar-chomping ward heelers scratching backs and passing fat envelopes full of something the color of the shamrock. With its high, 19th-century coffered ceilings and dark wooden booths like tall-backed pews, Doyle's is a church of good cheer whose guardian angel is no less than the late Mayor Curley himself.

BROOKLINE

Fueled in part by attractively upscale demographics, Brookline teems with neighborhood restaurants, mostly small, casual eateries with devoted local followings. If you're staying at one of the Brookline inns or guest houses, visiting the local historic sights, or shopping for Judaica among the Harvard Street shops, you'll find a

THE BOSTON DELI—NO, AS A MATTER OF FACT, IT'S *NOT* THE SAME AS A NEW YORK DELI

D isplaced or visiting New Yorkers seem dumbfounded that a city of Boston's stature should lack a good New York-style deli. Los Angeles, after all, has its deli barrio, down on Fairfax Avenue; Ann Arbor, Michigan, has Zingerman's. You can find Dr. Brown's sodas even in Oberlin, Ohio. So why not in Boston, already?

In fact, New York-style deli ventures just flat fail here. Boston has no shortage of delis, but it seems to stubbornly resist homogenization with New York (even if New Yorkers are buying up our newspapers and department stores).

The Manhattan purist will scoff, but, folks, we're not talking the difference between dishwater and seltzer. Unless you were weened on Zabar's silken smoked Nova Scotia salmon, there's no reason to let debate among deli scholars spoil your Boston bagel with lox. And, if nothing less than a Brooklyn bialy or big fluffy Brighton Beach knish will stop your kvetching, get on the MassPike westbound, hang a left at I-84, drive for four and a half hours, and start looking for parking.

significant family-friendly, budget-priced cluster of eateries at Coolidge Corner, the intersection of Beacon and Harvard Streets (and a stop on the Green "C" Line). Most of Boston's major food groups are replicated in Brookline, from international to traditional American, but standouts include Middle Eastern places, bagel bakeries, and kosher spots catering to the town's large Jewish population. Brookline is certainly unique in one respect: since 1995 it has banned smoking completely in both restaurants and bars, unless fully separate ventilated rooms are available.

Within Harvard Street's first two blocks south of the Coolidge Corner T stop is a typical mix, with Northern Indian, Chinese, and the fast-food **Zaatar's Oven,** offering Middle Eastern flatbreads and *sanbusaks,* a Syrian calzone. Next door, the dashing **Pandan Leaf,** 250 Harvard St., tel. (617) 566-9393, serves up a broad menu of Malaysian cuisine, from noodles to curries,

vegetables to seafood ($6.50-17.25). Experienced Southeast Asian diners will appreciate that for the most part the exclamation marks signifying spicy hot dishes are well earned. Open till at least 10:30 p.m. nightly.

Anyone looking to keep kosher should turn north from the T stop and head up past the Coolidge Corner Theatre to **Rami's,** a shoe-box-sized Middle Eastern counter-service joint whose limited menu is as delicious as it is cheap (and, man, is it cheap), or walk a few blocks farther to the more commodious glatt kosher **Jerusalem Café,** next to Kupel's Bagels at JFK Crossing, tel. (617) 278-0200 ($3.50-13.95). The same few blocks have a pair of quite decent Japanese restaurants and the vegetarian Chinese **Buddha's Delight Too,** for those in an Asian frame of mind.

CAMBRIDGE

Dining options in Cambridge cover the spectrum—from swish, upscale places that prompt normally conservative restaurant critics to effervesce like tipsy guests making toasts at a wedding, to chipped-Formica-and-paper-napkin joints where the Fryolator is king. Almost every ethnic cuisine available in the region can be found here, too. Among the specialties that entice people over the river or out of the suburbs: the minimall of Japanese sushi bars in Porter Square; the Indian, Creole, and Korean restaurants of Central Square; four-star hotel restaurants in Harvard Square; the brewpubs; and the coffeehouses. Nearly every named square has numerous choices within a small walkable radius. Cambridge's Harvard, Central, Porter, and Kendall Squares and—just over the line in adjacent Somerville—Davis Square are all easily accessible by the Red Line. Inman Square is a short hop by bus (#69 Lechmere) or cab from Harvard, or an easy 15-minute walk from Central.

Harvard Square

Student staples like pizza, sandwiches, espresso, and wraps (upscale, anything-goes burritos—a far cry from rice and beans) are well represented around the Square—you'll find everything from local-gone-national establishments like **Bertucci's** and **Au Bon Pain** to more famil-

detail of David Fichter's mural The Potluck

iar names like **Pizzeria Uno** and **Starbucks.** The Garage, on the corner of JFK St. and Mt. Auburn, is home to multiple fast-food options, as is the concourse of 10-story Holyoke Center, home to the Harvard Information Center and Harvard University Press bookstore. Hankering for grilled snapper with basmati rice and mango glaze and several piquant garlicky condiments in a red chili pepper tortilla? This and other fashionable wraps (along with smoothies) are exclusively at **Wrap Culture,** 71 Mt. Auburn, diagonally across from Schoenhof's Foreign Books. Health-conscious eaters will appreciate the full nutritional breakdown of the menu of tasty sandwiches and pasta salads at tiny **Santa Barbara Cafe,** 1 Arrow Street. Readers wanting to grab a good burger should follow their noses to **Mr. and Mrs. Bartley's Burger Cottage,** 1246 Mass. Ave., next to the Harvard Book Store. One of the last remaining off-campus haunts familiar to anyone attending their 35th reunion, Bartley's and its grilled burgers have few peers in or out of eastern Massachusetts. Inhale the heady aroma, enjoy the whimsical menu and time-capsule bumper-sticker decor, and then take a bite out of one of the fat, perfectly seared burgers—under $4 plain, over $6 "gourmet"—and see if you don't agree (closed Sundays).

Inexpensive ethnic food runs the gamut from Spanish **Iruña,** an unassuming but heartfelt little soup-and-paella cafe at the rear of 56 JFK St., tel. (617) 868-5633, to **Bangkok House Thai,** a good find in the basement of 50 JFK St. opposite the Galleria mall, tel. (617) 547-6666. Several Northern Indian restaurants inhabit the Square and environs, but none quite matches the Galleria's **Bombay Club,** tel. (617) 661-8100, a spacious and elegantly underlit second-story spot overlooking JFK St. and small Winthrop Park. The food, too, is a flight above most of the competition (on Sunday, the spotlight shifts to southern Indian cuisine). If you like Indian food but have limited tolerance for hot and spicy, the **Cafe of India,** 52A Brattle St., tel. (617) 661-0683, is for you—even their so-called hot selections are relatively mild, and the extensive selection greatly appeals to American palates. Lustrous copper goblets, individual chafing dishes brought to keep your food warm, and intricately carved chairs lend an air of sumptuous comfort ($8.95-17.95).

Harvard alumni who haven't returned for years will remember Brattle St.'s **Casablanca,** tel. (617) 876-0999, as a dim hangout with basic pub grub, superlative martinis, and signature murals of Bogart, Bergman, and other cast members from the movie. While it still occupies the lower level of Brattle Hall beneath the Brattle Theatre, still has the murals and martinis, and still seems relaxed enough for jeans to be as acceptable as professorial tweed—especially at the bar in the rear—the expanded restaurant now boasts one of Cambridge's most creative menus, prepared by one of the region's star chefs. Local seafood, ever-popular poultry, and reliable steaks are tinged with hints of the sunny Mediterranean, from North Africa to Turkey, and served with seasonal vegetables from the area's top organic farms. It's certain to be unlike almost anything you've ever tried before ($10-21).

Another stellar local chef holds forth at **Rialto,** in the Charles Hotel at the edge of the Square, tel. (617) 661-5050, a darling of restaurant critics and cosmopolitan gourmands with excess disposable income. To find out what the raves are about, it's best to book a reservation a couple weeks in advance ($20-29). The hotel's main dining room, **Henrietta's Table,** tel. (617) 864-1200, is Rialto's well-bred rural cousin, creatively interpreting traditional New England cuisine with the absolute freshest regional products available, in a bright clapboard decor reminiscent of fine old country inns. Pork chops with apple sauce, chicken pot pie, cod cakes, or grilled summer vegetables might be among the day's selections, which vary depending on what's available and in season; separate pricing for entrees ($10-12.50) and side dishes ($3.25) allow diners to mix and match to personal taste. The regional theme extends to the wine and beer list—dozens of New England brews are on tap. A produce market at the front of the restaurant nearly completes the illusion of being close to the farm rather than in the heart of a teeming metropolis.

Central Square

Through Central Square, Mass. Ave. seems strewn with half a dozen casual Indian eateries—sort of a less cohesive Cambridge version of lower Manhattan's 6th St. Indian restaurant row. Differences exist between them, but more apparent at first glance are the similarities: mostly northern Indian cuisine, mostly averaging around $10, and mostly served quickly by polite, quiet men in fairly simple storefront restaurants. **Ghandi,** at No. 704, is one of the better of the lot, with South Indian *dosa* added to the usual curries, korma, and vindaloo, and a good variety of vegetarian specialties. For good tandoori dishes, try the **Tandoor House,** 569 Mass. Ave., or the **Indian Globe,** 474 Mass. Ave. Across from Ghandi is Central Square's other inexpensive exotic, **Asmara,** tel. (617) 864-7447, serving Ethiopian-Eritrean cuisine. For timid companions who aren't attracted to the tender stewed

and sautéed meats and richly sauced vegetables—all served on the crepe-like *injera* bread that doubles as your flatware—there's a side menu of Italian dishes, a legacy of Ethiopia's colonial rulers ($6.75-8.95).

Although Chinese food hardly seems exotic anymore to American palates, **Mary Chung Restaurant,** 464 Mass Ave., tel. (617) 864-1991, has the highly unusual distinction of having its own Usenet chatgroup (alt.fan.marychungs). A favorite of generations of Internet-savvy MIT students, it sometimes seems as if those not currently residing on campus down the road seem to plan their get-togethers solely around Mary's peerless dun dun sesame noodles and steamed *suan le chow show*. These and the 150-plus other items on the Sichuan and Mandarin menu constitute a good, grease-free alternative to a trip into Chinatown. Prices are within reach of those hungry scholars, and everything is efficiently served in spotless, casual digs ($4.50-9.50).

While there's no law requiring Central Square eateries to make generous use of chili peppers and complex spice blends (the fast-food burger chains and donut shops provide proof), it seems that most do. **Rhythm & Spice,** 315 Mass. Ave. about a block past the Shell station, tel. (617) 497-0977, applies Caribbean heat in jerk-rubbed barbecue, curries, and marinated fish dishes, with relief provided by fruit chutneys, ice-cold island beers, and home-brewed sweet sorrel. The tropical palm-fringed decor and lively (often live) music seems to keep the sun shining even in the depths of a winter night.

One of the metro area's best Korean restaurants is found a few blocks north of the Central Square T station. **Koreana,** 154 Prospect St., tel. (617) 576-8661, is worth a trip just for its extensive menu of hotpots and sushi accompanied by the usual array of beautifully pickled vegetables and blazing *kim chee* (fermented chili-laced cabbage). Groups interested in sharing Korean barbecue can reserve one of the tables with built-in grills. Also on Prospect halfway between Mass. Ave. and Koreana is **Carberry's Bakery & Coffee House,** tel. (617) 576-3530, an ideal spot for a little elevenses, relaxing over tea and monster-sized scones while planning your next move, or for picking up tomorrow's breakfast. The great baked goods include Scandinavian pastries and about 30 varieties of traditional European-style breads, including hearty Icelandic *grøn,* a fiber-laden whole-wheat variety (open to 8 p.m. daily).

North of Harvard

Until refrigerated rail cars in the late 1870s undercut local abattoirs with cheaper processed meat from Chicago, the district north of Harvard Square was one of several cattle markets serving New England in the 18th and 19th centuries. One legacy of that era is the porterhouse steak, a cut named after a hotel that once stood in **Porter Square,** near the Red Line T station. Today, the Mass. Ave. neighborhood a mile north of Harvard is renowned even in Tokyo as a center of Japanese shops and restaurants. Aside from Sasuga, the Japanese and English bookstore on Upland Rd. just across Mass. Ave. from the T station, the biggest cluster of Japanese shops is inside the cream-colored art deco Porter Exchange building a block back down Mass. Ave. from the T. A string of open-kitchen, market-style eateries lines an inside hall, offering the sort of menu specialization common in Japan but rare among Japanese restaurants in the U.S. Among the selections, try fried tempura at **Tampopo,** noodles at **Sapporo Ramen,** *wasoku* (Western dishes reinterpreted for Japanese tastes) at **Cafe Mami,** macrobiotic fare at **Masao's Kitchen,** and sushi at **Kotobukiya.** There's also a Kotobukiya supermarket toward the rear of the building for cooks interested in trying some of these dishes at home.

Half a mile and one stop farther outbound along the Red Line, in the adjacent city of Somerville, is **Davis Square,** Somerville's answer to Harvard Square. Although utterly lacking in bibliophiliac attractions, Davis in many other respects recaptures the spirit of old, pre-chainstore Cambridge. The excellent Somerville Theatre and a couple of Irish bars and clubs draw numerous people in from outside the neighborhood, but diners looking for distinctive meals have reason to come, too. **Redbone's,** 55 Chester St. off Elm, two blocks south of the Somerville Theatre, tel. (617) 628-2200, for instance, has the hands-down best two-fisted, open-your-mouth-when-you-laugh Dixie ambiance of any barbecue joint in Greater Boston, if not all New England (cash only). Arkansas travelers, Texan tourists,

and Memphians missing a taste of pork amid all the multicultural highfalutin' New American fusion stuff should park themselves at the back counter by the mesquite cooker and breathe deeply for proof that New England isn't a complete lost cause. The advantage to this place over those back home is a superior beer selection, including a fluctuating set of two dozen fine microbrews on tap. It even manages to out-Cambridge Cambridge, by offering valet bicycle parking. The kitchen is open until at least 10 p.m. nightly ($5.95-13.95; cash only).

Davis Square is also home to one of the area's few classic diners. Serving decent meals and accessible to the T, just off Elm St. a block past Redbone's, **The Rosebud,** tel. (617) 666-6015, is a handsomely restored 1940s semi-streamliner from the Worcester Lunch Car Company, the state's preeminent diner manufacturer. Steak tips with honey barbecue sauce, char-broiled chicken breast sandwiches, pasta and meatballs for two, and other renovated standards fill the bill, along with great fluffy omelets and other breakfast dishes ($4.50-10.95; cash only). Tucked discreetly behind the smoked-glass storefront between the Rosebud and that better-than-average picante burrito parlor is one of Somerville's better upscale restaurants, **Gargoyles,** 215 Elm St., tel. (617) 776-5300. Its intimate interior and top-notch New American menu is more reasonably priced than many similar chef-owned spots six subway stops away in downtown Boston, thanks perhaps to Davis Square's lower real estate prices. Closed Monday for dinner ($11.50-16). Further inexpensive alternatives to Back Bay's creative cookery are found on the north side of the Somerville Theatre, including **Johnny D's Up-Town Restaurant & Music Club,** 17 Holland St., tel. (617) 776-2004, for modestly inventive comfort food and good vegetarian selections (half-price early bird menu Tues.-Fri.), and **Tallulah's Tap & Grille,** 65 Holland St., tel. (617) 628-0880, for "Floribbean and Calasian" fusion cuisine accompanied by 60 fine craft brews on tap.

If you do come by T, as you enter or exit Davis Square, be sure to look closely at the bricks beneath your feet. You'll find 11 poems inscribed on the subway platform, including ones by Emily Dickinson, Walt Whitman, and Elizabeth Bishop, and this favorite:

At 7 am watching the cars on
the bridge
Everyone going to work, well
Not me, I'm not
Going to work.

—JAMES MOORE

Millions of scuffing shoes and grit are causing them to fade, but they're worth the effort of deciphering.

CITY-WIDE SPECIALS

Ice Cream

On average, New Englanders consume nearly twice as many quarts of ice cream and frozen yogurt as anyone else in the country—despite spending half the year clad in wool sweaters and long underwear. But there's no mystery behind this passion—sample the quality of local ice cream makers and you'll double your consumption, too. **Steve's,** at the east end of Faneuil Hall Marketplace, isn't a bad place to start—use it to establish a baseline for comparison. After selling out to a major corporation, the founder, Steve Herrell, founded **Herrell's,** which is a decided improvement over his now-franchised first creation. Found in Allston at the corner of Harvard and Brighton Aves. and on Dunster St., in Harvard Square, Herrell's is particularly good for dense, chocolatey flavors. For liqueur-flavored ice creams and deceptively rich-tasting low-fat hard yogurts, **J P Licks** is the place to go, in Jamaica Plain, Coolidge Corner, and Back Bay. The JP location on Centre St. is easy to spot—just look for the life-size cow over the entrance (even more irresistible is the upper Newbury St. parlor, with tilework à la An-

---

IRISH PUBS

In addition to the downtown taverns and Boston's oldest Irish pub (Doyle's, in Jamaica Plain) cited in the text, the following selection constitutes a good place for anyone looking to crawl through Boston's stellar Irish pubs to begin. All feature regular live music (often, but not always, Celtic). Cover charges vary from nothing at all to big bucks for big-name talent. Most host a weekly *seisiun,* a traditional informal Irish jam session (which is how it's pronounced in Gaelic, too); if the day isn't listed below, call to inquire.

Around North Station and the FleetCenter:
The Irish Embassy, 234 Friend St., tel. (617) 742-6618. The varied musical bill of fare attracts a diverse young crowd, but the atmosphere is aided by lots of Irish accents on both sides of the bar (and better ventilation than most small places).

McGann's, 197 Portland St., tel. (617) 227-4059. Fancier than average, with lots of brass, varnished oak, a granite fireplace, and lighting that lets you see who you're talking to. Wednesday seisiun.

Grand Canal, 57 Canal St., tel. (617) 523-1112. Another place where antiques, wood trim, and draught microbrews are in far greater abundance than frat boys, baseball caps, and sports TV. Monday seisiun.

Farther Afield
(At Least a T ride from Central Boston):
Brendan Behan Pub, 378 Centre St., in Jamaica Plain, two blocks from the Perkins St. stop on the #39 Forest Hills bus, tel. (617) 522-5386. A tiny spot with a rich atmosphere, big 20-ounce Imperial pints, and, in keeping with its literary namesake, occasional poetry readings. Saturday and Tuesday seisiuns.

Plough and Stars, 912 Mass. Ave., in Cambridge, halfway between Central and Harvard Squares, tel. (617) 441-3455. More Cambridge than Dublin, it's still a venerable place as old as the hills.

The Druid, 1357 Cambridge St., in Inman Square, Cambridge, tel. (617) 497-0965. A TV-free zone with great Guinness and a nice Sunday brunch—all in a cozy neighborhood joint.

The Thirsty Scholar, 70 Beacon St., on the Cambridge/Somerville line, outside Inman Square, tel. (617) 497-2294. Attracts a convivial, energetic young crowd that appreciates the above-average pub grub.

The Burren, 247 Elm St., in Davis Square, Somerville, tel. (617) 776-6896. Huge, well-appointed, with a great sound system and Celtic music almost every night.

tonio Gaudí). Farther down Newbury, **Emack & Bolio's** makes the definitive Oreo ice cream, and **Ben & Jerry's** does the best job of matching flavors to pop cultural icons, but for the true pinnacle of the local ice cream scene, cross the river to Cambridge and find one of the three **Toscanini's** along Mass. Ave. (The one opposite Harvard Yard is easiest to find but is also the most expensive and limited in its selection; better are the original parlor, at the corner of Main St. and Mass. Ave., in Central Square, and the one in the MIT Student Center, opposite MIT's 77 Mass. Ave. entrance.) Toscanini's specialties are intense flavors like burnt caramel, malted vanilla, and seasonal fruit flavors, plus the occasional bit of whimsy (Guinness ice cream).

For those who find ice cream a poor substitute for the processed form of *Theobroma cacao,* all your chocoholic cravings will meet their most formidable challenge at the **Chocolate Bar,** an all-you-can-eat buffet of over 30 chocolate desserts presented each Saturday afternoon 1-3 p.m. Oct.-May at Le Meridien's Cafe Fleuri in the Financial District, tel. (617) 451-1900.

Coffeeshops and Hangouts

Boston once had its own distinctive high-end coffeeshop chain, but Starbucks, that Microsoft of the espresso bean, bought it, and thereby defused a much-anticipated East Coast-West Coast coffee war. Taking up where Boston left off, in fact, have been two more West Coast chains, Seattle's Best Coffee and Peet's. The former sells through suburban storefronts and campus pushcarts, the latter through a strategic alliance with Au Bon Pain bakery-cafes. Coffee (and tea) drinkers interested in sparks of individuality in the local market should look in either Cambridge or Boston's North End—although Back Bay's smattering of hangouts provide equally piquant alternatives to the sip-and-run storefronts.

A well-established trend in college-saturated and computer-savvy Boston is the Internet cafe, a place where you can browse the Web, cappuccino in hand, for a fee that's generally competitive with those charged for renting desktop computer time at copyshops like Kinko's. Defining the high end of this genre is **Cybersmith,** upstairs from the Border Cafe on Church St. in Harvard Square, tel. (617) 492-5857. Cybersmith's snaking neon, suspended halogen lamps, and scores of built-in terminals make it just your average corner patisserie designed by Braun and furnished by MacWarehouse. They've chosen some of the area's best sandwich, dessert, and coffee bean suppliers, though, so even if you feel like a Jetson you certainly don't eat like one. As an alternative to a computer arcade, check out any of the following places gathered around Harvard and within walking distance of one another: **Cafe Paradiso,** facing the Harvard Square Hotel, with gelati and shots of Italian syrups; **Cafe Algiers,** on Brattle St., one of whose specialties is a bracing Turkish coffee you can almost eat with a fork; or **Cafe Pamplona,** on Arrow St., near Baskin-Robbins, with uniquely intimate low-ceiling philosophers-club ambiance.

Although the Algiers' pot of sinus-clearing mint tea is warmly recommended, tea lovers may prefer the singleminded dedication of **Tealuxe,** a "tea bar" at Zero Brattle St., next to Urban Outfitters. Although a hip place for sipping and socializing, it's too cramped to be truly relaxing. On the other hand, it's a darn sight more affordable than either the posh high tea served at the Ritz in Boston (often to the accompaniment of a live harpist), or the equally ritzy tea service at the neighboring Four Seasons Hotel, overlooking the Public Garden.

The most Berkeley-like of Greater Boston's java joints is at Central Square, a stop away from Harvard on the Red Line. Named in honor of a long-vanished local jazz club (the actual street number is 757 Mass. Ave.), the **1369 Cafe** is a favorite haunt of local Moon authors, as the mellow staff, good tunes, giant scones, smoke-free atmosphere, and quality house joe all lend themselves to writing away an afternoon. Another tasty and laid-back spot to linger is **Carberry's Bakery & Coffee House,** 74 Prospect St., within two blocks north of the T station, open nightly till 8 p.m. If nicotine is critical to your caffeine enjoyment, try the smoker-friendly **Phoenix Coffeehouse,** 675 Mass. Ave., virtually atop the outbound side of the T station, whose hazy atmosphere helps mask the rather sterile plate glass and exposed brick of its former-video-store quarters. Good coffee and baked goods, if you can taste them through the carbon cloud.

No run-down of one-of-a-kind coffee stops would be complete without mention of the

Someday Cafe, in the heart of Davis Square, in Somerville. Just steps from the Red Line station, the Someday welcomes its predominately younger patrons with a "Sorry, we're open" sign, thrashing music (to keep cellphone-packing Sharper Image types away), no-nonsense espresso, and top-notch biscotti. Don't take the attitude personally, sit in the back room away from the stereo speakers, and you'll enjoy one of the hippest hangouts inside Rt. 128.

Across the river, in Boston, the self-conscious antidote to Back Bay's self-conscious yuppiness is **The Other Side Cafe,** 407 Newbury St., on the forgotten side of Mass. Ave., kittycorner from the giant Tower Records store atop the Hynes/ICA Green Line station. Here, the Joe Camel generation balances tar and nicotine with fruit and vegetable smoothies, wheatgrass shots, sandwiches, soup, veggie lasagna, decent desserts, and all manner of espresso drinks. It's a well-established hangout, and you'll enjoy it most if you like listening to Cranes or other college radio alternative music.

A block away, at 338 Newbury, the **Trident Bookseller Cafe** offers a more clean-cut slice of Bohemia—the kind you'd feel safer introducing to your mother. Against a backdrop of a very literary and political magazine selection and art and new-age books, readers in solitary reverie or couples in animated conversation linger over coffees, herbal teas, light meals, and lovely desserts. If you're in downtown's Theater District, you might mosey over to the very foot of Columbus Avenue, opposite the rounded point of the Statler Building (home to the Park Plaza Hotel), and check out the **Tar Bar,** a dark hangout favored by Emerson College performing arts students and other theater types.

Finally, there's the North End, whose main artery, Hanover Street, has a number of good cafes serving cappuccino and cannoli, chased perhaps with Sambuca or grappa. For a cross-section of what's available within a radius of thirty yards, sample the ever-lively mirror-covered **Caffè Paradiso,** modern **Cafe Graffiti,** or soccer-crazy **Caffè dello Sport.**

TRANSPORTATION

GETTING THERE AND AWAY

Planes

All the major domestic airlines, many smaller regional ones, and over 15 international carriers fly into **Logan International Airport,** making it one of the busiest airports in the nation. Competition is strong enough to keep most domestic fares on par with New York—about as low as it gets for transcontinental travel. Unfortunately, the cost of doing business at either city's airport has prevented cut-rate airlines from making more than minor inroads, robbing New York- and Boston-bound passengers of the significant competitive benefits associated with such short-haul and no-frills fliers as Southwest Airlines. To enjoy Southwest's savings, you must fly into T.F. Green Airport in Providence, Rhode Island—a $13.50, 90-minute bus ride from downtown Boston via Bonanza Bus Lines, tel. (888) 751-8800 or (401) 751-8800. Depending on the value you place on your time, you may be glad to ride that bus: on selected routes, *all* airlines flying into Providence will match or beat Southwest's fares, which can translate into literally hundreds of dollars of savings off a comparable flight into Boston. Similarly, Boston is often a significantly more expensive destination for international passengers than nearby New York. However, connecting from New York to Boston is either so expensive ($89-129 one way via the hourly airline shuttles) or time-consuming (minimum seven hours by bus or train, counting transit time from airport to the respective stations) as to thoroughly negate any savings.

Although few large cities boast such a major airport so close to downtown as Logan is to the heart of Boston, nobody inching through rush-hour tunnel traffic takes comfort in the fact that downtown and the airport and only a little over a mile apart. On the other hand, having the Inner Harbor lapping at the ends of the runways also means that no ground transportation quite matches the **Airport Water Shuttle**—for speed or sheer fun. From the Logan dock, it's just a seven-minute ride to Rowes Wharf at the edge of the Financial District (every 15 minutes weekdays, 30 minutes on weekends; $8 pp one-way, $14 roundtrip). Specially marked buses (#66) serve stops outside each terminal's baggage claim area and the Logan dock. For other harborside destinations, from South Boston's Black Falcon Cruise Terminal and World Trade Center to the North End's FleetCenter or even Charlestown, consider the **City Water Taxi,** on call daily from April to mid-October ($10 pp to or from Logan, $8 pp for parties of two or more, $5 between any two off-airport stops). Ask the driver of the dock-bound bus to radio ahead for a boat to meet you, or call (617) 422-0392 to schedule a pickup. If you're bound for the South Shore, **Harbor Express,** tel. (617) 376-8417, can take you from Logan to Quincy in 45 min-

utes ($10), or connect to the MBTA's **Hingham Commuter Boat** via the Water Shuttle (discounted joint fares available; inquire aboard the Shuttle or call 617/23-LOGAN).

Half a dozen bus companies ply long-distance routes between Logan and Cape Cod, Central Massachusetts, and the rest of New England, stopping first in downtown Boston; $6 lands you a comfortable and quick ride to South Station aboard any of these. Departures are typically every 15-30 minutes until 11:15 p.m. **Logan Express** buses operate between the airport and outlying suburbs and cities including Quincy, Braintree, Natick, Framingham, and Woburn ($6-8; every 30-60 minutes). Taxi rates for up to four people from Logan to downtown

---

GREATER BOSTON FESTIVALS AND EVENTS

All events are free unless otherwise noted.

APRIL

The third Monday of the month is **Patriots Day,** celebrating colonial armed resistance to the British at Lexington and Concord back in 1775. It's also Marathon Day—the Boston Marathon shares the holiday with the American Revolution. The Olympics-inspired footrace and reenactments of Paul Revere's and William Dawes' rides both begin mid-morning. The MetroWest area also hosts battle reenactments on April 19th; tel. (617) 536-4100.

MAY

The month begins with the annual **Harvard Square Book Festival,** tel. (617) 876-0786, which rouses hibernating synapses with three to four days of authors' readings, bookstore appearances, and a free outdoor book fair. It isn't until the third weekend that the city believes that spring isn't just a hallucination induced by collective cabin fever. That's the Saturday that the **Boston Kite Festival,** tel. (617) 635-4505, brightens the skies over Franklin Park with thousands upon thousands of kites. The day after that, the Arnold Arboretum celebrates springtime with **Lilac Sunday,** tel. (617) 524-1718, showcasing over 400 varieties of these showy flowers.

JUNE

On the Sunday closest to the new moon, the **Dragon Boat Festival** brings international competitors to

the Charles River near Harvard Square for a day of racing in honor of Qu Yuan (343-277 B.C.), a faithful minister to the King of Chu and exalted Chinese poet (one of the illustrated scrolls of his revered masterpiece, *The Nine Songs,* is in the collection of the MFA). Call the Dragon Boat Line, (617) 426-6500 x778, at the Children's Museum for the specific date.

JULY

For a solid week leading up to July 4th, Boston celebrates its waterfront with **Harborfest.** Brochures listing all the special tours, cruises, parades, concerts, Sunday **Chowderfest,** and the like are available from the various information booths around town, or call (617) 227-1528. On Independence Day itself, a sea of cheerful humanity lines the Charles River with motor boats and the banks with picnic blankets to hear the Boston Pops Orchestra perform their free annual Esplanade concert, with its climactic bell-ringing, howitzer-thundering, fireworks-exploding rendition of Tchaikovsky's 1812 Overture. Roads along both banks are closed to traffic, but the T runs extra trains. Loudspeakers are strung in trees so even MIT students in Cambridge can sing along with full symphonic accompaniment to that other 1812 wartime composition and Pops standard, "The Star-Spangled Banner." The evening ends with several tons of colorful pyrotechnica being detonated over the assembled and Back Bay typically run $12-20; Brookline, Allston, or Cambridge drop-offs may set you back $17-22 (these estimates include the $1.30 airport fee and $1 tunnel toll cabbies legitimately may add on to the metered fare). Fixed-schedule services such as **Back Bay Coach,** tel. (617) 698-6188, and **City Transportation,** tel. (617) 561-9000, make frequent rounds between Logan and a dozen downtown and Back Bay hotels for $7.50 pp (slightly more for Allston or Brookline). Or make an appointment with **U.S. Shuttle,** tel. (617) 894-3100, from the airport or Boston/Cambridge, or, from outside the 617 area code, (800) 714-1115 ($7 and up per person depending on destination), for door-to-door pick-up or drop-off anywhere in the greater metro area. To check whether your hotel or inn has an airport courtesy van, look for the phone-equipped displays generally tucked away to the side of each baggage claim area.

Next to courtesy vans, the cheapest of all the airport-city transit options is the **Blue Line subway** inbound to Government Center (85 cents!), with connections to the rest of the T's subway and trolley lines; catch the designated free bus (the #22 or #33) to the subway from outside the lower level of your terminal. Any hour of day or night, the latest fares and schedules of all these buses and boats—plus up-to-the-minute traffic reports on airport roadways—are just a touch-tone call away: **Massport Ground Transportation Information Service,** tel. (800) 23-LOGAN.

crowd, a good half-hour of high explosive entertainment visible and audible from almost anywhere around the lower Charles River Basin.

July 14, **Bastille Day,** is celebrated with a block party on Back Bay's Marlborough St. in front of (and inside) the French Library, tel. (617) 266-4351, at No. 53 (admission).

July also marks the start of the North End **Italian festivals,** tel. (617) 536-4100, a series of feasts and processions that run sporadically through September, each honoring a different saint or madonna.

AUGUST

The second Saturday of the month, the **Cambridge Carnival International,** tel. (617) 661-0457, spices up Central Square with a colorful parade, performance stages, and flavors of both the Caribbean and Latin America. Across the river, the giant **Caribbean Carnival** finishes out the month with an entire week of awards banquets, costume competitions, coronations, and parades through Dorchester (call Shirley Shillingford, 617-534-5832 x111, for details).

Chinatown celebrates the **August Moon Festival,** tel. (617) 542-2574, late in the month with a parade, music, and lucky moon cakes that help usher in an auspicious harvest.

SEPTEMBER

The Saturday after Labor Day, tens of thousands of people head down to the banks of the Charles between Harvard's Weld Boathouse and Western Ave. for the **Cambridge River Festival,** tel. (617) 349-4380, comprising music stages, a gospel tent, wandering street performers, a petting zoo, and a block-long gauntlet of ethnic food vendors.

On a midmonth Sunday, the Cambridge **World Fair,** tel. (617) 8868-FAIR, prolongs summer with a hot program of music and food around Central Square, showcasing another typically Cantabrigian range of cultures and tastes.

OCTOBER

The second Sunday of the month, a few blocks around Harvard Square are closed off for the annual **Oktoberfest,** tel. (617) 491-3434, with music, food, and lots of streetside shopping. Don't look for fountains of free beer, though—an oompah band is about as close to Munich as it gets. Since it's on a Sunday in a state with stiff blue laws, liquor stores are all closed, too.

The fourth weekend brings the **Head of the Charles Regatta,** tel. (617) 864-8415.

DECEMBER

On December 31, **First Night,** tel. (617) 542-1399, rings in the New Year with a huge panoply of arts and entertainment, including an afternoon Children's Festival, a sunset parade through Back Bay, evening concerts and shop-window performance art, ice sculpting, fireworks over Boston Harbor, and the countdown to midnight at the Custom House Tower clock. Special buttons grant admission to paid events; they go on sale at the beginning of the month; look for the special displays at local Starbucks, supermarkets, and other retailers. All MBTA trains and buses are free after about 8 p.m.

Trains

North and South Stations are the two main passenger rail terminals connecting Boston with New England and the nation. South Station, a magnificent building from the golden age of rail, provides **Amtrak** service to downtown Boston from western Massachusetts, Albany, and the Great Lakes, plus coastal Connecticut, New York City, and points south. For Amtrak info and ticketing, call (800) 872-7245 or visit the site www.amtrak.com. South Station is also where you can catch MBTA **Commuter Rail,** tel. (800) 392-6099 from outside Boston, or (617) 222-3200, to Worcester, Providence, and intermediate destinations throughout southeastern Massachusetts. North Station, on the ground level of the FleetCenter near the I-93 bridge over the Charles, provides Commuter Rail service to Concord, Lowell, Salem, Cape Ann, and other points on the North Shore and in the Merrimack Valley. It's also slated to provide Amtrak service to coastal New Hampshire and Portland, Maine, beginning in 1999. The two stations have no *direct* public transportation link between them, but both are on the T. Most New England destinations are served by several daily departures. For anyone staying in the Back Bay or South End, most trains to and from South Station also make stops at Back Bay Station, on Dartmouth St.

Buses

All major intercity and interstate buses arrive and depart from the **South Station Transportation Center,** the boxy modern building propped up over the far end of the train station's rail platforms. If arriving from the distant south or west, New York City is likely to be part of your itinerary, whether you like it or not. Springfield-based **Peter Pan Bus Lines,** tel. (800) 237-8747, www.peterpan-bus.com, has the most expeditious express buses (4.5 hours) from New York's Port Authority bus terminal, with additional express connections from Philadelphia, Baltimore, and Washington. Reliable **Greyhound,** tel. (800) 231-2222, also has "express" service from New York (which makes a 15-minute stop in Hartford, Connecticut), plus runs from Albany and points west. They also serve Connecticut's Foxwoods Casino. If you don't really care (within reason) how

long it takes to get here from New York and you want to enjoy the journey, book a space aboard the **East Coast Explorer,** tel. (800) 610-2680, a three-season, twice-weekly van service that spends an entire day meandering along a scenic route to and from Manhattan, stopping at half a dozen interesting sights along the way, all for only a few dollars more than the regular bus. They even drop off at hotels and hostels around town.

For travel within New England and upstate New York, Peter Pan Bus Lines is again recommended for local service to such regional destinations as Worcester, the Pioneer Valley, and Williamstown; Albany, New York; and Hartford or New Haven, Connecticut. If bound for Providence, Rhode Island, or Bangor, Maine, go with Bonanza. For Hanover, New Hampshire, Vermont, Maine, and Montreal, **Vermont Transit** is best: tel. (800) 451-3292. Central New Hampshire (including the AMC Pinkham Notch base camp on the Appalachian Trail, but excluding Hanover) and coastal Maine are served by **Concord Trailways,** tel. (800) 639-3317, while **C&J Trailways,** tel. (800) 258-7111, covers the New Hampshire seacoast with an intermediate stop on the North Shore at Newburyport.

Principal carriers within eastern Massachusetts include **Bonanza Bus Lines,** tel. (888) 751-8800, Web site www.bonanzabus.com, serving Fall River, New Bedford, and upper Cape Cod; **Plymouth & Brockton Street Railway,** tel. (617) 773-9401, Web site www.p-b.com, serving the South Shore and all Cape Cod; and **American Eagle,** tel. (508) 993-5040, to New Bedford and Fairhaven.

Despite its recent construction, the bus terminal is not particularly comfortable for long waits; if you have a lot of time to kill before catching a bus out of town, you may find the grand concourse and food court at next-door South Station more interesting.

Car Rentals

All the major national car-rental companies are represented around the metro area, mostly at Logan Airport and near downtown hotels. **Alamo,** tel. (800) 327-9633, and **National Car Rental,** tel. (800) 227-7368, have airport offices, while **Avis,** tel. (800) 831-2847, **Budget,** tel. (800) 527-0700), **Dollar Rent A Car,** tel. (800) 800-4000), **Hertz,** tel. (800) 654-3131, and **Thrifty Car Rental,** tel. (800) 367-2277, all have downtown and Cambridge locations in addition to their airport lots. Among the most widespread and affordable is **Enterprise Rent-a-Car,** with offices in downtown, Copley Square, Cambridge, Brookline, and outside Logan, tel. (800) 736-8222. Average rental rates are generally much higher than the southern or western U.S., plus there's a $10 fee per rental to help defray the cost of constructing the city's new convention center, so be prepared for sticker shock.

GETTING AROUND TOWN

Boston's small size compensates somewhat for the absence of an easily navigable street grid over most of the city—even when lost, you probably aren't too far from where you really want to be. City blocks in the shapes of trapezoids and triangles and streets that seem to be parallel and perpendicular at the same time all take some getting used to. However, just remember *not* to assume that four right turns will always bring you back to where you began and you'll at least be in the right frame of mind.

When asking directions, be warned: first, several major avenues are abbreviated when spoken (Massachusetts as "Mass," Commonwealth

---

BOSTON TAXI COMPANIES

Selected taxicab companies in Boston:
Boston Cab, tel. (617) 262-CABS
Checker Cab, tel. (617) 536-7000
ITOA, tel. (617) 426-8700
Red & White Cab, tel. (617) 242-8000
Town Taxi, tel. (617) 536-5000

And Cambridge:
Ambassador Brattle Cab, tel. (617) 492-1100
Checker Cab of Cambridge, tel.
   (617) 497-9000
Yellow Cab, tel. (617) 547-3000

For help locating property accidentally left behind in a Boston cab, call the Boston Police Hackney Hotline, tel. (617) 536-TAXI.

---

as "Comm," and Dorchester as "Dot"); second, many residents have no clue as to the names of the streets they use every day. In truth, it wouldn't really matter much if they did—signs are options rather than standard equipment in many parts of town anyway.

Since nearly every hotel, restaurant, university, and tourist attraction mentioned in this chapter is accessible via Massachusetts Bay Transit Authority subways, buses, trolleys, boats, or commuter trains, public transit is your best option for getting around Boston and 77 adjacent communities. Over 700,000 daily commuters who use the **MBTA** know that despite occasional delays and crowds, it beats sitting in gridlocked traffic or trying to find affordable parking. If you do decide to sacrifice peace of mind for the right to boast of having driven in Boston, be prepared to pay dearly: with 150,000 cars competing daily for only 9,000 metered parking spaces, parking garages—though pricey—are your surest bet. Don't be tempted to park illegally in residents-only spots or other questionable curbsites—the city tickets and tows with frightening efficiency.

Taxis are, of course, another option, and a less expensive one than in most other American cities. Service within 12 miles of downtown is charged by meter, but destinations outside the 12-mile radius are all assigned flat rates by the Boston Police Dept. So, if you're taking a cab to Cape Ann, Plymouth, Maynard, or other distant places, ask the driver for the predetermined rate. (Note that *all* of the communities and attractions mentioned in this chapter are within the meter limit.) For trips to Logan Airport, there are also vans that make the rounds of the major downtown and Back Bay hotels; ask at the front desk of your hotel for information.

Public Transit

Unless you're chaperoning a large family entourage, the MBTA—"**the T**"—is your most affordable means of getting around the city. Except for crosstown travel—that is, a route circumventing downtown, such as from the Museum of Fine Arts to Harvard Square—it's reasonably rapid and convenient, too. (The only crosstown service is by bus—usually more than one, but transfers aren't free.) The four color-coded Boston subway and trolley lines are well explained by schematic maps throughout the system and aboard each vehicle. Pocket-sized copies are also available at Park St. and selected other stations. Since the system is a "hub and spoke" design, with all fixed rail lines running to and from downtown Boston, there are two principal directions used on T signage and by anyone who may supply you with directions: *Inbound* trains head toward the system's downtown hub; *outbound* trains head away from downtown.

MBTA **Passports,** for unlimited one-, three-, or seven-day travel ($5, $9, or $18) on all but the suburban components of the system may be purchased daily at the Airport, Government Center, Back Bay, and Hynes Convention Center subway stations; at both North and South Stations; at the newsstand in the Alewife terminal of the Red Line in Cambridge (except Sundays); or from the downtown visitor center on Boston Common. Many hotel concierge desks sell them, too. Otherwise, the standard fare is an 85-cent token for the subway, 60 cents exact change for buses. Certain idiosyncracies should be noted: Green Line surface streetcars require a token or 85 cents exact change for inbound rides (more on the "D" branch, whose fare runs $1-2 on the aboveground portion), but *all outbound rides westward are free if you board aboveground.* The fares are higher for express buses to or from communities outside Boston, and on the Braintree branch of the Red Line; observe the signs explaining the fare, or ask the driver or token collector for details. Tokens are sold at collector's booths in subway stations, or at token machines (examine the LED text display on the machine before feeding it your bills—when machines are unable to give change they say so). At Prudential and Symphony stations, the collector's booth is no longer staffed, so proceed through the open gate by the turnstiles and pay at the farebox at the front of the trolley with exact change or a token.

The T does *not* run 24 hours; trains and trolleys generally start rolling 5-6 a.m. and operate through midnight or shortly after; buses start at the same time and usually run until about 1 a.m. Service is reduced on Sundays and

---

MBTA LOST AND FOUND PHONE NUMBERS

Blue Line, tel. (617) 722-5533
Green Line, tel. (617) 722-5221
Orange Line, tel. (617) 722-5403
Red Line, tel. (617) 722-5317

Mattapan High-Speed Line, tel. (617) 722-5213

Buses, tel. (617) 722-5607

Commuter Rail/North Station, tel. (617) 722-3600

---

holidays, except on the Blue Line, to and from the airport.

Red, Orange, and Blue Line subways are wheelchair accessible via elevators at many, but not all, stations; consult the system map available from visitor information booths to identify those that are. Wheelchair access to Green Line streetcars is planned but not yet available. All bus routes have at least some lift-equipped vehicles; to find out whether a lift bus is in service on a specific route—or to schedule one a day in advance—call (800) LIFT-BUS.

All MBTA subway, bus, and ferry schedules and fares are available by phone when there's a live operator available, generally until 8 p.m.; tel. (617) 222-3200 or, outside Boston, (800) 392-6100. Automated Commuter Rail departure and fare info, while rather tedious to extract, is available from the same number 24 hours a day. If you plan on being in the area for a while or you intend to rely on the T to get to many different parts of the city or region, you should invest in the handy book, *Car-Free in Boston: The Guide to Public Transit in Greater Boston & New England,* published by the nonprofit Association for Public Transportation, tel. (617) 482-0282. It's available in bookstores, newsstands, and information centers throughout the city.

THE BOSTON PASSPORT

Driving? You Crazy?

There's only one word of advice for anyone thinking of driving into Boston: DON'T. Most of the city was laid out centuries before the automobile existed, and it shows. Narrow, often one-way streets, adhering to long-buried footpaths and shorelines, routinely baffle drivers raised on the nice platted grids of most North American cities. Irregular intersections and infamous rotaries help terrorize novices, while an obstinate resistance to street signs and virtually no legal parking help to confuse and frustrate. To top it all off, Bostonians have a well-deserved reputation for driving as if it's a contact sport. All of which is why hundreds of thousands of residents daily use the best alternatives: their feet and the T. If you value your peace of mind, do likewise.

Since the ratio of cars downtown to on-street parking downtown is almost 20:1, competition for a metered spot is fierce. Paid parking lots will save you endless circling around the block, but be prepared to fork over a hefty chunk of change for the privilege: day rates of $6-10 plus $2 per hour are typical, and even after 6 p.m. parking near restaurant and theater hot spots often runs a flat $8-12. (An exception: the bargain-priced $6 evening rate in the underground Boston Common Garage, 4 p.m.-midnight) Even if others seem to be getting away with it, *don't* be tempt-

> For traffic conditions in the Boston area—including airport roadways and all numbered state and federal highways—call SMARTraveler, tel. (617) 374-1234.

ed into parking in a tow zone, and *never* think you can get away with sneaking into a resident-permit parking zone; while some scofflaws get lucky, the city's treasury reaps millions of dollars each year from fools whose luck ran out. If your car gets towed in Boston, call the Transportation Department Tow Line: (617) 635-3900; in Cambridge, call (617)349-3300; and in Brookline, call (617) 730-2230. If your vehicle was towed rather than stolen, you'll be told who has it and given a number to call for directions and terms of payment. If you're lucky, you'll have been towed by the City of Boston: their fees begin below $30, they accept credit cards, and their tow lot is within a couple dollars' cab ride of the T. Private tow companies charge $50-80 or more, typically won't take anything other than hard cash, and are often located in the most God-forsaken industrial limits of the metropolitan area. The towing fees are entirely separate from the bright hazard-orange ticket you'll find tucked under your windshield wiper. Lest you think of

HELL ON WHEELS: DRIVING IN BOSTON

So, you've chosen to ignore all the advice and drive in Boston anyway. In the interests of full disclosure, here's a sneak peek at a few favorite local driving maneuvers (don't try these at home).

Team Turning. A single car needing to make a left turn across traffic turns slightly, waiting for a break in the on-coming stream; using it as a shield, three other cars pull up beside it in parallel. When the break comes—usually just before a fast-moving truck or bus—all four cars leap in unison to complete their turn, trying to merge into the single lane before being broadsided by that bus or semi. A great spectator event.

The Smerge. Whenever a handful of streets merge into one another at acute angles, the resulting expanse of pavement is traditionally left unmarked, so that drivers may define their own lanes—and refuse to merge until at least two car

lengths after there is absolutely no other choice. In slow-moving rush-hour traffic, the result—a smerge—resembles an entire theater audience trying to exit through a single set of double doors. Once you've mastered the smerge, the next step is the high-speed rotary.

The Nose-First-Noodge. The solution to poor visibility around cars parked beside driveways or side streets, this fearless move simply involves boldly driving halfway into heavy cross traffic, forcing vehicles to swerve or screech to a halt—thus allowing a proper exit to be completed.

Eye Contact. Strictly *verboten*. An adversary who sees the whites of a fellow driver's eyes will seize the initiative. Make eye contact and one of you will have to blink first; avoid it and you'll be telling the truth when you tell the officer filling out the accident report, "I never saw it coming."

trying to collect a sheaf of them as souvenirs or to trade with friends, be warned that it takes only a few before your towed car will be wearing a Denver Boot—a giant yellow steel spur that renders driving impossible. Finally, if you accrue any Boston parking tickets during your stay, you may pay them by phone with a Visa card by calling (617) 635-3888.

Using Your Feet

In his rhapsodic *About Boston: Sight, Sound, Flavor, and Inflection,* poet David McCord wrote, "A pedestrian is a man in danger of his life; a walker is a man in possession of his soul." Where better to connect the sole of your shoes to the soul of your being than in "America's Walking City," where insouciant native Bostonians walk the way Parisians drive—striding between all traffic, stopped or in motion. To a walker, all those light-running cabbies and commuters, double-parked delivery vans, and irksome one-way streets are merely local idiosyncrasies to be savored. Get in a car and the flavor of this bedlam instantly sours. Walkers find views of the city no drivers can ever see without endangering life and limb. Walkers who make wrong turns simply turn around and retrace their steps; drivers who do this end up circling the Public Garden six times. Walkers in Boston experience serendipity. Drivers in Boston experience frustration and despair. But don't take my word for it—try walking around a little bit and see for yourself.

INFORMATION AND SERVICES

Local bookstores are the best source of additional information about Boston, from historic neighborhood guides and street maps to glossy coffee-table books. Otherwise, for a full supply of rack cards advertising commercial tours and attractions—or if you need directions to something around downtown—drop in on the Boston Common **Visitor Information Center,** tel. (617) 536-4100. Just don't expect this business-sponsored operation to help you stray far off the well-trod tourist path. Visitors who cross the river will find the **Cambridge Information Kiosk,** by the entrance to the Harvard Square T station, a much more informed resource, well equipped with excellent maps, event calendars, and a decent little brochure outlining a walking tour of Old Cambridge. (Don't be tempted by the free map offer at the usually adjacent sightseeing tour counter—the maps aren't even worth giving away.) Advance planners looking for the most comprehensive accommodations listings should call the **Massachusetts Office of Travel and Tourism,** tel. (800) 447-MASS, and request a copy of the state's *Getaway Guide.* Or point your Web browser to **www.boston.com,** a service of the *Boston Globe,* and follow the links for travel information.

It's impossible to recommend any all-encompassing Boston street map since none of the major brands commercially available—Rand Mc-Nally, Gousha, Arrow—has kept pace with the city's evolution. (To be fair, neither has Boston's own planning agency.) "Don't drive today with yesterday's map," declares one, trumpeting its inclusion of newly constructed airport roadways even as significant citywide alterations—some well over a decade old—continue to be omitted. The worst offender of all is the American Automobile Association's "downtown and vicinity" map, offered free to AAA members, possibly the most erroneous and carelessly rendered piece of cartography you'll find for the Hub. Comprehensiveness—it shows every street in Boston and surrounding communities—is its only saving grace. For consolation, in selected smaller portions of the metro area, look for Hedberg Maps' "Professor Pathfinder's" series of university-and-vicinity maps. Unsurpassed in accuracy, legibility, and graphic detail, they're available at most area bookstores and newsstands. Call (800) 933-6277 or e-mail HedbergMap@aol.com to find out where to obtain them in advance. Back Bay shoppers will want to keep an eye out for Hedberg's free "Newbury Street League" pocket map and business directory, available from League members and at various information kiosks around Boston. Harvard Square visitors should drop two bits at the Cambridge Information Kiosk for Hedberg's map of that lively ivy quarter of town.

FOREIGN EXCHANGE BROKERS

Exchange rates are quite competitive from one company to the next, typically varying by no more than one percent. But, if you want to be sure you get the best deal, do a little comparison shopping by telephone.

AMERICAN EXPRESS TRAVEL SERVICES

Fee ($1) charged for exchanging currency; 10 major currencies accepted. American Express traveler's checks are cashed for free; no other brands are accepted.

Offices:

1 Court St., downtown Boston, tel. (617) 723-3077; open Mon.-Fri.

39 JFK St., Harvard Square, Cambridge, tel. (617) 349-1818; open Mon.-Sat.

THOMAS COOK CURRENCY SERVICES

Fee ($4 or 2%, whichever is greater) charged for either exchanging currency or cashing checks; 120 currencies accepted. Fee is waived on Thomas Cook checks.

Office:

399 Boylston St., Back Bay, tel. (800) 287-7362 or, in Canada, (800) 561-4212; open Mon.-Sat.

BANKBOSTON

Fee (the greater of $2.50 or 1%) charged on all foreign currencies or checks. All major brands of dollar-denominated checks are cashed for free.

Offices:

1414 Mass Ave., Harvard Square, Cambridge, tel. (617) 556-6050; open Mon.-Sat.

175 Federal St., downtown Boston, tel. (617) 788-5000; open Mon.-Fri.

Logan Airport, Terminal C, tel. (617) 569-1172; open daily

Logan Airport, Terminal E, tel. (617) 567-2313; open daily

Mail, Faxes, Phones

There are **post offices** throughout the city, most open weekdays 9-5 and Saturdays until noon or 2 p.m. Selected high-volume branches stay open later (for example, the Harvard Square branch handles stamp sales weekdays until 7:30 p.m., Saturdays till 5 p.m.), but if the itch to write home strikes at a truly odd hour, head down to Boston's general mail facility, tel. (617) 451-9922, next to South Station: its full-service counter never closes.

For large parcels, the best one-stop shop for packing materials and delivery services is any of the dozen **Mailboxes Etc.** stores around town, which will arrange pickup by any of the major private couriers, from **UPS** to **Federal Express.** FedEx, tel. (800) 463-3339, and **Emery Worldwide,** tel. (800) 443-6379, also have their own network of drop-off centers, most conveniently downtown in the financial district; call for directions to the nearest one.

If you are reluctant to make collect calls home, you can purchase prepaid **phone cards** at almost any post office or convenience store in town. **Photocopying** and **fax** services are also nearly ubiquitous, from small mom 'n' pop markets to every copy shop in the city (these last are generally the least expensive and most reliable). Even e-mail isn't hard to find: several coffeehouses have **public Internet access** for a modest hourly charge, including Cybersmith, on Church St. in Harvard Square, and the Barefoot Café, on Centre St. in Jamaica Plain. Most Kinko's copy shops around town do, too; look for their 24-hour storefronts next to the Copley Plaza Hotel in Back Bay, across from Government Center downtown, in Post Office Square in the Financial District, and next to the Harvard Square post office.

Newspapers and Radio

The mainstream daily *Boston Globe* is the largest-circulation paper in the region and worth picking up on Thursdays for the "Calendar" section, which offers a preview of the coming week's events and activities. A subsidiary of *The New York Times,* the *Globe* fits well within its parent organization's conservative respectability; newcomers to its pages will find only faint traces of the liberalism that Kennedy-bashers might imagine and expect. At least it has some very good investigative stories on occasion, which is vastly more than can be said of most of the competition. The large, highly educated young demographic in the city would seem ideally suited to support a thriving alternative press, but, judging from the content of the various weeklies, infor-

COURTESY OF BOSTON PUBLIC LIBRARY, PRINT DEPT.

New England Telephone operators, circa 1915

mative journalism takes a back seat to personal ads and movie reviews, executive career moves, and society gossip. Visitors accustomed to the tradition of provocative alternative free weeklies such as are found in cities coast to coast will be disappointed to find the most provocative content in the local variant, *The Phoenix,* is its massive quantity of adult escort and phone-sex ads—which apparently make an insufficient subsidy, since the cover price is $1.50. (Nearly identical editions *are* available free in Worcester and Providence.) Still, *The Phoenix,* which hits newsstands on Thursdays, offers the most comprehensive band listings for clubhoppers keen to catch a few gigs by local musicians.

When it comes to radio, Boston displays a bit more evidence that it values diversity, vitality, and experimentation. The usual range of adult-oriented album rock, oldies, Top 40, and AM talk radio occupy much of the dial, but among the local FM stations are not one but two NPR affiliates (the classical-music-minded **WGBH 89.7** and the all-news **WBUR 90.9,** the home of "Car Talk") plus several college stations upholding their breed's national reputation for independence and nonconformity. Tune in to **WZBC 90.3** from Boston College for the best dose of truly alternative musical programming, or sample some of the runners-up: **WMFO 91.5,** from Tufts University, and **WMBR 88.1,** from MIT. Folk and acoustic listeners should turn the dial to the University of Massachusetts' station, **WUMB 91.9,** or, for a mix of acoustic, bluegrass, and classical, listen in on Harvard University's **WHRB 95.3.** None of these college stations have very strong signals, so your hotel's bedside radio may be inadequate, but it's worth a try.

COURTESY, ESSEX SHIPBUILDING MUSEUM, ESSEX, MA

NORTH OF BOSTON

Northeastern Massachusetts is the storekeeper of the state's stock-in-trade—early American history. Essex County, which covers most of the territory in this region, is chock full of sites related to its 17th-century settlement, maritime trades, merchant empires, and pivotal role in propagating the Industrial Revolution. But the 20th century has spawned cul-de-sac suburbs and executive office parks in strategical clusters along the city's radial interstates inland from what was once the Gold Coast of Boston's Brahmins.

Bostonians and regional residents refer to much of this area as "the North Shore," an increasingly elastic term that was once limited to the summer playground of well-to-do 19th-century Bostonians escaping the city. First applied only to communities south of Salem, then stretched to encompass most of the shore below Cape Ann, the term North Shore now designates the state's Atlantic coast all the way from Boston well nigh to New Hampshire. The massive popularity, in summer, of many of the region's swimming beaches and second-home communities is offset by plenty of protected parklands and wildlife refuges. Away from the ocean, too, are rural villages that don't fit into the urban commuter's equation of acceptable driving distances, and towns whose diminutive lot sizes still keep subdivision developers at bay. For a hint of this more sedate side to the region, stick to the smaller state roads along the coast, or local roads along either side of the Merrimack River valley, where the historic character of Essex County remains unmistakable. With a little serendipity and a wrong turn or two, you may even be fortunate enough to discover the hidden pockets that stay so willfully out of step with the modern age.

THE NEAR NORTH SHORE

Like a geode's hidden crystals, many of the North Shore attractions closest to Boston are concealed behind a thick rind of unsightly shopping centers and industrial zones. The almost historic, oversized tackiness of Rt. 1 from Boston through Saugus, a.k.a. the Saugus Strip, is a slight improvement over Rt. 1A, which runs through the tank farms of Revere. However, the speedy pace of traffic on Rt. 1 makes it difficult to appreciate the art deco WPA overpasses, the Leaning Tower of Pizza, the pair of palatial pagoda-styled restaurants, the plastic herd grazing at the Hilltop Steakhouse, and other Strip landmarks.

This is by no means an utter tourist wasteland. Real history buffs will find some nuggets in Saugus and Lynn, two blue-collar communities whose mere mention in a travel guide will choke most Massachusetts natives with mirth. North out of Boston along Rt. 1, look carefully and

you'll see small brown signs directing you to the first such nugget, the **Saugus Iron Works National Historic Site,** 244 Central St., tel. (781) 233-0050. In 1646 this integrated furnace and forge began supplying the Puritan-ruled Bay Colony with wrought and cast iron, thus becoming the first successful colonial iron work. Guided tours (April-Oct.) and year-round exhibits help interpret 17th-century life among the workers, whose number included indentured Scottish prisoners from the English Civil War. Even without the informative rangers, the great

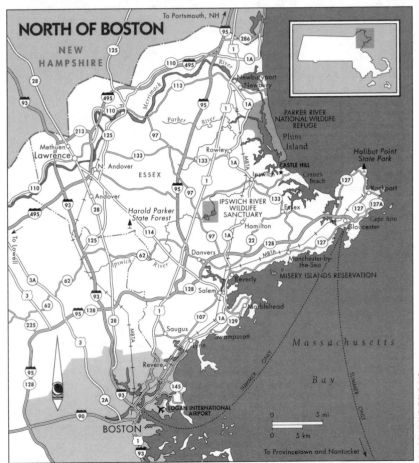

wooden apparatus and spacious grounds are a nifty and unexpected break from the surrounding built-up residential area.

If you take Rt. 1A north of Boston, overlook the auto dealerships and liquor stores and stop a while in **Lynn.** Despite being a national leader in the manufacture of jet aircraft engines and marshmallow fluff, Lynn suffers from a reputation low enough to have prompted a recent campaign to change its name to Ocean View. Foremost among the city's several worthy attractions is the **Lynn Heritage State Park,** in a renovated brick shoe factory at Washington and Union Sts., a block from the downtown commuter rail station, tel. (781) 598-1974. Similar to the state's other heritage parks, this one focuses on an industry that helped build Massachusetts—in this case, fashionable ladies' footwear. The industry gave Lynn the nickname "Queen Shoe City." The park is open Wed.-Sun. year-round, with ranger-led walks or special events featured most summer Saturdays. Follow the faded yellow footprints painted on the sidewalk beginning at the visitor center door; these lead you over Rt. 1A to the peaceful little waterfront park and marinas.

The **Lynn Historical Society,** a few blocks away at 125 Green St., tel. (781) 592-2465, also has a few modest exhibits (Mon-Sat.; $3), research library, and gift shop. Best of all the society offers seasonal house and walking tours in Lynn's historic neighborhoods (call for upcoming dates and fees). The Diamond District is the most well-known, and can be navigated on your own. Situated along Lynn Shore Drive beside the three-mile-long seawall and attractive park strand, the district is full of fine mansions with Atlantic vistas. Though of a wholly different character than San Francisco's hillsides of "painted ladies," some beautiful and well-preserved architecture does exist here, in styles popular between the Victorian era and the start of the Great Depression. Around early December, if you're braving the cold, the Diamond District B&B, at 142 Ocean St., sponsors an open house trolley tour of some of the more remarkable private homes in the neighborhood; call (800) 666-3076 for information.

No visit to Lynn is complete without a stop at the incomparable **Capitol Diner,** 43 Union St. opposite the Heritage State Park, tel. (781) 595-9314. This 1928 Brill diner, famous for the live chickens in the yard, earns its cheap-eats crown with sturdy American standards such as meat loaf, turkey with gravy, club sandwiches, and tried-and-true burgers. At lunchtime the line runs out the door. When the rush eases, the waitstaff will banter with regulars nursing their coffee by the window or along the Formica counter burnished with innumerable work-weary elbows. If you let drop your name, don't be surprised if everyone remembers it when you return two weeks later for one last order of pancakes.

MARBLEHEAD

Founded by fishermen from Cornwall and the Channel Islands who didn't see eye-to-eye with Salem's Puritans, Marblehead was the sixth most populous town in the American colonies in 1760, even larger than Baltimore. Though it still can claim one of the nation's largest historic districts, Marblehead is now a small community of barely 17,000 that lies off the beaten track. It's shielded from the curious—to the relief of many residents—by the standard Massachusetts practice of poor road signs and confusing one-way streets. Those who succeed in discovering quaint Marblehead will be rewarded with narrow lanes, closely packed wooden houses, interesting galleries, artful shops, excellent bakeries, and almost no parking on summer weekends.

Since before the American Revolution, when 1,000 of its men founded the Continental Army's only amphibious regiment, Marblehead has kept its feet in the ocean. (Washington crossed the Delaware aboard the regiment's boats to earn one of his only battlefield victories, in Trenton.) The town commissioned the first ship of the U.S. Navy (although nearby Beverly built it), and provided much of the crew for the USS *Constitution* during the War of 1812. Now with six yacht clubs and thousands of sloops, ketches, and schooners at anchor all around the peninsula, Marblehead easily rivals the California cities of San Diego and Newport as a center for sailing. (If you arrive by sea, call the Harbormaster for mooring or anchorage instructions: 781-631-2386.)

Sights

Marblehead's historic district is worth a stroll whether or not you have a keen eye for 18th- and 19th-century architecture. For a peek at the fine arts hidden behind some of those stately facades, visit one of the town's two public Georgian residences: the **King Hooper Mansion,** on Hooper St. at Washington, tel. (781) 631-2608, or the **Jeremiah Lee Mansion,** a stone's throw away at 161 Washington, tel. (781) 631-1069. Anyone who expects old things to be musty and boring should skip a visit to the Hooper property, which was built about 250 years ago by a wealthy Tory who earned his royal nickname from fair dealings and civic gifts. Its owner, the Marblehead Arts Association, maintains a busy year-round schedule of contemporary art exhibits, monthly opening receptions (to which the public is welcome), lectures, a handful of concerts in the grand ballroom, and art classes. There's also a shop selling members' wares. The 1768 Lee Mansion, home to the Marblehead Historical Society, also is not entirely frozen in time: rooms are furnished and decorated to represent several distinct periods from the Georgian through the 19th century, and from one visit to the next you may find items rearranged according to particular seasonal or historical themes. For a special treat, call ahead and time your visit with one of the special candlelight house tours. Small changing exhibits touch on local history, as do the society's regular walking tours of town. Open seasonally, from mid-May through the end of October; admission is $4.

Near the crest of Washington Street beyond the Lee Mansion is **Abbot Hall,** the sturdy red-brick building that houses the town offices. You can't miss the tall Victorian clock tower and swatches of patriotic bunting. The selectmen's meeting room and adjacent corridors hold the typical small-town assortment of flotsam. Abbot Hall's prize possession is a bit more out of the ordinary: a painting by Archibald M. Willard, commissioned during the U.S. centennial in 1876 by a printer of mass-market chromolithographs. Never heard of Willard? His humorous painting of a rabbit-chasing retriever, titled *Pluck,* was the 19th-century equivalent of the poker-playing dogs. As for his centennial piece, its subjects are as well-known as Uncle Sam: two drummers and a fife player in a pose Willard called "Yankee Doodle." The work was officially christened *The Spirit of '76* by popular acclaim. Willard himself produced several copies—one is in Ohio—but the original hangs here at Abbot Hall, in the company of paintings of Washington crossing the Delaware and busts of once-famous sons of Marblehead.

Lower Washington Street is where you'll find interesting shops such as **F. L. Woods,** 76 Washington St., tel. (800) 286-7568. Reflecting the town's prevailing passion, this is your best local source of nautical books, charts, flags, chandlery items, and that signal cannon you've always wanted. Nearby at the foot of Pleasant Street is **Much Ado,** filled floor to ceiling with used and rare books in an atmosphere redolent of old leather, paper, and the occasional batch of fresh-baked cookies. Specialty stores and art galleries on the surrounding blocks stand equally ready to turn window shoppers into gift buyers.

Don't leave town without paying a visit to **Marblehead Neck.** Peripheral Ocean Avenue offers beautiful views of boundless waves, small boats with taut sails scudding before the wind, and the Boston skyline 17 miles away. Fishing Point and Desmoulin are two of the dead-end lanes that permit you to park and clamber down the generally rocky shore to tide pools and surfcasting spots. At Castle Rock, there's even a small park with a playground and benches; for picnic tables and restrooms, go to the park at the peninsula's north end, where Marblehead Light flashes from atop its steel truss tower. Million-dollar views lie landward, too: the mansions that ring the Neck.

Boats and Beaches

July is a particularly busy month for local skippers. It starts off with the Wooden Boat Race and ends with Marblehead Race Week. Every odd-numbered year, the Halifax Race between Marblehead and Nova Scotia also hits town, commencing on the first Sunday in July. But throughout the summer sailors hone their skills with all manner of day races, easily observed from Castle Rock or the lighthouse park. If you have experience and wish to join in, check the various yacht clubhouse bulletin boards for crew-needed ads. Before and after most events you can also eavesdrop on crews as they relive the high points at local bars and restaurants throughout town—particularly at Maddie's.

Local boating isn't confined to offshore waters, either: for over a century model boat races have been held on Redd's Pond, near Old Burial Hill. You can usually catch them on summer Wednesday evenings and Sunday mornings.

Small swimming areas, some no wider than a few yards, are scattered at the ends of waterfront boat landings and public rights-of-way all around town, from the sandy harborfront beach at the bottom of the Parker Lane stairs on Marblehead Neck to modest Gashouse Beach. If you're staying at a local B&B, your host can clue you in to a swimming area close enough for a wake-up dip. A sandy break in the rocky shore of Little Harbor, Gashouse Beach is off Orne Street below Old Burial Hill (free but limited parking). Much larger and easier to find is **Devereux Beach,** the long, sandy margin beside the boulders lining the ocean side of the Marblehead Neck causeway. With bathrooms, a food shack, and a reasonable amount of parking (fee charged for non-residents), it's understandably the most popular swimming spot in town.

Accommodations

Marblehead is the bed-and-breakfast center of the North Shore, and many of its establishments still live up to the name—they're private homes whose owners accommodate guests with spare bedrooms and a morning meal, rather than small inns run by hired managers. Many are moderately priced, and most are too small to charge room tax. Most also are not actually oceanfront places, although water views are routinely advertised. (Accurately so, but how much time do you plan to spend in your bedroom looking out the window?) All but one are open year-round, and nearly all require a two-night stay at least on summer and fall weekends, if not the entire high season. The cooperative spirit that prevails among the B&Bs means a last-minute caller for same-day reservations can always depend on a referral to whomever in town has available rooms.

For character alone, try **Guest House at Lavender Gate,** tel. (781) 631-3243, an early 18th-century residence at the base of Summer Street with a decidedly literary bent. The two air-conditioned, book-filled suites, named after a pair of Victorian publishers, are comfortable and private enough to forget about going outdoors. (If

you're much over six feet tall, be sure to request the downstairs room.) The ample continental breakfast included in the $100 nightly tariff may be taken in your suite, in the common dining area (which features a framed pair of Eugene O'Neill's boxer shorts and a massive cookbook collection), or out in the small garden planted only with species cited in Shakespeare's plays.

Equally cordial hospitality amid more modern trappings prevails a couple of blocks away at **Brimblecomb Hill B&B,** 33 Mechanic St., tel. (781) 631-3172 (nights) or 631-6366 (days). Rooms that share a bath are $65; the queen-bedded room with private bath is $85. You'll find similar rates at **Stillpoint,** 27 Gregory St., tel. (800) 882-3891, an environmentally friendly, fragrance-free home with harbor views. Rooms with shared baths are $75, or reserve a private bath for $10 more. Also in the same price range—actually, a bit lower—is **The Nesting Place B&B,** 16 Village St., tel. (781) 631-6655, e-mail Louisehir@aol.com. Though farther from the Old Town shops and waterfront, this bright and airy turn-of-the-century home is close to the Five Corners business and restaurant cluster, and next to the bike path to Salem. The owner's passion for handpainting furniture adds a colorful, contemporary folk art accent to the place, while the jacuzzi out on the back deck helps guests relax even more. Rates are $65-70 with shared baths. Families with children are welcome.

For a spot actually on the ocean with private beach, check out the family-friendly **Tidecrest by the Sea,** on Spray Ave., tel. (781) 631-8153, a short drive away from the historic center and near Marblehead's southern edge. Oceanfront rooms with private baths are $125-150; a two-room family suite is $200. Open seasonally mid-May through mid-October.

The town's largest lodging option is the 20-room **Harbor Light Inn,** tel. (781) 631-2186, with comfortable rooms (many with working fireplaces and double jacuzzis), heated outdoor pool, continental breakfast, and the convenience of a 58 Washington St. address, smack in the center of the Old Town. Rates range from $95-150 d. A short drive down the coast toward Boston is another small property blending the best of hotel and B&B worlds. The **Diamond District Bed & Breakfast,** 142 Ocean St., tel. (800) 666-3076, is an 11-room inn overlooking

*the Capitol Diner,
a 1930s Brill model,
in Lynn*

the strand along Kings Beach in Lynn. Built in 1911 by a multinational shoe magnate who held a boot contract with the U.S. Army when WW I broke out, this spare-no-expense mansion offers some of the North Shore's most stately accommodations. There's a choice of rooms with either shared or private baths (a couple with fireplaces), plus suites. Business travelers will appreciate the color TVs, dual-line phones with modem ports, and voice mail. In a region where most B&Bs offer only continental breakfasts, this one maintains the only way to start off your morning right is with a full meal. Remarkably convenient to Logan airport, Salem, Marblehead, and the express bus to downtown Boston, it's a real find. Rates range between $80-110 Nov.-March, and $105-140 April-Oct.; for the two-room suite with fireplace, private deck, and two-person whirlpool bath, add about 50%. For additional lodging suggestions in the vicinity, including chain hotels and motels, consult "Accommodations" under "Salem," below.

Food

Marblehead, alas, conforms to the unwritten Massachusetts rule requiring prime waterfront locations to be wasted on establishments serving mediocre food. Most of the town's best meals aren't even from the sea at all. Italian restaurants, the old stalwarts of the pre-yuppie dining era, reign in Marblehead, as they do in Worcester and other central Massachusetts locales. (Come to think of it, Worcester even has a bet-

ter seafood restaurant.) This means that if you want great lobster or fish that isn't fried, continue north to Gloucester on Cape Ann.

This is not to say that Marbleheaders don't appreciate fine dining. *Au contraire*—the town has way more than its fair share of gourmet shops doing a brisk business in affordable take-out, usually until 6 or 7 p.m. So if you came in your own boat or can find a good perch in Crocker Park or Fort Sewall overlooking the harbor (remember, too, there are picnic tables out by Marblehead Light on the Neck), fetch something extraordinary from **Truffles,** 114 Washington St. at the end of Pleasant, tel. (781) 639-1104. Equally good but further from the harbor are **Delphin's Gourmandise Fine French Patisserie,** 258 Washington, over the hill at Five Corners, tel. (781) 639-2311, and, most reasonably priced of all, **Eat Your Heart Out,** in the Village Plaza on Pleasant and Besson Sts., tel. (781) 639-0244. The rich but modestly priced genoises and gâteaux at Truffles and Delphin's are to die for. When cold sesame noodles, grilled chicken salads, crab cakes with pesto, or marinated antipasti are too fancy for lunch on a rock, buy a hunk of fine cheese at Truffles, or Crosby's supermarket in back, and step across to **Iggy's Bread of the World,** 5 Pleasant St. (open daily except Christmas), for an excellent sourdough loaf to put it on.

Among recommendable restaurants, **Maddie's Sail Loft,** 15 State St., tel. (781) 631-9824, earns high marks for honest, fried and broiled seafood at fair prices with a casual, TV-over-the-bar atmosphere ($9.95-14.95). Across the street is **The King's Rook,** tel. (781) 631-9838, a wine bar and cozy little cafe ideal for philosophizing about the merits of oceanside living while wrapping your fingers around a mug of tea or coffee, sipping something from their extensive list of wines by the glass, or digging into their rich desserts. They also serve inexpensive salads, sandwiches, soups, and single-serving pizzas, all well under $10. Both Maddie's and The King's Rook are closed Monday evenings. For Italian, consider the local outpost of Boston-based **Trattoria Il Panino,** 126 Washington (enter around the back, below street level), known for its well-prepared pasta and gourmet pizzas ($7.95-15.95), or **Pellino's Fine Italian Dining,** 261 Washington St. at Five Corners, tel. (781) 631-3344, whose name is no idle boast.

When nothing less than waterfront dining will do, forget the tourist traps down on Front Street—except, perhaps, The Barnacle—and try **The Rockmore,** moored out in Salem Harbor, tel. (781) 639-0600. Weather permitting it's open daily from the end of May through Labor Day. Catch the red launch from the western end of Village Street (or from the Congress Street dock in downtown Salem). The food may not be terribly exciting—and since they often run out of selected items it's best not to expect more than a sandwich—but the location makes it an unbeatable place for seafood and fries, or just a drink at dusk. **The Barnacle,** tel. (781) 631-4236, is the one Front Street eatery worth a try for basic grilled fish, fried fish, or thick chowder, but come with plenty of patience and cash: they don't accept reservations or credit cards, and it's not cheap.

Cravings for something more exotic than Italian will be appeased by **Thai Thani,** 408 Humphrey St. (Rt. 129), tel. (781) 596-1820, actually south of Marblehead in residential Swampscott, across the street from the ocean. A couple of neighboring restaurants also capitalize on the supply of local fish but this is the only place that gets and deserves out-of-town loyalty. Besides seafood, all the standards from *pad Thai* to hot curries are present, complemented by friendly service, the obligatory glass-topped tables, and travel posters of far-away temples. Open for lunch weekdays and dinner nightly ($8.95-13.95).

Getting There

The only public transit to Marblehead are the MBTA #441 and #442 buses from Boston, originating from the depot above the Haymarket T station on the Orange and Green lines. The one-way fare is $2.25; trip time is about an hour. Both routes stop at the commuter rail station in Lynn. The frequency of service peaks during weekday rush hours, dropping back to once an hour evenings and Sundays.

Information

The **Marblehead Chamber of Commerce** operates a seasonal information booth on Pleasant Street a block north of the Warwick Theater. Besides offering a pleasantly thorough and price-specific accommodations list, they can tell you which, if any, of the listed inns and B&Bs have availability for that night. They will also offer valuable tips on where to find parking. To obtain information in advance of your visit, call (781) 631-2868, e-mail info@marbleheadchamber.org, or visit their homepage at www.marbleheadchamber.org.

SALEM

In light of the infamous Witch Trials of 1692, it may seem a tad ironic that Salem derives its name from the Hebrew word for peace, shalom. In fact, the village in which those 17th-century persecutions occurred erased the irony long ago by changing its name to Danvers. That's right, modern Salem isn't really the scene of the crime, so to speak. It isn't entirely disconnected from the trials, either—a judge lived here, and most of the victims were hung here. But fact and proportion are flimsy restraints, and given Danvers' renunciation of its dark past, it stands to reason that Salem's merchants would adopt the story of those old witches as their own. Contemporary ones are welcomed, too, so watch out for low-flying broomsticks and plenty of costumed phantasmagoria in October, when the city pulls out all the stops for Halloween.

History

The offspring of an abortive fishing venture, Albion, established in 1623 farther north at Cape Ann, the Salem area was among the earliest sites of English settlement in the northeast. When the backers in Albion pulled the plug on the unprofitable plantation, some of its members chose to move south to the Pawtucket Indian village of Naumkeag, whose scant survivors of European epidemics welcomed their new neighbors as protectors from hostile tribes to the north. By the time the Massachusetts Bay Colony was officially chartered in 1628, the newly rechristened town of Salem was a viable settlement. Its "Old Planters" were accustomed to both autonomy and relative religious freedom, from Church of England faithfuls to Separatist (e.g., Pilgrim) dissenters relocated from Plymouth. Both of these traits made Salem a very sharp thorn in the side of the fundamentalist Puritans, who alighted in Salem only long enough to depose Governor Endicott before moving south and making their capital in Boston under the rule of John Winthrop. The conflict came to a head when Salem chose Roger Williams as minister. Williams criticized as "a National sinne" the Puritan doctrine of total disregard of Native American land rights. Boston ultimately brought Salem into line by banishing the heretical Williams in 1636, on pain of death; but before being carted back to England, he escaped and founded the Providence Plantation—now known as Rhode Island.

Salem's 17th-century affair with witchcraft, a fever pitch of finger-pointing and snitching neighbors and veritable lynchings, seems to comprise the town's most enthralling historical episode, judging by the sheer quantity of commercial attractions based on it. The impact of the trials is disturbing: 19 men and women were hanged; one man was crushed under heavy stones; and an untold number died in jail, or, like the five-year-old child imprisoned for a year, were psychologically crippled for life. The shame lasted for generations. Nathaniel Hawthorne added a "w" to his family name to distance himself from his ancestor and trial magistrate John Hathorne. Embarrassment may yet be a reason the town of Danvers to this day doesn't publicize trial-related sights within its boundaries.

After the American Revolution, Salem rose to prominence in seaborne trade. Ships from Salem sailed east, monopolizing Africa, Arabia, India, Malaysia, Indonesia, and the Philippines, multiplying profits geometrically by trading at each port en route. The local fleet of nearly 200 "East Indiamen" traded Yankee rum, chocolate, salt cod, furniture, and flour for coffee, indigo, cotton, sugar, and a major slice of the Indonesian pepper crop. But Salem's days as a pepper potentate and coffee kingdom were numbered: President Jefferson's 1807 embargo on American overseas trade and "Mr. Madison's War" with England in 1812—foreign policies ostensibly designed to punish England for violating American neutrality at sea—cut off Massachusetts maritime trade at the knees. Sea trade began again after the war's end in 1814, but Salem's port never regained its former stature. By the middle of the 19th century, manufacturing overtook trade as Salem's economic breadwinner.

Sights

With over two dozen galleries in two buildings and nine historic houses, the **Peabody Essex Museum** is one of New England's largest museums, and the oldest continuously operating one in the nation. Reflecting both Salem's past

MARK SEXTON/COURTESY, PEABODY ESSEX MUSEUM, SALEM, MA

figureheads from the ship Talma, *the bark* Western Belle, *and the ship* Indian Princess, *in the Peabody Essex Museum's East India Marine Hall*

SAMUEL McINTIRE'S LEGACY

C harles Bulfinch gets (and deserves) the lion's share of the credit for originating the Federal style of architecture. But he was never its sole practitioner. In fact, some of the finest Federal structures in existence are the work of Samuel McIntire—a *Salem* builder.

A homegrown American variation on the prevailing English decorative style, Federal architecture emphasizes symmetry and two-dimensional ornament—square facades framed on the sides by flat pilasters, for example. The center doorway gets the most lavish treatment—a columned portico, perhaps; fanlight windows; sidelights sometimes. A distinguishing feature of most Federal houses is that the third-story windows are much smaller than those on either of the first two floors. Roofs are flat, rather than pitched, and usually have fancy railings running along the edge.

Ranger-led walking tours of McIntire's legacy start at the National Park Service's Salem Visitor Center. Or, to wander on your own, pick up a free Park Service guide to the McIntire District (centered in Chestnut St.), a couple of blocks west of downtown.

and the activities of its 18th-century founders, the strengths of the collections lie in maritime art and history, Asian and Pacific ethnographic art, New England architecture and decorative arts, and a peerless collection of Asian export art specifically crafted for foreign trade. Salem's globe-spanning commerce is amply illustrated with artifacts from every imaginable trading partner and then some. The legacy of indigenous New Englander's is also extensively documented within the museum's collections. You can study the infamous Witch Trials here, free of the dramatics that attend their description elsewhere in town, and examine some of native-born Nathaniel Hawthorne's personal effects. The two main buildings, tel. (800) 745-4054, www. pem.org, are on Essex and Liberty Streets near East India Square, both of which are open daily between Memorial Day and Halloween and Tues.-Sun. the rest of the year. The museum's historic houses are mostly in the block adjacent to the Essex Street building, although one, the Ropes Mansion, is at 318 Essex St., in the McIntire Historic District. Six are open seasonally to guided tours only, including the stately 14-room **Gardner-Pingree House,** whose three stories of red brick are widely regarded as the zenith of

Samuel McIntire's work. Some architecture critics even consider it the definitive example of the Federal style. Admission to the museum and the houses is $7.50 ($18 family of four).

Maritime and Literary Sights: Over a half dozen historic structures along the city's old commercial wharves have been preserved as part of the **Salem Maritime National Historic Site,** including Derby Wharf, the Custom House, and other buildings related to the East Indies trade. The sites are united by a waterfront park whose centerpiece is the *Friendship,* a functional replica of a 1797 sailing vessel. Start at the two-room Central Wharf Orientation Center on Derby Street for a video introduction to the site and a menu of ranger-led tours ($2).

The Custom House at the head of Derby Wharf is another of the many Massachusetts buildings Nathaniel Hawthorne helped put firmly on the map, this one by lampooning its functionaries in his prefatory sketch to *The Scarlet Letter.* The inspiration for Hawthorne's vinegary satire derived from his short term as a government surveyor, a patronage appointment wrung from his friend and Bowdoin College roommate, President Franklin Pierce, whose fawning campaign biography Hawthorne penned.

The National Park Service operates a spacious **Salem Visitor Center** in the old brick armory at the corner of Essex and New Liberty Streets, tel. (978) 740-1650, between the two halves of the Peabody Essex Museum grounds. A few displays and a very good film presentation put Salem's maritime pursuits into the wider context of surrounding Essex County, whose historical riches have earned it designation as a National Heritage Area. Pick up free guides to the county-wide Heritage Trails, or a walking tour brochure to Salem's own Heritage Trail, marked by a red line on downtown sidewalks. Restrooms, gifts, a wall full of well-selected books, and the chance to query the friendly ranger staff for suggestions or opinions about sights, restaurants, or the fastest routes out of town are all further reasons to visit the center, which is open daily 9 a.m.-6 p.m.

Four blocks east of Derby Wharf stands **The House of Seven Gables,** 54 Turner St., tel. (978) 744-0991. Celebrated as the setting for Nathaniel Hawthorne's eponymous novel, parts of this rambling waterfront mansion date back to 1668. Period gardens and several other 17th-century buildings, including the Salem house Hawthorne was born in on the Fourth of July, have been relocated here and are included in the guided tours (open daily; $7).

Witches, Wretches, and Pirates: Salem leads the state in cheesy sideshow-style entertainment venues masquerading as museums. Kids love 'em, and if you need to plan a birthday party for a bunch of 12-year-olds, you could do a lot worse than booking it at one of these. With one exception all are seasonal, generally open daily from April or May through Halloween or Thanksgiving. Admission fees are about $4-5 each; several knock off a dollar if you buy admission to their companion attraction. None are hard to find: stroll west along Derby and New Derby Streets from the wharfside Orientation Center and you'll pass a handful—**Salem's Museum of Myths & Monsters,** in the Pickering Wharf shops and the **New England Pirate Museum,** the **Salem Wax Museum of Witches & Seafarers,** and **Dracula's Castle,** on the pedestrian-only Marketplace. On the other side of downtown Washington Street is the **Witch Dungeon Museum,** 16 Lynde St., which at least gives you some live theatrics (loosely based on an actual witchcraft trial transcript) for your money. The **Salem Witch Museum,** on Washington Square across from the common, purports to be the most popular, but behind the photogenic stone facade, the amateurish diorama-with-lights show is truly the biggest disappointment of the whole lot. Stick to the gift shop. Despite the long swirling cape and tall, wide-brimmed hat, the statue in front is neither witch nor judge. It's Roger Conant, Salem's first European settler.

The *Real* Witchcraft Sites: Besides the grave of two of the witchcraft trial magistrates— John Hathorne's in Charter Street's old Burying Point behind the wax museum, and Jonathan Corwin's in the Broad Street burial ground—modern Salem has very little remaining

that's truly related to the infamous trials. The courthouse in which the proceedings were held is long gone; the site, beneath Washington Street in front of City Hall, is marked only by a plaque on the Masonic Temple. The jail, or gaol, in which the accused were incarcerated was also felled in the name of progress. Its site now belongs to a telephone company building. The location of Gallows Hill has never been conclusively identified, although a couple candidates are west of downtown off Boston Street. The principle surviving site from 1692 is Justice Corwin's home, popularly mislabelled **The Witch House,** 310 Essex St. at the corner of North, tel. (978) 744-0180. Tours focus on the First Period architecture, furnishings, and the life of the building's infamous owner.

It takes a car, but if you are determined to see where most of the Salem uproar really occurred, you'll have to drive west to neighboring Danvers. Although houses that belonged to people who testified at the witchcraft trials and the tavern in which preliminary hearings were held are now almost all private residences, there are a couple of notable exceptions. Foremost is the 1678 **Rebecca Nurse Homestead,** 149 Pine St., tel. (978) 774-0554, the house and farm of a devout septuagenarian whose standing within the community was high enough to give the witch trial magistrates pause before accepting the accusations against her. Although initially found not guilty, the fits of her accusers prompted judges and jury to reconsider their verdict; in July of 1692 she was hanged with four other alleged witches. Tours of the property are the most historically accurate of all the witch-related attractions, and do not pander to popular superstitions or the public thirst for over-simplified histrionics. Open Tues.-Sun. 1-4:30 p.m., June 15-Labor Day, plus weekends through the end of October. Admission is $4. Tours begin in the replica of the Salem Village Meetinghouse built for the TV movie *Three Sovereigns for Sarah,* which shares the homestead grounds with other farm buildings. The original meetinghouse, in which some of the pretrial examinations took place, sat on Hobart Street opposite Danvers' present pale granite memorial to the witchcraft victims.

The 1692 witch hysteria all began at yet another Danvers locale, the home of Reverend

Parris. He lived there with his oddly behaving daughter and neice, and Tituba, one of the family's two slaves and the children's alleged guide to satanic arts. Though long gone, the home's foundations may still be seen at the **Salem Village Parsonage Archeaological Site,** now a town park with a few interpretive signs to tell the tale. Despite billing itself as one of the most significant historical sites of colonial America, it is nearly inaccessible, located behind a private home at 67 Center Street. Foliage nearly obscures the only streetside sign, and no genuinely safe or legal parking is available. (Parallel park with two wheels a foot or so over the curb and leave your emergency flashers on if you do pay a visit.) To get there from the Nurse Homestead, continue north on Pine and make a left on Hobart (at the flashing yellow signal), and then a right where Hobart intersects Center. Number 67, a yellow-clapboard house whose owner doesn't take kindly to visitors, will come fairly quickly on the right after the bend.

Tours and Cruises: Whalewatching cruises on the North Shore have an advantage over operations in Boston and Cape Cod in that they can choose to head for a second, more northerly feeding ground, Jeffrey's Ledge, if early morning reports from the fishing fleet indicate whales are more numerous there than on Stellwagen Bank, which is due east of Boston. From Salem, the **East India Cruise Company** departs for where the whales are on weekends in May, daily June-Labor Day, Thurs.-Sun. the remainder of September, and weekends only through October. Tickets—$23 for adults, $16 for kids under 14—may be purchased from their office at 197 Derby St., tel. (800) 745-9594, at the head of the Pickering Wharf shops.

Typical tour trolleys and horse-drawn carriages, rare in Massachusetts, both ply Salem's streets through the high season months, and are easily located around Pickering Wharf. Combination land and water tours are the exclusive province of **Moby Duck Tours,** tel. (978) 741-4FUN, whose red ticket booth sits on the corner of Essex Street next to the visitor center. The narrated, 50-minute ride aboard their amphibious vehicle costs $12 adults, $8 children; departures are scheduled on the hour, daily 10 a.m.-4 p.m., May-Oct., weather permitting.

Accommodations
For proximity to the historical and maritime attractions of this former gateway to the East Indies, it would be hard to top the fine old **Hawthorne Hotel,** right smack on the common, tel. (800) SAY-STAY, recently restored to all its original polish. The ambiance is one of a small inn rather than a large hotel, although as the tallest building in the neighborhood most of its rooms afford good views. Doubles range from $80-125 Jan.-Mar. to $92-162 in summer and fall (minimum stay required over high season weekends). Typical of the half-dozen other inns and B&Bs within a few blocks are **Amelia Payson House,** Winter St., tel. (978) 744-8304, and the **Stepping Stone Inn,** overlooking the imposing Roger Conant statue in Washington Square, tel. (800) 338-3022. Both are expensive, as are nearly all the others. The only moderate rooms in Salem proper are at the motel-like **Clipper Ship Inn,** 40 Bridge St. (Rt. 1A), tel. (978) 745-8022. Moderate prices are also the rule at the **Days Inn,** on Rt. 128 Exit 24, tel. (800) 325-2525, next to Denny's and the Liberty Tree Mall. A seasonal campground exists on Winter Island, a former Coast Guard base. You'll find RV hookups along one wall of a hulking Depression-era seaplane hangar and tent sites scattered over the mostly bare grass, but unless you're capable of falling asleep to the flash of aircraft warning lights on the neighboring power plant's smokestacks, give the place a miss.

Food and Drink
Being a tourist hot spot hasn't overloaded Salem with witch-themed restaurants or fast-food franchises. Downtown has its share of bar-restaurant combos, where buffalo wings and steak tips reign supreme, but there are also some fine upscale New American places, and great ethnic spots. Folks desperate for an espresso fix will find a less-expensive alternative to Starbucks in the **Cafe Bagel Co.,** on Washington St. just south of Essex.

Popular with locals and tourists alike is Derby Street's **In a Pig's Eye,** tel. (978) 741-4436, a cheerful den a couple of blocks past the Custom House. The eclectic fare is a good match for the ambiance; skip the Mexican items (too far from the source) and you won't leave disappointed or hungry. It's open to midnight Mon.-Saturday. A slightly more '90s menu of brick oven pizzas, lots of things laced with chipotle peppers or dry-rubbed spices, and plenty of fresh veggies is found up the street at the **Salem Beer Works,** 278 Derby, tel. (978) 741-7088 ($10.95-15.95). All this is accompanied, of course, by a passel of beers brewed on the premises.

The **Thai Place,** inside the Museum Place shops on the Essex Street pedestrian mall, tel. (978) 741-8008, is Salem's reliable Southeast Asian offering. Everything's well-spiced, swiftly served, and reasonably priced ($8.75-12.95). Another prime Asian contender is **Asahi,** 21 Congress St., tel. (978) 744-5376, a very informal, often quite busy spot next to Pickering Wharf. Besides the usual sushi and sashimi—some of which arrives in lacquered bento boxes like little treasure chests—the fine tempura and a number of hotpot entrees are also deservedly popular ($9.50-18.95). Closed Mondays. Across the street at 26 Congress is one of the area's best restaurants, **Grapevine,** tel. (978) 745-9335. An elegant, relaxed oasis of mostly northern Italian cuisine, its chef spices up the menu of familiar dishes with unexpected flavors from other continents ($12.95-18.50). Dinner nightly; lunch Wed.-Saturday.

Several blocks south of the touristy Pickering Wharf area is **Red Raven's Love Noodle,** 75 Congress St., tel. (978) 745-8558. The scene behind the little maroon, flowery facade could teach Boston a thing or two about the cutting edge of cool. Open daily 5-10 p.m., the Noodle attracts a young, loud crowd hip to ethnic noodle dishes, lots of boldly seasoned appetizers, an extensive list of under-$20 wines, lots of dark sweet beers, ginseng elixirs, and fruit-based concoctions (entrées $10-15). Beware: "no credit cards or yuppies," and it's located in an urban edge neighborhood that draws customers into complicity with the owners' spirit of adventure. Though more upscale, **Red Raven's Havana,** tel. (978) 740-3888, the second sibling in the growing Raven family, almost manages to make Love Noodle look tame. The purple awning and heavily draped windows at 90 Washington Street, downtown, conceal an interior approximating a bordello

designed by Pedro Almodovar—beaded curtain at the entrance, animal print upholstery, artwork ranging from the Renaissance to Cubism, and a ripe, Batista-era big-band sound pouring out of the house stereo. The mixed drinks are named with such undisguised double entendre that if they were funded by the National Endowment for the Arts, Congress would pillory the artist who concocted them. The menu is divvied into three categories: spa (non- or low-fat), bourgeois, and gastronomique. The simplest entrée might be a vegetable paella with cumin-scented crisp bulgur bread; a more self-indulgent patron may prefer a spiced walnut-crusted rack of lamb. As you could guess, such a rich sensory experience doesn't come cheap: entrées run $14.75-24.75. If you feel any slight vibrations under your feet, don't worry—it's only Salem's Puritan founders spinning mightily in their graves.

Finally, though it's a drive from downtown, the **Salem Diner,** 70 Loring Ave. (Rt. 1A) near the intersection with Canal St., tel. (978) 744-9776, is well worth a detour for a good square meal or fine short-order breakfast (open to 7:45 p.m. weekdays, and to half past noon on weekends). Come for fluffy pancakes, tasty omelettes and home fries, steak tips, fried seafood, and all the excitement of watching the masterful staff juggle a score of meals in the aisle behind the Formica, with barks of "Order's up!" punctuating the bacon-sizzle and plate-clatter. Sit at the counter and Alex and Pete will show appropriately gruff concern for whether you enjoy your meal, but don't pay the guys any strong compliments. Too much praise and they might get some swell ideas, raise their rock-bottom prices, and start adding French accents to the menu, heaven forbid. Diner fans won't want to miss this place: it's one of a handful of Sterling Streamliners still in use, a 1941 model rounded at both ends in the sleek, aerodynamic style pioneered by their maker, the Massachusetts-based J. B. Judkins Company.

Getting There

Although only 16 miles from Boston, with bridge or tunnel traffic it'll take a good 40 minutes to drive to Salem from the Hub, and parking is free in city lots only on weekends and holidays. Alternatively, catch any train bound for Rockport or Ipswich on the MBTA commuter rail from Boston's North Station; in half an hour or less you can step off at Salem's Bridge Street depot, at the end of Washington Street on the edge of downtown. Roundtrip fare is $5; for daily schedules call (617) 222-3200 or toll-free within Massachusetts (800) 392-6100.

Information

The *Salem Visitor Guide,* listing additional restaurants, lodgings, and shops, is readily available from many attractions around town, or request a copy to be mailed from the **Salem Office of Tourism & Cultural Affairs** by calling (800) 777-6848. You can also visit their Web site at www.salemweb.com.

CAPE ANN

Cape Ann's lobster traps, buoys, and nets may seem to be more for tourist effect than indicative of the location, but since 1623 most of the settlers on this granite thumb have in fact earned their living from the ocean. In this century residents have relied on easels along with hooks for their livelihood. The nation's oldest artist colony makes its home on aptly named Rocky Neck across from downtown Gloucester, while adjacent Rockport has a fishing shack so picturesque, it is known simply as "Motif #1." All around the cape, granite ledges provide exactly the sort of setting that inspires people to quit their jobs and pick up a paintbrush or camera. Artists and summer vacationers notwithstanding, Gloucester is a working city first, with an industrial waterfront. Alas, the deadly overefficiency of its fishing fleets have added uncertainty to its future, which means tourist dollars are even more prized than before.

Although both Cape Ann and Cape Cod share an abundance of senior citizens, artists, seascapes, fish, and old architecture, the two are not as similar as one might think. Cape Ann's lack of white collar luxury-car owner retirees, coupled with Gloucester's double-digit unemployment, spares it from both the suburban condo villages and country clubs that have arisen on Cape Cod. With commensurately fewer attractions, little Cape Ann also has a more relaxed ambiance, and no amount of weekend traffic can seem to dispel its civility and good cheer. Even tiny Rockport, with its shops full of painted seascapes and salt-water taffy, can't hold a candle to the other Cape's rampant commercialism. Without a large-scale summer labor pool of students, Cape Ann's nightlife doesn't touch Cape Cod's, either. (Besides, Rockport is a dry town.) Lastly, there's the very land itself: the North Shore sits atop outcroppings of the granite spine of New England. It makes for a picuresque coastline that doesn't disappear into the ocean by the acre, as does the shifting sand of the other Cape's.

Not all of Cape Ann's industry is fish-related. Charles Fisk Organs are made here. The company is one of only two American pipe-organ builders whose wares are so good they are exported to Europe. Some of the largest pipe organs in the world are Fisk instruments.

SIGHTS

Hammond Castle

In Magnolia, on the west side of Gloucester harbor, is the Hammond Castle Museum, 80 Hesperus Ave., tel. (978) 283-2080 ($6), a grand medieval-looking stone mansion perched above the ocean, formerly home of John Hays Hammond, Jr. The main attraction is the sculpture, Renaissance art, and antiques collected by the man billed as "America's second greatest inventor." Hammond conceived hundreds of patented items, from shaving cream to electric toy trains. The setting, replete with secret passages, is ideal for late October's haunted house nights and July's Renaissance Fair. Year-round, the giant 8,200-pipe organ is put to good use in special concerts ($15-20). Open daily June-Aug., Wed.-Sun. September through Columbus Day, and weekends only Nov.-May (weather permitting). For more information regarding the castle, check out their Web site at www1.shore.net/~hammond/.

Downtown Gloucester

Except for the fact that too many of them sit idly at their piers for too long, the giant fishing

Leonard Craske's harborfront sculpture, The Fisherman, *also called* The Man at the Wheel

trawlers and storage facilities lining the waterfront of downtown Gloucester paint a clear portrait of a city too busy to pay attention to tourists. A block from the harbor, narrow, one-way Main Street largely confirms this impression—its miscellany of shops, from the chain pharmacy, family clothing stores, and career-counselling center to the Portuguese sweet breads at Virgilio's Italian Bakery, under the striped awning near the foot of the street, apparently dedicated to local needs.

Indeed, many visitors tend to shun downtown in favor of gallery-filled Rocky Neck, across the harbor in East Gloucester, or tacky shop-lined Bearskin Neck, in the heart of neighboring Rockport. But with the help of Sebastian Junger's *A Perfect Storm,* the nonfiction bestseller about a Gloucester fishing boat and crew lost in the No-Name gale of October 1991, downtown's handful of art- and gift-related shops have finally captured some overdue attention, as readers of the book (the Bookstore, at 61 Main, always has

copies on hand if you haven't read it) traipse around looking for the once-disreputable Crow's Nest, an upper Main Street bar and fishermen's hangout featured in its pages. While Junger's spellbinding story does a great job of portraying a side of Gloucester rarely seen by anyone not working in the fishing fleet, the self-guided *Gloucester Maritime Trail* walking-tour brochure is a handy, well-mapped alternate introduction for visitors, with four separate walks around "America's first seaport." The free brochure is widely available wherever local visitor information is displayed.

Perhaps the highlight of downtown is the **Cape Ann Historical Museum,** 27 Pleasant St., tel. (978) 283-0455. In addition to various historical artifacts, the museum holds works by noted artists who have lived in Gloucester at one time or another, including Winslow Homer, Milton Avery, and John Sloan. It also features the largest collection of paintings and drawings by Fitz Hugh Lane, the 19th-century romantic painter whose luminous seascapes have begun fetching millions at art auctions since the mid-1990s. Open Tues.-Saturday.

One of a mere handful of surviving two-masted Grand Banks fishing schooners—of the likes portrayed frequently by Lane—may be found berthed down past the Coast Guard station on the Harbor Loop, below the artist's granite house on the Loop's high center knoll. Now a designated National Historic Landmark, the 1926 *Adventure,* tel. (978) 281-8079, built in nearby Essex, opens its decks to visitors Thurs.-Sun. in summers (modest charge for tours). After Labor Day, the solidly built 121-foot "knockabout" moves over to its off-season berth, at the State Fish Pier, a half-mile east along the waterfront.

Although a couple of tiny parks are slotted amid the fishing fleet's piers, west of downtown toward Stage Fort Park (where the 1628 Puritan Fleet first set up operations), lies a great wide arc of greenspace. Here, benches are strategically positioned to invite contemplation of the harbor waters in all their infinite subtlety—without a foreground of rust-stained steel. Lunch from the Boulevard Ocean View restaurant, near the middle, deliciously complements the panorama. The half-mile waterfront strand along Stacy Boulevard and Western Avenue (Rt. 127) is marked in part by the patinated Fishermen's

Memorial, better known as the "Man at the Wheel," whose towering figure honors "they that go down to the sea in ships" (including, of course, the crew of the *Adventure* and thousands of her sister vessels).

Rocky Neck

Rocky Neck holds one of the nation's oldest art colonies. You'll also find plenty of galleries, shops, and several restaurants on this lovely peninsula. It's a good spot to walk around. In summer, CATA (Cape Ann Transit Authority) Water Shuttle ferries visitors to the Neck from Gloucester's Harbor Loop.

Beauport

At 75 Eastern Point Boulevard in East Gloucester, past signs reminding non-residents they don't belong here, is Beauport, a.k.a. the **Sleeper-McCann House,** tel. (978) 283-0800, a 26-room mansion now maintained by the Society for the Preservation of New England Antiquities. Built in 1907 as a summer home for a well-to-do interior designer, Henry Davis Sleeper, this oceanside extravaganza is aptly described as his "fantasy house." The structure demonstrates his design skills across every inch of its many rooms, alcoves, and towers. Frequently depicted in magazines, it epitomizes a pre-Depression age of leisure along the "Gold Coast," which still clearly exists in this neighborhood.

To reach the Eastern Point lighthouse, whose breakwater affords beautiful sunset vistas, turn in at the "Private—residents only" sign just beyond Beauport. Never mind the sign, the way is most certainly public.

Pidgeon Cove

With its exterior walls framed in ordinary materials such as wood and stone, the **Paper House,** on Pidgeon Hill Ave., seems at first to have been misnamed. Get close enough and you'll see it *is* misnamed: the 100,000 newspapers that in fact comprise those walls are so heavily shellacked it should be called the Lacquer House. Inside, the furnishings are likewise nearly all made of newspaper, a 20-year experiment in newsprint durability begun in 1922 by the uncle of the current owner, who lives next door at number 32. Paper House is located in a residential neighborhood of Pidgeon Cove. Look

for the uphill turn off Rt. 127 just north of the Yankee Clipper Inn, and then follow the hand-lettered signs. Admission is $1.50.

RECREATION

Hikes and Walks

The dramatic granite coastline of Cape Ann is best appreciated at Rockport's **Halibut Point State Park** (parking, $2). The Atlantic rolls in over the boulder-strewn beach, and the rocky promontories offer some of the North Shore's best sunset views—for which purpose many benches of Cape Ann granite (leftovers from the abandoned quarry here) have been strategically positioned to offer optimal vantage.

The park headquarters, built as a defensive lookout during WWII, is an interesting structure in its own right: a clapboard hip-roofed house was constructed around the base of the concrete observation tower to disguise the building's function. Owing to the winds off the point (which are indirectly responsible for the park's name—derived from the sailor's command to "haul about") and the swift currents just offshore, no swimming is allowed from the beach.

Roughly at the center of Cape Ann, **Dogtown Common** is a 300-acre town conservation area named for the poverty-stricken settlement of widows and children that inherited the rude dwellings of Gloucester's 17th-century fishermen. An extensive trail system—sometimes following old gravel lanes—wanders the boulder-strewn hills and blueberry-filled woodlands. There's even a boardwalk over a classic New England bog. Though only a few cellar holes remain today, old "Dogtown Square" is most notable as the upland end of the Babson Boulder Trail, where, in the 1930s, businessman Roger Babson engraved granite stones with inspirational messages for the Hooverville poor who once lived in this neck of the woods. Today, "Get a job," "Industry," "Respect Mother," and a dozen other simple exhortations and admonitions implore hikers to stop and reflect on more than the beautiful tree-covered topography. These inscribed rocks aren't all easy to find (when you see what a bumper crop of rocks the Ice Age sowed among these hills you'll know why), and, to forestall wandering aimlessly until the voracious evening mosquitoes come out, consider springing $5 for the Dogtown Advisory Committee's *Dogtown Common Trail Map*, available at several local shops and all local bookstores. Dogtown Common trailheads are found off Rt. 127, near a gravel pit north of the Babson home (now preserved as a museum), as well as at the end of Summit Avenue. But the easiest access to find is the well-signposted parking area off Cherry St. near the first Gloucester rotary on Rt. 128, just after crossing the Annisquam River (take the rotary exit marked Rt. 127 to Annisquam, immediately take the next right, and the first left is Cherry Street).

Gloucester's other major attraction for hikers is TTOR's **Ravenswood Park**, off Rt. 127 on the mainland part of town, two miles west of the Bynham Canal (the short 1640-era cut from the Annisquam River to Gloucester Harbor, which effectively turns downtown Gloucester and Rockport into an island). Offering a natural respite from the extensive oceanfront residential development endemic to much of the state's shoreline, this 500-acre hillside park is composed largely of mixed pine, oak, and hemlock hardwood forest. There's also a swamp filled with magnolia—the northernmost natural occurance of this Dixie native—and patches of great boulders dumped by retreating glaciers. Contrary to the old advice of some guidebooks, mountain biking is no longer permitted here.

Fun In and Under Water

Most of the North Shore is composed more of rock ledges and boulders suited to tide pool exploration than sandy beaches good for lay-on-your-back relaxation. But when sand does appear, it often comes up in spades, producing some of the state's best beachs. Named after the sound the sand makes underfoot, **Singing Beach,** in Manchester-by-the-Sea, is always one of those near the top of any North Shore beachgoer's list, despite its modest half-mile width and the 20-minute walk from the town's Commuter Rail station. Since non-residents must park in the station lot, driving won't get you any closer.

Much larger and more protected from heavy surf is Gloucester's **Wingaersheek Beach,** at the end of Atlantic Street. This beautiful dune-backed crescent at the mouth of the Annisquam

River doesn't come cheap, though: parking is $15 per car. When the tide is right, body surfers will find good breakers at Gloucester's **Good Harbor Beach,** on Rt. 127A facing the open Atlantic. Paid parking is available, and the beach is also served by both CATA Salt Water Trolley routes (see "Getting Around," below, for details on local public transit).

A very active community of **scuba** enthusiasts keeps the "diver down" flags flying around Cape Ann in all but the nastiest weather, 12 months of the year. Folly Cove, Cathedral Rocks, and a dozen other spots are frequented by shore divers. Scores of offshore sites, from walls of soft coral to wrecks such as Old Ironsides' sister frigate, the USS *New Hampshire,* attract boat divers. The best resource for anyone with scuba certification is **Cape Ann Divers,** on Rt. 127 in the Cape Ann Market Place between downtown Gloucester and Rockport, tel. (978) 281-8082. Full gear and wetsuit rentals and sales, summer weekend beach diving guides, and a daily, year-round dive boat (including weekly night dives) are more than enough reasons to pay them a visit. If you've got your gear in the trunk and just need a dive buddy, check out the Saturday Date-at-Eight, an ad hoc divers' rendezvous at the Burger King on northbound Rt. 128 just after Exit 19. A volunteer outreach service of the MetroWest Dive Club, the gatherings are held rain or shine at 8 a.m. year-round, and are designed in part to pair up nonmembers with divers experienced in local water and weather conditions.

Remember that below the thermocline, which separates warmer surface waters from colder subsurface waters, it's mighty chilly, often barely above 60° F in summer. Visibility is also very poor compared to diving on the world's great reefs, and nothing in these northern waters is as colorful as in the tropics. But if you've never tried cold-water diving before, it's highly recommended—especially here on Cape Ann, where it's as good as it gets in the northeast.

Island Hopping

Several islands off of Cape Ann are accessible in summer via public boat launches. The easiest to visit is small **Ten-Pound Island,** right in Gloucester Harbor. Once a Coast Guard seaplane base, the island has a modest yet picturesque lighthouse. Its proximity to Rocky Neck has made the island an inevitable subject for many Gloucester artists, most famously Winslow Homer, who even resided on Ten-Pound for a time. Catch the CATA Water Shuttle to the island from either Seven Seas Wharf (hourly on the hour) or from Solomon Jacobs Park on the Harbor Loop (hourly at half past the hour). It runs daily between late June and Labor Day, plus weekends through the end of September. One-way fare for the 15-minute ride is $1; call (978) 283-7916 for further information.

Farther south in Salem Bay lies **Misery Islands Reservation,** a pair of islands abandoned prior to the Depression after various uses as pasturage, country club, and summer cottage colony. Now maintained as public conservation land by The Trustees of Reservations, the Miseries are a favorite retreat for private boaters, with a good swimming beach, mowed paths, fragrant honeysuckle thickets, wild berries, and a freshwater pond. Various ruins mutely evoke the islands' past: a water tower's fieldstone pillars, foundations to a golf course clubhouse and barn, and the overgrown concrete floor of a WW I-era seaplane hangar. There's even rotting wooden frame timbers from an old steamship that was stripped and burned in Little Misery's shallows after being salvaged from its wreck site off the coast of Maine. On Monday and Tuesday from June-Aug., for $10 roundtrip ($8 TTOR members), a ferry shuttles visitors to the islands several times a day from Masconomo Park in Manchester-by-the-Sea. Bring all food and water, as there are no facilities of any sort on the island. Call (978) 356-4351 for further information and reservations, which are absolutely essential. Masconomo Park is on the waterfront off Beach Street, a block from the MBTA Commuter Rail platform and parking lot, and about three blocks south of Rt. 127 through downtown.

Whalewatching

Between spring and fall, humpback, northern right, sei, and fin whales come to feed in Massachusetts' offshore waters, either at Jeffrey's Ledge, east of Cape Ann, or on Stellwagen Bank, in Massachusetts Bay. Protected as a National Marine Sanctuary, Stellwagen attracts a million humans, too, who hunt the giant mammals with cameras. Cape Ann is home to four whalewatching outfits, all of which offer several daily departures (weather permitting) May-November. The four-hour trips are all similarly priced—around $23 adults, $14 kids under 16. Choices include West Gloucester's **Yankee Fleet Whale Watch,** 75 Essex Avenue (Rt. 133), tel. (800) WHALING, the only one not downtown on the waterfront; **Seven Seas Whale Watch,** on Seven Seas Wharf at the Gloucester House Restaurant, tel. (800) 238-1776; **Capt. Bill & Sons Whale Watch Cruises,** departing from the Star Fisheries pier, tel. (978) 283-6995 (or toll free within New England, 800-33-WHALE); and **Cape Ann Whale Watch,** Rose's Wharf, tel. (800) 877-5110. All have oodles of free parking.

Land and Harbor Cruises

Departing hourly from the Harbor Loop downtown off Rogers Street is **Moby Duck Tours,** (978) 281-DUCK. Riding in the company's distinctive amphibious vehicles, you get a street tour of Gloucester, which ends with a big splash—your mighty steel-hulled carriage drives right into the ocean for the finale, a tour of the inner harbor.

Summer cruises around parts of the Cape are offered by both motorboats and sailing vessels, most based out of Gloucester Harbor. **Harbour Tours,** tel. (978) 283-1979, conducts lighthouse cruises and lobstering trips aboard the *Beu,* departing daily from the Harbor Loop from mid-June to Labor Day, then weekends through Columbus Day. The fishing schooner *Thomas E. Lannon,* tel. (978) 281-6634, www.schooner.org, makes a number of two-hour sailing trips around the harbor daily as weather permits; tickets are $25 adults, $15 children 16 and under. The gaff-rigged, 65-foot boat casts off from Seven Seas Wharf. For more intimate sailing, book passage on the restored 1910 Friendship sloop *Chrissy,* tel. (978) 768-2569. Look for this trim little classic at her berth in Gloucester.

PRACTICALITIES

Accommodations

Drive around the perimeter of the Cape from Atlantic Road on the East Gloucester backshore to Folly Cove at the north end of Rockport and you'll pass most of the lodging options, from plain beachside motel blocks catering to beach-going, sun-loving families to spiffy B&B inns. Most lodgings open for summer only, shuttering up in the winter. In general, prices here are significantly less than comparable properties on Cape Cod or the Islands. Cape Ann accommodations are also a lot less expensive than those in Boston. Given the ease of catching the train to the Hub and of driving from Gloucester to anywhere north and west of Boston's Rt. 128 beltway, it's wise to seriously consider Cape Ann as a base for exploring northeastern Massachusetts.

Cape Ann Motor Inn, off Rt. 127 in Gloucester, tel. (800) 464-VIEW or (978) 281-2900, is one of the few year-round places. Kitchenettes are available for $15 extra. **Best Western Bass Rocks Ocean Inn**, on East Gloucester's backshore, tel. (800) 528-1234 or (978) 283-7600, closes late Oct.-late April. Though it's more than walking distance from any eateries, **Old Farm Inn**, 291 Granite St. (Rt. 127), tel. (800) 233-6828 or (978) 546-3237, next to Halibut Point State Park, does offer a very nice setting.

A grand place a bit removed from Rockport's center, **Seacrest Manor**, 131 Marmion Way, Rockport, tel. (978) 546-2211, includes a full breakfast with room rates. The **Yankee Clipper Inn**, 96 Granite St., north of the village in Rockport, tel. (800) 545-3699 or (978) 546-3407, is the place Katherine Anne Porter wrote her only full-length novel, *Ship of Fools*. This traditional, seasonal seaside inn, is rather grand yet by no means ostentatious.

If two yards of plain earth is all your budget can afford, check out **Cape Ann Camp Site,** tel. (978) 283-8683, on Atlantic Street beside the Jones River, a mile from Wingaersheek Beach. Tent and trailer sites run $16 for two with no facilities, $20 with electricity and water, and $24 with electricity, water, and sewer.

Food

Call it Gloucester soul food: the local specialty that's not to be missed is the solid Portuguese fare which reflects the ethnic and industrial roots of this working port. Given how hard the predominately Portuguese fishing fleet works to catch that mountain of seafood found on platters around Cape Ann, the least you can do is be polite, leave your jacket and tie in the car, and sit down for a real feast. A good place to start is at the plain-as-a-paper bag **Boulevard Ocean View,** facing Gloucester Harbor from 25 Western Ave., tel. (978) 281-2949, a stone's throw east of the Man at the Wheel sculpture. Try tasty portions of such standards as the *mariscada,* a meal-and-a-half pile of shellfish topped with a whole lobster, or tasty linguica and clams steamed in a beer broth, or plain old fish and chips. The no-frills setting is perfectly appropriate—it eliminates the need to be self-conscious about the mess made while dismantling those always-affordable crustaceans.

Gloucester's Main Street has a good range of other options, from solid Mexican to sophisticated French. Their south-of-the-border entry is **Jalapeños,** 86 Main, tel. (978) 283-8228. The extensive menu offers some 50 or more dishes, from such basics as sopas, quesadillas, enchiladas, fajitas, and flautas, to oodles of house specials such as tamales, richly sauced meats and poultry, and a half-dozen shrimp dishes ($6.75-15.25). Closed Monday. **Passports,** a block up Main St., tel. (978) 281-3680, has a more free-form international theme, with influences from the peppery Southwest to spicy Jamaica jazzing up the fresh vegetable pastas, seafood scampi, hand-pounded veal, seared duck, char-grilled filet mignon, and daily fish specials ($9.50-18.50). The narrow, artful storefront is open Mon.-Sat. for lunch till 2:30 and dinner till 9 p.m. For more cosmopolitan palates, the **Cafe Beaujolais,** a couple of doors away at 118 Main, tel. (978) 282-0058, speaks solid French, accented with carefully selected local fish and produce. The dining room's dark satiny wood and big picture windows frame elegantly presented bistro fare that is as creative as works from the local artists' colony. If the prospect of blowing your last ATM withdrawal on dinner for two is daunting, you can still enjoy the setting from the wine bar, regarded by oenophiles as one of the state's best. Open nightly, with live jazz most Tuesdays. Finally, if it's just a healthful lunch, fruit-filled smoothie, or scrumptious pastry you crave, check out the **Glass Sail Boat Cafe,** on Duncan St. around the corner from the 170 block of Main, tel. (978) 283-7830. Besides the pizzas and sandwiches, vegetarian entrees, and sweet stuff, this place doubles as a gourmet grocery, bulk spice shop, and laid-back coffeeshop. Open daily to 4 p.m. for cafe meals, or to 5-6 p.m. for drinks, desserts, and pay-by-the-pound salad bar.

In addition to its many sweet shops and the obligatory seafood restaurants, Rockport's specialties include several casual breakfast/lunch cafes, such as the thoroughly contemporary **The Greenery,** tel. (978) 546-9593, (breakfast on weekends and holidays only); chummy **Flav's Red Skiff,** tel. (978) 546-7647; or the more Californian **Flying Saucer Cafe,** tel. (978) 546-5130. All are within the two blocks south of Bearskin Neck. The Greenery also serves dinners with a New American spin, dressing up its grilled seafood and generous pasta with good fresh produce and bright flavors borrowed from beyond New England. It's open mid-April through mid-November. Of the three, only Flav's is open seven days a week year-round (Thanksgiving and Christmas excepted).

Getting There

Carless visitors bound for the Cape from Boston and intermediate points may rely on the MBTA **Commuter Rail** Rockport line for frequent daily departures from North Station, Lynn, Salem, Beverly, and Manchester. Of the three rail platforms in the Cape Ann area—in West Gloucester, Gloucester, and Rockport—only the last is well-connected with CATA buses for local travel (see below), although the Gloucester station is only four blocks from downtown. The roundtrip fare from Boston is $7.50-8, depending on where you get off; for recorded departures, dial the MBTA info line at (617) 222-3200, or (800) 392-6100 within Massachusetts.

Come summer, Cape Ann is also accessible by boat. **A. C. Cruise Lines,** tel. (617) 261-6633, offers a summer passenger ferry from Boston to Gloucester. The boat sails from Boston at 10 a.m. Tues.-Sun. late June through Labor Day (weekends only late May-June), arriving at 12:30 p.m. at The Studio Restaurant on Rocky Neck. Return trips depart at 3 p.m. A.C.'s pier in Boston is on Northern Avenue beyond the World Trade Center; limited free parking available. Roundtrip tickets are $18, one-way is $12, and bikes are an extra dollar each way. Anyone contemplating a true circle tour of eastern Massachusetts including Cape Cod should check out the

Gloucester-Provincetown Boat Express, tel. (978) 283-5110, operated by Cape Ann Whale Watch between late June and early September. It sails daily except Saturday at 9 a.m. from Rose's Wharf in Gloucester, returning from Provincetown at 3:30 p.m.; the fare is $22 one-way, $35 roundtrip. Reservations are required.

Getting Around

The Cape Ann Transit Authority (CATA), tel. (978) 283-7916, is your ticket to hands-free travel around the Cape, from summer boat launch service to year-round commuter buses. One-way fares range 50 cents-$1. Schedules are available from all information booths and aboard all buses. Of principal interest to visitors are the **Water Shuttle,** the **Rockport Park 'n' Ride** shuttle, and the two **Salt Water Trolley** routes. Trolley #1 runs Mon.-Sat. from downtown Gloucester's Harbor Loop to Rocky Neck and the East Gloucester beaches, to Essex and the Shipbuilding Museum, and to Magnolia, including Hammond Castle. Since the trolley only completes the loops of this route two or three times per service day, pick up a schedule so as not to miss your return ride. Trolley #2 shuttles daily between downtown Gloucester and Rockport via Rocky Neck, Good Harbor Beach, and the Rockport Commuter Rail station. Both trolleys operate only June-Labor Day and then weekends till the end of September, but you can still travel between Gloucester and Rockport Mon.-Sat. year-round on CATA's Red Line bus. Free parking, just a few steps away from marked bus stops, is available on Gloucester's waterfront at St. Peter Square and Rocky Neck.

From late June through September, the Water Shuttle links Gloucester's waterfront with Rocky Neck and Ten-Pound Island. Catch the boats from either the Harbor Loop, hourly on the half hour, or from Seven Seas Wharf, hourly at the top of the hour. Before Labor Day the shuttle runs daily 10 a.m.-6 p.m., then weekends only through the end of September. The Rockport Park 'n Ride bus operates on weekends and holidays from early June through mid-October. Buses pick up from the two free parking lots, which are clearly signposted for all incoming traffic. Weekdays, parking in Rockport is usually available on T-Wharf, parallel to Bearskin Neck.

Information, Maps, and Restrooms

Maps, additional accommodations listings, and other assorted brochures are available locally from Gloucester's seasonal **Visitors Welcoming Center,** tel. (800) 649-6839, at Stage Fort Park off Rt.127 on the west side of the harbor, or year-round from the **Cape Ann Chamber of Commerce,** tel. (800) 321-0133, on Gloucester's industrial waterfront at 33 Commercial St., opposite St. Peter Square. The chamber also maintains a Web site at www.cape-ann.com/cacc.

Both Stage Fort Park and the chamber have public restrooms. So do the Fitz Hugh Lane House in the Harbor Loop, Rose's Wharf, and Gloucester's City Hall, on Warren St. around the corner from the Cape Ann Historical Association. In Rockport public restrooms are available on T-Wharf next to the Fire Dept.

THE NORTH SHORE TO THE MERRIMACK RIVER

The granite bedrock ledges that dominate coastal New England from Cape Ann to northern Maine are briefly softened by the 17,000-acre Great Marsh. The marsh is protected in part by the huge Plum Island barrier beach at the mouth of the Merrimack River. While the area's centuries-old working relationship with the sea is celebrated in a couple of small but fascinating museums, the most obvious historical artifacts are the coastal towns themselves, with their 17th- and 18th-century homes, tall church steeples, and ancient burial grounds. The trophy homes found along the Gold Coast to the south are also evident here—predominantly along the inland stretch of Route 1A through Hamilton (the center of Massachusetts' horsey set). Along the shore, such houses are eclipsed by picturesque salt meadows gilded in afternoon light, antique stores brimming with the jetsam of the past, and long barrier dunes covered in summer with sunbathers from all around the region.

Hamilton's sprawling estate houses are mostly glimpsed through trees or at the ends of the broad pastures that open up on either side of the road. Telltale wooden fences often replace the usual old drystone walls in the surrounding pastures. With its frequent woodlots and occasional wetlands, the rolling landscape—the local variant on Kentucky's bluegrass horse farms—was a favorite of equestrian General George S. Patton (whose wife came from a socially prominent North Shore family of five-star Yankees). The area is still home to the Myopia Polo Club, tel. 978-468-7956, founded in 1888, whose tournaments inspire images of English royals having a romp on their ponies. Myopia's energetic games may be witnessed for a modest fee on Sunday afternoons from Memorial Day through early October. Don't forget to bring your own tailgate picnic.

Getting There

While a car provides the quickest introduction to this part of the North Shore, the curvaceous roads, easy availability of refreshment stops, and great variety of less-trafficked back roads offer great cycling, too. Until the Ipswich Line of the MBTA Commuter Rail, tel. (617) 222-3600, is extended to Newburyport, at the mouth of the Merrimack, in 1999, taking a train is recommended only for visitors who rent bikes in Boston and obtain the necessary permit to bring them aboard ($5 from the Pass Office on the underground concourse at Downtown Crossing T station, open Mon.-Fri. 8:30-4:15). Roundtrip fare tops out at $7, to the end of the line (a 52-minute ride from Boston's North Station); for daily schedules, call (800) 392-6100 or (617) 222-3200. Since space for bikes is limited on the trains, and the North Shore is such a popular destination for city cyclists, reservations are highly recommended.

ESSEX

At first glance, Essex seems to consist of little more than a couple of small clusters of shops and eateries on either side of the Rt. 133 causeway over the Essex River estuary. But Essex isn't only the antiques center of the North Shore and the birthplace of the fried clam, but also a major launching place for tidal marsh recreation.

ATMs and modern gas stations notwithstanding, there's also a fair share of historic buildings to provide a picturesque backdrop to the working boatyards along the riverfront. Eagle-eyed drivers may also notice the discreet signposts to oft-overlooked public conservation lands amid the salt marsh—the Stavros Reservation, north of the town center, and the Allyn-Cox Reservation, to the south—where visitors will usually encounter a blissful windblown privacy interrupted only by the splash of a duck, the whistle of a songbird, or the quiet plunk of a great blue heron stalking among the reeds.

Sights
Wooden boats have been built in Essex for over 300 years. In fact, in the age of sail, when ship construction required carpenters rather than steelworkers, nearly four percent of all vessels flying the American flag were built right here on the Essex River. Such a meager proportion might not seem worth boasting about today—with the Microsofts and Coca-Colas of the world routinely garnering huge "market shares" for their products—but, given the myriad American boatbuilders of the day, even one or two percent would represent a dramatic concentration of industry. At its peak, in the mid-1800s, little Essex's 15 boatyards launched scores of ships each year—predominantly two-masted fishing schooners for local use in the fisheries of the Grand Banks, off the coast of Nova Scotia and Newfoundland. Remnants of those glory days are preserved at the **Essex Shipbuilding Museum,** 28 Main St. (Rt. 133) next to the White Elephant antique shop, tel. (978) 768-7541. If the displays, models, and videos pique your interest in the art and science of wooden boatbuilding enough to try your own hand at it, you'll find plenty of ships' plans and how-to books in the small gift shop.

Stroll up Main to the museum-owned **Story Shipyard,** next to the Periwinkles restaurant, where the overhaul or construction of a wooden vessel is typically under way six to nine months of the year. Lectures by maritime historians, readings, concerts, and other special events are regularly held in the big garage-like Waterline Center, at the back of the yard, near the hulking remains of the 1927 *Evelina M. Goulart,* one of only five historic Essex schooners still extant. Open year-round, Thurs.-Mon.; admission is $3.

Anyone the least bit interested in indigenous decorative arts won't want to miss **Cogswell's Grant,** tel. (978) 462-2634, at the end of Spring Street near the center of Essex. Now maintained for the public by SPNEA, this big, red 18th-century farm was the summer home to Nina Fletcher and Bertram K. Little, whose collection of Americana is considered the largest and most significant in the nation. Evidence of the unique style and sweeping inventiveness of early American craftsmen, from Grandma Moses-style primitives to Shaker furnishings, whirligigs to duck decoys, fills every nook and cranny.

River Recreation
One way to experience nearby estuarine salt marshes and wildlife is with **Essex River Cruises,** based out of the Essex Marina, 35 Dodge St., tel. (800) 748-3706. As the small *Essex River Queen* motors around Essex Bay, your guide will provide narration that touches upon the town's historical past as a shipbuilding center and explains the wildlife flying or swimming nearby. Weather premitting, the 90-minute cruises are offered up to six times a day between May and October; tickets are $14 adults, $7 children, with discounts for the first trip of the day.

For those more inclined to combine an estuary tour with a physical workout, consider joining **Essex River Basin Adventures** (ERBA) for an introduction to sea kayaking. While you'll still see a zillion more sailors than paddlers in Massachusetts' coastal waters, this outfitter is patiently making enthusiastic converts of people who sample one of their repertoire of guided paddling trips. Offerings include the easygoing, three-hour Gilligan Tour, sunset paddles complete with clambake dinners, day-long offshore excursions, and moonlight trips with coffee and dessert. Prices start at $35 per person, for the bare-bones introductory tours, and go up to $75 for a full day with lunch. Trips run May-October. ERBA's tour office shares the Story Shipyard with the Shipbuilding Museum; call (978) 768-ERBA or (800) KAYAK-04 for additional information about what to bring and wear.

To Eat Clams or Not to Eat Clams
Essex's claim to culinary fame rests on the capable shoulders of Lawrence "Tubby" Woodman, who, in 1916, invented the fried clam.

Route 133 north and south of the Rt. 22 junction has several places that honor this landmark achievement, including the original **Woodman's,** tel. (978) 768-6451, whose order-here-and-we'll-call-your-number simplicity belies the worshipful praise bestowed by nearly all who speak of it. Such a classic creation can't be tampered with merely to suit modern health concerns, so the tons of tasty little mollusks churned out here are still fried in lard. Some iconoclasts believe nearby **Farnham's,** south on Rt. 133, has a superior fried clam, but it's best to judge for yourself: try 'em all. Woodman's stays open year-round; its smaller competitor is open from the first Friday in March through early November, and then Thurs.-Sun. till the week after Thanksgiving. Both establishments also fry other seafood items such as fish and squid, and Farnham's ladles up a nice silken chowder well-laced with juicy little clams.

If you'd as soon eat beef tallow as fried clams, a couple of alternatives exist. One, the **Conomo Cafe,** tel. (978) 768-7750, is almost directly across Rt. 133 from Woodman's. It may look as if it was once a seafood-in-the-rough sort of place, but with views across the salt marshes to the Essex River estuary, diners in jackets and skirts, and imaginative, seasonally adjusted cuisine attractively presented and attentively served, the only thing that's rough now is trying to leave room for dessert ($14-21). Closed Mondays. Along similar lines is **Jan's Encore,** at the Hamilton-Essex town line, on Rt. 22, tel. (978) 768-0000, although here the gourmet dining is complemented by a pub that firmly caters to the steak, ribs, and beer crowd. High-quality fresh fish and produce; influences from the bold-flavored cuisines of Asia, the Caribbean, and Louisiana; and a fine array of desserts ensure steady crowds throughout the year ($7.95-16.95). Lunch and dinner are served daily.

IPSWICH

The center of Ipswich comprises little more than a block or two of shops and a hellish, no-Stop-sign intersection called Five Corners, where the north end of the main street meets the foot of a steep hill. The view from the banks of the Ipswich River, which curls through town below the backsides of downtown shops and several old stone bridges, is worth seeking out, even when the water is so low that garbage catches up against the gravelly banks. It's worth strolling around town, too, to see the numerous First Period dwellings. Nearly every structure in the landmarked Historic District is identified by original owner and date of construction courtesy of the Historic Society, so you can easily brush up on your 17th- and 18th-century architectural vernacular.

The essence of Ipswich, though, like its inland neighbors, is outdoors, at its beaches and conservation lands. You won't find a surplus of eateries or lodgings here—look to Newburyport for the widest selection of both north of Cape Ann—but for long beachcombing walks or bird-watching in salt marshes, this town can't be beat.

Castle Hill and Crane Beach
Properly speaking, this Argilla Road property of The Trustees of Reservations is the **Richard T. Crane, Jr. Memorial Reservation,** tel. (978) 356-4351, but it's more widely and descriptively known as Castle Hill. Overlooking the ocean, Castle Hill is crowned by a dramatic 59-room English mansion known as **The Great House,** built in the 1920s by Chicago plumbing tycoon Richard Crane. For $5 per car, visitors can come admire the grand allée rolling to the sea, Italian gardens, bowling green, and wooded paths, all of which make the mansion a prime picnic destination and a great place for young kids to romp around. Weekly house tours are also featured on Tuesday afternoons (additional $5 for adults, $3 for children). The shoreline at the distant end of the cascading green lawns below the house is a small part of **Crane Beach,** a four-mile-long sandy stretch that handily accommodates large summer crowds undaunted by the summertime $9-15 parking fee (high price prevails on weekends; it's half price for TTOR members and for everyone after 3 p.m.). Given the long, gradual slope of the beach, body-surfers will have to look elsewhere for big waves. Remember, too, that late July and early August are the months of the biting greenhead fly; slather on the appropriate repellents.

On the backside of the peninsular barrier beach, across the brackish mouth of the Castle Neck River, is a series of islands belonging to the Crane Wildlife Refuge. The nearest and most prominent is **Hog Island,** whose photogenic fields and spectacular ocean view were featured in the 1996 film *The Crucible,* as the location of the tragically bewitched Salem village. The Trustees of Reservations sponsors daily guided trips to the island May-Oct., including a hayride and a visit to the 18th-century Choate House. Departures from the estate are scheduled in the morning, afternoon, and before sunset; the trip lasts 90 minutes. Tickets are $12, with discounts for kids and TTOR members.

Food

For victuals in Ipswich, there are a couple of Formica and paper-napkin pizza joints, a pub by the Choate Bridge (Rt. 133), and a small cafe under the pub, partially overlooking the river. The small craft brewers of **Ipswich Ale** are located at 25 Hayward St., near the Commuter Rail station, south of the center of town along the main drag, tel. (978) 356-3329. While too tiny to offer tours or a tasting room, they at least sell refillable "growlers." Between June and September, the **White Farms Ice Cream** on Rt. 133 near the Rowley town line, tel. (978) 356-2633, serves up giant portions of all your frozen dairy favorites, all made on the premises in dozens of flavor combinations and a range of fat levels. A side lunchroom offers choices from hummus to hot dogs for anyone in need of a hearty foundation for those desserts.

NEWBURYPORT AND VICINITY

While its sister ports of Salem and Boston hit the jackpot in overseas trade, Newburyport contented itself with interstate shipping up and down the Atlantic seaboard. When the city's aged waterfront buildings started becoming casualties of urban renewal, the citizenry rallied to save the historic center. As a measure of preservationist success, note how almost every business in the old brick-front waterfront district uses carved wooden signage—even the gas station.

Sights

Discreetly signposted off Rt. 1A, just seven-tenths of a mile south of the town line in neighboring Newbury, is the **Spencer-Pierce-Little Farm,** 5 Little's Lane, tel. (978) 462-2634. Surrounded by fields that have been under cultivation since 1635, this baronial mansion is atypical for its day, built mostly of stone in an era and locale where wood prevailed. Improved and enlarged by its occupants over time, the house now offers visitors a look back at domestic life throughout the generations, as well as glimpses, quite literally, into the very walls of the place. A portion of the long-distance Bay Circuit trail cuts across the property, providing birdwatchers easy access to nearby salt marshes. Open Thurs.-Sun. only, June-Sept.; $4.

Whalewatching

If you've yet to succumb to the temptation of paying a visit to the 50-ton giants of the deep supping on bait fish in offshore waters, you have another chance to take in this inspiring sight with the aid of **Newburyport Whale Watch,** 54 Merrimac St. at Hilton's dock (turn at the sign reading Passenger Boats & Fishing), tel. (800) 848-1111. Boats depart daily May-Sept., five days a week in October, and usually on weekends in April, as well. Rates are $23 adults, $16 for kids 16 and under. Allow around half a day, and remember that it's about 15 degrees cooler out where the whales are than on land.

Recreation

The Newburyport area's top outdoor attraction and most beautiful swimming is undoubtedly on **Plum Island,** particularly in the portion protected by the **Parker River National Wildlife Refuge,** tel. (978) 465-5753. While the refuge headquarters are on the end that has been wholly taken over by beachfront housing, pass through the refuge gates south of the island's only bridge from Rt. 1A and you'll discover over 4,600 acres of nearly pristine barrier beach backed by dunes, tidal pools, and salt marsh. Deer, fox, and hundreds of bird species—even yellow-bellied sapsuckers—reward the patient observer and contribute to the island's reputation as one of the nation's top birdwatching sites. At the southern end is a drumlin, a glacial deposit of clay and rock typically found along rougher shores. The drumlin's soils and elevation produce good conditions for the kind of woodland not normally found this close to salt water. The entrance fee is $5 per car, or $2 for

SEEING GREEN: THE BAY CIRCUIT

In the late 1920s, advocates of setting aside undeveloped land for the enjoyment of Boston's burgeoning population created an ambitious plan for a great semicircular park outside the city—a great green ring looping from north of Cape Ann clear to the South Shore. Events—including the Crash of 1929, world war, urban population loss to the suburbs, and construction of the Rt. 128 beltway—intervened and spoiled any chance that this "Bay Circuit" could ever be implemented as originally conceived. But the idea was never scrapped.

Finally, in 1984, a precedent-setting state bond, floated to finance conservation projects, revived the Bay Circuit's prospects. Bond money leveraged land acquisition and led to an overall plan, but economic recession and top-down intransigence on environmental initiatives (financing the purchase of open space was derided as "elitist" by the state's most recent Republican acting governor) has put the Bay Circuit in the position of being heavily outgunned by politically influential real estate developers. Still, the 200-mile trail is slowly being stitched together through the tireless efforts of grassroots proponents, town conservation agencies, and the Bay Circuit Alliance—the trail's dedicated cheerleader.

When completed, after the year 2000, the Bay Circuit will encircle Boston from Plum Island—at the mouth of the Merrimack River—in the north to the South Shore's Kingston Bay. Some 80 parks, forests, and sanctuaries and 50 towns will be connected by paths across rural, residential, and institutional property, along river banks, on paved rail trails, and even on roads. The result is intended less as an eastern Massachusetts equivalent of the Appalachian Trail than as an English-style cross-country ramble through towns and farms, meadows and woods, over hills and across highways, along gravel lanes and over wetland boardwalks. Sights are wonderfully varied: hidden forest parcels, Thoreau's famous Walden Pond, sleepy villages with welcome little stores selling cold drinks, downtown Lowell and its historic textile mills.

A couple of primitive campsites exist, but use requires prior notification of local police and fire departments. As a result, the Bay Circuit is best suited to day hikes. Each spring, a portion of the route is also chosen for a 50-mile foot race; for a registration packet contact the Bay Circuit Alliance, tel. (978) 470-1982, or e-mail baycircuit@juno.com.

Bay Circuit trailheads are identified with medallions of the Bay Circuit logo, but the route is mostly marked by white blazes roughly the size of a dollar bill (where the route follows a road shoulder or street for a ways, look for these on telephone poles). In places where the trail crosses a school campus or other private property, maps are usually posted at either end of the unmarked section directing walkers to where blazes resume.

The northern third of the trail contains the largest contiguous piece—the almost 60-mile **Rowley-Andover** portion. About eight miles follow road shoulders, and the rest runs through forests, old farmland, and occasional utility rights-of-way. The eastern end begins at Rowley's Prospect Hill Park, off Prospect Rd., the first left turn north of the White Farms Ice Cream stand in Ipswich. The western end is at Andover's Deer Jump Reservation, on the banks of the Merrimack River near the city of Lowell. In between are access points with parking at Harold Parker State Forest in North Andover; Boy Scout Park on Topsfield Rd. in Boxford; and Willowdale State Forest in Ipswich. **Wayne's Store,** the post office/general store/pizza parlor that constitutes rural Boxford's "downtown," is also a good intermediate trailhead, in part because the store sells copies of The Bay Circuit Guide to Walks in and Around Boxford, $10) with parking.

The drawback to the trail's being built by local entities is the lack of any dedicated end-to-end trail guide; instead, each participating town has a map or guide to its portion. In some cases, these are no more than hand-sketched maps available at a particular town hall, but a few communities have produced full-blown pocket guides ($5-10) to their segments, with detailed trail descriptions and fold-out maps. A preliminary visit to www.serve.com.baycircuit will provide a list of these locally produced resources, as well as links to a few rough on-line maps and trail descriptions.

By far the best overall description is contained in the Appalachian Mountain Club's AMC Massachusetts and Rhode Island Trail Guide, although the circuit isn't included in any of this handy volume's maps. Drop in on **Moor & Mountain,** 3 Railroad St. in Andover, tel. (978) 475-3665, for a sample of the most complete guide and map inventory for the entire route.

pedestrians or bicyclists. This is one of the last remaining barrier beach-salt marsh ecosystems in the northeast; to protect it, only 300 cars are allowed in at any one time, and even fewer between April and July when endangered nesting shorebirds prompt beach closures. If you're summarily turned back at the gate—a strong likelihood on any decently sunny day—you can still get a taste of all but the swimming at Massachusetts Audubon's **Joppa Flats Wildlife Sanctuary,** on the Plum Island Turnpike, back on the Rt. 1A side of the bridge, tel. (978) 462-9998. The small property includes a boardwalk into the salt marsh, plus an observation tower and bird blinds, which make it easier to see some of the large number of waterfowl that require the wetlands for their survival. As always, the on-site gift shop has all the books and field guides you need to identify those feathered inhabitants. Joppa Flats is also the northern terminus of the Bay Circuit trail, which presently runs for five miles (about half on road shoulders) to the Rowley town line before requiring a lift around the region's last missing link.

To see Plum Island from the water, consider spending a weekend learning to **sea kayak** with Zoar Outdoor, a seasoned western Massachusetts outfit with a full range of whitewhater rafting, canoeing, and kayaking expeditions, skills clinics, and tutorials. These two-day sessions, combining introductory lessons with plenty of ocean touring to develop paddling skills, are offered about half a dozen times over the summer for about $200, lodging not included. Call (800) 532-7483 for further information and reservations.

On the western side of Newburyport, isolated from the rest of town by I-95, is **Maudslay State Park,** tel. (978) 465-7223, a wonderful oasis for bikers, hikers, anglers, horseback riders, or cross-country skiers. Once part of a grand 19th-century estate—some of whose buildings and foundations still remain—this park protects a long stretch of undeveloped pine-covered acreage with beautiful views along the banks of the Merrimack River. In addition to the curious remains of the original owner's formal Italianate gardens and hedgerows, the property includes one of the state's largest stands of mountain laurel (access to which is closed to the public between November 1 and March 31). Free and open daily, the park is readily found by following signs from Rt. 113. Remember mosquito repellent in summer.

Food

Newburyport has a plethora of decent restaurants within easy walking distance of downtown Market Square, from the atmospheric Fowles Luncheonette (17 State St.) and the upscale yet affordable Scandia Restaurant (25 State) to casual Cajun up the block and above-average Asian around the corner. Right smack *on* Market Square, in the renovated firehouse arts center, is a good choice for casual Italian fare: **Ciro's Ristorante & Pizzeria,** tel. (978) 463-3335. Despite all the exposed brick, the decor leans closer to that of your local pizza parlor than to linen and sconces, but the decor hardly matters. Serving unusual pizzas, well-stuffed calzones, fresh tortellini, decent table wine, and more, Ciro's gives you good portions of good food at very reasonable prices. In summer, the outside tables are some of the most valuable real estate in town. Beepers summon you when you're table's ready, allowing you to wander while you wait. Open daily for lunch and dinner, to midnight on weekends.

For a table with a less pedestrian-filled view—and decent seafood, too—try the casual **Captain's Quarters,** 54 Merrimac St., tel. (978) 462-3397, overlooking the broad mouth of the Merrimack from beside Hilton's charter fishing and whalewatch boat dock. Forget fancy presentations and trendy vegetable accompaniments: the cooks here let good, fresh seafood speak for itself. Open daily for lunch and dinner, and Tues.-Sun. for breakfast.

MERRIMACK VALLEY

LAWRENCE

The mill town of Lawrence has undergone such major urban decay that it may be the only New England town to have experienced black flight as well as white. Site of the 1912 Bread and Roses Strike, the city that once wove "the world's worsteds" is not a destination for anyone seeking a tranquil New England townscape.

However, it is not without its points of pride—in addition to its industrial prowess. As an adolescent, Robert Frost moved here with his family and stayed until the end of his teens (and eventually married his Lawrence high school sweetheart). A jumbled stone fountain on the edge of the Common commemorates the former poet laureate's years here, its design inspired by his early poem "A Brook Through the City." The prolific, conspicuous warnings not to play on the rocks—i.e., Police Take Notice—are indicative of what has happened to the city since both Frost and the mills left.

And never let it be said that Lawrence has lost its ability to make a difference in the world. In 1987, Lawrence's own *Eagle-Tribune* (which,

in truth—like its readership—fled long ago to the suburbs) broke the story of Willie Horton, the Massachusetts murder convict who broke into a house while participating in a work-release program and tortured a Maryland couple unspeakably. For its coverage, the *Eagle-Tribune* won the Pulitzer Prize in 1988. But most people know the story today as the basis for George Bush's infamous (and highly successful) campaign commercials, which torpedoed Massachusetts' then-governor Michael Dukakis's presidential aspirations.

Lawrence Heritage State Park

Lawrence Heritage State Park, 1 Jackson St., tel. (978) 794-1655, is open daily 9 a.m.-4 p.m. Of the several cities on the banks of the Merrimack River that grew up around the early textile industry, Lawrence is remembered most for its labor history, particularly the seminal Bread and Roses Strike of 1912. This urban historical park illustrates the lives of the city's workers and immigrants, supplemented by guided interpretive tours past the massive old brick mills that bookend the downtown. A visitor's center is located in a restored 1840s boarding house.

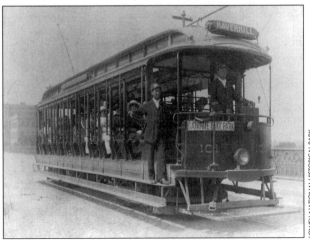

electric Merrimack
Valley interurban
trolley from Lowell to
Haverhill and Canobie
Lake Park (New
Hampshire)

LOWELL NATIONAL HISTORICAL PARK

Methuen Memorial Music Hall

Sandwiched between Lawrence and New Hampshire (talk about Scylla and Charybdis!), the small town of Methuen (m'-THOO-in) is famous among New England organists for the instrument housed in its Methuen Memorial Music Hall, on Broadway (Rt. 28), tel. (978) 685-0693, which was built specifically for the "Great Organ" within. Like town hall and several other civic buildings, the music hall was a gift of Edward Searles, a local Horatio Alger success story. Born in poverty on a local farm, Searles grew up to become a very successful interior designer for a major Boston furniture maker, a career that took him to California to work for the wife of San Francisco railroad tycoon Mark Hopkins. After she became a widow, they scandalized 19th-century Nob Hill society by marrying and returning east, where her money went to work building things that invariably have his name on them.

Organ concerts are performed every Wednesday at 8 p.m. beginning the first Wednesday in June and running through the end of September; there's also a Phantom of the Opera special on Halloween. A schedule is available on the Internet homepage, www.cybercom.net/~tneorg, of *The Northeast Organist,* a bimonthly magazine/concert calendar.

Food

Despite its legacy of arson, riots, and car theft, Lawrence does have a few eateries worth visiting, but don't expect portabello or radicchio. The two principal institutions in town are **Bishop's,** on Hampshire at Lowell, occupying most of a block between the police station, the downtown post office, and the fire department, and **Larry's Cedar Crest,** a few blocks away. About a block north of the main downtown drag (Essex St.), Bishop's is a long-standing family-owned place serving Middle Eastern and American fare. It features expensive, competent cooking and presentation and belly dancers regularly, and it's plush enough to draw wealthy surburbanites into the city—absolutely the only sit-down place in Lawrence that can make that claim. Everyone in town knows it and can give directions.

Larry's Cedar Crest is the only holdout from Lawrence's once-vibrant Italian community. There's a cheap lunch-counter-style side area in

addition to the main dining room. This is where Jackie O. used to take John-John when she'd visit him at Phillips Academy. The staff nearly all speak Spanish now, but it's still the best place in town to get "veal on a heel," local parlance for the breaded veal cutlet on a sub roll smothered in red sauce (served all over town). Nothing can beat Larry's for a taste of Lawrence atmosphere. It's on Broadway a couple of blocks north of Essex Street—you can't miss the big blocky facade and heavy wood doors.

Authentic and cheap Lebanese is available at **Mounir's** on South Broadway, over the river from downtown, and **Elsie's,** a block farther south past the Dunkin' Donuts, catercorner to the big Southern Beer and Wine store. Both are real neighborhood places, casual and friendly and doing a brisk take-out business. Some Syrian grocers remain around town, with deli counters that dish up great standards such as stuffed grape leaves, hummus, and more, but none are within walking distance of the Common.

For another true taste of local history, head to the bridge over the Great Stone Dam and step into **Lawton's Hot Dogs,** on the Broadway Street side. This Lawrence institution dates back to the Depression or earlier (it's in photos of the 1936 floods). Some say the grease hasn't been changed since then, either. The hot dogs are battered and then fried, or something equally delicious.

Several choices also lie around the classical mass of City Hall (recognizable for its nine-foot tall golden eagle perched over the south side of Campagnone Common), a couple blocks northwest of the Heritage State Park visitor center. **Ye Loft and Ladle,** 337 Essex St., tel. (978) 687-3933, is a burgers-and-beer joint frequented by lawyers from the District Court. For a taste of the city's dominant Latino culture, consider the nearby **Cafe Azteca,** 180 Common St., by the corner of Jackson, tel. (978) 689-7393. Behind the plain brick facade, it's a pleasant place in a Formica and plastic way—and not unreasonably priced. The food is anglicized enough that it doesn't intimidate the town's non-Spanish-speaking population, yet good enough to hint at the delicious possibilities of Mexican campesino fare. If you prefer cultural immersion along with your meal, try **Garcia Candido,** 291 Essex, tel. (978) 725-8077, which doesn't need any crossover dishes to broaden its appeal—it's already as popular among the Latino citizenry as any place in town. (Happily, it's also open daily 8 a.m.-11 p.m.)

ANDOVER

A prosperous bedroom community conveniently located beside the northern junction of Interstates 93 and 495, Andover is perhaps most famous as the home of Phillips Andover Academy—the oldest prep school in the nation. Though by no means unattractive, the historic, small-town New England grace Andover once had has been severely compromised by heavy traffic along Rt. 28—Main St.—and by peripheral malls, which killed off the sort of mom-and-pop markets and hardware stores that once inhabited downtown, leaving only banks and upscale boutiques.

Sights
Phillips Andover Academy has a near monopoly on sterling cultural attractions in town with its free **Addison Gallery of American Art,** tel. (978) 749-4015. Though the handicap entrance is off its rear sculpture garden, on Chapel Ave., opposite the Andover Inn, the main entrance is under a big classical portico overlooking the broad campus lawn lining Rt. 28. Historic ship models and diverse collections of 18th- through 20th-century American paintings, sculpture, and prints are among the notable holdings of this excellent museum, but possibly the most amazing feature is the photo collection. From Eadweard Muybridge and Matthew Brady to Theodore Roszak and Dawoud Bey, from 19th-century landscapes and Civil War photos to Man Ray's rayograms and Harold "Doc" Edgerton's stroboscopic freezing of time, it's an en-

cyclopedia of the medium. Open Tues.-Sat. 10 a.m.-5 p.m., Sunday 2:30-5 p.m. Closed holidays and all of August.

Though the general weight of Massachusetts' museums might lead to the conclusion that nothing of significance occurred before the *Mayflower* landed, exhibits at the Academy's **Robert S. Peabody Museum for Archaeology,** tel. (978) 749-4490, demonstrate that North America actually had a pre-Pilgrim history, too. In addition to both its permanent collection and a selection of artifacts on loan to it, this small museum, at the corner of Phillips and Main Streets (across Rt. 28 from the Addison Gallery), also hosts regular guest lectures by anthropologists and archaeologists of national stature. Only open noon to 5 p.m. weekdays, 10 a.m. to 1 p.m. on Saturdays, mornings by appointment.

Camping
The only state campground in the area is in neighboring North Andover in the **Harold Parker State Forest,** 1951 Turnpike Rd., signposted from Rt. 114. Its 130 campsites are available mid-April through mid-Oct. for $6, including full amenities (water, flush toilets, hot showers). The place fills up on weekends so plan to arrive early if you want a spot, or make advance reservations by calling (978) 686-3391. Camp sites are in pine woods planted in the 1930s by the Civilian Conservation Corps, mature enough to have a very high understory with next to no shrubbery, but rolling terrain and wide spacing keeps the number of neighbors' camp lanterns at a minimum. All those pine needles make for soft ground cover, and with no hookups, tents outnumber RVs, so generator noise isn't such a disturbance here, either. Besides hiking trails and bridle paths, the forest has a popular swimming pond.

Accommodations
This gift of a grateful Phillips Academy alumnus, the **Andover Inn,** on Chapel Ave., tel. (800) 242-5903, still draws upon the business of visiting parents—for whom it was built earlier this century—but many other guests have simply come to appreciate its singular grace and old-world charm as an alternative to the executive conference hotels along nearby I-93 and I-495. Expensive.

Alternatively, for the best value in a standard motel, head up I-93 one exit north of I-495 to the Andover flagship of the small, family-owned **Tage Inn** chain, tel. (800) 322-TAGE or (978) 685-6200, with rooms and amenities comparable to those offered by up-market nationally known hotels—but at a better price. Inexpensive.

Food

Most of Andover's best dining is clustered around the town center, at the intersection of Main (Rt. 28), Central, and Elm Streets. **Vincenzo's,** 12 Main, tel. (978) 475-7337, puts a creative twist on typical Italian menu items—walnut pumpkin filling for their tortellini, for example, or a ragout of wild mushrooms, and, of course, a fresh catch of the day (perhaps an herb-crusted mahi-mahi with artichokes). **Cafe Lafortuna,** 16 Post Office Ave. (the side street near Breugger's Bagels), tel. (978) 474-8788, of-

fers a small but upscale menu—seared tenderloin in a port wine sauce, veal-filled tortellini in a gorgonzola sauce . . . you get the picture—as well as the option of combining the day's specials into a three-course prix fixe dinner. The house bread is so good that customers have been known to request a loaf when they leave. Open Wed.-Fri. for lunch, Mon.-Sat. for dinner, till 9 (later on weekends).

During the week, the dining room of the distinguished old **Andover Inn,** tel. (978) 475-5903, is primarily a haven for refined Continental cuisine like Dover sole and shrimp scampi. But come Sunday, the influence of the Dutch innkeeper surfaces in the renowned Rijsttafel, an Indonesian-influenced buffet whose combination of sweet and savory flavors is quite different from the Asian cuisines with which most Americans are familiar. Just remember to come on the early side—the buffet ends at 8:30 p.m.

LOWELL NATIONAL HISTORICAL PARK

METROWEST

From the Native American powwow site in the forests below the New Hampshire line to western Norfolk County's strawberry farms, Metro-West roughly encompasses a fertile crescent of often affluent suburbs within I-495, Boston's outer beltway. Like the rest of eastern Massachusetts, rich pickings await even the most casual student of U.S. history: cornerstones of both the American and Industrial Revolutions (Lexington's Battle Green, Lowell's old textile mills) and landmarks of the nation's first literary age, from Walden Pond to the Wayside Inn.

As its name implies, this region is by no means all picturesque countryside, mossy old manses, and emigrant-rich old manufacturing towns on the mend. High-tech office parks and bedroom communities have sprung up around selected interstate exit ramps. These "Edge Cities" have their own constellations of townhome subdivisions and malls amid the long-abandoned and reforested colonial farmsteads. Yet even suburbia takes on a historical dimension here, since natural barriers to Boston's physical growth have prompted flight to the city's surrounding uplands since before the Civil War. (Boston had three rail lines ferrying commuters from its incipient western suburbs before London laid a single railroad tie.)

While the late 20th-century spread of four-lane arterials, acres of shopping, and countless residential cul-de-sacs has made many MetroWest towns indistinguishable from suburbs across the country, a few have attempted to preserve their 19th-century cores with ordinances against homogenous, auto-oriented commercial strips, and several have made great strides in preserving open space. As a result the region is able to frame historical attractions with a modest share of scenic ones, from lightly trafficked backroads well-suited for leisure cycling to state parks and wildlife sanctuaries appropriate for an afternoon hike. While most of these shouldn't distract nature-lovers on a tight schedule from heading for the dramatic waterfalls, rocky summits, and woodland trails of central and western Massachusetts, flatwater kayakers and canoeists will find such scenic MetroWest waterways as the Sudbury and Concord Rivers definitely worth visiting.

As in Greater Boston itself, public transit largely targets downtown commuters, so visiting several MetroWest attractions in succession without returning to Boston in between absolutely requires a car or serious touring cycle. Anyone staying in the Hub can hop a train to most of the major sights.

LOWELL

Over a century ago when Lowell was the envy of weavers worldwide, its factories and canals earned flattering comparisons to Venice, and became a compulsory stop on any foreign dignitary's American tour. A marvel of the Industrial Age, Lowell became one of its casualties, too, when the industry it long monopolized fled south. Today, the vast 19th-century mills and their working class neighborhoods have many interesting tales to tell now that they've been renovated into a city-sized museum, which highlights the nation's transformation into an industrialized society. And it's more than just a nuts-and-bolts story of technical innovation or shrewd capital management: the lives of the early "mill girls," the changes wrought by massive immi-

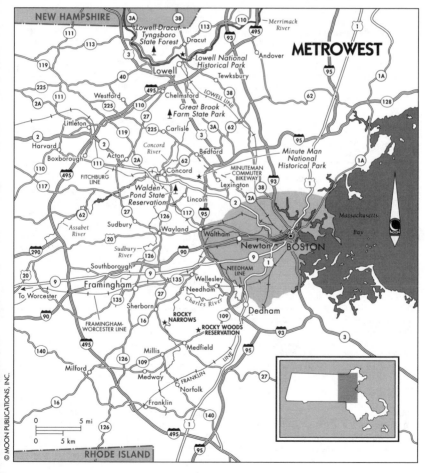

© MOON PUBLICATIONS, INC.

METROWEST FESTIVALS AND EVENTS

APRIL

On April's second Saturday, **Thoreau's Portage,** tel. (978) 934-0030, showcases a daredevil spirit in a set of professional canoe and kayak races over the cascades of the Concord River in Lowell.

The same weekend is also usually when Lowell's Southeast Asian community celebrates **Cambodian New Year,** with music, dance, food, and fun, at JFK Plaza next to City Hall. Call the Lowell Office of Cultural Affairs, (978) 441-3800, for details.

Midmonth, on or near Rama's birthday, a one-day round-the-clock performance of the **Ramayana**—the Indian epic that may be 2,000 years older than Homer's *Odyssey*—occurs at the Sri Lakshmi Temple in Ashland, at 117 Waverly St. (Rt. 135), very near the Framingham town line. The 17th-century South Indian composer Tyagaraja's "Five Jewels" is featured, too. Call (508) 881-5775 after February for the specific date.

JULY

Every Friday and Saturday throughout this month and August, enjoy great **live music** at Lowell's

Boarding House Park, downtown on French Street (nominal admission). Call the National Historical Park, (978) 970-5000, or the Lowell Office of Cultural Affairs, 441-3800, for schedule.

Set aside the last weekend of the month for the **Lowell Folk Festival,** a three-day extravaganza of music, food, and crafts.

OCTOBER

During the first weekend of the month, the **Pig 'n' Pepper Bar-B-Q Festival,** tel. (978) 369-0366, puts spice in the lives of thousands of happy carnivores in an appointed giant field off Rt. 110 on the Westford-Littleton town line, near I-495 Exit 31. Besides a dozen or so restaurant vendors, animal rides, balloon rides, and a bunch of famous live bands, this educational fund-raiser (admission) features a state championship barbecue contest sanctioned by the Kansas City Bar-B-Q Society, which connossieurs will recognize as the grand poobahs of pulled pork and ribs. Don't miss dairy-fresh desserts from Kimball's Ice Cream across the street, either.

gration, and the struggles for decent working conditions are given as much attention as the engineering and financial wizards whose names are on street signs and building facades.

Lowell may seem to be an old Rust Belt city that's rather well preserved but otherwise unremarkable. Look closely, though: the galleries and condos occupying those 19th-century factories, the Cambodian and Laotian influence in store windows and on local menus, *two* professional minor league sports teams, and the extensive calendar of local cultural offerings hint at how much more there is to this place then first meets the eye. While the city lacks the critical mass of quaintness conducive to B&Bs, national hotel chains are amply represented along nearby I-495. Hostelers and other car-free travelers needn't miss out, either, as Lowell is a reasonably cheap and easy commute from Boston.

History

The city straddles a sharp bend in the Merrimack River between Pawtucket Falls and the confluence with the diminutive Concord River, an

area that was a vital salmon fishery and trading site for the area's indigenous people thousands of years before either Christ or Columbus. When Samuel de Champlain sailed up the Merrimack in 1605, the two sides of the falls were occupied by a pair of Algonquian-speaking tribes in northern New England's Pennacook confederation—the Pawtucket and Wamesit tribes. The frequent presence of the Pennacook's supreme leader, Passaconaway, suggests the falls were a seat of government. Ravished by European plague and lethal raids by Mohawk and Abenaki warriors from the west and north, the confederation was in no position to resist to the English who soon came in Champlain's wake. By 1644 Passaconaway had signed a covenant with Boston's colonial government pledging fealty, unleashing a rash of laws regarding dress, behavior, religion, and just about everything else that could possibly distinguish Native Americans from Bible-thumping Puritans. After 16 more years of losing land to court-favored colonists, the once-great sachem and shaman, rumored to be over 100 years old, abdicated his power to his eldest son Wannalancit with warnings to followers that quarreling with the white man would bring certain destruction. The advice was misdirected: the Pennacooks were soon so decimated in a retaliatory raid against the Mohawks that they couldn't have joined King

Philip's War even if they'd wanted to. A village of Christianized Indians was established briefly after the war, but the encroachment of colonial farmers forced Wannalancit to sell the land and move most of his band north well before the end of the 1600s.

JACK KEROUAC, LOWELL'S NATIVE SON

San Francisco may have named a street for him, and Greenwich Village wouldn't have been the same without him, but Jack Kerouac always considered himself a Lowell boy. Patron saint of the Beat Generation—whose name he coined one long-talking night in 1948—and poster boy of bohemian excess, Jean-Louis Kirouac was born March 12, 1922, to a French-Canadian family living in the Centralville (say "Cennerville" if asking directions) part of town.

"Petit Jean" grew up to play sports at Lowell High well enough to win a football scholarship to prep school and then Columbia University in New York, where he met Allen Ginsberg, William S. Burroughs, John Clellon Holmes, and other writers of the postwar underground. Most of his next 25 years were spent outside Massachusetts—but as a measure of Kerouac's regard for Lowell, consider that of his 20-some books, five are semi-autobiographical novels based on growing up in "Galloway": *The Town and the City, Maggie Cassidy, Doctor Sax, Vanity of Duluoz,* and *Vision of Gerard.*

Kerouac died (of an abdominal hemorrhage, after watching an episode of "The Galloping Gourmet") in St. Petersburg, Florida. But his wake was held and he was buried in Lowell. His flat gravestone lies among those of his third wife Stella Sampas's family in Edson Cemetery, on Gorham St. (Rt. 3A), a couple of miles south of downtown (look for the altar-like pile of offerings beside Lincoln Ave. between 7th and 8th Sts., or follow the tracks if there's snow).

At **Kerouac Commemorative Park,** on Bridge St. downtown, excerpts from several of the author's more prominent works are inscribed on granite monoliths. When the golden late afternoon sun burnishes the red-brick backdrop of the Massachusetts Mills, this is one of Lowell's nicer urban oases.

Lowellians have had their share of ambivalence toward Kerouac, and some—with personal memories of his self-destructive lifestyle—question pay-

ing lofty tribute to such a role model. But if you're around during the first weekend of October, check out the **Lowell Celebrates Kerouac!** festival, with photo exhibits, walking tours, literary symposia, poetry readings, music, and much more—and judge for yourself what epithets or eulogies are worthy of the guy. To receive a festival calendar of events (which actually begin midweek), call the Greater Merrimack Convention & Visitors Bureau, (978) 459-6150, or write to Lowell Celebrates Kerouac!, P.O. Box 1111, Lowell MA 01853, or e-mail mhemenway@drc.com, and ask to be added to the mailing list.

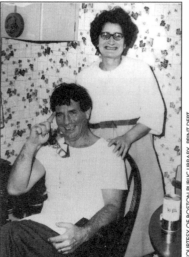

Jack Kerouac, 44, and his third wife, Stella Sampas, 48, at home after their wedding, in Hyannis, in November 1966

COURTESY OF BOSTON PUBLIC LIBRARY, PRINT DEPT.

East Chelmsford, as the township was then known, tilled the soil for nearly a century. As population outgrew arable land, residents turned to cottage industry and trade. East Chelmsford's transformation in particular was spurred by transportation improvements begun in the 1790s to provide access to New Hampshire timber. The 1.5-mile Pawtucket Canal was financed by shipbuilders at the Merrimack's mouth to circumvent the town's hazardous falls, and the 27-mile Middlesex Canal was built largely to bring logs from the upper Merrimack directly to Boston. In 1821 some Boston-area industrialists looked at these canals and saw horsepower waiting to be harnessed and a shipping lane for both raw materials *and* finished products. Within a year the Boston Associates began building a company town named after their founder, Francis Cabot Lowell. Though he himself didn't live long enough to enjoy the rewards, this Boston cloth merchant's successful development of a power loom (based on a mechanical design memorized during tours of English mills) was the final step to automating the whole textile manufacturing process under one roof, from cotton bale to bolts of finished cloth. Implementing the "Lowell system" on the Charles River at Waltham, just west of Boston, proved so hugely profitable that Lowell's partners quickly sought a place suitable for a massive expansion. They found it by the bend in the Merrimack at Pawtucket Falls; within a generation "Spindle City" was the second most populous community in Massachusetts, its 10 giant mill complexes employing over 10,000 workers. Lowell remained the nation's leading textile producer until almost 1880, when it was finally surpassed by Fall River in southeastern Massachusetts.

By the end of the 19th century, the success of the mills stopped trickling down to the workers. Massive immigration permitted wages to drop as competition among mills intensified, and both racism and the all-important need to uphold satisfactory profit margins forestalled any concern about worsening health and living standards. At various times throughout the 1800s, Lowell's mill workers went on strike for shorter work hours or to protest pay reductions, but each time some pool of poor newcomers were effectively used as strikebreakers. Cooperation across ethnic lines was finally acheived during the 1912 general strike, begun downstream in Lawrence, but victory was not sweet. By the time the Great Depression hit, those among Lowell's cotton capitalists who were deaf to innovation went bankrupt. The rest took their profits and ran to the South, which actively courted manufacturers with cheaper labor, lower taxes, and a hands-off attitude toward working conditions. With mills quiet and a fifth of its population gone in search of work elsewhere, Lowell eked by, down but never quite demoralized. A couple of short-lived reprieves during WW II and the early '80s heyday of computer maker Wang Labs helped preserve the immense facade of its former industrial glory, now recognized as a major physical, cultural, and historical asset to the city's future. The city's economy has even returned to a semblance of prosperity—*without* becoming dependent on a single major industry or employer.

LOWELL NATIONAL HISTORICAL PARK

Begin a visit to Lowell at the National Historical Park's Market Mills **Visitor Center,** on Market St., tel. (978) 970-5000, across the canal and trolley tracks from the neon mule at Haffner's "It Kicks" gas station. With free introductory slide show, helpful and well-informed park rangers, ticket desk for canal boat tours, self-guided walking tour brochures (ask about the Canalway and Riverwalk), local cultural events calendars, and an excellent bookstore/giftshop that even carries Kerouac, it's the best place to orient yourself to what's happening and where. Free ranger-guided walking tours are always worthwhile, but if at all possible call ahead and reserve a space aboard one of the boat trips through the city's historic waterways. Narrated tours offered almost daily between early June and mid-October range from the 75-minute trips along Pawtucket Canal to a wonderful series of two-hour excursions between the canals and the Merrimack, which may include helping test water quality, exploring the water-diverting gatehouses, or simply enjoying a sunset cruise. All are $4 ($7 with combined admission to the Boott Cotton Mills Museum). Due to enormous popularity advanced reservations are essential.

THE LOWELL FOLK FESTIVAL

The largest free folk festival in the nation takes hold of Lowell on the final weekend (Fri.-Sun.) of July. A score of music and dance performers appear on half a dozen stages set up all over downtown, from Boarding House Park on French St. and the JFK Plaza beside City Hall to smaller open spaces in and around Market Mills, on Market Street.

The event is truly international in scope. Past festivals have included gospel, zydeco, bluegrass, klezmer, tap dancing, Celtic button accordion players, Swedish fiddlers, Mexican-American mariachis, traditional West African kora music, ancient Vietnamese imperial court music, and Yup'ik (Eskimo) music and dance.

You can also count on being tempted by tons of ethnic food, home-made food, fast food, and more food. An outdoor concourse of craft demonstrations includes masters of traditional arts—Puerto Rican gourd carving, German *scheren-schnitt* paper cutting, and Russian lacquer painting, for example—and local occupational artisans in such fields as bookbinding, pipe organ restoration, brick carving, plaster molding, and locksmithing.

Despite the fact that the festival enjoys an attendance of hundreds of thousands of people, you won't feel like you're stuck at some huge stadium concert: the large number of venues and the grand scale of Lowell's mills promote a big, happy, block-party ambiance. Boston visitors can follow a Saturday morning parade from Faneuil Hall to North Station to catch the special noontime Festival Train up to Lowell (or hop any of the other hourly Commuter Rail connections to the Spindle City for only $7 roundtrip). Call festival co-sponsor Lowell National Historical Park, (978) 970-5000, for schedule or information, or visit www.nps.gov/lowe and follow the "Special Events" links to the latest Folk Festival homepage.

One could easily spend all day visiting the park's holdings, which are scattered around downtown—the map from the Visitor Center shows where—along with a variety of public artworks celebrating the city's heritage. Most exhibits are free, and share the Visitor Center's schedule of staying open daily year-round. An impressive working example of the water-powered flywheels that drove a whole company spins mightily amid a whiplashing of leather belts and pulleys at the Suffolk Mills, several blocks away on the banks of the Northern Canal. The human side to the lost factories, the original Yankee farm daughters who labored in them, and Lowell's many successive waves of immigrant workers are the subjects of exhibits at the **Mogan Cultural Center,** 40 French St., tel. (978) 934-4998, appropriately ensconced within a reconstructed 1830s boardinghouse dating back to the Boott Mills' paternalistic early days. With its octagonal clock tower and gilded yarn shuttle weathervane rising behind Boarding House Park, the 19th-century Boott complex is one of the most handsome of the sprawling brick edifices around town. Inside, the **Boott Cotton Mills Museum,** 400 John St. ($4), features the dramatic sight and sound of 88 vintage power looms clanging away like a mad mechanical version of the Anvil Chorus, along with interactive exhibits on the Industrial Revolution and the labor movement's rocky road to unionization. Take the elevator up to the **Tsongas Industrial History Center,** whose regular hour-long family programs ($3 per person over age 5) give young inventors and hydro-engineers props and guidance in practicing their professions, or ride to the 5th floor to visit the **New England Folklife Center,** tel. (978) 970-5193, showcasing traditional folk arts through both changing exhibits and an ethnic foodways program in their demonstration kitchen (Mon.-Fri., $1.50). Be sure to inquire for their free *Cambodian Neighborhood Walking Tour* brochure, too, if you want to get beneath the city's working-class veneer and witness how Lowell's latest—and largest—immigrant group has established a community.

While the National Historical Park's constituent parts are within walking distance of one another, from March-Nov. you can hop aboard the park's trolleys—meticulous reproductions of vintage 1901 and 1912 electric street railway cars used in eastern Massachusetts—for a step-saving free shuttle between the Visitor Center and the Boott Mills.

OTHER LOWELL ATTRACTIONS

The art and history of quilting, a classic New England domestic industry, are showcased at the **New England Quilt Museum,** 18 Shattuck St., tel. (978) 452-4207, a block from the Market Mills Visitor Center. Both antique and contemporary quilts are displayed, with galleries devoted to both the museum's permanent collection and changing exhibits highlighting the work of modern practitioners (would you believe photorealism in fabric?). Open Tues.-Sun. from May-Nov. and Tues.-Sat. in winter ($4). For something totally unrelated to mills, textiles, or waterpower check out the local branch of the multi-state **New England Sports Museum** across the street in the former 1886 W. A. Mack stovemaking shop, behind an eye-catching statue of Portuguese soccer star Eusebio. Offering interactive and seasonal exhibits on professional and amateur sports, the museum is open Tues.-Sun. till 5 p.m. year-round; admission is $4 adults, $2 kids, or $10 for a family of up to five.

George Washington Whistler was in charge of the locomotive and railroad works for the city's mills when his son, James McNeill Whistler, was born here in 1834. Although baby James never returned to Lowell after the family moved abroad (his father was hired to build a railroad for the Russian czar), the **Whistler House Museum of Art** on Worthen St. near towering City Hall, tel. (978) 452-7641, embraces Lowell's "native son" with examples of the expatriate artist's lesser-known prints and memorabilia. The collection also includes works by Whistler contemporaries, as well as artists with modern ties to Lowell. Open Wed.-Sun. from March-Dec. (closed Jan.-Feb.); admission $3.

A very long block south of the Whistler home is the **American Textile History Museum,** 491 Dutton St., tel. (978) 441-0400, occupying the enormous premises of the former Kitson Machine Shop. Don't worry about needing a map: there's only one way to circulate through the nearly 100 displays covering the history and diversity of American-made woven cloth and period clothing up through the mid-1900s. The museum, which relocated here in 1997, also houses one of the nation's largest and possibly most advanced labs for textile conservation. Given the modern installation and expert staff, it's a mystery why display labels aren't more informative; some even allow readers to infer that satin and damask are types of material like cotton and wool, rather than correctly identifying them as styles of weave. Nevertheless, the collection of fabrics, costumes, and tools is unparalleled, and walking through the display of spinning wheels is alone almost worth the $5 admission (Tues.-Sun.). Among the museum store's many gifts, books, and other textile-related wares are replicas of exhibit pieces, including some produced with the working machinery on display. A pleasant little cafe mercifully saves footsore visitors from having to walk back downtown to slake thirst or sate hunger.

SPORTS AND RECREATION

Bicycling

Visitors equipped with their own bikes should consider joining a two-hour ranger-guided ride around Lowell, as part of the National Historical Park's **Spindle City Bike Tours.** In spring and fall rides are scheduled each Saturday morning at 10 a.m.; come summer they begin on Thursday at 6 p.m., neatly avoiding the dehydrating afternoon heat. All tours are free, and each is different: one may venture into the city's 19th-century park-like cemetery, another may hit local Kerouac-related landmarks. Others visit historic city neighborhoods with a good anecdote or two to add to the Lowell story. Group size is limited, so register in advance at the Market Mills Visitor Center or by calling (978) 970-5000. Helmets required. As an alternative to urban cycling, consider coasting along the **Vandenberg Esplanade** on the north shore of the Merrimack upstream of Pawtucket Dam's rickety-looking wooden topboards. The two-and-a-half-mile riverfront park is a nice place to stroll or picnic, too, particularly in summer when the Heritage Farm Ice Cream stand is open, on Pawtucket Boulevard at the corner of Delaware Avenue. It's also one of Lowell's contributions to the Merrimack River Trail, which when complete will enable hikers to walk the length of the river from Canada to the Atlantic.

Whitewater Rafting

Given how much effort has been applied over the centuries to taming local rivers to suit the needs of mill owners, intuition suggests the only river recreation around short of going over a dam in a barrel would be flatwater boating. But in fact, the Concord River sports Class III-IV rapids during the spring runoff, earning favorable comparisons to New England's most famous whitewater, the Kennebec River up in Maine. The surrounding scenery isn't nearly as wild (here you even end passing through a centuries-old lock chamber, a thrill of a different sort) and the length of the runs aren't nearly as long, but for an adrenaline-boosting kick that's closer than the Kennebec at a fraction of the price, don't dismiss rafting on the Concord between April and early June. The **Lowell Parks & Conservation Trust** is the nonprofit sponsor, while rafts and guides are provided by Wilderness Plus, an outfitter whose commercial trips are found on a number of better-known rivers throughout New England. Since the intent is to heighten awareness about local water resources, prices are kept at a break-even $61, including everything but bathing suit, soakable sneakers, and dry towel. For further information or reservations, call toll-free (888) 375-1115.

Parks and Sanctuaries

Two nearby state parks also invite exploration by mountain bike or foot: **Lowell/Dracut/Tyngsboro State Forest,** straddling the northwest corner of Lowell and its two neighbors about three miles west of downtown, and **Great Brook Farm State Park,** about eight miles due south in the town of Carlisle, signposted off Rt. 4. The state forest, located on Trotting Park Rd. off Varnum Ave., offers six miles of trails for hiking and biking, plus a swimming beach on modest-sized Althea Lake. Most of its 1,150 acres were once included within the boundaries of the 17th-century "praying Indian" village of Wamesit, established by a compact with English colonists. Native American powwows are still held in it; the Greater Lowell Indian Cultural Association, P.O. Box 1181, Lowell, MA 01852, tel. (603) 878-1368, can provide information on these.

Great Brook Farm, tel. (978) 369-6312, is both state park and working farm, with farm buildings, farm animals, and farm stand selling fresh sweet corn in summer and cranberries from the county's last working cranberry bog, among other things. Miles of paths trace through the property's meadows, wetlands, and woods, looping around a canoe-able pond, low hills laced with wild berries, and over brooks both great and small. Seasonally there's an ice cream stand at the farm, but the product it sells is a commercial brand from southeastern Massachusetts, not homemade; for a more authentic farm-fresh summer treat visit the summertime **Kimball Farm Ice Cream** stand on Rt. 225 about 2.5 miles south of park headquarters and east of Carlisle center.

If a day in Lowell has whet your appetite for fascinating relics of our nation's industrial past, make tracks about 10 miles west to the town of Westford, at I-495 Exit 32. Hidden there in the **Russell Bird Sanctuary** is a beautifully well-preserved 1872 stone arch bridge over duckweed-covered Stony Brook, once part of the Red Line, a.k.a. the Nashua, Acton, and Boston Railroad. The mortarless 60-foot arch is one of the finest of its type remaining in the region, and despite being favored by adolescent smokers, hasn't been seriously defaced. Though the sanctuary is totally unmarked, the bridge trailhead is posted with a small sign on a tree in a pine grove on Cold Spring Rd. at the corner of Forge Village Road. (Turn north toward Westford at the bottom of the interstate ramp, then turn left a mile later at the corner of Main St. by the town common; Forge Village Rd. is the continuation of Main, and Cold Spring is just over a mile.) The bridge is unmistakable—it's half a mile from the trailhead and the town's huge buried reservoir. From the main path atop the abandoned old railroad bed, additional trails run around the sanctuary's wetlands; one even has strategically placed benches for spying on the many migrating waterfowl that frequent the place.

Minor League Pro Sports

Lowell proudly landed a pair of professional sports franchises recently, and has built a pair of spanking-new stadia to put them in. On the baseball front are the **Lowell Spinners,** a short-season, single-A Boston Red Sox farm team, whose mid-June to early October home games are played in the Edward LeLacheur Stadium at the foot of the Aiken Street bridge over the Merrimack. General admission tickets are always a bargain, just a few dollars apiece. Call (978) 459-1702 for this season's schedule, or visit www.lowellspinners.com.

Hockey fans can look forward to some energetic action in the Tsongas Arena, a couple blocks downstream behind the post office on Father Morissette Boulevard, when the American Hockey League's **Lock Monsters** take to the ice, October to mid-April. Call (978) 458-PUCK for a calendar of home games and box office information.

PRACTICALITIES

Accommodations

Both **Sheraton Inn**, tel. (800) 876-4586 or (978) 452-1200, smack downtown by the Pawtucket Canal's lower locks, and **Courtyards by Marriott**, tel. (800) 321-2211 or (978) 458-7575, on Industrial Ave. East, off the Lowell Connector between downtown and I-495, have footholds in Lowell. Both are moderate to expensive. A brief jot west along the interstate at Exit 34 in neighboring Chelmsford are a **Best Western Inn**, tel. (800) 446-4656 or (978) 256-7511, and a **Radisson Heritage Hotel**, tel. (800) 333-3333 or (978) 256-0800. The Best Western's rates are moderate to expensive; the Radisson, expensive. Within two miles east on I-495 in adjacent Tewksbury is a **Susse Chalet Hotel** at Exit 39, tel. (800) 5-CHALET or (978) 640-0700. Rates are moderate. Slightly farther afield on I-93 one exit north of I-495 is the Andover flagship of the small, family-owned **Tage Inn** chain, tel. (800) 322-TAGE or (978) 685-6200, with rooms and amenities comparable to an up-market nationally known hotel, but a better price. Inexpensive.

Solo budget travelers or Hostelling International members will find the nearest HI affiliate about 15 miles southwest of Lowell in the rural town of Harvard. Take I-495's Exit 29B to Rt. 2 west, immediately getting off at the next exit, Littleton/Boxborough. Make a series of three lefts—from the end of the ramp onto Taylor St., then Porter Rd., and finally at the stop sign, Whitcomb Ave.—and proceed another 1.5 miles until the large white clapboard home of **Friendly Crossways Conference Center** appears amid the pastoral scene (tel. 978-456-3649 be-

fore 9 p.m., e-mail friendly@ma.ultranet.com, or visit their homepage at www.ultranet.com/~friendly). Hostelling International members pay $12-17 per person (dormitory beds or semiprivate room), nonmembers $15-20. Private rooms for couples are available for $25, as well as family rooms for $40-50.

Food

One Lowell dining landmark is the **Southeast Asian Restaurant,** 343 Market St., tel. (978) 452-3182. A place that offers Laotian, Thai, Cambodian, Vietnamese, and Burmese food is rather rare even before considering that the owner is Italian, but this Vietnam vet and his Laotian-born wife know of what they cook. Whether or not the large Southeast Asian community in Lowell helps keep them on their toes, the net result is a casual place with great city-caliber ethnic dining at a small-town price ($5.95-11.95). The specialty of the **Công Ly Restaurant,** 124 Merrimack Street, tel. (978) 970-0740, is Vietnamese beef soup, or *pho.* It's very good and extra large, just as the menu says, and cheap—a complete meal for under $6. Besides the soup, the menu is full of inexpensive exotica: clay pot combos with seafood or poultry, spicy salads such as "tiger's tear" or "jumping squid," big bowls of vermicelli with grilled meats, and plenty of vegetarian treats. Lunch buffet and dinner Mon.-Sat. till 10 p.m.

Besides Southeast Asian places Lowell is enviably endowed with several gems of the dining car era, such as the 1930s **Club Diner** on Dutton St. nearly opposite the Market Mills Visitor Center, or the equally antique **Paradise Diner** on Bridge St. next to the Boott Cotton Mills Museum (open for breakfast and lunch only). But best of all is the **Four Sisters' Owl Diner,** a classic Worcester Lunch Car Company model on Appleton St. between the Commuter Rail station and downtown. Square meals don't get much better than this, which is why you may have to wait in line, particularly for Sunday brunch. Such a well maintained setting deserves huge Western omelettes, perfectly browned hash, silken turkey gravies, and decent coffee; happily, the masters of the short order grill deliver on all counts.

An abundance of history hasn't restrained the city from acquiring such modern accoutrements as the brewpub restaurant, the mulitplex, or the video arcade. In fact, someone has efficiently wrapped all of these under one giant old mill roof, throwing in a billiard parlor, sports bar, and indoor miniature golf course for good measure. It's **The Brewery Exchange,** 199-201 Cabot St., tel. (978) 937-2690, off Father Morissette Blvd. in the great limbo of parking lots and under-occupied buildings over the Northern Canal from downtown. Take a tour of the Mill City Brewing Company, sampling their wares in their taproom or at the **Brewhouse Cafe & Grille,** whose menu ranges from wild mushroom fettucine and salmon en croute to the more dependable burgers, beefs, scampi, and chicken parmesan, all reasonably priced ($5.95-19.95). Wildly popular, with frequent live music and lots of dating rituals, the Exchange is open daily.

For fancier fare, try the French-influenced cuisine of intimate little **La Boniche,** tel. (978) 458-9473, in the beautifully renovated old Bon Marché Building at 143 Merrimack St., an Art Nouveau landmark shared with Barnes & Noble. It's not cheap, but don't you deserve something special now and then? The appetizers are generous enough that almost any two will make a meal, especially if you wisely choose to leave room for dessert (entrees $15-21). Open Tues.-Sat. for lunch and dinner.

Getting There
Lowell's only passenger trains are those of the MBTA **Commuter Rail** from Boston, offering daily service from North Station ($7 roundtrip). Travel time is about 45 minutes; for a recorded schedule, call (617) 222-3200 (or toll-free 800-392-6100) and work through the touch-tone prompts. Lowell is also a stop on the Boston-to-Burlington, VT interstate buses of **Vermont Transit Lines,** tel. (800) 451-3292, departing Boston's Logan Airport and South Station several times a day. From New York City, **Peter Pan Bus Lines,** tel. (800) 343-9999, makes two trips a day to Lowell via Hartford, CT and Worcester. Whichever option you choose, you'll arrive at the Gallagher Transportation Terminal on Thorndike Street opposite the South Common. Though barely six-tenths of a mile walk from the Market Mills Visitor Center, Thorndike's particularly pedestrian-unfriendly interchange with Routes 3A and 110 will make it seem much farther; alternatively, catch the regular public shuttle bus to downtown (Mon.-Sat. only, and no evening service; 30 cents).

CRADLE OF REVOLUTION

On April 19, 1775, a British expedition to confiscate a suspected cache of colonial arms touched off the American Revolution. The magnitude of what that day wrought indelibly marks this upland region west of Boston, so much so that it's hard to speak of Lexington without Concord, or to think of either without recalling bits of America's collective national legend about bold minutemen, daring midnight rides, and those stiff-necked Redcoats put to flight by American marksmanship. A passel of historical sights help place the spark and its kindling in a wider context; see also the Booklist at the end of this guide for background readings about the Revolution and its origins.

Concord's contribution to the region also includes America's first native literature, transcendentalism, and that feisty iconoclast Henry David Thoreau. If you stayed awake through high school English class you'll recognize the other men and women such as Emerson and Alcott who gathered in this little town, a generation of writers whose homes now comprise the other half of Concord's tourist landmarks.

Minute Man National Historical Park
You can retrace the most eventful leg of the British troops' day in the country "alarmed and assembling," from Lexington to Concord and back again, by visiting some of the homes and taverns whose occupants played a role that April morning, by walking or cycling along nearly six miles of the "Battle Road" itself, by surveying key skirmish sites on foot, or by studying the exhibits in the two visitor centers at either end of the Minute Man National Historical Park. Descriptions of the highlights are divvied up across town lines, just as they are on the ground, from Lexington's Battle Green to Concord's North Bridge. For best results orient your-

self in advance to the lay of the land and the Revolution's chronology at the **Minute Man Visitor Center,** off Rt. 2A just west of Rt. 128/I-95 Exit 30.

The third Monday in April is observed as **Patriots Day,** a state holiday. April 18th and 19th's precipitous events, from the lanterns being hung in Old North Church in Boston to the confrontations between armed colonial militia and British Redcoats, are commemorated with lots of costumed finery, musket volleys, speeches, and hot beverages to ward away the predawn chill of the earliest events. (Lexington scrupulously observes the timing of the actual skirmish on their town green at daybreak; plan to arrive well before 5:30 a.m. if you hope to find both parking and a good position near the front lines of the large, sleepy-eyed crowd.) Concord has tended to be a stickler about reenacting their North Bridge battle at 9:30 a.m. on the 19th, if it falls during the weekend, rather than on the observed Monday holiday, so don't assume everything is coordinated around the same day. Schedules for the weekend's events are usually known to rangers at the Park Service visitor centers by the first week of April; tel. (978) 369-6993, ext. 6.

The respective centers of Lexington and Concord are accessible via public transit from Boston, but Boston-based visitors to the Minute Man park should take particular interest in the seasonal shuttle scheduled to serve Lexington's Battle Green and all the major Battle Road sights from the end of the MBTA Red Line in North Cambridge. Beginning on Patriots Day weekend, the narrated trolley will depart the Alewife Station busway every 20 minutes Sat.-Sun. only from mid-April through June, and then daily July to mid-October. The inexpensive fare grants riders a day's worth of reboarding privileges. Call (781) 861-1210 for more information. Cyclists, meanwhile, enjoy nearly direct access to nearly all the attractions of the national historical park—and then some—via the Minuteman Commuter Bikeway from North Cambridge. It runs right beside Lexington's small visitor center opposite the Battle Green, and connects to the Battle Road's paved 5.5-mile park-like path via Hartwell Ave. and Wood St., on the west side of the bikeway's bridge over Rt. 128.

LEXINGTON

Now a largely residential suburb on Boston's western edge, Lexington was the original destination of Paul Revere's famous ride, since two important leaders of the colonial independence movement happened to be in the parsonage a short distance from the town common. The town has preserved everything even remotely associated with the morning that royal British infantry inflicted the day's first casualties on the town's militia, killing two outright and six more as they fled. The common—now smaller, sown with a broad lawn, and renamed the Battle Green—is still watched over by Buckman Tavern, where Revere and fellow courier William Dawes took a thirst-quenching break. The Hancock-Clarke House, in which Sam Adams and John Hancock slept until Revere awakened them, also still stands. And if Lexington's sturdy mansions and tall church spires make gunfire between militia and Redcoats difficult to imagine, step into the chamber of commerce visitor center for a little prompting from their small diorama of the scene.

Museum of Our National Heritage

At the hilly junction of Rt. 2A and Rt. 225 east of downtown Lexington sits the northern headquarters of the Scottish Rite of Freemasonry. Adjoining the Mason's large, modern inner sanctum is a set of galleries featuring a permanent exhibit on Lexington's attitude toward the prospects of a rebellion against Mother England, plus changing exhibits on American history and contemporary culture. Past examples include exhibitions of Navajo weaving, fly-fishing, the history of the diner, the Vietnam Veterans' Memorial, Shakers—in short, a pleasantly eclectic variety, always well curated, and often accompanied by equally diverse lecture and live music programs. Open daily, the museum itself is always free, although special events may not be, tel. (781) 861-9638.

Around the Battle Green

Until cherishing American myths became such a major civic preoccupation, the Battle Green was the plain old village common. H. H. Kitson's statue, *The Minuteman,* now prominently

awaiting orders at a Patriots Day reenactment in Concord

marks the site where advancing British Regulars fired upon the three or four score armed militiamen gathered under Capt. Parker by Paul Revere's call to alarm. The **Buckman Tavern,** in which militia members debated how to greet the approaching threat, stands across the street from the musket-toting bronze figure. It's open to visitors daily from Patriots Day through Halloween, one of three historic houses whose role in April's drama is recounted by Lexington Historical Society guides (single house admission $4, or $10 for all three; $1-2 for kids 6-16). The other two are the **Hancock-Clarke House,** 36 Hancock St. about a block from the Buckman, and the **Munroe Tavern,** 1332 Massachusetts Ave., a few blocks east of the Battle Green, in which the retreating British ministered their wounded while Lord Percy's artillery-equipped reinforcements temporarily staved off the swelling colonial regiments. For more info on hours or occasional special programs, call the historical society at (781) 862-1703.

CONCORD

The steady headlong rush of traffic on Rt. 2 belies the sedate character of Concord's main village, in which small boutiques and gourmet coffeeshops nestle near homes whose parlors have hosted the men and women who presided over the "flowering of New England," as critic Van Wyck Brooks put it. Such a well-preserved small town doesn't need Little Women T-shirt shops or Minuteman Motels, but occasional historical plaques, readily available tourist brochures, and busloads of tourists paying pilgrimages to the place, all serve as frequent reminders that you can't throw a stick without hitting something associated with Thoreau, Emerson, or the Revolution.

Conservation land around the town captures some of the spirit of that earlier time, when transcendentalists looked for guidance in the simplicity of the natural world. The extent of wooded land also lends a peaceful air to the former battlefields, although in fact much of what is now tree-covered was wide open pasture, cleared for colonial farms that have long since gone the way of buckskin coats and horse-drawn plows. For a relic of this rural past of apples and asparagus, peaches and black cherries, look no further than the old drystone walls running through Concord's fields and forest.

By the North Bridge

Everybody who comes to Concord stops by the North Bridge off Monument Street, and so should you. Lexington may demur politely about whose act of resistance can be called the Revolution's start—even nearby Acton stakes a claim, since its minutemen were the first on the colonial side to return British fire—but here in Concord is unarguably where the first British casualties were inflicted. Over 500 well-trained colonial minute- and militiamen, assembled in regimental companies from Concord and three surrounding towns, advanced across the original "rude bridge" over the Concord River with a smart military precision that surprised the British. Though under fire from the Redcoats, these colonial "irregulars" displayed more order, taking aim before shooting and specifically targeting officers. To the surprise of all concerned, the King's troops broke ranks and ran. By sundown the British column limped across Charlestown Neck into the protective range of Boston Harbor's naval guns with over 270 killed, wounded, or missing. The colonial losses were about a third of that.

That first wooden trestle is long gone. Despite sometimes being called the "old" North Bridge this one, the fifth, was built in 1956. At the western end downhill of the North Bridge Visitor Center stands the iconographic *Minuteman* bronze by Daniel Chester French (of Lincoln Memorial fame), the young Concord artist's first statue. On its base is the first and most memorable stanza of Ralph Waldo Emerson's "Concord Hymn"—a celebrity endorsement, so to speak, of Concord's claim that the war began on her turf:

By the rude bridge that arched the flood
Their flag to April's breeze unfurled
Here once the embattled farmers stood
And fired the shot heard round the world.

The old colonial parsonage next to the North Bridge predates the Revolution by six years. Its builder, the Reverend William Emerson, supposedly stood in his fields rooting for his neighbors that fateful April morning while his family and his African slave, Frank, witnessed the skirmishes from an upstairs window. But the house derives most of its recognition from literature. Like most of the other historic homes open to the public around town, **The Old Manse** is known for the authors who lived under its weathered slate roof. The reverend's grandson, Ralph Waldo Emerson, briefly lived here after becoming a widower, penning his essay *Nature* before remarrying and moving across town. Nathaniel Hawthorne and his honeymoon bride Sophia rented the place for several years, scratching all sorts of love-tinged grafitti into the window panes with her diamond and writing the story collection from which the house got its name, *Mosses from an Old Manse*. The inscribed panes are still to be seen, along with rooms of 18th- and 19th-century furnishings, household artifacts, and hobby collections. The Trustees of Reservations, current owners, give guided tours daily except Tuesday from mid-April through October ($4.50; tel. 978-369-3909).

Other Historical Attractions

At the busy junction of Lexington Road and the Cambridge Turnpike, about 10 minutes' walk east of the town common, is the **Emerson House.** Here from 1835 until his death in 1882, Ralph Waldo Emerson wrote essays, organized well-attended cross-country lecture tours, and entertained scads of visitors. Here, too, the nascent Transcendental Club convened and created a wholly American literary movement. Knowledgeable guides conduct intimate tours of the prosperous-looking home Thurs.-Sun. and on Monday holidays between mid-April and the last full weekend of October ($4.50; tel. 978-369-2236). As you might expect, a small shop purveys copies of Emerson's works and related souvenirs.

The house isn't totally intact. Harvard University has most of Emerson's library, for example, while his original study is across the street at the **Concord Museum,** 200 Lexington Rd., tel. (978) 369-9609 (open daily; admission $6). The museum's wide-ranging historical collection also includes one of several incarnations of Thoreau's cabin, artifacts from his sojourn in the Walden woods, and plenty of Revolutionary War relics—including the only extant member of the "one if by land, two if by sea" pair of signal lanterns that some might say precipitated the wake-up shot to the world on the other side of town.

On Lexington Raod about a half-mile east of the Concord Museum stands **The Wayside,** home at one time or another to nearly all the town's leading literary figures. Bronson Alcott and his family—including young Louisa May—moved into the Lexington Road house in 1845, when it was already over 150 years old. Nathaniel Hawthorne bought the property, then called Hillside, from the financially strapped Alcotts, enlarged it, and lived in it until his death. As with several other houses around the state, it's his name for the place that has stuck. Later it belonged to childrens' book author Harriet Lothrop, known pseudonymously as Margaret Sydney. Now owned by the National Park Service, the house offers excellent daily tours from mid-April through October ($4; tel. 978-369-6975). The dreamy utopian (and perpetually vagabond) Bronson Alcott eventually returned as Hawthorne's chatty neighbor next door in the **Orchard House,** whose appearance will be familiar to any reader of his daughter Louisa's *Little Women*. Among the remnants preserved from the Alcotts' 20-year residency are drawings "Amy" left in her room at "Apple Slump." Come on the weekend closest to May 23rd and be a guest at eldest daughter Anna's wedding to John Pratt, or visit the week before Christmas and enjoy the living tableaux of family life, all in period costume. House tours are scheduled daily until 4:30 p.m. (except on weekdays Nov.-March, when the last is at 3 p.m.), mid-January through the end of December ($5.50 adults or $16 for family with up to four kids; tel. 978-369-4118). Advance same-day ticketing *is* available. Besides thematic knick-knacks and crafts, the small gift shop stocks every Louisa May Alcott book in print.

Concord's place in American letters even extends to its burial grounds. **Sleepy Hollow Cemetery,** on Bedford St. a short walk from the town common, is the final resting place for the Alcotts, Nathaniel Hawthorne (but *not* his wife—curiously, she's in England), the Emerson clan, and Henry David Thoreau. All are up on Author's Ridge, back against the cemetery's north side. For a little contrast to the disarming simplicity of these graves keep an eye out for the classical beauty of *Mourning Victory,* a memorial sculpture by Daniel Chester French, who was tutored in drawing as a lad by Louisa May Alcott's sister May.

Walden Pond

A deep kettlehole formed by a melted chunk of glacial ice, Walden Pond State Reservation has become a mecca for Henry David Thoreau readers, who are often spotted on the circumferential path deeply engrossed in dog-eared copies of *Walden,* Thoreau's philosophizing account of two years spent in the surrounding woods. The pond's reputation as a good swimming hole is well known to three million Bostonians, so you'll have to come at the crack of dawn or off-season if you want to park anywhere remotely within walking distance, or to find any hint of the solitude Thoreau enjoyed. A Commuter Rail line from Boston borders one side of the reservation, across the pond from the bath house and the most accessible (and therefore most crowded) part of the shore; between screaming kids and rumbling trains Thoreau fans may recognize some sort of ironic proof of Henry's critical fore-

sight. (To be fair, it's worth noting that the railroad actually predates Thoreau's Walden days.)

A replica of Thoreau's cabin may be found by the reservation's parking lot; here in summer daily ranger talks are held. The original house site, 15 minutes' walk into the woods on the pond's north side, is identified by an inscribed stone marker and an accretion of rocks representing over a century's worth of visitors. Ranger-led programs are offered in every season, from summer's regular living history interpreters or guided saunters with a Thoreau scholar to January's celebration of Martin Luther King's birthday with a walk drawing parallels between the civil rights leader's strategy and Thoreau's *Civil Disobedience*. Swimming, canoeing, and fishing are allowed, but mountain biking is not; May-Oct. the parking fee is $2. No more than 1,000 vehicles are allowed at any one time, so be prepared to be turned away at the gate if you drive up after 10 a.m. on any warm, sunny, summer weekend. Call (978) 369-3254 to find out if the lot's full or to ask questions of the friendly, patient park staff.

Whether you have a high school paper to research or simply a modicum of curiosity about the man behind the American myth of rugged individualism, consider dropping by the new multimillion-dollar home of the **Thoreau Institute,** the Thoreau Society's successor to their cramped little lyceum formerly located in Concord. Handsomely situated on an 18-acre wooded estate just over the town line in Lincoln, the institute welcomes the public to programs and exhibits drawn from the world's most comprehensive collection of anything and everything related to Thoreau. Since it's located at the end of a private road with limited parking, the institute's good-neighbor policy (contractual agreement, in fact) obliges people to call ahead before arriving; call (978) 259-9411 or drop by **The Shop at Walden Pond,** the Society-run gift and bookstore on Rt. 126 beside the state reservation parking lot, for directions and dibs on a parking space.

NEARBY SIGHTS

Sandwiched between and slightly to the south of Lexington and Concord is the beautifully rural and stunningly wealthy town of Lincoln. Along its rolling, wooded roads are several gems worth a detour. A cyclist can visit them all over the course of an eight- or nine-mile loop from Walden Pond, where one can finish with a swim. The supermarket in the back of the Mall at Lincoln Station on Lincoln Road makes a convenient refreshment stop, and **Lincoln Guide Service,** tel. (781) 259-1111, across the street rents mountain bikes, road bikes, tandem bikes, even high-end full-suspension bikes to those in need (rates start at $10 for two hours, $25 a day). For folks totally without their own wheels, MBTA **Commuter Rail** provides regular service from Boston's North Station to the whistle-stop platform that's shouting distance from the bike shop; for details see "Getting There" under "Battle Road Practicalities," below.

Attractively nestled among the farmlike estates along Sandy Pond Road, the **DeCordova Museum and Sculpture Park,** tel. (781) 259-3628, www.decordova.org (open Tues.-Sun.; $6 for the museum, sculpture park free), consistently presents challenging exhibitions by New England contemporary artists to compliment its permanent collection of 20th-century art, newly housed in the modern wing cascading down from the original benefactor's hilltop castle. Overlooking a large pond, the 35-acre grounds are a favorite destination of weekend cyclists, families, and picnickers who spend the afternoon amid the sometimes whimsical, sometimes interactive outdoor sculptures. Ceramic artist Robert Arneson's irreverent *Bench Head,* Sol LeWitt's conceptual *Incomplete Open Cubes,* and George Rickey's kinetic *Three Lines* are among the park's varied treats. A wooded open-air amphitheater hosts a popular summer music series; the entrance is near *The Musical Fence* by Paul Matisse, a work no man, woman, or child can resist. Adjacent Sandy Pond features circumferential trails through its surrounding public conservation land, including the Three Friends Trail historically enjoyed by Thoreau and his boon companions William Ellery Channing and Sterns Wheeler. The trail is thought to pass close to the place where Wheeler, another natural philosopher, built a hut in the woods for use during college vacations between 1836 and 1842. Thoreau wanted to try his experiment here by Sandy Pond, too, and for many years after begrudged the owner who re-

fused to give permission. Fortunately for posterity, his friend Ralph Waldo Emerson owned a woodlot beside another pond in the area, and was much more favorably inclined toward Henry's experiments.

A short distance west of the DeCordova sits the **Gropius House,** 68 Baker Bridge Rd., tel. (781) 259-8098, one of 45 unique properties under the care of the Society for the Preservation of New England Antiquities (SPNEA). Built in 1937 by Walter Gropius, founder of the original Bauhaus school in Weimar, Germany, this personal residence introduced the then-revolutionary Bauhaus design precepts to the American landscape. Boston-born skyscraper architect Louis Sullivan may be accorded the credit for declaring "form ever follows function"—a pithy summation of a millenia of architectural desires—but thanks to the profound impact of Bauhaus's modernism he and his predecessors have been roundly usurped by a new standard for functional design. That we now take sharp machine-tooled lines, planar surfaces, and mass-produced building materials so for granted can be traced back in part to this modest structure. Some of the furnishings are by Marcel Breuer, a fellow Bauhaus proponent and founding member, with Gropius, of The Architects Collaborative, one of the most influential practices in its field. Tours on the hour 11 a.m.-4 p.m., Wed.-Sun. between June and mid-October, and Sat.-Sun. the rest of the year ($5).

Another SPNEA property in the vicinity is the **Codman House,** a.k.a. "The Grange," on Codman Rd., tel. (781) 259-8843. The contrast to the Gropius House, a half-hour stroll through the woods to the north, is striking: the Grange is a 16-acre estate with English country gardens. The main house is a veritable dictionary of major 19th-century architectural styles, from Georgian to Colonial Revival. Interior furnishings are less eclectic; mostly they reflect the neoclassical tastes of Ogden Codman, Jr., the last owner of the place. In his day Codman and collaborator Edith Wharton guided the tastes of upper class England and America as profoundly as Emily Post would later influence etiquette; their book *The Decoration of Houses* was required reading in mansions on both sides of the Atlantic. Tours begin on the hour 11 a.m.-4 p.m., Wed.-Sun. from June through mid-October; admission is $4.

Drumlin Farm

Outside of a farmstay out in the western Massachusetts towns of Charlemont or Colrain, **Drumlin Farm Education Center and Wildlife Sanctuary,** tel. (781) 259-9807, is about as close as you can get to that increasingly rare Massachusetts artifact, the working farm. Doubling as headquarters for the Massachusetts Audubon Society (which is older than, and quite independent of, the national Audubon Society), Drumlin specializes in kids' programs of all sorts, from summer day camps to winter activities during school vacation. Hayrides, baby animals, and Harvest Days are among the seasonal highlights that appeal to families, while adults are drawn to the regular birdwatching and nature walks. As avid birders know, the combination of both wooded and open habitat—and the edges between the two—promotes a diverse set of species within what is a relatively small area. Located on Lincoln's South Great Rd. (Rt. 117) slightly east of Rt. 126, the farm is closed Monday. Admission $6 adults, $3 kids and seniors.

Garden in the Woods

Wildflowers are the star attraction of this woodsy acreage, owned and operated by the New England Wild Flower Society, a conservation advocate and partner in maintaining a seed bank for endangered wild flora. A lily pond, pine barren, wetland bog, and rock garden are among the habitats replicated in the garden, incorporating some 1,500 plant varieties. Two acres are also set aside to showcase over 100 rare and endangered species native to New England, nearly a third of which are found almost nowhere else on earth. The garden and its shop—which sells plants and books along with small gifts—are open year-round, daily from mid-April-Oct., Tues.-Sun. the rest of the year. In May, when many flowers are in bloom, the hours are extended to 7 p.m., otherwise plan to arrive by 4 p.m. to gain admission ($6). The easiest approach is from US 20 in Sudbury; look for the signposted turn south on Raymond Rd., between Wayland's attractive Congregational church at the Rt. 27 junction and Sudbury's heap of quaintly misnamed shopping plazas.

Appetites made large by nature walks may appreciate a detour to the sandwich and barbecue counter at **Gerard Turkey Farms,** tel.

(508) 877-2300, on Water St. in Saxonville less than two miles southeast of the Garden in the Woods. The poultry in the turkey burgers and barbecue chicken certainly beats US 20's fast food for flavor and freshness, and the salads aren't half bad, either. Open Mon.-Fri. to 6:30 p.m., Saturday to 4 p.m.

The Wayside Inn

The Wayside Inn may owe its renown to Longfellow's *Tales of a Wayside Inn,* but it owes its survival to Henry Ford, whose collection of landmark Americana now housed in Dearborn, Michigan, was partly inspired by this ancient hostelry. "History is bunk," Ford once said, but his actions spoke otherwise: after acquiring and finishing restoration of the historic inn, he added a series of other structures to create the atmosphere of a colonial settlement, from one-room schoolhouse (of "Mary Had a Little Lamb" fame) to tavern and grist mill. Ford even paid to move US 20 away from the growing complex in order to preserve its serenity. (Past experience with his own boyhood home had taught Henry that highway expansion was one of the principal threats to historic sites.) Preceding Virginia's Williamsburg restoration by a whisker, the Wayside became one of the earliest examples of that Disneyesque phenomenon, the museum village. Not to detract from the honor due the fine inn, the oldest parts of which date back to the early 1700s and include original furnishings, but most of the other structures are contrivances built in the 1920s to fit popular perceptions of New England's heritage. At this late date, even these stereotypes are well-nigh historic, and certainly instructional in their own fashion. Consider how well the rustic grist mill with its big water wheel fits your mental image for such things—despite being wholly unlike any such mill actually used in the region. As for the Depression-era chapel, it looks so like a genuine 18th-century Congregational church high atop a picture-perfect green knoll that it's one of the busiest wedding sites in the state.

The Wayside Inn itself, licensed in 1716 to serve teamsters and travelers along the Boston-Albany Post Road, continues to provide food and accommodations, even for horses. Just don't come expecting to sleep in a nearly 300-year-old bed, or eat in an atmospheric old tavern: the main dining room and eight of the 10 guest rooms are all in the rear ell added in 1929 by Henry Ford and extensively rebuilt after a distasterous 1955 fire. For $100-140 d, membership in the "Secret Drawer Society" (a running journal of guest impressions left in the drawers and cubbyholes of the in-room desks) is quite steep. The tried-and-true menu of prime rib, broiled swordfish, baked stuffed shrimp, and the like isn't for the pennywise, either ($15.95-21.95). If you want a taste of the Wayside's genuine past, have an 18th-century rum concoction in the old bar.

RECREATION

Paddle in the gentle wake of Henry David Thoreau's journey down the Concord River, or simply get the fish-eye view of where the embattled farmers fought in 1775 by the North Bridge when you rent a canoe or kayak from **South Bridge Boat House,** Main St. in Concord, tel. (978) 369-9438. Open daily April-Oct.; rates run from $7.75 an hour weekdays to $8.85 an hour weekends. The rental dock is on the Sudbury River just a few minutes' away from where the Assabet joins in to form the Concord River, so from South Bridge you have your pick of placid waters. Downstream to the north, the Concord flows through the Great Meadows National Wildlife Refuge. Upstream to the south, the Sudbury broadens out into lake-like Fairhaven Bay, beneath the brow of Lincoln's Mount Misery, an attractive parcel of conservation land whose public trails connect through to Walden Pond. If you're ferrying your own boat around, use the excellent put-in next to the Rt. 117 bridge over the Sudbury, on the eastern, or

THE OLD POST ROAD

Through most of the MetroWest region, US 20 carries some variant of the name "Old Boston Post Road"—a form of recognition of the colonial thoroughfare used by mail-carrying stagecoach traffic. Though some tourist guides refer to it simply as "the" Post Road, it is today a tiny fraction of the 2,400-mile Quebec-to-Florida post-road network inaugurated during Benjamin Franklin's 22-year career in the colonial postal service.

Like many of Massachusetts' well-developed colonial roads, the various postal routes from Boston to New York expeditiously followed preexisting Native American trails. First improved early in the 18th century, the route most closely coincident with US 20 followed a well-used trail, called the Bay Path, from Boston Harbor to a ford on the Connecticut River at the Chicopee Falls, continuing west to the Hudson River near Albany.

In 1769, this post road was one of the first to be calibrated with carved markers identifying the distance to Boston (another of Postmaster General Franklin's innovations). Only 17 of the granite milestones remain; among the best preserved and most readily identified actually lies north of US 20, on Rt. 117, in Lincoln.

1769 milestone on the Old Post Road, in Southborough, 27 miles from Boston

Lincoln, side of the river (Concord is on the western bank). The parking area is signposted discreetly enough that you may only spot it as you pass it; from the east it's about a mile from Rt. 126 (Concord Road).

BATTLE ROAD PRACTICALITIES

Accommodations

Lexington's overnight guests have a choice between a couple of executive-priced chains out on the interstate, a fusty downtown motor inn showing its age, or a handful of true B&Bs. Price ranges among all three options overlap considerably, so don't let budget stand in the way of trying the local hospitality. Consider **Occasional Larks,** tel. (781) 862-5275, a modern colonial-style home advantageously located in the Historic District, minutes' walk from the Battle Green, and adjacent to both park land and the Minuteman Commuter Bikeway to Cambridge. Good breakfasts, a welcome basket of fresh munchies, and cordial hospitality from your host and her dachshunds epitomize the reasons for choosing a B&B over a seen-one-seen-'em-all hotel. The higher-priced suite-sized room with private bath is an unbeatable value, but the shared-bath alternative isn't anything to sneeze at, either ($70-90 d, $10 less for singles, no tax or credit cards). Equally delightful is **Ashley's Bed and Breakfast,** in the Six Moon Hill neighborhood, tel. (781) 862-6488. Most people wouldn't associate historic Lexington with Bauhaus architecture, but in fact this subdivision was designed by The Architects Collaborative for their members—Fletcher Ashley among them. Textbook contemporary design and furnishings aside, the Ashleys are gracious and informative, and provide an above-average breakfast ($80 d, no tax or credit cards).

Several national chains catering to business travelers are found along exits off Rt.-128/I-95 in both Lexington and Bedford. At Exit 30 is the **Sheraton Tara,** 727 Marrett Rd, tel. (800) 325-3535, while spread along Rt. 4 (named Bedford St. in Lexington and Great Rd. in Bedford) west of Exit 31 are **Holiday Inn Express** tel. (800) HOLIDAY, **Ramada Inn,** tel. (800) 228-2828, and **Bedford Travelodge,** tel. (800) 578-7878.

At first blush Concord seems to offer a choice of either a modern **Best Western** at the Rt. 2 rotary west of Concord's center, tel. (800) 528-1234 or (978) 369-6100 (moderate to expensive), or any of several historic inns, but in fact most of what is advertised as historic really isn't. The town's most famous inn is a case in point: it's got a lot more motel in its bones than the exterior—or the prices—would have you believe. Why pay a premium for pretense when you can get geniune character and comfort for less? If you agree, call the **Hawthorne Inn,** 462 Lexington Rd. opposite The Wayside, (978) 369-5610, or the **North Bridge Inn,** 21 Monument St. next to The Nature Company store, tel. (978) 371-0014. Both range from expensive in winter to very expensive or luxury in summer and fall. The Hawthorne is a genuinely old 19th-century house, but the decor runs to eclectic ethnic and contemporary art: South American textiles, Asian masks, and sculptures by one of the owners. Writing desks and lots of books add an appropriately literary air, and resident cats, dogs, and kids add a jovial undercurrent. Rates include a continental breakfast of treats from the best bakeries in town, plus plenty of good advice on what to do besides the usual touristy things. The North Bridge Inn, at the heart of town, is a thoroughly modern, all-suites B&B inn that happens to look vaguely historic. Its six double-sized quarters are attractively decorated—no veneers or excessive frills, just solid wood, well-coordinated fabrics, and warm colors—and all equipped with at least partial kitchenettes. Rates include a full breakfast.

The most affordable option is the **Colonel Roger Brown House B&B Inn,** 1694 Main St. (Rt. 62) in West Concord, tel. (800) 292-1369 or (978) 369-9119. The facade may belong to a house that was being framed the day the American Revolution began down the road, but the interior is quite contemporary—as are the amenities, from private baths, TVs, and phones to full use of the fitness club and corporate services agency in the renovated 19th-century mill next door. Concord's major attractions are a short bike ride or drive away, while the commuter parking garage at one end of Boston's subway is under 20 minutes' drive. Just don't expect its semi-rural environs to ensure peace and quiet: Route 62, at the front door, is a major thoroughfare, rendering morning or evening jogs quite out of the question. Moderate.

Food

Top-drawer restaurateurs in nearby Cambridge and Arlington needn't be afraid of Lexington trying to lure away their customers, but if you're content with such staples as pizza, somewhat Americanized Thai, or Chinese, you won't have to venture out of downtown. **Bertucci's,** 1777 Massachusetts Ave., tel. (781) 860-9000, is the top pizza contender, solidly upholding this regional chain's reputation for wood-fired brick-oven pies with ample fresh toppings on thin, smoky crusts. Hearty salads, pasta, and calzones are also available, along with a kids' menu that stretches the umbrella of Italian cuisine to include peanut butter and jelly sandwiches. Across the street **Lemon Grass,** tel. (781) 862-3530 offers a safe introduction to Southeast Asian food, with a top-40 approach to delicious Thai dishes and a conservative hand on the chili peppers.

In Concord, the best fine dining—and essential stop for garlic lovers—is at **Aïgo Bistro,** 84 Thoreau St., tel. (978) 371-1333 (open daily), in the festively colored upper floor of the former Concord depot. Whether dressed to kill or slumming in your jeans, the staff will treat you to impeccable service, while the chef prepares excellent Mediterranean and Provençal-influenced cuisine. Prices are a tad on the high side compared to the competition for this level of quality from suburban places closer to Boston—most entrees are $18 and up—but if you're not counting change it beats hunting for a parking space in Harvard Square. Even more khakis and fewer ties are in evidence at casual **Walden Grille,** 24 Walden St., tel. (978) 371-2233, the town's other high-end choice ($14.95-21.00). Enjoy a hearty Tuscan-influenced menu with all the arugula and sun-dried tomato a gourmand might expect, yet enough grilled meats and potatoes for traditionalists. Like the Aïgo, Walden Grille has a broad selection of wines by the glass, and locally brewed Concord Junction beer.

With so many attractive spots for picnicking—Revolutionary battlefields, Walden Pond, the banks of the Concord River, even Sleepy Hollow Cemetery—a well-stocked gourmet store such as **The Cheese Shop,** 31 Walden St., tel. (978) 369-5778, open Tues.-Sat., makes a picnic hamper a viable alternative to sit-down dining. From raw ingredients to fully prepared deli meals-to-go, this place will furnish everything but the sunshine. In a similar vein, across Rt. 2, **Concord Teacakes,** 59 Commonwealth Ave., tel. (978) 369-7644, opposite the West Concord Commuter Rail platform, is ideal for high-quality sandwiches, soups, and sweets for eat in or take-out.

If basic burgers and fried fish would suit you more than smoked turkey and escarole on multigrain sourdough bread, head straight away to **The Willow Pond Kitchen,** on Lexington Rd. (Rt. 2A), the only small dingy-looking place with a Schlitz sign between Concord common and the Minute Man Visitor Center. Inside under the glassy stare of a mangy stuffed cougar, the clock seems to have stopped sometime during the decade after this place opened in 1944. The food won't earn any awards, but it's got character in spades, and nobody in town can beat the prices.

Getting There

Both Lincoln and Concord are on the Fitchburg line of the MBTA **Commuter Rail,** which departs Boston's North Station 8-12 times a day; fares are $6-6.50 roundtrip. Call (617) 222-3200 for recorded schedule info, or toll-free (800) 392-6100 from anywhere in North American outside Greater Boston. The historic center of Lexington is accessible by two MBTA buses, the #62 Bedford V.A. and the #76 Hanscom Field, departing from the busway atop Alewife Station at the end of the Red Line. Unfortunately for tourists, neither bus operates on Sundays, and when they do run it's with infrequent, mostly hourly service. However, as this book goes to press a tourist-oriented trolley shuttle is scheduled to go into service between Alewife, Lexington's Battle Green, and all the major Battle Road sights from the Minute Man Visitor Center west to Concord's North Bridge, operating weekends from mid-April through June, and daily July to mid-October. For one low fare of just a few dollars, you'll have a full day's worth of re-boarding privileges. Call (781) 861-1210 for more information.

THE CHARLES RIVER VALLEY

"Valley" may conjure up visions of a great V-shaped topographical feature with a river coursing down the middle like an oversized drainage ditch, but this watershed is nothing if not subtle. Rising in wetlands in the town of Hopkinton, the Charles River practices every dilatory move known to water as it wends its way to the sea. By the time it reaches Boston Harbor it has covered a full 80 miles, testing every point of the compass along the way. Any self-respecting crow could cover the same ground in about 26 miles (which is why the Boston Marathon coincidentally begins and ends where the Charles does).

This is the most densely populated watershed in New England, shot through with highways and houses and such a jumble of shops and signage that for the most part you'd never notice a river runs through it unless you knew where to look. Seek, and ye shall find: a general theme among the parks and sanctuaries highlighted in this section is that they abut, overlook, or include portions of the Charles River or one of its tributaries. As a happy consequence of waterways being superceded in importance by roads and rails, these rivers have become in modern times some of the region's best urban wilds, rich in flora and fauna. Several lakes and reservoirs in the area are also good for boating and swimming. If you're unimpressed by all the water-related activities, how about some long country walks? This, too, may run contrary to expectations raised by the obvious suburban sprawl, but nature doesn't quit putting out leaves, spinning webs, or singing up a storm just because some developer puts up another hundred custom-designed homes. Don't come looking for a Pike's Peak or Bridal Veil Falls: MetroWest lays no claims to exceptional wilderness or breathtaking natural wonders. Highlights here are birdwatching amid oak-beech forests, views of the distant Boston skyline from unexpected promontories, brilliant autumn colors in a woodlot across a meadow, signs of deer and coyote, spring peepers at a pond's edge, or simply the cooling scent of pine and juniper on an otherwise sultry afternoon.

ROUTE 135—
THE MARATHON ROUTE

Hopkinton
Every April sleepy little Hopkinton briefly becomes an international sports center as thousands and thousands of long-distance runners congregate around the world-renowned Boston

Johnny A. Kelley wins the 1935 Boston Marathon. Kelley ran "the Boston" 61 times, starting in 1929; he won twice and placed seven times. A statue dedicated to him, Young at Heart, stands in Newton.

COURTESY OF BOSTON PUBLIC LIBRARY, PRINT DEPT.

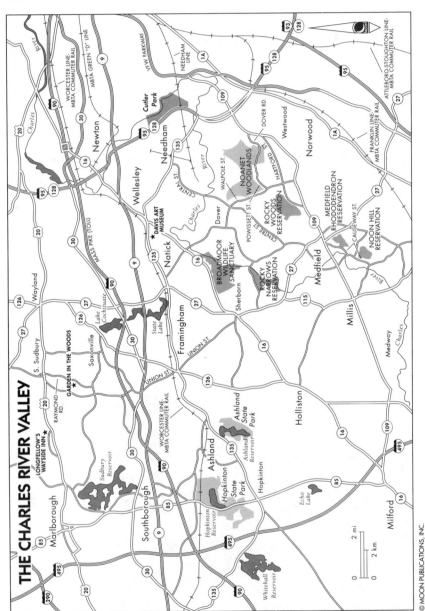

THE CHARLES RIVER VALLEY

© MOON PUBLICATIONS, INC.

Marathon's starting line beside the town common. Add a huge passel of spectators, race volunteers, traffic cops, photographers, and reporters and you have the makings of a major party—about the only thing missing is the Mardi Gras music. Outside of Patriots Day—the state holiday on which the race is always run—about the only reason to come to Hopkinton is for a dip in the large reservoir in **Hopkinton State Park,** off Rt. 85 between the center of town and Southborough ($2 day use fee), or for a hike around its 1,400 acres. (Bring mosquito repellent in summer.) With the aid of your trusty Eastern Massachusetts bicycle map from Rubel BikeMaps ($5.25 including postage from P.O. Box 1035, Cambridge, MA 02140), you can also plan a scenic day-long bike ride around the area.

Broadmoor Wildlife Sanctuary

East of Hopkinton, Rt. 135's semi-rural quality quickly evaporates as large houses set well back from the road are supplanted by a checkered array of multi-family dwellings, quick lube garages and car dealerships, gas stations and tire stores. Until Wellesley's obvious wealth restores a semblance of landscaping, Rt. 135 wallows in enough petroleum products and doughnut shops to make a wildlife sanctuary not only unlikely, but inconceivable.

Yet south of the Marathon route, the Charles River flows implacably onward amid a corridor of lush green. Once upon a time a pair of small mills used its waters to produce flour and lumber; now the long-abandoned site and its surrounding forests and fields are preserved for your enjoyment in the Massachusetts Audubon Society's Broadmoor Wildlife Sanctuary, tel. (508) 655-2296. Trails offer visitors a chance to catch a glimpse of many feathered and furry residents, from great blue herons nesting by the pond to field mice scampering around the meadow grasses. Don't miss the long bridge over Indian Brook, either. Programs are offered most of the year: natural history walks, canoe trips, bird counts and banding, and the ever-popular Mother's Day "Birds & Breakfast." Admission to the sanctuary is $3; special programs are extra (closed Monday). If you left your Petersen's at home, the small nature center and gift shop can sell you a new one, along with all the other field guides you might want. Located on Rt. 16 in South Natick near the Sherborn line. Call ahead for program reservations.

Wellesley

This small bedroom community straddling Routes 9, 16, and 135 also happens to be the most affluent college town in the state. The most widely known of its three institutions of higher education is **Wellesley College,** one of the nation's top-ranked liberal arts schools, whose graceful, hilly campus lies between Rt. 135 (Central St.) and Lake Waban at the west end of town. Often confused—in name only—with Connecticut's Wesleyan University, Wellesley has been an all-women's college since its doors opened in 1875, although men enrolled within a regional consortium of 12 colleges are accepted as exchange students for a semester or two. Marathon runners know they're reaching the halfway point of their ordeal when they hear the sound of students lining the race course, whose traditional tunnel of screaming encouragement lifts flagging spirits and speeds contestants into the marathon's toughest part—the Newton Hills.

Generally overlooked on the periphery of museum-rich Boston is the college's excellent—and free!—**Davis Museum and Cultural Center,** 106 Central St., tel. (781) 283-2051 (Tues.-Sun.), near the campus physical plant. Reflecting its benefactors' diverse interests, the Davis collection includes everything from classical antiquities and African art to works by Warhol and de Kooning. The world-class holdings are shown to further advantage by the building interior itself—a dramatic and light-filled space designed by the Spanish architect José Rafael Moneo. Aside from the museum and nearby science building, the campus is dominated by Gothic architecture, lending it a European air. This is reinforced by the view over Lake Waban: across from the college is a six-acre Italianate topiary garden on the private Hunnewell estate. (H. Hollis Hunnewell coined "Wellesley" from his wife's family name, Welles, when he acquired the property in the 19th century. The post office branch and college adopted the name, too, and his fellow townsfolk followed suit when they split from Natick in 1881.) The tiers of neatly shaped trees and shrubs are thought to be the nation's oldest such garden. Equally exotic are the tropical and desert fauna in the college's

Margaret C. Ferguson Greenhouses by the Science Center, tel. (781) 283-3094, open to the public daily until 4:30 p.m., year-round. While there's next to nothing in bloom in summer, the spring perennials and bulbs will enliven any visit Feb.-May. As for the tree collection, simply look about as you stroll the campus: the entire grounds constitute an arboretum, and nearly all specimens are tagged for easy identification. Free tours for prospective students and others are generally offered Mon.-Fri. year-round plus Saturday mornings during the academic year. Tours depart from the Board of Admission at Green Hall, whose square, cathedral-like tower dominates the campus. To confirm that student guides will be available the day of your visit, call (781) 283-2270.

ROUTE 135 PRACTICALITIES

Accommodations
Chain hotels comprise the majority of accommodations along the suburban half of the Marathon route, with the exception of the **Wellesley Inn on the Square,** 576 Washington St., tel. (800) 233-4686 or (781) 235-0180. Expensive.

A scattering of bed and breakfast homes exist in the area, too, almost exclusively available through reservation services such as **Bed and Breakfast Associates/Bay Colony, Ltd.,** tel. (781) 449-5302. Otherwise look to the heavily commercialized Rt. 9 strip through Framingham and Natick (roughly parallel to the Marathon route) for a half dozen national chain hotels.

Food
If hunger strikes near the starting line of the Marathon route, choose from **Hopkinton's pizza shop** on Main St. next to the savings bank, or head east to adjacent Ashland for a visit to **Udupi Bhavan,** on Rt. 126 next to the Pond Plaza Market Basket supermarket, tel. (508) 820-0230 ($4.25-11.95; closed Tuesday). The South Indian cuisine served here is so good it handily compensates for the sterile atmosphere of its strip mall location. Crepe-like *dosa,* frittata-like *uthappam,* and a-little-bit-of-everything *thali* banquets are all delicious, wholly authentic, purely vegetarian, and quite unlike the

ROUTE 9 ACCOMMODATIONS

These accommodations are listed in order from west (Framingham) to east (Natick).

Motel 6, 1668 Worcester Rd. (Rt. 9) at MassPike Exit 12, Framingham, tel. (800) 4 MOTEL6 or (508) 620-0500. Inexpensive.

Sheraton Tara Hotel, unmistakable half castle and half Tudor mansion also at MassPike Exit 12, Framingham, tel. (800) 325-3535 or (508) 879-7200. Very expensive.

Econo Lodge, 1186 Worcester Rd. just west of Framingham State College, tel. (800) 556-ECONO or (508) 879-1510. Inexpensive to moderate.

Red Roof Inn, 650 Cochituate Rd. (Rt. 30) just north of Rt. 9 near the Framingham Mall, tel. (800) THE ROOF or (508) 872-4499. Moderate.

Howard Johnson Hotel, 130 Worcester Rd., Framingham, tel. (800) I-GO-HOJO (508) 872-8811. Moderate.

Hampton Inn, at the Speen St. exit across from Sam's Club and the Natick Shopping Center, tel. (800) HAMPTON or (508) 653-5000. Expensive.

Crowne Plaza Boston/Natick, 1360 Worcester Rd., tel. (800) 465-4329 or (508) 653-8800. Very expensive.

Natick Travelodge, 1350 Worcester Rd., tel. (800) 578-7878 or (508) 655-2222. Moderate.

thick curry- and grill-oriented Northern cuisine featured at most Indian restaurants in this country. Ashland's Sri Lakshmi Hindu Temple (on Rt. 135 near the Framingham line) is the spiritual center for much of New England's Indian population, so expect long lines at the restaurant after weekend services. Meat lovers should head north of Hopkinton on Rt. 85, past the stone-gated entrance of the state park, to plain-looking **Ipanema,** just beyond the small railroad trestle in neighboring Southborough, tel. (508) 460-6144. In the typical manner of traditional Brazilian *churrascarias,* diners pay a single price for all the spit-roasted meat you can eat, plus a modest salad bar and side dishes largely based on Brazilian cookery's myriad preparations with manioc. If you've been fortunate enough to never have tried Brazilian *cachaça* before—a powerful fermented tequila-like drink—you can end your lucky streak here. Open Wed.-Fri. 5-10 p.m., Sat.-Sun. noon-10 p.m.

At the Wellesley end of Rt. 135, dining out generally means a casual counter-service cafe, pizza, or Asian food. The cluster between campus and Wellesley Square, the oblique intersection of Central and Washington Sts. (Rts. 135 and 16), gives a good taste of what's in store. Closest to campus is **Figs,** 92 Central St., tel. (781) 237-5788, an upscale Boston-based pizza and pasta joint highly recommended for their thin crusts, wood-fired oven, and gourmet toppings. On parallel Linden St. across the Commuter Rail tracks—turn off Central at Crest St. and you'll find it—is a more down-home local favorite, **Jimmy's Cafe,** 151 Linden, tel. (781) 431-7616. The hand-me-down furnishings instill a warmth mirrored in the food, which has plenty of high-toned touches—wild rice and fresh fruit chutney, garlic mashed potatoes and Dijon glaze—without either the attitude or the price. For ingredients as fresh these, the under-$10 average is a steal, no matter how much your chair wobbles. No corkage fee for folks who bring their own beer or wine, either. Closed Monday. If it's lunchtime and you just want something to go, consider the fine fresh fare available up the street at **Captain Marden's Seafood,** 279 Linden, suppliers to some of Boston's finest restaurants. Try a sandwich with whole clams or lobster salad for a proper bit of New England flavor.

Back in the center of the Square is another great inexpensive option, **EatSmart,** 555 Washington St., one of a new breed of cafes serving fast food with flair (open only to 9 p.m. most nights). Blonde maple decor, gourmet coffee, fruit smoothies, fresh vegetables, and ethnic flavors are the standard here, with items such as Jamaican jerk chicken or poached salmon and veggies in a spinach tortilla, or maybe just a generous helping of pasta tossed with pesto. Everything's under $10, and the staff doesn't make you feel like you're the billionth customer they've served. A block away is the local Thai contender, **Amarin,** at 27 Grove St. just off the Square, tel. (781) 239-1350. All your favorite curries, seafood sautés, beef with macadamias and watercress, and a smattering of vegetarian selections are served up with quiet alacrity in an attractive space at reasonable prices ($6.75-14.75).

Getting There

Wellesley College is relatively easy to reach via the MBTA **Commuter Rail** from Boston's South Station. Multiple departures are available daily (tel. 617-222-3200 for recorded schedule, or 800-392-6100 within Massachusetts); board trains serving the Framingham/Worcester line, and get off at Wellesley Square ($5 roundtrip). Campus is on Central Street (Rt. 135), about a 10-minute walk west from the rail platform (take a left at the top of the stairs, a right on Central, and you'll see the college entrance past the next set of traffic lights).

ROUTE 109— WESTERN NORFOLK COUNTY

As most commuters who ride this spoke to Boston know, Rt. 109 is often a forgettable claptrap of commercial signage, but don't let inauspicious beginnings keep you from delving beyond the clutter. In Dedham at the east end, the auto dealerships, muffler shops, and household furnishings stores come thick and fast, but farther from Boston, up in the M's—Medfield, Millis, and Medway—open land and even a few working farms appear along the route, and greenery becomes thick enough to obscure the extent of suburban sprawl. The gentle hills of the area are the trailing edge of the eastern Massachusetts uplands; south of I-95 and the Norfolk County line the land flattens out into the sandy-soiled, pine-covered coastal plains. Historically this section of tripartite Norfolk County, whose southern edge marks the boundary between the old Puritan and Pilgrim colonies, was a leading supplier of straw bonnets for the northeastern United States. From its beginnings as a cottage piecework business producing cheaper oat-straw knock-offs of fancy northern Italian millinery, the straw hat production became as centralized, machine-driven, and high-volume as the state's textile and shoe industries. Thanks to changing markets and one too many factory fires, Norfolk County bonnets and straw goods manufacturing followed buggy whips into oblivion by the early 1900s.

There's not much in the way of dining out here beyond the occasional fast-food outlet on Rt. 109, although for a special treat during June don't miss out on strawberry season. **Jane & Paul's Farm,** 41 Fruit St. in Norfolk (Rt. 109 to Rt. 115 south, left on Cleveland St., look for sign on left), tel. (508) 528-0812, offers pick-your-own usually until July 4. Those looking to stay overnight in this slice of the MetroWest region have a choice between a few national chains in Dedham within two exits of the Rt. 128/Rt. 109 interchange: **Comfort Inn,** tel. (800) 244-8181 or (781) 326-6700, and **Holiday Inn,** tel. (800) HOLIDAY or (781) 329-1000, both at Rt. 128 Exit 15 (and both ranging in price from moderate to very expensive); or the high-priced **Hilton at Dedham Place,** tel. (800) HILTONS or (781) 329-7900, at Exit 14. The best lodging value is found on the other end of Rt. 109 at the **Tage Inn—Milford,** just west of I-495 Exit 19, tel. (800) 322-TAGE or (508) 478-8243. Inexpensive. Though not nearly as close to Boston as the hotels on Rt. 128, the Tage Inn is only two interstate exits north of the Forge Park station at the end of the Commuter Rail's Franklin line, with up to 16 daily departures to Boston's Back Bay and South Station, about an hour away. You couldn't drive into the city any faster, even if there wasn't another car—or cop—on the road, and the roundtrip fare of $7.50 plus $1 for parking at the commuter lot is still a better deal than most city parking, hands down.

Noanet Woodlands

Protecting the headwaters of Noanet Brook (no-ANN-it), a tributary of the Charles River, are extensive woodlands with over 30 miles of trails through tall white pines and mixed hardwood forest, around four ponds, and to the 387-foot crown of namesake Noanet Peak, whose 20-mile vista includes Boston's skyline. By late spring the pond lilies have put forth their showy white blossoms, painted turtles sun themselves on branches, and warblers trill among the trees. Slough away summer's heat-induced lethargy with shaded walks beneath rustling birch and oak, or explore the rebuilt stone-faced dam

whose original incarnation helped power the Dover Union Iron Company's forges back when Illinois still belonged to Indians and machine-made cotton cloth was a novelty. After September's broadwings migrate past eager hawk-watchers atop that hill, autumn's bright chemistry paints the woodlands with maple-leaf reds and beech yellows, and squirrels have a field day hiding acorns for the winter. Although the property is split between The Trustees of Reservations (TTOR) and privately managed **Hale Reservation,** mountain bike permits ($15 for a calendar year) are available for the whole woodlands from either Noanet's ranger station (staffed on weekends and holidays only), or from the Hale main office (open 8 a.m.-8 p.m. daily, late May-early Sept.), or by calling The Trustees of Reservations regional office at (781) 821-2977. Admission for hikers is free; parking and trail-head access is at Caryl Park in the town of Dover, on Dedham St. between Dover center and the Charles River. The main office for Hale Reservation, tel. (781) 326-1770, is signpost-ed from Dover Rd., off Rt. 109 in Westwood. Hale Reservation is a privately run tract that operates day camps on a large pond, with water sports and a swimming beach available by membership only ($565 per year).

Rocky Woods Reservation

Immediately east of Noanet over the Medfield town line is one of TTOR's most popular holdings, nearly 500 acres of forested wetlands and hills aptly known as Rocky Woods. Hike for an hour or an afternoon on the dozen miles of paths and trails that wander into every corner, or visit in winter for wonderful cross-country skiing. A self-guiding nature trail interprets the reservation's geology, flora, and fauna. Admission is free weekdays, $2.50 weekends and holidays; entrance and parking is off Hartford St. about half a mile east of where it intersects Rt. 109 in Medfield.

Gates of the Charles

For most of its length the Charles River winds through a broad floodplain, but at the boundary between Middlesex and Norfolk Counties it cuts between sharp granite cliffs backed by wooded hills. These "Gates of the Charles" are protected as part of TTOR's **Rocky Narrows**

THE METROWEST LEG OF THE BAY CIRCUIT

The 200-mile Bay Circuit around Boston is still very much a work in progress, but you'd never guess that from a hike through its completed MetroWest sections. In large part, this is because the route incorporates so many well-established conservation properties. Here are three of the best local bits, with directions to the trailheads.

Acton-Sudbury (17 miles); runs south through Concord's beautiful Estabrook Woods, an ecological study area partly owned by Harvard University, around Walden Pond, and through a small but very attractive corner of Lincoln. Maps covering portions of the trail include the Lincoln Land Conservation Trust's guide to all Lincoln walking trails and the New England Orienteering Club's map of Estabrook Woods—both available from the Shop at Walden, the Thoreau Society's store, at the entrance to Concord's Walden Pond.

Sherborn (11 miles); hike either south from Barber Reservation, whose entrance is signposted from Western Ave., or north from the TTOR Rocky Narrows Reservation. Perfectly beautiful section, this. If you want to carry a natural history guide, pick up a copy of *Sherborn Walks,* by Arthur Schnure ($10), at the gift shop at the Massachusetts Audubon Society's Broadmoor Wildlife Sanctuary.

Medfield-Sharon (9 miles); begin from the north at TTOR's Noon Hill Reservation, in Medfield (signposted off Causeway St. a little over a mile south of Rt. 109), or from the south at Massachusetts Audubon Society's Moose Hill Wildlife Sanctuary, on the east side of I-95 between Exits 10 and 8. From Exit 10 catch Rt. 27 north to Walpole, and turn on Moose Hill St. before crossing over the interstate; from Exit 8, head east on Main toward Sharon, and turn, within a mile, on Moose Hill Street. Includes a primitive campsite (you must notify the Walpole police and fire departments before using).

Additional information about the Bay Circuit and a list of available trail guides may be found on the Internet at www.serve.com/baycircuit.

Reservation, along with gravelly eskers, a wonderful picnic spot known as King Philip's Overlook, and some of MetroWest's prettiest Bay Circuit mileage. Spring is unmistakable for the migrating songbirds that fill the forest and wildflowers that fill the open pasture. Summer vacation brings the usual complement of hot weather, late afternoon mosquitoes, and the occasional radio-controlled airplane hobbyist to the fields across the river from that high overlook. As days grow shorter the buzzing aerobatics are replaced by the dry rustle of unseen mammals scampering about in the fallen leaves; come winter's snow and cross-country skiers will at least see tracks of those that don't hibernate. The reservation's trailhead is in a tiny parking area off Rt. 27 in Sherborn, on the Dover-Medfield line 3.5 miles north of Rt. 109.

Noon Hill

Despite appearances, the Trustees of Reservations aren't the only stewards of open land in this region, but they certainly do the best job of providing access to what land they do own. Medfield's Noon Hill Reservation is akin to their other properties within the Charles River watershed, with its shade-tolerant, moisture-loving birch and beech below a tall canopy of pine, general topography of hills abutting floodplains, and miles of trails fit for peaceful wandering. But the wetlands here are truly extensive, augmented by a sizable acreage maintained as a natural floodwater storage basin by the Army Corps of Engineers. This reservation also shows more evidence of its early agricultural use, with old drystone walls encompassing long-overgrown fields made fertile by the seasonal whims of the Charles and Stop Rivers, back before dams were built at the mouth in Boston. In addition to its autumnal display of colorful foliage, the property is the scenic access point for a quite varied stretch of the Bay Circuit. Parking and trailhead are signposted off Causeway St. a little over a mile south of Rt. 109. Also off Causeway St. just south of Rt. 109 is the marked parking area for TTOR's **Medfield Rhododendrons,** a small parcel on the north side of the Stop River with a short trail through a colony of native rosebay rhododendrons. Though familiar as a garden ornamental, in the wild this gaudy July bloomer is one of New England's rarest shrubs.

WILLIAM ALLEN WALL/OLD DARTMOUTH HISTORICAL SOCIETY/ NEW BEDFORD WHALING MUSEUM

SOUTHEASTERN MASSACHUSETTS

With the exception of a few towns on the southern fringe of Boston, and the eastern side of Narragansett Bay, southeastern Massachusetts comprises the original Plymouth Bay Colony of 1620. The fur-trading Pilgrims who staked out the "Old Colony" would undoubtedly be a tad dumbfounded by the subdivisions now blanketing their old plots of herring-fed corn. Extensive highway and rail connections with Boston, Providence, and the MetroWest industrial and office parks have made the relatively cheap land too good to pass up for thousands of home buyers; consequently, backroads are more residential than bucolic. A landscape dominated by glacially flattened coastal outwash plains and scrubby pitch-pine barrens means vistas are constrained rather than panoramic, and lack much of the blazing autumnal colors found west of Boston.

The region's decidedly uneven economic history has resulted in an equally uneven preservation of the region's rich natural and architectural heritage. Yet beguiling New England villages exuding colonial charm do exist, along with meandering rural byways, miles of sandy public beaches, and decent public campgrounds, too, although you often have to run the gauntlet of suburban housing and strip malls to reach them. Unless you have local friends or family to guide you through the density of commercial and residential development concealing the fruits of this region's interior, stick instead to the coastal areas, where natural and historical assets have been appreciated by tourists for over a century.

All the urban destinations described in this chapter are accessible from Boston and elsewhere via some form of public transit, although certain destinations—e.g., Plymouth—lack any weekend service of any use to tourists. Fortunately, attractions, restaurants, and—with some exceptions—accommodations at all these destinations are predominately within walking distance of the local intercity bus terminals. Getting around to outlying sights, on the other hand, requires a car, or plenty of cycling; if you choose

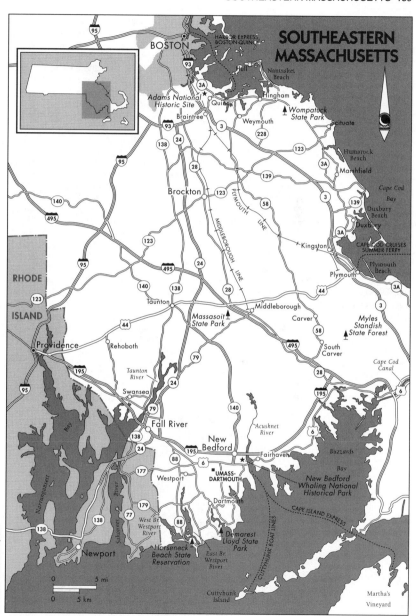

BOSTON

HARBOR EXPRESS
BOSTON-QUINCY

Hull

Nantasket
Beach

Adams National
Historic Site

Quincy

Hingham

Braintree

Weymouth

Wompatuck
State Park

Scituate

Humarock
Beach

Marshfield

Brockton

PLYMOUTH LINE

Cape Cod
Bay

Duxbury
Beach

Duxbury

MIDDLEBOROUGH LINE

Kingston

CAPE COD CRUISES
SUMMER FERRY

RHODE

Plymouth

Plymouth
Beach

ISLAND

Taunton

Massasoit
State Park

Middleborough

Carver

Myles
Standish
State Forest

Providence

Rehoboth

South
Carver

Taunton
River

Swansea

Cape Cod
Canal

Fall River

Acushnet
River

New
Bedford

Fairhaven

Buzzards

Westport

UMASS-
DARTMOUTH

Bay

New Bedford
Whaling National
Historical Park

Dartmouth

CAPE ISLAND EXPRESS

West Br.
Westport
River

Newport

Horseneck
Beach State
Reservation

East Br.
Westport
River

Demarest
Lloyd State
Park

CUTTYHUNK BOAT LINES

Cuttyhunk
Island

Martha's
Vineyard

0   5 mi

0   5 km

© MOON PUBLICATIONS, INC.

the latter, anticipate having to bring your own bike, as rentals are next to nonexistent.

HISTORY

The last few centuries of southeastern Massachusetts' history may be largely summed up in these words: industry shaped by candlewax and textiles. Going further back in time are the disenfranchised religious fundamentalists in a marriage of convenience with nationalistic venture capitalists, i.e., passengers on the *Mayflower* and their ilk who sought political asylum. Before *that* is the 10,000-year history of Paleo-Indians and their Native American successors. Unfortunately the biographies of these early native residents have been largely overshadowed by the Pilgrims' powerful documentation and broadcasting skills, which trumpeted *their* achievements so loudly the echoes ring in our ears even today. Science is finally filtering out the noise of past indifference and reconstructing what was never recorded in diaries, prayerbooks, and letters. The voice of pre-contact Indians lingers most in place names such as Scituate and Acushnet, Titicut and Manomet, Noquochoke and Nantasket. Contrary to popular belief, Native Americans never completely disappeared, although the region's Herring Pond and Ponkapoag bands of the Wampanoag confederation are still invisible in the eyes of federal bureaucracy.

So long as ships were the link between producers and consumers, settlement of the Old Colony was largely near water. First along the coast, where deep-sea fishing fueled the export trade to England and the West Indies, and then along rivers, which became the primary transportation and trade routes in much of southeastern Massachusetts.

After American independence, cotton mills became the nucleus for massive regional growth, abetted by President Jefferson's 1807 Embargo and the War of 1812, both of which strangled maritime trade, giving boatbuilders and fishermen reason to work for the textile mills that sprang up in Taunton and Fall River. Only New Bedford's whaling fleet—which as early as the 1750s comprised dozens of vessels voyaging as far as South America—could match textiles for profitability. Fall River profited so well during the Civil War, having had the foresight to stock up on cotton beforehand, that by the U.S. centennial a decade later, the city was in the midst of a dizzying rise as a textile center. It produced one half of New England's cotton printcloth. Only Manchester, England, spun and wove more cotton than Fall River's 43 factories and 30,000 looms. Location helped: coastal humidity improved the elasticity of cotton fiber, allowing mills to specialize in the fine-textured, high-quality cloth that brought higher profits than the coarse material produced in the Merrimack Valley. And its portside location yielded a slight edge over inland competitors by cutting out overland trans-

child laborers in the spinning room of the Cornell Mill in Fall River, circa 1912

LEWIS HINE/LIBRARY OF CONGRESSS/LC-SZ62-58600

SOUTHEASTERN MASSACHUSETTS FESTIVALS AND EVENTS

JUNE

If you can't make it to the Mississippi Delta—or if you want to whet your musical appetite for a future trip—come check out the annual **City of Presidents Blues Festival,** at Quincy's Memorial Stadium, on the last Sunday of the month. A roster of blues bands from around New England headlines. The sounds are as convincingly authentic as anything heard on the banks of the Sunflower River down south—even if there aren't any fried tamales nearby and the humidity is only half as high. Call (617) 376-3676 for ticket prices and more information.

JULY

The first Sunday brings the **Pilgrim Breakfast** to the Harlow Old Fort House, Plymouth, tel. (508) 746-0012.

SEPTEMBER

One midmonth weekend, the **Eisteddfod Traditional Arts Festival,** tel. (508) 999-8546, comes to the University of Massachusetts, on Old Westport Rd. in North Dartmouth, south of I-195 Exit 12 (follow Faunce Corner Rd. south across US 6; the UMass-Dartmouth campus will be on the right).

Jousting, jesting, feasting, magic, music, animals, crafts, and 500 performers fill every weekend between early September and late October as the Renaissance festival **King Richard's Faire,** tel. (508) 866-5391, brings the 16th century alive in the woods of South Carver, southwest of Plymouth on Rt. 58. Followers of the national "Rennie" circuit know each has a reputation for excelling in some particular; this one is known for period authenticity and professional acting. Admission is $18 adults, $7.50 kids; parking is free.

portation costs. Fall River also capitalized on steam, which had become cheaper, easier, and faster to build and expand than the canal-fed hydraulic systems employed by Lowell and its sister cities up north. Enjoying the same advantages, New Bedford joined the textile bandwagon from the 1880s until after WW I, surpassing Fall River but finally succumbing, as did all of New England's early industries.

This bygone mill era has left a mixed legacy. The need for more hands to tend acres of spinning frames and power looms attracted a steady supply of poor immigrants from overseas, out of which arose the multicultural heritage of the region, as Irish, Germans, French-Canadians, Syrians, Portuguese, and—almost exclusively to New Bedford—Cape Verdeans swelled city populations. Expanding populations spawned the two-story wooden tenements and three-story triple deckers, which impart a distinct look and feel to the coastal cities even today. The wealth accumulated by the mill owners also left its mark in elaborate civic structures such as theaters, city halls, banks, and museums; city parks with bandstands; and neighborhoods of fancy mansions.

THE SOUTH SHORE

As in nearly every other area within an hour's commute of Boston, the South Shore of Massachusetts Bay down to Plymouth has witnessed explosive growth in the state's postwar era. Despite urbanization, several South Shore communities have continued to uphold their reputations as summer resorts, with public beaches, grand seaside homes, sailboats at anchor off town piers, and a small corps of Fryolators and soft-serve ice cream machines working overtime on July and August evenings. Unfortunately, outside of a few notable exceptions, finding public access to the shoreline requires such detailed maps or other local guidance as to be effectively out-of-bounds to out-of-towners.

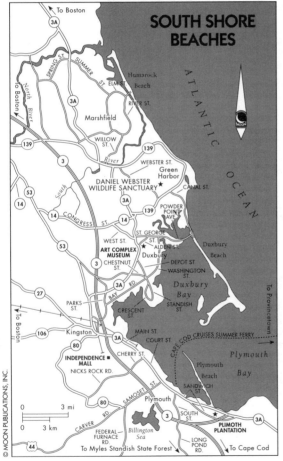

Getting There

Speaking of access, the South Shore's principal connection to Boston, Rt. 3, suffers some of the most intractable rush hour traffic tie-ups in eastern Massachusetts—something to keep in mind if you've elected to make Boston the base for your day-trips by car. Alternatively, Braintree-bound trains of the Red Line T run from Cambridge and downtown Boston to within blocks of Quincy's main historic sights, and should definitely be your top transit choice if that's the extent of your South Shore interests.

QUINCY

Spread along the South Shore between the Neponset and Weymouth Fore rivers, Quincy (QUIN-zee) has essentially been a Boston suburb since the early 1600s. It certainly has that satellite look: lots of residential neighborhoods, shopping plazas, edge-city-style executive office parks on the perimeter, a modest downtown, and stores that cater mostly to the immediate community.

When it comes to history, Quincy's page in the books is

guaranteed, largely by virtue of being the birthplace to much of the great Adams dynasty, wellspring of several generations of prominent public figures. The Quincys, relatives and neighbors of the Adams as well as descendants of the city's namesake settler, also merit notice, having produced three generations of influential Boston mayors. (They were among the last of the blue-blooded Yankees to hold the job.) With such a pedigree one might think that the "City of Presidents" butters its bread with patrician grace, but actually its industrial history is about as long as the Adams' family tree, and filled with as much distinction.

The city's exposed bedrock helped make Quincy a leader in the nation's granite industry for nearly 200 years. At the height of the business, its high-quality hard stone was known to builders and pavers worldwide. Quincy also built ships: wooden ones for the local fishing trade in the 1700s, and eventually steel ones for the Navy during and after WW II. The mighty Fore River Shipyard, now slated for building supertankers rather than destroyers or aircraft carriers, has the distinction of being Massachusetts' last significant heavy industry.

Quincy is the location of several of New England's earliest colonial settlements—fishing and fur-trading enterprises begun in the 1620s. All were short-lived, and they illustrate how the colonists were often their own worst enemies. The first, Wessagusset, was comprised of 60 indentured servants and a handful of overseers sent over in 1622 by one of the original financial backers of the Pilgrims to the south. The disputatious bunch fell apart over Indian relations (some robbed and abused them, some lived with them quite amicably), and finally went back to England after the Pilgrims came and "rescued" them by killing local sachems (which naturally invited retaliations). Six months later another group came to Wessagusset, and while the leader lacked the endurance for a New England winter, the remainder either stayed behind or scattered themselves around the north and west rim of Massachusetts Bay. (Reverend Blaxton, who was an influential farmer, was one such pioneer.)

The decade's most notorious lot of would-be homesteaders was the third settlement, another group of indentured servants with but four

masters, who arrived in 1625. After two years of no profits, *their* leader, a Capt. Wollaston, left for Virginia with his lieutenant to traffic more rewardingly in servants for the Jamestown settlers. One of the principals left behind, Thomas Morton, booted out the fourth overseer by appealing to the servants to cast off their bonds and join him in a community of equals. Morton mischievously christened their settlement Ma-re Mount, erected a maypole for traditional English festivities, and became successful enough in civil and trade relations with neighboring Indians that the Pilgrims no longer could find anyone to barter with for corn or furs. Furious at the unorthodox disregard for class differences, unholy Mayday revels, and—perhaps most important—the liberal-minded friendship with the Massachusett tribe, Plymouth raided Morton's settlement and deported the "Lord of Mis-rule" back to England. Morton soon returned, this time scandalizing his new Puritan neighbors to the north. After a second deportation, the righteous English of Boston and Plymouth were rid of their disruptive, free-thinking competitor. It's perhaps unfortunate that Quincy's forerunners couldn't prevail over their nervous neighboring countryfolk; as one scholar has noted, it's interesting to speculate how New England would have developed had a more secular community free of religious zealots established a successful foothold in the region.

The Adamses

Home to four generations of Adamses, including two American presidents and their heirs, the **Adams National Historic Site,** 135 Adams St., tel. (617) 770-1175, is brimming with history. This large 1700s-era Georgian Colonial with its lovely flower beds and orchard was christened "Peacefields" by George Washington's vice-president and successor, John Adams—but was known as "The Old House" to his family. The property retains traces of the lawyers, diplomats, politicians, and academics who occupied it for a century and a half. John's wife Abigail mockingly called the place a "wren's nest" after returning from ambassadorial life abroad. Come, and decide for yourself whether her criticism was warranted. Among the free special programs offered at the site are condensed reenactments of historical events in which Adamses took part, including defending the British soldiers accused in the Boston Massacre (program held on Patriots Day, the third Monday in April); passage of the Declaration of Independence (July 4th); Congressional debates over southern secession (Gettysburg anniversary, mid-August); and passage of the Constitution (Constitution Day, September 17, and the nearest Saturday). Visitors are supplied scripts to take part, and are rewarded with refreshments.

The grounds are open year-round, but the house is only open for scheduled tours between Patriots Day (the third Monday in April) and Veterans Day (November 11); tickets are sold at the small National Park Service visitor center a short walk away on Hancock Street, in the Galleria shops of Presidents Plaza. The $2 admission includes validated parking in the plaza's garage, guided tours at both the Old House and the two presidential birthplaces (a mile away on Franklin Street), and free connecting transportation between them all by trolley—a real bargain. If your appetite for early American decorative arts and architecture isn't sated by these, ask the rangers for directions to the historic homes in which Abigail Adams was born, in neighboring Weymouth, or to the two homes of the Quincy family (the Dorothy Quincy Homestead and the Josiah Quincy House), all of which are seasonally open to the public for a price.

If driving from the north, take I-93 Exit 8 and follow the National Park Service arrowhead logo to downtown Quincy, a circuitous route past homes, an overgrown hillside, and a couple of shopping plazas. The logo signs unfortunately disappear, but at the foot of the eight-story Stop & Shop office building, turn left and follow traffic around the gold-domed, gray-granite First Parish Church, turning left again at the Harvard Community Health Center. The park visitor center is in the multistory building next door; parking is at the rear. From the west or south take Rt. 3 Exit 18 and follow the Burgin Parkway north; in just under two miles and a little ways past a large T station, make the indicated right turn at the sign for the visitor center, and then the next unsigned right onto downtown Hancock Street. The visitor center will be on your left. By T from Boston or Cambridge, take any Red Line Braintree-bound train (*not* an Ashmont one) to Quincy center (*not* Quincy Adams) and follow signs out the Hancock Street exit. The visitor center is on the ground floor of the six-story building straight ahead. The Park Service's site maps, available to visitors, have clear pedestrian directions to all the historic Adams houses.

USS *Salem*

As an anodyne to all the decorum and decorative arts of that Adams clan, follow the signs from Rt. 3 or Rt. 3A a couple of miles south of downtown Quincy to the berth of the vintage USS *Salem* at the Fore River Shipyard, tel. (617) 479-7900. Over 40 years old and over two football fields long, this huge successor to the battleships of WW II is the nucleus of a hoped-for museum to U.S. naval shipbuilding, a business with which Quincy is intimately acquainted. From late May-Oct. 1 the ship is open daily 10 a.m.-4 p.m.; wander at will during the week or join the guided tours on weekends. Since the vessel is staffed by volunteers year-round, off-season visitors won't be turned away, just ring the bell if nobody's on the quarterdeck, and someone will come and let you aboard. Keep in mind that the amount of indoor heating is very limited. Admission is $6 adults, $4 seniors and kids ages 4-12.

The shipyard may inadvertently have been the source for arguably the most widespread piece of graffiti ever produced: "Kilroy was here." Throughout WW II an equipment inspector named James J. Kilroy allegedly scrawled that famous tag on war materiel inspected by his work gang.

If you don't have a car, the shipyard is accessible from downtown Boston via the **Harbor Express** commuter ferry, operating daily (except Thanksgiving and Christmas) from the north side of Long Wharf, behind the Marriott Hotel. Travel time is about 30 minutes, and puts you within steps of the USS *Salem*. The one-way fare is $5.

Practicalities

Quincy is close enough to Boston to keep accommodation prices high, although parents hoping to attend Cambridge graduations may find the **Best Western Adams Inn,** tel. (800) 368-4012 or (617) 328-1500, on Rt. 3A at the foot of the Neponset River bridge, to be a relative bargain, despite its small rooms. Doubles are $94-

114 during high season and $84 Nov.-mid-April. As compensation for its isolated setting, parking is free, complimentary on-call airport pick-up and drop-off are available, and the North Quincy Red Line T station is only a 10-minute walk (or short free van ride) away. Since even the **Motel 6,** tel. (800) 4 MOTEL6 or (718) 848-7890, a couple of miles south of Quincy at Rt. 3 Exit 17, is $72 d in high season, thrifty travelers will have to look farther southwest to the junction of Interstates 495 and 95 to find a double room regularly under $60 even in high season (specifically, the Motel 6 in Mansfield, tel. 508-339-2323). Alternatively, there's a home hostel in Plymouth; see below for details.

Destination dining is certainly not one of Quincy's strengths, although visitors to the Adams sights will find at least as many eateries downtown along Hancock Street as salons for doing your nails. From donuts and bagels to pizza and gyros, most of the choices are local variants on fast-food, although Mando's Italian Cafe, Siam House Thai Cuisine, and the Blackboard Cafe offer some worthwhile variations within the blocks immediately south of the National Park visitor center.

SOUTH SHORE BEACH TOWNS

Every city and town from Boston south to Cape Cod has some sort of public beach. The ones worth a visit—those with fine sand, nearby parking for nonresidents, and enough breadth to accommodate the crowds that flock to them—are in the towns of Hull, Marshfield, and Duxbury, all about 45-75 minutes' drive south of the Hub via Rt. 3 and local roads. Only Hull's beach is directly accessible on public transit from Boston—via a summer-only ferry from Long Wharf on the downtown waterfront—but cyclists can reach the other two towns with a head start on Commuter Rail. For only $8 roundtrip, the Old Colony Line from South Station will put you at either Kingston or Plymouth station—within a 6-12 mile ride of every public beach from Duxbury to Marshfield. Bike permits (they're good for four years) to bring your wheels aboard the train are available from all of Boston's Commuter Rail terminals for $5. (Alternatively, disembark at the Plymouth end of the line and walk half a mile south on Rt. 3A to

Martha's Bicycles & Fitness, tel. 508-746-2109, the region's only rental shop remotely close to public transit.) Along with sunscreen, remember to pack a copy of the *Eastern Massachusetts Bicycle and Road Map* from Rubel BikeMaps, available at better bookstores (and bike shops) throughout Boston, Cambridge, and the rest of the region; it'll help you find the most bicycle-friendly road to your final destination.

Hull
Poking out into Massachusetts Bay with a long, crooked finger like a miniature Cape Cod, Hull has been a seaside resort for city dwellers since the 19th century. The face it presents to the sea is **Nantasket Beach,** over three miles of broad sand and wide breaking waves backed by video arcades, fried food, ice cream, a classic 1928 carousel, a handful of bars, and a renovated Art Deco bathhouse. More than the beaches to the south, Nantasket has a well-earned reputation for being a real cruisin' beach, though you'll see as many retirees and families with small kids as 20-something buff stuff in Speedos and thong bikinis. From Rt. 3, take Exit 14 and follow Rt. 228 to the end; you won't miss the 1,000-car parking lot beside the ocean when it finally comes up (parking $2).

Dining choices lean heavily toward pizza or fish-and-chips, with the exception of **La Dalat,** a Southeast Asian place on the block with the Dream Machine arcade. If you come prepared—a reservation would help, for a start—consider the nouvelle northern Italian comfort food hidden behind a little beach-shack exterior of **Saporito's Florence Club Cafe,** tel. (781) 925-3023, 11 Rockland Circle off George Washington Blvd., several blocks southwest (uphill) of the beach. Entree prices average around $15, but portions are generous and the seasonally changing preparations are usually quite interesting: meaty heirloom beans from Pescadero, California to accompany a veal scaloppini, for example, or a slab of smoky grilled ricotta boldly paired off the subtle sweetness of a pan-fried bass with chilled corn and peas. Add oversized desserts that nearly outshine the entrees and service warm enough to make you feel like a regular, and you know this is one place that clearly takes customer satisfaction seriously from start to finish. (There's even dental floss in the bathroom.)

Open Wed.-Sun. 5-9 p.m. (10 p.m. on Friday and Saturday), Tuesday, too, in summer. Since it's been discovered by Zagat's, those reservations are all but mandatory. Casual dressers will face a gauntlet of thinly veiled stares from the Talbots-wearing crowd, so change into that blazer or long skirt before coming in off the beach.

Marshfield

The South Shore's "Irish Riviera" is a largely residential community whose year-round population of 21,000 nearly doubles each summer with second home-owners and cottage renters drawn to the ocean. Besides the relative affordability of land and the upward mobility it put within reach of Boston's postwar working classes, Marshfield is blessed with miles of sandy, public beaches, from one end of town to the other. The finest, a long barrier beach beside the South River, actually belongs to neighboring Scituate, but Mother Nature (and the storm of 1898) rearranged the river's opening to the sea, giving Marshfield sole access. Coincidentally, Marshfield also has the only access to next-door **Duxbury Beach,** too (unless you're a Duxbury resident or on bike). In sum, if you're interested in catching some South Shore sun and surf, Marshfield is the place to be.

Three-mile-long **Humarock Beach** is that prize won from Scituate, and finding it can be a little tricky: from Rt. 3 Exit 12 take Rt. 139 east and turn left on Willow St., just before the Marshfield Plaza and the junction for Rt. 3A south. Follow Willow northeast through its various name changes until you hit the village with its fast-food joints, general store, and Sea St., which crosses South River to the beach. All the other beaches are found off Rt. 139 in the town's southern half, where it makes a looping "D" along Ocean St. and Dike Rd. east of Rt. 3A. Quiet **Rexhame Beach** and long **Breakwater Beach,** for example, are located at the end of Standish St. and Surf Ave.; nonresidents park in designated spaces along Rt. 139 or in the Surf Avenue lot. **Brant Rock Beach** is more pebbles than sand, but the views and strolls are fine. Park on the ocean side of Ocean St. between Hancock and Samoset, in the lot on Dike Rd., or at the VFW Esplanade in the village. Immediately to the southwest across the mouth of the Green River is **Green Harbor Beach,** running almost unbroken south to Duxbury. Turn off

Rt. 139 at Beach St., and pray there's still parking available in the lot at the end by Bay Avenue. Enclosing Duxbury Bay to the south is Duxbury Beach, one of the South Shore's nicest set of barrier dunes, five miles of clean sand with nothing but the rolling surf between you and the Azores. If you don't want to walk from Marshfield, look for the signposted turn off Rt. 139 onto Canal St. and follow it to the enormous parking lot at the end ($5 weekdays, $8 weekends). Cyclists coming from the south—the Kingston Commuter Rail station, for example, or Plymouth—can access this beach more expeditiously over the Powder Point Bridge from Duxbury Village; your bike map will show the way.

Except for Brant Rock, all these beaches have restrooms, and both Green Harbor and Duxbury have showers. Most have snack bars, too, although for a much better value try the fish at **Antonio's by the Sea,** 915 Ocean St. (Rt. 139) between Breakwater and Brant Rock.

Marshfield has more up its sleeve than sand and salt water. The Massachusetts Audubon Society has a pair of small properties in the town, the larger of which is the **Daniel Webster Wildlife Sanctuary** at the end of Winslow Cemetery Road. Once the productive farm of the famous jurist and statesman whose rhetoric could outfox the Devil, these fields and woodlands around the Green River estuary are well-suited for short walks and bird watching, with nesting boxes, gourds for purple martins, an osprey pole, and comfortable guidebook-equipped observation blinds overlooking a wetland frequented by ducks, geese, herons, and egrets. Open daily year-round (admission $2), the sanctuary is signposted with the Massachusetts Audubon tern logo from Webster St., both ends of which are crossed by Rt. 139 as it makes its loop through southern Marshfield.

Though he served in Congress as senator from New Hampshire, and is firmly remembered there for his contributions to his alma mater, Dartmouth College, Webster was born in Marshfield, returned here in his twilight years, and is buried in that fenced enclosure with the flagpole passed by sanctuary visitors headed down Winslow Cemetery Road. His law office is also preserved at the 1699 **Winslow House,** tel. (781) 837-5753, open summer afternoons Wed.-Sun. to the public on the southern junction of Rt. 139 and Webster

Street. The namesake of house, road, and cemetery is about the only other mark on Marshfield's otherwise unblemished historical slate: Edward Winslow, Pilgrim, *Mayflower* passenger, and four-time governor of the Plymouth Colony, founded Marshfield in 1640. Admirers of old gravestone art will find members of the 17th- and early 18th-century Winslow clan under the solitary red cedar behind Webster's little wrought iron stockade. The governor himself was buried at sea, but there's a marker for him, too.

Duxbury

If there's one attraction in this seaside village besides the beach that's worth a detour, it's the **Art Complex Museum,** tel. (781) 934-6634, on Alden St. just off Rt. 3A a jot south of Rt. 14, particularly on the last Sunday of each summer month when a public tea ceremony is performed in the traditionally designed Japanese garden. The eclectic permanent collection includes Asian art and Shaker furniture, while changing exhibits regularly feature the work of outstanding contemporary New England artists. The museum is open Wed.-Sun. noon-4 p.m. only; admission is free. Call for information on current or upcoming exhibits. Anyone with a yen for exquisite sweets should also check out **French Memories,** on Washington St. in Duxbury Village near the post office, whose fruit croissants, petit fours, fancy fruit tartlets, and miniature gateaux are all exceptional and quite reasonably priced. The meringues—try the almond-orange, bursting with citrus flavor—are without peer. The sandwiches are a tad on the small side and too restrained with the fillings for the price; stick to the confections and pastries. The fact that this place has a gourmet ice cream and candy shop, imported wine seller, and antique store for its neighbors precisely conveys what sort of average household income lies within this quaint-looking village.

PLYMOUTH

Historic Plymouth, where New England's first successful English settlement took root in December of 1620, didn't draw serious interest in its preservation until the 1800s. Now, after another century of practice, this town could teach Walt Disney a thing or two about marketing Pilgrim-related trinkets and mementos. While history may be the town's trump card, it has a good hand of other activities, including water sports, whale-watching, and antiques. Appropriately enough for the home of America's first Thanksgiving, Plymouth is also one of the leading lights in the cranberry industry, processing tons of the tart fruit from bogs found along many of the more rural state roads in the surrounding county. Great blooms of red dot the autumn-browned landscape during the year-end harvest as bogs are flooded with water and millions of floating berries are corralled for trucking to Plymouth.

Pilgrims Progress

On sloping ground overlooking Plymouth Bay from beside Rt. 3A south of downtown, some 20 thatched structures sit within the stockade of the **Plimoth Plantation,** a carefully studied reproduction of the early 17th-century Pilgrim village. Within the timber walls time is frozen at 1627 as costumed interpreters replicate the quotidian lives of actual villagers, English dialects and all. Though recounted in modern terms, an equally thorough view of 17th-century Native American life is provided at **Hobbamock's Homesite** along the adjacent Eel River. The interpretive staff are very well informed, and while they understandably don't waste their capabilities on those who simply try to trick them into confessing how much time they spend watching TV, anyone who shows the least bit of genuine interest in the lives of their characters are treated to bravura performances.

If you were raised on the usual pabulum served up in school, you may be quite surprised by what the Saints and their Merchant brethren really believed. (Abandon all political correctness ye who enter here—it has no currency in the 17th century.) It's also pleasantly challenging to answer *their* questions about *your* life, when you must resort to analogies or concepts familiar to someone who predates nearly every technology you know by over 350 years, but do try, it doubles the fun. Elsewhere in the complex are museum exhibits, a crafts center where-

costumed interpreters doing work around a Plimoth Plantation animal pen and thatched storage hut

TED CURTIN/COURTESY OF THE PLIMOTH PLANTATION

in artisans produce colonial-style works for sale, food service, and a well-stocked gift shop with quite the comprehensive book selection. Open daily April-Nov., admission to the Plantation alone is $15 adults, $9 for kids 6-17. If you intend to visit both the village and the *Mayflower II,* it pays to buy a combined general admission for $18.50 adults, $11 kids. With validation from the Plantation Visitor Center, tickets may also be used for a second day. Call (508) 746-1622 for more information, including a schedule of such upcoming special programs as the popular harvest dinners, prepared according to 17th-century recipes and techniques.

Two and a half miles away on the harbor waterfront, the *Mayflower II* stands at anchor. Since no detailed description has ever been found for the ship that brought the Pilgrims to New England—even its name went unmentioned until three years after landing—this vessel is a generic rather than specific reproduction of a 17th-century sailing ship. The costumed interpreters who greet you on board, on the other hand, like their Plantation counterparts, are modeled after passengers and crew known to have made the 1620 voyage. Admission, if separate from the Plantation, is $5.50 adults, $3.75 children. Days and hours of operation are the same as at the village.

While there isn't any public transportation shuttling between the downtown and the Plimoth Plantation, weekday commuter buses of the **Plymouth & Brockton** line stop off at the Plantation weekdays on their run from Boston's South Station. (You can effectively use them as a shuttle if you catch 'em at their stop in front of the CVS pharmacy in downtown Plymouth.) Only two departures allow enough time to take it all in without being stranded; call (508) 746-0378 for automated schedule and fare info.

Other Pilgrim-Related Sights

In the shoreline park beside the *Mayflower II* stands a grandiose columned vault, inside of which lies one of most famous thresholds in American history: **Plymouth Rock.** The claim in favor of this surprisingly diminutive stone (which "isn't worth, at the outside, more than 35¢," cracked Mark Twain) being the welcome mat for some reconnoitering Pilgrims back in 1620 rests on the second-hand recollections of a 95-year-old gent who identified the artifact in 1745. Both the surrounding park and "Brewster Gardens," a block south and across the street along Town Brook, are good spots to ponder the ironies of hanging so much American myth on such a small hinge. That brook, barely more than a little freshet for ducks, and its accompanying path run west to the Jenny Grist Mill, a replica of the Pilgrim's 1636 wind-driven cornmeal grinder anchoring a tiny "village" of shops, including an ice cream stand and the aptly named Run of the Mill Tavern.

Rising sharply above Plymouth Rock is Cobb's Hill, on which the earliest Pilgrim settlement was built. Plaques on the houses along Leyden Street and its neighbors tell the early Pilgrims' tale in bite-sized morsels of names and dates. If piecing them all together, adding the Massasoit statue at the hill's seaward edge, and salting with the inscriptions from the adjacent Pilgrim burial marker is still too flavorless for your tastes, check out the **Plymouth National Wax Museum,** there behind Massasoit at 16 Carver St., tel. (508) 746-6468. This, too, is entirely a matter of taste, but at least it leaves nothing to the imagination. Open daily March-Nov.; admission is $5.50, but be sure to inquire about AAA and other discounts, or look for coupons in the various tour brochures at the nearby waterfront visitor information center.

When **Pilgrim Hall Museum** first opened its doors, James Monroe was in the White House and Thomas Jefferson was still throwing parties at Monticello. With the largest extant collection of Pilgrim-related artifacts, it's the town's second must-see for anyone seriously interested in the lives of those 17th-century European immigrants, though it also makes an honorable effort at accurately interjecting a dose of Native American history, too. Among its treasures are the only portrait of a *Mayflower* passenger—Edward Winslow—and the hull of the *Sparrow-Hawk,* one of several vessels that carried the immigrants to these shores, its frame a collection of improbably bandied and spavined tree trunks. The museum's granite Greek Revival facade can't be missed at 75 Court St., tel. (508) 746-1620, where it's open daily till 4:30 p.m. Admission is $4.

Be sure not to pass up on a visit to **Burial Hill,** rising steeply west of Main St. behind the First Church in Town Square. Besides being the one place where the Pilgrims identified their dead, it offers a fine panorama of town and harbor. Plymouth also has a half-dozen 17th- and 18th-century homes open seasonally to the public, including one from 1667 that actually housed some Pilgrims. The friendly folks at the visitor information center on Water Street can supply directions and information on each one.

Prevents Scurvy, Too
Everything you always wanted to know about cranberries—and then some—is found at **Cranberry World,** sponsored by industry-dominating Ocean Spray, 225 Water St., tel. (508) 747-2350. Daily from May-Nov. their visitor center offers displays on the plant's life cycle, the history of its cultivation, and examples of products made from cranberries through the years. Try samples and take home recipes, too. Like everything at Cranberry World, it's all free.

Of course, to really taste the full potential of that bright red berry head over to the **Plymouth Colony Winery,** off Rt. 44 three miles west of Rt. 3 Exit 6, tel. (508) 747-3334. As you could probably guess from the acres of fertile bogs surrounding the place, cranberry wines are the specialty, but other locally grown fruits are featured in the line-up, too. Free tours and tastings are available daily, April-Dec., and weekends in March. Massachusetts blue laws regarding beer and wine sales apply only to retailers, not producers, so you may arrive on a Sunday confident of being able to buy whatever strikes your fancy.

PRACTICALITIES

Camping
The South Shore boasts two attractive public campgrounds, both of which are fairly close to Plymouth. The nearest is in the **Myles Standish State Forest,** southwest of downtown on the Plymouth-Carver line, tel. (508) 866-2526. Nearly 500 campsites are spread out around four completely separate ponds, with water, fireplace grills, bathhouses including showers, and a dumping station (no hookups). Open mid-April-mid-Oct., $5-6. Selected sites are also available to RVs throughout the winter for a discount. To the north in Hingham about halfway between Quincy and Marshfield is **Wompatuck State Park,** with 400 campsites also amid pine forest, albeit amid more hilly terrain. Wompatuck matches Myles Standish in amenities, but also offers electrical hookups for a couple of dollars over the base site fee of $6. The season is also

the same, mid-April-mid-Oct., but here there are no off-season exceptions. Wompatuck does, however, take reservations: tel. (781) 749-7160. To reach the park, take Rt. 228 east about three miles from Rt. 3 Exit 14, and follow signs from the turn onto Free St. Don't be put off by the amount of suburban development leading up to the front gate—it's a different world inside.

Accommodations

Given all those big bus tours that roll through, it should come as no surprise that Plymouth's average room rates aren't much lower than Boston's, although families may appreciate not having to pay extra for their kids or their cars. Inexpensive rooms aren't totally unheard of, though, thanks to the **Bunk & Bagel,** tel. (508) 830-0914, a backpackers' B&B of sorts whose owners retired from many years of operating an AYH/Hostelling International affiliate elsewhere in the state. Located just a couple of blocks from downtown, it's the best deal in the region for single travelers: $15-25 pp for a bed in one of three shared, single-sex rooms. Couples should inquire about the availability of a room of their own.

Only one national chain is represented locally, although there's a small cluster of others halfway to Boston (priced accordingly), among the South Shore office parks about a mile west of Rt. 3 Exit 14. Otherwise Plymouth offers a number of small motels, the sort of family-run places that used to beckon vacationers along every two-lane highway across America in the pre-interstate era. For additional accommodation suggestions, including a list of the town's many modest B&Bs, drop by Plymouth's **Waterfront Information Center** down on the harbor and pick up a *Plymouth Area Motel Guide,* also available by phone, tel. (800) USA-1620, or on the Internet at www.plymouth-1620.com.

Food

Eating out in Plymouth is like voting in a Congressional race: outside of a few exceptions most of the choices are either unremarkable or downright disappointing. This is the home of the BLT, veal parmesan, chicken fingers, seafood Newburg, and shrimp scampi. Do you miss your Stovetop stuffing and glossy squares of Velveeta? Rejoice—you can quench all such homesickness right here, with a waterfront view no less. No-surprise dining is also available at a variety of fast-food places familiar from home and on the road; besides those along Rt. 3A through town check out the food courts at the huge Independence Mall beside Rt. 3 Exit 8 in adjacent Kingston.

Anyone in need of an eye-opening breakfast should make a beeline for **Persy's Place,** also in Kingston, at Dempsey's Country Store on Main St. (Rt. 3A) just east of Rt. 3 Exit 9, tel. (781) 585-5464. If the number of the menu items doesn't get your attention, the Homeric portions will. Down-home and family-friendly, Persy's is open for lunch, too. When it comes to fried or broiled fruits of the sea, head for Plymouth's town wharf, home to several seafood-in-the-rough places, each of which has a loyal following that will only grudgingly admit to the strengths of the opposition. Trading its lack of waterfront tables for a slight edge on price, **Souza's Seafood,** tel. (508) 746-5354, is at least equal to its neighbors on the fried shellfish front, but the dish that dusts the competition is the lobster bisque: thick, rich, flavorful, and not to be missed. Open daily in summer till 10 p.m., cutting back in winter to Thurs.-Sun. until late afternoon or early evening, depending on business. Alternatively, a few miles south of Plimoth Plantation on Rt. 3A is **Star of Siam,** tel. (508) 224-3771, a Thai take-out joint of surprisingly good quality.

PLYMOUTH ACCOMMODATIONS

Sheraton Inn Plymouth, 180 Water St., tel. (800) 325-3535 or (508) 747-4900; restaurant, indoor swimming pool; $105-165 d.

Governor Bradford Motor Inn, 98 Water St., tel. (800) 332-1620 or (508) 746-6200; heated outdoor swimming pool; $58-89 d.

Cold Spring Motel, 188 Court St. (Rt. 3A), tel. (508) 746-2222; open April to October; $49-89 d.

Pilgrim Sands Motel, on Rt. 3A opposite the entrance to Plimoth Plantation, two miles south of downtown, tel. (800) 729-SAND or (508) 747-2800; the only lodgings in Plymouth with a private beach at its door; $65-115 d.

Finally, if you crave a classic fine dining experience, make reservations at the **Crane Brook Restaurant-Tea Room,** 229 Tremont St. in South Carver, tel. (508) 866-3235. Located about 10 miles southwest of downtown Plymouth (take Summer St. west to Federal Furnace Rd. south, which becomes Tremont across the town line), this establishment is widely regarded as the South Shore's finest restaurant, the kind of place that discreetly attracts business tycoons and heads of state passing through Boston. It's priced to match: dinner for two with a modest wine will top $100.

Getting There
Anyone without a car will find Plymouth's public transportation gateway is almost strictly via Boston. Although any glance at a Commuter Rail map will temptingly show a nice direct line southward out of the Hub, Plymouth's station is unfortunately some two miles north of downtown at the Cordage Park Marketplace on Rt. 3A. Furthermore, service is strictly off-peak: for maximum appeal to Boston-bound commuters doing the 9-5 thing, rush-hour service skips Plymouth entirely and substitutes the

Kingston station, near the Independence Mall on Rt. 3. With over 1,000 parking spaces available for only $1, the Kingston station is, however, a good choice for visitors based in the Plymouth area and planning only a daytrip up to Boston. Call (800) 392-6100 or (617) 222-3200 for Commuter Rail schedules and fares. Unfortunately, until some sort of year-round shuttle between the Cordage Park depot and downtown is established, it makes no sense to recommend the train for car-free visitors *to* Plymouth. In the meantime **Plymouth & Brockton Street Railway** bus service is the ticket, albeit a weekday-only one. (Their weekend Boston-Cape Cod service stops in Plymouth, but only at the Industrial Park out by Rt. 3, a couple of pedestrian-unfriendly miles from any local attractions. Or call Mayflower Taxi: 508-746-7887.) The nearly hourly Mon.-Fri. downtown-to-downtown buses pick up passengers from Boston's South Station bus depot and all Logan Airport terminals; to the center of Plymouth it's a 75-minute ride with lots of local stops along the way. Call (508) 746-0378 for automated schedule and fares, or visit them on the Web at www.p-b.com.

NEW BEDFORD AND VICINITY

If any one place deserves recognition for having propelled whales to the brink of extinction, it's New Bedford. With its deep-water port, proximity to inland markets, and financial capital from a Nantucket man, Joseph Rotch, the city overtook its island competitor early in the 1800s. By the middle of the 19th century, New Bedford sent more whalers a-whaling than all other U.S. ports combined. Discovery of Pennsylvania crude oil in 1859 and predatory Southern raiders during the Civil War put a severe damper on the whale oil business, forcing a shift away from lighting and lubrication to the sale of baleen, a natural plastic. The loss of a large number of New Bedford's fleet in the Arctic ice pack during the winter of 1871 and the nationwide Panic of 1872 dealt two more crippling blows to the industry; and when finally spring steel was invented in 1905, the market for baleen evaporated almost overnight.

A dozen years before the bottom dropped out of the whale oil market, the Wamsutta Mills had commenced to build up its reputation for cotton sheets, called percale to distinguish them from the lower-quality goods of northern mills. Buoyed by consumer demand and then WW I, textile manufacturing grew fast enough through the early 1900s so that the local economy hardly hiccuped when the baleen business went belly-up. Similarly, by the time the mills started to shut down for good, the city had enough invested in cod fishing to soften the fall from the textile throne. After two near misses, New Bedford finally became too dependent in this century on a single industry, namely, New England's largest commercial fishing fleet. Plundering the seas since the 1977 Magnuson Act established America's 200-mile territorial limit has resulted in forced closure of the fisheries by federal regulators belatedly reacting to two decades of shortsightedness. Needless to say, the grounding of hundreds of vessels has had a profound impact on the local economy.

Despite the city's troubles the immutable charm of the downtown historic district remains, with its cobblestone streets and brick facades virtually unaltered since Herman Melville shipped out in 1847 aboard a whaler bound for the Pacific. For a good orientation to the area, drop by the well-stocked **Waterfront Visitor Center,** tel. (800) 508-5353 or (508) 979-1745, on State Pier at the base of the big pedestrian bridge over the four-lane Downtown Connector (Rt. 18 South).

SIGHTS

A-Whaling We Go
You'll find the best orientation to the area from the **New Bedford Whaling National Historical Park** visitor center, tel. (508) 996-4469, in the handsome brownstone 1853 District Court building (the Old Savings Bank), on the corner of William St. and N. Second. Browse all the same flyers found down at its pierside cousin, join a city resident for one of the free hour-long walking tours offered daily July-Aug., inquire about ranger-guided activities, or pick up brochures for one of a handful of self-guided architectural walks (meticulously researched by the New Bedford Preservation Society) around town.

The city's foremost attraction, and rightfully so, is the excellent **New Bedford Whaling Museum** atop of Johnny Cake Hill, tel. (508) 997-0046. Fanciful carved ship figureheads, a large scrimshaw collection, historic photos, paintings, tools and artifacts of the industry that made the city famous on the seven seas, an 89-foot model of a fully rigged sailing vessel, and changing exhibits about modern maritime pursuits are just a few of the highlights. Maintained by the Old Dartmouth Historical Society, the museum is open daily until 5 p.m.; admission is a bargain $3.50. Across the cobblestone street is the **Seamen's Bethel,** an attractive clapboard sanctuary featured in a chapter of *Moby Dick*. More frequented now by tourists than "moody fishermen shortly bound for the Indian or Pacific oceans," the 1832 "whaleman's chapel" otherwise remains much as Herman Melville de-

The crew of a whaleboat off the Wanderer *heaves to at the oars as the man in the bow prepares to throw the lance.*

scribed it. Open Mon.-Sat. late May-early Sept.; off-season the Bethel is locked, but when available the staff next door at the Mariner's Home, tel. (508) 992-3295, are happy to let you in. Admission is by donation, but "nobody will look at you funny if you don't put anything in." Since it *is* a working church, the Bethel is unequivocally closed to visitors during weddings, funerals, and selected other commissioned services.

Schooner *Ernestina*
Generations before electronically-guided overfishing, twin-masted wooden schooners such as the *Ernestina* flocked to Newfoundland's cod-rich Grand Banks with decks full of small dories from which the crew would hand-trawl for their catch. After years of service in the Gloucester fishing fleet under the name *Effie Morrissey*, this 1894 "Banker" saw duty as an Arctic explorer, naval base supplier, and transatlantic packet. It's tempting to say they don't build 'em like they used to, but while the *Ernestina* is one of a mostly vanished breed, the Essex boatyard that built her and hundreds of her sisters does continue to operate under the auspices of the Essex Shipbuilding Museum. In 1997, it

even launched a hand-sawn double-frame schooner not unlike this one, for use in daysailing and charters out of Gloucester.

A floating National Historic Landmark, the *Ernestina* is also engaged in tourism and education, regularly calling on seven of the state's ports for dockside tours and daysailing trips during its May-Oct. season; call (508) 992-4900 to check on the schedule, or visit the vessel's Web page: www.umassd.edu/specialprograms/caboverde. When moored at the State Pier next to the Cuttyhunk ferry, admission for dockside visits is $3. Sailings, for which reservations are recommended, are typically $40-50 for a half day.

ACROSS THE ACUSHNET RIVER

For much of the past century families have signaled their improving lot by moving up out of New Bedford's grim mills and wharves and across the harbor to **Fairhaven** (Fair HEY-ven), within spyglass view of Johnny Cake Hill. From the palatial Italianate high school to the monumental gothic-spired Unitarian Memorial Church with its Tiffany stained glass, this small town is plainly cut from different cloth than its sister city across the harbor. The look of the place is almost entirely the work of one man, Henry Huttleston Rogers, a native son and robber baron who made a small mountain of money as a president of half a dozen of John D. Rockefeller's Standard Oil companies. The school and church are but two of a half-dozen opulent buildings donated by Rogers between 1885 and 1904 to his grateful hometown. Stop by the marvelous Millicent Library on Center Street—named after Rogers' daughter, and accurately described as "a heaven of light and grace and harmonious color and sumptuous comfort" by his good friend Mark Twain—for a Fairhaven **walking tour** brochure (also available at the town **Visitor Center,** a block west of the library by the corner of Main and Center, tel. 508-979-4085). Besides epitomizing the spirit of the Gilded Age in which it was built, the Millicent's Romanesque stonework, detailed woodwork, and stained glass convey the church-like appreciation once accorded to public libraries in this country.

While at the library you may care to peruse the displays about Fairhaven's sister city of Tosashimizu, Japan. It's a relationship that grew out of the fact that the first Japanese resident of the U.S., "John" Manjiro Nakahama, settled in Fairhaven in the 1840s after being brought there by the whalers who rescued him from a Pacific shipwreck.

SOUTH TO THE SEA

Detached from the rest of Massachusetts by I-195, the nubbin of land drained by the Apponagansett, Slocum, and Westport Rivers south and west of New Bedford is one of the state's lesser-known gems. Which is only to say that it's on the dark side of the moon as far as Bostonians are concerned. But to Rhode Islanders, local residents, and yachties who knock around Buzzards Bay, the two towns comprising this area—**Dartmouth** and **Westport**—are a familiar and highly prized morsel indeed. The strip mall development along US 6, parallel to I-195, and heaps of adjacent low-density commuter suburbs will leave you totally unprepared for the idyllic villages along the coast, the sort once found on Cape Cod before it was overwhelmed by commercialism.

Historically this has been farming country, to which the old drystone walls and weathered barns so eloquently bear witness. The tourist trade and summer homes are no strangers to the area either, having roots in the 19th century, but the landscape is most visibly shaped by the working farms that still remain. Some have found a niche raising high-value organic or specialty meat and produce, but the agricultural product gaining the most attention in the area is *vitus vinifera:* the traditional grape of fine wine. The results of both may be sampled locally; try **Worden's** on Water St. in Padanaram Village, tel. (508) 999-4505, for a very expensive but very good introduction to local baby greens, herbs, Macomber turnips, fish, ostrich, and wine, among other things. (The meat of ostrich, which are raised at Pokanoket Farms across the bay on Gulf Raod, does *not* taste like chicken—it's rather more like alligator.) The surrounding village **Padanaram** (PAY d-NAREM) barely occupies more than two blocks, but both are a window-shopper's delight, with antiques, art, Shaker-style contemporary furniture, Aussie women's clothing, and good eateries about every five yards. Bring a full wallet; there're no ATMs here.

Padanaram is by tradition the center of South Dartmouth, a formerly precise marker of geographical and social standing dating back to the days when New Bedford was known as Old Dartmouth. These days South Dartmouth is the post office's shorthand for both Padanaram Village and the Slocum River to the west, whose wide, irregular estuary begins at Russells Mills Village—ostensibly little more than an 18th-century general store and nearby pottery shop—and ends at **Demarest Lloyd State Park.** The park's protected beach opens out onto Buzzards Bay (day use $2; showers available). Those "buzzards" are actually ospreys, whose preferred habitat includes much of the Slocum's salt marsh. You can try and catch sight of these fast-diving raptors from the trails or indoor observation room of the **Lloyd Center for Environmental Studies,** on wooded Potomska Rd. along the east side of the estuary, tel. (508) 990-0505. The grounds are open daily year-round; the center itself is open Tues.-Sun. and Monday holidays. Admission by donation. Naturalist-led trail walks and canoe trips are also available, for a fee; call ahead for schedules and reservations. Additional walking trails and paddling suggestions are to be found in a local publication called *Recreation Guide to Dartmouth,* available at Padanaram's **Village Bookshop,** 294 Elm St., or by mail ($9); to order call (508) 991-2289.

Over the town line west of Russells Mills Village lies Westport's wine country, whose rocky soil and temperate climate, similar to the northern Burgundy region of France, are particularly suited for white and sparkling wines. **Westport Rivers Vineyard & Winery,** 417 Hixbridge Rd., tel. (508) 636-3423, has used these natural advantages to become New England's largest grower of *vinifera* grapes—chardonnay, riesling, pinot noir, pinot meunier—and arguably its most acclaimed winery. Massachusetts wine may have been an oxymoron once, but stop by for a sample of this historic farm's vintages and discover firsthand why California isn't the last word in premiere American wines. The tasting room and shop is open daily April-Dec., and weekends only Jan.-March. Winery tours are offered on weekends year-round (free), and every quarter is laced with special events pairing fine food with Westport wines (definitely not free).

For all those whose personal maxim is closer to "I'd rather be surfing" than "in vino veritas," Westport also has **Horseneck Beach,** almost six miles due south of the winery. When prevailing summer southwesterly winds get a little frisky, this broad, two-mile stretch catches some good strong breakers off the Rhode Island Sound. Day-use fee for the beach, with snack bar, bathhouses, and showers, is just $2.

PRACTICALITIES

Camping
The area's nearest public camping is along the coast to the southwest, in **Horseneck Beach State Reservation** at the end of Rt. 88 in Westport, tel. (508) 636-8816. Open mid-May-mid-Oct., fees are generally $6, or a dollar more for waterfront locations. Despite the lack of hookups the campground is very popular with the big homes on wheels, which, when combined with the lack of any vegetation higher than your ankles, means the place bears an often uncanny resemblance to a dealers' used RV lot. But with the ocean only a hop, skip, and jump away (and hot showers for your après-surf pleasure) who's complaining? Tent campers will want to give serious consideration to the weather before choosing one of the waterfront sites in front of the dunes: if strong, gusty winds are in the overnight forecast you'll be feeling and tasting crunchy for days. All 100 sites are available on a first-come, first-served basis, but from shortly after opening until after Labor Day it can be tricky trying to find a vacancy; arrive early or call ahead to check on availability.

Accommodations
The warmest welcome and greatest convenience to downtown attractions and restaurants is **The 1875 House B&B,** tel. (508) 997-6433, on Seventh St. in the historic district within walking distance of the Whaling Museum. Three comfortably decorated rooms with private bath and continental breakfast are $55-65 (no credit cards). Equally convenient to downtown at-

tractions and restaurants is the 17-room **Spouter Inn,** tel. (800) 691-9066 or (508) 997-7771, in a fortress-solid old granite building on the downtown waterfront. Doubles run $90-120 including a continental breakfast in the rooftop restaurant overlooking the fishing fleet. Least convenient for tourists—unless you want an indoor pool to occupy the kids—is **Days Inn,** on Hathaway Rd. by the airport, at I-195 Exit 13B, tel. (800) DAYS INN or (508) 997-1231. Usually a promotional rate around $65 d is available, although members of various hotel discount schemes hoping to land a bargain will find regular rates are actually around $94 d.

A mile away across the Acushnet River in Fairhaven lay several more possibilities, all of which are actually closer to downtown than that Days Inn. Right at the eastern end of the Middle St. bridge is the **Seaport Inn,** tel. (800) 835-7678 or (508) 997-1281, while over by I-195 Exit 18 is a **Hampton Inn,** tel. (800) HAMPTON or (508) 990-8500. Both are moderate. There's also the aptly named **Edgewater Bed and Breakfast,** tel. (508) 997-5512, in Fairhaven's oldest neighborhood a couple of blocks from both the resting place of the town's earliest white settler and the launch site of the *Spray,* a refitted little oyster boat whose landmark 1895-98 voyage is beautifully chronicled in Capt. Joshua Slocum's autobiographical *Sailing Alone Around the World.* Originally a store selling all sorts of imported goods from the West Indies, the large cedar-shingled home at the end of Oxford Street now offers hospitality in a range of rooms and fireplace-equipped suites, all with modernized private baths, carpeting, and cable TV. Prices range from $65-95 including a filling continental breakfast. For something close enough to make strategic forays into the city but rural enough to allow a walk to the beach or a country ramble by bike, look to the handful of B&Bs in Padanaram Village and South Dartmouth, all no more than six miles from downtown New Bedford. These include **The Saltworks,** tel. (508) 991-5491, e-mail quickshole@aol.com, a friendly, art-filled, fireplace-equipped manse a short stroll from the center of Padanaram, $95 d (closed mid-December through late January); and **Salt Marsh Farm,** tel. (508) 992-0980, in the countryside of South Dartmouth, $70-90 d. Both feature private baths, full breakfasts, and the kind of

hospitality that prompts returning guests to reserve rooms months in advance.

Food

Diner fans on the lookout for big breakfasts or blue-plate lunch specials will appreciate New Bedford's pair of offerings in this department. Easiest to find is **Angelo's Orchid Diner,** a 1951 O'Mahoney stainless-sided model on US 6 at Rockdale; its menu is solid short-order fare enlivened by a Portuguese influence. For a traditional Greek hand over the grill, check out the pristine **Shawmut Diner,** another '50s O'Mahoney on Shawmut Ave. at Hathaway, near Rt. 140 and the airport. Open daily 5 a.m.-7 p.m., with a neon Indian that's almost worth a visit in itself. (A third mint-condition O'Mahoney, **Jake's Diner,** can be found beside the Pasta House on Alden Rd. in Fairhaven, north of the big Fairhaven Commons shopping plaza on US 6.)

On the other end of the lunch spectrum—and within walking distance of the Whaling Museum—are the sorts of places familiar with raspberry vinaigrette and romaine lettuce: **Phoebe's Restaurant,** for example, on S. Sixth St. at Union (closed Monday), in a pleasantly airy 19th century space behind a hefty granite facade; or **Freestone's,** at the corner of William and N. Second St. near the National Park visitor center, with its specialties of steak and seafood. The latter is also open daily for dinner, until 11 p.m.

Given that you're in a city that's 60% Portuguese, you should consider acquainting yourself with this local cuisine, although if you're a light eater bring along a pair of friends to finish your meal. Best known around town is **Antonio's,** on Coggeshalle and N. Front slightly northeast of the I-195/Rt. 18 interchange (Exit 15), tel. (508) 992-7359. Industrial-strength fare at a minimal (cash only) price are the rule at this bar-cum-dining room, whose plainness doesn't detract one whit from the boisterous enjoyment of the never-ending crowds. Buried equally deep in a mixed commercial-residential neighborhood on the opposite end of downtown is **Vasco da Gama,** on Dartmouth at Washington, a block south of Metro Pizza, look for the 7-Up sign over what's essentially a plain brickfront bar. Kale soup, rabbit or shellfish swimming in spicy tomato-based sauces, and of course *bacalhau* (salt cod) are typical menu items at both places, in portions designed to stoke a boat crew until their return.

If the screeching of the seagulls around downtown is whetting your appetite for seafood, consider **Davy's Locker,** tel. (508) 992-7359, way out on E. Rodney French St. at Billy Wood's Wharf, where the ferry for Martha's Vineyard departs. There outside the rocky seawall you can watch the wheeling gulls over the harbor as you dig into some of the freshest fish in town, grilled, broiled with butter and bread crumbs, or fried, and served as it has been since the place opened in 1966, with mashed potatoes, canned vegetables, and red jello for dessert. There's also a short menu of "light, healthy" meals to give peace of mind to that half of the clientele that has to regularly visit a cardiologist.

Next to fragrant, belt-stretching Portuguese cookery, the most exciting menus are on the city's outskirts. One of the hands-down best places for seafood in the area is across the harbor in Fairhaven: **Margaret's,** tel. (508) 992-9942, at the corner of Main St. and Ferry, a block from the water. Run by the Isaksens, descendants of a Norwegian family attracted by the local maritime trades, this cozy little rough-cut gem also has the most difficult hours: Monday and Wed.-Sat. 7 a.m.-2 p.m. for breakfast and lunch, Friday 5-9 p.m. for dinner, and Sunday 7:30 a.m.-noon for breakfast. Breakfasts include fruit-filled Norwegian pancakes; lunches lean toward sandwiches, pasta, baked or fried seafood, and a soul-stirring chowder. Catch that Friday dinner and your choices might include grilled tuna with tropical salsa or Thai chili sauce; oven-roasted fresh salmon; or shrimp, prosciutto, and chevre baked in phyllo. If there are deep-sea scallops on the menu—probably fresh off the family's own boats—don't pass them by.

In the opposite direction, out on commercial US 6 west of the city, is **Not Your Average Joe's,** a brick-oven gourmet pizzeria. (It's actually just over the Dartmouth line.) Walls adorned with art of Calderesque simplicity, bold Santa Fe colors, and light wood trim set the scene, that roaring oven, and the young, casu-

al staff set the tone, while dishes like herb-marinated steak tips with wild mushrooms or artichoke- and marscapone-stuffed spinach pasta set off the rave reviews. With as many pasta, barbecue, and grilled meat dishes as pizzas, this isn't just a hip alternative to Domino's. Top-notch desserts (try the seasonal fruit crisp, or the perfectly tart key lime tarte), excellent beers (from the nearly local Tremont Ale on tap to the elusive Mackesson XXX stout in bottles), extensive wines by the glass, bottomless soda, and the ability to add your name to the waiting list by phone all add up to one thing: this one's a winner. If you need to while away some time before your table is ready, step next door to **Baker's Books,** the area's best bookstore.

Getting There and Away

Frequent daily express bus service is available between Boston and New Bedford via **American Eagle Motor Coach,** tel. (508) 993-5040. Daily service from Cape Cod, New York city, and Providence, RI, is also available with **Bonanza Bus Lines,** tel. (800) 556-3815 or (401) 751-8800. All buses arrive at New Bedford's downtown transit terminal on Pleasant St. between City Hall and the post office, two blocks from the National Park visitor center at 33 William St., four blocks from the Whaling Museum, and just over six blocks from the Cuttyhunk ferry.

Between mid-May and mid-October, the **Cape Island Express,** a.k.a. the M/V *Schamonchi,* tel. (508) 997-1688, has 1-4 daily departures from New Bedford to Martha's Vineyard. The 90-minute trips start from Billy Wood's Wharf just outside the hurricane barrier on the city's southern peninsula; from I-195 Exit 15 or Rt. 18 south, simply follow the ferry signs. Year-round, the Elizabeth Islands are as close as a ride aboard the **Cuttyhunk Boat Lines'** doughty little *Alert II,* which departs from downtown Fisherman's Wharf from twice a week in winter to daily mid-June-mid-September. The one-hour ride is $15.75 roundtrip, plus $5 for bikes. Call (508) 992-1432 for a detailed schedule.

FALL RIVER AND VICINITY

Even if you've never heard of Fall River, you probably know a small but memorable bit of Fall River history. You learned it at school: "Lizzie Borden took an ax/And gave her mother 40 whacks…" Yes, Miss Lizzie Andrew Borden, a wealthy financier's daughter (and Sunday school teacher) accused of double murder in 1892, was a Fall River gal. A jury of Miss Borden's peers returned a verdict of *not guilty*. But you probably knew that, too.

Before Lizzie Borden made Fall River famous, the town was king of fine printed cotton, material suitable for dresses, lingerie, and other quality apparel. European revolutions and crop failures swelled the city with immigrants from across Europe and Canada. Besides the Portuguese, whose presence is still abundantly evident in city menus and Portuguese-language ATM instructions, the city gained large numbers of both French Canadians and Lebanese Christians, who were able to share French-language church services. In its ascendancy, over 85% of its workforce was employed in textiles, a percentage unrivaled by any other industry in any other Massachusetts town. The problem with such lopsided concentration became apparent as soon as textile firms made their exodus to the low-wage, anti-regulatory southern states: there was no other industry to pick up the slack. Fall River swiftly became one of the leading casualties of the Depression. Manufacturers' flight, compounded by a devastating downtown fire and the stock market crash of 1929, propelled the city into a decade of bankruptcy. The giant brick mills have only recently reawakened from their decades of boarded-up slumber, re-animated by the factory stores that contribute to Fall River's new stature as southern New England's discount retailing center.

SIGHTS

Battleship Cove

Beneath the huge I-195 bridge spanning the mouth of the Taunton River lies a small armada of old naval vessels. The centerpiece is the USS *Massachusetts,* known to her crew as "Big Mamie," a 46,000-ton battleship that dwarfs the WW II-vintage destroyer, submarine, and PT boats at anchor nearby. The $8 admission covers the whole fleet, and you're free to explore the all, from the massive gun turrets to the below-deck quarters, where local Boy Scout troops are treated to special slumber parties. Open daily; for further information, call (800) 533-3194 or (508) 678-1100.

Often sharing the cove is the anachronistic HMS *Bounty,* a vessel more often associated with the South Pacific than southeastern Massachusetts. Scrupulously reconstructed from the original Admiralty blueprints, this replica of the original 18th-century Royal Navy tall ship—slightly enlarged to accommodate movie cameras—was built for the 1962 MGM version of the famous mutiny against the infamous Capt. Bligh. A gift to the city, the boat during the week performs a special brand of seaborn education, but come the weekend it throws open its gangway to visitors; admission $4. Costumed staff are on hand to answer questions, give demos, and explain why the captain's decision to reserve precious fresh water for his cargo of breadfruit trees—cargo vital to feeding slaves that worked England's Caribbean plantations—was among the sparks that kindled the 1789 mutiny. Occasional port calls are made elsewhere in New England, so phone ahead, tel. (508) 673-3886, before making any special detour to see it.

Adjacent to the mothball navy is the **Fall River State Heritage Park,** tel. (508) 675-5759, whose exhibits commemorate the city's textile history. Lewis Hine's photos documenting child labor in the local mills, part of a body of evidence that helped establish the nation's first child labor laws, are not to be missed. Open daily 10 a.m.-4 p.m., summers until 6 p.m.; admission is free. The boardwalk esplanade along the water's edge is a good place to soak up some rays over a picnic lunch if the weather is cooperative, but for a loftier view of the broad Taunton River be sure to climb up the belltower beside the visitor center entrance. Between late May and early September you'll notice a small fleet of Mercury daysailers awaiting customers at the park boathouse; if you're experienced, the only thing between you and a day of tacking about Mt. Hope Bay is a test demonstrating your skill to the boathouse staff and $15 for a season pass. Novices can stick around for a couple of weeks' worth of classes. If you haven't that much time, as consolation you might try to catch one of the free summer **Heritage Park Concert Series** performances in the meadow behind the visitor center, usually on Sunday afternoon or evening.

Hulking steel ships, squealing seagulls, and grainy recollections of life during the Industrial Revolution aren't all that draws visitors to Battleship Cove. The park is further augmented by the antique **Fall River Carousel,** under the interstate bridge, whose hand-painted mounts were the work of Philadelphia Toboggan Company craftsmen. Puppet shows, face painting, and other activities are usually on hand, if young riders get tired of their steeds. Open daily May-Oct.; rides are under $1. And across the street from the petite merry-go-round is the **Old Colony and Fall River Railroad Museum,** tel. (508) 674-9340, a collection of railroad miscellany housed in a pair of rail cars, one of which bears the livery of the long-defunct namesake passenger line. Open afternoons daily late June-Labor Day, and weekends only mid-April to early December.

Last but by no means least is **The Marine Museum at Fall River,** two blocks south at 70 Water St., tel. (508) 674-3533. The 28-foot model of the RMS *Titanic,* built for the eponymous 1953 movie is just the tip of the iceberg at this cavernous museum, whose curious and sometimes surprising highlights include a huge collection of *Titanic* memorabilia, numerous detailed ship models, and artifacts from the steamers that ferried Fall River textile tycoons to and from New York City. Open daily; admission $3.50.

The Highlands Historic District

Historically, the social geography of Fall River has been based on The Hill. The worlds "above the hill" and "below the hill" were always separated by more than elevation. While today the fashionable Victorian homes built by Fall River's captains of industry don't stand quite as tall over their downhill neighbors as they used to, the Highlands district still has plenty of well-preserved reminders of the city's zenith. A walking tour brochure identifying the area's most notable unaltered mansions is available from either the public library on N. Main St. at Franklin, or from the **Fall River Historical Society,** tel. (508) 679-1071, whose hilltop mansion headquarters sits behind the fancy iron fence on the corner of Rock St. and Maple. Inside, the society has captured a glimpse of the neighborhood's golden years with opulent furnishings, ornate interiors, and a stunning collection of some 2,000 Victorian costumes. And yes, morbid curiosity-seekers hooked on the celebrated 1892 Lizzie Borden trial will find that the forensic evidence used in court, including the alleged murder weapon, are also part of the society's collections. Souvenir Victorian plates, Christmas ornaments, and toys are available in the gift shop, along with a variety of books on local and regional topics. Open Tues.-Fri. April-Dec. plus weekends in summer; admission $3.50.

PRACTICALITIES

Accommodations

On I-195 from Swansea, west of Fall River, to Dartmouth, east of town, you'll see the signs for most of the area's available accommodations—all national chains. For an inexpensive bed and breakfast—one of the best-priced accommodations in the state outside of hostels and campgrounds—try **Gilbert's Tree Farm B&B,** tel. (508) 252-6416, less than eight miles away, in rural Rehoboth. Its three rooms run $32-50 with shared bath and full country breakfast.

Food

Hot dogs are to Fall River what coffee is to Seattle. Buy 5 Get The 6th Free! signs adorn tiny storefronts on seemingly every block of the city. Aficionados of the steamed frank are often found downing a few inside the classic little 1956 **Nite Owl Diner,** tel. (508) 673-6335, on the corner of Pleasant and Eastern at the far east end of The Flint. And who can pass up the triple crown of "dogs, donuts, desserts" at the modern **Doo-Right Dogs,** tel. (508) 676-8605, on Pleasant and Quarry, a block from the Tower Mill outlets? In a similar vein, on the south side of town is **Hartley's Original Pork Pies** way up on the

FALL RIVER AREA ACCOMMODATIONS

The following are listed as they appear traveling on I-195 between Fall River's western and eastern neighbors:

Quality Inn, on the south side of I-195 Exit 4 in Somerset, tel. (800) 228-5151 or (508) 678-4545; free continental breakfast, restaurant, indoor swimming pool; $54-99 d.

Hampton Inn, beside US 6 at the Fall River/Westport line, I-95 East Exit 9, tel. (800) HAMPTON or (508) 675-8500; restaurant; $64-99 d.

Best Western Fall River, Airport Rd., Rt. 24 Exit 8 (five minutes north of I-195), tel. (800) 528-1234 or (508) 672-0011; restaurant, indoor swimming pool, fitness center; $49-79 d.

Comfort Inn, in Dartmouth, less than 10 miles east of downtown Fall River, at I-195 Exit 12, tel. (800) 228-5150 or (508) 996-0800; $60-100 d.

1700 block of South Main (Rt. 138) opposite the big fluorescent-lit Crosson gas station. Hartley's is a genuine unvarnished taste of one of Fall River's earliest contributions to American cookery, dating back to the days when this was the city of "hills, mills, pork pies, and dinner pails." Don't be put off by appearances; steel yourself and go through that door. Anyone nagged by second thoughts en route can opt for the **Ukrainian Home,** tel. (508) 672-9677, a local institution known far and wide for its hearty Eastern European stick-to-your-ribs soups and meats. Located on Globe Street catercorner from the Dunkin' Donuts at the Y-intersection of Broadway and South Main, the "Uke" is open for lunch and dinner daily except Sunday.

If you've sworn off franks, that's okay, but you will truly do yourself an injustice if you don't try some fresh Lebanese flat bread while in town. Called *lavash,* when cold they're as plain as a pita, tortilla, or Indian roti, but when freshly baked and adorned with savory or sweet toppings, wow, *there's* something wonderful. Sold open-face or folded into triangular pies, these treats are eagerly snapped up straight out of the ovens from shops that tend to appear as if they were once someone's garage. Case in point: **Sam's Bakery,** tel. (508) 674-5422, occupying the white shed-like addition off the back of a single-family house on residential, one-way Flint Street, just off Pleasant (turn at the sign of "The Big Five," the Fall River Five Cent Savings Bank). Ten pie variations, from traditional *menich* (m'NEESH, a mix of sesame seeds, parsley, and *zaatar,* or sumac bark) to Portuguese *chouriço,* fairly fly out the door while supplies last or until the 1 p.m. closing, whichever comes first. For well under a dollar each, these concoctions are a bargain take-out lunch that can't be beat. Closed Monday and Thursday. Exactly one block west on parallel Harrison is **George's Lebanese Bakery,** tel. (508) 672-8218, a good second if you're early enough to catch their pies still warm from the oven. Unlike Sam's, which continues baking until the lunch crowd gathers four deep at the counter, George's shuts down the assembly line while the clock still reads a.m.

Portuguese restaurants are another fixture across the city, for the most part seven-day-a-week lunch-and-dinner places specializing in such flavorful ingredients as *chouriço,* pan roasted potatoes, peppery cumin-laced tomato sauces, and of course *bacalhau,* dried cod. One of the finest of these restaurants is **Estoril,** 1577 Pleasant St. at Everett near the Comercial dos Azores, tel. (508) 677-1200. White table linens, subdued atmosphere, attentive service, and an extensive menu—including a favorite borrowed from the other side of the Iberian peninsula, *paelha a Valenciana*—make for an excellent introduction to the cuisine, at prices that stay firmly on the underside of $10. Similar dishes and prices prevail at **Terra Nostra** on Rodman at Hartwell, tel. (508) 677-9879, although the setting leans more toward the sleekly modern than the traditionally romantic. The bar up front seems to draw guys with expensive cars and suits. Downtown at 408 South Main Street is the most casual option, the **Tabacaria Açoriana Restaurant,** tel. (508) 673-5890, more widely known as simply the T.A. Specials may be written in neon pen on a backlit dry-board and the menu may include hot dogs and BLTs, but stick to such items as the shrimp Mozambique or marinated chicken *Alentejana* and you won't be disappointed.

Portuguese bakeries are almost as numerous as Portuguese restaurants, although the best are all some distance outside the downtown area. **Lou's Bakery,** for example, at 379 East Main, tel. (508) 672-5795, makes sweet bread even your Lisbon-born grandmother would approve of, if you have one. A good runner-up is across the river in Swansea: the **Continental Bakery,** 198 Pinehurst Ave., tel. (508) 672-8521.

A more recent arrival on the local restaurant scene is Cambodian cuisine, exemplified by the **New Phnom Penh Restaurant,** tel. (508) 324-4909, in Angkor Plaza, a cluster of businesses catering to the city's 4,000 Cambodians. Found on Quequechan St. next to the big Wampanoag Mill factory outlet center, the New Phnom Penh also serves good Thai, Vietnamese, and even Chinese food. One can't complain about the bare bones decor, either, when only a handful of the 300 dishes costs more than $7.50. Closed Monday.

Short of stocking up on Sam's spinach pies, the **Waterstreet Café,** tel. (508) 672-8748, in the nondescript, single-story brick building down by Battleship Cove between the railroad and marine museums, is nearly the only place in the city to acknowledge the existence of either vegetarians or cosmopolitan palates. Influenced by the Middle Eastern and Mediterranean heritage of the owners, the reasonably priced menu is revised daily to reflect whatever is most fresh off the farm or boat—scallops with walnut pesto, veal with wild mushrooms, autumn squash and apple soup. Waterstreet doesn't shirk from standards such as sirloin, clam chowder, or pork medallions, either, which are anything *but* standard when dressed up with the day's best market produce, fresh herbs, and uncommon starches such as cous-cous or orzo rice. Complemented by the warm decor of antique wood cabinets, rich colors, and original art, lunches are served Tues.-Sat. 11 a.m.-4 p.m., dinners Thurs.-Sat. 5-9 p.m. There's also a popular Sunday brunch 10:30 a.m.-3:30 p.m.

Food mavens have one other option, though it's a bit tricky to find and only open Fri.-Sat. 5-9 p.m. But **Puerini's Cafe/The Pasta Factory,** tel. (508) 678-1030, rewards diligent searchers with excellent Italian dinners featuring their own top-quality fresh pastas fleshed out with choice meats and fresh seafood (bring your own beer or wine). If you have access to a kitchen, go simply to pick up some great pasta from their outlet shop, open Mon.-Saturday. To find it, follow North Main St. away from downtown and turn on Weaver St., the last possible left before crossing Rt. 79. Where Weaver St. ends take another left and thread through the former Border City mill complex, zig-zagging where needed but essentially continuing straight. Puerini's is at the end beside the Carpet Brokers warehouse.

Finally, in the same direction but with longer hours and only half as far from downtown is a classic '50s diner, **Al Mac's,** tel. (508) 679-5851, on US 6 at the base of President Hill at the junction with elevated Rts. 79 and 138. With eye-catching neon, jukeboxes, and plenty of shiny surfaces, this local institution will satisfy all your comfort food cravings, from the four-egg omelettes and chicken rice soup to veal parmesan and tapioca pudding. Yes, there's meatloaf, and homemade pies, too (try the banana cream). It's also open till the wee morning hours Wed.-Saturday.

Getting There

About a half dozen buses to Fall River depart daily from Boston, New York, Providence, Rhode Island, Newport, Rhode Island, and Cape Cod (via New Bedford). All belong to **Bonanza Bus Lines,** tel. (800) 556-3815 or (401) 751-8800, whose Fall River terminal is located at 221 Second St. near downtown. Although close to local restaurants and not all that far from waterfront attractions, local accommodations are all a cab ride away.

CAPE COD

Of Cape Cod, to which he made several visits in the 19th century, Henry David Thoreau wrote, "A man may stand there and put all America behind him." Jutting 40 miles into Atlantic, this relatively young fishhook of sandy soil and pitch pine forest, appreciated by Thoreau for its desolation, has become one of the nation's pre-eminent seaside resorts; its 15 towns and hundred-odd beaches draw millions of summer residents and visitors each year. The Cape once lived off the sea, but it now depends on people who come merely to dip their toes in it.

In recent decades, new residential subdivisions, timeshare condos, summer cottages, and sprawlmarts set amid acres of asphalt have metastasized across the Cape—giving first-time visitors, with no clear sense of what it *used* to be like, plenty of reason to wonder what all the repeat customers from southern New England and Canada see in the place. The quaint gray-shingled and white-clapboard villages so typically associated with Ye Olde Cape do still exist, but much is of more recent vintage than you might imagine—deliberately built or renovated to fulfill the expectations of tourists who came first by rail and steamer and later by car. The neocolonial style is now old enough to be historic in its own right, of course, but if you can't be bothered with imposters, pay close attention to your Historical Society walking-tour brochures, for that 18th-century house you're admiring may actually be a product of someone's 1920s—or 1980s—nostalgia.

Of course, the big attraction for many visitors—even those drawn by childhood familiarity or the fact that if grandma doesn't live in Florida she lives on the Cape—is not so much the land as what's around it. Like sailors responding to the call of the sirens, the sybarite hidden within every New Englander just can't resist all those beaches and all that water rolling over them. Admittedly, the call of the sizzling deep-fryers is pretty seductive, too, but even Spam on stale crackers might not seem so bad if you could enjoy it while stretched out on one of the Cape's better beaches. The big drawback for short-time visitors is that most beach parking requires either a resident sticker or a fee up to $10 per day—something to factor into any decision about how much of a premium to pay for being within walking distance of the water. But even the most popular beaches with either free or inexpensive parking can can offer a soupçon of privacy if you remember that about 90% of the Cape's would-be sunbathers are weighed down with coolers, chairs, kids, and toys and don't walk more than 20 minutes from their cars. Though swimming is out of the question for most warm-blooded mortals after September, the parking restrictions are lifted then and the crowds thin to a relative trickle, leaving the tide's treasures and the sumptuous sunrises and sunsets to those hardy beach-walkers who put off their vacations until just this time of year. (Having a fireplace and hot bath waiting back at the B&B helps.)

Any time of year, the Cape's local conservation lands and privately managed sanctuaries also offer an antidote to ringing cash registers and creeping traffic. A few other possibilities that will help counter impressions of the Cape as a monotonous landscape of pitch pine forest and sandy house lots: kayaking along a salt marsh estuary among blossoming white shadbush, sitting beside a kettle pond listening to a kingfisher's rattle, spotting redwing blackbirds among the cattail reeds of an abandoned cranberry bog, or encountering bright lady's slippers (Cypripedium acaule) scattered amid the moist coolness of a maturing stand of oaks.

GEOLOGY: A DANCE OF SAND AND SEA

Compared to the billion-year-old landscape of most of Massachusetts, Cape Cod is a veritable newborn—a long limb of glacial drift pushed around by the great Laurentide ice sheet between 14,000 and 20,000 years ago. It also has a relatively short life expectancy for a landmass: the Atlantic Ocean may erase the Cape from New England's rocky coast within another 5,000 years. That's based on an extrapolation of today's rate of loss, but rising sea levels caused by global warming could cut that figure dramatically. In fact, rising seas currently claim nearly three times as much acreage every year as surf erosion, and predictions are that over the next decade the storm tides will produce increasing flooding in such low-lying areas as downtown Provincetown.

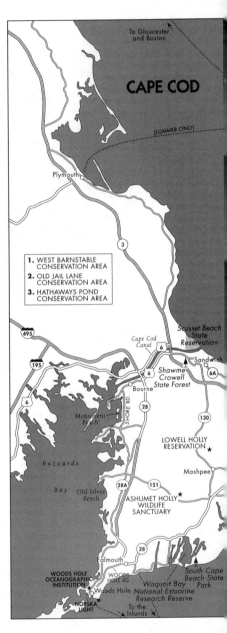

CAPE COD

1. WEST BARNSTABLE CONSERVATION AREA
2. OLD JAIL LANE CONSERVATION AREA
3. HATHAWAYS POND CONSERVATION AREA

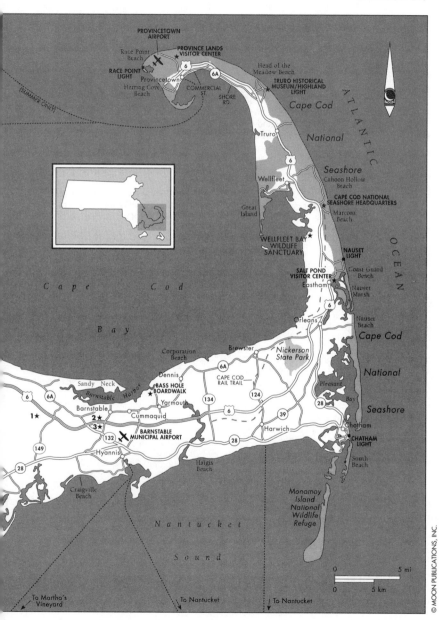

© MOON PUBLICATIONS, INC.

As for the erosion, if it happened any faster it would be like watching Alaskan glaciers calving icebergs; the 14-mile stretch of cliffs and barrier beaches along the Cape's outer shore already recede an average of several feet a year. For a graphic illustration of how dynamic these shorelines really are, check out the short film presented at the Cape Cod National Seashore's Province Lands visitor center, or the Cape Cod Museum of Natural History's before-and-after photos of Chatham's storm-punctured outer bar.

The advancing and retreating glacial lobes of the last ice age are responsible for giving the upper and middle Cape its rocky spine of unsorted stone and sediment. As it moved south during a brief period in its 15,000-year meltdown, the thick ice sheet bulldozed this end moraine into its present location. The ridge, known as the Sandwich moraine, is now topped by the Mid-Cape Highway, US 6, and in selected conservation areas its uneven slopes provide the region's most challenging mountain biking. South of the moraine, the landscape is characterized by outwash plains formed after the glacier resumed melting, releasing everything from fine-grained clay to gravel and larger boulders. (Think of a 1,000-foot-thick ice sponge that's been wiped across all of New England, sopping up a sample of every bedrock surface it crosses. When that ice melts, it's just as if you gave that sponge a squeeze.) Some of the material deposited has been matched to unique bedrock formations, such as the Brighton volcanics—igneous rocks dating back to the ancient heyday of a Boston-area volcano. These are good indicators of the path of the original glacial advance, southeast from Canada.

PRACTICALITIES

A Vacationer's Gazette and Calendar

Forget the compass. When someone with a good sense of direction but an abiding faith in highway signage takes a turn marked "south,"

For current Cape-wide weather information, call the WQRC-FM forecast phone at (508) 771-5522.

---

only to realize that it actually goes *north,* it's very, very discombobulating. The operative principle on the Cape is up and down. "Up-Cape" means westward—toward the Upper Cape and that big hummock known as "off-Cape" to locals and "North America" to everyone else. "Down-Cape" means eastward—toward the Outer Cape, Provincetown, and Portugal. These terms make more sense if you're a sailor, or have a passing familiarity with the Greenwich Prime Meridian: degrees of longitude descend as you head east, increase as you head west. (Which also explains why New York yacht owners go "down East" to get to their Maine summer cottages.)

Further important distinctions are made between the three sides of the Cape's bent arm: **"bayside"** refers to the entire rim of Cape Cod Bay, from the Canal at Sandwich down to MacMillan Wharf in Provincetown. The first half comprises historic and picturesque Cape villages, as venerable as Thanksgiving, along what was once the "Old King's Highway" (now Rt. 6A). The **"south shore"** faces Nantucket Sound, between Buzzards Bay and the Cape's "elbow," at Chatham. Blatantly commercial Route 28, as casual as a beer belly over the barbecue and as gaudy as the Fourth of July, is the main artery of this side. And the **"backside"** denotes that segment that braves the open Atlantic from the Chatham elbow to the "fist" of Provincetown; most of which is preserved for posterity by the Cape Cod National Seashore.

Successfully navigating the Cape is as much a matter of timing as of geography. Between Memorial Day weekend and Labor Day weekend, the millions who converge on the Cape spawn legendary traffic jams, long lines at restaurants, and a plethora of "no vacancy" signs at local lodgings. With a gazillion vehicles trying to cross the two bridges over the Cape Cod Canal on any given summer or holiday weekend, the 50-mile journey from the South Shore to, say, Woods Hole can actually take as long as the 300-mile drive to Canada. July begins the flood of families, predominately to the south shore beachside motels; August brings flocks of psychiatrists, lawyers, doctors, and other professionals to Chatham, at the Outer Cape's southern extremity, and to bayside towns from West Barnstable to Wellfleet. State-run public campgrounds are usually full throughout the summer—even midweek and in bad weather—in part because nine-month apartment leases and four- or fivefold increases in rents during high season forces more marginal Cape residents to spend their summers in tents and camper vans.

Despite the disadvantages, high season is also when everybody is open for business—seven days a week, morning, noon, and night. Out of season, businesses close up (not because the visitors disappear—fall and spring are quite popular with a discerning few hundred thousand people—but because the employees do). In high season, if it wasn't for the army of teenagers, college students, and Irish citizens on temporary work visas, the Cape would seize up like a car without oil. After US schools start, in September, only the Irish remain—and *they* stay only until *their* classes begin, in October. (The corollary to this seasonal dependence on outside labor is that some places may still be closed when high season kicks in because they haven't finished hiring the necessary staff.) While the "30% off" signs start appearing in front of T-shirt and beachwear shops as early as the last weekend of August, don't expect accommodations, car and bike rentals, or other services to significantly lower prices until after New Year's.

Accommodations

You may as well forget about taking advantage of your half-price hotel cards or airline-hotel frequent-flyer alliances on the Cape—barely more than a dozen properties, out of over 400, belong to any of the national chains. This is the land of the vintage motel, the bed and breakfast inn, and the small, at-home B&B, both plain and fancy. While many of Rt. 28's motel courts externally evoke Nabokov's descriptions in *Lolita,* most are perfectly tidy family-run places, albeit rather dated in their decor. Others have been modernized inside to the point of having more beige fabric, blonde veneer, and bland clip-art framed over the beds than the most generic chain motel in the land. Like exterior appearances, brand affiliations are not reliable indicators of what's inside, either: the Ramada Inn Regency in Hyannis, for example, is one of the dreariest, amenity-free accommodations available in the region, despite prices implying oth-

erwise. If you're shopping around in person, look at your room before signing the credit card slip.

Minimum stays during summer weekends are becoming more the rule than the exception at inns and B&Bs, but it never hurts to ask—especially on short notice—in case scheduling gaps or cancellations arise. And while hundreds of accommodations dot the region, most close for some or all of the off season, so don't anticipate any glut of vacancies waiting to be snapped up for a song at the end of summer.

The only easy generalizations about the region's bed and breakfasts are that (a) most are found along bayside Rt. 6A and the Outer Cape, up through Provincetown, and (b) Portuguese strata (a delectable savory bread pudding with cheese) appears on more breakfast menus here than in any other part of the state. Otherwise, you'll find enormous variety in decor, quality and quantity of breakfast, convenience of location, and extra amenities, even though most places price themselves within the same narrow range ($85-115). To find one that suits your needs, consider using a reservation service such as **Orleans Bed & Breakfast Associates,** tel. (800) 541-6226 or (508) 255-3824, for homes on the Outer Cape; or **House Guests Cape Cod and the Islands,** tel. (800) 666-HOST or (508) 896-7053. The small fees such agents charge are liable to be less than what you'd spend on the phone hunting up a place with a vacancy, especially if you're searching during the summer.

For a fairly comprehensive list of where to lay your head for the night, pick up *The Accommodations Directory* from the **Cape Cod Chamber of Commerce,** tel. (508) 362-3225, whose visitor information booth is at the rotary on the off-Cape end of the Sagamore Bridge (you can also visit the chamber on the Web at www.capecod.com/chamber).

The Strange Case of the Hungry Gourmet

Most people can probably remember a favorite little restaurant which promptly hit the skids as soon as it became wildly popular. At least, *you* thought the quality ran out the back door; the people lining up outside every night, for some odd reason, failed to notice. Many vacation resorts suffer from this syndrome on a grand scale: millions of people spend millions of dollars every year on food that no self-respecting airline would serve. For proof, look no farther than the Rt. 28 side of the Cape, where cottonseed oil is king. If the food isn't fried, it's "continental"—which means that whatever isn't put under the broiler is buried in bleu cheese dressing. Of course, food may only be a mere afterthought to a day spent basking in the sun or splashing in the surf: some carbohydrates, some icy liquids, and you're a happy camper. But anyone who values both variety and quality will find it a marvel that the Cape—with supposedly more restaurants per capita than any other part of New England—is so *average.* Good, fresh seafood is a rare and delicious thing, and it should be a crime to subject it to the same salty batters and gooey sauces that are used back home solely to hide the fact that back home, the seafood isn't fresh. Yet thousands of kitchens on Cape Cod commit their daily misdemeanors to the acclaim and apparent satisfaction of millions. Go figure.

If you don't love seafood, don't worry—burgers are plentiful and poultry is always an option, albeit typically a second-rate one. Vege-

tarians had better be prepared to consume plenty of pasta and pizza; only a smattering of Cape restaurants understand that iceberg salads with croutons and julienne cheese strips won't earn a page in the next Moosewood cookbook. Early-bird specials are offered by more restaurants here than in any other region of the state, making significant savings possible for those who work up an appetite before 6 p.m.

Diners with a conscience will be dismayed at the amount of plastic and paper that is casually consumed by restaurants here; if you want to minimize your contribution to the daily garbage train hauling the stuff off-Cape, firmly refuse the well-intentioned attempts to serve you better with huge handfuls of paper napkins and complete place settings of plastic—even when all you order is french fries. Those soda cans and bottles may often be returned to where you bought them, whether or not they carry a cash deposit (most do); now that most towns accept recyclables like glass and metal, many take-out counters and shops have begun in-house collections. Those that haven't may think twice about their environmental apathy if enough customers seem to expect action, so don't hesitate to speak up.

CAPE COD CLAMS

Shellfish are a specialty of Cape Cod and Massachusetts' Islands, from Wellfleet's oysters to Martha's Vineyard Cape Poge Bay scallops. But the most ubiquitous bivalve mollusk on Cape menus is the clam.

Two species prevail: hard-shell clams *(Venus mercenaria),* called quahogs (a Wampanoag word, pronounced KO-hogs, or K'WOGS), and steamers *(Mya arenaria),* soft-shell clams. When small, quahogs are called "littlenecks" or "cherrystones" and are best eaten raw with a squeeze of lemon or Tabasco. When mature, their robust flavor makes them the stars of clambakes and chowders. By their very name, steamers are self-explanatory regarding how best to eat them (for maximum effect, however, accompany them with drawn butter and "liquor"—the broth drained from the clams themselves). Blended with sour cream and cream cheese, cooked steamers become clam dip; drenched in batter and lightly fried, they become the Cape's most familiar offering to the hungry summer tourist.

RECREATION

Scores of beautiful beaches line Cape shores, and from the end of June through Labor Day, in early September, hardly a single one has free parking. In most instances, you pay a daily fee to a gatekeeper to gain entrance, but some beaches reserve parking exclusively for residents, or for guests who purchase special weekly stickers or season passes at the appropriate town hall (bring vehicle registration and proof of local property rental or motel or B&B stay). Except in the National Seashore, walkers and bicyclists get in to all beaches free. Since applicable fees are collected only until 5 p.m. but most beach parking is kept open in summer until at least sunset (and as late as midnight in some towns), there's a nice window of opportunity for those who care more about catching a quick swim or a good sunset than a day of tanning. Individual town information kiosks (all prominently placed at strategic highway junctions or right downtown) can provide a fairly thorough list of local

CAPE COD NATIONAL SEASHORE

a group of men and women, equipped for clamming, aboard the day-sailer Elsie

beaches, but the ones most welcoming of non-residents are also well-signed from major roads, such as Rts. 28 and 6A.

The heaviest (and coldest) surf is from the Atlantic Ocean piling up along the backside beaches of the National Seashore. Summer's prevailing southwesterly winds can fatten up the waves on the south shore, too, but in general the Nantucket and Vineyard Sound beaches (and Buzzards Bay) are either more sheltered, shallower, or otherwise kinder and gentler than those on the Outer Cape. By virtue of the great tidal flats extending far from shore, bayside beaches are most serene in summer and relatively tepid. Offshore, the Bay is actually colder than the surrounding Atlantic Ocean, because the northern Labrador current, coming down along the coast of Maine, gets embayed by the Cape's hook, while the Atlantic is warmed by the Gulf Stream 100 miles to the southeast.

Before undertaking certain shore hikes (at the Namskaket Sea Path in Nickerson State Park, for example, or Great Island in Wellfleet), digging clams, windsurfing, or ocean kayaking, it would be wise to check for the high and low tides. Consult the tide tables printed in any of the local Cape daily papers, or pick up a handy free chart from the outdoor enthusiast's year-round friend, the Goose Hummock Shop, located at the Town Cove in Orleans on Rt. 6A, and at Rt. 28 and Main in Hyannis.

The Nasty Stuff
Before you go striding off through marsh reeds or bushwhacking through the woods in spring, summer, or fall remember that the Cape is the home to both wood and deer ticks. Thoroughly checking yourself after summer outings may help you find the former, but the latter are so tiny they're essentially invisible. Better to adopt preventative measures such as wearing light-colored clothing that covers you from neck to toe and wrist, keeping a hat on in the woods, slathering on tick repellent, and staying on paths. If you notice the symptoms of a deer tick bite (the distinctive bull's-eye rash, for starters, which sometimes doesn't appear for many weeks), seek medical attention promptly—it's a vector for several potentially serious but quite treatable illnesses, including Lyme disease.

Poison ivy is another native resident worth avoiding. Growing as either a plant or vine, it's often found amid beach grass, where it exacts revenge on those who ignore dune-climbing restrictions. It's recognizable by its three leaves on woody or hairy stems, sometimes accompanied by clusters of small, off-white berries.

TRANSPORTATION

Getting There
The obvious way, of course, is to drive—but the arguments against that option are legion (see above). The most affordable year-round alternative to driving is to take a bus. **Bonanza Bus Lines,** tel. (800) 556-3815, offers direct service from New York City (or Albany) to Hyannis, via coastal Connecticut (or western Massachusetts), Rhode Island, Fall River, and New Bedford. Bonanza also has service from Logan Airport and Boston's South Station bus terminal directly to the Steamship Authority dock at Woods Hole, where the ferry departs for Martha's Vineyard. To reach Hyannis from Logan or Boston, take the **Plymouth & Brockton Street Railway,** tel. (508) 771-6191. P&B's

CYCLING TO (AND ON) THE CAPE

Experienced bike riders looking for a long-distance cycling opportunity may want to try the Claire Saltonstall Bikeway—also called "Bike Route 1"—a 135-mile marked bikeway from Boston to Provincetown (with a 20-mile spur to Woods Hole). Sharing urban and secondary roads through Boston's southeastern suburbs, the route passes through Plymouth and over the Sagamore Bridge, then roughly shadows US 6 to the Outer Cape. Summer riders will find three public campgrounds and two Hostelling International affiliates along the way, plus—for a relaxing finale—a pair of ferries from Provincetown back to either Plymouth or Boston.

Every year, HI's Boston hostel organizes group rides along the route; call (617) 536-1027 for information. HI also publishes the *Claire Saltonstall Bikeway Map*, available at their Boston retail store, 1020 Commonwealth Ave., at the west end of Boston University, tel. (617) 731-5430.

On-Cape cyclists who prefer the security of riding among their own kind can take advantage of several paved bike paths, including ones on either side of the Cape Cod Canal; the scenic **Shining Sea Bike Path,** from the center of Falmouth directly to the Woods Hole ferry dock; and a few short paths scattered through the National Seashore on the Outer Cape. The biggie, however, is the **Cape Cod Rail Trail,** stretching for more than 25 miles between Dennis and South Wellfleet. This granddaddy of Massachusetts rail trails follows the right-of-way of the Old Colony Railroad, an early beneficiary of the summer tourist trade. With parking at either end and five spots in between, the trail makes its scenic way through pitch pine forest, coastal grass plains, and alongside glacial kettlehole ponds. You'll find trailside rental shops (mostly seasonal) in Nickerson State Park, downtown Orleans, and at the Wellfleet end, beside US 6. Free rail trail maps are available from the ranger station at the entrance to Nickerson State Park, and at various town information booths. The *Cape Cod & North Shore Bicycle Map*, available at almost any bike shop or bookstore in the region, provides a complete cyclists' map of the entire Cape, identifying all paved offroad trails and highlighting roadways conducive to biking. (For a copy by mail, send $5.25 to Rubel BikeMaps, P.O. Box 1035, Cambridge, MA 02140.) This map also identifies B&Bs and inns that welcome bike-touring guests, and the many resident-parking-only beaches that are utterly free to cyclists (which, in summer, should be incentive enough to start pedaling).

buses continue from Hyannis to Provincetown and points in between. Don't assume buses and boats coordinate their schedules: long layovers are more the rule than the exception, and some buses from both Boston and New York arrive in time to miss the last ferries of the day entirely. Whether or not you connect straight through to a waiting ferry, both these companies sell bus and boat tickets at the same time.

On summer weekends, **Amtrak,** tel. (800) USA RAIL, runs a single roundtrip train from Providence to Hyannis; it leaves on Friday evening and returns Sunday afternoon. Like nearly all New England train travel, it is, alas, neither cheaper nor faster than the buses that ply the same route—but it *is* more spacious, scenic, and, by reason of its deliberate speed, a magnet for people who still believe the subtle pleasures of travel lie in the journey as much as the destination. Conveniently, the depot in Hyannis (shared with the Cape Cod Scenic Railway) is right downtown, opposite the nexus of local ground transportation, the P&B bus station.

For travelers at the other end of the speed spectrum, or fans of *real* flying—the kind where you can watch the wheels leave the ground, or even look over the pilot's shoulder, rather than stare over the heads of two hundred peanut-crunching passengers—Barnstable Municipal Airport in Hyannis is well connected to the off-Cape world. Predictably, Boston is the principal originating gateway, with year-round flights offered by **Cape Air,** tel. (800) 352-0714, and **Business Express/The Delta Connection,** tel. (800) 345-3400, and additional summer commuter "express" service from **Continental Airlines** tel. (800) 525-0280, and **USAirways,** tel. (800) 428-4322. From New York City, **Continental Connection** (formerly Colgan Air, whose name still adorns the planes), tel. (800) 272-

5488, is the only carrier offering year-round non-stops into Barnstable Municipal, supplemented in summer by USAirways and Business Express. From Newark, try Colgan/Continental Connection, which is seasonal.

Visitors looking for alternatives to the ferries for a return from Martha's Vineyard and Nantucket have a choice of Cape Air, **Nantucket Airlines,** tel. (800) 635-8787, or tiny **Island Airlines,** tel. (800) 248-7779, the last two flying exclusively between Nantucket and Hyannis.

If you're coming on your own boat, you'll find nearly every Cape harbor has at least a couple anchorages or berths for visitors. Marinas and yacht yards able to accommodate at least a few dozen cruisers are found at Cataumet, on Buzzards Bay; Falmouth, Osterville, and Hyannis, on the south shore; and Provincetown. Smooth sailing is aided by a good guide to local waters. For Massachusetts generally, the traditional sailor's companion (after the don't-sail-from-home-without-it *Eldridge Tide and Pilot Book,* sold at marine stores from Maine to Florida) is the *Cruising Guide to the New England Coast,* recently updated by Roger F. Duncan, Paul W. Fenn, W. Wallace Fenn, and John P. Ware (New York: Putnam). Despite its obvious appeal to power-boaters and amateurs, diehard yachties shouldn't overlook *Embassy's Complete Boating Guide & Chartbook to Rhode Island, Massachusetts, & New Hampshire,* either (Lexington, MA: Embassy Marine Publishing; tel. 781-860-0430). With its NOAA coastal charts, GPS waypoints, extensive anchorage descriptions, and marine service summaries for every harbor in the state, the latest spiral-bound edition must make the AAA's Triptik designers pea-green with envy. If you can't make your way through local waters with either of these detailed compendiums, you belong on Amtrak.

Getting Around

If you don't have a car, don't worry. With just patience and a pocket full of quarters it's possible to reach almost every town on the Cape with one or more of the Cape Cod Regional Transit Authority's three year-round bus lines and five summer trolleys, in combination with the all-season P&B and Bonanza buses mentioned above. (The most notable missing link is Sandwich. When it comes to bus travel, you can't get there from here.) Plymouth & Brockton provides local service from the Mid-Cape (Hyannis) to Provincetown via all the bayside and Outer Cape communities, while Bonanza makes local stops in towns along the western edge of the Upper Cape, from the Cape Cod Canal down to Woods Hole. The CCRTA serves every south shore and backside town between Woods Hole and Orleans with its **SeaLine, Villager,** and **H2O Line** bus routes, which operate Mon.-Sat. year-round (the H2O Line also operates on Sundays). In addition, local shoppers' and beach-goers trolleys loop around each of the five south shore towns daily late June-early September. Though Hyannis is the hub of the system, connections in Orleans make it feasible to do a circle trip around the entire Mid-to-Outer Cape area.

Fares on the Villager line and all summer trolleys are $1 per ride (75¢ if you buy discounted tokens in advance) or $3 for an all-day pass. CCRTA bus fares are $1-3.50, depending on distance (though discounted passes give you 20 rides for the price of 15). All passes may be purchased directly from the driver, but discount trolley tokens are sold only at the P&B terminal in Hyannis and at local chambers of commerce. While some of the trolleys run well past sundown, the CCRTA's three buses favor daylight hours. For a complete system timetable, pick up the CCRTA *Cape Cod Trolley & Bus Guide* at the P&B terminal, town information booths, or almost anywhere you see racks of tourist brochures. Or you can call the CCRTA directly, tel. (800) 352-7155 or (508) 385-8326, and press the appropriate buttons to get prerecorded schedules.

Cyclists should note that all the CCRTA vehicles are also equipped with bike racks—unlike the Bonanza and P&B buses, which only take bikes as last-priority baggage (i.e., if there's room and so long as no risk is posed to other luggage). Most are also wheelchair accessible.

THE UPPER CAPE

One of the great attractions of the Cape is the diversity of its towns. Behind the uniform weathered gray shingles and simple little saltbox houses, clam shacks and soft-serve ice cream machines, pitch pine and scrub oak forests, subscriptions to *Bassmaster* and *Modern Maturity,* lie such fundamental differences in history, politics, and demographics that a taxonomist could easily find evidence for separate species. This certainly holds true of the four Upper Cape towns, which by turns embrace and ignore tourism, are highly commercialized and nearly rural, and feel country clubbish and working class. With about one-third fewer lodgings than any of the other parts of the Cape, it's an area often bypassed by visitors bound for the motel-lined shore of the Mid-Cape and inn-saturated streets of Provincetown, and by all the hopefuls headed to the Woods Hole ferry. Which only means that the people who do stop here can start enjoying a Cape vacation while other holiday-makers are still stewing in traffic on US 6.

The Upper Cape also benefits from having a nearly forgotten side to it: the Buzzards Bay shore. Although only a couple of the beaches here are open to outsiders who come by car (one, Monument Beach, even has free parking!), simply driving or cycling the route closest to the bay is as good an introduction as you can get to the sedative charms of the Cape landscape. Though it led the region in catering to summer tourists in the late 1800s, with fancy beachfront hotels along the then-new railroad to Woods Hole, the area has since slid gently into a lower residential gear. A few garish new suburban-style subdivisions have slashed big openings atop the hills offering water views, but more often the road passes modest old homes tucked behind trees, marsh-edged inlets, undeveloped woods, and signs for boatyards. Bumper boats, miniature golf, T-shirt stores, taffy shops, and other cheesy Cape cud are nowhere to be found—arguably because low-clearance railroad bridges keep buses and RVs away (the bridges are something to keep in mind if you have bikes mounted on your car roof). And while parallel, four-lane Rt. 28 effectively draws south-bound drivers more intent on their destination than on the scenery, this is one of the few places on any of the Cape shores where puttering along won't instantly produce a 25-car entourage of impatient tailgaters.

SANDWICH AND VICINITY

Sandwich, settled by a group of 60 families from north of Boston in 1637, was the first town to be established on the Cape; adjacent Bourne, which split from Sandwich in 1894, was the last. The area also had one of the only Indian settlements to have survived to the end of the colonial era, a place called Comassekumkanet until its residents, members of the Herring Pond band of Wampanoags, succumbed to the preaching of missionaries. Although the resulting "praying Indian" reservation was eventually absorbed by Sandwich, the band is memorialized on the north side of the canal by the namesake Herring Pond Recreation Area, a small turnout with parking and picnic tables off US 6 in Bournedale. The site is popular in spring when thousands of alewives (members of the herring family) return to the pond to spawn; come in mid- to late April to watch the run at its peak.

Despite the proximity of generally intolerant authorities in nearby Plymouth, early Sandwich became a haven for Quakers and other religious groups who disagreed with the Pilgrims. This acceptance became a hallmark across Cape Cod, whose various towns were about the only ones in provincial Massachusetts to let go ministers who didn't suit their congregations (off-Cape ministers usually served lifetime appointments). Perhaps it also foreshadowed an aloofness from the orthodoxies of the following century, too, when the strong patriotism boiling over in Boston and elsewhere in New England failed to kindle much passion on the Cape.

As terminus of the Plymouth stagecoach in the early 1800s, Sandwich was one of the earliest towns on the Cape to attract tourists. These early pioneers of the region's now-dominant industry were usually men of wealth or consequence from nearby Southeastern Massachusetts or Boston (like Daniel Webster), who were drawn to Sandwich for sport hunting in its deep woods. The town now has its sights set on motorists flocking over the Sagamore Bridge, and it snares them with its exceedingly well-turned, almost manicured historic district on the banks of Shawme Pond, at Main and Water Streets (take US 6 Exit 2, or turn south at the traffic light on the Sandwich stretch of Rt. 6A).

Cape Cod Canal

The Cape used to be separated from the rest of the state by a valley with two opposite-flowing rivers, the Manomet and the Scusset, whose headwaters came to within a mile of each other. Indians portaged between them, and so did the Pilgrims—who recognized as early as the 1670s that a canal between them would be a good idea. Over the next 200 years, it seems as if every engineer and surveyor in the U.S. was hired or consulted at one time or another to review the prospects for a canal between the Cape Cod Bay and Buzzards Bay. All praised its suitability, but it wasn't until 1884 that anyone ventured to actually start digging. A couple of decades of stops and starts, political slapstick, lawsuits over contracts, and other diversions ensued, but finally, in 1909, construction began in earnest, fully financed by private capital. The first vessels passed through the completed eight-mile canal in July 1914. The passage never proved profitable for its builders—navigating the narrow channel was dangerous, and vessels kept hitting the drawbridges. The Federal government bought the canal in 1928, nearly doubled its width, and built the two huge highway bridges that now provide the Cape's principal link to the rest of the nation.

The 6.5-mile service roads on the banks of the canal are paved for use by skaters, joggers, and cyclists; expect lots of slowpokes and great views of the canal's ship traffic. When you tire of battling headwinds as stiff as the currents through the canal (the tidal difference between the bays at either end is over five feet), consider hooking up with Shore Road in Bourne (parallel with the west end of the Cape-side path) and riding a short distance west to the beaches at Gray Gables, facing the canal, or Phinney's Harbor, on the causeway to Mashnee Island. Parking is limited to residents at the former and is nonexistent at the latter, so biking is about the only way to experience either one in summer.

Parking lots that give access to the canal's north side are mostly located beside speedy US 6 westbound, and appear with so little warning that you'll probably have to turn around and try a second time. On the Cape side, parking is available at the east (Sandwich) end beside the big, boxy Canal Electric generating station off Rt. 6A (turn on Tupper Rd. and follow signs with the US Army Corps of Engineers logo), and at the west (Bourne) end off Shore Rd., by the railroad lift bridge that resembles two Towers of London. **Bike rentals** are available from Sandwich Cycles, tel. (508) 833-2453, on Rt. 6A a jot west of the Stop & Shop plaza.

The Origin of an Empire

Wall Street may be the seat of America's capital markets today, but if you want to see the "Birthplace of Free Enterprise in America," you'll have to pay a visit to the **Aptucxet Trading Post Museum,** tel. (508) 759-9487, beside the canal bike path in Bourne. There, off Shore Rd. west of the Bourne Bridge, is a replica of the seasonal 1627 trading post in which local Pilgrims, Native Americans, and Dutch from New Amsterdam dickered, bargained, and bartered to change wampum into furs and vice versa. There's also a salt works, windmill, and the minuscule private depot President Grover Cleveland had built when he used to escape malarial Washington D.C. to visit his "summer White House," the home he bought and named Gray Gables, at the mouth of what was then the Manomet River (now open Tues.-Sun. May through mid-October, daily July-Aug.; admission $2.50).

Historic Sandwich Village

"Quaint" is a word much abused on the Cape, so to refrain from adding to its abuse, let me define this and another important term: places that are "quaint" are exceptionally akin to postcards come to life. They fit a romanticized image of what historic New England towns "should" look like, and very often try hard to conceal how truly commercial thay are. "Cute" (in these pages only) refers to a quaint place where real people live and work. The village of Sandwich—with its restored 1640 grist mill grinding cornmeal for tourists, its classically inspired Town Hall and meetinghouse, its Christopher Wren church on a hill, and its carefully crafted imitation stagecoach inn—almost epitomizes quaintness. By the same token, it is such a dainty morsel, such a small-scale sample, that fault-finding is out of the question. There simply isn't enough there to saturate the senses, even though you could spend the better part of a day (and a fair amount of money) examining the various collections of things carefully maintained around the town.

One of the early gents who came to Sandwich for the hunting was Deming Jarves, who recognized in the woods a potential source of fuel for a glass factory's furnaces. (Daniel Webster, for one, complained that the consequently diminished forests were no longer adequate for "good sport.") For much of the 19th century, his Boston & Sandwich Glass Company dominated the nation's nascent glassmaking industry, turning an expensive import item into a domestic commodity well within the means of most Americans. At the **Sandwich Glass Museum,** tel. (508) 888-0251, in the single-story clapboard building on Main St. opposite the Town Hall and First Church, gallery after gallery of samples illustrates the evolution of this early mass-produced glassware. While the factory's artisans were capable of remarkable personal work, it helps to have a collector's interest in the cut saucers, plates, lamp chimneys, and other household items displayed in such great numbers. Open Wed.-Sun Feb.-March and Nov.-Dec., daily April-October. Admission is $3.50.

In the 1833 meetinghouse, a block farther up Main St., is the lilliputian world of the **Yesteryear's Doll Museum,** tel. (508) 888-2788. Thousands of dolls, some older than the United States, others as young as Barbie, fill the building's two floors. From European crèche figurines to Walt Disney products, the collection—supplemented by doll houses, toys, and other miniatures, plus a large gift shop that even stocks antiques—truly showcases the Western dollmaker's art. They also have an appraisal service (but no catalogue for mail orders). Open Mon.-Sat. mid-May through mid-October; admission $3.50. Across the street, past the handsome public library, is **The Weather Store,** 146 Main, tel. (508) 888-1200, whose inventory of weathervanes, whirligigs, thermometers, barometers, and the like shows as much single-minded dedication as any of the town museums, but charges no admission.

About three-quarters of a mile south of Town Hall, at Grove and Pine Sts., is the Sandwich king of collecting, the **Heritage Plantation,** tel. (508) 888-1222. You'll find this Americana by the acre, a diverse assemblage encompassing antique autos, military miniatures, Currier & Ives prints, landscape paintings, trade signs, and carved cigar-store figures, just to name a few of the items. A working 1912 carousel is among the larger specimens in the collection, though even the gallery buildings themselves are architectural showpieces, and the grounds are a horticultural gallery of show gardens. The famous hybrid rhododendrons alone draw busloads of gawkers when in flower (the first half of June). Added highlights include changing art exhibits and a summer concert series; call for details. Open daily mid-May through October, admission $8.

Camping

Sandwich has two state campgrounds to its credit. If you need a place to hook up your RV, try **Susset Beach State Reservation,** on Cape Cod Bay due east of the Rt. 3 traffic rotary at the foot of the Sagamore Bridge; follow the signs. It may look as if you'll be plugging straight into an outlet in the wall of the hulking gas-fired power station, but it's actually on the opposite side of the canal from the camping area—just close enough so those blinking aircraft warning lights on the tall smokestacks will be as reassuring as stars twinkling in the night's dark firmament. Five tent sites are tucked in among the scrubby little trees at the back of the campground and are available mid-April through mid-October for $8. The other 98 sites are available year-round to self-contained vehicles for $8 in season, $5 otherwise.

If sleeping next to a utility company isn't your idea of what camping's all about, try the **Shawme-Crowell State Forest,** off Rt. 130 (Main St.) in Sandwich proper, tel. (508) 888-0351. No RV hookups are available, but the campground has a dumping station, full bathhouses with hot showers and all modern conveniences, and even a store selling firewood and minor supplies. The 280 sites, generously spread throughout the pine woods, are available April-Nov. (barring blizzards) for $6 a night. A couple dozen spaces are also open to RVs through the winter. Although overnighters are granted free day use of Scusset Beach (a $2 savings), this property's distance from the Cape Cod Rail Trail and the National Seashore ensures that it never fills as quickly as Nickerson State Park, on the Outer Cape, the region's only other public campground reachable without a boat.

Accommodations

Outside of the three hostels on the Outer Cape and Provincetown, some of the most affordable rooms on the whole Cape are found at the **Spring Garden Motel,** near milepost 7 on Rt. 6A in East Sandwich, tel. (800) 303-1751 or (508) 888-0710. Open year-round, the 11 pine-paneled rooms facing a bird-filled marsh are only a half-mile walk from a bayside beach. (There's also a shallow in-ground pool.) At their July-Aug. peak, prices are $71-75 d, but they drop to below $60 in the shoulder months and under $50 in winter (that includes complimentary bagels and donuts in the morning).

You'll find a half-dozen other small motels and cottages, none as inexpensive, along Rt. 6A west and east of the Spring Garden. There's also a **Best Western,** tel. (800) 528-1234 or (508) 759-0800, in neighboring Bourne at the foot of the Cape side of the Bourne Bridge, with high-season doubles for $89-99 ($55-65 Nov.-April). At those rates, you could also try one of the handful of bed-and-breakfast places in the center of Sandwich's historic village—especially if you don't need the motel-standard extra double bed for your kids, or such unromantic amenities as in-room TVs and telephones. Most of the B&Bs are found on Main St. within a short stroll of the scenic grist mill on Shawme Pond. **The Summer House,** tel. (800) 241-3609 or (508) 888-4991, is an 1835 home with unfussy decor, painted hardwood floors, fireplaces in most rooms, and a barn for bike storage. The late-May-through-October rate of $95 d includes both a generous full breakfast and afternoon tea and cakes; off season, the quiche, French toast, and omelets are just as filling, and the rate drops $10. Up the street is the very Victorian **Isaiah Jones Homestead,** tel. (800) 526-1625 or (508) 888-9115, behind whose wicker porch furniture lie a handful of rooms decorated

in authentic late 19th-century style—floral chintz fabric here, a full canopy bed there, and everywhere fresh flowers and candles. As a concession to modern romance, a couple of rooms have gas-fueled fireplaces and whirlpool baths; cyclists can park their trusty steeds in the carriage house out back. Rates are $85-160 d June-Oct., including full breakfast (with a strata if you're lucky) and afternoon refreshments; off season savings are up to 30% on the luxury end. Nearby, on Jarves St., **The Belfry Inne & Bistro,** tel. (508) 888-8550, exemplifies that contemporary, design-magazine blend of Victorian manor house, selected antiques, abstract art, and ultramodern plumbing, including a two-person jacuzzi in one of the high-end rooms. The eight guest rooms range in price from $95-165 June-Oct., including a full breakfast. Off season rates are 10-20% less.

Food

A good bet for any meal of the day is the home-style **Marshland Restaurant,** tel. (508) 888-9824, a combination bakery/eatery on Rt. 6A at the Citgo gas station, 1.5 miles east of the Bourne-Sandwich line. (Their T-shirt logo: "Eat here and get gas!") Escarole soup, fish 'n' chips, spaghetti and meatballs, veggie stir-fry, veal parmesan, and homemade desserts (try the "Pilgrim pie"—apple-cranberry with walnuts—if you visit in autumn) are examples of the rib-sticking fare—and prices are low enough to produce lines of patient diners on summer weekends. Two people can eat breakfast for under $10, and other meals are just as friendly to the wallet. Open daily till 9 p.m. in season. An equally good value for lunch and dinner is the **Sagamore Inn,** on Rt. 6A at the Bourne-Sandwich line; look for the white clapboard building whose roadside sign proclaims, "Family Restaurant–Native Seafood–Steak–Lobster." Inside the main dining room, the maple floors, ancient wooden booths, and coffered tin ceiling refract the sounds of many happy families, creating an atmosphere of a big, clamorous party. Though the menu offers strictly Italo-American and New England basics, the broiled and fried seafood is done simply and well, and the boiled lobsters are always priced for residents rather than tourists. In true roadhouse fashion, this place also serves an armload of homemade pies daily—made by someone who knows the secret of a good, tender crust. The whiskey-chocolate-pecan, for one, outshines yuppie restaurants from Boston to the Berkshires. Open daily except Tuesday 11 a.m.-9 p.m.

A number of restaurants by the Cape Cod Canal have good water views, but if you're looking for a meal to match the panorama, you've got to go to the **Chart Room,** tel. (508) 563-5350, overlooking Red Brook Harbor from the Kingman Marine boatyard in the Bourne village of Cataumet. The place serves traditional surf and turf, from broiled swordfish and baked stuffed lobster to steaks and lamb chops, but prepares them to a higher standard than most Cape waterfront places, which seem to believe that you pay for the view rather than the food. Reservations are nearly essential; ask for a porch table if you want the best seat for a Buzzards Bay sunset. Open Thurs.-Sat. in May and October, daily in between.

For a meal more likely to feature grilled fresh fennel than french fries, and phyllo-wrapped salmon rather than batter-dipped scrod, drop in at **The Belfry Inne & Bistro,** 8 Jarves St. in Sandwich, tel. (508) 888-8550. A casual summer lunch and early dinner menu is available Wed.-Sun. May-Oct. (with desserts and coffee until 11 p.m.), while more formal prix-fixe dinners are served weekends through the off season; reservations advised.

FALMOUTH

Steamer connections to Nantucket and Martha's Vineyard made Falmouth a conduit for both island-bound Sunday day-trippers and resident "summer folk" as early as 1836—the dawn of offshore tourism. But it wasn't until the railroad came down the Buzzards Bay coast to Falmouth's portside village of Woods Hole in 1872 (ostensibly to serve the guano industry based there) that the town started to capture some of the tourism pie for itself. When the railroad inaugurated "Dude Train" service from Boston in 1886, Falmouth siphoned off even more of the summer trade, prompting construction of a series of grand Victorian resorts, mostly along Grand Avenue overlooking the Vineyard Sound. Visitors would come for weeks or months at a time, many traveling from New York via the luxurious Fall River Line, disembarking across Buzzards Bay and completing their journey by train. Side by side with the tourists came the summer-home owners, who invested in property along the shore. All of the old hotels are gone (along with the railroad they relied upon for customers), but the turn-of-the-century real estate developments remain and are a defining visual element of the town's south shore.

Boughs of Holly

Falmouth and adjacent Mashpee sport separate preserves bearing the mark of "the Holly Man," Wilfrid Wheeler, the State Secretary of Agriculture who gained fame during the first half of this century as one of the world's leading propagators of holly trees. His personal collection, donated after his death to the Massachusetts Audubon Society, is now the **Ashumet Holly and Wildlife Sanctuary,** at the corner of Ashumet and Currier Rds. off Rt. 151 in East Falmouth. The 65 varieties of holly from around the world now occupying the few dozen pondside acres were all planted by Wheeler, along with a number of other exotics such as Japanese umbrella pine, a Manchurian dawn redwood, and a late-flowering Franklinia, garden offspring of a Georgian native now extinct in the wild. Besides summer natural history programs on the property, the sanctuary sponsors naturalist-guided trips to the Elizabeth Islands, including occasional outings to some not served by the usual public ferries or tours; tel. (508) 563-6390 for information. Open Tues.-Sun. year-round (plus major Monday holidays), Ashumet is free to Massachusetts Audubon members but $3 for everyone else.

Wheeler's other bit of handiwork is the **Lowell Holly Reservation,** on Conaumet Neck, jutting out between a pair of joined ponds on the Mashpee-Sandwich town line. Unlike Ashumet, this 135-acre peninsula already had a large stand of native American holly, for which Cape Cod marks the northern edge of its natural range; Wheeler supplemented the indigenous population with new trees selected for their fruitfulness. But what's unique about this property of the Trustees of Reservations is that it's the Cape Cod equivalent of an old-growth forest, untouched by brush fires, chainsaws, or plows since at least the Revolution. As such, it's one of the few places on the Cape whose mix of trees suggests how the region's landscape might have appeared to its early inhabitants. Not that the place is wholly untouched: its previous owner introduced a number of flowering shrubs to provide a showy floral display each spring. Open year-round, the reservation is found on South Sandwich Rd. off Rt. 130, adjacent to Sandwich's Ryder Conservation Lands; turn at the cursive-script white sign for Carpe Diem (the private residence shares TTOR's driveway), and follow signs. Memorial Day to Columbus Day, parking is $6 on weekends and holidays, due to the popularity of the swimming beach on the Ryder side of Wakeby Pond.

Waquoit Bay

If you study the Upper Cape shoreline on a map, you'll notice how the sea, rising after the end of the Ice Ages, has pushed up the water table and flooded the valleys carved by glacial meltwaters through the coastal sandplain along Falmouth's southeastern coast. The largest of these finger-like valleys breached by Vineyard Sound is now largely protected within the state-owned **Waquoit Bay National Estuarine Research Reserve,** tel. (508) 457-0495, whose visitor center is on Rt. 28 down the street from Edwards Boatyard. A vast open-air laboratory of ponds, salt marsh, barrier beaches, and a large wooded island, the reserve is used in part to study the effects of non-point-source pollution. This is the collected runoff from a wide area of petroleum-stained pavement, over-fertilized yards, and leaky septic systems—which adds up to a major environmental hazard, as serious as any pipeline spill or untreated factory discharge. The effects are ominous: algae blooms, fish kills, and declining eelgrass beds, for a start. (Eelgrass is a vital nursery habitat for shrimp, crabs, and over a dozen fish species, including such commercial varieties as flounder, pollack, and hake. If there's no eelgrass, there are no baby fish.) Waquoit Bay is hardly alone in these problems—from sea to shining sea, the nation's wetlands and the fisheries they support are seriously threatened—but it's one of the few being subjected to careful study. On the outreach side, the reserve sponsors a number of seasonal interpretive programs to inform visitors of the bay's special qualities and raise awareness about watersheds. You can also explore on your own: some five miles of trails run through the place, including boardwalks in the marshes. After your ecology lessons, take a break at the **South Cape Beach State Park,** at the mouth of the bay. Accessible from the end of Great Oak Rd. in South Mashpee, its parking is a mere $2. The reserve also has 10 primitive, public campsites on 300-acre Washburn Island ($4), but you'll need a boat to reach them (by canoe or kayak, it's a 20-minute paddle), reservations are required year-round, all fresh water has to be packed in, and no campfires of any sort are permitted (the risk of their getting out of control on the windblown island is just too high).

WOODS HOLE

Woods Hole has the distinction of being Massachusetts' only seaside college town. This isn't just any college, either: the tiny village at the Cape's "other tip" is home to the Woods Hole

Before writing Silent Spring, *Rachel Carson served as chief publications editor for the US Fish & Wildlife Service, in which capacity she joined the crew of the Woods Hole-based R/V* Albatross *on a 10-day trip to Georges Bank— breaching a barrier against female oceanographers' participating in overnight research cruises.*

COURTESY OF THE BOSTON PUBLIC LIBRARY, PRINT DEPT.

Oceanographic Institution (WHOI, or "hooey"), a private, largely federally funded research center known most widely for the work of its pioneering little deep-sea submersible, *Alvin.* The US Geological Survey (USGS), the National Marine Fisheries Service (NMFS), the Marine Biological Laboratory (MBL), the undergraduate Sea Education Association, and other environmental think tanks are also based here in whole or in part, making Woods Hole the 800-pound gorilla in the world of marine science and education. Though the presence of the Martha's Vineyard ferry gives the village all the trappings of the Cape's other tourist towns in summer—overflowing parking lots, scores of cyclists, eateries crowded with out-of-towners, strolling shoppers—during the off season, the community of some 1,500 scientists and students reveals its true nature—essentially that of one big academic campus.

That heavy volume of summer traffic to the Steamship Authority ferry and the dearth of even paid parking around the village can make a peak-season visit frustrating for drivers. One solution is to take advantage of the acres of free parking back in Falmouth at the Falmouth Mall (on Rt. 28, east of downtown) and from there hop aboard the regular Woods Hole Shuttle (WHOOSH). Running daily until early evening (and until 10 p.m. on Fri.-Sat.) late June through early September, WHOOSH trolleys are a service of the Cape Cod Regional Transit Authority, meaning that all-day CCRTA trolley passes are valid (standard adult fare is $1 otherwise). A second option is to bike to Woods Hole via the three-mile **Shining Sea Path,** a paved rail trail beginning at the intersection of Woods Hole Rd. and Mill St. (south of Main) in the heart of Falmouth and ending right at the Steamship dock. Bike rentals are available from several shops in Falmouth, including downtown **Corner Cycle,** 115 Palmer Ave. (Rt. 28) a quarter-mile north of the path, tel. (508) 540-4195; and the seasonal **Holiday Cycles,** 465 Grand Ave., tel. (508) 540-3549, among the inns and motels along Falmouth Heights. More dedicated cyclists may want to try the longer, equally scenic route along Buzzards Bay, following Sippewisset Road from West Falmouth to Woods Hole. Along the way are houses nestled in trees like elfin cottages, glimpses of the bay through people's backyards, and the Knob—a sanctuary at the end of Quisset

Harbor Road with breathtaking views out at the end of its causeway. Rent a bike for this route at **Art's Bike Shop,** on the corner of County Rd. and Old Main in North Falmouth (slightly west of Rt. 28A), tel. (800) 563-7379 or (508) 563-7379.

The Undersea World of Woods Hole

The work of the Woods Hole's scientific community isn't concealed entirely behind closed lab doors or beneath distant oceans. The **WHOI Exhibit Center,** in a chapel-like clapboard building on School St. a block north of Water, tel. (508) 289-2252, has two floors of displays and videos on coastal ecology and discoveries made through WHOI-sponsored research, from understanding the lives of jellyfish in local Atlantic waters to strange lifeforms around the ocean floor's hydrothermal vents. The center also showcases the tools of the oceanographer's trade, including a full-sized mock-up of the remarkable titanium-sphered *Alvin,* 30-some-year-old pioneer of deep-sea exploration, discoverer of the *Titanic,* and doorway to the world of 4,500 meters (14,700 feet!) under the sea. A small gift shop sells selected books, magazines, and journals. Open Tues.-Sun. till 4:30 p.m. May-Oct. (daily during high season), and Fri.-Sun. in April, November, and December. Admission is $2. As a complement to these exhibits, the WHOI News & Information Office, on downtown Water St., sponsors guided hour-long walks around its campus, giving a general overview of the institution's history while taking in the dockside ship operations and even, if you're really lucky, a laboratory. Offered late June through early September, the walks commence at the Information Office and are by reservation only; call (508) 289-2252.

The village center is shared by shops, restaurants, and the buildings of the **Marine Biological Laboratory,** a private nonprofit which hosts marine-related undergraduate and graduate programs for students of two East Coast universities, as well as the sponsored research of hundreds of scientists from around the world. Free tours are available weekday afternoons July-Aug., starting at their gift shop in the Candle House on Water St.; look for the half-hulled ship model poking out of the facade. Reservations are strongly recommended, as space on the tours is limited; tel. (508) 289-7623. Two blocks farther west is the **National Marine Fisheries Service Aquarium,** on Albatross St. near the end of Water., tel. (508) 548-7684. You've seen their names on laminated menu cards at sushi bars, but here's where you can see what cod, haddock, yellowtail flounder, salmon, octopus, and other denizens of local waters *really* look like. The creatures in this free exhibit of the village's oldest science institution (the NMFS's forerunner established a collecting station in Woods Hole in 1871) are all the subjects of the facility's research into fish biology and fisheries resource management—so they may change to reflect what's turning up on twice-weekly sampling trips. Some scene-stealing harbor seals in the outdoor pool by the entrance, too, but these also vary, depending upon who's been rescued from shore strandings and is being fattened up or allowed to regain flipper strength before being released again into the wild. Open daily to 4 p.m. mid-June through mid-September, and weekdays the rest of the year.

If you're not content just looking, you can get wet with a hands-on 90-minute tour by **Ocean-Quest,** tel. (800) 37-OCEAN. Making the rounds of collection points in the harbor, naturalists use handling tanks aboard the vessel to bring up critters for examination—and the day's catch serves as an introduction to topics in marine ecology. Weather permitting, up to four departures are scheduled each weekday in summer from the dock opposite the MBL Candle House, next to the pleasant waterfront park filled with salt-spray roses. Tickets are $15 adults, $10 kids 12 and under, and may be purchased or charged at the dock.

Accommodations

A trio of small seasonal motels flanks Woods Hole Road as it enters the village from Falmouth: the **Sleepy Hollow Motor Inn,** tel. (508) 548-1986, the **Nautilus Motor Inn,** tel. (800) 654-2333 or (508) 548-1525, and the **Sands of Time Motor Inn,** tel. (800) 841-0114 or (508) 548-6300. All are open mid-April through mid-October or early November. The last two have almost identical rates ($95-140 d mid-June through mid-September, with a drop of $10-20 in the spring and fall), while Sleepy Hollow is as low as $85-115 in summer and $65-95 in the shoulder months. Alternatively, about three

miles away from the heart of the village—conveniently close to the start of the Shining Sea Path just south of Falmouth center, and on the route of the summer WHOOSH trolley to Woods Hole—is the year-round **Woods Hole Passage B&B Inn,** tel. (800) 790-8976 or (508) 548-9575. Rates are $90-115 April-Oct., $75-85 Nov.-March, and include private baths and full breakfast.

Falmouth proper, on the other hand, oozes with accommodations. Several familiar national chains are found on or near Rt. 28 as it bends through the center of town, including, from north to southeast, **Quality Inn,** on Jones Rd., tel. (800) 228-5151 or (508) 540-2000; **Ramada Inn on the Square,** 40 N. Main, tel. (800) 2-RAMADA or (508) 457-0606; and **Best Western Falmouth Marina Tradewinds,** off East Main on Robbins Rd. a few hundred feet from the Island Queen ferry to Martha's Vineyard, tel. (800) 528-1234 or (508) 548-4300. The first two are open year-round, while the Tradewinds closes January through early March. All are expensive to luxury in summer, and only moderate before mid-June or after Labor Day. For moderate prices in high season, about your only option is one of the small motels around Falmouth Heights: **Hotel Falmouth,** 359 Main St., tel. (800) 544-3613 or (508) 548-3613; **Town & Beach Motel,** 382 Main, tel. (508) 548-1380; **Flagship Motel,** 24 Scranton Ave., tel. (800) 457-5567 or (508) 548-1110; or the **Island View,** 375 Grand Ave., tel. (508) 540-1080.

Food

On Water St. around the corner from the Steamship Authority ferry ("262 *leisurely* paces" from the gangplank) is **Fishmonger's Cafe,** tel. (508) 548-9148, which, despite the name, is one of those extremely rare Cape establishments that openly embrace vegetables. The regular dinner menu initially looks like your typical college-town cross-cultural blender: gazpacho, chicken California, Middle Eastern plate, fish and chips, broiled sirloin with garden salad and brown rice. But daily specials push the menu into eclectic New American territory, with offerings such as pumpkin-sage ravioli, osso buco, and grilled tuna with Barbados black beans. The owner has an admirable way with pies, too. Most entrees and specials are under

$16; veggie selections rarely top $10. Open for breakfast and lunch, too; closed Jan.-Feb.

Two other good options are just across the street: the almost-year-round **Captain Kidd,** tel. (508) 548-8563, half casual dining, half turn-of-the-century sailors' bar; and the more ethnically influenced **Black Duck Restaurant,** tel. (508) 548-9165, open March-Nov. or early December.

MID-CAPE

HYANNIS

One of the Cape's early resorts, Hyannis and the neighboring villages of Hyannisport and Osterville have been known since the 1920s for their oceanfront estates. Today, Hyannis is the most urban of Cape towns (pop. about 41,000), a major commercial center attracting Mid-Cape visitors and residents to its big shopping plazas along busy Rt. 132. Come summer, it's an absolute boom town, filled with families spending summer at Grandma's, renting kitchenette-equipped "efficiencies" by the week, or joining the ant-like streams of island-bound passengers making their way down to the ferry docks from satellite parking lots.

It may not have much in the way of museums or historic sights, but in addition to having the most passenger rail, bus, boat, and airline connections to the off-Cape world, Hyannis boasts the region's highest concentration of guest rooms, with over 40 motels, hotels, and inns around town. It's also a hub for Cape nightlife, with bars, cafes, and nightclubs drawing the legion of young summer workers who flock to the region to earn next year's college money. While the party abates after summer ends, this is still about the only Cape town where you can schmooze over some brews with the under-35 single set off season.

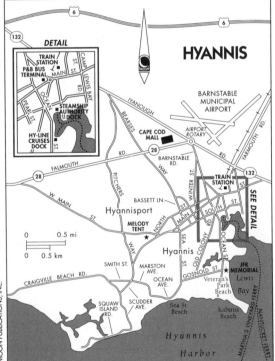

Get to Know Jack

Fans of the Camelot years in the American presidency—and anyone else wanting to trip lightly down the path of nostalgia—should be sure to check out the JFK photos and videos on display at the **John F. Kennedy Hyannis Museum,** on the ground floor of Main St.'s bunting-draped Old Town Hall, tel. (508) 790-3077, covering the years he spent vacationing at the local family spread, from the 1930s until his death in

© MOON PUBLICATIONS, INC.

COURTESY OF BOSTON PUBLIC LIBRARY, PRINT DEPT.

Kennedys—Patricia, Teddy, Rose, Bobby, Eunice, and Jack—hold court in Hyannisport, July 23, 1940

If you're in town around the Fourth of July, catch the **Cape Cod Symphony** on the Town Green, where they perform their annual free summer concert the Saturday of that holiday weekend. The Boston Pops Esplanade Orchestra also puts in an annual appearance on the Town Green, the first Sunday evening in August; tickets for this special **Pops by the Sea** concert are sold in advance through the Hyannis Area Chamber of Commerce, 1481 Rt. 132, tel. (800) 4-HYNNIS or (508) 362-5230.

Tours

Taking the **Cape Cod Scenic Railroad,** tel. (800) 872-4508 or (508) 771-3788, through the varied topography of the Upper Cape is a relaxing alternative to stewing in traffic, and the railroad right-of-way is pleasantly free of the commercial clutter that increasingly mars sightseeing by car. Roundtrips from Hyannis include stops in historic Sandwich and at the Cape Cod Canal; some trips include dinner or guided marsh walks. Regular scenic trips are offered Tues.-Sun. and Monday holidays June-Oct., weekends in May and December (no set schedule for November); fare is $11.50 adults, $7.50 kids. Dinner trains and other special excursions—wine-tasting trips, for example—are available at additional cost and begin on weekends in late March, expand to Wed.-Sun. June-Oct., and then return to weekend operation through New Year's Eve. Trains depart from the downtown railroad station at 252 Main St., across from the P&B bus terminal and next to the miniature golf course.

1963. Open daily in summer, Wed.-Sun. off season (closed January); admission is $3. There's also a **JFK Memorial** on Ocean St. past the ferry staging area, overlooking sheltered Veteran's Park Beach next to the yacht club (fee for beach parking in summer). The famous Kennedy Compound—whose nucleus is the much-expanded 1902 cottage that Joe and Rose Kennedy and their nine kids used for a summer home—is located in the well-heeled residential neighborhood of Hyannisport, south of downtown. But, given the frequent traffic restrictions, voyeurs are better off taking one of the several cruises that parade past the compound's waterfront, out by the harbor breakwater. The excursion with the most historical resonance is **Catboat Rides,** with 90-minute sailing cruises to Hyannisport and beyond aboard a classic catboat, a type of sloop indigenous to the Cape. At the Ocean St. docks, look for the boat with the grinning Cheshire-like puss on the sail; reservations tel. (508) 775-0222.

Music al Fresco

Throughout the summer, you can catch up with America's aging (or ageless?) pop, rock, and country-western stars at the **Cape Cod Melody Tent,** on West Main, tel. (508) 775-9100. The venue is certainly more intimate than any Vegas stage, and ticket prices aren't stratospheric, either.

Combination land-sea excursions are the province of **Cape Cod Duck Tours,** tel. (508) 362-1117, one of several outfits around the Massachusetts seaboard that have sprung up in the wake of the stupendously successful Boston Duck Tours. This local Cape variant doesn't use the war-surplus DUKWs so renowned in Boston, but their amphibious vehicles are just as capable of negotiating both downtown pavement and harbor waters. Departing four to seven days a week late spring through mid-October from the Duck Inn Pub, at 447 Main, the 45-minute tours cost $12 adults, $8 kids under 12; tickets may be purchased in advance (recommended).

Since the best local place to spot whales is in the waters off the other side of the Cape, **Hyan-**

nis **Whale Watcher Cruises** departs out of Barnstable Harbor north of Hyannis.

Accommodations

While a handful of no-frills B&Bs and guest-houses are to be found on Sea and Ocean Streets north of the harbor (in the company of **The Inn on Sea Street,** tel. 508-775-8030, and **The Simmons Homestead Inn,** tel. 800-637-1649 or 508-778-4999—both definitely a cut above the rest), Hyannis is first and foremost a motel town. The half dozen establishments sharing the waterfront district can legitimately claim to be within walking distance of the beach, but the other 35 are more likely to offer views of asphalt than water. Most of the national chains found on the Cape are here in Hyannis, as well, generally along mall-lined Rt. 132. Much more affordable (and within walking distance of Main St. restaurants, shops, and all forms of local transportation, including bike rentals on the premises) is the very modest **Cascade Motor Lodge,** 201 Main St. opposite the train station, tel. (508) 775-9717, open year-round.

Food

American diner-style fare may be overly abundant in these parts, but not all vendors of the stuff are equal. If you want to rub elbows over breakfast

---

ADDITIONAL HYANNIS ACCOMMODATIONS

Days Inn, 867 Iyannough Rd. (Rt. 132), tel. (800) DAYS INN or (508) 775-3011; $45-150 d.

Cape Cod Hyannis Hotel, 707 Iyannough Rd. (Rt. 132), tel. (800) 989-9827 or (508) 775-6600; $58-139 d.

Radisson Hotel & Conference Center, 287 Iyannough Rd. (Rt. 28), tel. (800) 771-7200 or (508) 771-1700; $60-129 d.

Super 8 Motel, 36 East Main St., tel. (800) 800-8000 or (508) 775-0962. Outdoor swimming pool; $32-130 d.

Howard Johnson Express Inn, 447 Main St., tel. (800) I GO HOJO or (508) 775-3000; $59-129 d.

---

with residents rather than day-trippers, head up-Cape to Marstons Mills, one of the rural Barnstable villages about eight miles west of downtown Hyannis. There you'll find the **Mills Restaurant,** on Rt. 149 next to the Mobil station, tel. (508) 428-9814, an extremely popular place known for its solid country breakfasts (including a couple of vegetarian omelet choices), weekend brunches, and great prices. Open Tues.-Fri. till 2 p.m. (with a half-hour break between breakfast and lunch), and till 1 p.m. Sat.-Sun.

Both decent lunches and late-night cheap eats are available from **Spiritus Café & Pizzeria,** 500 W. Main St., Hyannis, tel. (508) 775-2955, which is quite the hangout for local teens and summer's transient crop of McJob holders. Foccacia sandwiches, veggie soup, garden salads, pizzas, and fountain items (including great Emack & Bolio's ice cream, from Boston) are counterbalanced by the status-priced espresso drinks. The hours (daily to 11 p.m. or midnight) can be a lifesaver, though, particularly off season. However, if it's just pizza you're after—or if you prefer not to eat in a room full of smoldering cigarettes—you'll do better at **Jack's,** 373 W. Main St., tel. (508) 775-0612. This is a local spot par excellence, as down-home comfortable as you'll find; prices are as reasonable as the staff is friendly. It's also open year-round until 1 a.m. daily.

You can get pizza at the lighter-fare back room of the **Roadhouse Cafe,** at 488 South St., tel. (508) 775-2386, too, but most folks wisely choose to sit up front, amid the nautical tchotchkes, and order lobster or steak. Red-meat eaters seeking relief from the relentless barrage of fried seafood can also put an end to their "we're not in Kansas City anymore, Toto" lament with a thick slab of prime rib beneath the crew racing paraphernalia decorating the **Black Cat Tavern,** on Ocean across the street from the Hy-Line ferry landing, tel. (508) 778-1233. Of course, seafood lovers won't go unrewarded. If you hesitate to drop in excess of $20 per person by the time the night is done, you can always belly up to the bar and have a simple burger or bowl of chowder while jawing with the friendly barkeep over a decent microbrew. Closed Monday off season.

For more surf and less turf, in family-friendly surroundings (and featuring lower prices), try

Mildred's Chowder House, by the airport on Rt. 28 opposite the Radisson Hotel, tel. (508) 775-1045. Whether broiled, fried, stuffed, baked, or served over linguine, the seafood is the star here, though there's always something in the meat and chicken department. As for that chowder, four varieties are routinely offered, and all are rich enough to lend credence to the menu's boast that Mildred's is the number-one cream-consuming restaurant.in New England. Go ahead, live it up—you can count calories when you get back home. (Or penitently order the Jell-o for dessert.)

For a seafood meal with a tad more sophistication in the accompaniments than iceberg salads and baked or fried potatoes, choose **Penguin Seagrill,** 331 Main St., tel. (508) 775-2023. Nobody has fresher fruits from the sea, and that wood-fired grill does a mighty good job of bringing out the best flavors in all of them. Whether you have rack of lamb or mushroom risotto, Portuguese seafood stew or nut-crusted salmon with fruit salsa, you'll be getting your money's worth. (And yes, it costs a pretty penny: most entrees are over $16.)

Finally, though Cape Cod isn't known for multicultural dining, places such as **Pavilion Indian Cuisine,** downtown at 511 Main, tel. (508) 790-0985, are helping change all that, chipping away at the ubiquity of fried seafood and pasta with such familiar Indian dishes as mulligatawny soup, lamb vindaloo, and tandoori chicken. Good portions, a perfect willingness to turn up the spiciness upon request, and prices that don't aim to gouge the tourists are the rule here, all year round. Serves lunch, too, Sun.-Friday.

Getting Away

As the year-round Mid-Cape gateway to the island of Nantucket, Hyannis Harbor bustles with the horn-blasting boats of **Hy-Line Cruises,** tel. (508) 778-2600, and the **Steamship Authority,** tel. (508) 477-8600. If you'll be taking the bus to Hyannis, intending to connect straight to an outbound ferry, you can save yourself a wait in line by purchasing your ferry ticket when you pay your bus fare. Drivers will notice that all directional signage avoids mentioning either company's name. If you want the Hy-Line, follow signs to the Ocean St. docks; for the Steamship, follow signs to South Street. If you have time to kill, next to no luggage (or can drop someone off to watch it), and don't mind walking a fair piece, the cheapest parking is east of the Steamship dock. Don't let the authoritative, red-flag-waving guys with the too-cool shades dupe you into turning into the super-expensive lots immediately opposite the Hy-Line passenger drop, as you can save several bucks a day (and be just as close to the ferry) by simply taking the next left.

Both companies offer a choice between fast and expensive or slow and cheap ferries to Nantucket, while Hy-Line adds a seasonal vessel to Martha's Vineyard.

Getting Around

The P&B terminal serves as an endpoint for all three Cape Cod Regional Transit bus routes: the **SeaLine,** running west to Falmouth and Woods Hole; the **Villager,** heading north to Barnstable Harbor via the Rt. 132 malls; and the easterly **H2O Line,** connecting Hyannis to Orleans via Rt. 28 through Yarmouth, Dennisport, Harwich Port, and Chatham. Saquetucket Harbor in Harwich Port, the departure point for the Freedom Cruise Line boat to Nantucket, is one of the possible stops along this last route. Also from Hyannis, the **Yarmouth Easy Shuttle** (YES) operates hourly in summer along Rt. 28 with stops at a couple of south shore beaches and an onward connection with the **Coach of Dennis.** Call the CCRTA toll-free at (800) 352-7155 for schedule and fare info, or pick up their system timetable at the bus terminal.

If you're coming by boat (your own), you'll want to call ahead and reserve a slip at the Hyannis Marina, tel. (508) 775-5662. There, on the inner harbor across from all the island ferries, you'll find all the repair, rigging, pump-out, hookup, shower, and laundry facilities you could want. Trolley service to Main St., too.

ROUTE 6A: BARNSTABLE TO DENNIS

Although recent decades have inundated Cape Cod with ever-increasing numbers of summer residents and retirees whose housing and shopping needs are making much of the Cape indistinguishable from the average American suburb or strip mall, there are still a few places that capture the look and feel of yesteryear—or of the last century. The Mid-Cape portion of Rt. 6A passes through a number of these throwbacks, winding between one after another of the historic villages along the protected shores of Cape Cod Bay. Shingle-sided saltbox or steep-roofed Cape houses, white clapboard churches, and fancy Federal or Greek Revival captains' mansions abound—as do B&Bs, art galleries, antiques shops, and pottery studios. Unfortunately, traffic is so heavy and fast most of the year that you won't have time to dawdle over the roadside views unless you stop and park. But the route isn't conducive to strolling pedestrians or leisure cyclists, either, as the road is generally narrow and buildings abut it quite closely. If ever the Cape adopts the Bermuda model—forcing tourists to ride around exclusively on slow little mopeds or slow big buses—perhaps the charms of Rt. 6A will become more apparent to more than just a small circle of local residents. In the meantime, you'll have to either drive the road at sunrise on Sunday or take it on faith that the stuff you can glimpse through your windows as that sport utility vehicle tries to climb into your back seat is well worth a longer look, if you can manage it.

Sandy Neck

On Cape Cod Bay by the Sandwich-Barnstable town line is the largest salt marsh ecosystem north of Chesapeake Bay and its accompanying six-mile beachfront of creeping barrier dunes. Though access to Sandy Neck isn't cheap (nonresident parking is $10 mid-May through mid-October), a visit pays many dividends: hours of potential walking along the shore, with its wrack line of tide-borne curiosities and its busy population of shorebirds; discovering coyote tracks in the arid swale between the parallel formation of protective dunes, whose accreting sands, augmented by eroded material from the western rim of Cape Cod Bay, are slowly closing off Barnstable Harbor. Or the sight of tree swallows swooping through the Great Marsh behind the dunes, snapping insects out of the air (plenty of leftovers remain, however, so bring repellent). Early-summer visitors may also see the carefully monitored nests of the endangered piping plovers and least terns, two tenative but regular visitors to the Cape's shores. To reach

Sandy Neck from Rt. 6A, turn north on Sandy Neck Rd. in East Sandwich, between the Sandy Neck Motel and the Sandy Neck Restaurant, and proceed to the ranger station and parking lot at the end.

Inland Walks

The town of Barnstable has much more to offer than austere coastline and spongy peat mats in tidal wetlands. Inland of Barnstable Harbor are several municipal conservation properties encompassing portions of the glacially formed moraine underlying US 6. The hilly upland woods are choice spots for hiking on days too cool for the beach. You can also leave the crowds behind and find out how dry and hot a pitch pine forest can get in summer. The largest is the 1,100-acre **West Barnstable Conservation Area,** bounded by US 6, Rt. 149, a small airport, and the town of Sandwich; look for parking off Rt. 149 south of US 6 Exit 5, on Popple Bottom Rd. nearly opposite the Olde Barnstable Fairgrounds golf course. (Popple is an old colloquialism for poplar trees.) Two smaller parcels sandwich the Mid-Cape Highway from beside Phinneys Lane, slightly east of Exit 6 and due south of the one stoplight on Rt. 6A in Barnstable: **Old Jail Lane,** with parking beside the eponymous access road on the north side of US 6, and **Hathaways Pond,** a popular freshwater swimming beach on US 6's south side ($4 parking fee in summer). All three welcome mountain bikes as well as hikers, and offer the kind of terrain that justifies having one along. (Since there are no rental shops in the immediate vicinity, you have the choice of tacking on a road ride or renting a car rack from down-Cape's seasonal **Idle Times Bike Shop,** on Rt. 6A at the entrance to Nickerson State Park in Brewster, tel. (508) 896-9242 or, within the area, (800) 924-8281 (call to confirm the availability of those racks). **Art's Bike Shop,** on County Rd. in North Falmouth, tel. (800) 563-7379 or (508) 563-7379, also has car racks for their rental customers.

Excellent computer-generated and GPS-tested topo maps and pocket-sized interpretive booklets to these and four other town conservation properties are available free from the Barnstable Conservation Commission, 367 Main St. in Hyannis, tel. (508) 790-6245. Pick up *A Hiker's Guide to Town of Barnstable Conser-*

vation Lands weekdays in person, or send a self-addressed five- by ten-inch envelope with enough postage for five ounces to the above address (zip code is 02601).

Whalewatching

The only whalewatch excursions available between Plymouth and Provincetown are the **Hyannis Whale Watcher Cruises,** out of Barnstable Harbor off Rt. 6A, tel. (800) 287-0374 or (508) 362-6088. Daily May-Oct., the company's speedy boat departs the Millway Marine boatyard for Stellwagen Bank off the tip of Cape Cod in search of Stellwagen's most frequently sighted species: the finback, blue, sei, humpback, and North Atlantic right whale, all of which are endangered (as is the minke whale, a seasonal visitor). Reservations are advised; tickets for the four-hour outings are $20 adults.

Cape Cod Museum of Natural History

Well signed on an otherwise undeveloped stretch of Rt. 6A a few hundred yards west of Paine Creek Rd. in West Brewster is the Cape Cod Museum of Natural History, tel. (508) 896-3867 or, in Massachusetts, (800) 479-3867, with two floors of aquariums showcasing aquatic flora and fauna of the local waters (salt and fresh), plus a pair of interpretive trails behind the museum offering views of a salt marsh, cranberry bog, and beech grove. Numerous items cater specifically to kids, from the live, glass-enclosed beehive to the big rockinghorse-like whale vertebrae; adults, meanwhile, should check out the museum's nature trips, scheduled throughout summer and fall. Cruises around Nauset Marsh, day trips (and rustic overnights) to Monomoy Island's National Wildlife Refuge, and guided full- or half-day canoe trips are among the various options; all require preregistration. The museum is open daily mid-April through mid-October, Tues.-Sun. otherwise; admission is $3.50.

Accommodations

Most of the score of small inns and B&Bs in this area are readily visible to passing motorists along Rt. 6A between Rt. 132 in Barnstable and Union St. on the east side of neighboring Yarmouth Port. No two are alike, although the prevailing theme is colonial rather than Victorian. If you want a nice romantic B&B or comfortable inn within a block of a beach, head to the south shore on the other side of Rt. 28 (but expect to pay at least half again as much as you would here, where the entry price point for a room with private bath and full breakfast is around $90).

A good example of what you'll find in this area is **The Acworth Inn,** a mid-19th-century home in the Barnstable village of Cummaquid, tel. (800) 362-6363 or (508) 362-3330. Light-filled rooms, here and there with antiques and painted furniture, and a generous breakfast that, though billed as continental, includes much more than just a buffet of cereals and beverages. You couldn't ask for more congenial hosts, either—these are quite willing to share their love and knowledge of the area. Rates are $85-95 mid-May-Oct., $10 less off season (except the Cummaquid Room, which you should request if you like to warm yourself by a fire). A couple of miles east, in Yarmouth Port, is the **One Center Street Inn,** tel. (888) 407-1653 or (508) 362-8910, a former parsonage built in 1824. Each tastefully decorated room, whether under the upstairs eaves or in the attached carriage house, takes full advantage of the space, so that even the smallest is able to include comfortable seating and a good reading lamp (a feature all have in common) without feeling the least bit cramped. Stay for a week and you still won't exhaust Karen's breakfast repertoire—though you'd certainly have a fine time trying: the morning's baked goods alone could qualify her for *Bon Appétit.* All this for $85-100 mid-May through mid-October, $75 with a shared bath; off season, subtract $10. The two-room suite with fireplace is $110 year-round. The long Bass Hole boardwalk out over Yarmouth's bayside tidal marsh—a favorite sunset viewing spot among mid-Cape residents—is a two-mile jog or bike ride from the door of the inn; beside it is tiny Gray's Beach, the only free saltwater beach on the Cape in high season.

If you're just not a B&B person, or you require TVs and telephones by the bed, you can't beat the value of a stay at **The Colonial House Inn,** on Rt. 6A at the corner of Strawberry Lane in Yarmouth Port, tel. (508) 362-4348. The rambling structure, parts of which date back to the 1730s, has 21 rooms of various sizes and sleeping capacities, but all have private baths, a/c, and canopy beds. Cyclists will apreciate the covered storage space and the chance to soak tired muscles in the small indoor pool or jacuzzi. The dining-room fireplaces, the overstuffed armchairs with lace antimacassars in the bar, and white wooden chairs on the terrace all contribute to the comfortable air of a classic, unstuffy country inn, presided over by one of the best innkeepers in the business. The only surprises with the solidly traditional seafood, steak, and pasta meals are that they're included in the bill—the $95 d summer room rate (late June-Labor Day) includes breakfast *and* dinner. In winter, rates drop to $70-85.

Food

If for some reason you wanted a second breakfast—or you're staying in one of the inns that doesn't serve one—pay a visit to **Jack's Out Back,** behind 161 Main (Rt. 6A) in Yarmouth Port, tel. (508) 362-6690, amid the short cluster of shops next to the two ATM-equipped banks. A true local institution, Jack's features square meals (no omelets) at low prices, although the real attraction is Jack himself, an irascible fellow beloved by people for his sharp tongue. When a regular calls out, "How ya doin', Jack?" upon entering, Jack may yell back sourly, "Working my ass off." To a customer chatting at the counter, Jack isn't unaccustomed to issuing reprimands: "Eat your breakfast—it's getting cold." And you have to do everything (except cook) for yourself—directions for filling out an order, getting your own beverages, and cleaning up are taped to the counter. Bus your own dishes or your sloth will be proclaimed to the next customer looking for a table. And mind your little ones: "Unattended children will be sold as slaves." Jack's is also open for lunch.

For just a snack, step into **Hallet's,** the old-fashioned ice-cream parlor on the same block. If Mary Hallet Clark, daughter of the shop's founder, is behind the counter (she usually is—she hasn't been off-Cape in over 20 years), you'll have the fortune of listening to a real undiluted Cape accent. The apothecary cabinet along the wall is a real beauty, with Latin names inscribed on the brass drawer pulls, and the malted frappes are darn good, too. Open spring through December.

Between Jack's and Hallet's is the Japanese restaurant **Inaho,** occupying the ground floor of a historic house at 157 Main, tel. (508) 362-5522. Perhaps no restaurant on the Cape shows off the fresh bounty of the local waters like this small establishment, whose sushi, tempura, and whole-fish dishes are served in the welcoming atmosphere of a private home. The flourless chocolate cake is one of the best desserts in the region, too: light and not too sweet. Dinner is served year-round six nights a week off season, seven nights in season (except when the owners take their winter vacation).

For more traditional New England seafood, try **Mattakeese Wharf,** on Barnstable Harbor, 271 Mill Way (turn at Rt. 6A's traffic light east of Barnstable Village), tel. (508) 362-4511. The atmosphere may be as casual as at a mall restaurant, but no mall has such a fine portside location, and few have fish of this quality. The preparations won't knock your socks off, but they're more than competent: no-nonsense seafood, pastas, meat, and poultry. Enjoying bouillabaisse on the covered deck while watching the small marina in late evening's golden light is the quintessential way to end a Cape summer afternoon. Not that foul weather should be any deterrent: moody gray becomes the harbor as much as brilliant sun, and the porch seating areas are fully enclosable if necessary. Open May-Oct. for lunch, dinner, and Sunday brunch.

THE OUTER CAPE

Most of the human settlement of the Outer Cape, right up to this century, has come from its proximity to excellent fishing grounds. (The Cape's name, of course, reflects this.) Native Americans spent summers fishing and gathering shellfish, 15th- and 16th-century European fishing vessels put ashore to dry fish and engage in minor trade, and post-*Mayflower* colonists built a fishing industry from these exposed shores. But what the sea giveth, it can also taketh away—like a video on fast forward, the effects of wind, tide, and erosion are probably more visible on the Outer Cape than anywhere else along the Massachusetts coast, not only from year to year, but sometimes from day to day. The barrier beaches and backshore cliffs that bear the brunt of this process make up the diadem in the region's crown of natural wonders: the 27,000-acre Cape Cod National Seashore, extending the length and sometimes the breadth of the Outer Cape.

CHATHAM

Situated at Cape Cod's "elbow," Chatham presides over the hazardous waters whose "dangerous shoulds and roring breakers" sent the *Mayflower* scurrying for the protection of Provincetown harbor. Now that the Cape's economy has shifted from harvesting cod and trading with Cathay to marketing quaintness, this old sea captains' town of about 6,500 year-round residents has become one of the Cape's best gifts to the tourist trade, with clapboard mansions, boutiques, art galleries, summer concerts in the old bandstand, and historic lighthouses. Nor does it shut down and turn out the lights when the tourists go home. One of the Cape's most fashionable addresses, Chatham is even coveted by the sea itself; unfortunately for oceanfront homeowners, negotiating with Poseidon is an extremely one-sided deal. Since the protective outer barrier beach was breached in a 1987 winter storm, the town's coastline has been more dramatically altered than perhaps anywhere else on the Cape; see the results for yourself at the vast South Beach, in front of the Coast Guard station and lighthouse on Shore Road, which once was separated from town by the harbor.

Monomoy National Wildlife Refuge

Monomoy Island (actually two separate islands a short boat ride south of town) used to be a peninsula connected to town, as South Beach is now, with bus service down to the lighthouse station at its tip. A 1958 storm breached the sandy strand, and today the only residents of this National Wildlife Refuge are birds, a winter colony of harbor seals, and several hundred gray seals, year-round residents since 1991. Like some tourists, these last seem to have liked what they saw, and not only came to stay, but told a lot of their friends—most of whom seem to be Canadian bachelors from Nova Scotia's Sable Island, home to 90% of North America's gray seals. Needless to say, Monomoy is great birdwatching territory, and good for strolls on the beach without stepping over thousands of sunbathers.

The Cape Cod Museum of Natural History, tel. (800) 479-3867, operates day trips to both North and South Monomoy ($40-65, May-Oct.), and overnights with rustic camping in the restored lighthouse-keeper's house ($120 including dinner and breakfast, June-Oct.). Massachusetts Audubon also offers trips to the refuge ($30-55 depending on duration); call or drop by their Wellfleet Bay Wildlife Sanctuary, off US 6 in South Wellfleet, for reservations. Call (508) 349-2615 for schedule.

As a property of the US Fish and Wildlife Service, the islands are open to the public so long as you observe certain guidelines with respect to their ecology and inhabitants. If you don't have your own boat and don't wish to tramp about with a naturalist guide and company, you can hire someone to ferry you across, or even rent a boat of your own. Keith Lincoln's **Monomoy Island Ferry,** tel. (508) 945-5450, operates daily on demand in summer (weekends in spring and fall) from the beach below the Refuge HQ on Morris Island Rd. Simply head down and look for him; if he's not there in good weather, wait a few minutes—more than likely, he'll turn up, fresh from dropping a boatload of passengers off on the beaches. Passage costs $10-14 and takes seven to 30 minutes, depending on where you want to go. John McGrath, Jr., runs a similar service, the **Water Taxi,** from the Fish Pier in Chatham, tel. (508) 430-2346, and charges $11-45. John, however, operates year-round, in case you're stoic enough to brave winter's blasts to get a good gander at those harbor seals in December. Both skippers drop you off and then return to fetch you at an agreed-upon time and place. McGrath also rents boats, if you prefer.

A final note: between early June and the last full moon in August, the north island in particular is overrun by greenhead horse flies whose voracious appetites are not to be underestimated. Take all the usual precautions—covering every inch of exposed skin with clothing and bug repellent, for example—but recognize that no matter what you do, you're likely to meet that one cloud of greenheads who lap up DEET like slugs do beer.

Accommodations

Quaintness enhances the price of lodgings everywhere on the Cape, and Chatham is no exception. The dozen small inns and B&Bs within a reasonable stroll of downtown are all very expensive in summer, though before mid-June or after Labor Day the rate spread on some of the larger properties dips under $100. For ex-

ample, **The Moorings Bed & Breakfast,** 326 Main St., tel. (800) 320-0848 or (508) 945-0848, has doubles for $95-128 in spring and fall—rooms which in peak season run $125-158. (They also have rooms with kitchenettes, two-bedroom suites, and a rental cottage.) Arguably, you get your money's worth: besides being within a stroll of shops, restaurants, concerts at the town bandstand, and the beach, the Moorings has free bikes for guests, beach chairs, and a creative full breakfast unlike anything you'd make at home. If triple digits still make you wince, the only lodgings with moderate prices in high season are a mile west of the village center: the **Chatham Guest House,** on Queen Anne Rd. just off Rt. 28, tel. (508) 945-3274. The Chatham Chamber of Commerce can give you the skinny on what else is available—and usually even has an idea about who's got last-minute availability; visit their seasonal info booth next to the town hall on Main St., or call (800) 715-5567 or (508) 945-5199.

Food

If you aren't staying in a B&B and need an eye-opening meal, you could grab some overpriced croissants from one of the gourmet provisioners in the center of town, or you could drive west on Rt. 28 to **Larry's PX,** 1591 Main in West Chatham, tel. (508) 945-3964, and join the local fishermen over an early breakfast. If it's lunchtime or later, consider a visit to that king of the fried clam, **Kream 'N' Kone,** up the road at 1653 Main,

County Road in Truro at the turn of the century

TRURO HISTORICAL SOCIETY

tel. (508) 945-3308. This signature Cape dish may have been born in Essex, on Boston's North Shore, but it tastes as if it's achieved satori in the fryers of this small fast-food joint across from the A&P supermarket. Open March through late October or early November, or as long as the customers keep coming. For a sweet finish, head farther west to **Marion's Pie Shop,** 2022 Main St., South Chatham, tel. (508) 432-9439. Fruit pies, pecan pies, and lemon meringue pies are among the offerings (all for take-out only), from family size down to mini two-person portions. (If you have a kitchen at your disposal, Marion's also serves heat-and-serve quiches, casseroles, and savory meat pies.) To say the lemon meringue is Massachusetts' best is awfully faint praise given the lack of competition, so let's be more specific: the crust is perfectly crisp and flaky; the filling has a nice custardy texture, not too sweet; and the meringue is lofty enough to reach from your chin to your nose. In sum, it's as good a commercial variety as exists outside of the midwestern Pie Belt. Open Tues.-Sat. till 7 p.m. from mid-March to Christmas, plus Sunday 7 a.m.-2 p.m. in summer.

When the tourists leave at the end of summer, quite often the stellar chefs do, too, leaving slim pickings for the off season. Chatham is lucky in having excellent dining year-round at **Christian's,** in an old captain's house at 433 Main St., tel. (508) 945-3362. The fresh ingredients, handsome presentation, friendly atmosphere, and lively upstairs piano bar make this local landmark one of the best values for your dining dollar east of the Cape Cod Canal ($9.50-19.50). If nightly specials like crispy roast duckling with pear-peppercorn sauce or local haddock sautéed with julienne shiitake mushrooms and perfectly steamed vegetables is too rich for your blood, stick to the grilled steaks, broiled fish, amazing meatloaf, or movie-themed pizzas and pastas (including a pair of quite good vegetarian selections). Head upstairs if you want to try snagging a seat in one of the great book-lined booths. Open for lunch and dinner daily year-round except Tues.-Wed. in Jan.-March.

Also open year-round for lunch and dinner is **The Impudent Oyster,** steps off Main St. at 15 Chatham Bars Ave., by the bandstand, tel. (508) 945-3545. This irresistibly named place is sure to have been recommended by your innkeeper or

B&B host, which is partly why dinner reservations are absolutely mandatory throughout high season. The seafood selection is quite good, portions are more than generous, and the soothing classical music, sable-hued wood, and white linen makes for a delightful setting. Whether all this will compensate for the iceberg salads, plain presentation, and bread-pudding-textured pies is up to you; the popular vote, though, is a resounding yes. (Of course, most Chathamites also voted for Ronald Reagan.)

For a place that prefers preparing its fresh fish and fine meats on a wood grill rather than in a sauté pan, and with herb-infused reductions more than rich cream sauces, look for **The Bistro,** tel. (508) 945-5033, on the second floor of a small shopping arcade near the Rt. 28 rotary. If the contemporary decor doesn't assure you that this isn't your father's Cape Cod restaurant, the multiethnic influences and attention to vegetables certainly will. Open for lunch and dinner daily in summer.

ORLEANS AND EASTHAM

Two of the smallest towns on the peninsula, Orleans and Eastham (pronounce both syllables; it's not East'm), share the pivot point in the Outer Cape, where the tributaries of Cape Cod Bay and the Atlantic come within half a mile of each other and all the major up-Cape highways merge into the single strand of US 6. Both towns were once united with their neighbors in a much larger township named after the native Nauset Indians, one of several bands residing around inlets on the Cape's back shore. The Nausets' home turf was much visited by European explorers and would-be colonists in the early 1600s, partly because of a navigational impediment that once stretched eastward from today's shore, forcing vessels to take shelter in the area from unfavorable winds or to make repairs to broken rudders. "Tucker's Terror," as it was branded by English captain Bartholomew Gosnold in 1602, may even have been the reason the Pilgrims were forced to abort their southward journey along the Outer Cape shore en route to the mouth of the Hudson. The Nausets' encounters with these various newcomers neatly synopsizes their experience with Europeans in the New World: amicable relations soured by the newcomers' prejudice and greed; kindnesses and hospitality repaid with suspicions; amends made and strained again; and, ultimately, the winning combination of microbes and weapons reducing an indigenous population to a bunch of poetic place names.

Lacking sufficiently deep harbors to attract the shipbuilding and other maritime industry adopted by many other Cape towns, this area remained invested in agriculture well into the early 1900s. Eastham, in particular, enjoyed a reputation for being the farmer among its seafaring neighbors, with its farms supplying produce, dairy products, and even grain to the region. Today, Orleans provisions and outfits the area with its shopping centers, while Eastham has become the gateway to the National Seashore, whose main visitor center is within the town limits. Between them, the two towns boast dozens of accommodations options and a range of fine beaches offering either bayside serenity or backside intensity.

Nauset Marsh

The salt marsh estuaries protected by the Nauset barrier beach are a world often unseen by Cape visitors: calm, unpaved, with nary a traffic tie-up in sight. The vast majority of this large salt marsh is actually in neighboring Eastham, but seasonal boat access is available from the Town Cove in Orleans, courtesy of guided trips sponsored by the Cape Cod Museum of Natural History (CCMNH), tel. (800) 479-3867 or (508) 896-3867, and the Massachusetts Audubon Society, tel. (508) 349-2615. Aboard the CCMNH pontoon boats, you'll learn about marsh ecology and the importance of wetlands, with strands of local human history woven in. There are trips for both adults and families; on the latter, kids are given a chance to handle marine specimens. Offered daily in July and August, and on weekends and occasionally midweek late May through mid-October, the price is $24 adults, $16 kids age 4-14. Preregistration and advance payment is required.

The National Seashore

Begin your visit to the Cape Cod National Seashore at the **Salt Pond Visitor Center,** beside US 6 about three miles north of the big Or-

leans rotary. Open weekends and holidays Jan.-Feb., then daily March-Dec. (except Christmas), this center and its helpful staff and handy publications will orient you to what's available in the park, from historic lighthouses to abandoned cranberry bogs, beautiful beaches to rigorous bike trails. Forearm yourself with a briefing on the park's natural history from the museum exhibits, pick up a field guide from the small shop, and most definitely inquire about the tempting lineup of ranger-guided activities. Wading around playing amateur naturalist in muddy salt marshes, learning to surfcast, canoeing one of the park's kettle ponds, listening to campfire storytelling, and making after-dark wildlife searches are among the many programs offered daily and weekly in high season. Reservations are occasionally required, and fees may be charged, especially where equipment is provided; call (508) 255-3421 for advance details.

One of the attractions that northbound drivers will pass prior to reaching the visitor center is the 1867 **Captain Edward Penniman House,** on Fort Hill Rd. off US 6. In sharp contrast to the plain Cape houses that were the prevailing standard, this whaling captain's fancy Second Empire-style mansion and its ornamental carpentry illustrates how lucrative a seaman's career could be in the days when the nation's lamps were lit with whale oil. And yes, that front gate is indeed a pair of whale jawbones. Open daily in season. Birdwatchers and anyone curious about what remains of the Nauset tribe that once lived here should walk the short trail around panoramic Fort Hill just beyond the mansion, overlooking Nauset Marsh.

Beaches

Orleans has one beach on its ocean side and one on its bay side, and both are available to visitors for a fee of $6-8 (free to cyclists and walkers). Bayside Skaket Beach is, of course, the warmer and calmer of the two—and the cheaper to visit. Nauset Beach, on the other hand, is considered one of the best on the Cape: mile after mile of sandy shore, with nothing beyond those waves until you hit the Iberian peninsula. In summer, it often appears as if every day-tripper on the Cape has ended up here, but determined walkers can generally find some space way down the beach.

Unlike many Cape towns, Eastham permits outsiders to use all nine of its fresh- and salt-water beaches. These beaches also among the least expensive ($5 a car; free to cyclists and walkers except in the National Seashore, where you'll pay$3). Note that Coast Guard Beach has such limited parking that in season cars must use the satellite lot on Doane Rd. past the visitor center, and take the bus shuttle or walk the remaining half mile.

Camping

The only public campground in the Outer Cape is in Brewster's **Nickerson State Park,** west of Orleans on Rt. 6A. The 418 sites are broken up into many small cul-de-sac clusters throughout the park's dense pine- and oak-covered hills, whose stones and sand are well carpeted with a comfortable mat of pine needles. Though a number of sites are rather too close to their neighbors, most are adequate—you won't feel as if you're sleeping under the flags, signs, and laundry lines some of the more settled-in residents use to stake out their perimeters, and a few choice spots—#32 in Area 7, for one—are quite secluded indeed. Though no hookups exist, a dump station is available, along with full bathrooms, showers, camp store, and bike rentals (next door) for use on the park's many paved trails or the on Cape Cod Rail Trail, which crosses Rt. 6A beneath Nickerson's front entrance. All campsites are open mid-April through mid-October for a fee of $6, and 55 are available to self-contained RVs through the winter. Reservations are accepted; tel. (508) 896-3491.

Accommodations

Accommodations in Orleans are about evenly split—half are on Rt. 28 from downtown south toward Chatham, and half are in East Orleans, near the popular Nauset Beach. Eastham's are concentrated along US 6, with a dozen others scattered close by. For the most affordable digs in the area, check out Hostelling International's **Mid-Cape Hostel,** on Eastham's Goody Hallet Dr. off Bridge Rd. near Rock Harbor, tel. (508) 255-2785. Tucked into the woods on the Orleans-Eastham line, next to the fancy Whale-walk Inn and one-quarter mile from the Cape Cod Rail Trail, the hostel comprises eight small bunk-filled cabins. Six sleep eight people each;

the other two are reserved for groups and families and have the only double beds on the premises. These are cozier than they are rustic, despite the outdoor shower. Reservations are definitely recommended, but outside of July and August weekends, anyone looking for same-day accommodations may get lucky. (Given the distance to the nearest transit, *don't* just walk in without calling ahead.) Open early May through mid-Sept.; $15 pp non-members, $12 pp HI members. As at most HI-affiliated hostels, the registration office is closed during the day, 10 a.m.-5 p.m.

There's a year-round Sheraton **Four Points Hotel,** tel. (800) 325-3535 or (508) 255-5000, on US 6 in Eastham about a mile north of the Salt Pond visitor center, but for something more moderate in price try the comfortable **Ocean View Motel,** also on US 6 diagonally across the highway from the 1680 windmill in Eastham's center, tel. (800) 742-4133 or (508) 255-1600. Open late February through October; rates begin at $78 d late June through Labor Day, $47 d off season. For about the same high-season price, B&B fanciers can land a spacious room with a true ocean view at **Cedar Bank B&B,** tel. (508) 255-2398, a contemporary home above nearby Nauset Marsh. Bicycles for guests, a small motorboat for dinking around the marsh, the National Seashore's Coast Guard Beach only a mile away, and a hearty breakfast add up to good value for only $80 d, year-round (no credit cards).

In addition to B&B homes, a number of highly regarded B&B inns are also found in this area. One that is sure to please is **The Parsonage Inn,** on Main St. in Orleans opposite Fancy's Farm, a mile and a half from Nauset Beach, tel. (508) 255-8217. Friendly, casual comfort is the rule at this 1770 Cape-style house and its rambling additions, amid country antiques and fascinating souvenirs of East Africa. No vicar could make you feel more welcome and at ease than owners Ian and Liz Browne, either. Open all year; rates are $90-120 d June-Oct., $70-95 d in winter, including full breakfast and happy hour refreshments. Also high on the hospitality index is the **Nauset House Inn,** a mile farther east on Beach Rd, tel. (508) 255-2195. Besides a plant-filled conservatory, painted furniture, whimsical trompe l'oeil, and extensive quilts, this place has an insidious fun streak running through it—the kind that gives rise to dangerous thoughts about quitting your job and moving to the Cape to putter around enjoying yourself, entertaining friends, and sharing your life with tourists. If you catch yourself thinking what a delight it would be to run an inn like this, you better pack up and leave right away—don't even *think* of staying around for that big breakfast smorgasbord. Open April-Oct.; rates run $95-115 d with private bath, $65-75 d shared, and $55 for the small single room with shared bath. Full breakfast is $5 extra, continental is $3 extra.

Further B&B accommodations, both local and elsewhere on the Outer Cape, can be booked (for a nominal fee) through **Orleans Bed & Breakfast Associates,** tel. (800) 541-6226 or (508) 255-3824.

Food

Wake up to a tried-and-true white bread breakfast at **Nonnie's Country Kitchen,** opposite the Mobil station on Rt. 6A at Main St. in downtown Orleans, tel. (508) 255-1415, where the only questions needing any reply are, "How d'you want those eggs?" and, "Need a refill on that?" Though hunched with age, Nonnie is as dedicated as ever. The decorative plate collection on the walls will turn flea-market archaeologists pea-green with envy.

When it comes to batter-dipped seafood cooked in hot oil, Orleans has two of the Cape's best purveyors. Try the perfectly fried sweet scallops at **Sir Cricket's Fish & Chips,** for example, a hole in the wall on Rt. 6A south of the rotary and next to the Nauset Lobster Pool, tel. (508) 255-4453. Or savor that delicate sea-salty essence still lingering over the juicy fried clams from **Kadee's Lobster & Clam Bar,** an always-packed, roughhewn shack on East Main, tel. (508) 255-6184. Kadee's is only a summer operation, but Sir Cricket's is open daily year-round.

For a good dinner, try to land a table at the year-round **Nauset Beach Club,** on East Main two doors past Kadee's, tel. (508) 255-8547. Though after 6:30 in season there's almost invariably an hour's wait for a table (no reservations for parties of fewer than six), the reasonably priced food is worth it ($12-18.50). Robust dishes like veal saltimbocca, lobster vermicelli, and risotto are prepared with fresh, high-quality ingredients (no iceberg lettuce here), accompanied by good wines and imported brews, and served in an attractive, intimate dining room free of pretense. Open nightly mid-May through Columbus Day, Tues.-Sat. thereafter.

WELLFLEET

As one of the least commercialized towns on the entire Cape, Wellfleet is a window to what must have been the rule rather than the exception as recently as a single generation ago. Once home port for one of the largest cod fleets in 19th-century New England, and a top oyster producer for over 40 years, the town is now more of an enclave for writers and psychiatrists than fishmongers. Most tourists, anchored by the more extensive accommodations in neighboring Provincetown or Orleans, know only of Wellfleet's ocean beaches—if they know the town at all—but those who do make the short detour from the highway will find a pleasantly becalmed community of small art galleries, a working pier, and almost no T-shirt shops.

Instead of competing with the motel room and retail capacity of its neighbors, Wellfleet prefers to be an oasis for the long-term rental crowd, with restaurants and shops sprinkled among—or in—old houses and town offices on narrow, meandering streets. You won't find much artificial quaintness here either: like fading jeans worn chamois-soft, this place feels lived-in.

While Wellfleet had some early ups and downs in fishing, shipbuilding, and coastal trading, its lasting fame comes from its oysters. The foot-long specimens gathered by Native Americans—so plentiful that Champlain named the harbor after them when he charted Wellfleet waters in 1606—died off before the American Revolution, but imported stock kept "Wellfleet" synonymous with "oyster" well into the Victorian era (quite appropriate for a town whose namesake was an English village known for *its* bivalves). Virtual monopoly over New England's supply of this alleged aphrodisiac was attained in the middle decades of the 1800s, abetted by the newly arrived railroad, fast schooners, and fussy tycoons who could afford to be particular about their Wellfleets on the half shell. The oysters' popularity was such that by 1870 as many as 40 vessels were engaged in ferrying Virginia seed to the Outer Cape for a proper upbringing. Chesapeake's partisans may choose to focus on this Southern pedigree, but chefs and gastronomes claim Wellfleet's water imparts the agreeable and incomparable flavor to its shellfish. A deadly parasite known as the oyster drill devastated the industry in the early 1900s, but renewed interest in aquaculture may restore the Wellfleet *Cassostrea virginica* to its lost throne.

Songs of praise for the oyster aside, the town was no slouch in the fishing industry back in the days when cod and mackerel outnumbered tourists. A few working boats still exist, along with plenty of good clam-digging mudflats (required permits are sold at the Town Pier), but these days Wellfleet is better known for its cluster of art galleries and pottery studios than for what it fetches from the sea. Fortunately, despite shifting demographics, the town retains some of the look and feel of a place in which mending nets is more important than peddling knickknacks to tourists—a true anachronism on the Cape of the 1990s.

Besides more than a dozen galleries—almost all of which lie within the triangle formed by Main, Commercial, and Holbrook—a couple of interesting bookstores, shops stocking items such as used silk kimonos or Afrocentric art (Eccentricity, on Main), and an exceptional fish market (Hatch's, behind Town Hall), this place is also summer home for the small **Wellfleet Harbor Actors Theater.** Favoring topical contemporary drama over retreads of old Broadway chestnuts, WHAT performs in a plain building on Kendrick Ave. between the Town Pier and Mayo Beach, but the box office, tel. (508) 349-6835, is on Main St. next to the newstand.

If you spend much time within earshot of the First Congregational Church, listen carefully whenever its bells chime and perhaps you'll figure out how to use "ship's time." According to *Ripley's Believe It or Not,* this is the only town clock in the world that uses this two-, four-, six-, and eight-bell system for marking the hours.

Beaches

Between the last weekend in June and Labor Day, most of Wellfleet's 10 saltwater beaches are off limits to anyone without a resident permit (available to visitors with proof of local lodging

from the booth at the end of Commercial St. in the Town Pier parking lot; $25 a week or $75 for the season). Exceptions include three of the five long backside beaches—Marconi, White Crest, and Cahoon Hollow ($5-10 parking fees in season, $3 bikes/pedestrians at Marconi)—and the always-free Mayo Beach along Kendrick Ave. near the Town Pier. Windsurfers, by the way, aren't particularly welcome here; Wellfleet restricts sailboarding to certain hours in only one area—Burton Baker Beach, which is restricted to resident sticker holders. Likewise, surfboards are allowed only on the Atlantic's White Crest Beach.

Permit or no, parking is never guaranteed—unlike the ticket you'll get if you flout the No Parking signs. Since parking restrictions don't have to be posted in rural areas, confirm where it's safe to stash your car when buying your beach sticker.

Great Island

Thanks to the continual reshaping of the Outer Cape, this former island has grown an umbilical to the hilly shore west of Wellfleet's village center, and has thus become one of the more exceptional hiking spots in the National Seashore. Since walking the length of the island can easily take a full afternoon, visitors generally enjoy great solitude even on the most frenzied summer holiday weekends. It's a good place to do birdwatching, and an excellent spot to play amateur naturalist, like Thoreau. The farthest part of the trail, out to Jeremy Point, gets submerged at high tide; know when this occurs or be prepared to do some wading. Since summer's prevailing southwesterly winds can be brisk and unabating, extended wading isn't as pleasant as you might think, unless it's a really hot day. The National Seashore visitor centers can help plan an outing, or you can join Park Service rangers for their free guided tours in season; call (508) 255-3421 for schedule.

Marconi Station

In 1903, President Theodore Roosevelt sent greeetings to King Edward VII of England via the magic of Guglielmo Marconi's wireless telegraph—a historic event made possible by an enormous set of radio masts erected two years earlier at this Wellfleet cliff. The antennae are long gone—coastal creep has undermined the site, although a couple of the concrete anchor posts remain at the cliff's edge—but a small pavilion holds a model and interpretive signs recalling the facility and explaining the scientific achievement it represented. Here, too, is the trailhead for the National Seashore's Atlantic White Cedar Swamp Trail, an easy 45-minute ramble through an ecosystem more typical of the wetlands along the southern New England coast than the Cape's well-drained, sandier glacial moraine. Along with the towering native pines, the rot-resistant white cedars were aggressively harvested by European settlers as building material. Imagine the specimens along this trail replaced by mammoth trees five feet wide and you'll appreciate why the early colonials felt their prayers had been answered.

Numerous ships have been wrecked on the shoals off this stretch of shore, but none as famous as the *Whydah*, a pirate ship that sank here in 1717. Black Sam Bellamy and over 100 of his crew washed up, dead, but no treasure was recovered until 1985, when salvager Barry Clifford located the first of the ship's artifacts. As of this writing, the millions of dollars worth of recovered coinage and hardware are still looking for a permanent public home.

Wellfleet Bay

Salt marsh, ponds, and moors, home to numerous species of terrestrial and marine animals, are part of the landscape found within Massachusetts Audubon's **Wellfleet Bay Wildlife Sanctuary**, whose entrance and parking are located off US 6 just north of the Eastham-Wellfleet town line. Turtles, horseshoe crabs, migratory and nesting birds, bats, and owls are among the denizens of the sanctuary's 1,000 acres, which include what was once some of President Grover Cleveland's favorite duck-hunting habitat. Brush up on your wetland ecology at the visitor center, or join one of the guided walks or birding programs scheduled during the busiest months of the year (prepaid reservations required). More active events are also sponsored, such as snorkeling around the bay in search of crabs and snails, twilight canoeing, and various off-site excursions to places like Pleasant Bay estuary south of Orleans, Monomoy Island, and offshore to the fishing grounds of the Atlantic aboard a commercial trawler. All require advance registration; fees run from under $10 to over $70, depending on the program. Open daily until sunset; admission is $3.

Camping

Are you a tenter tired of ending up sandwiched between a pair of patio furniture dealers equipped with enough lanterns and charcoal lighter fluid to outshine a Texas oil refinery? Relief is at hand at **Paine's Campground,** on Old County Rd. east of US 6 in South Wellfleet, tel. (800) 479-3017 or (508) 349-3007. Located in pine woods a couple of minutes' ride north of the Cape Cod Rail Trail terminus, most of Paine's 150 sites are strictly for tenters and pop-up trailers. Better yet, they provide wholly separate areas for families, groups, couples, and singles and young couples. Reservations recommended; rates are around $20 for two people. Open mid-May through late September. Alternatively, head for the scenic and spacious **Horton's Camping Resort,** on S. Highland Rd. in North Truro, tel. (508) 487-1220. Open May through mid-October, Horton's 220 sites include a generous number for tenters, as well as some reserved for campers without children. There's even a fully accessible bathroom fo visitors with disabilities. Rates are $16-20 July through Labor Day (reservations essential; three-night minimum may be required), more for hookups, less at the beginning and end of the season. Located between Highland Light and the FAA's big transatlantic air traffic control radomes east of US 6; turn at the blue "camping" sign about 5.5 miles north of the Truro-Wellfleet line and proceed another mile.

Accommodations

Wellfleet has scores and scores of weekly rental cottages and kitchen-equipped efficiency units, about a dozen B&Bs (most with one or two rooms), and a half-dozen motels, all of which are along US 6. Moderate room rates are fairly abundant in these parts, too, although minimum-stay requirements are as widespread as everywhere else. Before mid-June and after early September, most motels go straight into their inexpensive off-season rates—ideal for the budget traveler. The **Wellfleet Chamber of**

Commerce, tel. (508) 349-2510, will happily provide you with a brochure that lists every one. Call to request a copy or drop by their seasonal information booth beside US 6 in South Wellfleet, beside the northern end of the Rail Trail.

The area's only non-camping budget option is **Hostelling International–Truro,** at the end of North Pamet Rd. (take the Truro Center/Pamet Roads exit from US 6, and stay to the east of the highway). Though hardly convenient to any local transit—the P&B bus stop on the Hyannis-Provincetown route is two miles away, by the Truro post office, and Provincetown's ferries are a windblown 10-mile trek to the north—this 42-bed hostel packs a full house throughout its short, 11-week season, late June through Labor Day, and no wonder: the former oceanside Coast Guard station in the Pamet River valley is a seven-minute walk from beautiful Ballston Beach, where parking is otherwise restricted to residents with beach stickers. (Geographical aside: the beach is a few hundred yards from the headwaters of the Pamet River, which drains west to the Cape Cod Bay; when the ocean succeeds in breaching this gap—as it temporarily has during past winter storms—the northern tip of the Cape becomes an island.) It's also got plenty of common space, a decent kitchen, very cheerful management, and superb second-floor views (for the women, that is; men get to share two basement rooms big enough to ensure at least one snorer in each). No private rooms for couples here, and no family rooms unless space is available. Rates are $15 pp nonmembers, $12 pp HI members, and reservations are essential; call (508) 349-3889 and have your credit card handy.

Among the motels on US 6, South Wellfleet's **Even'tide Motel & Cottages,** tel. (508) 349-3410 or, in state, (800) 368-0007, is one of the three that's open year-round. Located near mile marker 98, it's right on the Rail Trail, which makes it possible to get to local beaches without messing with either highway traffic or resident parking restrictions. In-room mini-fridges and all the usual motel amenities are standard, plus there's a heated, indoor, 60-foot pool. Peak-season rates begin at $72 d, late June through Labor Day, then promptly drop back to below $50 d. Off-season rates for in-the-woods two-bedroom A-frame cottages equipped with kitchens and fireplace stoves are a steal: as low as $69-75 with a two-night minimum. (The summer rental rates on these are $625-690 per week.) For something more like a low-key country inn, with simple furnishings, clawfoot tubs, nappy white bedspreads, and rustic rough pine walls in some quarters, check out the 1813 **Inn at Duck Creeke,** 70 Main St. just off US 6, tel. (508) 349-9333. Overlooking Duck Pond under half a mile from the center of town, this breezily informal place has its own tavern and is next to two fine restaurants. Open mid-May through mid-October; rooms with private baths are $75-90 d in the peak period (late June through Labor Day), $50-70 d in spring and fall. Rooms with shared baths are $10-15 less. All rates include continental breakfast.

If you'd rather stay only a walk from the town's center, **Brehmer Graphics Art Gallery B&B,** on Commercial St., tel. (508) 349-9565, is a fine year-round choice just a stroll from galleries, shops, and dining. Within the white clapboard walls and mansard roof of this 19th-century captain's home is a pair of comfortable rooms with shared bath, lots of heirlooms and artwork (owner Bethia is a printmaker), full homemade breakfasts, and a warm welcome for people and their pets (this is one of the few animal-friendly B&Bs in the region). Rooms are $75-85 July-Aug., $65 June and September, and $55 off-season. If you'd prefer a more rural retreat, consider the friendly **Cahoon Hollow B&B,** tel. (508) 349-6372, a rambling 1842 house two miles from an ocean beach. Its two comfy suites, full breakfasts, and guest bicycles cost but $85-90 d year-round.

Food

While location a step or two off the beaten track has its advantages at the height of summer, off season it almost guarantees everything shuts up tight for the duration. This is certainly true of Wellfleet, where one of the only winter eating options is the local branch of Box Lunch, the Cape chain of rolled-pita sandwich shops. Fortunately, there's also **finely JP's,** on US 6 in South Wellfleet about a mile north of the Wellfleet Drive-In theater, tel. (508) 349-7500. The plain, pine-paneled roadhouse appearance (inside and out) belies the quality of what issues from the kitchen: delicious local oysters or clams on

Inn at Duck Creeke, tel. (508) 349-3003. "Simple food in a funky place" is owner Kate Painter's credo, apparently in reference to the fact that her preparations favor marinades over complicated cream sauces, and presentation strives to be appealing rather than architectural. But Kate cut her teeth at top-drawer joints like Jeremiah Tower's Stars, in San Francisco, and Lydia Shire's Biba, in Boston, and it shows—in the sure hand behind some unusual pairings (juniper berries dressing a thick slab of fresh tuna, or tequila lime chili butter for grilled oysters), and the respect for freshness, in vegetables and meats alike. The results are impressive. Dinner served nightly in summer and Thurs.-Sat. at the margins; breakfast also daily in summer. There's a "studio bar" upstairs, too, usually with live music, where you can kick back with friends.

If you didn't come to the Cape to eat avocado or crostini, head straight for the **Bayside Lobster Hutt,** on Commercial St., tel. (508) 349-6333, in the barn-like building with the big wooden dory on the roof. Take a peek at your dinner in the holding tank, then take a seat at the picnic tables and gorge on the fruits of the sea—steamed, broiled, or fried—for a moderate tariff. Open for dinner daily late May-Oct., and lunch July-August. For a sweet finish to your meal, stop at the back of the parking lot at **Just Desserts.**

the half shell, warmed spinach and scallop salad, spicy calamari or garlicky sautéed shrimp over pasta, hearty vegetarian lasagna, and pork medallions with apples and goat cheese. Even the pizzas are made with a gourmet flair. Nothing very fancy, but darn good—and priced to match the veneer rather than taste or portion size (nothing's over $15). Open year-round for dinner.

If the leaves are back on the trees and you're seeking one of the more imaginative menus on the Cape, try **Painter's,** on Main St. next to the

PROVINCETOWN

Where once the sea sustained Provincetown—as trading center, whaling village, and fishing port— now the summer does. Clinging to the inside shore of the outermost arm of Cape Cod, contemporary "P'town" is a salty mix of tourists, artists, fishermen, and gays, a place whose population mushrooms by a factor of 12 between the off-season calm and the high-season carnival. Here is where the *Mayflower* Pilgrims first came ashore, plundered caches of Indian corn, and then left for the mainland in search of an adequate source of fresh water. Subsequent centuries saw a hardscrabble fishing village take hold amid the dunes—a place whose bargain cost of living and beautiful light proved a big draw to painters and playwrights in the decades before WW II. In 1901, Charles

Hawthorne, fascinated by the Mediterranean feel of the dilapidated harbor village and all its Portuguese fishermen, opened an art school here. Greenwich Village Bohemians followed, a fashionable flock that included the likes of John Reed and Eugene O'Neill, whose Provincetown Players made theater history. John Dos Passos, e. e. cummings, Edward Hopper, Sinclair Lewis, Jackson Pollock, Mark Rothko, Norman Mailer, and Edward Gorey (still living in Yarmouth Port) are some of the other luminaries who have lived here at one time or another. Now that the cottage-filled town has become a major seaside resort, its narrow streets overflowing each summer with T-shirt-shopping, taffy-eating, Teva-wearing sun-seekers, bargains are scarcer than parking spaces. At least the sunsets are free—and still one of the best shows in town.

SIGHTS

Views Past and Present

Only one place in town combines both a figurative overview of local history and a literal overview of local geography: the **Pilgrim Monument and Provincetown Museum**, on High Pole Hill, tel. (800) 247-1620 or (508) 487-1310. The hill is off Bradford St. behind Town Hall; the monument is the thing on top visible from 40 miles away. Besides displays reminding modern visitors that Provincetown, not Plymouth Rock, was where the Pilgrims spent their first five weeks in the New World, modest exhibits range from a model of the original Provincetown Playhouse, which launched Eugene O'Neill's career, to artifacts gathered during the 15 Arctic expeditions of native son Donald MacMillan. Sticklers should be forewarned that the museum's depictions of Native Americans and assertions about Norse explorers are a bit dubious, and in general the early-history exhibit suffers from sloppy editing (discrepencies in the number of *Mayflower* passengers, misnamed vessels, that sort of thing). Take it as a gentle reminder that so-called history is almost invariably less a collection of facts than a point of view.

A view that's undisputable is the one from atop the 255-foot granite tower rising over the museum, which in clear weather unequivocally makes up for the lack of an elevator. Museum and tower are open daily April-Nov.; admission $5.

Show and Sell

P'town is chock full of art—even without counting artist-run boutiques selling unique clothing, jewelry, cards, and other artifacts (see the Susan Baker Memorial Museum Franchise at 379 Commercial St. for an eminently affordable sample). Galleries range from experimental spaces to established storefronts featuring established local artists, and well-attended openings year-round demonstrate the vitality of the local visual arts. To check out both the deep roots of this community and its emerging new shoots, visit the **Provincetown Art Association & Museum**, 460 Commercial St. in the East End, tel. (508) 487-1750. Founded in 1914, PAAM has a large permanent collection representing both famous American artists who've worked in P'-town over the decades, as well as others who've lingered less forcefully in the annals of art history. Changing exhibitions drawing from this repository are staged throughout the year, mixed with exhibits of new work by living local artists. Open daily till 9 p.m. late May through early October, and at least weekends through the off-season; admission $2.

The Province Lands

The northernmost of the three National Seashore visitor centers overlooks the Province Lands, whose name is a reminder of the Province of Massachusetts' explicit title to the area both before and after the town's 1727 incorporation. Now lightly wooded or covered in beach grass, the Province Lands' wind-driven dunes once upon a time threatened to bury the settlement at their watery margin. When the Pilgrims landed in 1620 they found "excellent black earth" when they probed with their shovels, "all wooded with oaks, pines, sassafras, juniper, birch, holly, vines, some ash, [and] walnut." In defiance of laws enacted as early as 1714 to save it, this tree cover was so thoroughly clearcut by colonists that the topsoil blew away, freeing the sand to migrate toward the harbor. Two centuries after the Pilgrim landfall, Thoreau claimed there wasn't enough black earth to fill a flower pot, "and scarcely anything high enough to be called a tree." Efforts to stabilize the dunes were begun a generation prior to Thoreau's visits and continue to this day. Besides visitor center exhibits on the landscape's fragility, a variety of ranger-guided activities are scheduled throughout the summer, from beach walks and mountain-bike rides to talks at the Old Harbor Life Saving Station on the back shore; call (508) 487-1256 for schedule. Staff dispense advice and interpretive brochures, too, for trails in the vicinity. Located on Race Point Rd., the visitor center is open daily April 15 through Thanksgiving. Weekdays the rest of the year, National Seashore info is available from the Race Point ranger station, at the end of the road.

Most visitors to the Province Lands, like Cape visitors generally, come for the beaches. Mile after mile of coarse sand pounded by the long breakers of the open Atlantic Ocean make **Race Point Beach** a great spot for walking, body surfing, and just lazing under a summer sun. Walk far enough west and you'll reach **Race Point Light,** a short cast-iron tower whose steady white flash—now visible from some 11 miles at sea—has warned vessels away from the northern end of the infamous Peaked Hill Bars since 1876. Though its predecessor was undermined by storms, this is the only backside lighthouse not threatened by erosion—P'town's beaches are actually the beneficiaries of sand swept up the coast from the south.

Right at the end of of US 6 close to town is **Herring Cove Beach,** whose westerly orientation makes it the best place to watch the sun setting fire to the waters of Cape Cod Bay. When the sun's up, it's also a nice spot for swimming in gentle surf. Lifeguards are present and bath houses are open at both beaches July through early September, at which time the National Seashore charges $5 for parking, $3 for bicycles and pedestrians. The rest of the year, the beaches are free.

Whalewatching

The southern edge of Stellwagen Bank, a prime feeding area for finback, right, minke, and humpback whales, happens to be just offshore of Provincetown's breakwater—making it a prime destination for whalewatchers from mid-April through the end of October. Several outfits offer the three- to four-hour excursions, all for about the same price of just under $20 adults and about $15 kids. At the start and finish of the season, you'll find just one or two trips a day, but by summer some operators run as many as nine daily departures from MacMillan Wharf. The **Dolphin Fleet of Provincetown Whale Watch,** tel. (800) 826-9300 or (508) 349-1900, originated East Coast whalewatching, in 1975, and stands out among local excursion operators for its use of naturalists from the local Center for Coastal Studies—one of New England's handful of cetacean research organizations. Or choose from among the **Portuguese Princess Whale Watch,** tel. (800) 442-3188 or (508) 487-2651; **Provincetown Whale Watch,** tel. (800) 992-9333 or (508) 487-3322; or **Cape Cod Cruises,** tel. (508) 747-2400 (the only one that departs from Fisherman's Wharf rather than MacMillan).

PRACTICALITIES

Provincetown is the only place on the Cape whose accommodations run the gamut from campgrounds and hostels to resort motels, hotels, timeshare condos, guest houses, fancy B&Bs, and romantic, spare-no-expense little inns. The only place that can book you a space in just about any of them is the **Provincetown Reservations System,** tel. (800) 648-0364 or (508) 487-2400, which is also a full-service travel agent and theatrical box office. (They can even make your restaurant reservations, if you like.) They're open year-round—9 a.m.-9 p.m. daily in high season—and are friendly, helpful, very well informed, and free.

Camping

Two private campgrounds are on the edge of town: **Dunes' Edge Campground,** tel. (508) 487-9815, and **Coastal Acres Camping Court,** tel. (508) 487-1700. Reservations at both are highly recommended July-August. Dunes' Edge is beside mile marker 116 on US 6, at the perimeter of the National Seashore and a short distance from Nelson's Bike Shop, Deli & Market, on Race Point Rd., a seasonal rental outfit just yards from the Province Lands bike trails. Among the 100 mostly wooded sites is a secluded tenting area, and electrical and water hookups for RVs. Open May-Sept.; base summer rate is $20 for two people (slightly less beyond peak summer months). Coastal Acres is beside Shank Painter Pond, near the very end of both US 6 and Rt. 6A; turn at their sign on Bradford St. Ext. (Rt. 6A) in the West End, next to Gale Force Bike Rentals. Catering more to RVers than tents—almost two-thirds of the 120 sites have power and water hookups—this campground also has one of the longer seasons around, staying open from April 1 to November 1. Rates for two people are $20-27, exclusive of hookups.

Accommodations

A **Holiday Inn** on Rt. 6A, tel. (800) 422-4224 or (508) 487-7458, and a couple of franchises of the **Best Western** brand, tel. (800) 528-1234, bookend the town. All are open only seasonally, May-October. Except for families, who will find most

*beach cottages from
the 1930s, North Truro*

B&Bs unable to accommodate kids in the same room as their parents, or travelers with disabilities, who require the accessibility of the Holiday Inn, the luxury rates at these national chains are hardly a good value—especially since you'll have to shuttle back and forth to shopping, dining, and entertainment in the center of town. More affordable and attractive rooms are found among P'town's many small B&B inns and guest houses, which, while predominantly expensive June through Labor Day, are often moderate in spring and fall, when the weather still makes being outside—if not in the water—tolerable, and restaurant lines have all but vanished. A high proportion of places stay open year-round, too, if you need a winter getaway at a good price—and a few even offer in-room fireplaces.

The only budget choice for summer visitors is the bare-bones **Outermost Hostel,** on Winslow St. just past the entrance to the Pilgrim Monument's parking lot, tel. (508) 487-4378. Comprising four virtually historic cabins—epitomizing the height of tourist convenience back before Holiday Inn revolutionized the business—each with six or seven beds and a full bath, the Outermost is undeniably short on frills, but for $14 pp with free parking, it's also an unbeatable value. Anyone who's ever enjoyed the hospitality of the Huck Finn hostel in St. Louis may be surprised to find owner Tom Cochran is the man behind this joint, too, but you may be sure he's as reliable a guide to P'town as to the Gateway City of the West.

In the East End, about 10-15 minutes' stroll from the ferry, is **Three Peaks,** 210 Bradford St. beside the Berta Walker Gallery, tel. (800) 286-1715 or (508) 487-1717, a well-appointed example of year-round B&Bs. This handsome 1870s Victorian has been divvied up into a handful of rooms and a pair of kitchen-equipped efficiencies, all with private baths, small color cable TVs, and either small or full-size refrigerators. Rates are $85-95 d mid-May through mid-September ($20 more for the apartments), including continental breakfast. Winter rates are as low as $55-65 d. Late October through mid-June, the third night is free (except on holidays). A block west at the next corner, **The Inn at Cook Street,** tel. (888) COOK-655 or (508) 487-3894, a carefully restored 1836 home, combines lots of decks, an inviting pocket-sized garden with fishpond, and a variety of rooms and suites, as well as a cottage with kitchenette and loft bed. Attractively furnished, with mattresses and towels of perceptibly better quality than is customary, this inn also features a more substantial breakfast than is typical around town. June through mid-September, rates are $90 d, $100-125 cottage and suites, dropping to an eminently reasonable $65-75 in fall and $50-65 for winter-spring.

Food

If popularity is any measure, P'town's best breakfast is at **Cafe Edwige,** upstairs of 333 Commercial St. across from the public library, tel.

(508) 487-2008. Given the food-savvy palates in this town, acclaim like this is no small thing. Among the touches that explain the approving chorus are a choice of tabouli or home fries with the big fluffy omelets, pots of honey for tea drinkers, broiled flounder among the usual pancake and egg options, and fresh flowers on each table. Though its's only seasonal, if you miss a table for breakfast you can try again at dinner Thurs.-Sun. (Try for a window table—it's one of the best people-watching seats in town.)

For a snack, sip, slice, or salad, it's hard not to like **Spiritus Cafe & Pizzeria,** Commercial St., tel. (508) 487-2808, which is even more funky than its Hyannis progenitor. The chrome proboscis of a cherry-red Chrysler pokes out of the ceiling, the tables are adorned with painterly decorations, and the wide front steps are perfect for fraternizing. Around closing time in the busy season—when the bars are emptying out and the last pizza slices are being scarfed up by dance-happy club-goers, the pheromones are nearly as thick as the ice cream. Open April 1 through early November (Men's Weekend), daily till 2 a.m. in summer. Another satisfying choice is **The Purple Cactus,** in the Old Aquarium Building in the 200 block of Commercial St., tel. (508) 487-4432, open 11-11 daily in season. It's a burrito bar with good pedigree—the chef worked in Santa Fe and San Francisco before coming to this bastion of fried seafood. In the same arcade, **Flying Cups & Saucers,** tel. (508) 487-3780, constitutes one of the far-flung outposts of Seattle's Best Coffee, along with trays of tempting baked things and a view from the deck out behind the building, overlooking the bay. Open daily in season till 11 p.m. weekdays, midnight weekends. If coffeehouse atmosphere isn't as important as a sample of local tradition, check out the **Portuguese Bakery,** 299 Commercial, tel. (508) 487-1803. Despite the impression given by restaurants around town, Portuguese cuisine isn't all tomato, onion, and cumin-flavored fish stews, simmered slowly all day. A good dessert tradition exists within the cuisine, too, as this storefront bakery amply and ably demonstrates. Try the *trutas* (sweet potato fritters), or the almond meringues for a real Portuguese treat. Open daily March-October.

Speaking of fish stews, don't leave town without trying one. **The Lobster Pot,** 321 Commercial St. just east of Macmillan Wharf, tel. (508) 487-0842, is a fine place to start, especially since it offers two immediate advantages: its waterfront view and the fact that upon entering you must pass the kitchen, inhaling a foretaste of the palate-tickling fare that awaits. Platters of seafood in bread-sopping sauces more than measure up to that evanescent preview, as do the clambakes, lobsters, and vegetarian pastas ($14-19). It's open for lunch and dinner daily except for a few shuttered weeks in winter, so you have little excuse for missing out.

If you want to take advantage of P'town's healthy variety of creative and ethnically influenced cuisine, you would do well to consider **Lorraine's,** 229R Commercial St., down the alley near the Pennsylvania Co. store, tel. (508) 487-6074, whose New American menu is spiced up with a hint of old Mexico. Or go completely south of the border at the **Iguana Grill,** as centrally located as you can get in this town, at the corner of Bradford St. and Standish, tel. (508) 487-8800, whose lunch and dinner menus sport a blend of Dominican and Mexican preparations. Across the street is the local king of cross-cultural blending, **Napi's,** tucked away at 7 Freeman St., sort of behind the Tedeschi convenience store on Bradford, tel. (508) 487-1145. One of the few all-year stalwarts, its diverse globe-trotting menu includes spicy Oriental noodles, Greek caponata, Thai chicken, Brazilian steak, and, of course, plenty of seafood . Though not cheap ($12 for a veggie burrito dinner, for example, and generally $13-23 for entrees), it's also one of the few spots to please serious vegetarians. (Pass on the forgettable, overpriced desserts.) Decor reflects the owners' passion for objects with a past—from art to building timber. Serves dinner daily, lunch Sept.-April.

Finally, if you have a need to really wow a date, only the **Martin House,** 157 Commercial St., tel. (508) 487-1327, will do. This 18th-century structure is probably the most romantic setting in town, with fireside dining available in every one of its cozy parlors. The chef is no slouch, either, although you'll of course pay for the privilege of eating such dishes as rabbit loin stuffed with olives, pignoli, basil, and watercress, or steamed clams in a tamarind broth (entrees $14-26). Great desserts, too.

TRANSPORTATION

Ferry Facts

Crossing Cape Cod Bay off season requires a friend in the fishing fleet, but come summer you have your pick of several passenger ferries up and down the Massachusetts coast. The largest and slowest among them is Boston's **Bay State Cruise Company,** tel. (617) 457-1428 or (508) 487-9284, with daily 9 a.m. departures mid-June through early September, plus weekends (Fri.-Sun.) at the head and tail of the season, late May and early October. Tickets are $16 one-way or $29 for same-day roundtrips. Board the boats at the Commonwealth Pier in South Boston, beside the World Trade Center; take Bay State's 8:30 a.m. shuttle boat ($1) from Long Wharf, by the New England Aquarium, or practice your race walking down the length of busy Northern Ave.—about a mile. Bikes are an extra $5 each way. If only the ship were equipped with hammocks or reclining beach chairs instead of hard plastic seats, it wouldn't matter so much that between leaving Long Wharf and returning again, you'll spend seven hours in transit and a little over three ashore in Provincetown. But if this ratio is less than satisfactory, consider making your P'town excursion part of an overnight visit to one of Boston's neighboring ports to the north or south, where you'll find much faster boats, comparable ticket prices, and free dockside parking.

North of Boston, **Cape Ann Whale Watch,** tel. (800) 877-5110, runs a boat Friday, Sunday, and Monday late June through early September from Gloucester to P'town for $22 one-way, $35 same-day roundtrip. The two-and-a-half-hour excursion leaves downtown Rose's Wharf off Rogers St. at 9 a.m. and returns by 6 p.m. (later if whales are spotted en route). From the South Shore, Cape Ann runs the very same boat midweek from Quincy's Marina Bay, for a slightly lower price. Both routes almost invariably sell out, so advanced reservations are advised; cyclists in particular should book ahead, as there is only space aboard for 10 bikes ($3 extra roundtrip).

Historic Plymouth is the departure point for **Cape Cod Cruises,** a.k.a. Cap't John Boats, tel. (800) 242-2469 or (508) 747-2400. With a 90-minute crossing and five full hours in

Provincetown, this is the only choice that offers day-trippers more time on land than on water. Service begins on weekends in late May, runs daily mid-June through Labor Day, and wraps up with Tues.-Wed. and weekend departures the rest of September. Catch the boat from the State Pier opposite the *Mayflower II*—and be back on Plymouth Rock by 6 p.m. Fares are $14 one-way, $22 for same-day roundtrip, and $2 roundtrip for bicycles.

Whichever boat you choose, call to confirm departures if the weather is unsettled—occasionally trips are canceled due to rough seas.

Get on the Bus

Year-round bus service from Boston and the South Shore is provided by **Plymouth & Brockton Street Railway Co.,** tel. (508) 771-6191, with connections in Hyannis to **Bonanza Bus Lines,** tel. (800) 556-3815, serving southeastern Massachusetts, Providence, Rhode Island, and points west to New York. Of P&B's dozen daily Cape-bound departures from Logan Airport and Boston's South Station, two to four run all the way to the Lower Cape—at least a four-hour trip from downtown to P'town. Bonanza's Providence-Hyannis route is fed by frequent daily nonstops from Manhattan's Port Authority Bus Terminal, as well as coaches from Albany, upstate New York, and Canada, the Berkshires and southern Vermont, Springfield, and Hartford. With optimum scheduling, a trip from New York to P'town takes about eight hours and costs just under $50. An intrepid rider from Toronto could make it in about 20 hours.

By Plane

Short of sprouting wings or taking your Gulfstream V out of the hangar, the only scheduled air service to P'town is **Cape Air,** tel. (800) 352-0714, which flies year-round from Logan International. Their fleet of nine-passenger Cessnas makes the 18-minute flight three to seven times daily, depending on season. Besides joint ticketing and baggage arrangements with all major US and European carriers serving Logan, Cape Air often has attractive joint fares, too—check with your carrier before flying into New England. P'town's seasonal shuttle bus doesn't run to the airport, but there's always a taxi to meet your flight (flat $5 to anywhere in town).

Getting Around

Since P'town is a couple of miles long and barely that many blocks wide, one of the best alternatives to driving is using your feet. In warmer weather, bike shops also open for rentals. The best selection is found at **Arnold's,** 329 Commercial, tel. (508) 487-0844, where your average 18- to 21-speed hybrid all-terrain bike rents on a sliding scale for from $3 an hour to $65 for a whole week, or $15 for a workday (8:30 a.m.-5:30 p.m., May 15 through late October). **P'town Bikes,** 306 Commercial, behind Skin Leather, tel. (508) 487-6718, has comparable rates, comparable bikes, but longer business hours (8 a.m.-8 p.m. April-Oct.), plus a second location at 42 Bradford St., tel. (508) 487-TREK, which stays open on a limited basis into the off-season. If for some reason you can't find satisfaction at any of those shops, try **Gale Force Bike Rentals,** on Bradford St. Ext. in the far West End, tel. (508) 487-4849, whose selection of three-, 10-, and 18-speed bikes are available at least 9-5 daily May-Oct. for roughly the same rates everyone else charges. Or, if you're driving into P'town for a day-trip, take advantage of the free customer parking at **Nelson's Bike Shop,** 43 Race Point Rd. out toward the National Seashore visitor center, tel. (508) 487-8849. The challenging Province Lands bike trails start only 100 yards from their door, and they have all the provisions you need before or after your ride. All shops provide locks (free) and helmets ($1 a day).

If you want someone else to do the driving, look for the **Summer Shuttle,** ($1.25) a big yellow school bus pressed into service on an hourly schedule 8 a.m.-midnight between the end of June and Labor Day. Flag it at any Bradford Street intersection for a ride between the east and west ends of town and, from 10 a.m.-6 p.m., to Herring Cove, the nearer of the two National Seashore beaches. Or call a cab: **Atlantic Sam's Taxi,** tel. (508) 487-7777; **Cape Cab,** tel. (508) 487-2222; **Martin's Taxi,** tel. (508) 487-0243; **Mercede's Cab,** tel. (508) 487-9434; or **Schatzi's Taxi,** tel. (508) 487-1827. All are open year-round, but some of them do take breaks between bar closing and daybreak.

Parking Woes

On-street spaces are at a premium in this small town, so drivers should anticipate paying big-city rates to park in one of the flat-rate or per-hour lots within walking distance of all the good stuff. You can slowly circle the Town Hall waiting for someone to give up a precious metered space—if you're patient, winter will roll around, everyone will go home, and you'll get lucky. If you do, note that the quarters-only meters run 8 a.m.-midnight *daily.* However, you *can* feed them for a full 10 hours ($5) at one pop. If you cave in and are willing to pay for a space in an attended lot, expect anywhere from a flat rate of $4-6 dollars for all-day farthest from downtown to $1.50 per hour at the most central lot, on MacMillan Wharf. Alternatively, stash your car for free on the outskirts of town—follow the signs—and hop on the **Park & Ride–North Truro Shuttle** into downtown.

INFORMATION AND MEDIA

Get the latest word about goings-on around town at the Chamber of Commerce information booth in Lopes Square, and have a look at their racks of colorful brochures and flyers for information on possible diversions and amusements. (To request a sampling of this material in advance, call 508-487-3424.) Or peruse a copy of *Provincetown Magazine,* a free weekly published March-Dec. and distributed beside many local cash registers. The magazine's restaurant ads, gallery listings, and community calendar page will give you a rather complete snapshot of the town's commercial, retail, and entertainment possibilities.

NANTUCKET HISTORICAL ASSOCIATION

THE ISLANDS: MARTHA'S VINEYARD AND NANTUCKET

Most southern New Englanders lump Martha's Vineyard and Nantucket together familiarly as "the Islands," and, historically, the islands have felt the impact of many of the same forces, from glaciers to tourism. Yet two personalities could hardly be more distinct.

Martha's Vineyard (or just "the Vineyard")—larger, more populous, more multiracial, and more accessible—may be best known for big-name celebrities and yacht owners, but it also has a thriving young slacker scene in summer and, while not inexpensive, doesn't completely thumb its nose at budget travelers.

Nantucket—a pretty little pearl of rose-draped cottages hugging narrow lanes and low, shrubby moors ringed by wide, sandy beaches—eschews both populism and diversity, and although it welcomes day-trippers of all stripes from the mainland, its long-term appeal is almost exclusively for those who *never* have to ask, "How much?"

Common to both islands is the summer crush of tourists and renters. There are subtle variations in the onset of full-bore high season, but

generally it runs from Memorial Day to Labor Day. Island populations swell tenfold; roads, stores, beaches, and restaurants are at their most congested; and anything fit for a night's sleep commands a princely ransom. Vacationers with more leeway in their schedules may prefer the shoulder seasons—particularly mid-week after Labor Day, when water and weather remain warm but the crowds largely disappear.

THE LAND

Like Cape Cod, Nantucket and the Vineyard are principally artifacts of the last ice age, formed by the advance and retreat of the Laurentide glacier during the closing stage of the Pleistocene epoch, 14,000 to 21,000 years ago. Three discreet lobes from this continental ice sheet covered Cape Cod and what's now the surrounding continental shelf; Nantucket, Martha's Vineyard, and the Elizabeth Islands around Buzzards Bay are evidence of these lobes' farthest advance. Like a carpet wrinkled by sliding heavy furniture across it, sedimentary layers up to 100 million years old in the glacier's path were folded into ridges, or moraines, that are now the backbone of these islands. When the two-mile-thick glacier finally began to melt faster than the icebox up north could replenish it, the runoff spread outwash plains of glacial drift—all the rocks, sand, and soil scraped up and ferried southward in the great ice sheet—like skirts around the hips of these terminal moraines.

Bicycles are probably the best way to experience these glacial features: you can actually *feel* them (in your leg muscles). On Martha's Vineyard, for example, most of the paved bike paths inscribe the great level outwash plain filling the island interior, but ride out of the port of Vineyard Haven and you can't miss the slope of the plain's eastern edge, collapsed after the retreat of the glacial ice like a shelf of books that have lost their bookend.

Outwash deposits give Nantucket, too, a low, flat profile—but there's actually a big difference between the island's oldest plain, spread evenly in front of where the glacier's leading edge used to be (a clear shot on a bike from Nantucket Town east to Siasconset), and the dips and curves of the younger plain on the western end of the island, along the bike path to Madaket. This more varied terrain was formed

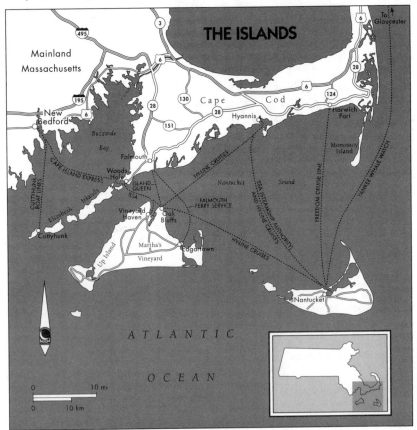

THE ISLANDS

© MOON PUBLICATIONS, INC.

as the receding Laurentide glacier shed enormous chunks of ice and then buried them in glacial drift too heavy to be borne out to the coastline (then some 70-80 miles south) by meltwater streams. As these big ice cubes melted, the surface of this newly formed plain was left with kettles—holes and pockets of subsidence, sometimes many acres in size—which, when deep enough to reach the water table, form distinctive, nearly circular ponds, such as Nantucket's Gibbs Pond and Head of Hummock, or the Vineyard's Old House, Uncle Seth's, and James Ponds.

As the ice age ended, rising oceans swollen from melting ice inundated the conifer- and tundra-covered continental shelf around the islands, submerging habitat once roamed, according to dental records dredged up offshore, by mastodons and mammoths. By about 6,000 years ago, the ocean had filled Nantucket Sound and begun biting away at the islands' moraines, creating prominent marine scarps at Nantucket's Sankaty Head and the Vineyard's Gay Head Cliffs. The geologic record revealed at these sites is hardly as accessible as in the walls of the Grand Canyon, though: at Sankaty Head, the Laurentide glacial deposits are tossed with sands a good 100,000 years older, while Gay Head interleaves folds of Tertiary and Cretaceous strata five million to 75 million years old.

Although the rate at which the oceans are rising has slowed considerably over the last few thousand years, the water is still creeping upward (and may in fact accelerate if predictions about human-induced global warming prove accurate). The shorelines of Nantucket and Martha's Vineyard already lose an annual average of about 30 feet to the tides and winter storms; by some estimates, tiny Nantucket will be a mere shoal under the waves within the next 700-800 years. (Land loss isn't even or gradual, by the way: some shores may be stable for years, then lose a hundred yards in a single storm season.) In the meantime, the islands are migrating slowly toward Cape Cod, as northbound currents relocate a portion of the material eroded from beaches and shore cliffs. This "longshore drift" is most visible in the lengthening of the finger-like sandbars at Nantucket's Great Point and the Vineyard's Cape Poge.

FLORA AND FAUNA

Great grassy meadows once flourished along southern New England's sandy margins, but coastal development has all but eradicated this globally rare ecological community. Most of the planet's remaining acreage of this sandplain grassland is found on the islands—an estimated 90% on Nantucket alone. Unlike that island's distinctive heaths (a shrub-dominated community that's also disappearing across the region), sandplain grasslands visually and botanically resemble midwestern prairies more than their geological twins, the sandplain pine barrens between Rhode Island and Cape Cod. Asters, wild indigo, goat's rue, and bluestem grass are typical of these oft-overlooked meadows; so is Nantucket shadbush, a feathery-white May bloomer common to both islands but a rarity anywhere else.

Sandplain grasslands are rich in other rare or endangered wildflowers such as bird's foot violet, sandplain flax, New England blazing star, and bushy rockrose—and insects such as the tiger beetle, American burying beetle, and moths so uncommon that they are known only by their Latin names. The terrain is also vital habitat for northern harriers (marsh hawks), short-eared owls, and grasshopper sparrows—ground-nesters made rare on the mainland by territory lost to housing subdivisions and eggs lost to raccoons, skunks, and other mammals. (Consider yourself particularly lucky to catch site of the owls: only a couple dozen breeding pairs remain in all New England.)

Human activity hasn't been exclusively detrimental to the grasslands, by the way. At Katama Airfield—a historic 1929 grass-strip "airpark" on Martha's Vineyard visited by Charles Lindbergh—the sandplain grasses have been unwittingly perpetuated by the mowing and burning used to keep runways clear of invasive shrubs and seedlings; now conservationists on both islands practice controlled burns to try to aid the survival of this diminishing landscape.

As on Cape Cod, plants more common to Chesapeake Bay flourish here on the islands, too—at the northern limit of their range—thanks to the temperate, ocean-warmed climate. Examples include Maryland meadow beauty, Eastern silvery aster, St. Andrew's Cross, and post oaks (more common on the Vineyard than Nantucket), which in these latitudes grow only knee-high to their stout Dixie cousins. Even more unusual are Arctic species, such as broom crowberry and caribou moss that advanced ahead of the ice age glaciers and then adapted sufficiently to survive after the big thaw. The moss will be familiar to architectural students and model railroaders: when dried, its tiny tree-like branchings often serve as lilliputian shrubbery.

Although separation from the mainland for 5,000 years has given rise to some endemism—there's a species of vole on Nantucket's Muskeget Island, for example, that is found nowhere else—there are more noticeable differences in what's missing on the islands. Mammals such as the red fox and the wily coyote, who's even trotted across the Cape Cod Canal bridges and swum to the Elizabeth archipelago, haven't yet figured out the ferry schedules to Nantucket or the Vineyard. Nantucket doesn't even have raccoons or skunks. There are no poisonous snakes here, either—the shy little red-bellied *Storeria occipitomaculata* you may chance to see are dangerous only to slugs and worms.

The ancient oak, cedar, and beech trees whose huge proportions amazed the earliest English explorers to these isles were long ago felled by settlers' axes. Their successors have largely been fast-colonizing species able to thrive in depleted soils and desiccating salt air (which "burns" most deciduous trees' fragile leaves where unprotected by topography or other trees). The most abundant survivors are the salt- and fire-resistant pitch pine (native to the Vineyard, introduced on Nantucket), well adapted to the task of securing sandy ground laid bare by overgrazing and firewood gathering, and the even more salt-tolerant scrub oak, which seeds rapidly and germinates in even the poorest soil. With its superior growing conditions, the Vineyard has re-acquired some of the diversity described by those 17th-century English—and both islands have acquired a whole host of introduced species: ornamentals such as cockspur thorn, Russian olive, and purple loosestrife; seafaring souvenirs or old-country natives including Japanese black pine, Scots pine, and English oak; and others, such as the red pine, planted for their economic value in reclaiming damaged land and providing a source of new timber.

The islands routinely rank among the nation's top birdwatching destinations thanks to very active local birders; a closely packed array of diverse habitats, from shore and marsh to woodlands and meadows; and to its situation on a migratory flyway used by over 300 species of song and shorebirds. Plenty of terns, cormorants, gulls, herons, osprey, and other seafood eaters are resident in both summer and winter, as are cardinals, woodpeckers, mourning doves, and some finches. Spring and fall see the largest number of migrants pass through, from Canadian geese and gannets to song sparrows and warblers. Some—particularly shorebirds like the plover and sandpiper—come all the way from Mexico specifically to spend the season munching fly larvae on the islands' beaches. Winter brings large flocks of sea ducks down from Canada: scoters, scaup, mergansers, goldeneye, bufflehead, and thousands of mollusk-loving eiders (North America's largest duck). Some years, when their winter food supply in northern New England gets skimpy, even snowy owls from the Arctic put in an appearance on local shores.

The increase in offroad-vehicle use in the last 20 years has made piping plovers and least terns the most endangered beach-nesters, although protection programs on the islands (and the Cape) have caused their numbers to rebound. Curiously, the very success of the beach-driving restrictions has brought pressure to relax them; adopting the kind of weird logic that would suggest seat belts and airbags are no longer necessary now that they've saved so many lives, the state has tried to open up beaches to plover-squashing Jeeps and dune buggies again.

White-tailed deer are the largest animals on the islands. You may catch them at dusk browsing in fields, munching tulip buds in the back yard of your B&B, or risking a dash through your high beams on some back road far from town. Harbor seals also frequent some coastal areas, and signs of elusive river otter and muskrat can be found at certain ponds on the Vineyard.

In most guidebooks, the islands occur almost as an afterthought to the more heavily visited Cape Cod. This makes them decent all-in-one values for hikers or cyclists, but a major disappointment for anyone interested in plant and animal identification. Island-specific field guides for trailside flora and fauna are so rarely stocked by Massachusetts bookstores—even on the Cape—that your best bet is to simply do your book-buying after you arrive on the islands. The independent retail bookstores in Nantucket, Edgartown, and Vineyard Haven are particularly worth visiting, although for the widest range of natural history titles you would do well to check out Nantucket's Maria (ma-RYE-a) Mitchell Association gift shop;for the Vineyard, stop by the store at the Massachusetts Audubon Society's Felix Neck Wildlife Sanctuary. If you're the consummate prepare-ahead traveler, check the Booklist for mail-order info on some harder-to-find island-related titles.

CLIMATE

Weather on the islands, like that on the Cape, is governed by the ocean. Slow to heat up, and equally slow to cool down, the surrounding salt water acts as a vast heat sump that keeps island temperatures from hitting the extremes recorded around the rest of the state—much the same way that the air in your home dilutes the effect of holding open the door of either your freezer or oven. This briny reservoir is itself warmed by the 50-mile-wide Gulf Stream current, which comes pouring up the eastern seaboard from the Caribbean and brushes within a few dozen miles of the islands' southern shores en route to northern Europe. Despite the islands' being surrounded by water, humidity is kept at bay by the sea breezes that both residents and innkeepers rely upon to make even August heat waves quite tolerable—which is why many island lodgings offer no air conditioning.

Spring, a quiet season of daffodils and days that call for a sweater, comes earlier and lasts longer here than on the mainland, with average temperatures in the upper 40s and low 50s. Summers are ideal, with the average high for July and August pegged at 80° F on the Vineyard and in the mid-70s on Nantucket, although increasingly stifling traffic conditions will make drivers feel anything but cool and relaxed. Early fall is valued not for its foliage but for its tranquillity, as the hectic hordes of summer visitors return to school and jobs. Discerning or contrarian folks, who don't mind that restaurants

may be short-staffed or that the public shuttles no longer run, will find their stay rewarded with warm weather (in the 60s and low 70s), slightly fewer rain days than in the rest of the year, and water temperatures nearly unchanged from palmy August. After October, cool nights become downright chilly, and short days usher in brisk lashings of winter. December boasts the lowest lows—down to 0°. While January features a brief warm spell, it and February are overall the coldest months, with temperatures dipping down to the 20s through early March. Though usually spared the heavy snowfalls that routinely blanket roadways from Boston to the Berkshires, the islands receive rough compensation from ferocious *northeasters* (called "nor'easters" more by folksy meteorologists than by locals) and their accompanying storm surges. These huge waves—amplified by winter's high tides and the storm's own low-pressure center, can turn beachfront homes into beached rafts, punch holes in barrier beaches, take mammoth bites out of shoreline dunes and cliffs, and otherwise demonstrate the impermanence of oceanfront real estate. Needless to say, even the 400-ton island ferries tend to batten down in their snug Cape Cod harbors when these North Atlantic Valkyries come calling.

Hurricanes occasionally hitch rides up the Gulf Stream between July and October, the fast-moving columns of rising air sustained by the current's warm waters, but the cold-air phenomenon known as the "Bermuda High" keeps most of these Caribbean interlopers from ever making it this far north. The downside of this neighboring high-pressure cold is that it can keep summer thunderstorms stalled over the islands for a few days at a time, too. Otherwise, storm fronts blow quickly out to sea, so while precipitation is evenly spread across the calendar (with most months averaging 10-12 days of rain or light snow), it's unusual to have more than a couple of days in a row spoiled by wet weather.

Since clouds, fog, and lower temperatures are more prevalent where the cool sea breezes come ashore, bathers may wish to keep in mind that the prevailing winds in summer are south-westerly, which means that the protected beaches on the lee side of the islands—e.g., the north shores—are apt to be sunnier and warmer than those on the windward side. Sometimes the differences are quite sharp: passengers disembarking from the ferry in Vineyard Haven can be squinting in the sun and reaching for their shades at the same time that frustrated beachgoers on the other side of the island are wondering who brought the pea-soup fog. When the wind swings around to the northwest in summer it brings sultry, sticky weather from the mainland, and in winter it delivers blasts of Canadian-chilled air—"Alberta clippers." Bathers should note, too, that no matter what the provenance of the offshore Gulf Stream, local waters are warm compared to the Gulf of Maine, not to Miami Beach. While the Nantucket and Vineyard Sounds are diminutive enough to heat up a good 10-20 degrees more than the open ocean in summer, swimming in this latitude of the Atlantic is otherwise guaranteed to cool you off, often quite briskly. The goosebumps raised by waves in the mid-50° range lapping on each island's southern shores, for example, can be the perfect antidote if you (or the children) have overheated.

Given the risk from northeast storms, any circumnavigating sailor crazy enough to winter over in these islands rather than farther south should haul his or her boat into dry storage—unless it's a weathertight Great Lakes trawler with enough bow and stern anchors to keep from becoming a waterborne bulldozer in a gale. But for temporary refuge from passing summer depressions, Vineyard Haven Harbor is as well protected a hurricane hole as you could ask for in these parts.

Newspapers from Boston to the Cape print daily island forecasts year-round. Although there is no recorded weather information specifically available for them, the WQRC-FM **Forecast Phone**, tel. (508) 771-5522, at least apprises you of the general weather in the vicinity (e.g., Hyannis). Just bear in mind that temperature and humidity on both islands are typically lower than at this Mid-Cape radio station.

RECREATION

Summer recreation here is virtually synonymous with at least some time in or on the water. Luckily, both islands are well equipped to to offer aquatic fun-seekers a busy time aboard a wide variety of human-, wind-, wave- and engine-powered inventions. Underwater sports are another matter: the marine life of the temperate zones is too monochromatic to interest most casual snorkelers, and no outfitter currently offers a dive boat to any of the worthwhile shipwrecks in the vicinity. Hardcore dive rats may be able to get a fix by making friends with local boat owners knowledgeable about the local waters (places rent gear on both islands), but most recreational scuba and snorkel divers should probably leave the fins and masks at home and use the luggage space for something more useful, like sunscreen or a stash of fine wine.

Don't want to get wet? Dry land also offers plenty of diversions, almost none of which will cause vertigo. Birdwatching is a major occupation on both islands, but you don't have to know or care that the nearby songster is a rufous-sided towhee to enjoy the back-country walks and bike rides. A mountain bike or a slick-tired hybrid comes in handy for negotiating the islands' sandy backroads—and Nantucket Town's cobblestones—but, given all the miles of

ISLAND FESTIVALS AND EVENTS

APRIL

On the last full weekend, Nantucket trumpets the real arrival of spring with its annual **Daffodil Festival.** Garden Club and Art Association events, inn tours, an antique and classic car parade, a tailgate picnic contest, and some three million daffodils are among the highlights.

MAY

Each Memorial Day weekend, the **Figawi Race** fills the waters between Hyannis and Nantucket with the largest sailboat race on the East Coast. The race's current size and respectability belies its colorfully rum-soaked origins, the only remnant of which is the name (an homage to the slurred morning-after query of hungover racers: "Where th' figawi?").

JUNE

During the second weekend, Nantucket pulls out all the stops for its **Harborfest,** tel. (508) 228-1700, with all manner of nautical exhibits, tours, and demonstrations, plus the ever popular Chowder Contest.

Midmonth, try **A Taste of the Vineyard,** at the Old Whaling Church, Edgartown, tel. (508) 627-4440.

On the Sunday following the 16th, celebrate **Bloomsday** at Vineyard Haven's Katherine Cornell Memorial Theatre, tel. (508) 627-4120, with a night of music, drama, and recitations inspired by James Joyce's *Ulysses.*

The last weekend of the month belongs to good listeners as the annual **Festival of Storytelling,** tel. (508) 693-4986, returns to the Vineyard's Union Chapel in Oak Bluffs.

JULY

In the middle of the month, yachties swarm the Vineyard to race in the **Edgartown Regatta,** tel. (508) 627-4361.

The third weekend brings a flavor of the Vineyard's Portuguese heritage to Oak Bluffs in the form of **The Feast of the Holy Ghost,** tel. (508) 693-1564, held both outdoors and at the Portuguese-American Club on Vineyard Avenue.

AUGUST

Around the third weekend of the month, the Martha's Vineyard Agricultural Society sponsors its annual **Livestock Show and Fair,** tel. (508) 693-1343, at the West Tisbury Fairgrounds (also called the New Ag Hall), with old county fair-style fun and good food and music.

That same weekend, Nantucketers turn out for the **Annual Sandcastle and Sculpture Day,** tel. 508-228-1700, at Jetties Beach, while sailors compete in the **Opera House Cup Race,** tel. (508) 228-2121, outside Nantucket Harbor.

SEPTEMBER

On the second Saturday after Labor Day, the Vineyard town of Oak Bluffs takes its final bow of the season with **Tivoli Day,** named for a once-grand but now long-gone Victorian dance hall.

OCTOBER

The weekend after Columbus Day, Nantucket holds its annual **Cranberry Harvest Festival,** tel. (508) 228-1700, featuring tours of the berry-filled bog and tasty accompaniments from local kitchens.

DECEMBER

During the first full weekend of the month, shoppers are lured out to Nantucket by its annual **Christmas Stroll,** the most eventful day of the month-long "Nantucket Noel."

The Vineyard follows suit with **Tisbury's Twelve Days of Christmas,** from the first to the 12th, in Vineyard Haven, and **An Old Fashioned Christmas in Edgartown,** on the second Sunday of the month.

On New Year's Eve, the Vineyard celebrates **First Night** tel. (508) 693-0085, with arts performances in all the down-island towns capped off by fireworks over Vineyard Haven Harbor at 10 p.m.

---

well-paved roads and bike paths, there's little reason to rent fat tires if you have your own skinny-tire touring cycle at hand. Serious mountain bikers won't find this terrain as challenging as that on the mainland; off-road island cyclists face more deep sand than steep grades. The fragility of the open land also means that the damage done by even one or two bikes lasts an entire season (or longer), so heed restrictions where they exist.

A Gentle Reminder

When you spend time outdoors on Massachusetts' islands, remember to take precautions against poison ivy and wood and deer ticks, all of which are native to the islands. Nantucket in particular has a high population of deer ticks, those nasty little *Ixodes dammini* no bigger than any of the commas in this sentence, which can carry Lyme disease, babesiosis, and human granulocytic ehrlichiosis, or HGE. Easy preventative measures include wearing light-colored clothes (the better to spot dark-colored ticks), long sleeves, long pants tucked into socks or gaiters, hats, and tick repellent, and staying on paths rather than romping through tall grass. Since it generally takes one or two days for a tick to transmit bacterial and parasitic agents to its host, quick removal is also usually an effective defense, but be sure to use the proper technique (see "Health and Safety" in the On the Road chapter).

PRACTICALITIES

Caveat Emptor

Historical interest to one side, the fact that the Islands are among the nation's oldest summer resorts is significant for one big reason: it means that your vacation budget is going to be ambushed by an industry that's patiently trained for your arrival since before you were born. The odds are distinctly in the house's favor: you can't escape to the mall McDonald's when you need a break—there are no malls, let alone golden arches; neither will Motel 6 leave the light on for you here—the chain has never gained a toehold, and probably won't until the day Nantucket asks Wal-Mart to come pave its wetlands (that is, a few decades—or more—*after* hell freezes over). What *is* available comes at a considerable premium, which may explain why so many islanders are expatriate New Yorkers: ex-Manhattanites are the only people within 3,000 miles accustomed to such a usurious cost of living.

The defense most often given is that most Island merchants must make an entire annual income in one short season—summer. In fact, only year-round residents (plenty of whom truly live on the economic margins) are entitled to this excuse; others raking in the money from "summer people" are themselves part-timers, who either vacation all winter on their earnings or go south to work other seasonal jobs skimming the same cream from some other captive resort audience. The hordes of students in the summer labor pool (principally on the Vineyard) have the most legitimate right to defend the high prices (which trickle down to them in tips and wages), since most are genuinely trying to earn enough in three months to last the other nine (although you wouldn't always guess it from the number who end up blowing their paychecks on food and accommodations, just like everybody else).

In short, the Islands are a playground most enjoyable for the $200-a-day crowd; if you're more interested in staying below $80, make sure your Hostelling International membership is paid up before you come, and bring the appetite of Tom Thumb. And if you want to kvetch about how little your dollar buys, you may as well just stay home altogether—sympathy is in shorter supply than change for a $20.

What a Difference a Season Makes

The rampant overpricing makes for a fine line between mediocrity and robbery—when a gourmet cafe charges $6 for yesterday's stale dessert, or a B&B inn sees nothing wrong with serving a supermarket-doughnut and coffee continental breakfast to guests paying $155 a night. Every attempt is made in these pages to highlight establishments offering good value, but neither this nor any other guide can predict the rapid shifts in quality from one year to the next—the result of extremely high turnover in staff and even ownership, particularly among restaurants. Consider the parable of the Martha's Vineyard burrito parlor in Oak Bluffs. Its first season, the food was unique for its great taste, quality ingredients, and budget friendliness; a homemade mix of alternative rock and Elvis Presley tunes blared from the kitchen boombox; customers caught up on back issues of *Mad* Magazine; and the counter staff sowed rumors that Elvis was living in Edgartown. But the fabulous founders soon abdicated the kitchen to someone who raised prices and lowered quality—perhaps hoping that sunshine and celebrity sightings around town would distract patrons from noticing the Velveeta in the newly anorexic $9 burritos. Alas, a similar fate could befall any of the places cited here.

However, the corollary to that, of course, is that frogs can become princes, too.

Accommodations

With one high-priced exception, you won't find any familiar interstate hotel names on either Nantucket or the Vineyard, but you *will* find scores of character-rich small hotels, inns, B&Bs, and B&B inns (that blurry category of establishments which dress a motel's economies of scale in B&B frills and ruffles). Predictably, none of these places participate in the various half-price hotel schemes promoted by credit card issuers. Discounts of any kind, in fact (including those for AARP or AAA members, or for corporate travelers), are rare, but, as always, it never hurts to ask.

The Islands aren't completely devoid of cheap places to sleep, though: there's a fine pair of Hostelling International-affiliated hostels, one on each island, plus three privately operated campgrounds in the Vineyard's interior. Nantucket takes a dimmer view of sleeping under the stars; the fine for camping there is a hefty $200.

Whether romantic or rustic, many island B&Bs eschew air conditioning, offering fans instead. First-time visitors—Southerners in particular— are skeptical about booking a room without a/c, but island nights really *are* bearable—especially near the water—during all but the muggiest dog days of August. Just leave those flannel pajamas at home. And consider the upside of screen windows (the islands' most popular cooling system): if you've slept in air-conditioned houses all your life, you've probably never had the pleasure of being awakened by songbirds perched outside your open window singing a gentle morning reveille.

Ferry Service

Nantucket and Martha's Vineyard are connected to Cape Cod by ferries throughout the year, but, understandably, the greatest variety of service blossoms between May and October. Out of the summer high season, Vineyard-bound passengers have but one option, the community-governed

Steamship Authority, at Woods Hole (eight sailings daily in winter, 45 minutes), while anyone going to Nantucket must leave from Hyannis, choosing there between the Steamship Authority's pokey car ferry and **Hy-Line Cruises'** deluxe, passenger-only, high-speed catamaran. Weather permitting, the Authority has at least three daily crossings in winter (twice that in summer) from its South Street docks on Hyannis Harbor to Nantucket's Steamboat Wharf, a two-hour-and-twenty-minute journey. Hy-Line's fast cat makes at least five roundtrips between Ocean Street in Hyannis and Straight Wharf, and justifies its premium price with a travel time of only one hour.

All Steamship Authority vessels carry vehicles, but car owners—particularly those bound for Nantucket—are strongly urged to leave them behind on the Cape. If you actually enjoy spending your vacation in what by summer often resembles the roll-off line of a Detroit assembly plant, by all means fork over that $76 to the Vineyard or $202 to Nantucket (summer roundtrip price—over and above the cost for driver and passengers) and you, too, will be able to savor life in a quaint seaside parking lot. On the other hand, for the same amount of money and hardly any less convenience, you can hire taxis as necessary on Nantucket, or choose between a couple weeks' worth of shuttle bus tickets, several days of bike rentals, and a handful of cab rides on the Vineyard. Sure, a car-less vacation in America is almost worthy of *Ripley's Believe It Or Not,* but unless you're traveling in winter, staying at a rural Vineyard B&B, or carting around quintuplets, there's little excuse for adding to the congestion of the Islands' roadways.

If, after all this, you still can't be parted from your car, then at least do yourself the favor of planning ahead. Auto reservations, tel. (508) 477-8600, are mandatory for Vineyard-bound traffic every weekend (Fri.-Mon.) during the summer high season and the whole week after July 4; they're accepted up to a half-hour before sailing, but keep in mind that some popular weekends have been known to sell out months in advance. Whenever reservations are *not* required, show up and try your luck in the daily standby lines; call (508) 548-3788 to inquire about the length of the wait for the Woods Hole boats, tel. (508) 771-4000 for standby conditions in Hyannis. Up-to-the-minute service bulletins—plus the latest schedule and fare info—are also available from Boston-based SMARTraveler, a traffic monitoring service, tel. (617) 374-1234 (then press 72-star). As a further disincentive to car-owners with inflexible

---

ISLAND FERRIES

All fares are one-way unless noted. Tickets for children under 12 are generally half the adult price—except on Hy-Line's high-speed service to Nantucket.

TO MARTHA'S VINEYARD

Steamship Authority, tel. (508) 477-8600 for schedule and advance auto reservations, (508) 477-SHIP for same-day reservations, 693-9130 for on-island advance auto reservations, 693-0367 for on-island same-day standby conditions

- **Wood's Hole-Vineyard Haven:** passengers $4.25 off-season, $4.75 in-season, bikes $3, cars (does not include driver or passengers) $27 off-season, $38 in-season; parking $7.50 a day ($6 Jan.-Mar.); daily service year round

- **Wood's Hole-Oak Bluffs:** passengers $4.75, bikes $3, cars $38; parking $7.50 a day; daily service May-Oct.

Hy-Line Cruises, tel. (800) 492-8082 in MA, (508) 778-2600 for schedule, (508) 778-2602 for guaranteed tickets and parking, 693-0112 on-island

- **Hyannis-Oak Bluffs:** passengers $11, bikes $4.50, no cars, parking $10 a day; daily service May-Oct.

Island Queen, tel. (508) 548-4800

- **Falmouth-Oak Bluffs:** passengers $6 ($10 same-day roundtrip), bikes $3, no cars, parking $10 a day; daily service late May through early October

Falmouth Ferry Service, tel. (508) 548-9400

- **Falmouth-Edgartown:** passengers $12.50 ($22 same-day roundtrip), bikes $3, no cars, parking $8 first day (min. $5); daily service mid-June through early September

Cape Island Express, tel. (508) 997-1688, 693-2088 on-island

- New Bedford-Vineyard Haven: passengers $9 ($16 same-day roundtrip), bikes $2.50, no cars, parking $6 a day; daily service mid-May through mid-October

TO NANTUCKET

Steamship Authority, tel. (508) 477-8600 for schedule and auto reservations; 228-0262 on-island (information only); (508) 495-FAST regarding new high-speed passenger service

- **From Hyannis:** passengers $10, bikes $5, cars $77 off-season, $101 in-season, parking $7.50 a day; daily service year round

Hy-Line Cruises, tel. (800) 492-8082 in MA, (508) 778-2600 for schedule, (508) 778-2602 for guaranteed tickets and parking, 228-3949 on-island

- **From Hyannis (standard service):** passengers $11, bikes $4.50, no cars, parking $9 a day; daily service May-Oct

- **From Hyannis (high-speed service),** tel. (508) 778-0404 for reservations (essential): passengers $29 ($52 roundtrip), bikes $4.50, no cars, parking $10 a day; daily service year-round

Freedom Cruise Line, tel. (508) 432-8999

- **From Harwichport:** passengers $14.50, bikes $5, no cars, parking first day free ($8 each add'l); daily service May-Oct.

Yankee Whale Watch, tel. (800) WHALING

- **From Gloucester:** passengers $50 ($69 roundtrip), bikes free, no cars, parking free; weekly service July-September

INTERISLAND (June through mid-September)

Hy-Line Cruises, tel. (800) 492-8082 in MA, (508) 778-2600 for schedule, 228-3949 on Nantucket, 693-0112 on the Vineyard

- **Oak Bluffs-Nantucket:** passengers $11, bikes $4.50

schedules, be warned that if the ferry for which you hold a reservation is canceled by bad weather, you'll be stuck on standby for the next one with the exact same status as someone driving up reservationless to try his or her luck. Depending on how many vehicles get bumped, how heavily booked the boats are when they start moving again, and whether you're willing to sit in parking lots for hours on end, even *after* routine service resumes you can easily get stranded on-island for a couple of *days*.

Passengers sensibly leaving their cars behind should allow some extra time. For example, Woods Hole is so small that in high season, ferry parking is usually available only in satellite lots in Falmouth, a few miles away. (Signs posted along Rt. 28 coming from the Bourne Bridge will give you advance warning when the dockside parking is full.) Free passenger vans shuttle from these outer lots to the docks daily, and a van for bicycles and baby carriages is also provided Fri.-Sun. between Memorial and Columbus Day. Cyclists may enjoy a beautiful four-mile ride along the paved "Shining Sea" path from Falmouth direct to the ferry landing.

If you spend the night in Hyannis before or after catching one of the ferries there, be sure to inquire from your motel or innkeeper about reduced-rate parking—it can cost appreciably less than the ferry company lots. And if you arrived at either Hyannis or Woods Hole by bus—and intend to return the same way—don't forget that the ferries and buses are not fully synchronized; be careful not to end up marooned for the night after getting off the boat.

Between May and October, several other companies weigh anchor with their own passenger-only services, departing from Upper and Mid-Cape ports as well as southeastern Massachusetts. Most competitive with the Steamship Authority's Vineyard run in both price and speed is the **Island Queen,** making the 40-minute trip from Falmouth's Pier 45 to Oak Bluffs at least five times every weekday and up to eight times a day on weekends. If you want to be strolling around Edgartown within the hour, head down the block to Pier 37 and catch one of **Falmouth Ferry Service's** four to six daily departures. They also have ample parking for a sliding fee ($8 for the first day and $1 less each of the next three days, to a minimum of $5).

Hy-Line Cruises supplements its zephyr-like catamaran with slower summer boats out of Hyannis to both Nantucket and the Vineyard (the latter a one-hour-and-45-minute trip from the mainland, up to four times a day), but if you want to avoid the crush of traffic around the Hyannis docks, consider either the under-two-hour trip aboard the **Cape Island Express,** (a.k.a. the M/V *Schamonchi*), with as many as four departures from New Bedford to Vineyard Haven, or Harwich Port's **Freedom Cruise Line,** with three daily roundtrips to Nantucket in summer and one a day in both spring and fall, from Saquatucket Harbor on Rt. 28.

With proper planning, reaching the islands by boat doesn't require going anywhere near Cape Cod. Visitors to Nantucket, for example, can take a truly novel approach to the island by embarking from Massachusetts' other cape, Cape Ann, courtesy of **Yankee Whale Watch,** tel. (800) WHALING. Weekly from mid-July to mid-September their boats circle the Outer Cape in the footsteps of Nantucket's earliest European settlers, departing Gloucester Monday night and arriving in Nantucket first thing Tuesday morning. After spending the full day ashore, you return to Gloucester (where the parking is free!) Tuesday night, arriving back early Wednesday morning. Accommodations aboard the boat are youth-hostel simple, just bunkbeds and shared bathrooms, no showers or private cabins. (Yankee's boat, by the way, comes to Nantucket for extra-long whalewatching trips to the Great South Channel; overnight passengers can tag along for a discounted price.)

Some final tips: Fridays and Sundays see the most sailings from Cape and Island ports, with evening or nighttime departures (as late as 10:45 p.m. for the Steamship Authority) added to regular weekday schedules. The reason for the extra boats, of course, is the extra demand; be prepared to face larger crowds, shorter tempers, and less parking if you choose to travel on these days. As a rule, phone reservations are *not* accepted for passengers on most boats (with the exception of certain early and late sailings on the Falmouth Ferry, and Hy-Line's high-speed Nantucket service), and tickets purchased in advance don't always guarantee seating. All sailings are, of course, dependent upon the weather; if in doubt, call ahead.

Bus Connections

Bus service to the Steamship Authority pier in Woods Hole is available year-round from Boston, Providence, and points west (New York City, Albany, Springfield) via **Bonanza Bus Lines,** tel. (800) 556-3815. Buy your ferry ticket along with your bus fare and you'll save having to stand in line a second time. Except for its Boston buses, Bonanza also serves the P&B Terminal in Hyannis and both the Hy-Line and Steamship docks. The Boston-Hyannis bus route is operated by the **Plymouth & Brockton Street Railway Company,** tel. (508) 771-6191, which also stops directly at the ferries. Car-free travelers can also reach Freedom Cruise Line's Harwich Port dock by using the Cape Cod Regional Transit Authority's H2O Line; call the CCRTA, tel. (800) 352-7155 or (508) 385-8326, for details and information.

Winging It

The quickest way to the Islands, of course, is by air—a flight to either takes but minutes. From within Massachusetts, the most frequent all-season service to both islands is provided by **Cape Air** and its sister, **Nantucket Airlines,** with up to a dozen daily departures from Boston

in summer and a plethora more from Providence, Rhode Island, New Bedford, and Hyannis—as well as between the Islands themselves. In fact, a veritable airborne conveyor belt runs out of Hyannis: Nantucket Airlines offers 22 daily flights between Barnstable Municipal and Nantucket Memorial Airports *year-round.* Its competitor, **Island Airlines,** does the same, helping Nantucket rack up more take-offs and landings than many of the nation's major cities. If you're going to make this run frequently, you should ask about books of ten unrestricted one-way coupons, offered by both companies for a slight discount over the advance-purchase roundtrip fare. Cape Air also offers discounted one-day roundtrips on nearly all its routes and joint fares with nearly all major foreign and domestic airlines flying into Boston. Airport parking in Hyannis is $10 a day, in New Bedford $5 a day.

Other contenders with year-round service from Boston include **USAirways Express,** to both islands, and **Business Express/The Delta Connection,** just to Nantucket. Business Express also flies year-round between Hyannis and Nantucket, while USAir adds flights between Hyannis and the Vineyard in summer.

THE AIR CHARTER OPTION

If you've ever wished you could call on an airplane like a taxi (and skip the trip to the big metropolitan airport), if your transcontinental arrival comes in too late to meet the last scheduled commuter flight, or if you've just heard a report that the traffic jam down to the Vineyard ferry landing is five hours and growing, maybe you should be looking at chartering a plane. Sound pricey? If you're traveling with another couple or two, chartering a plane to the Vineyard or Nantucket from Long Island, Philadelphia, Washington, or New Bedford might actually be cheaper than flying the scheduled big-name alternative. Even when nothing can beat the price of that 14-day advance fare with the 45-minute layover in Boston, the sheer convenience of a direct flight that leaves right when and where you want may more than make up for the difference.

Charters charge by the hour, and the meter's running from the minute the plane leaves its home

field to the minute it returns. Obviously, the most cost-effective method is to use an outfit whose home base is the beginning or end point of your trip. Small, propeller-driven planes are the norm for the charters available around Massachusetts, though there *are* companies out there with executive jets for hire.

Here are a few folks whose service will make you feel like a CEO: **Air New England,** tel. (508) 693-8899, has three-, five-, and seven-passenger planes based on Martha's Vineyard. While the northeast corridor from Virginia to New Hampshire is their bread and butter, they're fully capable of handling business all over the U.S. and Canada. **Direct Flight,** a solo operation with a single five-passenger plane, is also based on the Vineyard. **Ocean Wings,** tel. (800) 253-5039, has a handful of planes for five to nine passengers based in Nantucket, which is also home to seaplane-flying **Brisco Air,** tel. (508) 824-3729.

AIRLINES SERVING THE ISLANDS

All of the following airlines serve Nantucket; those also serving Martha's Vineyard are marked with an asterisk:

American Airlines (seasonal) (800) 433-7300

Business Express/Delta Connection (800) 345-3400

*Cape Air (800) 352-0714

Colgan Air (Continental) (800) 272-5488

*Continental Express (seasonal) (800) 525-0280

Island Airlines (800) 248-7779

Nantucket Airlines (800) 635-8787

*USAirways Express (800) 428-4322

Plenty of carriers vie for pieces of the summer bonanza between New York City and the Islands, but the only year-round flights are on **Continental Connection** (formerly Colgan Air) between LaGuardia and Nantucket. Outside the summer months, Vineyard-bound passengers from the Big Apple have to connect through Boston. Between June and October the options multiply: Business Express and **Continental Express** add seasonal service to both islands, the former from LaGuardia, the latter from Newark. USAirways and **American Airlines** (weekends only) add summer nonstops from LaGuardia to Nantucket. USAirways provides limited inter-island service in summer, too. The prices on direct flights from New York aren't always a better deal than connecting through Boston, by the way, and given that Cape Air shares its terminal at Logan International with USAirway's LaGuardia Shuttle, the difference between direct and indirect flight paths isn't necessarily as great as you might think, either.

You'll have your pick of a handful of car rental agencies and taxis at either island airport (count on paying at least $7 to get to town on Nantucket, up to twice that on the Vineyard), but only the Vineyard's terminal is also on the route of public transportation. The Gay Head Shuttle, tel. (508) 693-1589 (complicated recorded recital of pickup times; $2.25-4.75 one-way), stops at the airport seven or eight times in each

direction about 10 a.m.-6 p.m., on weekends only from late May through late June, then daily until early September.

Sailing to the Islands

The Islands are one of the world's yachting centers, so if you're coming in your own boat, book a mooring in advance. For an extended anchorage, consult the local town harbormasters, who generally deal in season-long leases; transients, meanwhile, are better off calling the private mooring rental companies. The cost of an overnight mooring to sober up from shore leave before braving the infamous rips and shoals of Nantucket Sound ranges from a low of $25 per night in Vineyard Haven Harbor to $50 per night at Nantucket.

In Nantucket, the Town Pier's Harbormaster, tel. (508) 228-7260, can either help you directly or refer you to an appropriate private marina such as the Nantucket Boat Basin at Swain's Wharf, tel. (800) NAN-BOAT. On the Vineyard, you can choose between anchorages in each of the bustling down-island towns or a more sedate berth amid the small up-island fishing fleet at Menemsha. The numbers for their respective harbormasters are: Vineyard Haven, tel. (508) 696-4200 or 693-7792; Oak Bluffs, tel. (508) 693-4355; Edgartown, tel. (508) 627-4746; and Menemsha, tel. (508) 645-2846 or 645-2220. Transients visiting the Elizabeth Islands should call Cuttyhunk's harbormaster, tel. (508) 990-7578, for advance info on public moorings.

Since all fuel sold here has to be shipped in from off-island, budget-conscious cruisers will want to top off their tanks at a mainland marina if at all possible. Launch services, haul-out, dry storage, and all manner of repairs are available on both islands, but don't count on public showers or dockside pump-out facilities at all moorings. Not that there aren't compensations: on summer mornings, the Vineyard Haven Launch Company, tel. (508) 693-7030, for example, makes the rounds of that harbor's mooring field with bagels, muffins, juices, the *Boston Globe,* and assorted other essentials.

No cruiser should venture into local waters without a proper reference book near the chart table. Favorites for sailors include the *Cruising Guide to the New England Coast,* by Roger F. Duncan, Paul W. Fenn, W. Wallace Fenn, and

John P. Ware. An equally valuable work, more specific to the islands, is the latest edition of Lynda and Patrick Childress's *Cruising Guide to Narragansett Bay and the South Coast of Massachusetts* (Camden, ME: International Marine, ISBN 0070163049). For the encyclopedic approach there's also *Embassy's Complete Boating Guide & Chartbook to Rhode Island, Massachusetts, & New Hampshire* (Lexington, MA: Embassy Marine Publishing, tel. 781-860-0430), from the makers of Maptech electronic navigation software.

MARTHA'S VINEYARD

You're already aware that, to sound as if you're in the know, you need to forget about Martha and call this place "The Vineyard." Now, if you dare, take it a step further and partake of the practiced effrontery of long-time residents, who barely acknowledge the existence of nearby Nantucket—call this simply "the Island."

By any name, it's a peach: big enough to have quiet spots even in the busiest season, small enough that you can get to know it quickly, slightly more democratic than its neighbor in matters of room and board, and far more accessible to day-trippers. This is the island of seaside naps and lazy days in chaise longues, of sailboats and bicycles, lighthouses and gingerbread cottages, artists and professors, carpenters and movie stars, presidential advisors and, occasionally, presidents. Water sports, historical exhibits, and nature trails provide alternatives to the beach, while abundant seafood and all manner of sweets lay to rest that austere summer diet you fleetingly considered in order to fit into last year's swimsuit.

Up-Island and Down

The Vineyard's 100-plus square miles are neatly divisible into "up-" and "down-island"—as on Cape Cod, a holdover from days of whalers and sailors that make sense if you remember that degrees of longitude ascend from east to west. Up-island—the southwestern corner farthest from the Cape Cod ferries, comprises the predominately rural towns of West Tisbury, Chilmark, and Gay Head—home to only a smattering of small restaurants and stores. Many of the area's undulating country roads are lined with great *alleés* of oak, like antebellum plantation driveways, and the woods are filled with the drystone walls of bygone sheep farms. The up-island hills—the Vineyard's highest ground—offer great views en route to their abrupt tumble into the sea beneath the steady sweep of the beacon in red-brick Gay Head Light (hugely popular with the organized bus tourists). While even this section of the Vineyard does depend on "summer people," it also relies on agriculture and fishing; its working roots are especially visible in pic-

LIBRARY OF CONGRESS/LC-USZC4-1345

1920 Martha's Vineyard travel poster, by John Held, Jr.

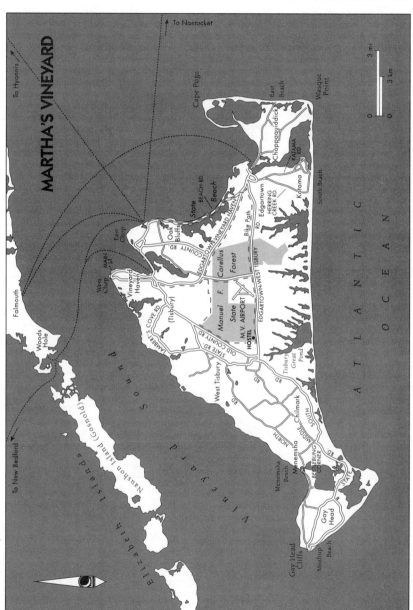

MARTHA'S VINEYARD

To Nantucket

To Hyannis

To New Bedford

Woods Hole

Falmouth

Elizabeth Islands

Nashon Island (Gosnold)

Vineyard Sound

ATLANTIC OCEAN

Cape Page

Chappaquiddick

East Beach

Wasque Point

KATAMA RD.

Kalama

South Beach

State Beach

BEACH RD.

Oak Bluffs

East Chop

West Chop

MAIN ST.

Vineyard Haven (Tisbury)

LAMBERT'S COVE RD.

STATE RD.

OLD COUNTY RD.

West Tisbury

EDGARTOWN-VINEYARD HAVEN RD.

COUNTY RD.

Manuel F. Corellus State Forest

M.V. AIRPORT

HOSTEL

EDGARTOWN-WEST TISBURY RD.

Bike Path

Edgartown

HERRING CREEK RD.

Tisbury Great Pond

NORTH RD.

MIDDLE RD.

SOUTH RD.

STATE RD.

BEETLEBUNG CORNER

Chilmark

Menemsha

Menemsha Beach

Gay Head

Gay Head Cliffs

Moshup Beach

3 mi

3 km

© MOON PUBLICATIONS, INC.

turesque Menemsha harbor—home to more groundfish draggers and lobster trappers than luxury yachts—and at the regular farmers' market in West Tisbury.

Since touring up-island generally requires owning or renting a set of wheels (two or four), most visitors never get farther than the Vineyard's pedestrian-friendly down-island threshold: Vineyard Haven, Oak Bluffs, and Edgartown. The leafy sanctuary of up-island's hidden lanes may be fine for a country B&B stay or a fortnight of housekeeping and cooking in a self-contained cottage far from the madding crowd. But if being within walking distance of good food and nightlife is important, if you want the flexibility of catching a ferry at a moment's notice, if you prefer the comforting glow of streetlights over a chorus of crickets when you go to sleep at night, then you want to be down-island. Even nature-lovers needn't worry: along with a near monopoly on knickknack shops, sweet treats, and Black Dog T-shirts, down-island offers plenty of scenic beauty and is home to over half of the Vineyard's two dozen public beaches.

In Season and Off

Geography isn't the only area in which the Vineyard can seem downright binary. The other big one is The Season, the mixed-blessing phenomenon of the summer, which has carried the Vineyard economy now for more than a century. It's a fairly well-rehearsed course: after a practice gallop over the Memorial Day weekend, *in season* does a few light warm-up laps through June before finally bolting out of the gate in a breakneck frenzy on the Fourth of July. Careening like a tornado through Labor Day, it finally slows to a canter by Columbus Day—the semi-official end of the race and the point at which most owners retire to tally up their winnings. Lingering momentum and clement weather can prop up off-season weekends through Thanksgiving, but then the island finally becomes again the property of its year-round residents, who savor the calm until their memory of the last blockbuster summer becomes so distant that they grow impatient for the sequel. (Not all locals cope well with the annual shift from traffic jams to cabin fever: the draught-flood-draught resort economy, coupled with intense isolation, is believed to strongly contribute to the high local in-

cidence of alcoholism. Visiting 12-steppers who don't like to miss meetings need not worry; there are plenty to choose from here.)

The biggest difference between in season and off is, as you might expect, a sudden increase in the availability of just about everything. By the same token, it's also at this point that the restaurants, buses, ferries, accommodations, and shops all start to scale back their operating hours. Beach buses and public shuttles between up- and down-island are the first to cease, stopping promptly after Labor Day weekend (not to resume until the following mid- to late-June). By mid-October, most up-island restaurants and half the B&Bs in West Tisbury, Chilmark, and Gay Head have followed suit. By autumn, down-island towns start to roll up the rugs, cover the furniture, and forward the mail, too—but they have enough year-round residents to at least keep a few restaurants open all year. Last, but not least, there's Vineyard Haven; thanks to four-season ferry service, it actually retains a passing resemblance to a fully functioning small town, even at the nadir of winter.

The off season brings with it certain requirements—double-check restaurant hours, for example, and rely more on driving than you would in the longer and warmer days of summer. But these are more than outweighed by advantages such as being able to choose lodgings upon arrival (rather than sight-unseen three months in advance) and dining when ready, without waiting in line for an hour or making do with a fifth-choice reservation. While the *early* off-season is most prized, anyone looking for a cozy weekend escape to an austere Winslow Homer landscape shouldn't rule out December, or even February.

What you should *not* expect from the off season is significant savings. Innkeepers' supply costs are as high in winter as in summer, and off-season business is too sparse to be worth a price war. Yes, some room rates may drop almost 50% between summer and winter, but that simply reflects the fact that July prices are stratospheric; they return in January to the realm of the average Ramada Inn.

Like resort destinations all over the country, the Vineyard struggles with the pressures of popularity. Realtors talk about three-acre minimum lots as the balm for fears of over-development, but look closely as you come in on the ferry from Woods Hole and you'll see what land conservationists are concerned about: the wooded Vineyard shore is filling with rooftops. The development issue grows ever more urgent as summer traffic in down-island towns approaches your average metropolitan rush-hour gridlock. (You can be part of the solution rather than the problem by leaving your car on the mainland if at all possible, and taking advantage of the summer shuttle buses, extensive bike paths, taxis, and your feet.)

HISTORY

Early Visitors

Martha's Vineyard is generally said to take its name from an abundance of native wild grapes and the daughter of Bartholomew Gosnold, the English captain who spent the late spring of 1602 around Buzzard's Bay and the Elizabeth Islands (which he named in honor of his Queen), in what was then known as "the North part of Virginia." However, given that Gosnold didn't have a daughter named Martha and that his mother-in-law, Martha Goulding, helped finance his voyage, it is more plausible he was honoring *her*. According to the "Briefe and true Relation"

of the voyage, by one of its members, John Brereton, Gosnold actually applied "Marthaes vineyard" to a very small, uninhabited island overgrown with various fruit-bearing shrubs and such "an incredible store of Vines . . . that we could not goe for treading upon them." Probably this was what's now aptly called Noman's Land, a naval gunnery range-turned-wildlife sanctuary off Gay Head's south shore. By 1610, cartographers assigned the name to the much larger adjacent island (which for decades was widely called by its first English settlers "Capawack," probably from the Algonquian word for harbor, *kuppaug*), where it remains

The lure for Gosnold, as for other captains who ranged the New England coast in the early 17th century, was sassafras. The safrol in the leaves is now known to be a carcinogen, but to Gosnold's contemporaries the plant was widely believed to be a cure-all. "The roote of sassafras hath power to comfort the liver," enthused one 1597 herbal encyclopedia, "and to dissolve oppilations, to comfort the weake and feeble stomacke, to cause a good appetite, to consume windiness, the chiefest cause of cruditie and indigestion, stay vomiting, and make sweete a stinking breath." Perhaps more important to the gentlemen of Europe—whose demand for the stuff kept the price (and profit margins) so high—

THE LEGEND OF MOSHUP

The first Indian who came to the Vineyard, was brought thither with his dog on a cake of ice. When he came to Gay Head, he found a very large man, whose name was Moshup. He had a wife and five children, four sons and one daughter; and lived in the Den [Gay Head's circular depression]. He used to catch whales, and then pluck up trees, and make a fire, and roast them. The coals of the trees, and the bones of the whales, are now to be seen. After he was tired of staying here, he told his children to go and play ball on a beach that joined Noman's Land to Gay Head. He then made a mark with his toe across the beach at each end, and so deep, that the water followed, and cut away the beach; so that his children were in fear of drowning. They took their sister up, and held her out of the water. He told them to act as if they were going to kill whales; and they were all turned into killers

[killer whales]. The sister was dressed in large stripes. He gave them strict charge always to be kind to her. His wife mourned the loss of her children so exceedingly, that he threw her away. She fell upon Seconet [Sakonnet Point, RI], near the rocks, where she lived some time, exacting contribution of all who passed by water. After a while she was changed into a stone. The entire shape remained for many years. But after the English came, some of them broke off the arms, head, &c. but most of the body remains to this day. Moshup went away nobody knows whither. He had no conversation with the Indians, but was kind to them, by sending whales, &c. ashore to them to eat. But after they grew thick around him he left them.

(As told by Thomas Cooper, Gay Head Indian, to Englishman Benjamin Basset in 1792) was the belief that it could cure "the French Poxe" (i.e., syphilis).

They Came, They Saw, They Converted

When Gosnold's ship, *The Concord,* anchored in local waters, the Vineyard was well inhabited by Native Americans related to the Wampanoags of coastal Massachusetts and Rhode Island—a federation of Algonquian-speaking bands whose ancestors had occupied *Noe-pe* (the land "amid the waters") for at least 9,000 years. The 17th-century Wampanoags were farmers and fishermen organized in close-knit villages around *sachems* (hereditary leaders) and *pauwaus* (religious leaders and physicians, or medicine men). When the first white settlers arrived, in 1642, four sachems presided over the island's estimated population of 3,000 indigenous people.

title page of Experience Mayhew's 1709 translation into Wampanoag of the Psalms of David

These first immigrants were farmers and shepherds from the Boston area led by Thomas Mayhew, Jr., a missionary, and his father, a merchant. For 40 pounds and a beaver hat (about three times the price allegedly paid for Manhattan 15 years earlier), Mayhew, Sr., had purchased from the Earl of Stirling the patent to all islands then unoccupied by the English off the south shore of Cape Cod—and, importantly, beyond the boundaries of both the existing Pilgrim and Puritan colonies. Bypassing the sandy heaths of Nantucket and the too-small Elizabeth Islands as ill suited to the homesteading needs of their party, the Mayhews settled on the Vineyard.

The Wampanoags accepted them—despite previous experience that included an English captain's kidnapping a sachem for zoo-like display in London. Mayhew, Sr., assured the Indians that his master, King James, though superior to their sachems, "would in no measure invade their Jurisdictions." Surprisingly, he kept his word, paying for property rights as his settlements expanded or—as in the case of Nantucket—before he resold possessions granted him under his original royal patent. Such honesty merits special mention because it stands out so much from the shameless deceits of Mayhew's mainland contemporaries, but tolerance may have begun as a form of détente: the Wampanoags could not have forgotten the ruinous Pequot War, ended just five years before, and the devastation it brought that tribe in nearby coastal Connecticut for getting in the way of the English. And Mayhew's thirty-odd homesteaders would have been conscious of being far from the assistance of authorities in either the Massachusetts Bay or Plymouth colonies. In any event, the Indians' mortality rate and acculturation made hostilities or illegal land grabs wholly unnecessary. Beginning with a nasty plague outbreak a few years after the settlers' arrival, European diseases reduced the Wampanoag population by over 70% within as many years. Devoted missionary work by both Mayhews (capitalizing in part on the pauwaus' inability to stem disease-related deaths) converted many more Indians into model subjects of English law. Some were so thoroughly assimilated that the English islanders paid to send them to Harvard to be trained for the ministry.

After Mayhew, Jr., was lost at sea on a fundraising trip to England, Mayhew, Sr., effectively ran the island as the private Manor of Tisbury, with himself as Lord and Chief Justice. Intolerant of dissent, the Governor-for-Life jailed or exiled his fellow landowners as he saw fit, until finally succumbing to nature's term limits at the age of 85. Nine years of squabbling later, in 1691, the Vineyard was annexed to the new Province of Massachusetts formed by monarchs William and Mary after the various colonial charters were revoked by an English parliament impatient with their subjects' unruliness.

Population Pressures

Frothy politics aside, the remainder of the 17th century and most of the 18th were marked most by rapid population growth among whites—more from new births than new immigrants. Predictably, this had side effects: when J. Hector de Crèvecouer wrote, in his *Letters from an American Farmer,* that travelers to the Vineyard couldn't avoid becoming acquainted with all its principal families, he was complimenting island hospitality, but he might as well have been satirizing the islanders' inbreeding. At the time of his visit, in the 1770s, almost every new island marriage was between cousins of some kind; by the mid-1800s, half the island's population had one of only a dozen surnames. Until settlement by off-islanders in this century introduced new blood (and disapproval of cousinly marriage), there was no stigma attached to the high incidence of deafness among newborns—particularly in the rural up-island towns. Until after WW I, not surprisingly, sign language was widely spoken here.

The most pressing problem posed by the high birth rate, though, was that, like an infestation of weevils in a small garden, people proceeded to strip their patrimony bare, forcing a shift from sheep-shears, milking stools, and plowshares to oars, nets, and harpoons. Turning from their deforested, overgrazed hills (and later from an economy completely KO'd by English raids and embargoes during the American Revolution), an estimated 20% of the Vineyard's men—Wampanoag and white alike—became expert whalers and merchant seamen, as highly prized by captains and ship owners as their Nantucket brethren. "Go where you will from Nova Scotia to the Mississippi," wrote de Crève-

couer, "you will find almost everywhere some natives of these two islands employed in seafaring occupations."

But this didn't last, either. By the 1840s, local whale-oil merchants faced stiff competition from mainland producers (who were closer to their consumers), and local wool producers were edged out by cheaper foreign imports. In the year of John Brown's pre-Civil War raid on the federal arsenal at Harper's Ferry, whale-oil prices were shot down by cheaper Pennsylvania crude; by the end of the war, the whale fleet had been scrapped, sunk, or was rotting at the wharves. The Vineyard's whaling days were over.

"We'll Camp Awhile in the Wilderness"

As seafaring fortunes waned, the newest and most lasting transformation of the Vineyard was taking root in the Second Great Awakening, a nationwide resurgence of Methodist revivalism. In 1835, southern New England Methodists began holding revival tent meetings in an oak-shaded meadow they christened Wesleyan Grove, erecting a small village of huge "society tents" each August to house the crowds who came to experience a week of Bible-thumping preaching and religious conversion. The year the market for whale oil nosedived, 1859, some 12,000 souls turned up at the camp meeting, seeking salvation in 400 tents.

These tent revivals were such a magnet for tourists that they were featured in the *New York Times* travel section and in illustrated weeklies such as *Harper's.* The great congregation-sponsored tents were gradually replaced by fanciful wooden family cottages whose occupants soon set aside as much time for parlor entertainments, croquet, and promenading along the seashore as for hymns, gospel, and prayer. A speculative group of investors, the Oak Bluffs Land and Wharf Company, began constructing a summer resort around Wesleyan Grove, deliberately mirroring the camp meeting grounds' informality, capitalizing on the impeccable reputation and high moral character of the revival gathering (as opposed to the liquor-soaked haven of high society across Vineyard Sound at Newport) and targeting the same sober Christians as the camp meetings. Out of this emerging middle class of shopkeepers, blacksmiths, carpenters, watchmakers, and other artisans seeking both a hard-

VINEYARD ETIQUETTE

The list of past and present Vineyard residents (their names frequently recited in a rosary of off-hand vanity, as if the lifestyles of the rich and famous will trickle down to everyone simply by sharing the same beach) includes Spike Lee, Beverly Sills, Mike Wallace, Carly Simon, Denzel Washington, Alan Dershowitz, Ted Danson, Diane Sawyer, Henry Louis Gates, Jr., Jimmy Cagney, Sharon Stone, James Taylor, Walter Cronkite, André Previn, Art Buchwald, John Belushi, Jackie O. Maybe the sun *does* shine a little brighter on these people, but don't come to the Vineyard expecting to bask in it yourself.

Local wisdom holds that the Vineyard attracts celebrities precisely because locals have either too much Yankee sense or Puritan humility to make a fuss over cultural icons in the flesh. This legendary discretion has become the cornerstone of Vineyard etiquette, which declares that celebrities are to be allowed to go about unmolested by photographers or autograph seekers. Should you see Somebody, you should feign indifference instead of, say, crossing the street to get a better look. If Somebody sits at the next table in a restaurant, you are requested to act nonchalant instead of pulling out your camcorder.

You *can* do otherwise, of course, but then many trees' worth of *Vineyard Gazette* newsprint will be expended by local vigilantes clucking their tongues over another tourist who "just doesn't get it." Anyway, you're wasting your time driving Chilmark's back-roads hoping to catch some box-office headliners schmoozing over a barbecue; most of those Very Important People stay so well out of sight that the closest you'll get is Webb's campground—which is directly in the flight path of their chartered jets.

---

earned reprieve from sweltering cities and safe recreation for their families, "Cottage City"—eventually renamed Oak Bluffs—was born.

Over the last century, the Vineyard has continued to cultivate its reputation as a summer resort, although the demographics of both the visitors and their hosts have changed. The 1960s and '70s saw a rise in VW owners and McGovern voters coming to roost here permanently, accompanied by a handful of celebrities looking for a place to avoid the limelight. Both have been followed by the seasonal tide of college students seeking good parties and a wave of professionals, academics, and business execs on a spree of second-home buying. These days, media moguls and A-list movie stars are plunking down millions for secluded beachfronts and pedigreed estates. Besides sending high-end property values toward the moon, this latest trend has drawn star-gazers who either don't know or don't care about the local etiquette. Old-timers may rightly wonder whether the "good and happy grocer" of the camp meeting years would see the Vineyard of today as the piece of heaven he had sought or the profligate high-rolling resort he had sought to escape. But if you weren't here in the mellow hippie years, you have nothing to mourn. Local letter-to-the-editor writers may perennially wring their hands over the changes, but until all the old stone walls crumble to dust and the lighthouses fall into the seas, there will be enough uniquely New England flavor here to keep comparisons with Vail, Sun Valley, or Beverly Hills firmly at bay.

VINEYARD HAVEN

This is the island's largest year-round community and only year-round ferry port. But by all appearances, it's just your average small seaside town of about 4,300 stalwart souls, with a little light industry near the wharf, tree-shaded residential streets overlooking the harbor, and a small commercial downtown. White clapboard and gray shingle descendants of the venerable, sharp-gabled, Cape-style house rub shoulders with old captains' mansions. The automotive spectrum ranges from rust-flecked old American sedans to teenagers in their parents' mid-'80s hand-me-downs, from pickup trucks that clearly earn their mudflaps to mirror-polished German imports. Whatever its varied occupations the rest of the year, come summer the town has its hands full playing host and maître d' to the 20,000 visitors swarming through it.

Once known by the Wampanoags as *Nobnocket* (place by the pond), the port was known to later generations of sailors as Holmes Hole, after a 17th-century landowner. Early in the Victorian era, image-conscious citizens changed the name after deciding they preferred living in a place that sounded closer to heaven than hell. Since then, the harborside village has grown indistinguishable from Tisbury, the 17th-century township of which it was once just a part—but, aside from legal documents and town stationery, both general usage and the Post Office now favor "Vineyard Haven" for the whole.

Visitors disgorged by the ferries will find restaurants, shops, accommodations, car and bike rentals, ATMs, and (in the Steamship Authority Terminal beside the pier and, seasonally, above the A&P parking lot across the street) public bathrooms—all within a few blocks' walk. The one amenity you needn't bother looking for is a liquor store; by law, Vineyard Haven, and all the other up-island towns, is dry.

Since "the Great Fire of 1883" destroyed its center, the town's oldest buildings are found on upper Main Street north of the Compass Bank building (whose distinctive facade, a cross between craftsman-style stone and Mediterranean tile bungalow, occupies the grounds of the harness shop where the fire may have begun) and a block farther up from the harbor along William Street. Many of the fifty-odd houses included in the Historic District along this quiet street were built on the backs of the great whales or the decks of the "coasters," packet ships engaged in trade between Boston and New York

before the railroad came and spoiled the profits. Befitting the wealth of their builders, some of these houses typify the Greek Revival style now most commonly associated with old banks.

Plenty of New England's most attractive civic architecture has been inspired as much by religion as commercial profit, as some of this town's present and former churches attest. Tucked along side streets crossing Williams are three worthy examples: the classically inspired **Tisbury Town Hall,** a former Congregational/Baptist Church on Spring St. that's also known as Association Hall; the newer United Methodist **Stone Church,** on Church St., built early this century to replace its demonstrably flammable predecessor; and, opposite, the former 1833 Methodist meetinghouse, now **The Vineyard Playhouse,** the island's only professional theater. Association Hall is also home to a performance center, the **Katharine Cornell Memorial Theater,** a fully accessible space used by various local groups.

Seamen's Bethel

On Beach Rd. between Main St. and the traffic-tangling Five Corners, by the Black Dog Bakery, is the Seamen's Friend Bethel, tel. (508) 693-9317, a charitable organization founded a century ago to aid destitute mariners, some of whom are buried beneath evocative, weather-wizened old planks in the hard-to-find Old Sailors' Cemetery off Edgartown Road. These days, the Bethel's former chapel—more like a one-room

the mooring grounds, Vineyard Haven Harbor

schoolhouse than its church-like cousin in New Bedford, made famous by Herman Melville—displays a collection of historic photos, artifacts, and souvenirs donated by appreciative sailors and their families. The prize of the lot, a lifebelt from the *Titanic,* has unfortunately been expropriated by the organization's Boston branch, where it sits far from the curious eyes of tourists—but the remaining nautical tchotchkes are worth a quick look. As for some of those photos, they may look like just a bunch of old boats to you, but for most of this century islanders have had a visceral attachment to their ferries—the same sort of affection farmers used to reserve for their most reliable draft horses. So those photos of the *Nobska* and her sister steamers are like the family snapshots people keep in their pocketbooks and wallets. Open most weekday mornings until noon or 1 p.m., other hours by appointment or chance (free).

Shops and Galleries

An abundance of craftspeople and commercial artists consider the Vineyard their year-round home, and Vineyard Haven has its fair share of boutiques displaying their work. Specialty stores abound as well, offering everything from Kilims and incense to English country antiques and Native American jewelry. No need to shop on an empty stomach, either: you can grab a quick sandwich or snack around almost every corner.

One of the first sights to greet passengers disembarking from the Woods Hole ferry is **The Black Dog Bakery,** tel. (508) 693-4786, on Water St. across from the A&P Market. Although the counter staff often seem to have taken too much Thorazine (perhaps to cope with the crush of tourists) and the muffins seem to have shrunk in proportion to their popularity, the Dog is still a mighty contender in the island's baked goods sweepstakes. The related tavern on the beach behind the bakery was famous even before President Clinton and family stopped in for a bite while vacationing here a few years back, but the place now seems determined to clothe half the planet in its trademark T-shirts—which is why part of the bakery may at first glance look like a sportswear store. If you're interested in seeing what, besides clothing, the owners have chosen to put their logo on, from black lab dinnerware to pawprint drawer pulls, stop in at the **General Store,** tel. (508) 696-8182, behind the bakery.

Five Corners, there by the bakery, is easily the Vineyard's busiest (and most aggravating) intersection, and the side street that dead-ends down at the Black Dog Tavern probably holds some sort of Vineyard record for pedestrian traffic. Yet just a few steps away from both is one of the island's most hidden spaces, a set of **artist's studios** on the second floor over the Wintertide Coffeehouse. Most of the occupants welcome visitors, although irregular hours mean you never know whose door will be open. Hats, floorcloths, batik lanterns, and fabulous painted ceramics are some of the treasures to be found up here.

Up on Main St., past the gauntlet of candy stores and outdoor cafes, is **Paper Tiger,** tel. (508) 693-8970, with cards and prints by several local photographers, watercolorists, and collage artists among its many paper products—a must-stop if you owe notes to friends back home. If you'd like to see what others have written about this island, don't miss **Bunch of Grapes Bookstore,** across the street, tel. (508) 693-2291; besides plenty of Vineyard-related titles—including Philip Craig's series of Vineyard-based mystery novels—the shop is well stocked with much more than the latest bestsellers. After buying your books, why not just settle in for the summer and read? The real estate office up the street can help you choose the house, but **Shaw Cramer Gallery,** on the second floor of the building bearing the Vineyard Dry Goods sign, tel. (508) 696-7323, is the place to go to put some serious pizzazz into your dinnerware or pillowcases; among the functional and decorative contemporary furnishings are locally made textiles and handmade paper books. If $80 scarves or $2,000 hand-finished wooden sideboards aren't in your budget, there's always the **Thrift Store,** next door, tel. (508) 693-2278; some amazingly high-quality merchandise has been known to turn up on the racks, making shopping here a little like playing the lottery.

For the complete antithesis to the ersatz cheer of sunlit seascapes and floral still lives, check out **The Cricket Gallery,** across the street near the corner of Main and Union, tel. (508) 696-7772, the first retail outlet for an Atlanta-based dealer in original art from animated films and television. Yes, Ren and Stimpy, large as life—

and framed! Pencil drawings and limited-edition screen prints are available, but the specialty of the house is a huge collection of original production cels—hand-inked frames from all the major studios: Disney, Hanna-Barbera, Warners, MTV—and, yes, animé fans, even from the Japanese. (Open Memorial Day-Columbus Day.)

Tucked out of sight at 89 Main, down the little walkway next to the Compass Bank (follow the sign to their ATM) is the studio-cum-gallery of **Travis Tuck,** metal sculptor, tel. (508) 693-3914, whose unique repoussé (French for "pushed from the back," referring to how they're made, not how they work) weathervanes sell for prices starting in the low four figures. Browsers are warmly welcomed, and it's always fun just to watch Travis tattooing a good mambo on his latest work-in-progress, or to flip through his portfolio books of past work. While a Steven Spielberg-commissioned velociraptor and many other of Tuck's works adorn off-island homes, you'll also find the sculptor's designs atop a couple of local town halls, supermarkets, the *Gazette* offices in Edgartown, and the hospital. If it's uniqueness that you're after and cost isn't an issue, don't miss **Midnight Farm,** tel. (508) 693-1997, Carly Simon's shop, full of very beautiful but very expensive art, housewares, personal care products, and one-of-a-kind tchotchkes, on Cromwell Lane behind Bowl & Board and the A&P.

As a port of some renown, Vineyard Haven has the usual complement of marine-related services on Beach Road around the many boat repair shops. It isn't all outboard motors and anti-fouling paint, though: at the edge of the shipyards, **C.W. Morgan Marine Antiques,** tel. (508) 693-3622 (open April-Dec.) has a treasure chest full of ship models, ship paintings, old nautical devices and instruments, scrimshaw, and assorted other curiosities. More along the lines of a flea market is the array of consignment material at **Pyewacket's Flea Circus,** tel. (508) 696-7766, in the yellow clapboard house on Beach Rd. between the shipyards and the Tisbury Market Place mini-mall.

State Road, heading southwest from downtown, is the province of shops geared mostly toward errand-runners, but past the dry cleaning and home appliance centers, past the miniature golf and bowling alley, past the Lake Tashmoo scenic overlook, sits a place that any art-savvy visitor will find more than worth the mile-and-a-half trek from Main Street's busy sidewalks. The Vineyard is said to be home to over 40 art galleries, but if you disqualify places selling handmade T-shirts, crafts, and hotel-room faux Impressionist landscapes, there's really only a handful of galleries exclusively exhibiting fine art by serious artists. One of the oldest of these, **The Vineyard Studio/Gallery,** tel. (508) 693-1338, a nonprofit cooperative on State Rd. across from Lower Lambert's Cove Rd., is also the most museum-like—thanks to the 18th-century gray-shingled barn's high walls, good light, and absence of any pressure to make sales. In fact, thanks to the residential zoning of the neighborhood, no sales are even permitted on the premises (though arrangements can be made directly with the artists. Open daily 2-6 p.m. June 1 through late September, with receptions every other Sunday.

If by this time all the window shopping and art-critiquing requires more substantial sustenance than shortbread from downtown's **Scottish Bakehouse** (in the little walkway off Union St., parallel to Main) or butter-smooth fudge from **Murdick's,** on Union St., ignore that deli beckoning from 90 Main (unless you're a fan of iceberg lettuce and skimpy portions) and try a hefty turkey Gobbler from **Bob's Pizza,** on Main, or anything from the eminently affordable **Sandwich Haven,** on Cromwell Lane facing the back of Bowl & Board. (Real sit-down restaurants are described below.)

West Chop

Vineyard Haven's V-shaped harbor is protected on either side by jaw-like hunks of land known as East and West Chop. Upper Main Street runs along West Chop to a separate village of Tisbury, located at the end; East Chop belongs to neighboring Oak Bluffs.

About two miles up Main from the downtown shops is the 19th-century **West Chop Lighthouse,** sitting beside the road for photographers' convenience, though not open to the public (it's a private Coast Guard residence). The current 1891 brick tower is the third incarnation in a series of lights at this location that have guided seafarers since James Monroe sat in the White House. The white beacon, visible on the mainland, shows red if you get too close to the shoals off the end of the point.

West Chop Park, by the turnaround loop at the end of Main, is favored for watching the sunsets over Vineyard Sound, but any time on a clear day it offers a nice view out over what was once one of the world's busiest coastal waterways. Before railroads and the 1914 completion of the Cape Cod Canal siphoned away most of the cargo and passengers, this area was second only to the English Channel in boat traffic. Two hundred years ago, you could have counted scores of sails belonging to coastwise packets bound for Boston or New York and merchant vessels bearing West Indies molasses, South American hides, Sumatran spices, and Arabian coffee. Until technology enabling precise calculation of a ship's longitude became widely available, in the 19th century, most "East-Indiamen" put in at Vineyard Haven or Woods Hole before negotiating the great extended hook of Cape Cod; to set a course for Boston or Salem directly from the Caribbean or South Atlantic would have otherwise risked a fatal snag on Nantucket South Shoals.

OAK BLUFFS

Although even the meadow voles in the most remote acre of the island must by now recognize the tremors of the Season, possibly no place is as utterly transformed by the summer crowd as Oak Bluffs. From its chaste beginnings as host to great Methodist tent revival meetings, "OB" has evolved into the most honky-tonk town on the Vineyard, thanks to its after-dark appeal to the under-25 crowd.

Blueblooded Nantucketers, raised to see the Vineyard as a mongrel cross between Coney Island, Kmart, and a sailors' bar, get goosebumps just thinking of what goes on here, but it's no Ft. Lauderdale or Virginia Beach—or even Santa Cruz. Compared to the rest of the Vineyard, though, there's no denying that on summer evenings this joint jumps: cars prowl along "the Circuit" (Circuit Avenue, downtown's main drag), the small handful of nightclubs and bars pulse with music and pheromones, and even underage kids get giddy in the swirl of yearning, strolling up and down the Avenue with gossipy enthusiasm, eyeing members of the opposite sex, and lapping up lots of ice cream. Week-

enders and tourists, meanwhile, shop and enjoy the carnival atmosphere. At summer's end, the instigators of all the fun vanish as quickly as they arrived, returning to schoolyards and campus quads and leaving the town as quiet as a banquet hall after a big wedding. Gone are the circles of teenage hackysack players, the guitarists gently strumming Kurt Cobain songs, the cross-legged rows of tie-dyed sidewalk sitters. Gone are the lines at the two cinemas, and the crowds on the dance floors. Although the music still blares and the doors stay open until at least Columbus Day, more often than not it feels as if staff outnumber patrons as Daylight Saving Time rolls around. The rapid exodus of the town's spirited lifeblood makes OB the first down-island town every year to roll up its summer finery and shutter its colorful facades. Restaurants and accommodations nearly all close by the middle of October, with the pleasant exception of the least expensive eateries, several of which remain open year-round.

But OB's appeal isn't confined to the young. On the contrary, all but the most rural-minded travelers may find it to be the best base for exploring the whole Vineyard. By bus, car, or bike, it's as favorably connected to the rest of the island as you can get, and has ferry connections to more ports—including Nantucket—than any other island town. Its restaurants and accommodations fit all price ranges—which is more than can be said of any other place on either the Vineyard or Nantucket. It offers some of the most interesting street fairs and special events, from winter's Chili Contest to summer's Jazzfest. Its delicious ice cream emporium—**Ben & Bill's,** on Circuit Ave.—is the island's most affordable, and possibly the most fanciful (try the lobster flavor for proof, or "moose droppings"). Even the beach and brewpub are but a stroll from your room. All this, plus a fanciful Victorian frame of Gothic Revival and Queen Anne architecture.

Flying Horses Carousel

It doesn't take a kid or a carousel buff to appreciate the craftsmanship of the landmark Flying Horses, tel. (508) 693-9481, a contemporary of Coney Island's first merry-go-round. The 22 colorful steeds, adorned with real horsehair, were carved in 1876 by C.W.F. Dare. (Although it claims to be the nation's oldest working carousel,

Rhode Island has an 1870 contender for the title.) Rides are $1, and if you grab the brass ring you get another ride for free. Located on Lake Ave. smack between downtown and the harbor, the carousel is open weekends from Easter Sunday through early May and then daily through early October; between Memorial Day and Labor Day, it stays open to 10 p.m. nightly.

The Camp Ground

Just behind the commercial storefronts along Circuit Ave. lies a carpenters' jigsaw fantasia of the former Wesleyan Grove, now formally known as the M.V. Camp Meeting Association grounds, whose tent revivals begat both OB and the island's tourist industry. Stroll through the Arcade on Circuit Ave. and you'll discover a riot of colorful little cottages encircling Trinity Park and its large, open-sided Tabernacle like wagons drawn up around a campfire—hidden from downtown by design (the tall fence and limited entry points were originally intended to restrict the secular influences of the resort community springing up right in the pious campers' backyard). The closely packed cottages—which truly deserve the name, unlike the extravagances perched upon the seaside cliffs of Newport—evoke the intimacy of the tent encampment, whose early years were dominated by big tents shared by whole congregations (the steeply pitched roofs and twin-leaf front doors are deliberate allusions to the A-frame tents and their entrance flaps). If the Camp Grounds seem too neighborly for comfort by modern suburban standards, remember that in the 1860s, when most of these were built, the average huge hotels in America's most popular resorts were about as communal as you could get, with just about every waking hour spent in the company of fellow guests. For these happy campers, the mutual lives and close ties to their neighbors was not only customary, it was a source of their security. The ethos of the private car and private bath was still over half a century away when most of these little houses were built, and it shows.

With the exception of the 1879 wrought-iron and sheet-metal Tabernacle the Camp Ground is a celebration of the power woodworking tools newly available in the latter half of the 19th century. The gingerbread, porch railings, and window shutters are a catalogue of imagination, from the decorative (arabesques and French curves) to the narrative (a hunter and hound chasing a hare). Stop by the **Cottage Museum,** 1 Trinity Park, tel. (508) 693-0525 (10 a.m.-4 p.m. Mon.-Sat., mid-June to mid-Sept.), for some advice on locating the architectural highlights. For $1, you can also check out the museum's collection of furnishings—typical of the Camp Ground's Victorian heyday. Some nights in summer, the Tabernacle is used for musical performances, from Wednesday evening community sings to weekend concerts; if you're visiting in August, check the events listings in the local papers for information.

One of the early secular alternatives to gospel preaching was **Illumination Night,** begun by the Oak Bluffs Company in 1869. Houses in both that company's resort development, outside Wesleyan Grove, and the Methodist Camp Ground itself were bedecked with Japanese lanterns and banners that humorously commingled the sacred and the profane in such messages as, "We Trust in Providence, Rhode Island." Now, on an undisclosed date each August, Trinity Park and the surrounding cottages perpetuate the lantern-hanging tradition as part of a community event sponsored by the Camp Meeting Association. (Don't look for any advance notice—there is none, on account of past problems with crowd control, including an apocryphal drunken slumber party years ago in Ocean Park when thousands of day-trippers were supposedly stranded for a lack of late ferry sailings. If, by coincidence, you do find yourself in town on this special eve, for heaven's sake don't steal bikes and run them off the piers, or take laundry from people's lines for swaddling while you swill your beer in the park overnight, or you may get tourists banned from the event once and for all.)

Ocean Park

Fronting Nantucket Sound, surrounded by the turrets and balconies of OB's most spacious mansions, seven-acre Ocean Park is the focal point of many festivities. An ornate bandstand, built in anticipation of President Grant's 1874 visit, sits on the huge lawn like a fancy stickpin on a bolt of green felt; here in July and August, free concerts by the Vineyard Band are held on alternate Sunday evenings. Here, too, are the best seats in the house for August's end-of-season fireworks display, which doubles as a fundraiser for the local fire department. Other times in summer, it harbors basking couples, Frisbee players, and small kids running themselves silly. Admirers of Victorian architecture can stroll the park boundary and find a textbook of picturesque stylings: hints of a Tuscan villa here, a Swiss chalet there; Queen Anne towers and piazzas; craftsman- and shingle-style influences; and the ubiquitous fancy roof and porch trim deriving from the town specialty—carpenter gothic.

In the small portion of the park near the police station stands a monument to the end of the Civil War: "The Chasm is closed," begins its inscription. This gift of a local resident and veteran of the 21st Regiment of Virginia was originally a bronze Union soldier (notice the "U.S." on his belt buckle), but when the statue became too weathered, it was painted in its present vivid, wax-museum colors. As a result, the Yankee is now clad in a uniform of Rebel gray—which is perhaps entirely fitting given the tablet dedicated "in honor of the Confederate soldiers" on the pedestal.

East Chop Light
At the suburban tip of East Chop along East Chop Drive sits the East Chop Light, originally the island's only private lighthouse. In 1869, Captain Silas Daggett ventured his own money to build the navigational aid, then solicited contributions for its support from fellow captains, ship owners, and marine insurance companies. Besides alleged difficulty collecting after vessels had arrived safely, the civic-minded captain's first tower also burned down and had to be replaced—at no small expense. Eventually, the U.S. government bought the whole thing off Daggett. Finding his lantern building to be "little better than a shanty," the Federal Lighthouse Board approved construction of the cast-iron present structure in 1878. The name on the sign, Telegraph Hill, predates the light by a generation: in the early 19th century, a semaphore tower occupied the spot and sent shipping news from the island to Woods Hole for relay to owners and underwriters in Boston. In the middle of the century, that tower was replaced by an underwater telegraph cable.

Now leased from the Coast Guard by the local historical society, the light is open to the public for sunset viewing on summer Sunday evenings late June through mid-September, from 90 minutes prior to sundown to 30 minutes after; admission is $2.

Shops and Galleries
Anyone disembarking from the ferries at Oak Bluffs Harbor will be forgiven for initially thinking that T-shirt, postcard, and candy shops are the only retail trade on offer in downtown OB. In spite of the fact that some of the stores contain the word "gallery" in their names, the only art in the Dockside Market Place by the Hy-Line pier is strictly of the tourist variety. Away from the harbor, past the bars and grills, the main drag becomes slightly more recognizably part of a real town, with diner-like lunch counters and general merchandisers holding back-to-school sales in the fall. Amid all the shops competing for your attention, it isn't hard to pick out the vivid and whimsical window display at **Craftworks**, 149 Circuit, tel. (508) 693-7463, one of the rare specialty shops to stay open well into the off season (mid-March through late December, daily until 9 p.m. in high season). From bold Marisol-style folk art to the kind of pottery Keith Haring might have kept around his loft, even their functional crafts exude fun. If brass temple bells, Peruvian woolens, or things made of kinte cloth are more your style, check out the **Third World Trading Company**, a few doors up the block. There's apparel at **Cousen Rose Gallery**, tel. (508) 693-6656 (June-Sept., open mornings and evenings), too, past the pottery store at the top of the avenue, but it earns its name with its range of monoprints, pastels, watercolors, and other small painterly work. Don't miss the collection of children's books, either.

Among the most underrated shopping options on the islands are estate auctions, which typically take place off season here, Sept.-June. Whether or not you can make it to one of the "Good Riddance Girls" liquidation sales (always held on Sunday—consult the newspaper listings under "yard sales"), you can visit the group's store, **The Now and Then Shop**, 176 Circuit, tel. (508) 696-8604, and hunt for some overlooked treasure amid the eclectic jumble of furnishings and curios (year-round).

About a quarter mile from the harbor on Dukes County Ave., around the corner of Vineyard Ave., is a small cluster of artsy businesses, from interior designers to a recording studio. Among the storefront galleries and shops are the **Dragonfly Gallery,** tel. (508) 693-8877, whose exhibitions of contemporary fine art usually reflect more ethnic and international diversity than is usual in this business (12-7 p.m. Thurs.-Mon., April-Dec.); the Martha's Vineyard Center for the Visual Arts' **Firehouse Gallery,** holding group shows in a renovated gray-shingled fire station opposite Dragonfly; and the adjacent **Periwinkle Studio,** tel. (508) 696-8304 (April-Nov.), selling unique hand-block-printed clothing mostly for women. Thirsty shoppers and cyclists will find plenty of refreshment in the coolers at Tony's Market, just down the street—along with pizza slices and huge double-stuffed deli subs.

Thimble Farm

Besides being one of the increasingly rare chunks of down-island open land that hasn't been turned into house lots, this farm deserves special mention for the fact that it's the only place on the island where you can pick a basket of succulent strawberries or raspberries *and* a bouquet of flowers to go with them. The flowers—a range of perennials and annuals—run all summer long. Strawberries start around the second week of June and continue at least until the end of the month; by the time you read this, owners Bud and Patricia Moskow may have succeeded in timing their crops to bear fruit throughout July as well. Raspberries—both red and black—arrive in two waves, late July through mid-August and late August through mid-September. Call (508) 693-5441 to check on the pickings; open 10 a.m.-5 p.m. Tues.-Sun. Their farm stand—open until Columbus Day—also sells their own hydroponic herbs and tomatoes. Straddling three townships—West Tisbury, Tisbury, and Oak Bluffs—Thimble Farm is most easily reached from the OB side; take the signposted turn off the Edgartown-Vineyard Haven Rd. (about a quarter mile northwest of Barnes Rd.) and follow Stoney Hill Rd. another half mile west. Don't pay attention to the "Private" sign at the gates of the fancy "Iron Hill Farm" housing development, by the way—maybe it helps justify adding another digit to the purchase price of those pondside estates, or is a minuscule deterrent to the moped-riding sixpack-toting teens who used to hang out here, but the road is most assuredly public.

EDGARTOWN

With more than 350 years of history, staid old Edgartown is the antipode of youthfully energetic adjacent Oak Bluffs, which is why skateboarders and Rollerbladers should be aware of the $20 fine for venturing downtown. Yachting is the only true sport here, and if you can't afford to maintain a boat for the season, you can still adopt the local dress code of ruddy pink pants and brass-buttoned blue blazer—or a full outfit of tennis whites prior to cocktail hour—and pretend one of those sleek-hulled vessels swinging out there on its mooring is yours.

Called Great Harbor by the English (who made it their first island settlement) and then Old Town, after a second community was carved out of

the Old Whaling Church (1843)

ODE TO A VINEYARD CHICKEN

If you visit the Vineyard Museum, in Edgartown, be sure to pause a moment and pay your respects at the two verse-covered headstones in the Carriage House. Nancy Luce, the West Tisbury woman who had these memorials erected before she died, in 1890, would surely appreciate the visit. And so, no doubt, would the bantam hens honored by the tablets: Ada Queetie, Beauty Linna, and Poor Tweedle Dedel Bebbee Pinky.

Poor little Ada Queetie,
She always used to want to get in my lap
And squeeze me close up, and talk pretty talk to me.

She always used to want I should hug her up close
*   to my face,*
And keep still there she loved me so well.

When she used to be in her little box to lay pretty egg,
She would peak up from under the chair,
To see her friendy's face. . . .

Poor little Ada Queetie has departed this life,
Never to be here no more,
No more to love, no more to speak,
No more to be my friend,
O how I long to see her with me, live and well,
Her heart and mine united,
Love and feelings deeply rooted for each other,
She and I could never part,
I am left broken hearted.

Luce was one of the island's best-known "characters," an eccentric who wrote a volume of poetry, *Poor Little Hearts,* for her beloved chickens. She sold copies of the book—and postcards of her brood—to 19th-century tourists who passed her farm (she also happily gave recitals for a small tip). Her own grave, toward the rear of the West Tisbury burying ground, off State Rd., bears a simple marker without any epitaph.

control over all the dry land off the southern New England coast, from Long Island to Nantucket.) The most enduring legacy of old Mayhew's rule is Edgartown's continuing role as the seat of regional government—named with anachronistic English pomp the "County of Dukes County" and comprising both Martha's Vineyard and the Elizabeth Islands. But the Lord of Tisbury might take a pace-setter's pride in the town's per-capita income (highest in the region) and feel a kinship with the town's many registered Republicans (the largest percentage on the island). For the visitor, however, probably more interesting than the modern abundance of country squires is the testament to the wealth accumulated by captains and ship owners in the heyday of whaling—Edgartown's abundant neoclassical architecture.

Historic Buildings

Three of the town's architectural treasures are owned by the Martha's Vineyard Preservation Trust, which maintains one as a museum and keeps all three open for scheduled seasonal tours. The Trust's headquarters occupy the **Daniel Fisher House,** 99 Main St., tel. (508) 627-8017, an elegant federal-style mansion built in 1840 by one of the island's most successful whale-oil tycoons. Superb though its symmetry may be, the good Dr. Fisher's home was upstaged three years later by his next-door neighbor, the **Old Whaling Church,** a Greek revival eminence whose giant columns and broad pediment evoke the Parthenon's temple front. The Trust-owned building now does double duty as the Edgartown Performing Arts Center with a broad variety of secular events complementing the Methodist ser-

Indian lands to the west, Edgartown (named in tribute to the young son of the Duke of York) was finally incorporated in 1671, the same year the Duke gave his approval to Thomas Mayhew, Sr.'s private Manor of Tisbury. (Getting the ducal wink and nod was crucial—just a few years earlier, the restored Merry Monarch, King Charles II, had sown great confusion by giving the Duke's Manhattan-based colony nominal

vices still conducted each Sunday beneath the graceful chandeliers. Befitting such a true community center, its 92-foot clock tower is also a landmark for boaters out in Nantucket Sound.

In utilitarian contrast to this pair's grandeur is the **Vincent House,** a simple, south-facing example of early New England's homegrown "full Cape" style—i.e., a steep-roofed, story-and-a-half box with pairs of windows flanking a central door. Built in 1672, it's the island's oldest surviving residence and retains its original masonry, nails, hinges, handles, and woodwork. It's also the Preservation Trust's museum to island life, open daily 10 a.m.-3 p.m. Memorial Day through Columbus Day; $3. During this same season, guided tours of all three Trust properties are available daily on the hour 11 a.m.-2 p.m., starting from (and including admission to) the Vincent House; $5.

Streets intersecting Main near the center of town—School, Summer, Winter—are all worth roaming for a good look at the full range of island architectural styles, from old saltboxes and half-Capes to spare Congregational meeting houses and Tiffany-windowed Catholic churches, while Water St. is the island's premiere showcase of federal and Greek revival. Wander in either direction past Water Street's shops and the verandas of downtown inns and you'll quickly come to numerous 19th-century captains' and merchants' houses lined up along the harbor and looking, with their black shutters and white siding, like so many piano keys. In this street-sized textbook of neoclassical architecture, you should have no trouble spotting either the restrained federal style of the early 1800s (pilasters framing nearly square facades; columned porticos, fanlight windows and sometimes even sidelights framing the front doors; smaller third-story windows; and fancy, turned balustrades crowning flat roof lines) or the bold Greek columns of the successive style, which came into vogue following the widely reported expeditions of British Lord Elgin to Athen's Acropolis. If these concrete expressions of that era's love of Greek and Roman civilization don't inspire noble resolutions to read your Ovid or Aeschylus, perhaps you'd prefer to sit at the base of the 20th-century **Edgartown Light,** at the end of North Water St., and entertain more modern sentiments about the inconstancy of sun and tide.

By the time the cast-iron present tower was brought, early in WWII, to replace its 111-year-old predecessor, shifting sand had filled in around what originally was a stone pier set a short way from shore; where once the lighthouse keeper had to row to his post, now you may simply stroll through salt-spray roses.

Vineyard Museum

At the corner of School and Cooke Streets, a couple blocks from downtown's commercial bustle, sits a collection of buildings filled with a better-than-average potpourri of historical relics—from scrimshaw and whaling try-pots to costumes, domestic furnishings, and old farm implements. The Martha's Vineyard Historical Society curates the museum and also presents changing exhibits drawn from the society's large collection of historical photos and ephemera. Genealogists who fancy some connection to past islanders will want to visit the society's library, which also sells copies of the *Dukes County Intelligencer,* the society's quarterly assemblage of articles on island history and lore.

Perhaps the museum's most prominent exhibit is visible even before entering through the corner gatehouse—sitting in the yard is a large piece of lighthouse technology over 140 years old, an example of the huge Fresnel lens, whose invention revolutionized coastal navigation. The view from inside the lens may seem disorienting, but these concentric prisms totally reversed the illuminating efficiency of 19th-century lamps; whereas before, only one-sixth of a parabolic reflector's light could be seen by mariners, Augustin Fresnel's "dioptric apparatus" concentrated as much light in its high-powered beam as had previously been lost. In a reminder that red-tape bureaucracy is hardly a modern affliction, the U.S. government dithered for 30 years, despite the proven efficiency, making scientific studies and committee reports before finally adopting the French-made lens. One of the earliest Fresnels installed by the U.S. Lighthouse Service, this particular lens faithfully flashed its light over Gay Head for nearly a century before being replaced with an electric lamp.

The Museum, tel. (508) 627-4441, is open 10 a.m.-4:30 p.m. Mon.-Sat. in summer only; Wed.-Sat. Columbus Day to Memorial Day. Admission in season is $5, $4 off season (but one of the major display areas—the Thomas Cooke House, that tidy 18th-century Colonial—is closed for lack of heating then).

Shops and Galleries

Despite Edgartown's high-end demographics and an affected gentility unsullied by crass neon and billboards, each new season seems to find another of the city's expensive boutiques turning into another T-shirt shop indistinguishable from those found in every tourist town the world over. Holdouts against this trend include one of the island's most prominent galleries, plus a few purveyors of eye-catching, offbeat, or just plain unique gifts and indulgences.

While you'll find the most interesting gift and souvenir shopping around the harbor, long-term visitors on errands in cars prefer the commercial plazas on Upper Main St. between the A&P and The Triangle (the local name for the split between Main and the roads to Vineyard Haven and Oak Bluffs). The narrow, one-way downtown streets are great for pedestrians, but summer drivers should take an extra dose of hypertension medication before trying to do the same.

Foremost among the harborfront art venues is the **Old Sculpin Gallery,** on Dock St. opposite the ramp for the Chappy Ferry, tel. (508) 627-4881 (summers only). Housed in a former boatbuilders' workshop, this is the Vineyard's oldest operating gallery, run by the nonprofit Martha's Vineyard Art Association. In season, expect the customary artist openings every Sunday evening. A block up from the harbor, at the corner of N. Water and Winter Streets, is the **Christina Gallery,** tel. (800) 648-1815. The two floors of paintings and photographs are often quite predictable, but venture upstairs past all the sundrenched beach, cottage, and sailing scenes and you'll find a trove of antique charts and maps. For something more in the vein of a colorful folk-art trivet or vase, check out **Once in a Blue Moon,** in the adjacent Nevin Square shops opposite Darlene's Kitchen on Winter St., tel. (508) 627-9177. The hand-painted furniture beneath all those bright collectibles is for sale, too.

As if to prove that the full flavor of New England can be gift-wrapped right here in Edgartown, there's **The Vermont Shop,** at the corner of Winter and N. Summer. A world away and

half a block closer to Main is **The Golden Door,** 18 N. Summer, specializing in art from the Far East. It isn't nearly as incongruous as you might think: carved pachyderms, shining Buddhas, and mandala-like print fabrics were just the sort of worldly souvenirs whaling captains brought home a century and a half ago.

Doorways of the Far East are also found at the back of **In the Woods,** at the corner of N. Summer and Main, tel. (508) 627-8989. Past the Adirondack chairs, birdhouses, wooden toys, kitchen utensils, and assorted other forest products lie some pillars and paneled doors straight out of *The Man Who Would Be King*, every inch covered with intricate carving. They are, in fact, from the old Kingdom of Swat, now in northern Pakistan. Kids and Shakers may prefer the handsome and scrupulously simple pony-sized rocking horse.

Crew members on 19th-century whalers usually couldn't afford fancy trinkets for the loved ones *they* left behind. To keep from returning empty-handed, they used slack time over the course of their three- or four-year voyages to produce handmade gifts of scrimshaw, or carved whale ivory. The **Edgartown Scrimshaw Gallery,** on the right side of the bookstore, kittycorner from In the Woods, tel. (508) 627-9439, offers both antique and modern examples of the scrimshander's art (practiced these days mostly on the fossilized tusks of Siberian woolly mammoths, American mastodons, and walruses). Nantucket lightship baskets, lightship basket jewelry, wooden whales, and nautical art also crowds the walls and cases of this tiny shop, and friendly commentary is freely dispensed to the curious; open year-round (daily in high season, reduced schedule in fall, and Saturdays through winter). Whaling tales of a different sort—plus sailing stories and all manner of island-related reading matter—are found in **Bickerton & Ripley Books,** next door, tel. (508) 627-8463, year-round suppliers of good reading for beach chairs drawn into the shade or armchairs drawn up to the fire.

Chappaquiddick

The Wampanoags' descriptive name for Edgartown's sibling chunk of tree-covered sand means "separated island," but modern inhabitants have no time for all those syllables; it's "Chappy" now, to one and all. But the full name endures in infamy after what happened in 1969, when a car accident proved fatal to a young woman and nearly so to the career of the state's then-junior senator, who was behind the wheel. Kennedy-bashing may be a popular recreation back where you come from, but it's not here; nothing brands a visitor as an off-island yahoo more quickly than chasing after vicious gossip about the nation's foremost political dynasty. Of course, plenty of islanders privately suspect tourists are all yahoos anyway, so questions about the "Kennedy car wash" are widely anticipated.

Sparsely inhabited and infused with rural end-of-the-road isolation, Chappy feels as if it's far off the map even when the waiting line at the ferry clearly proves the opposite. Visitors are lured by the superb beaches at Wasque and Cape Poge, but canoeing, birdwatching, bodysurfing, surf-casting, hiking, and walking are equally good reasons to join that ferry line.

Means of access to the island (which isn't quite separated anymore) are limited to the Chappy ferry (also called the "On Time") or a good swim across the narrow entrance to Edgartown's inner harbor. The ferry runs every day of the year from the waterfront downtown, beginning at 7:30 a.m. Rates and schedule are posted at the landings, but in brief you can count on continuous service to midnight in season (June 1-Oct. 15), to 6 p.m. otherwise; after 6 p.m. off-season, three periods of service are spread out over the evening and the final run leaves at 11:10 p.m. Cars and their drivers are $4.50, passengers and pedestrians $1 each; bikes and riders are $2.50. All fares are roundtrip and are collected in full upon first crossing. Because of the maze of narrow one-way streets approaching the Edgartown waterfront, even bicyclists should follow the "Chappy Ferry" signs.

UP-ISLAND

In a place that's already about as laid-back as New England gets, up-island is where the Vineyard truly goes barefoot and fancy-free. Yet the relative seclusion of the up-island villages have traditionally meant that they are the purview more of the summer resident or cottage renter (and celebrities seeking true rural privacy) than

day-trippers or weekenders (despite the hordes of bus tourists flocking to the renowned Gay Head Cliffs). "Out of sight, out of mind" seems to be up-island's best disguise: trailheads look a lot like just more private driveways, their flora and vistas hidden from view. Visitors dedicated to maximizing beach time give scant thought to the up-island forests, and people who spend the big bucks to bring their cars across seem most likely to use them to avoid exercise rather than to explore the nooks and crannies where public shuttle- and tour-bus riders can't go. In short, for a variety of reasons even many up-island regulars never bother to explore the unheralded hilltops, ponds, and meadows virtually in their own backyard. All of which means that if you're able to spare the time and expense to get around up-island at your own pace, you have the chance to still discover the quiet, down-home place that exists for most down-island residents now more in memory than in fact.

West Tisbury

Oak Bluffs may boast greater diversity, but the most politically liberal town on the island is this 1896 splinter from next-door Tisbury. Familiarly known as "West Tis" (rhymes with "fizz"), the community had no qualms about allowing hippies to set up camps in the woods back in the first reign of the bell-bottom and the fringed halter. Even today, the area sets a standard for island liberals: in addition to the still-common colonial office of fence viewer (whose modern mandate is to arbitrate boundary disputes), for example, West Tis elects a "Community Right-To-Know Committee," an EPA-mandated oversight group that most towns resist on the grounds that industry is good for you.

Although this was one of the fastest-growing towns in the entire state during the go-go years of the 1980s, agriculture is still a vital part of West Tisbury's economy and landscape. From onions and lettuce to strawberries and cream, if you partake of an island-grown meal there's a good chance its components were cultivated here. Most of the upscale restaurants around the island in fact make a point of using local produce wherever possible, but for a true taste of the Vineyard's truck gardens, look no farther than the **West Tisbury farmer's market,** in and around the **"Old Ag Hall,"** a picture-book 1859 gothic revival shingled and gabled barn on State Rd. in the town center. There are farm stands down-island, too (Edgartown's Morning Glory Farms, at the corner of Machacket Rd. and Edgartown-West Tisbury Rd., about a mile from Main St., is in a class by itself), but between mid-June and Columbus Day weekend, the Old Ag Hall is *the* place to go, as much for the ambiance as for the fruits of the earth. Besides affordable vine-ripened tomatoes and enough cruciferous vegetables to make even the Surgeon General happy, there're always a few vendors selling fresh-cut flowers, a few masters of the Mason jar selling pickles and preserves, a few bakers with homemade desserts, and even fresh-spun yarn from just-sheared sheep's fleece. If you have someplace to store the leftovers—not that there are likely to be many—Eileen Blake's pies are legendary. In recent seasons, fresh coffee and homemade Vietnamese spring rolls have also made appearances. The market is held on Wednesday afternoons 3-6 p.m. and Saturday mornings 9 a.m.-noon; needless to say, Saturdays are mobbed.

Up-island's other celebration of its agrarian lifestyle, August's annual **Livestock Show and Fair,** raises the rafters of the "New Ag Hall" with a Vineyard version of the standard county fair; expect oyster shucking contests and great live music along with those horse pulls and tables of homegrown or homemade food. Also known as the Fairgrounds, the new hall is on Scotchman's Lane about half a mile north of the old one.

Like a page of Norman Rockwell's sketchbook, the village around the farmer's market is exemplary 19th-century picket-fence New England, from the handsome Congregational Church and well-trod porch of Alley's General Store to the proper old homes on tree-lined Music St. (this leafy residential way was once known to some as Cowturd Lane; "Their savage eyes turn'd to a modest gaze by the sweet power of music," perhaps, Tisbury residents renamed the street back in 1800s for the piano-playing daughters of a resident whaling captain and six of his neighbors). Those old ivories are long silent but the visual arts live on, in and around **The Field Gallery,** next door to the Council on Aging center and wonderful new town library, tel. (508) 693-5595 (daily mid-June-Columbus Day). As at most other island galleries, exhibits here are condensed for the summer rush, so each Sunday evening is opening night for the new art of the week. If you can't wait around for the wine and cheese, **Back Alley's,** across the street, has a smart line-up of reasonably priced deli sandwiches and baked goods (try those snappy ginger cookies), plus dirt-cheap coffee refills for folks who supply their own cups.

Half a mile away, on Old County Rd. at Scotchman's Lane, is the large **Granary Gallery,** tel. (800) 472-6279 (daily late May-early Oct., weekends in shoulder seasons from Easter through Christmas), which has the distinction of being the Time-Life Gallery of Photography's sole New England representative. So, in addition to locally produced artwork in a variety of media (painting, sculpture, and sometimes textiles), you can browse—or buy—limited editions, mostly signed, of museum-quality prints by the likes of Alfred Eisenstadt, Margaret Bourke-White, Andreas Feininger, Carl Mydans, and others whose contributions to *Life* magazine have become some of the nation's most recognizable cultural images.

North Tisbury

Within 25 years of their arrival, the English outgrew their settlement at Edgartown and moved up-island to this fertile area between Priester's Pond and Lambert's Cove Road. It was known to the Wampanoag as *Takemmy,* which is usually translated as "place where people go to grind corn," but may actually be from *touohkomuk,* or "wilderness." The English shepherds called the settlement Newton (Edgartown then was Old Town), and later Middletown. Now named after the post office station sandwiched into a storefront beside the incomparable Biga Bakery & Delicatessen, this part of West Tisbury township includes a couple of arty shops along State Rd., most notably **Martha's Vineyard Glassworks,** opposite the garden nursery, tel. (508) 693-6026, where the art of shaping attractive, functional items out of molten glass is on view daily between early May and Halloween. Nearly opposite the turnoff for Menemsha is a small nondescript cabin called the **Vineyard Foodshop Bakery** but known island-wide as Humphrey's, whose sugary trove of cookies, eclairs, and big fluffy croissants are snapped up by discerning neighbors and sharp-eyed passersby.

Christiantown

Although the Puritan founders of the Massachusetts Bay colony had obtained their royal patent by promising that "the principall Ende" of their settlement was to convert the indigenous people to "the Christian Fayth," the evangelical magistrates in Boston were so busy prosecuting heretics and building a profitable mercantile trade that it was in fact here on the Vineyard—outside their jurisdiction—that the first New England mission to the Indians began. The year after the Mayhews settled their parish in Edgartown, a Wampanoag named Hiacoomes became the island's first voluntary convert to Christianity. Within a decade, over 10% of the Vineyard's Indian population had signed a covenant with the proselytizing Thomas Mayhew, Jr.; within a generation, a majority of the Wampanoag on both the Vineyard and Nantucket had not only converted but had also resettled themselves into a series of 15 Christian communities modeled after the English style, a move heralding the profound change colonization wrought upon both Wampanoag culture and the Indians' relationship to the land.

One such town stood in North Tisbury on what's now Christiantown Rd., off Indian Hill Road. With the blessings of Thomas Mayhew, Sr., Wampanoag converts consecrated their first Christian church and burial ground here in 1659, on a parcel of land rented from a pair of up-island sachems. Besides the small number of descendants denied Federal tribal recognition, all that's left of Christiantown now is tiny little Mayhew Chapel, an 1829 replacement of the original; the mostly unmarked tombstones opposite; and abandoned 19th-century cellar holes and stone walls along the peaceful loop trail through adjacent **Christiantown Woods Preserve.** About a quarter-mile walk past the parking lot (follow the road and take first right; this is not driveable) is a state-maintained **fire tower.** When the tower is staffed—which is only when fire danger is high—you are welcome to go up and enjoy the fine 360° views.

Chicama Vineyards

While most island farmwork happens far from the curious eyes of off-islanders, an exception exists here, at the state's first legitimate winery, which offers tours up to five times a day in season. Year-round, taste from a variety of red and white table wines made from European vinifera grapes, including chardonnays, zinfindel, cabernet, a cranberry dessert wine, and the occasional sparkling wine. Chicama also bottles its own line of gourmet flavored oils, mustards, vinegars, chutneys, and other condiments. All, like the wines, are for sale in the gift shop-cum-tasting room (daily mid-May-Christmas, Fri.-Sat. only the rest of the year). Winery and shop are a mile down sand-and-gravel Stoney Hill Rd. from the signposted turn off State Rd.; call tel. (508) 693-0309 to check on the reduced off-season hours.

Chilmark

Sparsely populated Chilmark (whose year-round population is less than 700) once resembled a little corner of New Zealand, with more sheep than humans. The resemblance stopped at labor and farm expenses, though: before Down Under's huge sheep stations put the kibosh on profitability, back in the mid-19th century, Chilmark wool had been second only to whale oil in importance to the island economy. (The whalers themselves made use of the wool in the form of heavy-duty satinet coat fabric milled in neighboring West Tisbury.) Dozens of miles of drystone walls, all built from up-island's limitless supply of glacial till, lie half-hidden in the now-forested hills, quiet reminders of the loose-footed flocks of black-face sheep that once dominated the local landscape. If you've taken a close look at these sorts of walls elsewhere in New England, you'll notice that the Vineyard has a distinctive "lace wall" in its repertoire—a rickety-looking style with big gaps between the stones. The usual explanation has been that these perforated walls were built to accommodate stiff ocean winds raking over the once-treeless up-island hills, but Susan Allport, author of the exceptional *Sermons in Stone,* suggests the design may be a Scottish import. Although there is no written record one way or the other, a nearly identical style of see-through stone wall in Scotland—called a Galloway dike—was built to look deceptively precarious specifically to frighten bold sheep from attempting to leap over them.

Despite having its trees and vegetation shorn to the ground by its early "husbandmen," Chilmark still boasts some of the island's best soil, even if these days artists and telecommuting professionals far outnumber local farmers (though farms still seem to outnumber retail shops). The center of the village is the intersection of State (alternately known in Chilmark as South Rd.), Middle, and Menemsha Cross Roads (named Beetlebung Corner, after the stand of tupelo trees whose hard wood was valued by ships chandlers for making mallets—beetles—and cask stoppers—bungs). On the east side of the intersection is the Chilmark Library, whose "Island Room" is an ideal rainy-day destination for anyone whose appetite has been whet by the morsels of history presented here. Also hard by the corner is the **Chilmark Store,** a worthy pit stop for cyclists and others in need of a sandwich or slice of pizza (don't be put off by the prices—the portions more than justify them). If your consumer impulse runs to something more stylish than groceries and minor housewares, check out the town's popular **Flea Market,** on the grounds of the Community Church (8:30 a.m.-3:30 p.m. Wednesday and Saturday, end of June through late August or early September), where mostly professional craftspeople, artists, and antique dealers market seconds or blemished wares passed over by regular retail buyers at prices which, while not a steal, are generally well discounted.

With the exception of the village of Menemsha, most of Chilmark is rather leery of tourists. Summer's hordes may pay the bills but

that hasn't alleviated the Not In My Back Yard syndrome. (If you've never thought of yourself as the vanguard of the great unwashed, just attend a local town hearing the next time someone proposes creating a public beachfront reserve and listen to the dire predictions of how you'll ruin the neighborhood. You'd think tourists are just Hell's Angels in beach gear.) But not all Chilmark's inhabitants are loath to receive visitors; nothing's going to faze Lillian Hellman or John Belushi, for example, at their eternal residences in **Abel's Hill Burying Ground,** on South Rd. just under three miles from the West Tisbury's town line. While they're probably the most famous tenants, anyone with an eye for good epitaphs and fine stone carving will take greater interest in the many historic 18th- and 19th-century markers.

Menemsha

Anyone who wants proof that some of the people around here make a living off something besides the tourists can come to this Chilmark village and admire the Coast Guard station poised above the water in the golden light of a late summer afternoon. But the bigger attraction is the fishing fleet in Menemsha Basin, whose catch ends up on tourists' plates all over the island. Watching guys in rubber boots shovel fish into barrels against a backdrop of buoy-covered shacks crowned with whale-shaped weathervanes is undeniably picturesque—especially compared to down-island's retail barrage—but

a fisherman packs the day's catch, Town Pier, Menemsha

it resists any use of the word "quaint." If this place is an anachronism, it's only because so much of the region no longer soils its hands with anything other than cash register keys or touch-tone telephones.

Besides watching sunsets framed by the boat basin's thicket of swaying masts, Menemsha's summer visitors come for hiking, swimming, and seafood in the rough. Cyclists looking for a shortcut to Gay Head—and a chance to avoid some of the hills and punishing headwinds encountered on State Rd.— won't want to miss the **Menemsha Bike Ferry** ($4 one-way, $7 roundtrip, discount for Hostelling International members), which shuttles across Menemsha inlet to West Basin, near the east end of Lobsterville Beach. It operates on demand daily 8 a.m.-6 p.m. from June through early October, weather permitting, but before you make a descent to the Menemsha inlet, check the signs at any of the approaches in Chilmark, West Tis, or Gay Head to confirm whether the ferry is indeed running.

Gay Head

The most remote of the island's six towns, rural Gay Head (year-round pop. 260) seems to stand in sharp relief against the fortunes of its sister communities. The only island town to actually *decline* in population during the 1980s (the rest of the Vineyard posted double-digit percentage gains), Gay Head has an unemployment rate nearly three times the statewide average, and the lowest average household income in all of Massachusetts. By the numbers, it would seem to belong in Appalachia rather than on one of New England's most star-studded resorts (although if the Wampanoag Tribe Council of Gay Head ever obtains legislative approval to build a huge casino on the mainland, you can bet some of those statistics will rebound faster than a lottery winner can yell "Jackpot!"). The numbers, however, don't tell the full story: most of the town's property owners are summer people whose incomes boost the statistics somewhere else—if their accountants let the government know about it at all. Many other residents thrive on an underground economy of cottage artisanry, cash contract work, or investment income that escapes the attention of labor statisticians. With vacant land selling for $50,000-100,000 an acre and Gay Headers' kids tending to go to prestigious colleges and graduate schools, the town might be called many things, but "poor" isn't one of them.

Along with Mashpee on Cape Cod, Gay Head is one of two Massachusetts communities with a significant Native American population—over 35%, according to the last national census. Most are Wampanoags of the Gay Head band, one of the remaining handful of the 50 or so bands that once made up the Wampanoag nation; descendants of two other bands, the Christiantown and Chappaquiddick, also live in the community, although their cultural identity hasn't been maintained well enough to receive the same recognition. If every tribal member lived in Gay Head, they'd outnumber their non-Indian neighbors by more than four to one, but half of the 700-plus-member band lives off-island, and most of the rest live down-island.

In the 17th century, this area belonged to the sachemship known as Aquinnah ("high land"), and most of it stayed under Indian ownership until the 19th century, when condescending schemers pressured or duped native landowners into quite literally giving away the farm. After lengthy legal action, a few hundred acres were finally returned to the Gay Head Wampanoag after they obtained federal recognition in 1987, but there's no reservation—the restored acres came with some strings attached. Not surprisingly, accepting less than full control over a parcel of ancestral land much smaller than hoped for was a controversial price to pay for tribal recognition.

For anyone interested in the Wampanoags' history, the **Gay Head Public Library,** on State Rd. at Church St., tel. (508) 645-9552 (5-7 p.m. Monday, Wednesday, and Friday, and 9:30-1:30 Saturday), has a room devoted to books about and by Native Americans; ask the librarian to suggest a few of local relevance.

Gay Head Cliffs

Declared a National Natural Landmark in 1966, 130-foot high Gay Head Cliffs have been a tourist attraction for as long as tourists have come to the Vineyard. Cliff-climbing is *definitely* off limits—it's dangerous and accelerates the severe erosion of the unanchored clay—but you can admire the antediluvian strata from above or below, depending on whether you take a five- or fifty-minute walk from the parking lot. On clear or partly cloudy evenings, the clifftop overlook provide exceptional front-row seats for watching the sun extinguish itself in the ocean off Rhode Island.

Adding to the photogenic view from the cliffs is the 19th-century red brick **Gay Head Light,** tel. (508) 645-2211, whose alternating red and white flashes warn ships away from the Devil's Bridge, a treacherous line of partially submerged offshore rocks that prompted construction of the original 1799 beacon. Tricky currents and bad weather still sank many a sailing vessel on these rocks, even after the dim lanterns of old were replaced with the powerful Fresnel lens now seen in the yard of the Vineyard Museum; worst among these various disasters was the wreck of the *City of Columbus,* on which more than a hundred of its sleeping passengers died in a few minutes of a winter's night in early 1884.

Although the immediate grounds of the light are fenced off from public access throughout most of the year, on summer weekends (Fri.-Sun.) between June's solstice and September's equinox, the tower and grounds are opened for self-guided sunset tours ($2, free for anyone over 12, free to everyone on Mother's Day). The gates open 90 minutes before sundown and close 30 minutes after. Tours are canceled if the weather is so lousy that the sun can't be seen.

With the exception of a few tacky little gift sheds and fast-food stalls on the path to the clifftop overlook and the homey **Gay Head Gallery,** on State Rd. a short distance west of Lobsterville Rd., tel. (508) 645-9092 (Tues.-Sun. June-early October, weekends off-season), Gay Head is blissfully lacking in commercial attractions. Hungry visitors looking for something other than burgers, fried fish, or diner fare from a lofty cliffside perch have to bring it themselves.

GUIDED TOURS

Tours by bus, boat, and foot are all available in season, and since only one outfit serves each category, you're even spared having to shop around.

The white, pink, and turquoise old school buses of **Martha's Vineyard/Gay Head Sight-seeing** (a.k.a. Island Transport), tel. (508) 627-TOUR, 693-1555, or 693-0058, rendezvous with all incoming ferries in both Vineyard Haven and Oak Bluffs daily until 4 p.m. in season (May-Oct.). You can buy your tickets ($11.50 adults, $3 ages 12 and under) at the Steamship Authority terminal in Woods Hole, or aboard the Hy-Line, Falmouth, and New Bedford ferries en route to the island, and start off your Vineyard holiday with a two-hour narrated trip around all six towns, including a 25-minute stop at the Gay Head Cliffs. The buses pay only a cursory visit to the down-island towns, however, and the tour guides are typically off-island college students whose knowledge of the Vineyard may barely exceed your own. When it comes to identifying celebrity driveways or explaining what happened at Chappaquiddick in 1969, take what they say with a good dash of salt.

For an island tour by boat, try **Captain Gosnold Cruises,** tel. (508) 693-8900 or, in Massachusetts only, (800) 693-8001. Their ticket office is at the Tisbury Market Place, the cluster of shops on Beach Rd. opposite their berth at Pier 44, the same dock used by the New Bedford ferry. On Tuesday, Thursday, or Saturday you could start off the day with a six-hour trip to Cuttyhunk ($40 adults, $20 ages 14 and under) and spend about two and a half hours exploring that tiny capital of the Elizabeth archipelago. Or try the sunset cruise to Menemsha Harbor ($20 adults, $15 kids), with the option of having a fine seafood dinner from that fishing village's fine Home Port Restaurant ($20) delivered to the boat. On Wednesday and Friday, you could try the other trip out along the North Shore to the Gay Head Cliffs (also $20 and $15). A one-hour lobster cruise specifically pitched to kids ($15 and $10) covers the natural history of this snappy crustacean and includes pulling up live specimens for closer look.

Vineyard History Tours offers daily historical walks in season as weather allows ($5-8, depending on tour), by appointment any other time of year. Call (508) 627-8619 for current departure times and starting points. Tours of Edgartown's three Preservation Trust-owned properties and Oak Bluffs' Camp Ground are part of the current repertoire, but, of course, anyone burning with curiosity about the Kennedys will want to catch the "Ghosts, Gossip, and Downright Scandal" tour.

HIKES AND RAMBLES

Nearly a thousand Vineyard acres are available for your recreational use, mostly in the form of small preserves with simple trail systems winding through fields and forests, around ponds and wetlands, and along shorelines and streambeds. All but a handful are free, and nearly all are open dawn to dusk year-round, except during deer hunting week (beginning after Thanksgiving). An excellent, free, island-wide map identifying all accessible conservation properties is available by mail from the Martha's Vineyard Land Bank Commission, P.O. Box 2057, Edgartown 02539, or pick up a copy in person from their 167 Main St. office in Edgartown, tel. (508) 627-7141. Trail maps to individual properties are usually posted at the trailheads nearest car and bike parking; if no map is present, the trail is most likely a straightforward loop or something equally self-evident. For the ultimate peace of mind, pick up a copy of Will Flender's thorough *Walking Trails of Martha's Vineyard,* in local bookstores or directly from the Vineyard Conservation Society (VCS), an advocacy group headquartered at the Mary Wakeman Conservation Center on Lambert's Cove Rd. (RR1 Box 319X, Vineyard Haven 02568; tel. 508-693-9588). Several other land-saving organizations—the Sheriff's Meadow Foundation, The Nature Conservancy, and Vineyard Open Land Foundation—share office space with the VCS at the Wakeman Center; besides selling Flender's book and dispensing free information about their individual missions, the center hosts workshops and fundraisers and is the starting point for anyone interested in hiking around the adjacent 22 acres of ponds and cranberry bogs.

In addition to guided programs held in season at selected properties listed below, both the VCS and the Land Bank conduct off-season monthly walks on island conservation land. The VCS series (every second Sunday, Oct.-March) typically includes at least one hike on privately owned,

VINEYARD LAND BANK — MARTHA'S — COMMISSION — EST. 1986

undeveloped land not otherwise open to the public; the last event of the season is an island-wide beach clean-up on Earth Day in April. The Land Bank series (every first Sunday, Nov.-May) showcases the organization's own fine properties until their culminating full-day cross-island hike on National Trails Day, the first Saturday in June.

Both island weeklies, the *Vineyard Gazette* and the *Martha's Vineyard Times,* announce starting times and meeting places a few days before each walk, or you can get the skinny straight from the friendly staffers at either organization. When choosing your apparel, by the way, remember that these hikes are often wet or muddy.

Final notes: *all* town, county, and private conservation properties ban mountain biking on their trails. Only the State Forest allows it.

And anyone interested in gathering live shellfish at any of the pond- or bayside properties must obtain a town license from the shellfish warden at the appropriate Town Hall.

Felix Neck Wildlife Sanctuary

This Massachusetts Audubon Society property lies on a neck of land jutting out into Sengekontacket Pond, a large windsurfer and waterfowl habitat whose salt water ebbs and flows with the tides in adjacent Cow Bay. A good cross-section of the Vineyard's landscape is found here, from open meadows to woodlands. There's a small freshwater pond attractive to black ducks and mallards, and a bird blind to make their nesting and feeding easier to watch; similarly, patient observers can spy on the spring nesting of fast-diving ospreys—also known as buzzards—atop poles strategically placed in the open margin of the peninsula's pine groves. Throughout summer and fall, there are various scheduled walks with naturalists to introduce you to the sanctuary's wildflowers, birds, turtles, and marine life. Other program highlights include canoe trips, stargazing, snorkeling in Sengekontacket Pond, and even cruises to the Elizabeth Islands (for current events, call 508-627-4850). The entrance is a sandy lane signposted on the Edgartown-Vineyard Haven Rd.; admission is $3. Open daily only in season; between November and May, it's closed Mondays (like most other Mass Audubon sanctuaries).

Mytoi

Midway along Chappaquiddick's sandy Dike Road, the scaly trunks and tangled branches of pitch pine suddenly give way to the improbable sight of a little Japanese-style garden. The creation of Mary Wakeman, a well-known local conservationist, Mytoi (me-toy) is now one of the small gems in the crown of the Trustees of Reservations. Despite sustaining tremendous damage in 1991's Hurricane Bob—including the loss of over 100 mature shade trees—the garden still exudes tranquillity. Even at the zenith of summer, the pond inspires philosophical thoughts; cross the arched bridge to the islet at its center and feel them rise up like morning light. In spring—when the slopes are blanketed with bold daffodils, rhododendrons, dogwood, azaleas, and roses—the windswept beachgrass-covered dunes at the end of the road might as well be halfway around the world. But much work has to be done. Though entry is free, contributions toward the site's restoration are encouraged (note the metal money drop before you get to the pond). A water fountain and bathroom provide amenities rarely found on such rural properties; also, take advantage of the recycling bins for disposing of those empty cans and bottles rolling around your backpack or back seat.

Wasque and Cape Poge

The Trustees of Reservations also own nearly the entire east shore of Chappaquiddick, from the southern end of Katama Bay to Cape Poge Bay, from whose waters are taken some 50% of the state's annual bay scallop harvest. **Cape Poge Wildlife Refuge** encompasses over four miles of this barrier beach, accessible via Dike Bridge at the end of Dike Rd., while **Wasque Reservation** (WAY-skwee) protects a couple more miles of dunes and grassland around Wasque Point. Admission to either or both is $3 (free ages 12 and under) plus $3 parking, June-September, free the rest of the year. Bathrooms, drinking water, and recycling bins for beverage containers are all found at Wasque; at Dike Bridge there is nothing but a pay phone beside the attendant's shack.

Oversand vehicle permits are necessary for driving beyond the parking areas ($110, or $85 for TTOR members; tel. 508-627-7689; air for re-inflating tires is available at Wasque and Mytoi), but be aware that access may be totally denied (even if you have permits) if the endangered piping plover and least tern are nesting on the beach. The dunes are quite fragile, too, anchored by those wisps of beachgrass; since destabilized dunes are more likely to wash or blow away—or choke up the saltmarsh that helps support the rich shellfish beds—you'll notice many warnings posted to stay on existing jeep tracks and boardwalks. If you hate having your freedom circumscribed by such silly sounding restrictions, be warned that nature is the enforcer here as much as any ranger: the beachgrass is riddled with poison ivy.

The summer crowds come mostly for the swimming and surf-fishing (beware of the undertow), but any time of year this shore is unmatched for the simple pleasure of walking until there's nothing but breaking waves and scuttling little sanderlings to keep you company. Birdwatching has gained a steady following, too, with osprey nesting on the pole at the northern end of the refuge, great blue herons stalking crabs through the tidal pools behind the dunes, oystercatchers foraging with their flashy orange bills at the edge of the surf, and ragged formations of sea ducks skimming across the winter ocean. The cedar-covered portions of Cape Poge provide browse for deer and small mammals, most of whom remain invisible but for the occasional footprint or scat pile; if you're lucky, you may catch a glimpse of one of the resident sea otters slipping into a pond on the way up to the 1893 **Cape Poge Light.**

Thanks to the unremitting erosion along Chappaquiddick's outer shore, this is the Vineyard's most transient lighthouse; already, the present wooden tower has been moved three times this century, most recently in 1986. Before being automated in WW II, this lonely post was the one of the many spoils available to the political party controlling the White House: whenever the Presidency changed hands, so, too, would the nation's lighthouses. (Cape Poge's first keeper was appointed by Thomas Jefferson.) Ninety-minute **lighthouse tours** from the gatehouse at the Dike Bridge are offered between Memorial and Columbus Day ($12 adults, $6 kids) at 10 a.m. and 2 p.m. The beacon is also included on three-hour **Cape Poge natural history tours,** tel. (508) 627-3599 ($30 adults, $15 kids), start daily at 8:30 a.m. and 4 p.m. from the Chappy side of the "On Time" ferry. Preregistration is required for these—space is limited. Both tours use special "safari" vehicles to reach the lighthouse.

Naturalist-guided **canoe trips** around Cape Poge Bay or Poucha Pond (poach-a) are another option, priced and scheduled exactly the same as the natural history tours. **Canoe rentals** are also available for the do-it-yourselfer; they're at the Dike Bridge gatehouse for use in Poucha Pond ($25 per half day, $38 per full eight-hour day).

Manuel F. Correllus State Forest

This forest was originally set aside to protect the dwindling population of the heath hen, a relative of the prairie chicken extinguished on the mainland through hunting and habitat loss. But the gesture was undermined by a big forest fire and continued hunting. By 1932, the hen was extinct. In spite of a legacy of tree farming, a blight that's killing off the remaining stands of red pine, and proximity to the island's airport, some trail-savvy islanders consider the state forest a hidden gem. Hikers interested in the Vineyard's floristic communities won't find any better place to sample the island's pitch pine barrens and scrub oak bottoms, for example—and mountain bikers can crisscross the forest on miles of fire roads. If you happen to visit during a snowy winter, you'll find good cross-country skiing through the property, too. Pick up a map and advice from the helpful staff at the forest headquarters, off Airport Rd., tel. (508) 693-2540.

Long Point Wildlife Refuge

Big waves along an exceptional South Shore beach are the draw for summer visitors to this isolated up-island spot ($3 per person plus $7 parking June-Sept.), but birdwatchers and wild blueberry lovers may prefer the trails around the grasslands and shrub-covered heath opposite the high-season parking lot on Long Cove Pond. Interpretive trail guides to the mile-long barrier beach-and-grassland loop are available year-round at the parking-lot bulletin boards, along with the latest schedule of ranger-led tours. The other mile-long trail visits the freshwater marsh along the edge of Long Cove, where in spring and summer you might hear frogs singing for sex, see herons stalking their supper, or spot river otters before they spot you. Spring is also a good time to catch migrating ducks feeding on the ponds and songbirds scouting nesting sites in the woods. Fall is impossible not to love: as the last papery pink salt-spray roses start to fold, the bayberry and huckleberry bushes impart a warm burgundy glow to the heathlands, and the waterfowl stop over again on their way south. On good summer swimming days, you'd do well to consider biking in to avoid being turned away when the parking lot fills, but off season this is a good place to be alone with your thoughts and brisk ocean breezes. In summer, by the way, the 6 p.m. closing is strictly enforced, so don't expect to hang around for sunset views over distant Gay Head unless you sign up for one of the after-hours tours.

Summer access is via Waldron's Bottom Rd. off the Edgartown-West Tisbury Rd.; follow the signs to the high-season parking lot by the beach (fresh water and bathrooms available). Off season, the gate at road's end is closed; mid-September through mid-June, visitors should then use the heavily potholed, single-lane dirt track called Deep Bottom Rd. (again, follow the signs) to get to the facilities-free parking area near the caretaker's cottage.

Sepiessa Point Reservation

Like nearby Long Point, this Land Bank reservation protects some of the planet's last remaining acres of sandplain grasslands, backed by a large swath of woodlands along the edge of Tiah's (rhymes with wise) Cove, one of many slender inlets to Tisbury Great Pond. Since the only public boat access to the Great Pond is via the reservation's cove-side canoe and boat slides, most islanders familiar with this unheralded place know of it by the cove's name instead of the peninsula's. The property sports a short stretch of hard, sandy beach along the pond edge, too, but heed the posted warnings about the broken oyster shells, which are about as friendly to tender, unshod feet as discarded metal sardine cans. At a small pull-out near the reservation entrance—the only parking available to hikers and swimmers (each boat slide has its own handful of spaces)—a signboard identifies the trails that loop through pine-oak woods and converge on the grassy meadows about a mile away. Though quite plain for most of the year, the meadows are good wildflower territory in spring—the bushy rockrose, Nantucket shadbush, and other rare sandplain plants blossom throughout May and June. Summer's insects and autumn's berries bring birds out of the woods to forage throughout the rest of the high season, and if you look carefully before they all get eaten, at the end of summer, you may spot fruit-bearing creepers of the wild grape vine that supposedly inspired the island's name. Northern harriers, another of the state's rare species, have occasionally been sighted hunting in the meadows for rodents and insects.

Free year-round, Sepiessa Point is signposted with the Land Bank logo along Tiah's Cove Rd., a dead-end fork off New Lane in West Tisbury. Only about a mile and a quarter from the Edgartown-West Tisbury Rd., the reservation is accessible to most bikes and even up-island shuttle riders who request a stop at New Lane, almost across from the volunteer fire station.

Cedar Tree Neck

Ask your innkeepers or island hosts to recommend their favorite hiking spot and nine times out of ten they'll nominate this property of the Sheriff's Meadow Foundation. Located on West Tisbury's North Shore, it fully earns its reputation with nearly two miles of looping trails through woods, wetlands, and dunes; along a brook; along a morainal ridge; and along the beach. A kid-friendly pamphlet—available in the map kiosk at the parking lot—provides interpretive detail on one trail; others are summarized on memoranda posted in the kiosk by the property managers. The trails were designed in part by Anne Hale, whose locally published book *From Moraine to Marsh: A Field Guide to Martha's Vineyard* is the best natural history companion for walks around the Neck.

Swimming is prohibited along the property's gorgeous Vineyard Sound shoreline, and a summer attendant enforces this restriction—part of the terms that made the land public. As is the case nearly everywhere on the Vineyard, neighboring houses are never far from sight, but the beauty of the Neck will put them clean

out of your mind. In fact, don't be surprised if a scant half hour of soaking up the views from the beach has you forgetting your *own* home. Located at the end of Obed Daggett Rd., off Indian Hill Rd., Cedar Tree Neck is free all year. A bike rack is provided, but bathrooms aren't.

Waskosim's Rock Reservation

Straddling the West Tisbury-Chilmark town line near the headwaters of pristine Mill Brook are nearly 200 acres almost straight out of the 19th century: abandoned farmland bordered by drystone walls, the ever-encroaching forest, and wetlands that feed that brook, a vital tributary of Tisbury Great Pond. The waters of the brook are so clean that they're home to the brook lamprey, a species whose hypersensitivity to pollutants has made it widely endangered.

Presumably named after a local Wampanoag, Waskosim's Rock is a giant cracked boulder that marked a 17th-century boundary between English and Indian lands. Natural forest succession has obscured the views once afforded from the rock itself, but fine down-island vistas may yet be found by the cleared fields rising out of the Mill Brook valley and from occasional breaks in the hilltop forest. Since much of the abutting private property is equally undeveloped, trails through the reservation's varied habitats are as good for birders as for anyone looking for a glimpse of Vineyard Haven's water tower. Conspicuous summer visitors include flickers, cuckoos, blue jays, and ovenbirds (in the dry oak forest at the southern, high end of the property); cedar waxwings, swallows, song sparrows, and white-eyed vireos (out on the old pastures); and northern parula warblers (around the scrubby red maple swamp near the trailhead).

The reservation's entrance, and parking for both bikes and cars, is signposted with a discreet Land Bank logo beside North Road a few hundred feet on the Chilmark side of the Chilmark-West Tisbury boundary.

Fulling Mill Brook

Although drivers on Chilmark's Middle Road will most likely miss its small trailhead parking lot, the relaxing half-mile walk through the Fulling Mill Brook Preserve is worth turning around for. The quiet, lazy trout stream grows garrulous and boulder-strewn as it runs through mixed hardwood forest down the shoulder of Abel's Hill, part of the morainal ridge that runs between Tisbury and Gay Head. Shrubby savanna interspersed with oaks and a spot of wildflower-filled meadow occupy some of the slopes over the stream.

The brook takes its name from the mill that used its waters in the process of "fulling" cloth—making it heavier through shrinking and pressing—back in the 1800s. In the 1700s, several tanners treated hides in this neck of the woods, too. Today, decaying leaf litter and fresh breezes have replaced the tannic scent of curing leather. In summer, woodland songbirds abound along the brook's path, but proximity to those drier upland habitats means you're as apt to hear mourning doves and song sparrows as the quiet call of the whippoorwill.

While cars are limited to the Middle Rd. lot, cyclists can take advantage of a second bike rack, on South Rd., at the preserve's lower end, beside an impressive stone and wrought-iron gateway.

Peaked Hill Reservation
Three of the island's highest points (some especially good vantages for Gay Head sunsets, views over the Elizabeth Islands to the Southeastern Massachusetts coast, and hawkwatching) include the old WW II garrison site Radar Hill and 311-foot Peaked (two syllables, not one) Hill. Both crown ridges whose slopes were once nearly girdled with luxury homes but whose timely acquisition by the Land Bank preserved them for public enjoyment. Numerous large moss- and lichen-covered glacial erratics, chunks of granite gouged out of mountains or exposed bedrock farther north and deposited here during the last ice age, dot the wooded trails. Some of the stones form the panoramic ledges; others are distinctive enough to have their own names (such as Wee Devil's Bed) or serve as reminders of the late 18th- and early 19th-century farmers who cleared much of this land (their pin-and-feather technique for splitting huge boulders into gateposts and foundation slabs is writ large on the edges of unused stones).

The military has also left some marks here, too. They're mostly steel-and-concrete tower footings and broken asphalt, but notice, too, the full-grown tree grown up through the old Radar Hill fencing, its trunk indelibly tattooed by the rusty chain link. The reservation now plays host to a large herd of white-tailed deer, whose distinctive bite can be seen in the severed ends of lower branches on small trees and shrubs all over these 70 acres. The rich forest understory and dense thickets also provide vital cover for numerous small mammals and birds, including an array of finches, sparrows, swallows, warblers, and woodpeckers. Conspicuous but locally uncommon species such as yellow- and black-billed cuckoos, killdeer, and bluebirds have been sighted here, and the relatively high elevations attract red-winged hawks and American kestrels during both breeding and migration seasons.

The entrance turnoff is signposted on Tabor House Rd., a half mile from Middle Road. Parking, maps, and a bike rack are located eight-tenths of a mile up the potholed dirt lane—always take the right fork or you'll have to back out of several private driveways.

Menemsha Hills
Part of the reason the vista from the shoulder of Peaked Hill is so attractive is that the wooded hills bordering Vineyard Sound on the other side of North Road are protected by TTOR's Menemsha Hills Reservation. Several miles of trails offer walkers oak tree shade, hilltop views, and bracing winds along the lip of the 150-foot marine scarp over Vineyard Sound. Ruminate over the landscape, where sheep once grazed within the property's drystone walls; watch birds gorge themselves on the heath's summer berry crop; or pretend you're Thomas Hart Benton, the Missouri-born painter who summered here in Chilmark for 56 years, and stroll the rocky beach (no swimming!) with an artist's eye for the play of light and water upon the rough coast. In late fall or winter, you might spot harbor seals basking on the rocks or bobbing in the surf offshore.

A TTOR white-on-green sign marks the reservation's parking lot off North Rd. in Chilmark, a little over half a mile west of the junction with Tabor House Road. Admission is free.

CATCHING WIND AND WAVES

Beach Basics
When it comes to beaches, the Vineyard has a little something for just about everybody, from

body surfers to wading toddlers. Most, but not all, of the island's two dozen beaches are free and open to the public. Several on private conservation land charge seasonal access fees, and five town-owned beaches are restricted in summer to local residents and guests. Parking is not a given: some places have little or none, and some charge up to $20 for the privilege.

There's no nude beach per se, although discreet naturists are tolerated in select areas. Private ownership extends down to the low-water line, though, so respect beach fences, No Trespassing signs, and community standards for shedding your Speedo.

As a rule, the strongest surf is found along the Atlantic-facing south shore, since there's no land between here and Hispaniola to dampen the ocean swells. These beaches are the first to close during foul summer weather, when prevailing southwesterly winds propel huge waves up the shore. In their wake are new underwater sandbars that build the kind of tall breakers beloved by serious boogie-boarders but hazardous to windsurfers and their equipment. Parents and timid swimmers should also be mindful of this shore's strong undertow.

Until the onslaught of winter northeasters, the east shore—facing Nantucket Sound—and the north shore—facing the Vineyard Sound—are milder. As a rule, they're also warmer. North shore beaches are reputed to have the clearest water and definitely feature the best sunsets.

Vineyard Haven Beaches

Vineyard Haven has five public beaches, three of which are within a mile of downtown. Tiny **Owen Park Beach** is only a block from the Steamship Authority (SSA) dock, but it gets more use as a boat launch than as a serene spot for catching rays. Since the breakwater keeps the surf away, it's probably best appreciated by really small kids—but if you have some time to kill before catching the ferry, it's good for soaking tired feet. The area to the left of the wooden town pier is private, by the way. From the SSA, either cut through the parking lot behind the bank, or step up to Main and follow the one-way traffic one block to the bandstand; that's Owen Park. The beach is at the bottom of the hill.

Farther up Main St., about three-quarters of a mile from the cinema, is the **Tisbury Town Beach,** (also called Bayside), an 80-foot sliver of sandy harbor shoreline between stone jetties at the end of Owen Little Way, from which you can watch the comings and goings at the Vineyard Haven Yacht Club next door. Free swimming lessons are given here in summers. On the other side of the harbor, about three-quarters of a mile along Beach Rd. toward Oak Bluffs, is **Lagoon Bridge Park,** on Lagoon Pond. This, too, is enjoyed more by waterskiers and windsurfers than sunbathers. (It's also the only one out of the town's four beach parks without any parking.)

Vineyard Haven's most attractive swimming beaches are about two miles from downtown near the west end of Lake Tashmoo. Facing Woods Hole and the Elizabeth Islands across Vineyard Sound (that's big Naushon stretching away to the left and tiny Nonamesset almost opposite), the ocean portion of **Wilfrid's Pond Preserve** is exemplary of the north shore: little to no surf, light winds if any, no audible motorized boats, and water that stays relatively warm and shallow for some distance from shore. It's also quite small, which is why parking (free) is limited to space for five cars. Wilfrid's Pond itself is *not* open to swimmers, but the bench overlooking its brackish waters is a fine spot to forget worldly cares. Another half mile past Wilfrid's, at the end of the same heavily gullied and potholed lane, is **Tashmoo Beach** or Herring Creek Beach (also with free parking). At first glance, it's disappointingly small, but walk back along the sandy lakeshore and you'll find the part favored by regulars. To reach either beach, make a right at the end of Daggett Ave. on the better-maintained of the two sandy tracks there by the fire hydrant.

Oak Bluffs Beaches

Running discontinuously below Seaview Avenue's sidewalk promenade is the **OB Town Beach,** the most central of OB's four. Except when low tides expose a decent swath of sand, it's narrow and often gravelly—especially at the northern end, between the harbor entrance and the ferry pier at Ocean Park. Near the foot of huge, grassy Waban Park is the most pleasant and popular part, nicknamed the Inkwell, with lifeguards and swimming lessons in summer. South of the Inkwell, the **Joseph A. Sylvia State Beach** stretches in a broad two-mile crescent between OB and Edgartown (which calls its end

Bend-in-the-Road Beach). Backed by the windsurfing haven of Sengekontacket Pond, facing the gentle kid-friendly waves of Cow Bay, and easily accessible by the paved OB-Edgartown bike path, State Beach is deservedly one of the island's most popular.

Facing Vineyard Haven Harbor is calm, clear little **Eastville Beach** (minimal parking) beside the Lagoon drawbridge and riprap-lined channel underneath. Although lacking the sheer beachcombing breadth of State Beach, it's a good dipping spot for cyclists or neighboring cottage renters, and a prized spot for sunset views. The truly handkerchief-sized beach at **Sailing Camp Park** (a former Lagoon Pond girl-scout camp off Barnes Rd. in the wooded residential edge of town), is only recommendable as a put-in for windsurfers—despite the diving raft offshore.

Edgartown Beaches

When it comes to public beaches, Edgartown is arguably the most well endowed on the island, with surf of all sizes and miles of sand. Plenty of athletic-looking, bronze-bodied young surfers and swimmers make **South Beach** the Vineyard's answer to Southern California, although easy access from town ensures that everybody can see and be seen on this lively three-mile strand (by the way, the security guard at the far western end of the beach should convince anyone skeptical of the idea that some islanders enforce their waterfront property rights rather rigidly; he no longer packs a sidearm, but that's a small improvement). Swimmers who don't want to battle the undertow may prefer the warmer waters of enclosed Katama Bay, accessible from **Norton Point,** the narrow barrier that divides bay from ocean at the eastern end of the beach, or **Katama Point Preserve,** a small, sandy chunk of Land Bank property adjacent to the town landing on Edgartown Bay Road. County-owned Norton Point, by the way, is the only part of the Vineyard outside of Chappaquiddick that permits off-road vehicles (required $50 ORV permits are available from the Treasurer's Office in the County Courthouse on Main Street).

Facing Nantucket Sound on the combined outer shores of Chappy's Cape Poge Wildlife Refuge and Wasque Reservation, **East Beach** and **Chappaquiddick State Beach**—still known to many locals as Leland Beach—constitute

Edgartown's other breathtaking waterfront. Over four miles of austere, unspoiled barrier beach backed by fragile grass-covered dunes, salt marsh, and salt ponds await swimmers and beach walkers. Between early June and early September, expect to pay admission ($3 adults, free for ages 15 and under) and parking ($3), and expect to find some bird-nesting areas roped off. Since the 1995 opening of a new bridge over Poucha Pond at the end of Dike Rd., each end of the shore now has its own access point, although if misguided Kennedy souvenir hunters steal enough chunks from the new timber span it may eventually be necessary to go back to a single entrance—down at Wasque Point. Swimmers should, however, stay far from the Point itself due to the dangerous riptides.

For anyone seeking watery relief within easy walking distance of downtown should make a beeline for **Chappy Point Beach,** an attractive, calm-water outer harbor spot on Chappaquiddick, about twice as long as a football field and within a short stroll of the "On Time" ferry. Flanking the squat tower of Edgartown Light on Starbuck Neck are two more beaches—**Lighthouse** and **Fuller Street**—half a mile of mostly sand, weather depending, as suited to views of the historic Edgartown Inn or close-up portraits of the lighthouse as to sun-bathing or swimming. Watch for broken glass, though—the salt-spray

Chappaquiddick's East Beach, Cape Poge Wildlife Refuge

rose bushes along the access paths have traditionally been a place for inconsiderate drinkers to toss their empties.

Up-Island Beaches

For the duration of summer, up-island towns restrict most of their beaches to residents or renters. (Guests of area B&Bs and inns *may* also be able to obtain beach permits; inquire at check-in. Don't think the permits apply only to cars: beach attendants will check them no matter how many wheels—or feet—you come in on.) So **Lambert's Cove**, in West Tisbury; **Lucy Vincent** and **Squibnocket** Beaches, in Chilmark; and **Philbin** and **Head of the Pond** Beaches, in Gay Head, are thus off-limits to most visitors from June through September—although at gorgeous Lambert's Cove, nonresidents are free to come catch the sun's last golden rays 6-9 p.m. But despair not: the publicly accessible alternatives are by no means negligible.

West Tisbury, for example, has a pair of conservation properties along the South Shore whose mix of pond and ocean beaches amply reward the effort of reaching them. **Long Point Wildlife Refuge**, another property of TTOR, has half a mile of dune-backed beach along the Atlantic that rarely gets congested—thanks to the strict limit on the number of vehicles admitted (arrive early on hot, clear days, and walk west from the parking lot for more elbow room). June through early September, admission is $3 for anyone over 15, plus $7 parking; TTOR members get in free. To get there, turn off the Edgartown-West Tisbury Rd. onto Waldron's Bottom Rd. (look for the TTOR sign) and then follow the arrows. Just west of Long Point is the Land Bank's **Sepiessa Point Reservation**, with a small beach along the edge of Tisbury Great Pond (watch for sharp oyster shells on the beach). The pond itself is a body of salt water and marsh now hemmed in on the ocean side by barrier dunes (private) that are breached twice a year to maintain the pond's salinity, vital to maintaining its shellfish population. This place is virtually unknown even to most Vineyarders, so don't be surprised if you have it to yourself. Though free, parking is extremely limited; beachgoers should use the first trailhead pullout and leave the southerly ones for folks who have boats to schlep. The walk to the beach from the upper trailhead is just over a mile, mostly through woods.

Menemsha Beach is Chilmark's most accessible—a big, family-friendly north shore spot with plenty of parking, food, restrooms, and views of the local fishing fleet returning to adjacent Menemsha Harbor; from the village center, follow signs for Dutcher Dock. By contrast, the Land Bank's **Chilmark Pond Preserve**, off South Rd. opposite Abel's Hill Burying Ground, offers what's tantamount to a private beach club, with the lesser of 10 vehicles or 40 people allowed onto the property at any one time. The preserve's small piece of the south shore lies just east of permit-only Lucy Vincent Beach. Lucy Vincent is regarded by some as the island's finest beach, but don't get your hopes up—to even reach the ocean dunes, you must bring a canoe or kayak and paddle diagonally across Chilmark Pond (be sure to read the lengthy posted explanations of where you can and cannot land on the opposite shore). In the end, it's one plum that may stay tantalizingly out of reach, despite being free and public.

Arguably the best public swathe of south shore surf and sand is at the Land Bank's **Moshup Beach** and adjacent **Gay Head Public Beach**, just a scant half-mile or so from the famous Gay Head Cliffs. Limited parking is available—for a punitive $20 in summer—in the lot at the State Rd. loop atop the cliffs, near the public restrooms (where, incidentally, the down-island shuttle bus stops). Cyclists will find free racks down Moshup Trail at the beach itself. East of the well-marked Land Bank property line is residents-only Philbin Beach; in the other direction, toward the base of the cliffs, is the island's principal nude bathing area. Up until a few years ago, it wasn't uncommon to see people giving themselves all-over paint jobs with the richly colored clay from the cliffs, but lately enforcement of the prohibition against all climbing, digging, and souvenir-taking from this Wampanoag-owned National Landmark has been sharply increased. The strict rules are not the work of mere spoilsports: clay removal artificially hastens erosion. Simply walking around the base of the spectacular marine scarp, however, is perfectly legit.

Gay Head's only other public shore is sheltered **Lobsterville Beach**, a mecca for surfcasting anglers. The absolute ban on parking on Lobsterville Rd. makes access difficult, however. Gay Head house renters and inn guests who obtain town parking permits (and the lucky few who snatch up the three or four spaces available for nonresidents) can park a mile away in the small lot at the end of West Basin Rd., just across the narrow channel from the fishing boats in Menemsha Basin; otherwise, it's a two-mile walk from the Gay Head bus stop up at the clifftop loop.

By far the best non-automotive approach is via the Bike Ferry from Menemsha, when it's operating (June-Oct.). Of course, if it's swimming rather than fishing that you want, save yourself a mile walk or ride and stick to state-owned **West Jetty,** at West Basin; despite the protection from prevailing southwesterly winds, Lobsterville is generally much too rocky to stretch out a towel on (although it should be pointed out that the offshore eelgrass and crab beds aren't everyone's idea of tactile pleasure).

Windsurfing, Sea Kayaking, and Canoeing
Though not the cheapest, Vineyard Haven's **Wind's Up!,** on Beach Rd. past the big gas tanks, tel. (508) 693-4252, is the island's best all-around source for hourly rentals of sailboards, sea kayaks, canoes, bodyboards, and just about anything else that can skim across water under power of wind, wave, or paddle. The friendly folks at this we've-got-everything emporium at Lagoon Harbor Park also offer lessons for nearly everything they rent or sell, provide car racks if you want to try the waters in another town, and can arrange delivery to anywhere on the Vineyard for stuff you rent by the week. A small-group introductory windsurfing lesson is $45, while a full eight-hour "certification" course—two days of coaching plus three additional practice hours scheduled at your leisure—runs $90. Sailboard rentals range from $14 an hour to $175 a week (more for expert-level boards), with a 10-hour rental card for $85. Sea kayaks rent for $12 per hour, $50 per day, or $150 per week (slightly more for tandem models); lessons are $25-45 per hour depending on whether you join a group or opt for one-on-one instruction. Canoe rentals run $14 per hour, $40 per half-day, $60 per day. Lifejackets are included in the rental prices—so

are wetsuits, for windsurfing lessons and hourly rentals.

Of course, if you're serious about becoming a sea kayaker, you probably want to take lessons from a serious paddler committed to the sport rather than simply someone cashing in on a hot new trend. You may want to try and book a lesson at **John Moore's Kayaks of Martha's Vineyard,** tel. (508) 693-3885. Two- to two-and-a-half-hour beginner's lessons ($25 per hour, plus $25 for a boat) cover all the basics—equipment, strokes, safety and rescue—but he'll tailor lessons to suit your skills (and rent or even sell equipment for use after completing a course). Ask about his intensive full-day workshops in August if you're hooked and can fit them into your schedule. John's business is mobile, so just phone to arrange an appropriate outdoor classroom. Off-season requests aren't a problem, either—he's a year-round resident, and even has drysuits for arctic souls who want to play in nippy April or November.

After mastering the basics, consider joining Rick Floyd's **Island Paddle Tours,** tel. (508) 693-7104, for a three-hour guided sea kayak trip (May-Oct., $45 per person). He's got equipment for hourly rentals, too ($12 for the first hour, $10 for each additional hour, $60 per day). As another mobile businessman, he can also make down-island deliveries and pick-ups free of charge.

Lagoon and Sengekontacket Ponds are the best spots on the island for beginning and intermediate windsurfers; they're great for kayakers, too. Good winds and safety from big ships make them a pair of two-mile-long playpens—although Sengekontacket can get too shallow at really low tides and Lagoon sometimes buzzes with waterskiers. Each is accessible from the adjacent public beaches. (If you brought your own rig to the island by car, Sailing Park Camp in OB is the only Lagoon Pond public access with parking.)

Strong currents and prevailing offshore winds make Cow Bay (in front of State Beach) and enclosed Katama Bay (accessible from the town boat ramp on Katama Bay Rd. in Edgartown) the province of more experienced windsurfers and paddlers; the waters of Vineyard Sound off Menemsha Beach are also generally too choppy for novices. And Vineyard Haven Harbor is strictly for experts, given the heavy ferry traffic.

Whether you bring your own canoe or the means to transport a rental, you'll find several fine salt- and freshwater ponds worth exploring, including Tisbury Great Pond, at Sepiessa Point, and Poucha Pond, at Wasque Reservation. Town-maintained landings provide access to three more bodies of salt water: Lake Tashmoo (ramp and pier at end of Lake St.); Katama Bay (small landing at Katama Point, off Edgartown Bay Rd.); and Menemsha Pond (boat ramp at the end of Lobsterville Rd. in Gay Head, but parking requires resident permit). Guided canoe outings (including canoe) are also scheduled in summer by the Massachusetts Audubon Society, tel. (508) 627-4850, and the Trustees of Reservations, tel. (508) 627-3599, at Felix Neck and Cape Poge wildlife sanctuaries, respectively.

Sailing

Local waters are a day-sailor's delight. If you've left your yacht in San Diego, you can rent or charter something here, from a little Sunfish to a big sloop—or catch a scheduled cruise with one of several operators. The king of the roost is undoubtedly the Coastwise Packet Company's square topsail schooner, Shenandoah, but unless you're a Vineyard fifth-grader taking part in the vessel's sailing program for island schools (or can afford to book the entire ship for a week), consider boarding Coastwise's meticulously restored pilot schooner, the Alabama, built in Pensacola in 1926, for one of two daily summer outings. Visit the Coastwise office on Vineyard Haven Harbor by the Black Dog Tavern to book a spot ($50), or call (508) 693-1699 for reservations or more information.

Several other boats sail out of Vineyard Haven Harbor: the Violet, for example, tel. (508) 693-5597, a 1911 gaff-rigged ketch (three-hour cruises thrice daily in summer) that observant film students may recognize from its appearance in Martin Scorcese's Age of Innocence. The 54-foot ketch Laissez Faire, tel. (508) 693-1646, a classic John Alden-designed wooden beauty, is available for half-day, full-day, or overnight sailings ($60-300 per person). Designed and built on the island, the 40-foot gaff-rigged sloop Liberty, from Spindrift Charters, tel. (508) 693-4400, also schedules a couple of outings each day from June through October, often including a sunset trip ($65 per person).

If you want more than just a little three-hour cruise on which you're served nothing but cheese and crackers and someone else plays skipper while you feel the wind and spray, you're looking for a term charter. ("Bareboat charters," the arrangement whereby you flash your skipper's license and sign a lot of expensive pieces of paper and walk away with a big boat at your command for a week, aren't available on the Vineyard.) Gannon & Benjamin Marine Railway, in Vineyard Haven, tel. (508) 693-4658, specializes in wooden boat construction and repair and offers term charters from May through October aboard their 64-foot schooner, When and If; call for a brochure or visit their busy office in the M.V. Shipyard on Beach Rd. By the day or week, they'll provide boat and crew if you provide the passengers (up to 15).

Edgartown's **Mad Max Sailing Adventures,** 31 Dock St., tel. (508) 627-7500, offers cruises around Nantucket Sound aboard its 60-foot catamaran. So does the schooner Good Fortune, tel. (508) 627-3445.

Prefer solo sailing—or beginners' lessons on something you can haul out of the water without a crane? **Wind's Up!,** 95 Beach Rd., tel. (508) 693-4252, rents Sunfish and similar-sized boats for $16 per hour, $65 per day; or slightly larger catamarans for $22 per hour, $95 per day. Private instruction runs $45 per hour (five lessons for $180), or two people can split the $55 per hour price of a lesson ($110 per person for five lessons).

Power-Assisted Water Sports

Mark Clarke of **Martha's Vineyard Parasailing & Waterskiing,** tel. (508) 693-2838, is the man to call if you have an itch to sail over water: for $50 ($85 for two rides), he'll rig you up on a platform on the back of his turbo-powered boat and tow you up 600 feet in the air over Vineyard Haven Harbor for a good 10-15 minute ride. Since dips in the water upon returning to earth are entirely optional, you can bring your camcorder without fear of submerging it and give the folks back home a satellite view of New England, including the Newport Bay Bridge in Rhode Island on the western horizon, 25 miles away. If you'd rather stay on the surface of the water, he can take care of that, too, with everything from beginner's lessons to trick waterskiing tips, regular skis, kneeboards, Bump & Ride inner tubes . . . you name it, from $100 per first hour, $80 for each additional hour. Catch him at the dock in Vineyard Haven's Owen Park daily in good weather from Memorial Day to Columbus Day.

Soaring

Katama Airfield, off Herring Creek Road, is where you'll find the island branch of **Soaring Adventures of America,** tel. (508) 627-3833 or (800) SOARING (Mon.-Fri. only), a national outfit (with 100 locations coast to coast). On clear days June through August, your enthusiastic pilot, Rob Wilkinson, will give you a gull's-eye view of the Vineyard from his self-propelled sailplane, or motorglider.

ENTERTAINMENT AND NIGHTLIFE

A variety of groups keep the performing arts alive on the island, often in casual surroundings such as local churches and school auditoriums. Professional theater, however, does have a home of its own: **The Vineyard Playhouse,** on Church St. in Vineyard Haven, box office tel. (508) 696-6300, off-season 693-6450, presents some half-dozen mostly contemporary works by mostly American playwrights on the main stage between late June and Labor Day (performances 8 p.m. Tues.-Sun.; $25), followed by such perennial off-season events as a fall new-play competition, a winter holiday show, and a spring short-play festival. The Playhouse also stages a couple of classics—such as Shakespeare and Greek drama—in the outdoor **Tisbury Amphitheater,** near the corner of W. Spring St. and State Rd., beside beautiful Lake Tashmoo, in July and August (5 p.m. Tues.-Sun., under $10). Previews of all indoor shows are half price, by the way, and rush tickets are discounted $10, so if you happen to catch an early dinner in town, it's a cinch to stroll by after and see if there's a pair of good seats left for dessert.

Named after the local resident and Broadway star whose philanthropy made it possible, nearby **Katharine Cornell Memorial Theater,** in Vineyard Haven's town hall, on Spring St., hosts community theater, chamber music, and an occasional film that isn't commercial enough to make it to the island cinemas. Consult the island papers or check the display case in front of the building to find out what's currently playing.

Modern dance is the bailiwick of **The Yard,** an up-island artists' colony founded in the early 1970s and located off Middle Rd. in Chilmark, close to Beetlebung Corner, tickets and schedule, tel. (508) 645-9662. Their Barn Theatre hosts a season of dance performances by colony residents at least one weekend a month from May-September, often including premieres of improvisational works that will next appear (at much higher prices) in New York City. Real traditional New England **contra and square dances,** sponsored by the Country Dance Society, tel. (508) 693-5627 or 693-9374, take place monthly off-season, Sept.-May, at the Chilmark Community Center and West Tisbury's Old Ag Hall. Beginners are welcome; call for schedule and dates, or consult newspaper calendar listings.

Diversity is the adjective for Edgartown's **Performing Arts Center,** in the Old Whaling Church, tel. (508) 627-4442, whose calendar typically ranges from big names in acoustic and spoken performance—such as Arlo Guthrie and Spaulding Gray—to antiques auctions and assorted other community events. One regular on the church schedule is the **Martha's Vineyard Chamber Music Society,** tel. (508) 645-9446, whose series of weekly concerts in July and August are performed once (on Monday nights) in Edgartown and then (on Tuesday) at the Chilmark Community Center.

Another frequent contributor to the high season cultural mix is Oak Bluff's octagonal Union Chapel, on the upper end of Circuit Ave. Free organ recitals, tel. (508) 645-2767, fill the warmly resonant wooden interior on summer Wednesdays at noon, while a variety of other musical offerings—from Shaker songs to piano jazz, tel. (508) 693-5350—fills up many an evening between the end of June and the end of August.

Clubs and Pubs

The Vineyard's answer to Planet Hollywood sits out on the airport's entrance road: the **Hot Tin Roof,** tel. (508) 693-1137, is a local institution (a former hangar) made famous as a low-rent dive featuring intimate performances by friends and contemporaries of co-owner Carly Simon. After passing through other hands and eventually into bankruptcy, the Tin Roof was resurrected in 1995 by Simon and a few other local luminaries whose collective influence and bankroll ensure that big-name national performers continue to make use of the state-of-the-art stage and sound system behind the meticulously restored exterior dilapidation and a wall-sized evocation of Thomas Hart Benton's Vineyard paintings. Local bands; comedy; and reggae, jazz, and R&B groups drawn from the mainland also appear. The place also offers memberships: for a few thousand dollars you can avoid being excluded by the guardians of the gate. Handicap accessible and smoke-free, the club is open Thurs.-Sat. in May and through mid-October, and seven nights a week mid-June through Labor Day. Call for the latest performance schedule.

Unshaken by the Tin Roof's celebrity appeal, "The A.C.," or **Atlantic Connection,** on Circuit Ave. in OB, holds its own with a young crowd interested in live club bands and deejays—and occasional appearances by emerging major-label artists on regional tours. Adjacent **Seasons** and the **Rare Duck,** the **Lampost,** and **The Ritz,** across the street, are all bars that do their utmost to uphold lower Circuit Avenue's reputation as a party street, sometimes against a background of live music, but more often against loud conversation and ESPN. After the summer crowds abate, Seasons trades some of its dining tables for pool tables; the Lampost and Rare Duck close down completely.

Several island restaurants are known for their musical offerings, particularly **Lola's,** the Southern-styled restaurant at the Island Inn on Beach Rd. in OB, tel. (508) 693-5007 or 693-5946, whose "Back Room" offers plenty of live blues and jazz year-round (nightly in season, Thurs.-Sat. off). Summer Sundays, the whole restaurant gets its spirits raised and its soul saved with a rousing Gospel brunch. For more of a piano-bar atmosphere—albeit an occasionally rockin', R&B piano bar—check out **David's Island House,** tel. (508) 693-4516, also in OB on Circuit Avenue. For a taste of the acoustic cafe scene, head to the **Wintertide Coffeehouse,** at Five Corners, in Vineyard Haven, for some of the best in folk music, from big names on tour to up-and-coming artists just gaining a following—all at affordable prices—year-round. A nonprofit, volunteer-driven, community-supported place, the

Wintertide also accommodates improv comedy, open mike nights, and, on Sunday afternoon, free jazz. True folkies will want to stick around until after Labor Day to reap the fruits of the annual Singer/Songwriters Retreat, in late September. Besides being the kid-friendliest club on the island, the cafe is alcohol- and smoke-free. Call (508) 693-8830 to hear the calendar of upcoming concerts, 693-8832 to make reservations with the box office (they'll hold tickets for off-island arrivals up to an hour before showtime).

Celluloid and the Spoken Word
The usual major commercial releases fill the screens of the island's four first-run movie houses throughout the summer. Come fall, Oak Bluff's downtown Strand and Island theaters go dark, leaving the off-season cinemaniac beholden to Vineyard Haven's intimate Capawock theater, on Main St., or Edgartown's completely modern two-screen Entertainments Cinemas, 65 Main St. above the Main St. Diner, tel. (508) 627-8008. All the island's movie schedules are listed in the weekly papers, or call (508) 627-MOVY for the three besides Edgartown's.

The Vineyard's creative community includes plenty of writers and poets who take to the bully pulpits of the public libraries on a fairly regular basis, or pop up for the occasional bookstore appearance and charity benefit. Again, the calendar of the Martha's Vineyard Times is the best resource for specific announcements of upcoming readings.

ACCOMMODATIONS

Any skeptic who doubts the Vineyard's hot-spot reputation obviously hasn't tried to book a room here in summer—when the island's 100-plus inns, B&Bs, motels, hotels, guest houses, and resorts are as full as Las Vegas on a Saturday night. Demand is strong enough to keep many innkeepers busy playing their annual game of brinkmanship with visitors, ratcheting up room rates and lengthening minimum-stay requirements until customers cry uncle. So far, most visitors aren't blinking, so some two-thirds of the island's rooms now easily top $100, and about the same fraction won't accept single-night bookings (and not only in high season but also on weekends and holidays most of the year). If these stats make *you* blink, don't give up hope—just modify your expectations. Staying flexible with your travel dates, sharing a bathroom, accepting smaller quarters, and settling for rooms without views are all tactics for maximizing your chance of locating lodging. Leaving junior at home may help, too, since most B&Bs and small inns cultivate a kid-free atmosphere; as a rule, the fewer antiques or the larger the establishment, the more likely it welcomes families.

Speaking of expectations, traditional B&B lovers should be warned that full breakfasts are possibly the island's rarest amenity, thanks to various local business and health codes. Barely a dozen places on the entire island serve something more than muffins and beverages with a side of fruit or cereal. If waking up to eggs Benedict, fresh fruit pancakes, or crepes is why you're choosing a B&B, inquire carefully about what's for breakfast *before* guaranteeing that three-night reservation with the non-refundable deposit.

Looking for a place with a private beach? You can count the number of candidates on your hands (and most of the beaches are like small sandboxes on busy boat-filled harbors anyway). As an alternative, consider up-island accommodations that afford guests the privilege of visiting large, beautiful, town beaches restricted to local residents—or try for one of the many rooms basically across the street from Oak Bluffs' or Edgartown's broad public beaches. Off-season's popular object of desire—the bedroom warmed by a nice crackling winter fire—is likewise available at just a dozen or so properties, although a score more have hearths in living rooms or other common areas. Can you sit by the fire and watch Neptune hurl waves against the shore outside? Only from a distance: this island is made of sand, not stone; any lodging built that close to any coastline not reinforced by concrete would wash away in a year. Private fireplaces and full breakfasts? Again, mostly no, but two exceptions (Aldworth Manor and Thorncroft Inn) are cited below.

Budget: under $35

The Vineyard's only true budget accommodation is West Tisbury's **Hostelling International Martha's Vineyard** (April 1-Nov. 15; $12 members, $17 nonmembers), a rambling, cedar-shin-

gled Cape-style structure at the edge of the state forest on an isolated stretch of the Edgartown-West Tisbury Road. For anyone unfamiliar with the concept, many hostels now offer private rooms for families and couples, but when this one was designed, in the 1950s (it's the first American youth hostel built specifically for the purpose), the prevailing ethic called for stacking hostelers like kids at summer camp—20 or more per room. So until someone endows this fine old place with a massive capital renovation budget, its big, bunkbed-filled dorm rooms, slightly rustic common spaces, and woodsy locale will remain the archetype of hostel life—especially when the huge downstairs bunkroom is filled by some exuberant school group. The bottom line is that when all 78 beds are full, it's a bit zoo-like, despite manager Chris Crowell and staff's superhuman efforts. Off-season, it's one of the most welcoming—and well-run—hostels in the business. Advance reservations are absolutely essential in summer, highly recommended off season; call (508) 693-2665. Although accessible by bike path, car, and summer shuttle buses, the hostel is three miles from the nearest decent market, so if you plan to use the spic-and-span kitchen, you may want to shop ahead for groceries.

The only other budget option for overnight stays is camping. Since none of the island campgrounds offers much of a back-country wilderness experience, fiscal austerity is about the only reason to camp. **Webb's Camping Area,** on Barnes Rd. in Oak Bluffs, tel. (508) 693-0233, is the most scenic, with more trees to lend campers a modicum of privacy. Women traveling solo may wish to ask about the women-only area. Open mid-May through mid-September; $28-30 for one or two adults, plus $8 for each extra adult, $1 for each child age five and up. Also in OB is the rather funky, near-communal **Atlantis,** on County Rd. next to the Trade Winds grass airfield, tel. (508) 693-1923; look for the rock at the foot of the driveway—it's painted with a dolphin logo and the legend, "Karma begins here." Although it caters primarily to seasonal island workers who want to save on rent, it's always worth a call to find out if one of the handful of tent and trailer spaces is available. Open April-Oct., sites start at $20 for two people. On Edgartown Rd. in Vineyard Haven, not too far from Webb's, is the **Martha's Vineyard Family Campground,** tel. (508) 693-3772, which attracts plenty of RV-style campers. Open mid-May through mid-October, its rates start at $26 for tent sites for two adults.

Inexpensive: $35-60

For two people in high season? On the Vineyard? You *must* be joking. Try Motel 6 on the mainland.

Moderate: $60-85

At first blush, Oak Bluffs visitors are among the island's most fortunate, since a sizable fraction of the town's accommodations squeak in under $85. What do these lucky super-savers get for their money? B&Bs and guest houses with shared bathrooms; no air conditioning; and fewer frilly fabrics, heirlooms, and soundly insulated walls than typically found at higher prices. One of the least-expensive options, **The Attleboro House,** 11 Lake Ave., tel. (508) 693-4346, across from OB's yacht anchorage, vindicates that old saw about location, location, location—its small, convent-simple, wood-paneled rooms and tiny, old-fashioned hall baths (three showers for 11 rooms) will set you back $65-75 d, $45 s. Open from the week before Memorial Day through the end of September, the Attleboro is one of a declining number of places that accepts single-night stays in summer—a relative luxury made possible, perhaps, by the many regulars and families who, preferring a bargain over firm box springs, book by the week. Other immaculately maintained variations on this rustic breed include **The Tucker Inn,** 46 Massasoit Ave., tel. (508) 693-1045 (year-round; $55-65 d summers); the **Narragansett House,** 62 Narragansett Ave., tel. (508) 693-3627 (May-Oct.; $55-65 d summers); and **Titticut Follies,** 43 Narragansett Ave., tel. (508) 693-4986 (May-Sept.; $55-75 d). Regular year-to-year patrons lend such places a certain family-reunion atmosphere, quite fitting for such casual throwbacks to a pre-Holiday Inn era. If you have an appreciation—or nostalgia—for the early postwar decades, you may especially enjoy Titticut's trundle-bed, partial-bath apartment units ($70-95 per night, $285-495 per week), whose kitchens wouldn't look out of place on *Leave It to Beaver.*

Up-island's epicenter of affordability is West Tisbury, where nearly half the lodgings belong to various descendants of old Thomas Mayhew himself—none of whom seem interested in fleecing visitors. Thus, you'll find such comfortable yet affordable B&Bs as **The House at New Lane Bed & Breakfast,** on seven attractive acres just off the Edgartown-West Tisbury Rd., tel. (508) 693-4046 (year-round; $65-85 d cash only, $20 more for one-nighters), and **The Blue Goose,** on Old Courthouse Rd., off State Rd. in North Tisbury, tel. (508) 693-3223 (May-Oct.; $85-90 d). Authors searching for inspiration may particularly appreciate the creative vibes around **The Cleaveland House,** on the Edgartown-West Tisbury Rd. at the corner of New Lane, tel. (508) 693-9352, home to a mother-daughter writer-poet pair. The circa-1750 house is full of character, with creaky old floors, two fireplace rooms, and plenty of cozy places to kick back and think up excuses for your editor after the surrounding acres' beauty distracts you from your muse. Open year-round; $60 s or $75 d in high season (two-night weekend minimum; no credit cards), $10 less from mid-November to mid-May.

Expensive: $85-110

This is *not* a very plentiful category in summer, but the short high season of many of the pricier larger inns and housekeeping motels means that some of them—the Crocker House, Dockside, Katama Shores, Point Way, and Menemsha inns, for example—usually offer something in this range until at least mid-June and again after late September. Catching pricey places in their slower seasons is about the only way you'll get a room with private shower, too—the most common feature of the under-$100 selections (besides the absence of TVs and telephones) is the prevalence of shared bathrooms.

Vineyard Haven has one of the friendliest and most convenient of this category: **Nancy's Auberge,** 102 Main St., tel. (508) 693-4434. Nancy Hurd is as sweet and hospitable as they come—an avid baker whose breakfasts put the island's typical continental offerings to shame. Though not located on the water (or priced like places that are), it *is* just across the street from Owen Park's town beach and only minutes from the Steamship terminal and downtown, close enough to watch the Woods Hole ferries, all lit up at night like big birthday cakes, from the front bedroom. B&B purists should put this place at the top of their lists. Open year-round, its three rooms run from $88 (twin beds and shared bath) to $118 (queen bed, private bath, and adjoining kid's room) in high season, $10 less off-season.

Built back when President Jefferson was welcoming Lewis and Clark home from their river trip, **The Look Inn,** at the corner of William and Look Streets, tel. (508) 693-6893, offers a casual antidote to the stereotypical B&B's dust-ruffled, four-poster decor. "No bows," vow hosts Cathee and Freddy of their restored farmhouse. Their aesthetic leans instead toward futons and contemporary prints in tasteful chintz-free rooms with sinks tucked in corners to make sharing the bath that much easier. The serenity of the breakfast table beside the garden's little ornamental fish pool will make Main Street's bustle seem much farther away than the few blocks it really is—which is only fitting for the home of a yoga teacher and massage therapist. Open year-round; $90 d in season, $75 d off.

If you're aiming to stay around Oak Bluffs, the next step up over the bare-bones guest house is one of the B&Bs arrayed among side streets off Seaview Ave., near the town beach and Edgartown bike path. **Bradys NE SW Bed & Breakfast,** 10 Canonicus Ave., tel. (888) 693-9137, is a good example. Its name reflects the blend of New England's seaside cottage-style, white wood-slat walls and the owner's penchant for Southwestern poster art. Open year-round, the porch-wrapped Victorian has shared baths,

MARTHA'S VINEYARD MOTELS

The vast majority of the Vineyard's lodging choices are small inns and adult-oriented B&Bs. If you prefer a private bath and free HBO to, for example, small talk over breakfast with strangers, make a beeline for the **Vineyard Harbor Motel,** on Vineyard Haven's Beach Rd. opposite the Citgo station, tel. (508) 693-3334. Open year-round, with its own private stretch of harborfront beach; doubles here run $90-100 late June through Labor Day (three-night minimum), $60-65 in shoulder seasons, $45-50 mid-October through early April. Rooms with full kitchens are only $5-10 higher.

Edgartown's South Beach is where you'll find another of the few places that deserves to advertise its beachfront status, the **Katama Shores Inn** (May through Columbus Day), tel. (508) 627-4747. It's a large, family-friendly motel with refrigerators in every room, TVs and telephones, kitchenettes in the larger quarters, an outdoor pool, tennis courts, gas grills, a playground, even shuffleboard. Rates are $99-179 d in summer ($1,075-1,500 per week for the cottage suites), $59-119 in spring and fall. The on-site seafood restaurant, **The Dunes,** is worth a visit even if you don't intend to stay the night.

Also in Edgartown, at 227 Upper Main, is the modern **Edgartown Heritage Hotel,** tel. (508) 627-5161, a Clarion Carriage House Inn, is the only chain representative on the Islands. From the full-sized, air-conditioned rooms (with color TV) to the Sizzler-style family restaurant, it's exactly what you'd find nationwide. The prices, however, are all Vineyard: $175 d July through Labor Day, $135 in late spring and early fall, $85 d from mid-October through Memorial Day.

private verandahs, and a warm welcome for just $88-98 d in summer, $55-65 in winter.

Very Expensive: $110-150

Some Vineyard accommodations seem to target people who would sooner empty their wallets than sit on the same porcelain as strangers. Others earn their higher rates with more than just a private commode and complimentary basket of tiny shampoo bottles. Consider Vineyard Haven's **Crocker House Inn**, tel. (800) 772-0206, on Crocker Ave., a quiet harborside street off Main, about five minutes' stroll from downtown shops. Each room has a distinct personality—from the white wicker and seafoam green of one to the brass bed and fireplace of another—reflecting the attractive Victorian inn's devotion to indulging guests (predominantly couples on getaways). Open only April-Oct., prices in high season run $85-160 d, with a three-night minimum. Romantic comfort is also the object of the **Twin Oaks Inn**, 20 Edgartown Rd., tel. (800) 696-8633 (year-round; $90-145 d summer), which coddles guests with its antiques-filled rooms, inviting porch, and an atmosphere that makes you feel right at home. A couple of blocks away, **Aldworth Manor**, 60 Mt. Aldworth Rd., tel. (508) 693-3203, is even more upscale, with its antique beds, fireplace rooms, landscaped acreage, afternoon tea, and extras such as beach gear (coolers, towels, chairs) for all guests. Hacker tourists will appreciate each room's direct-dial phone (with voice-mail). Food mavens will love the breakfasts (among the few that can't be confused with an after-school snack or dieter's regimen); stay for two weeks and you still wouldn't exhaust all the chef's menus. Rates run $129-169 d mid-June to mid-September (two-night minimum on weekends); $109-159 d from September through June. Not only are these well below comparable properties around town—they're lower than some (such as the Lothrop Merry House) that aren't in the same league.

Over in neighboring OB, **The Oak Bluffs Inn** (May-Oct.) on Circuit Ave. and Pequot, tel. (800) 955-6235, honors the town's decorative pedigree downstairs, but upstairs a soothing lack of Victoriana reigns, making the comfortable, high-ceiling rooms seem even more spacious. A four-story tower with a rooftop cupola gives late-Au-

gust guests a skybox seat for the town's end-of-season fireworks display (and simply a great view at any time). Rates are $120-150 d June-Sept., $110-120 in the pre- and post-season (not including the 11% tax and "gratuity" surcharge). At the other, extended end of Circuit Ave., opposite the harbor, **The Dockside Inn**, tel. (800) 245-5979 (April-Oct.), tips its hat to the Victorian beach resorts of a century ago and the colorful carpenters gothic cottages all around town. Wide, wrap-around verandas, detailed woodwork, period fabric prints, and furniture stylings all allude to the belle époque (without succumbing to chintz), but modern amenities and spaciousness abound, thanks to the inn's true age (it was built in 1989). Put this within just minutes' walk of all downtown, a beach, and four summer ferries and its high-season rates of $125-175 make it a good value. Come before mid-June or after Columbus Day, when rates drop about 30%, and you'll have yourself an even better bargain. Having your kids share your room adds $10-20, but cribs are free.

When it comes to accommodations, Edgartown generally costs more than any of its neighbors—witness the $175 summer rates for standard doubles in the island's only chain hotel. One of the few exceptions to such inflation is the **Ashley Inn**, occupying a shipshape old captain's home at 129 Main St., opposite small Cannonball Park, tel. (800) 477-9655. From mid-June through late September, $115-210 gets you a room of comfortable size (no tripping over your traveling companion's belongings) with unpretentious, tasteful decor; wonderfully friendly innkeepers; TVs and telephones; and a huge yard that invites curling up in the hammock with summer reading, far from the madding crowd. Prices drop $25-60 in spring and fall, and by half over the winter; the three-night minimum only applies to high-season weekends, too. One- and two-bedroom townhouse suites with jacuzzis are also available for anyone wishing to lie in the lap of luxury (five-day minimum in summer, at $325 per night, but winter rates are about a third of that—even less on slow nights).

Up-island has quite a variety of places in this price range, from an inn built around a 1790 farmhouse to modern lodgings built in the 1970s. West Tisbury's **Lambert's Cove Country Inn**, tel. (508) 693-2298, is the former, a secluded estate set way back in the woods at the end of a sandy lane off upper Lambert's Cove Road. Informal yet tasteful—a contented cat dozing on the library's Oriental rug sets the tone—this popular inn features all-weather tennis courts, TV- and phone-free rooms, a lot of private decks, highly regarded fine dining, and passes to lovely Lambert's Cove Beach. Open year-round, $135-175 d in summer (three-night minimum), $95-135 d in spring and fall, $85-125 d Thanksgiving to March.

Though equally rural, **The Bayberry,** on West Tisbury's Old Courthouse Rd., tel. (508) 693-1984, offers the more intimate atmosphere of a five-room B&B inn, a place where guests often linger over breakfasts, and deer come browsing through the backyard orchard. Though gilt around the edges with Staffordshire china and matching linens, the Bayberry exudes a wholesome country charm, warm and inviting as one of owner Rosalie Powell's handmade quilts. Small rooms with private baths start at $95 in winter and run up to $175 in summer; shared baths run $85-125.

For something more like either a motel or a private cottage, look no farther than the **Menemsha Inn,** off Chilmark's North Rd. at the Menemsha Cross Rd. junction, tel. (508) 645-2521 (May-Oct.). Fairly contemporary in design and decor, the inn offers a choice of 15 well-appointed doubles and suites ($115-170 d summer, $85-100 d spring and fall; no credit cards) or 12 one- and two-bedroom, fully equipped housekeeping cottages spread around the 10-acre hillside above Vineyard Sound (by the week only in summer, $1,075-1,475; two-night minimum the rest of the year, $120-135 d). Beautiful sunset views of Gay Head and Menemsha Bight, thoughtful extras such as beach coolers and outdoor barbecue grills, and guest passes to Chilmark's exclusive town beaches make this a deservedly popular place. Book early.

Luxury: $150+

Tucked in the West Chop woods on Vineyard Haven's upper Main St. is the **Thorncroft Inn,** tel. (800) 332-1236, the island's only four-diamond establishment. With private fireplaces and jacuzzis and full breakfasts worthy of that designation, it may come as no surprise to find room rates starting at $169 d (and topping out at over twice that). Closer to the vitality of downtown is the equally deluxe **Martha's Place,** 114 Main, tel. (508) 693-0253, whose four rooms (one with *two* fireplaces) strive to set a benchmark for local opulence (albeit with only a continental breakfast). Antiques everywhere, crystal chandeliers, Oriental carpets, Egyptian cottons, fresh flowers, jacuzzis, beach towels, coolers, and even complimentary bicycles give high-rollers good reason to part with $175-300 in summer (double occupancy only, two- to four-night minimum on weekends and holidays). Come at the tail end of Martha's off-season, Jan.-May, and take advantage of $125-250 bargain rates.

In Oak Bluffs, **The Oak House,** on Seaview Ave. between Narragansett and Pequot, tel. (508) 693-4187, is a former summer home of the state's fourth Republican governor; it's been turned into the quintessential B&B—a seaside Victorian with a picket fence and peaked roof, rocker-filled porches for afternoon tea and lemonade, and sunny balconies overlooking the beach across the street. Whether clad in solid oak paneling or coordinated around more feminine yellows and pinks, the 10 rooms and suites are almost exactly as you'd imagine a B&B *should* look, from antiques and gauzy curtains to the occasional painted brass bed or Oriental rug. (Unlike in most B&Bs, rooms here also come with TVs and telephones.) Open May-Oct., the standard room rates range $140-185 d at the height of summer, $100-130 in spring, and $115-155 in fall, with a two- or three-night minimum most of the season. Two-room suites run $170-275 for up to four people.

Stately old Edgartown offers a number of large, luxurious inns carved out of elegant 19th-century homes. Among the most notable is the **Point Way Inn,** on Main, at Pease's Point Way, tel. (508) 627-8633, in part because most of its decent-sized rooms include working fireplaces. It also has a way with memorable details: afternoon refreshments, small decanters of sherry in each room, pre-stamped envelopes for correspondence, beach chairs and towels, a shower-equipped bathroom for late-departing guests to use after checkout, a regulation-size croquet lawn. To top it off, there's a car available for guest use *free* (first-come, first-served). Stay more than the required two nights on weekends and the continental breakfasts may become repetitious—but if you make use of even half the available amenities it'll be hard to quibble with the nightly tariff ($150-195 d mid-June through mid-September weekends, $100-165 shoulder seasons, $90-125 winter; $20-90 more for suites).

Possibly the best place to go for broke is **The Tuscany Inn,** 22 N. Water St., opposite Murdick's Fudge smack in the town center, tel. (508) 627-5999. Ample and delicious breakfasts, elegant surroundings, and affable, attentive, hands-on owners have earned this handsome 1860 Victorian mansion a devoted year-round following undeterred by $200 (twin) to $325 (king) summer room rates (three-night minimum). Nov.-April, the prices drop in half, but Laura's fresh focaccia tastes just as good in front of the dining-room fireplace as in the garden hammock on a dreamy July morn. If you've a yen to learn the secrets of northern Italian cooking, ask about the winter culinary workshops.

Canopy beds also abound two blocks away at **The Victorian Inn,** 24 S. Water, tel. (508) 627-4784, where well-trained staff and generous four-course breakfasts are topped only by the views from the third-floor private balconies overlooking the garden court and harbor beyond. The nightly tariff ranges from $125-265 between mid-June and Labor Day (two-night minimum) to $70-145 November through March. Nineteenth-century antiques aren't out of place at **The Shiverick Inn,** either, on Pease's Point Way, tel. (800) 723-4292, one of the state's relatively rare Second Empire mansions (whose mansard roof and cupola are actually additions to the original 1840 house). The grace and simple refinement of that earlier age are borne out in the high-ceilinged rooms, cozy library, and formal gardens—where one may take one's afternoon tea (or morning granola, toast, and fruit) when weather allows. The inn's many fireplaces make it a romantic winter retreat ($120 queen, $175 suite Nov.-April), but even in summer modest size and the innkeeper's deft personal touch keep the high-season pandemonium at bay ($195-280, mid-June to mid-October, two- or three-night minimum). A B&B-style warm welcome is also a feature of Edgartown's newest deluxe property, **The Jonathan Munroe House,** 100 Main St., opposite the Old Whaling Church, tel. (508) 627-5536. Its handful of generously sized rooms (half with fireplaces and whirlpool

tubs), ample breakfasts, afternoon wine and cheese, and dedicated staff offer year-round comfort for $110-165 d off season, $150-200 d June-August (two-night minimum).

FOOD

Unlike Cape Cod, the Vineyard doesn't consume its weight in frying oil each day. Fish and chips are available if you want them, but most Vineyard eateries compete for either the country-club surf-and-turf set or upscale palates accustomed to fine comestibles at high prices. Local epicures have come to expect fresh herbs, organic greens, bottled water, and meat-free menu selections (if it isn't on the menu, ask). Even delis and fried-seafood shacks cater to health-conscious herbivores with veggie or "garden" burgers. If you enjoy wine with your dinner, remember that OB and Edgartown are the only Vineyard communities where you can buy alcohol in stores or restaurants. If you're dining in one of the island's "dry" towns, be sure to bring your own—and expect a small corkage fee to be added to the bill.

Most places stay open seven days a week in season, then cut back days and hours when business becomes more uneven. Beyond June-August, confirm that your destination restaurant is open before making any pilgrimage.

Vineyard Haven

Probably the most famous Vineyard restaurant is **The Black Dog Tavern,** next to the ferry staging area in Vineyard Haven, behind the Black Dog bakery-cum-clothing store full of Black Dog-brand wearables, tel. (508) 693-9223. The T-shirts have been sighted from Patagonia to Nepal, and if you're grabbing a snack at the bakery counter you may marvel that global fame hasn't brought about tremendous price hikes. Ah, but any comfort given by the bakery's prices will be quickly dispelled by the tavern's: entrees run $20-30. Such prices are typical of the island's best dining spots, but this isn't one of the best dining spots—not for dinner, at any rate. Better to come for breakfast, when you can enjoy the harbor view and nautical mementos without breaking the bank. Open year-round, it's absolutely mobbed in summers; no reservations accepted. While it doesn't have the full menu of the downtown location, the Black Dog's satellite Bakery Cafe, on State Rd., at the southern edge of town, nearly opposite Spinnaker Lanes candlepin bowling, is a good alternative for up-island visitors who want to sample the muffins, chowder, or burgers but avoid the morass of Five Corners traffic.

For a genuine sample of superior local dining, walk over to **Stripers,** 26 Beach Rd., tel. (508) 693-8383, opposite Ace Hardware on the industrial side of busy Five Corners. Contemporary blond wood and bold South Florida colors set a lively, informal tone at this intimate spot—and foreshadow the vivid flavors and presentation of the meals. With an emphasis on seafood, dishes such as shrimp and green papaya salad on a bed of Asian cellophane noodles, or roast cod and clams with orzo, spinach, and capers compete with the fine harbor view for your undivided attention ($16.95-26.95). Open for dinner daily mid-May through early October, and for Sunday brunch.

The season's bounty is also reflected on the short New American menu of **The Dry Town Café,** on Main St., tel. (508) 693-0033, opposite the Capawock Theatre. Fresh ingredients are appealingly combined to highlight local and seasonal products—whether fish, fowl, or vegetable. And don't worry about nouvelle portions; you won't leave with an empty stomach (your wallet may not be so lucky, however—as with others of this echelon, $10 appetizers and $25 entrees are typical). Open year-round. Hearty appetites with smaller budgets should seek out **Sandwich Haven,** in the lane next to Bowl & Board, tel. (508) 696-8383. Middle Eastern, all well under $10, is the specialty here: soft pitas wrapped around a half-dozen fillings from falafel to ground lamb *kufta,* entrees such as stuffed cabbage or highly seasoned Lebanese chicken with pine nuts and rice; salads; bagels; pastries; pies—all in a come-as-you-are cafe-casual setting that won't make families with young ones feel self-conscious. Open year-round.

But for the ultimate seaside vacation meal, try a bluefish sandwich and soft-serve ice cream from **Sandy's Fish & Chips,** tel. (508) 693-1220, open summers only at the corner of State Rd. and Martin, in the same building as John's Fish Market. While Sandy's can certainly fill your beach basket, picnickers who prefer to play Dagwood and build sandwiches from scratch are best served by the friendly **Tisbury Farm Market,** tel. (508) 693-6700, across from Cronig's Market, on the very busy stretch of State Rd. almost a mile from the harbor. You'll find imported cheeses, olives, and other fixin's—and high-quality (from up-island Biga Bakery) baguettes, focaccia, and other fresh loaves to put 'em on.

Oak Bluffs

When died-in-the-wool Nantucketers threaten their offspring with visions of the bogeyman, slumming at the Subway on Circuit Ave. is what they have in mind. This sub-sandwich parlor and Edgartown's Dairy Queen are the only toeholds national fast-food chains have made on the Vineyard. But they don't have a monopoly on the island's cheap eats. Subway's neighbors include **Linda Jean's,** 34 Circuit Ave., tel. (508) 693-4093, where sturdy breakfasts, lunches, and early dinners transport patrons back to simpler days and square meals, when coffee came only decaf or regular and Cool Whip had cachet. Open year-round. More contemporary breakfast and lunch choices (including fajita omelets, lox, latkes, and veggie quesadillas) are found down around the corner facing the boat anchorage at **Dee's Harbor Café,** on Lake Ave. next to Sun 'n' Fun car and moped rentals, tel. (508) 693-6506. Although nearly as inexpensive as Linda Jean's—everything's well under $10—Dee's is only open May through early October. Back up on Circuit Ave., **Papa's Pizza,** tel. (508) 693-1400, is the year-round answer to the question of where to find the island's best pizza, from pepperoni to pesto, thin-crust or deep-dish, whole wheat or regular—all at off-island college-town prices. Sandwiches, a couple of dinner entrees, and simple salads are also available, in a setting that has just enough wood and natural light to dispel any resemblance to your average plastic-and-fixed-seat pizza joint. Hearty, thick-crusted pizza is also available at **Giordano's Restaurant, Clam Bar & Pizza,** open in summer opposite the Island Theatre at the foot of Circuit Ave., tel. (508) 693-0184. But the real reason to come here is the robust and inexpensive (no credit cards) red-sauce Italian meals.

If your island holiday plans don't call for carbo-loading on pasta and pizza, consider **Something Fishy,** next to Ben & Bill's Chocolate Emporium, in the walkway between Circuit and Kennebec Aves., tel. (508) 693-6903. Between late April and October, this informal pocket-sized sushi bar presents Japanese favorites, from snapping fresh sashimi to an extensive list of specialty *maki* rolls, plus the usual combo platters, teriyaki, and crispy tempura—all priced only modestly higher than on the mainland. (Seafood fanciers who believe that fish out of water belong in deep fryers should cross the street to the **Hungry Whale.**)

For a real splurge, try **The Sweet Life Cafe,** on upper Circuit Ave. opposite the Oak Bluffs Inn, tel. (508) 696-0200. The elegance and intimacy of the residential interior and back garden provide the perfect backdrop for the kitchen's very 1990s approach to classic continental cuisine, pairing fine meats, fresh fish, and pick-of-the-crop vegetables with flavorful herbed broths, glazes, and wine reductions ($17-26). Pan-roasted salmon with mushroom polenta and rosemary jus, an autumnal rack of pork in port wine sauce with pumpkin risotto, or a spicy shellfish-and-sausage penne pasta with garlic bruschetta are just a few examples—each plate arranged with an architectural flourish. The expertise also extends to the desserts—life doesn't get any sweeter than this. Open through New Year's for lunch and dinner in high season, and even breakfast on summer weekends.

In a class by itself is **Lola's Southern Seafood,** tel. (508) 693-5007, on Beach Rd., at the Island Inn. Although it's a trek from downtown OB if you're walking, Lola's gives you more than enough reason to *need* that 1.3-mile walk back to Ocean Park and the Steamship dock. Lola left the idea of portion control behind in Louisiana. Forget ordering a full entree for every adult—each platter come with enough side dishes (starches and greens) to choke a horse. Pony up the fee for splitting a plate (or stick to the appetizers) and you'll still pay less and eat more than in almost any other island restaurant. Anyone lacking a teamster's appetite may want to stick to the pub, where a saner sense of proportion prevails (along with plenty of second-hand cigarette smoke). Serving breakfast, dinner, and Sunday brunch daily year-round, plus lunch in summer.

Edgartown

Good quality take-out or counter lunches, baked treats, and liquid refreshments are best obtained from **Espresso Love** (Apr.-Dec. only), on S. Water St., opposite the Edgartown National Bank ATM, or **Darlene's Kitchen,** 33 Winter Street. Vegetarians will find that the **Edgartown Deli,** at 52 Main St., makes a fine garden burger, and subscribers to the efficacy of the banana ice cream diet won't want to miss adjacent **Vineyard Scoops.** Fried seafood fans, meanwhile, should step down to the **Quarter-deck Restaurant,** on Dock St. by the harbor (lunch and dinner May-Oct.). You could grab a bite at the Navigator nearby ("the Nav" to locals), but come for evening drinks and entertainment instead and you get to savor the fine view. Brunch lovers—or anyone in search of a good full breakfast—should make haste for the dining room at **The Daggett House,** 59 N. Water St., tel. (508) 627-4600.

One of Edgartown's most affordable and dependable restaurants is **The Newes from America,** in the Kelley House inn at the corner of N. Water and Kelley Sts., tel. (508) 627-4397. Lower prices don't mean inferior food: the Newes' family-friendly menu of seafood, pastas, burgers, and bratwursts keep the casual crowd happy, as does the great selection of microbrews (in bottles and on draught). Open for lunch and dinner all year except on Christmas, when they close for lunch. Across the street, behind one of the porches of the rambling Colonial Inn (where Somerset Maugham sat out WW II), **Chesca's,** tel. (508) 627-1234, serves up fine Italian-influenced cuisine with a blend of paper-napkin informality and the hardwood, clapboard dignity of an old New England resort. The dining room's contented murmurings aren't due just to the catchy mood music: the food is inspiringly fresh, seasoned with a bold hand, and prettily garnished (a bit Jackson Pollock-like) with fresh herbs, flaked vegetables, and ground nuts. The restaurant doesn't stint on the desserts, either, as anyone who believes the more sugar the better will happily discover. With entree prices well under $20, dinners here are a relatively good value. Open for dinner Oct.-April, all three meals in the height of summer. Equally reasonable, less-embellished Italian dining is also available out by South Beach at **The**

Dunes Restaurant & Tap, in the Katama Shores Inn, tel. (508) 627-5353 (summer only), where fresh lobster ravioli and pesto crostini coexist with chicken parmigiana and char-broiled sirloin. If all it would take to make you happy is some decent pizza, stop by the **Fresh Pasta Shoppe,** on upper Main St. near The Triangle, tel. (508) 627-5582, as you bike in or out of town.

When it's time to impress your traveling companion with white table linen, soft lighting, *and* a fine meal—maybe sautéed foie gras on peach and fig chutney, followed by rosemary-crusted red snapper with orange butter sauce, or grilled rib-eye with portabello and radicchio salad and asiago potato lasagna—you couldn't do much better than **Savoir Fare,** behind the county courthouse on Main St., tel. (508) 627-9864. Open from late spring through New Year's, but weekends only off-season.

Up-Island Eats

Despite having a hostel full of them in its midst, the rural end of the Vineyard is not very kind to budget travelers. The foot-thick topsoil seems to yield not only fresh produce but fancy, destination dining. Nothing stays open past Thanksgiving out here, and most places start paring back their days and hours after September. Also remember that all three up-island towns—West Tisbury, Chilmark, and Gay Head—are dry, so stop at an OB or Edgartown package store if wine is vital to your dining pleasure.

Up-island's only reasonably priced eating is almost exclusively take-out—from grocery-store deli counters (Back Alley's in West Tisbury and the Chilmark Store at Beetlebung Corner), Biga Bakery & Delicatessen in North Tisbury, or, in Menemsha, small summer-only fish shacks such as **The Menemsha Bite,** on the road to Dutcher Dock and the village beach, tel. (508) 645-9239, or **The Galley,** at the dock itself, tel. (508) 645-9819. These last two are open daily until at least 7 p.m. You can also dine for under $20 at the **Aquinnah,** the gift shop-cum-eatery on the top of the Gay Head Cliffs, tel. (508) 645-9654, but come for the view, not the food.

Inquire after the best lobster on the Vineyard and residents most often steer you to the **Home Port Restaurant,** at the end of North Rd. in the heart of Menemsha, tel. (508) 645-2679. This is

a taste of New England, deliciously unadorned; no gelatinous cream-clotted chowder here, for example—just the rich taste of clams in a broth as smooth and flavorful as fine bouillabaisse. Since entrees come with appetizer, salad, and dessert, prices are reasonable. To make it even easier on your pocketbook, go around to the kitchen door off the parking lot and get take-out ($10-20) for a sunset picnic on the beach nearby. Open May-Oct. for dinner only.

Each of the other prime up-island restaurants offers innovative, upscale cuisine in settings that range from self-effacingly casual to stylishly contemporary. "Casual" doesn't quite do justice to **The Red Cat,** a chef-owned place on State Rd. in North Tisbury, tel. (508) 693-9599, by all appearances a simple roadhouse cafe replete with potholed parking lot and squeaky screen door. Once you're inside, the local art gracing the walls gives a clue of what's to come—and it ain't no roadhouse fare: lobster, fennel, and pear wontons in a small pool of vanilla citrus sauce, for example, or baked yellowfin tuna with wild mushrooms and juniper berry sauce, or a risotto singing with the flavors of the freshest local vegetables available. Herb-infused oils, sauce reductions, unusual pairings of fruits and savory meats, and fish that swam in the ocean that morning are typical of the notes sounded throughout the ever-changing menu ($19-28). Reserve for early evening, though, or you'll discover that the joint does *sound* like a roadhouse once it's full of happy diners.

By contrast, the shellacked pine and wicker simplicity of **Theo's,** 2.5 miles away at Chilmark's Inn on Blueberry Hill off North Rd., tel. (508) 645-3322, evinces a country squire's easy elegance, helped in no small measure by the inn's pine-shaded grounds and lichen-covered stone walls. Reservations in hand, you can disregard the signs unkindly warning away visitors and join the well-dressed devotees of the prix-fixe multi-course meals served within these softly lit dining rooms ($37-50). Off-season, the painterly presentations of classic cuisine—braised meats; seafood baked in parchment; lightly sauced pastas; rustic bisques, tarts, and pâtés; and salads served after the main course—are available à la carte. Sundays off-season, four-course dinners are offered at about the same fixed price as an average entree at other island restaurants of equal caliber—in short, a stunning bargain not to be missed. Whatever the season, request a table on the screened porch for the sublime addition of a lovely sunset, neatly visible through the strategically trimmed trees.

To make your up-island choices even more difficult, consider **The Feast of Chilmark,** next to the Chilmark Store at Beetlebung Corner, tel. (508) 645-3553. Spacious and modern, with an open kitchen, cordial service, and large prints by the island's most famous living photographer on its walls, the Feast's emphasis on taste cuts straight to the marrow of cooking. No cantilevered constructions of garnishes across your plate here, or whimsical dustings of color-coordinated herbs. Even a seemingly simple marinara sauce comes alive with a bite of fresh basil and a nip of pepper, potentially leaden codfish cakes brighten beneath a rich horseradish mayonnaise, and a chicken cutlet ventures beyond basic in a medley of three mustards ($16.95-32.95). Desserts are excellent, too, and the place even displays a very uncommon appreciation for good tea.

bike ferry

GETTING AROUND

In summer, all three down-island towns are connected to the mainland by ferries and to each other by shuttle buses and paved bike paths. Here the great concentration of food and lodging, mostly within walking distance of each other and transportation, makes it entirely practical (even eminently sensible) to arrive without a car.

By Bicycle

Vineyard Haven, Oak Bluffs, Edgartown, and parts of West Tisbury are linked by more than 15 miles of paved bike paths, so cycling around the island is a snap even for riders normally intimidated by traffic. The only major portion of the island lacking segregated bikeways is the southwest corner, but the beautiful tree-canopied roads there make for lovely riding nonetheless. And what better way to work off those calories from last night's dinner?

Over a dozen shops rent bikes—three on Circuit Ave. Ext. next to Oak Bluff's harborside ferry docks, three within a block of Vineyard

Haven's Steamship terminal, two within a stone's throw of Edgartown's central Main St.-Water St. intersection, and a couple more at the Triangle on Upper Main St. in Edgartown. Guests of B&Bs and inns away from the town centers can take advantage of the free bike delivery and pick-up offered by such rental outfits as **Martha's Bike Rentals,** on Lagoon Pond Rd., in Vineyard Haven, opposite the Post Office, tel. 508-693-6593; **Vineyard Bike & Moped,** next to the Strand moviehouse in OB, tel. 508-693-6886; or **Wheel Happy,** opposite the Harborside Inn on S. Water St. in Edgartown, tel. 508-627-5928. Most rental fleets are trendy mountain bikes and hybrids, but retro three-speeds, tandems, lighter road bikes (perfectly adequate if you intend to stick to pavement), and trailers for towing kids are also widely available.

If you've brought your own wheels and need repairs, several rental shops double as fix-it stops: Vineyard Haven's year-round **Cycle Works,** 105 State Rd. next to Cronig's Market, tel. (508) 693-6966; **Anderson's Bike Rental,**

Circuit Ave. Ext. in OB, tel. (508) 693-9346; or
R.W. Cutler Bike Shop, 1 Main St. in Edgartown, tel. (508) 627-4052.

By Bus or Taxi
Early May through late October, the privately
owned **Down-Island Shuttle** provides regular
daily service between Vineyard Haven (picking
up from the Steamship terminal and Beach Rd.'s
New Bedford ferry pier), Oak Bluffs (Ocean
Park), and Edgartown (Church St. Visitor Center). The shuttle's repainted school buses basically run every 30 minutes 9 a.m.-5 p.m. for the
first and last weeks of the season; 8 a.m.-6 p.m.
(and Fri.-Sat. to 11 p.m.) mid-May through June
and September through early October; and every
15 minutes 7 a.m.-midnight at the peak of the
season, late June through early September.
Fares are $1.50 per leg, cheaper when pur-
chased as a round trip. Anyone bound for the
airport, West Tisbury, Chilmark, or Gay Head
will have to rely on the same company's **Up-Island Shuttle,** whose white-and-pink school
buses operate weekends Memorial Day through
late June, then daily through early September.
This shuttle makes about eight runs between
10 a.m. and 6 p.m., mostly to and from Oak
Bluffs, the rest from Edgartown (connect at either
to Vineyard Haven via the Down-Island Shuttle), with a fare of up to $8.25 roundtrip. A record-
ing of departure times (rattled off too quickly to be
much use) is available by calling (508) 693-1589.

Daily 9 a.m.-5:30 p.m. mid-June to mid-September, the Martha's Vineyard Transit Authority
provides a **South Beach shuttle** from downtown Edgartown to the big surf off Katama.
Board the motor trolley at the visitor center, or
flag it down on its route along Pease Point Way
and Katama Road (every 15 minutes in good
weather, every hour in bad; $1.50 one-way).
The MVTA also operates the **Edgartown Trolley** and **Vineyard Haven Park N' Ride Shuttle,**
providing nearly continuous service mid-May
through mid-September to their respective
downtowns from free peripheral parking lots on
State Rd. in Vineyard Haven, by the Triangle
in Edgartown, and at the Edgartown elementary school on West Tisbury Road.

For island-wide door-to-door convenience,
choose from among the many available taxi
companies. Rates from the Steamship docks

**MARTHA'S VINEYARD
TAXI SERVICES**

AdamCab, Edgartown, tel. (800) 281-4462
All Island Taxi, VH, tel. (800) 693-TAXI
Anthony's Taxi, VH, tel. (508) 693-9611
Atlantic Cab, OB, tel. (508) 693-7110
Harbor Taxi, OB, tel. (508) 693-3705
Jon's Taxi, Edgartown, tel. (508) 627-4677
or -5298
Marlene's Taxi, VH and OB, tel. (508)
693-0037
Martha's Vineyard Taxi, OB, tel. (508)
693-8660
Patti's Taxi Service, VH, tel. (508) 693-1663
Tisbury Taxi, VH, tel. (508) 693-7660
TobyCab, West Tisbury, tel. (800) 360-TOBY
Up Island Taxi, Edgartown, tel. (508)
627-4566
Your Taxi, OB, tel. (800) 396-000

---

in either Vineyard Haven or OB can run as high
as $35 or more to Gay Head, $12-15 to the hostel in West Tisbury, but between down-island
towns you'll usually get change for a $10. After
midnight, fares rise 50%—and after 2 a.m., the
fare is totally at the driver's discretion.

By Car
If you're staying down-island in summer, you
really want to avoid driving. You may not think so,
as you imagine all the luggage you have to carry
and all the shopping you want to do—but if it's a
vacation you're after, seriously consider your
determination to drive; you're letting yourself in
for a slow, stop-and-go crawl through intersections packed with 20,000 other cars, not one of
which will yield to your left turn. If you're coming
in the off season or intend to spend most of your
time up-island and have never ridden a bicycle,
it's a slightly better idea. Just mind all those cyclists, and the deer at night—particularly on
curvy, shoulderless up-island roads.

If you decide to rent a car, be prepared for
rates that fluctuate wildly: ever-popular Jeeps
and convertibles that rent for over $150 a day on
any midsummer holiday, for instance, may drop
back to $50 off season unless the weather is

spectacular and demand is strong. Don't expect anyone but the major chains to quote prices over the phone—the independent operators prefer not to commit to anything that may scare off potential business. Remove any diamond jewelry you may be wearing and don't introduce yourself as a doctor and you'll find these indie outfits are prepared to haggle—so long as (a) you're mellow and not too pushy, and (b) they can see that the competition across the street still has a car or two in the lot. By the way, before you pay a massive premium for renting one of those macho four-wheelers, remember that driving on Vineyard beaches is restricted to privately owned vehicles with valid permits. (Oversand vehicle permits for Chappaquiddick are $110 from TTOR, tel. 508-627-7689; for Norton Point—the only other part of the Vineyard's coast open to off-road vehicles—the requisite permits are $50 from the Treasurer's Office in the County Courthouse on Main St. in Edgartown.)

By Thumb

Despite the rips summer congestion is rending in the fabric of the Vineyard's small-town life, the island has a well-deserved and enviable reputation as a great hitchhiking spot, a small vestige of the 1970s preserved here thanks to the large proportion of pickups and sport utility vehicles and the island's small size (no need to worry about making conversation for just a couple of miles). If you've never tried thumbing a ride, this is a good place to start; if you mourn the passing of safe hitching in the rest of the US, you'll find this a welcome time warp. (Which isn't to say you shouldn't trust your instincts: if you aren't comfortable with someone who's stopped to offer a lift, decline the ride.) Since the preservation of this casual anachronism depends on visitors as well as residents, don't think that just because you don't know your way around, you aren't eligible to contribute—if you have extra capacity in your car, share it.

INFORMATION AND SERVICES

If you like to peruse racks of promotional flyers or want more accommodations to choose from, drop in on the **Martha's Vineyard Chamber of Commerce,** on Beach Rd. in Vineyard Haven, opposite the fire station. Or call (508) 693-0085 ahead for a free copy of their Visitor Guide. In high season, staffed information booths in all three down-island towns (marked on the relevant close-up maps) are able to give directions, provide dining and lodging information, and answer most general tourist questions. Edgartown's booth also sells postcards and stamps, accepts mail, and vends snacks.

Public Restrooms

The only year-round bathrooms open to the public are at the Steamship terminal in Vineyard Haven and the Church St. Visitor Center in Edgartown. In summer, a number of other facilities open up all over the island: in the parking lot next to Vineyard Haven's A&P market, at the Steamship dock and on Kennebec Ave. in Oak Bluffs, at South Beach in Edgartown, in West Tisbury's Old Ag Hall on State Rd., and at the bottom of the loop drive atop Gay Head Cliffs. Showers are also available (for a fee), at the bathhouse beside Oak Bluffs Harbor and the Tisbury Inn Health Club in downtown Vineyard Haven, next to the Chamber of Commerce.

MARTHA'S VINEYARD CAR RENTAL AGENCIES

AAA Island Auto Rentals, tel. (508) 627-6800—Edgartown

Adventure Rentals/Thrifty, tel. (508)693-1959—VH

All-Island Rent-A-Car, tel. (508) 693-6868—airport

Atlantic Rent-A-Car, tel. (508) 693-0480—VH

Bayside Auto Rental, tel. (508) 693-4777—VH

Budget, tel. (508) 693-1911 or (800) 527-0700—airport, VH, OB

Hertz, tel. (508) 627-4728 or (800) 654-3131—Edgartown

Holmes Hole Car Rental/Rent-A-Wreck, tel. (508) 693-8838—VH

Sun-N-Fun, tel. (508) 693-5457—OB

Vineyard Classic Cars, tel. (508) 693-5551—OB

Media

For the most up-to-date arts and entertainment suggestions, check out Thursday's *Martha's Vineyard Times,* which includes night club live music listings in its calendar of events. Last-minute yard sales and estate auctions, on the other hand, are more likely to be found in the classifieds of Friday's more patrician *Vineyard Gazette,* regarded as one of the finest small-town newspapers in the nation—and possibly the most quaint: its oversized page, aphoristic masthead, and columns devoted to bird sightings all betoken a bygone era in journalism.

On the radio dial, WMVY-FM, 92.7, is the local gentle pop album rock station (think REM and Timbuk 3 plus the Who and Earth, Wind, and Fire) and best up-to-the-minute source for local beach and ferry reports. *All Things Considered* junkies who can't leave NPR behind, even while on vacation, can try tuning in Boston's WGBH-FM, 89.7, which usually comes in quite clearly over much of the island.

Money

You won't ever be far from an ATM in the down-island towns, but up-island is a different story. Avoid all **Compass Bank** cash machines unless you have an account with the bank or enjoy paying for the privilege of using its ATMs. Forunately, this sort of Las Vegas-style tourist tax hasn't caught on with any of the other Vineyard banks, each of whom has a cash machine within a block or two of Compass in Vineyard Haven, Oak Bluffs, and Edgartown.

Anyone carrying foreign currency had better make the necessary exchanges prior to arriving—none of the banks here handle such transactions.

Medical

For speedy clinical care of illnesses and minor injuries **Vineyard Medical Services,** on State Rd. opposite Cronig's Market, accepts walk-in patients weekdays 9 a.m.-1 p.m. Or, to make an afternoon appointment, call (508) 693-4400.

NANTUCKET

. . . Nantucket is no Illinois.
—HERMAN MELVILLE,
MOBY DICK

Known as the "Grey Lady" for the color of its cedar-shingled houses, stripped to a fine silvery gray by exposure to the sea air, Nantucket is barely more than a sandy mote in Neptune's eye. Two hours by ferry from the Cape, the island that was once one of the world's leading whaling ports is now a preserve of affluence, the lovely and narrow cobblestone streets of Nantucket Town lined with expensive boutiques and elegant restaurants. Decades of capitalizing on its blue-chip reputation for quaintness have produced a movie-set perfection bordering on preciousness. (Heck, the whole town—2,400 buildings—is a registered historic district, and the entire *island* is a National Historic Landmark.) Whereas Martha's Vineyard isn't self-conscious about mismatched chairs on the porch, peeling paint, or broken screen windows stacked up on the back step awaiting storage or rainy-day repair, the Grey Lady never appears in public without every window shutter and porch railing perfectly in place. Homeowners even supply their own cute captions: names like Serendipity, Whispering Pines, Ain Wee Hoose, and Latest Rumour decorate cottages all over the island. Yet for those who can take the time to explore it, this Ice Age remnant's 54 square miles offer a singular atmosphere of contemplative fogs, dusky green heathlands, garden gates laced with bright flowers, and picturesque lighthouses.

Sometimes, the island's port and business center is called Nantucket Town (just "town" suffices for verbal directions), to distinguish it from several named localities—from Wauwinet to Madaket—and the tiny, mostly residential village of Siasconset on the eastern shore ("Sconset" to locals). But town and island are actually one and the same. "Nantucket" also denotes one of the commonwealth of Massachusetts' 14 counties, comprising the eponymous main island and three smaller, privately owned ones to the west—tiny Esther, now apparently permanently attached by a sandy umbilicus; Tuckernuck; and Muskeget. In all its jurisdictions, Nantucket is small enough and its major attractions concentrated

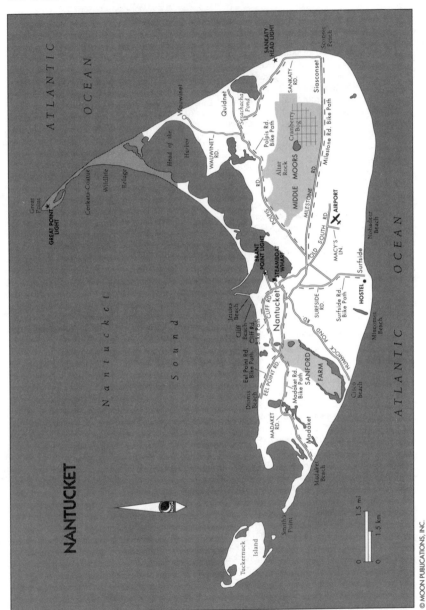

NANTUCKET

© MOON PUBLICATIONS, INC.

enough so that you shouldn't be deterred from a visit by either the high tariff on cars or accommodations—day-trippers on foot or bike can easily sample much of what the island has to offer.

HISTORY

The Good Old Days
At least half a dozen 16th-century European navigators—from Portuguese explorer Miguel Cortereal in 1502 up to English captain John Hawkins in 1565—are known to have passed in the vicinity of Nantucket, and at least a couple of them are believed to have espied its low cliffs. The earliest unequivocal evidence of an overseas visitor laying eyes on the island indicates that in 1605, George Weymouth, following up on the success of Gosnold's voyage to the Vineyard, sighted the pale marine scarp at Sankaty Head. Like many a vessel—even in the age of GPS and depth-sounders—Weymouth's *Archangel* was so bedeviled by Nantucket's myriad confusing rips and shoals that he sailed clear up to Maine before making another attempt to put ashore.

Navigational hazards may have spared the island's large Native American population early contact with Europeans and their infectious diseases, but by the middle of the 17th-century, land deals with Vineyard founder Thomas Mayhew brought the first permanent colonial settlement into their midst. Within a year of relocating from the Merrimack River region, Thomas Macy and Tristram Coffin had acquired most of the west end of the island for a small group of proprietors, and secured grazing rights to all Indian

lands to the east. These "first purchasers" and their partners initially believed sheep-raising would be their economic livelihood, but as the once well-wooded island was gradually denuded for crops and pasture, soil-blowing wind and leaf-drying salt air took their toll. Within a generation of settlement, the colonists (like their Vineyard compatriots) were forced by poor stewardship of the land to turn their attentions to the riches of the sea.

Gone Fishing
Nantucket wasn't the only port in Massachusetts—or New England—to outfit itself for the whaling industry. Neither did it have the biggest fleet. And it put away its harpoons and quenched its try-pot fires even as mainland neighbors were still unfurling their sails for further voyages. But no other port has come close to Nantucket in capturing the popular modern imagination with its whaling adventures—perhaps because no other port was so wholly dependent upon "blubber-boilers" for its livelihood. "The Nantucketer, he alone resides and rests on the sea," wrote Melville "He alone, in Bible language, goes down to it in ships; to and fro ploughing it as his own special plantation. . . . With the landless gull, that at sunset folds her wings and is rocked to sleep between billows; so at nightfall, the Nantucketer, out of sight of land, furls his sails, and lays him to his rest, while under his very pillow rush herds of walruses and whales."

The island's Nauset Indians had long been known to harpoon right whales that came close to shore—a technique English settlers also practiced through the 1600s—until they discovered the existence of the sperm whale with its head

OLD DARTMOUTH HISTORICAL SOCIETY/
NEW BEDFORD WHALING MUSEUM

The Capture *(of a sperm whale), by Albert Van Beest*

full of oil so fine that to this day no synthetic has equalled it. By 1730, Nantucketers were using a couple of dozen small ships to chase these creatures and bring them ashore for rendering; on the eve of the American Revolution, a generation later, whaling was the island's economic mainstay, employing a third of its population aboard some 150 vessels roaming the Atlantic from Greenland to Brazil.

Despite the Quaker-dominated island community's solemn declaration of neutrality during the Revolution (or perhaps because of it), both warring factions accused islanders of consorting with the enemy (which was true—with no local supplies of food or fuel, Nantucketers dealt with whomever they could to get whatever they needed). By war's end, all but one or two of the island's fleet had been burned or captured. Faced with prison or unable to return home, scores of island mariners also sailed under British and French flags; it was under the Union Jack, in fact, that Nantucketers first went whaling in the Pacific. Government incentives to revitalize the whaling industry after the war produced competition from ports up and down the new United States; resourceful islanders responded by pushing farther than ever for their quarry, outfitting huge vessels of several hundred tons' capacity for three- to four-year voyages to "the remotest secret drawers and lockers of the world," in Melville's words. The ink was barely dry on the newly ratified Constitution before Nantucket whalers were chasing whalespouts off the coast of Chile. One Nantucket captain discovered the whaling grounds between Easter Island and the Equator in 1818; two years later, another inaugurated the hunt off the coast of Japan; and in 1835, a Nantucket ship became the first non-Inuit craft to capture right whales off the coast of Alaska. It was even a Nantucket whaler who discovered the fate of the mutinous H.M.S. Bounty crew by putting in at Pitcairn Island for fresh water. By the middle of the 19th century, the Pacific seemed to be crawling with Nantucketers, most of whom saw every island from the Azores to Tasmania before setting foot again in Boston.

They left their names on such remote atolls as Starbuck, Howland, and Baker. They left their offspring and venereal diseases among Polynesian island women; and they left their graves, too, in places like New Zealand, where Americans who chance to examine the old cemeteries are sometimes surprised to see New England place names on the aged stones. All in the name of taking the greatest mammals of the deep and boiling them down for English, French, and American lamp oil, candle-wax, and cosmetics. They took so many in such short order that within a few decades, the populations of a half dozen major species had been reduced to insignificance. Profit margins on a successful voyage could still exceed 200-300%, thanks to the pittance paid to the crews and the lack of a reliable supply of cheaper substitutes for $1.77-a-gallon sperm oil, but in 1859, the party came to an abrupt end. A hole drilled in Titusville, Pennsylvania, hit petroleum and sank Nantucket's whaling industry. As the world lit its lamps with kerosene, Nantucket's own candle guttered and died.

Making Do with Quaint

After the demise of its major occupation, some of Nantucket's wealthiest citizens simply moved away; others surveyed New Bedford's textile mills, Provincetown's cod fishery, and the Vineyard's summer-cottage trade, and sank their money into resort developments. Most of these failed for a variety of reasons, not the least of which was a misunderstanding about what made the island attractive to visitors. Nantucket's tourists, it became clear, wanted neither Falmouth's fancy seaside hotels nor Oak Bluffs' cheek-by-jowl gingerbread cottages. Tradesmen stopped off at the Vineyard for boardwalk diversions; professionals came to Nantucket to listen to characterful old salts tell of their whaling adventures, and to soak up the primitive ambiance of derelict wharves and hollowed-out villages. Amid a general revival of national interest in all things colonial, Nantucket's visitors wanted to bathe in the island's past. If an antique-filled island frozen in the 1840s was what visitors would pay good money to see, then the island's citizens were happy to build it. (And they still are: local ordinances stipulate that all new houses continue to resemble centuries-old saltboxes or Capes, with cedar-shingle siding and steep pitched roofs.)

God's Country

Nantucket has taken great pains to ensure that its built environment conforms to the amalgam of myth and history it sells to visitors. Besides historic district guidelines regulating nearly every facade and fencepost on the island, local bylaws and groundwater protections control growth and strictly limit new housing construction. Ten nonprofit groups and government agencies have conserved thousands of acres of open land, aided in part by the nation's first local land trust, funded by real estate transaction fees. These measures go a long way toward preventing tacky suburban sprawl and preserving the island's look and feel, long recognized as its most marketable commodity. On the other hand, the property values have been driven up by the rich people who want in on this pristine economic equivalent of a gated community, spendthrift summer tourists, and the retailers who want to cater to both—pushing local shopkeepers out of town and forcing many less affluent residents to do their shopping "in America" (as the mainland is traditionally known). Careful land-use planning and zoning may preserve the look, but whether the feel can overcome off-season's vacant downtown and the colonization of island business remains to be seen.

SIGHTS

Museums, Museums, Museums

Ferry passengers disembarking from the Steamship Authority at Steamboat Wharf are greeted a block off the gangway by hints of Nantucket's two principal attractions—recreation and history. Beyond the bike shops beckoning from the foot of Broad St. is the **Whaling Museum,** tel. (508) 228-1736, where Nantucket's eminence in the whaling industry is recollected through art, tools, specimens, and dramatic narratives delivered with gusto by museum volunteers. Appropriately, the museum occupies a former candle factory, whose tapers were made from that most prized of whale oils, spermaceti. Open April through early December (Fri.-Sun. only starting in late April and ending the first weekend of December, daily late May through mid-October; admission $5). If the try-pots and whale tales whet your appetite for related books, toys, or even scrimshaw, be sure to visit the well-stocked museum shop. Next door, the **Peter Foulger Museum,** tel. (508) 228-1655,

provides a glimpse into the island's past through special exhibits culled from the Nantucket Historical Association's stash of treasures (same hours and days as the Whaling Museum; $4). Changing exhibits from the NHA's collections are also featured a few blocks south at the **Fair Street Museum,** tel. (508) 228-5205, next to the historic 1838 Quaker Meetinghouse. Open daily late May through early October; admission is $3. A combined ticket good for single admission anytime over the course of a season to any of the NHA properties, including these three museums, may be purchased for only $10 adults, $5 children 5-14.

The Maria Mitchell Association

In 1831, the King of Denmark offered a prize to the first discoverer of a comet by telescope. Sixteen years later, Maria Mitchell, daughter of a multitalented local educator, won the gold medal with the aid of a telescope she and her father shared on the roof of the former Pacific National Bank. At a time when, as she mused to her diary, "the needle is the chain of woman, and has fettered her more than the laws of the country," Mitchell quickly became an international celebrity. She learned astronomy from her father, whom she aided in his sideline business of calibrating navigational chronometers (note the inscribed stone markers used for this work at the curb beside the bank at 61 Main St., and a block south on Fair St.). After being lionized for her discovery—she became the first woman elected to the American Academy of Arts and Sciences—Mitchell undertook a career in mathematics and astronomy, eventually spending 20 years on the faculty at Vassar before ultimately retiring to Nantucket, where she lies buried in Prospect Hill Cemetery. Today, the Maria Mitchell Association promotes astronomy and the natural sciences through public lectures, classes, the **Maria Mitchell Aquarium,** on Washington St. near the Town Pier, tel. (508) 228-5387 (Tues.-Sat. June-Aug.; $1), a **Science Library,** on Vestal St., tel. (508) 228-9219 (year-round), and the preserved wildflowers and stuffed critters displayed in the adjacent **Hinchman House** at the corner of Vestal and Milk Sts., tel. (508) 228-0898 (Tues.-Sat. June-Aug.; $3). Among the prizes of this latter's herbarium is the great amateur naturalist

NANTUCKET TAXONOMY

Thanks to its size and physical isolation, and the high-minded ideals of the Victorian era, Nantucket's entire plant community—from sandplains to cedar bogs—is possibly one of the nation's best-catalogued landscapes.

Darwin's 1859 *On the Origin of Species* ushered in an age of scientific rationalism that was felt from London's Royal Academy to America's drawing rooms. As study of the natural sciences was becoming a middle-class fascination (tabloid dailies covered scientific expeditions, and Jules Verne took readers 20,000 leagues under the sea), Nantucket was becoming a popular Victorian resort, and the island's visitors heeded the encouraging call of island publicists, who promoted study of the local "vegetable and animal life." Anyone who suffered

through high-school biology may find it hard to believe, but pigeonholing the natural world with Linnaean binomials was once the stuff of proper leisure.

The personification of Victorian taxonomy was probably Eugene P. Bicknell, a 19th-century New Jersey banker who amassed the island's largest inventory of plants, a ledger-perfect collection now held by the Maria Mitchell Association. Bicknell's dedication and precision are sorely missed today: a 1996 inventory of the island fell a full 26% short of the 1,200-plus species collected by Bicknell and others. While ecologists don't doubt that some species have disappeared over the years, it is hoped that most of the missing simply went undetected and await the arrival of a new generation of Bicknells to ferret them out.

Eugene Bicknell's exhaustive, unrivaled collection of Nantucket plants, meticulously gathered around the turn of the century. The building also houses the association's gift shop, an excellent place to pick up field guides to local flora, fauna, and ecology. Or, for expert guidance in the flesh, inquire about the nature walks and birdwatching trips sponsored by the association.

Across Vestal St. is the **Maria Mitchell Birthplace,** tel. (508) 228-2896, restored with family possessions and other artifacts to illustrate the domestic life of a 19th-century Quaker family such as the Mitchells (tours Tues.-Sat. June-Aug.; $3).

If you intend to visit more than one of the association's properties, invest in a combined admission pass for just $5. And if you're staying overnight during the summer, inquire about the popular Open Nights at the association's research-oriented **Loines Observatory,** out on Milk St. Ext., tel. (508) 228-9273, for a free peek into the heavens.

Historical Houses

In addition to its varied museums, the Nantucket Historical Association maintains a number of carefully restored old buildings, from one of its oldest surviving houses to the 1805 Old Gaol, off Vestal St. past the Maria Mitchell complex. Several (such as the jail) are free, but most charge admission of $2 or $3 each (waived for holders of the NHA's all-inclusive $10 ticket) and offer

guided tours daily in season. All are open briefly for Memorial Day weekend, reopen a week later and stay open daily through Columbus Day, then cut back to only Fri.-Sun. until early December. For inquiries about any of the properties, call the NHA's main office, (508) 228-1894.

Pick up a museum guide from any of the staffed NHA properties and follow its suggested half-day walking tour for a thorough stroll through the ages, starting with the 1686 **Jethro Coffin House** on Sunset Hill, 10 minutes' walk from the center of town. Canonized over a century ago as the island's "Oldest House" (actually the oldest survivor on its original site—a few older structures have all been moved and modified), this simple farmhouse required extensive refurbishment in the 1870s, thanks to early tourists' practice of carving their names in the walls and stealing souvenir shingles. A wedding gift for a marriage that helped end a major family feud on the island, the house's design (with its central chimney, hall, and parlor) marks an ambitious improvement over that of the First Period dwellings (with one or two rooms and chimneys on the ends of the buildings) more typical of the region. At the other end of the spectrum is one of the NHA's youngest properties, the **Hadwen House,** 96 Main Street. Commissioned by William Hadwen, a silversmith turned whale-oil dealer, this handsome 1845 mansion embodies 19th-century ostentation as much as the Coffin

House, in its rudimentary way, set the standard for high living 160 years earlier. The Ionic-columned Hadwen and its Corinthian-columned neighbor are known as "the Two Greeks," in counterpoint to "the Three Bricks, " an exceptional trio of transitional federal-style homes built across the street by Hadwen's father-in-law.

Among the NHA's other highlights are the **Macy-Christian House,** an 18th-century merchant's home on Liberty St.; the island's first public school, on Winter St.; an 1886 neighborhood fire station, with its antique pumper, on Gardner St; and the photogenic 1746 **Old Mill,** on South Mill St., whose wind-driven millstones are still put to work producing cornmeal for sale in season whenever the weather allows. A different perspective on the history of some of these sites is offered by the **Black Heritage Trail** brochure, available at the Whaling Museum or the Visitor Services office at 25 Federal St., among other places.

Rise Above It All

Outside of a trip to Altar Rock in the Middle Moors, the best panorama of the island is found atop the steeple of the 19th-century **First Congregational Church & Old North Vestry,** 62 Centre St., tel. (508) 228-0950. The hike up all the stairs is amply rewarded by the view over rooftop widow's walks, a vantage from which weathered shingles, rose-covered trellises, and "catslide" roofs (shorter in back than in front) can be appreciated as textures of the landscape rather than as architectural details. Open Mon.-Sat. mid-June through mid-October; donations suggested for admission.

Lighthouses

Three lighthouses grace Nantucket's coast, but if you're keen on seeing all three you'll have your work cut out for you. Turn-of-the-century **Brant Point Light** is the easiest to visit: it's the diminutive wooden nubbin at the end of Easton St.—the one around which the ferries arc into the harbor. At only 26 feet, it's the nation's shortest lighthouse, but being small hasn't spared it the ravages of the elements: recurring fires and storms have required the original 1743 light to be rebuilt nine times.

About six miles to the east, at the end of the Milestone Rd. bike path, is **Sankaty Head Light,** both the island's oldest and the only one that

hasn't had to be rebuilt. Erected in 1849, the distinctive red-belted light towers 150 feet over some of the region's most treacherous waters, its flashing beacon nearly reaching Cape Cod 30 miles away. Although it kept mariners away from the beach, in the 50 years after its construction many of the 2,000 ships that went aground on Nantucket's shoals did so off this shore—on Rose and Crown, Great Rip, Old Man, and other of the many named hull-scraping rocks and shallow bars. These days it makes a prominent target for landlocked navigators cycling across the hummocky Middle Moors, suspended on the wind-blown horizon like a tantalizing heat-mirage.

Most difficult of all to see close up is **Great Point Light,** way out at the end of the Coskata-Coatue Wildlife Refuge. The newest of the island's lights, the present youthful incarnation is the replacement for the historic stone tower utterly destroyed by a violent winter tempest in 1984. So that this one may possibly beat its predecessor's 166-year tenure, its reinforced concrete walls are five feet thick at the base.

OUTDOORS ON THE MOORS

Middle Moors

Though much of Nantucket's interior has historically been described as "moors," any resemblance to Scotland's peat-based landscape is purely superficial. While some acidic peat-soiled bogs do exist here, Nantucket's moors are mostly combinations of grassy sandplains and dry shrubby heathlands—two very distinct (and increasingly rare) plant communities here intermingled nearly to the point of interchangeability. The Middle Moors, a great expanse of undeveloped land between Polpis and Milestone Roads east of town, is a good example of this grass and heath mixture—and also illustrates the probable fate of the island's heathlands, which are being overrun by native scrub oak. This sort of plant succession is entirely natural and would eventually return the island interior to the wooded state it was in when Europeans arrived. But prior to colonial settlement, the heaths flourished close to shore—where salt air put trees at a disadvantage—and in forest openings created by fire. Homeowners covetous of ocean views cleared muchy of that away, and fires are now suppressed to prevent property damage, so the heaths and their dependent ecosystem of insects, birds, and small mammals are headed toward extinction.

Altar Rock, a glacial erratic in the overgrown ridge (Saul's Hills) defining the moor's northern edge, affords the best panorama over the huckleberry, false heather, and intruding scrub oak barrens. Though a mere 100 feet above sea level, this rock and the four other hills in the ridge that share the same elevation are among the highest points on the island. Only Sankaty Bluff (at a skyscraping 109 feet), Folger Hill (at 108), and part of the $28 million Rees Jones golf course to the east are higher. Altar Rock also offers one of a declining number of island vistas whose foreground isn't speckled with vacation homes. The most direct route to the rock is via the signposted sand track off Polpis Rd., exactly opposite the Quaise Rd. turnoff; head toward the radio antenna. To identify other trails through the moors, pick up an all-island *General Information & Properties Map* from the Nantucket Conservation Foundation, 118 Cliff Rd., tel. (508) 228-2884 (open Mon.-Fri. only). Thirty miles of sandy roads accommodate mountain bikers—although to reduce erosion, bikers are requested to stay off trails blocked by posts or obviously narrow and suited only for walkers. Like all NCF holdings, the Middle Moors are distinguished from private land by the organization's gull/waves/hills logo, affixed to maroon posts at the boundaries.

Cranberry Bogs

Cranberries are as native to Nantucket as are thick fogs, but only since the mid-1800s have they been cultivated. The cranberry's high wholesale price makes it a prince among farm commodities, but on Nantucket land for houses commands kingly sums. To keep the island's surviving commercial cranberry bogs from disappearing beneath more cedar-sided saltbox summer homes for the rich and famous, they've been purchased and donated to the Nantucket Conservation Foundation. Through the NCF, **Windswept Cranberry Bog,** off Polpis Rd. opposite the Wauwinet turnoff, and **Milestone Road Cranberry Bog,** about five miles east of town along the Sconset bike path, remain working farms with over 200 acres under active cultivation and hundreds more acres of marsh, ponds, and forest open to the public. The mix of floristic communities makes for good birdwatching throughout the warmer months, and budding naturalists will find plenty of blossoms lending their colors to the landscape, from subtle little crowberry blooms to the more showy pink crane-like cranberry flowers. A trail map specifically for the Windswept property is available at the NCF office on Cliff Road.

Come mid-October, the fruits of these acres star in the annual Cranberry Harvest Weekend. Shuttles bring visitors from town to watch mechanical "water reels" plow through submerged bogs beating the cranberry vines, creating great crimson oceans of floating berries in their wake. The crop gets vacuumed up for shipment off-island, where the berries are turned into the jellies and sauces you may be buying for Thanksgiving. (Wet-harvested berries are never sold raw because the water starts breaking down their natural waxy coating, eliminating any chance of a viable retail shelf-life.) As you'd expect, the harvest allows local bakeries and restaurants to demonstrate the versatility of these tart treats in all manner of sweet and savory dishes.

BOB RACE

Coskata-Coatue Wildlife Refuge

One of TTOR's many fine properties, Coskata-Coatue (ko-SKATE-ah ko-TWO), tel. (508) 228-0006, encompasses Nantucket's longest barrier beach, largest salt marsh, a cedar forest, and—at the far north end of that beach—Great Point's lighthouse. Tidepools hold plenty of shellfish such as scallops, clams, and mussels, while wild roses and the elusive beach plum grow amid the dunes. To protect the fragile dunes from wind erosion, you're strongly discouraged from climbing them. And swimming isn't recommended, due to dangerous riptides. With over 10 miles of shoreline on three bodies of water—the Atlantic, Nantucket Sound, and the enclosed harbor—this is the place to take long meditative walks on the beach. Depending on how the bluefish are running, you may find a lot of serious surfcasters out at Great Point contemplating how to tempt a fish to swallow a hook. When not restricted for beach-nesting plovers and terns, four-wheel-drive vehicles with the proper permits may use designated roads out to the lighthouse. Permits ($85 a year for private vehicles, $20 per day for rental vehicles), information, and maps are all available May-mid-Oct. from the Wauwinet Gatehouse on Wauwinet Rd., the access point for the property.

The Sanford Farm

On Madaket Rd. about two miles west of the waterfront on the Madaket shuttle route is a small parking area and trailhead for the former Sanford Farm, now one of several contiguous parcels of public conservation land stretching nearly three miles to the South Shore's Cisco Beach. Several miles of trails traverse a varied set of habitats bounded on one side by Hummock Pond, whose waters fill a narrow glacial outwash valley. Swamps and sloughs where you might see turtles napping in the sun, old fields surrendering to bayberry and wild grape, grassland meadows known as the "Ram Pasture," woodlands browsed by white-tailed deer, and plenty of wild blueberries are among the treats for walkers and cyclists (others are described on the 26 interpretive markers spread along the six-mile loop to the ocean). If you can't spare a few hours to go the whole way, at least go as far as the barn—about 30 minutes' walk from the Madaket Rd. gate—for great views to the ocean.

FROLICKING IN SAND AND SURF

Beaches

About a dozen named beaches dot the island's shore, from kid-friendly **Children's Beach,** a few blocks north of Steamboat Wharf to the rough breakers at **'Sconset,** between the village and the Coast Guard's LORAN navigational radio masts. In general, beaches facing south or east receive the big breakers, strong currents, and fine sand, while those facing Nantucket Sound to the north are more calm (though also more pebbly). In summers there's a shuttle bus to 'Sconset from Nantucket Town (Washington St. at the corner of Main); for sustenance after arriving in the village, look to the 'Sconset Cafe by the Post Office.

Besides Children's Beach, harbor swimming spots include modest **Francis Street Beach,** out toward the end of Washington St. Ext., and **Brant Point,** by the lighthouse. The first is placid as a pond, but the Point boasts a stiff current (swimmers beware). Safer conditions prevail at the two north shore favorites, **Jetties Beach** and **Dionis,** both of which feature seasonal lifeguards and restrooms. With its windsurfing concession, beach volleyball, snack shack, adjacent public tennis courts, and connecting bus service to town, Jetties is *not* the place to seek splendid isolation. On the other hand, Dionis is a three-mile bike ride out Madaket and Eel Point Rds. and is a good half-mile wide—so anyone unburdened by kids and coolers stands a chance of finding some elbow room.

The south shore's magnet for the young, blonde, and bronze (and everyone else who feigns indifference to holes in the ozone layer) is **Surfside,** at the end of the eponymous road and bike path. Restrooms, showers, and unremarkable food are all available in season, as is shuttle bus service from downtown. Surfside is huge, but it still fills up; walk east a mile and you can join the lighter ranks of surfing enthusiasts who favor the big breaks at **Nobadeer Beach;** or walk west and eventually you'll join the often clothing-optional crowd at **Miacomet.** The other two beaches with southern exposure are **Cisco,** at the end of Hummock Pond Rd., and **Madaket,** as far west as the island's shuttle buses and bike paths go. Besides invigorating waves that leave you feeling like a sock in the spin cycle, Madaket is as good a seat for those lovely ocean sunsets as you're going to get without buying land out on Tuckernuck or Muskeget.

Water Sports

Windsurfers and surfer-wannabees who aren't headed to the Vineyard (where equipment rents for half what it does on Nantucket) should make tracks for **Force 5 Watersports** at Jetties

ISLAND ANGLING

It should come as no surprise that the islands constitute an angler's heaven. Whether fly-fishing for "bones" (bonito); trolling deep waters for mackerel, tuna, and swordfish; or jigging for flounder and pollack near coastal rocks, there's plenty of variety to keep beginners and experts occupied. But most prized by local fish fanciers are two species favored by surf casters—striped bass and bluefish.

Stripers are nocturnal feeders who school up in local waters starting around mid-May. Blues tend to start their runs past the islands in mid- to late June. Blues are like oceanic pit bulls, making slash-and-run attacks in their paths—from flesh to fishing tackle (if you get bitten, you won't suffer as much as the bait—but you'll definitely feel it). Schools of blues are easily detected by the tremendous commotion of other fish leaping out of the water to escape their high-speed pack attacks.

Both species have felt the impact of overfishing and pollution—stripers in particular were nearly wiped out in the region a few years ago—so limits have been set on size and quantity. Consult local tackle shops for current restrictions on keepers.

Martha's Vineyard visitors will find a dozen or more tackle shops, boat charters, guides, and equipment rental places listed in the Yellow Pages and the Chamber of Commerce *Visitor's Guide.*

On Nantucket, anglers will find sportfishing boats such as the *Just Do It Too,* tel. (508) 228-7448, and the *Herbert T,* tel. (508) 228-6655, ready and waiting down on Straight Wharf. Or call Mike Cody's **all over it,** (508) 325-6043, for an on-shore fishing expedition, from $100 (surf) to $150 (fly), including all equipment and transportation (discounts for parties of two or more).

Beach, tel. (508) 228-0700. Throughout the summer, you'll find plenty of sailboards, kayaks, Sunfish, and surf- or boogie boards for rent, starting at $15 per hour for kayaks, $25 per hour for windsurfers, and $30 per hour for Sunfish. Three-hour introductory group lessons for any of these items are $100 (private instruction is more, of course). To rent just kayaks or canoes (or "surf bikes," an update on the old amusement-park pedal boat), friendly **Sea Nantucket** is the place to go, at the Francis St. Beach, tel. (508) 228-7499. Non-rollable single and double kayaks are ideal for beginners—who have the entire protected length of Nantucket Harbor to play around in, from Coatue's gull rookeries east to Wauwinet. The company also handles deliveries, if you want to row around inland waters like long, narrow Hummock Pond, west of town, or large Sesachacha (se-SACK-atcha) Pond, on the eastern shore by Quidnet Beach. Open Memorial Day through early or mid-October; prices run from $15 an hour to $50 a day, slightly higher for double kayaks.

If you're making yourself at home on the island for the whole summer, you can work on that tan *and* learn how to sail courtesy of **Nantucket Island Community Sailing,** tel. (508) 228-6600. For a $150 membership and $160 course fee, you get 10 hours of instruction over five days; pass the qualifying exam at the end and you'll earn sailing privileges with N.I.C.S. boats for the remainder of the season. If you already know how to sail, you can rent boats for day sailing at **Nantucket Harbor Sail,** on Swain's Wharf, tel. (508) 228-0424.

The Community Pool

Year-round, if inclement weather or ice-cold water keeps you away from the shore, you can still swim laps at the Nantucket Community Pool at the intersection of Atlantic and Sparks Aves. next to the high school, tel. (508) 228-7262 (reachable on the NRTA "South Loop" shuttle). The Olympic-sized, heated, indoor facility offers a varied schedule of adult, senior, and youth lap swims, water aerobics classes, open family swims, and other organized programs. Day users pay $4.75; bring your own towel and lock for your belongings.

Whalewatching

Although nearly all Massachusetts' whalewatching tours head for the easily reached Stellwagen Bank portion of Massachusetts Bay, north of Cape Cod, whales can be spotted wherever there are enough fishy snacks to satisfy their outsized appetites. Nantucket's Great South Channel is one such place—its depth, currents, and water temperatures make for the kind of shallow, fertile feeding ground perfectly tailored to lunching leviathans and, consequently, curious humans. Veterans of Massachusetts Bay whalewatching may be interested to know there are some species here off Nantucket—pilot whales, for example—almost never seen on trips from mainland ports. Weather permitting, each week between mid-July and mid-September, **Yankee Whale Watch,** tel. (800) WHALING, brings one of their special vessels down to Nantucket from their home port, north of Boston, to spend a full day observing whales out there in the channel. The seven- to eight-hour trips ($65 adults, $30 kids under 16) depart Tuesday mornings at 9:30 a.m. from Straight Wharf, bringing you back in time for some dinner of your own.

TOURS

If you would like a guide to present Nantucket for you, try one of the small van tours available in season. Each of the following offers all-island tours lasting less than two hours for about $10 per person and picks up from any in-town guest house or inn (or from the ferries, if you let them know which one you'll be arriving on): **Ara's Tours,** tel. (508) 228-1951; **Gail's Tours,** tel. (508) 257-6557; and **Robert Pitman Grimes Tours,** tel. (508) 228-9382. Some folks would say the best way to get the lay of the land is from offshore, where Nantucket's true nature as a fragile outpost amid the waves is all the more manifest. Whether you need such a fancy excuse to getting out on the water, several sailing boats offer cruises in local waters, including the reasonably priced Endeavor, a gaff-rigged Friendship sloop that makes trips of up to three hours around the harbor and Nantucket Sound. The same friendly folks operate a reproduction classic whaleboat, the *Wanderer,* for harbor charters, too. For reservations or information about either, call (508) 228-5585, or visit the office on Straight Wharf.

ACCOMMODATIONS

Affordable accommodations are an oxymoron on Nantucket—even more oxymoronic than affordable dining. Scores of the town's 18th- and 19th-century houses have been converted to inns, many of which epitomize the traditional, frilly stereotype of the Olde New England B&B, brimming with wide wood flooring, tchotchke-laden mantelpieces, lacy curtains, stenciled walls, and period antiques. But snoozing in canopy beds under handmade quilts in this living museum of Colonial and Early American decorative arts doesn't come cheap—especially June-Sept., when two- and three-night minimums prevail and even rooms with shared baths can run more than $100. A handful of simple guest houses and a dwindling number of small, highly personal B&B homes, most of which are found on the outskirts of town or midisland, offer some relief, but most real savings don't arrive until the warm weather is gone.

You'll find many more staff-run inns than archetypal owner-operated B&Bs. This means, of course, that you can end up paying luxury hotel rates for places presided over by inexperienced summer-only staff. Of course, there are a number of exceptions, and not just in price—places whose impeccable taste or authenticity, consummate professionalism, or sincere attention to your comfort justify every dollar they charge. For the most comprehensive aid in booking a room or renting a cottage, consider a reservation service such as **Nantucket Accommodations,** tel. (508) 228-9559.

In general, the difference between expensive and very expensive or luxury is in the details: mirrors over the sink (try shaving with a mirror two feet from the faucet to appreciate how important this is), nightlights and hair dryers, umbrellas or beach towels for guest use. When choosing, weigh in-town convenience against out-of-town serenity: mopeds buzzing by your downtown window at 7:30 a.m. may not be the wake-up call you want on your vacation, and over-loud voices of late-night drinkers may not be the evening serenade you anticipated. Of course, if you're the one doing the carousing, or getting up early to hit the beach, such considerations hardly matter.

As on the Vineyard, bed and breakfast homes and inns almost all serve continental breakfasts, so if you want more than cereal, muffins, and fruit without leaving the premises, you'll have to stay at one of the dozen luxury-priced, full-scale hotels with restaurants, or at the exceptional Union Street Inn (value-conscious travelers will

ADDITIONAL NANTUCKET ACCOMMODATIONS

Anchor Inn, 66 Centre St., tel. (508) 228-0072; an 1806 captain's home with canopy beds, private baths, and continental breakfasts; open year-round. Very expensive in summer, moderate and inexpensive in winter.

Ayers Guest House, 6 Union St., tel. (508) 228-0245; private baths; open April through mid-October. Expensive in summer, moderate in the shoulder months.

Great Harbor Inns, tel. (800) 377-6609; three different inns—the Great Harbor, Fair Gardens, and Brass Lantern—offer a range of well-appointed rooms in centrally located historic homes, all with private baths and continental breakfasts; some rooms available year-round. Very expensive to luxury from late June through mid-October, moderate to expensive off-season.

Lyon Street Inn, 10 Lyon St., tel. (508) 228-5040; e-mail lyon@nantucket.net; historic home with working fireplaces, plenty of antiques, tapestries, and Oriental carpets, private baths, and continental breakfast; open late April through early December. Very expensive to luxury in summer, moderate off-season.

Nantucket Inn & Conference Center, on Macy's Lane by the airport, tel. (800) 321-8484; open year-round, it's the closest thing to a modern hotel in ambiance, amenities, and decor; pool, restaurant, hourly downtown shuttle, and cour-tesy pickups for Steamship passengers available only in season (which is why off-season rates drop to $55). Luxury from late April through late October, inexpensive otherwise.

Paul West House, 5 Liberty St., tel. (508) 228-2495; no credit cards accepted; some shared baths; open year-round. Expensive.

Stumble Inne, 109 Orange St., tel. (508) 228-4482, e-mail romance@nantucket.net; a pair of typically historic houses done over in country Victorian, with private baths and continental breakfast; open April-December. Expensive to luxury late June through mid-October, moderate to expensive off season.

The 1739 House, 43 Centre St., tel. (508) 228-0120; no credit cards accepted; shared and private baths, continental breakfast; open late May through Halloween. Expensive.

The White Elephant, 50 Easton St., tel. (800) IS-LANDS; classic seaside resort beside the harbor boat basin, with patios and porches under striped awnings, pool, upscale cosmopolitan restaurant, and lounge entertainment; open May-October. Luxury (i.e., $295-495 in peak season).

Walker Guest House, 5 Fair St., tel. (508) 228-0213; no credit cards accepted. Early 19th-century captain's home filled with antiques; open late May through mid-October. Expensive (shared bath) to very expensive (private bath).

want to take advantage of the off-season drop in rates at such high-end places). As for awakening to a view of boats swaying gently at their moorings, don't get your hopes up too high—valuable waterfront views are more prevalent among weekly cottage rentals than small inns. Finally, if you're after a romantic off-season getaway curled up in front of a crackling fire, be sure to inquire closely about inns claiming to have working fireplaces in their rooms: given the liability insurance for historic wooden buildings, many places restrict guests to using compressed firelogs rather than kindling real, roaring wood fires.

Budget: under $35

The only budget option on the island is **Hosteling International Nantucket,** out at the end of the Surfside bike path, on Western Ave., tel. (508) 228-0433. Common rooms, dining, and kitchen facilities occupy a handsome 1873 former lifesaving station with Victorian gingerbread trim; guests sleep in separate, single-sex dorms. Despite the lack of rooms for couples and families, the staff's good humor more than makes up for the occasional nights in a room full of snorers; open late April through late October, $12 HI members, $15 nonmembers (reservations essential most of the season). Since the nearest market, Peter Piper's, is almost two miles back on the edge of town, pick up groceries before arriving.

Inexpensive: $35-60

The only summer candidate in this category is **Claire's B&B,** on Skyline Dr., out by the airport, tel. (508) 228-8966: $55 d per night for stays of two nights or longer (single-night stays are $15 extra) in rooms with shared baths (cash only). Claire also has several bikes she rents to guests ($10 per day). Open mid-April through October or early November. If you're traveling by yourself and don't mind shared baths, the year-round **Martin House Inn** offers singles in summer for as low as $50-55, and its neighbor, the **Centre Street Inn,** has some for $45-50 up to late June and after late September. (See "Expensive," below, for details on both.)

Moderate: $60-85
Between Memorial Day and Columbus Day, the only place with rates that let it into this category is **The Nesbitt Inn,** 21 Broad St., tel. (508) 228-0156. The oldest purpose-built inn on the island, this 1872 Victorian encourages society rather than seclusion, with a common-room game table, backyard swingset for kids, and a warm hospitality that makes all guests start to feel like family. There are no private baths for any of the standard rooms—which is why this is one of the island's most affordable inns. Doubles start at $70 in season, singles $60. Off season, prices drop about $10.

Expensive: $85-110
Lower Centre St. is thrice blessed: it's quietly separate from yet quite close to downtown boutiques and restaurants, it's home to the beautiful First Congregational Church, and its inns offer eclectic room configurations spanning a wide price range. Two prime examples sit nearly across from one another: the **Martin House Inn,** 61 Centre St., tel. (508) 228-0678, e-mail martin@nantucket.net, and the **Centre Street Inn,** 78 Centre St., tel. (800) 298-0199. Behind the latter's cheerful yellow clapboard sit more than a dozen rooms, from cozy singles with shared baths (as low as $40 off-season, $65-75 in summer) to spacious rooms with queen beds, private baths, and fireplaces ($145-195 summer, $90-125 late spring and early fall, $80-115 off-season). In between are double and twin rooms with shared baths for $95-115 summer, $65-80 spring and fall, and $55-65 off-season. Though built in the mid 1700s and furnished accordingly, this former merchant's home is no museum—hospitality comes first, and the own-

ers take great care to make guests feel right at home. Open early April through early December. Guest quarters at the year-round Martin House also run the gamut from queen canopy bedrooms with private baths (and some with fireplaces) to doubles, twins, and singles with shared baths. The house is beautifully furnished from bottom to top, and the large dining room makes a most welcome spot to linger over breakfast or socialize with other guests. Rates are similar to those at the Centre Street Inn, but about 10% lower.

Very Expensive: $110-150
Built around the end of the American Revolution, the **Corner House,** 49 Centre St., tel. (508) 228-1530, has the expected complement of antiques and hardwood floors, but renovations have also exposed some the structure's evocative handhewn beams, and the whole is highlighted with contemporary colors and fabrics. The model ship collection adds a distinctive grace note. The rooms, actually spread among the main house and a pair of ancillary cottages, run $100-185 in summer, drop about 20% in late spring and early fall, and bottom out around $65-115 in the off season. All have private baths. Besides continental breakfast, rates include afternoon iced tea (or hot cider, as weather demands) and baked treats. Also open year-round is the smack-in-the-center-of-town **Hawthorn House,** 2 Chestnut St., tel. (508) 228-1468, e-mail HHguests@nantucket.net. July-Aug., doubles run $125 with shared bath, $150 private, but before Memorial Day and after September, these drop to $65-95 depending on the day of the week, and as low as $55-65 in the dead of winter. During peak season, an $8 coupon is given to guests for breakfast at either of a couple local eateries nearby.

Luxury: $150+
Occupying a 1770 home a block off Main St. is the **Union Street Inn,** 7 Union St., tel. (800) 225-5116, e-mail unioninn@nantucket.net. Attractively restored and furnished as befits its colonial heritage, the warm tones of the wood paneling and floors, subdued fabric, and classic nautical prints surely would earn approval from the Quaker captain who built the place. Half the 12 rooms include working fireplaces, and all

have fully modern private baths. Best of all, it's the *only* B&B-style property on the island to offer an honest-to-goodness breakfast with the bed. Between Memorial Day and mid-October, doubles run $140-200, then drop sharply for the shoulder month on either end. In winter, rates start at $80 (closed January).

Spend enough time visiting Nantucket inns and the variations on 19th-century decorative themes begin to blur together, until along comes an eye-opener like **Four Chimneys Inn,** 38 Orange St., tel. (508) 228-1912. Summery gardens-of-Giverny colors play off dark solids and bright whites, nicely framing rather than competing with patterned wallpaper and beautifully crafted antiques. Since the 10 very spacious rooms are available only late April through the end of October, there's little call for the five guests who have them to use the fireplaces, but you'll find plenty of reason to use the private porches (on the most expensive rooms), the rooftop cupola, or the attractive Japanese garden. Rates peak in July-Labor Day at $165-275 for two people (the strict limit per room), dropping back about 10% in the shoulder months. Continental breakfast is included.

FOOD

It's lamentable, but the days when a fine meal and a night at the inn didn't practically require pleading for an increase in your credit limit are gone. Heck, even the locals—most of whom live outside of town anyway—find it cheaper and often faster to order take-out from Cape Cod, which they pick up at the airport when the half-hourly flights from Hyannis come in. If paying $100 for dinner for two—without wine—isn't in your budget, stick to the pizza-and-beer joints.

An excellent breakfast may still be had without breaking the bank if you step on over to **Black-Eyed Susan's,** 10 India St. at Center (no phone; mostly year-round; cash only). The food is creative, fresh, and filling, and the ambiance is closer to that of a college town cafe than a fussy old Nantucket institution. Another local sit-down favorite is **Arno's at 41 Main Street,** open year-round. Or go next door, to **Congdon's Pharmacy,** for some fine muffins and a decent cup of coffee from their old-fashioned soda fountain. If

great cinnamon buns sound better, head over to the **Fog Island Cafe,** 7 S. Water St., which also serves reasonably priced omelets, fruit pancakes, cheddar-laced veggie homefries, and other fine egg dishes and griddle fare.

If you're staying on the fringes of town, you needn't go all the way into the center for good chow: **Something Natural,** 50 Cliff Rd., north of the Oldest House (April-Oct.), **Nantucket Bake Shop,** 79 Orange St., several blocks south of Main (open through December), and the **Nantucket Bagel Company,** near the Milestone Rotary, are all worthwhile stops for take-out coffee and breakfast bakery goods, or to pick up some fancy sandwiches for lunch at simple mainland prices. Any one of these makes a good lunch detour for day-trippers wandering among downtown's historic sights, or stop by **Provisions,** on Straight Wharf, for decent chowder, salads and sandwiches, and a cookie big enough to be a meal in itself.

Dinner won't consume your travel budget if you stick to **The Tap Room,** in the Jared Coffin House, at the top of Broad St., tel. (508) 228-2400, a year-round antidote to the island's sophisticated big-ticket cuisine ($8.95-18.95). During tourist season, the Jared also has an all-you-can-eat seafood buffet in their main dining room on Sunday and Wednesday—an outstanding value at about $25 a head. Equally reasonable but far less traditional is the menu down Centre St. at **Black-Eyed Susan's,** 10 India St. at Center (no phone; cash only). Like the breakfasts, dinners reflects the chef-owners' appreciation for fresh veggies and ethnic spices: world music for the mouth. Seafood lovers and vegetarians who care about challenging tastes more than candlelight and starched linen will be enchanted. Susan's also boasts a commendable policy of offering plenty of dishes in generous but money-saving half portions (BYOB).

Surrounding blocks are full of high-priced showcase restaurants, places where entrees run $20-30. Some are disappointingly ordinary (and as a result ridiculously overpriced) but the following handful should enhance any serious food-lover's day—or stay—on the island. Reservations are recommended in peak season for all, although waiting for your table at the bar is a good introduction to a major part of Nantucket nightlife. Among the strongest contenders for elegance and good eating without making you feel you have to whisper or wear black tie is **Cioppino's,** 20 Broad, tel. (508) 228-4622. Personable, attentive service and conversation-friendly small rooms in a beautiful old house—or breezy tables on the patio—are a perfect match for such flavorful dishes as blackened fresh halibut over red pepper rice, or a real San Francisco-style cioppino (seafood stew). The prix fixe three-course early-bird specials are a great way to save money, too, without resorting to sandwiches or pizza. Open seasonally, May through October. Open year-round is the **Boarding House,** 12 Federal, tel. (508) 228-9622. While the bar and bistro scene here is a cornerstone of island gay social life, the relaxed dining room is at the forefront of contemporizing classic dishes with light but intensely flavored stocks and sauces, perfectly prepared fresh vegetables, and presentations as wonderful to look at as to eat. Up the street, **21 Federal,** tel. (508) 228-2121, is one of the better local practitioners of New American regional cooking, emphasizing seafood and New England fare (April-Dec.). Regional cooking is also the star at **American Seasons,** 80 Centre St., tel. (508) 228-7111, a few blocks north of this downtown trio. Skillful renditions of dishes drawn from the traditions of different parts of the country and wines to match are offered indoors or out at this modest home among the graceful old inns at the foot of the First Congregational Church (April-Dec.).

Off the day-trippers' beaten path are a couple of prized local favorites: the **SeaGrille,** 45 Sparks Ave., out by the Milestone Rotary, tel. (508)325-5700, and nearby **Moona,** 122 Pleasant St., tel. (508) 325-4301, around the corner from the shuttle stop in front of the Chicken Box, or about a 20-minute walk from Main Street. Both are open year-round. The former is a family-friendly surf-and-turf place (specializing, as the name suggests, more in the surf), but the pasta and veal are handled as well as the lobsters, fillets, chowders, and steamers. Moona, meanwhile, is probably the hottest ticket of the last few seasons, and you'll see why with one look at the jazzy, art-filled space, the copper-top tables and painted burlap wallcoverings, the simple yet tantalizing menu, and the prices. The sensory stimulation at Moona certainly ranks as one of the island's best buys—especially if you graze on a selection of the assertive appetizers, several of which are as large as the entrees. If you get stuck with a table back by the kitchen, you can entertain yourself by watching patrons guess the genders of the silhouettes on the bathroom doors (not everyone gets it right).

Pizza, Burgers, and Beers

If you'd prefer to hoist a few cold ones over a burger plate or fish and chips rather than decide between garlic ginger broth and dried cranberry zinfandel sauce, you should check out the **Rose & Crown,** 23 S. Water St., tel. (508)228-2595. After a square meal at a great price, hang out at the lively bar with scads of young seasonal workers (April-Dec.). Instead of a TV in the background, the **Brotherhood of Thieves,** 23 Broad St. (no phone), accompanies its pub grub with regular live folk music. Named after a riot-inciting 1842 accusation leveled against island clergy by abolitionist Stephen Foster, this 19th-century whalers' bar-cum-bohemian hangout is a true local institution. The burgers, sandwiches, and seafood are eclipsed by an extensive bar menu of cordials, spiked coffees, cognacs, single malt Scotches, and other fine spirits. Closed Feb.-mid-March.

Finally, while most of the pizza passed off on tourists down by the ferry piers is a waste of your time and money (you're much better off waiting until you get back to Hyannis), cheapskate writers and other impatient pizza lovers would do well to bike out to **Foood For Here & There** 149 Lower Orange St., near the Milestone Rotary, tel. (508) 228-4291. Low prices, classic combos, and the kind of mostly takeout ambiance that makes you feel comfortable even in your cut-offs are reason enough to make the journey, but the place also delivers.

GETTING AROUND

Bike Rentals

By far the best way to avoid the frustration of summertime traffic is to avoid contributing to it. Bicycles are justly popular, given the relatively short distances you're likely to be traveling: from the steamship piers, every beach is within a nine-mile radius, and most lodgings are within just a mile or two. Level terrain and five paved

NANTUCKET HISTORICAL ASSOCIATION

bike paths radiating in all directions from town are added inducements. Mind the stiff winds, though: they speed dehydration, and a thirsty cyclist is soon a very exhausted cyclist (you'll find fountains on two of the bike paths, but a personal water supply is always a good idea). Rentals are available right off the boat: **Young's Bicycle Shop,** on Steamboat Wharf, tel. (508) 228-1151, and **Nantucket Bike Shop,** on both Steamboat and Straight wharves, tel. (508) 228-1999. Ever-friendly and helpful, Young's is open year-round (Nantucket Bike Shop closes between Nov.-March), offers hourly rates (it's the full day rate or nothing at all with their neighbor and competitor), and tosses in the helmets for free (next door, they're $3 per adult). A few blocks from the wharves—but close to lodgings north of Broad St.—is **Holiday Cycle,** 4 Chester St. at Cliff Rd., tel. (508) 228-3644, a small, friendly shop whose prices are always a dollar or two lower than anyone else's. No matter from whom you rent, anticipate shelling out from $15 a day for a classic Mary Poppins-style upright with a basket to $20 a day for 18- or 21-speed mountain bikes. Young's also offers free road service if you get a flat near a phone booth, and discounts for Hostelling International members. Most rent mopeds and scooters, too, for about twice the price of their bikes.

Shuttles and Cabs

Between June 1 and September 30, the **Nantucket Regional Transit Authority,** tel. (508) 228-7025, revs up regular public bus service around town and to either end of the island. Buses out to Madaket depart every half hour

from Broad St. in front of the Peter Foulger Museum (every half hour after July 1), while 'Sconset buses depart hourly on the half hour from in front of the famous compass rose painted on the side of the building at Washington Street and Main. Around the corner toward the back of the building, on Salem Street next to Ayers Guest House, is the stop for Miacomet and South Loop shoppers' shuttles, which run every 10-15 minutes to various peripheral commercial and residential areas. Find route maps almost everywhere tourist brochures are displayed. Shuttle stops are marked with gray poles with red and maroon stripes. All routes operate until 10:30 p.m. or even later, depending on the route; fares are 50 cents in town and $1 for long-distance destinations. If you intend to hop on and off a half-dozen times a day over a long weekend, inquire about the three- to seven-day ($12-20) passes (which entitle holders to discounts at various stores and eateries). Tired or out-of-shape cyclists will be happy to know all the NRTA buses are equipped with bike racks.

Warm weather also prompts the NRTA to commence its **beach shuttles** to Jetties and Surfside beaches from in front of the Peter Foulger Museum. These are weather dependent: rain keeps them grounded, and a cold spell may delay their start time. Ideally, however, shuttles run daily, hourly, 10 a.m.-6 p.m., mid-June to Labor Day at least.

Taxi rates are comparable to those in any big city, though after 1 a.m. surcharges are added to basic rates (up to an extra $5 3-5 a.m.). If you need to be fetched from outside of town, it wouldn't be uncommon to find yourself waiting an hour, so schedule pickups as far in advance as practical. You'll find cab stands at the airport and both ferry piers; a list of over 30 taxi operators—including those which take bikes—is available from Visitor Services.

Car Rentals

In addition to nearly all the downtown bike shops, which double as car and jeep rental agencies, several national chains are found in the airport terminal or on Macy's Lane between the airport and adjacent Nantucket Inn, including **Hertz,** tel. (800) 654-3131; **Budget,** tel. (800) 527-0700; **Thrifty,** tel. (800) 367-2277; and **Nantucket Windmill Auto Rental,** tel. (800)

228-1227. Other names in the business: **Don Allen Auto Service,** on Polpis Rd., just west of the Rotary, tel. (800) 258-4970; **Preston's Rent A Car,** on Somerset Rd. out Miacomet way, and at the Nantucket Inn, tel. (508) 228-4150; **Affordable Rentals,** 6 South Beach St. in town, tel. (508) 228-3501; and **Barrett's Tours,** 20 Federal St. opposite the Visitor Services office, tel. (508) 228-0174. Everyone picks up free almost anywhere on the island. Summer rates hover around $60 a day for a compact to $140 a day for a 4X4 sport utility vehicle; off-season, everybody halves their prices. Toys such as Jeep Wranglers are generally off limits to anyone under 30. Four-wheeling on any beach requires a permit between May and October, either from the local police at their S. Water St. headquarters, tel. (508) 228-1212 ($20), or, for driving within the Coskata-Coatue Wildlife Refuge, from The Trustees of Reservations ($85 a year or, for rental vehicles, $20 a day). TTOR permits are available from the Wauwinet Gatehouse at the Refuge entrance, tel. (508) 228-0006. Even with all the proper permissions, beach driving may be heavily restricted or even completely denied in some areas through mid-August, when endangered shore birds finally leave their nests.

INFORMATION AND SERVICES

ATMs
Automated teller machines with 24-hour access are found at 20 Federal St. opposite the Visitor Services building; at the Nantucket Bank offices (one on Orange St. around the corner from Main and the other at 104 Pleasant St.); and in the Steamship Authority terminal (except when the night watchman is out doing his 15-minute rounds). During regular business hours, additional ATMs are found in the Pacific National Bank on the main square, at both the A&P and Finast supermarkets, and at the airport.

Newspapers and Information
To immerse yourself in local news, pick up one of the two island weeklies, both owned by an off-island newspaper chain: Thursday's *The Inquirer and Mirror* (known to some as the "Inky Mirror") or *The Nantucket Beacon.* If all you want are listings of restaurants and activities—with a rudimentary map of town thrown in for good measure—pick up the free *Nantucket Map & Legend* from lobby racks at all the customary points of entry to the island, or in doorways or by cash registers of many shops and eateries around town.

The **Nantucket Chamber of Commerce,** upstairs at 48 Main St., tel. (508) 228-1700, should top your itinerary if you're looking for brochures. The very polished *Official Guide* makes an attractive free keepsake (or you can call ahead and order a copy for $5 postage and handling within the US) and a help in scoping out other accommodations. Many of the same brochures and lodging listings are also available at the **Visitor Services & Information Bureau,** 25 Federal St., tel. (508) 228-0925.

Finally, if you prefer literature over advertising, check out the extensive selection of local-interest books available from the Whaling Museum and the Maria Mitchell Association gift shops. Beach-blanket or fireside reading matter abounds at both **Nantucket Bookworks,** next to The Brotherhood of Thieves on Broad St., and **Mitchell's Book Corner,** 54 Main St.

Medical Emergencies
The island's only year-round, round-the-clock, full-service health-care provider is **Nantucket Cottage Hospital,** 57 Prospect St., just west of the Old Mill, tel. (508) 228-1200.

THE ELIZABETH ISLANDS

Politically, the Elizabeth Islands constitute Gosnold township—the only part of Dukes County not on Martha's Vineyard. But much of the archipelago is privately owned by the Forbes family (yes, *that* Forbes—the former presidential candidate and other relatives of the late Harley-riding plutocrat Malcolm). **Cuttyhunk** is the only one of the 16 islands that has public access (although certain tour groups often get permission to go ashore some of the others, and Naushon Island's Tarpaulin Cove is a favorite anchorage for cruising sailors). Birdwatchers on Audubon Society-sponsored trips frequent the island, as do nature enthusiasts on winter sealwatching cruises (Jan.-May, $16; tel. 508-992-1432 or 992-6076). Sport fishermen angling for Vineyard Sound's stripers, blues, and bonito are also regular visitors to the island's shores.

Fewer than 100 people consider themselves year-round residents of the islands, which is why high-school students have to board on the Vineyard and the fire department is a boat ride away in New Bedford. In summer, Cuttyhunk's household population swells to almost 300, augmented by as many as 500 motor cruisers and sailboats over the course of a typical July. Tourism has deep roots here: the privately held islands were stocked by a wealthy Bostonian in the late 1600s with deer and fowl in the tradition of the English private hunting estate. Under the Forbeses, sheep were introduced for wool, and later retained for controlling ground cover; but since the early 1990s, when coyotes with an appetite for fresh mutton swam over from Woods Hole, they've been largely replaced by more coyote-resistant cattle. Gosnold's history is rife with interesting anecdotes, from Captain Kidd's 1699 visit in his pirate days to Teddy Roosevelt's surfcasting for trophy-sized game fish. Paul Cuffee, the founder of the nation of Sierra Leone, was born in the Elizabeths, and before becoming an African nationalist he cruised local waters as one of the nation's earliest black captains of a New Bedford whaler. Even more frequently overlooked is Gosnold's 16 years as home to Massachusetts' leper colony; now, nearly 80 years after the colony's

close, the island it occupied, Penikese, is home to a special state-accredited boot-camp-style school for juvenile delinquents.

Attractions

Cuttyhunk has nice, sometimes pebbly beaches; an Audubon nature trail along a cliff on the southeast side; and an old tercentenary monument in the pond at the southwestern end commemorating the camp of Bartholomew Gosnold, whose ship brought the first European visitors to these shores in 1602. There are also plenty of ruins to explore: bunkers from WW I on the western shore above Gosnold Pond, the old life-saving station at the northeastern end, and, most prominent, the WW II submarine-spotting tower on central Lookout Hill. From this open platform, one can discern the rusty remains of a giant wind-powered generator erected by an energy-conscious islander in the 1970s (the town declined to continue the upkeep). The view also takes in many of the other islands in the chain, whose fluid names—Naushon, Nashawena, Uncatena, Weepecket, Nonamesset, and Vekatimest, among others—are the only legacy of their earliest indigenous occupants. But the strongest attraction is the pace of life: golf carts are the major form of transportation, dogs sleep in the middle of the roads, and occasional deer nose around yards in the late afternoon. If you want to unwind a notch, there's no better place to do it than here on Cuttyhunk.

Practicalities

Signs along the road from the ferry pier will keep you from getting lost looking for a bite to eat. **Cuttyhunk Breakfast & Sandwich Shoppe,** known simply as "the Bakery," has a good deli, and is the island's only breakfast spot. The **Cuttyhunk Store,** usually open daily through September, also has deli sandwiches, plus a few provisions for picnickers who neglected to bring their own from the mainland. In summer, the fish dock has a string of small food stalls vending everything from hot dogs and fried fish to raw oysters; the Bakery also runs an annex here. After Labor Day, you'll have to settle for a cup of coffee and biscotti from the gift-filled **Corner Store,** which stays open mid-April through mid-October. (Small Fry, next door, is also open outside the peak season, but you'll pay dearly and your meal is made of frozen Icelandic fish, Canadian scallops, and limp french fries? McDonald's in New Bedford does better than that.) The only real restaurant is summer-only **Peg Legs,** with ribs, pizza, and all the broiled fresh fish and lobster dinners you'd expect in a town surrounded by the sea. If you have a place to cook it, you can buy your own fresh fish in season directly from the fishermen filleting their catch right on the dock.

You can rent a cottage for a week or sleep on a boat if you have one, but there aren't any overnight accommodations—or any camping—on Cuttyhunk. But day trips are easy aboard the regular ferry from New Bedford operated by **Cuttyhunk Boat Lines,** or on tour boats from Martha's Vineyard. The *Alert II* departs

from downtown New Bedford's Fisherman's Wharf year-round: twice a week in winter, five days a week in spring and fall, and daily mid-June through mid-September; on Fridays and Sundays in July and August, there are even two daily departures for the little island. The one-hour ride costs $15.75 roundtrip, plus $5 for bikes. Call (508) 992-1432 for a detailed schedule.

If you have your own boat, the little marina inside the protected harbor is a good place to stop and meet other cruisers; call the Town Wharf/Cuttyhunk Marina at (508) 990-7578 to arrange a mooring ($20) or discuss the location of a safe anchorage. Be warned, though, that it's foolhardy to sail around the Elizabeths without some knowledge of the tides—differences between the rise and fall of Buzzards Bay and Vineyard Sound waters create riptides between the islands powerful enough to overwhelm small craft.

BLACKSTONE RIVER VALLEY NATIONAL HERITAGE CORRIDOR

CENTRAL MASSACHUSETTS

It's a well-established truism of Massachusetts cultural geography that for millions of metropolitan Bostonians living inside the ring of Rt. 128, the state might just as well end at that highway's southbound shoulder. Even residents of the MetroWest suburbs pay scant attention to anything past *their* outer concrete ring, I-495. Since half the state's residents equate "west a' Worcestah" with *terra incognita,* the bright side is that most of this area, between I-495 and the Quabbin Reservoir, remains firmly off the beaten tourist path. Don't be deterred by the lack of good regional road maps or the absence of corner espresso shops: there are plenty of rewards for the determined traveler, from classic diners and quirky museums to pick-your-own fruit orchards and attractive wildlife sanctuaries. Admittedly, for every quaint village common or wooded subdivision of six-figure custom homes there's a down-at-heels old manufacturing town rife with vinyl siding and rusty Plymouths. But beyond the strip malls and thrift stores you'll find both historic 18th-century farms and stands of deep forest which have never been felled—by either ax or chainsaw.

HISTORY

Long before the mill dams, water wheels, orchards, and malls materialized, Central Massachusetts was home to the Nipmucks—"people of the freshwater places." The region's contemporary outline closely corresponds with the historical territory of Algonquian-speaking Nipmuck nation, which was bounded peaceably by small tribes along the Connecticut River; Pennacooks to the north, along the Merrimack River; the Massachusett confederation around Boston; and such coastal tribes as the Pequot, Narragansett, and Wampanoag to the south. Afflicted by plague and conflicts with marauding Mohawks from the Hudson Valley, the Nipmucks were in decline by the time early colonial observers recorded impressions of them (although other tribes still spoke of their former greatness). Through the 17th century, the diminishing Nipmuck bands split among various political alliances with more powerful neighbors. In 1675-78, some even joined Metacom (King Philip) in his failed bid to rid the region of the English.

The Hassanamisco (still living in the Blackstone Valley) and the Charbunagungamaug bands (in Webster, nearer to Sturbridge) together account for the majority of the 1,600 Nipmuck still living in this country. Except for them, though, most of the local Native Americans are gone. (Fruitlands, in the Nashoba Valley, is nearly the only museum or visitor center in the region that pays any due to their presence or that of their ancestors.) Like other lost tribes throughout New England, the vanquished Nipmuck bands—the Nashua, Quaboag, Wachusett, Nichewaug, and Manchaug, among others—are almost entirely memorialized only in place names.

GETTING THERE AND AROUND

Central Massachusetts is served by a regional airport and Amtrak depot—both in Worcester—and by interstate bus stations in Worcester, Fitchburg, and Gardner. The airport only receives "lifeline" service from a single scheduled carrier (Continental), and Amtrak's Lake Shore Limited, from Chicago and Albany, is the only rail connection that doesn't originate in Boston, so most travelers to the region will end up coming through the Hub. The Fitchburg line of the MBTA **Commuter Rail** connects Boston's North Station with the cities along Rt. 2, on the region's northern edge, while the Framingham/Worcester line links Boston's South Station with, as you might expect, Worcester. Since the local urban bus systems only run from the Commuter Rail to adjacent residential and commercial zones, experiencing the best of central Massachusetts really requires a car.

Serious backroad explorers looking for a detailed guidance to the region should look for the Central Massachusetts bicycle map from Rubel BikeMaps. (Alternatives are a full set of USGS topos, or an expensive Worcester County atlas aimed at real estate buyers—unhelpfully alphabetized by town and all to different scales.) Luckily, the natives out in these parts are generally more helpful toward strangers than the average Bostonian, so trusting to serendipity and pointers from locals is a fine strategy.

THE BLACKSTONE VALLEY

From Millbury in the north to Millville in the south, the Blackstone Valley was once a showcase of Yankee manufacturing. Echoes of the huge impact of 19th-century industry still sound in the names of the region's full roster of company towns: Bramanville, Wilkinsonville, Saundersville, Fisherville, Farnumsville, Whitinsville, Wheelockville. As the state's economic foundation has shifted from assembly lines to MBAs, these factory-filled villages and their rural neighbors have been bypassed by all the research lab spin-offs, business school start-ups, and other elements of knowledge-based, information-age service sector growth.

Were it not for the preservation efforts of a precedent-setting National Park called the Blackstone River Valley National Heritage Corridor, the region might still be a forgotten footnote to the Industrial Revolution. Straddling the Massachusetts-Rhode Island line, this unique federal and state collaboration encompasses (and augments with a rare but welcome consistency in interpretive signs and visitor information) nearly all the attractions, both historic and scenic, described below.

This special park explicitly recognizes the Blackstone's rich and varied history, but you must disabuse yourself of any expectation that you'll find the artifacts of such a legacy all quaint and well cared for. They aren't. If you hurry through on the main roads, you'll see that gas stations seem to have replaced churches as the focal points of village life. Or perhaps you'll marvel at how a National Park can end up including dilapidated houses with laundry drying on the front porches, old cottages converted to nail and tanning salons, and Wal-Mart. But if you take the time to explore the valley's back roads, to walk its trails as you visit its attractions, it's hard not to come away with a far more positive impression.

If you *are* rushed for time, consider, instead, paying a visit to a place like Sturbridge Village, where you can soak up history and scenic landscape in one easily strollable package.

Besides telltale reminders of both the rise and fall of its industrial heritage, the Blackstone's landscape also illustrates history—in other, less obvious ways. The influence of pre-existing Indian trails is evident in many of the Blackstone's winding country roads, which, like those ancient footpaths, follow topographical contours and waterways. The 17th-century towns and early frontier farmsteads—some still intact, though whittled down in size—are all strategically located on hilltops above the river valley, clearly demonstrating the colonial settlers' wariness about their Native American neighbors. (King Philip's War, which leveled every white settlement in the region, helped perpetuate this bunker mentality well into the next century.)

The late colonial period is visible in the few turnpikes that cross the region, Federal-era toll roads whose straight lines and bridges illustrate how surveying and engineering were applied to the needs of interstate mail and commerce. In some respects, the valley's timeline seems to have been arrested there in the 1700s: thousands of forested acres have reclaimed the pastures and fields abandoned in the great western migration of New England's 19th-century farmers, deer are more numerous than at possibly any time since before Columbus, and even a mountain lion seems to have taken up local residence (attracted by all that fresh venison). In other respects, the industrial modern age is poised to reassert itself on the valley with a vengeance. Presently the predominant visual emblem of the post-war era is in the prefab chain stores—the fast-food franchises, gas station mini-marts, and big-box discount retailers—whose garish fluorescence stands out vividly against the prevailing 19th- and early-20th-century residential and industrial architecture. But skyrocketing land values in Eastern Massachusetts' most sought-after suburbs are rewriting all the old rules about acceptable commuting distances—causing modern tract housing to mushroom in places that would have been unthinkably inconvenient just a couple years ago. Such evocative subdivision names as "Oak Knoll" and "Deer Run" may soon become the sole reminders of what the Blackstone's back country looked like prior to the developers' blitz. The economic clout of tourists who appreciate scenic vistas and open land may be the Blackstone's last, best hope. So pay this place a visit

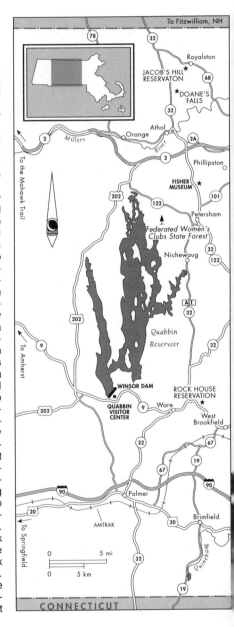

CENTRAL MASSACHUSETTS

NEW HAMPSHIRE

To Peterborough, NH

12 · 202 · Winchendon · 119 · Ashby · Squannacook River · 31 · Townsend · Pepperell · 111

Lake Dennison State Park · 101 · Willard Brook State Forest · Pearl Hill State Park · 119 · 111 · Groton · 40 · To Lowell

Otter River State Forest · 12 · Ashburnham · 13 · 225 · 495 · 110

140 · 101 · 12 · 31 · Fitchburg · Lunenburg · FITCHBURG LINE–MBTA COMMUTER RAIL

Baldwinville · 202 · 68 · Gardner Heritage State Park · 2A · 2 · 13 · Shirley · Ayer · 2A · 110

2 · Gardner · Templeton · 2A · Westminster · 31 · Leominster · 110 · Littleton · 2A · To Concord

68 · Leominster State Forest · 2 · Harvard · 111 · 119

Wachusett Mountain State Reservation · 140 · 70 · 2 · 495

Hubbardston · 31 · 12 · 117 · 190 · Lancaster · 110

62 · Princeton · 62 · Sterling · Bolton · 117

WACHUSETT MEADOW WILDLIFE REFUGE · 85 · 62

Barre · 32 · 122 · Rutland · 68 · 31 · 140 · 110 · 70 · Wachusett Reservoir · 62 · 20

122A · 190 · West Boylston · 12 · Boylston · 290 · 20 · 495 · 85 · 90

56 · 140 · 30

Moore State Park · 31 · Paxton · 68 · 70 · Shrewsbury · 135 · 9 · 135

67 · ST. JOSEPH'S ABBEY · 122 · 9

North Brookfield · 31 · 9 · Worcester · 122 · 30

East Brookfield · 31 · 56 · 290 · 146 · North Grafton · 90 · 85

Brookfield · WORCESTER LINE–MBTA COMMUTER RAIL · 20 · Grafton · 16

49 · MASS PIKE (TOLL) · Auburn · Millbury · 122 · 126

Wells State Park · 20 · 395 · 12 · Sutton · 122A · 140 · 495

Oxford · 146 · 122 · 16

20 · Sturbridge · Purgatory Chasm State Reservation · Whitinsville · 140 · 495

River · OLD STURBRIDGE VILLAGE · Manchaug · 16 · RIVER BEND FARM · Uxbridge · 126

84 · 31 · 131 · Webster · 16 · Douglas · 146 · 122 · Millville

Dudley · 197 · 395 · Lake Chargoggagoggmanchauggagoggchaubunagungamaugg · Douglas State Forest · Blackstone

To Hartford, CT · 12 · Woonsocket · RI

© MOON PUBLICATIONS, INC.

(before it's too late), and perhaps you'll have a hand in its salvation.

While many sights in the area deserve special recognition, when it comes to bed and board, the pickings are slim: a few small motels, a handful of attractive B&Bs, some characterful local restaurants, and a lot of fast food. Not to panic, though: there are plenty of places to sleep and eat just outside the area, principally in Worcester. Just don't put off dinner until 9 p.m.—most restaurants in the region keep more conservative hours than even those in sensible old Boston.

THE NATIONAL HERITAGE CORRIDOR

Like the more renowned National Historical Park in Lowell, the tongue-twisting **Blackstone River Valley National Heritage Corridor**, tel. (401) 762-0440, seeks to preserve and interpret a variety of historical attractions related to the Industrial Revolution. But instead of being clustered in one city, the sights are scattered among a score of towns along the 45-mile Blackstone—once considered "the hardest working river in America." More precipitous than the Colorado River, the Blackstone's steep 438-foot drop over its relatively short length spawned a nearly unbroken string of water-powered "manufactory" centers from its Worcester headwaters to its confluence with the brackish Seekonk River in Pawtucket, Rhode Island. While the 19th-century vestiges of the great mills, historic civic structures, prominent mansions, and worker housing form the Heritage Corridor's primary attractions, old farms are also among its treasures, complementing the obvious themes of mechanical innovation and labor history with a less-heralded one about the transformation of the New England landscape and evolution of market agriculture. Perhaps most evocative of the area's past are the remnants of the short-lived Blackstone Canal—still visible from old towpaths (or, most intimately, from a canoe). Completed in 1828, after overcoming years of obstruction from Boston merchant and maritime interests, who fought the prospect of diversion of inland commerce through rival Providence, the canal indeed helped boost business in both Worcester and Rhode Island by halving the costs of ship-ping freight overland to Boston. But operational problems and wrangling among mill owners over water rights kept the canal from ever becoming profitable for its investors. When the even-cheaper Providence & Worcester Railroad opened in 1847, it put the canal and its horse-drawn passenger and freight boats out of business within a year.

Three separate visitor centers guide travelers through this large chunk of history and real estate with all sorts of ranger-guided activities and a panoply of well-designed free brochures, including town-by-town walking tours and a detailed *Canoe Guide for the Blackstone River.* Two of the visitor centers are in Rhode Island—one at Pawtucket's **Slater Mill Historic Site** off I-95, the other at Woonsocket's excellent Museum of Work and Culture, about a mile south of the state line. In Massachusetts, a fourth center is slated to open eventually in Worcester, but in the meantime visitors to the northern half of the Corridor should drop in on the Blackstone River & Canal State Heritage Park, off Rt. 122 in North Uxbridge. Descriptive National Park maps and more perfunctory Corridor-related information is also available from MassPike (I-90) visitor centers, the Worcester Historical Museum, the Willard Clock Museum, and the Broad Meadow Brook Wildlife Sanctuary, among other places.

Touring by Car, Boat, Bike, and Foot

The quickest way to shuttle from one end of the Blackstone to the other is via Rt. 146, a fast, divided highway running the length of the Corridor from Worcester and the MassPike (Exit 10A) to Providence. To meander at a more deliberate pace among the old mill towns, use Rts. 122 and 122A. Various local roads traverse the Corridor from east to west and connect Rt. 146 with Rt. 122 to permit a wide variety of looping or figure-eight routes. The National Park map is the best planning tool for such trips.

Canoe and kayak rentals can be found on either side of the Blackstone valley, in either Sutton or Upton. On southbound Rt. 146 in Sutton, a half mile past Honeydew Donuts, is the **Great Canadian Canoe Company**, tel. (800) 98-CANOE or (508) 865-0010, e-mail www.greatcanadian.com. Several sizes of touring kayaks and fiberglass canoes are available

($25 a day and up—inquire about weekly rates— including cartop carriers, all essential paddling and saftey gear, and recommendations on where to go); closed Sunday. The company also carries a complete selection of appropriately topical books, from the Appalachian Mountain Club's excellent quiet-water and river guides to the aforementioned Blackstone River brochure from the National Heritage Corridor. Eastward across the river is **Fin & Feather Sports,** tel. (508) 529-3901, in the big red building on Rt. 140 a short distance south of downtown Upton. The $21 day rate includes car rack—and for an extra charge staff will deliver and pick up, too. On beautiful summer weekends, the rental fleets at either outfitter often go quickly, so consider confirming a phone-in reservation with your credit card.

If paddling sounds like too much exertion, perhaps you'd prefer cruising aboard the **Blackstone Valley Explorer,** tel. (800) 619-BOAT or (401) 724-1500, a barge-like riverboat operated on weekends April-Oct. by one of the Corridor's local tourism councils. Though most trips stay wholly within Rhode Island, a few venture into Massachusetts waters.

A dedicated bikeway is in the planning stages—it will roughly adhere to the route of the old Blackstone Canal towpath. But if the state's past record is any measure of future performance, it could be years before results appear. An abandoned railroad right-of-way identified on the Heritage Corridor map as the future Southern New England Trunkline Trail is also passable between river crossings—at least on a mountain bike. Someday, it, too, may become a full-fledged rail trail for bikes. (It's actually a combination of the Southbridge & Blackstone and Norfolk County Railroads (the trail's namesake, the never-finished Southern New England subsidiary of Canada's Grand Trunk Railway, followed a close but separate route). In the meantime, many of the roads in the more rural hills, away from the populated riverbanks and busy commuter routes, offer great cycling. The National Park map or—better yet—the Central Massachusetts bicycle and roadway map from Rubel Bikemaps (e-mail bikemaps@ziplink.net) will prove handy for picking routes and destinations. Or you can consider joining the Narragansett Bay Wheelmen on one of their

weekend bike tours. Ranging from 15 to 75 miles in length, this club's year-round rides within the Corridor visit different areas in both Massachusetts and Rhode Island. Call the Wheelmen's hotline, (401) 435-4012, for start date and directions to their next scheduled ride (not all of which are Corridor-related), or to leave a message requesting a copy of their latest seasonal calendar.

The National Park Service complements the Corridor's self-guiding tour brochures with additional weekend ranger-led walks—a list of which is available free at visitor centers or by mail from the National Heritage Corridor headquarters, tel. (401) 762-0440. Also listed are seasonal hikes, sponsored by the private nonprofit **Blackstone Canal Conservancy,** along the route of both the old canal and the proposed trail. For more info about the Conservancy's activities or membership, write to it in care of the Blackstone River Valley National Heritage Corridor Commission, One Depot Square, Woonsocket, RI 02895.

SIGHTS IN THE CORRIDOR

Museum of Work and Culture

Rhode Island's border city, Woonsocket (pop. 44,000), is characteristic of many of the Blackstone Valley towns. Though headquarters to a couple of major regional service and retail corporations, the place is steeped in its working-class industrial past. With thrift stores, a tattoo parlor, a boxing gym, and vacant storefronts along Main St., you won't have to risk too many consumer temptations as you motor through town. On the other hand, don't let the dearth of cute boutiques keep you from venturing down to Market Square, on a bend in the Blackstone at the south end of Main St., where you'll find the **Museum of Work and Culture,** tel. (401) 769-WORK. Within the renovated brick mill between Mulvey's hardware store and the Riverview Furniture building are two floors of exhibits focusing on the lives of the textile workers who brought prosperity to the Blackstone in the 1800s. Ingenious state-of-the-art interactivity brings to life issues surrounding unionization, management of an immigrant workforce, and the conservative influence of the church in perpetuating barriers between social classes. The little-known saga of *La Survivance*—the relocation of fully one-quarter of Quebec's population to New England's mill towns during the latter half of the 19th century—is also detailed here in photos, text, video, and walk-through displays. The flight of these predominantly poor, rural French-Canadians from farms to factories had a greater impact on Woonsocket than other New England communities in which they settled, turning it into *la ville la plus française aux États-Unis,* the most French city in the US. Although Francophone newspapers and broadcasting are things of the past, at one time all English-speaking residents had to become bilingual in order to survive among the French-speaking shopkeepers and mill workers. Descendants of the Quebecois still account for over half of the population, and a local French dialect may still be heard in passing on the street or on certain weekend radio shows.

Admission to the museum (open daily until at least 4 p.m.) is $5 adults, $3 students and seniors. To reach Market Square, follow signs with the Heritage Corridor logo from Rt. 146A, or take Rt. 122 into downtown until it runs into Main Street. If you're coming from I-495, catch Rt. 126 south from Exit 18 or King St. west to Rt. 126 from Exit 16, and simply follow Rt. 126 until it merges with Main St. by the classic (1926) Stadium Theater. The square (essentially a large parking lot for a small shopping plaza) is roughly straight ahead, two traffic signals beyond the Providence & Worcester Railroad overpass.

You may also want to check out the park behind the museum, with steps down to the river, or cross the square to the overlook beside the Thundermist dam across Woonsocket Falls, whose 30-foot drop now powers hydroelectric turbines instead of spinning frames and weaving looms. For commentary on these and other sights in the neighborhood, pick up a Woonsocket walking-tour brochure from the Heritage Corridor rack in the museum entrance.

There are simple eateries on Main St., but you'll also find plenty of local flavor a couple blocks up the hill from Market Square at sport-themed **Box Seats,** on High St., by the corner of Arnold. Or check out **Chan's,** on Main, almost beneath the railroad overpass, tel. (401) 765-1900, a Chinese restaurant whose incongruously bright facade also happens to conceal one of the region's premier nightclubs for cool jazz and hot blues.

Blackstone Gorge

Straddling the state line northwest of Woonsocket is the only part of the Blackstone River left largely in its natural state by early mill owners. Even with the spillway dam at its head, the 80-foot cliffs and the boulder-strewn bed of the Blackstone Gorge presents a wild little prospect—one that hints at what the river looked like prior to being subjugated by industry. The centerpiece of the eponymous double-state park, the gorge (with its pleasant half-mile hiking trail) is accessible from the end of County Rd. in the town of Blackstone; look for the Heritage Corridor sign at the bend in Rt. 122 as it runs through this tiny town on the Massachusetts side of the state line. While the gorge offers a morsel of *A River Runs Through It,* paddlers who come exploring during low water will also get a taste of *Modern Times* in the oversized mechanical hydropower apparatus by the old Tupperware Mill, just downstream.

Less than a mile north of the gorge on Rt. 122 is the tiny town of Millville. If you picked up a walking-tour brochure from one of the Corridor visitor centers, you can easily find the remains of Blackstone Canal lock #21, the best-preserved of all those remaining aboveground (Woonsocket has one in mint condition, but it's buried beneath the Market Square parking lot). Otherwise, turn southwest on Central St. from Rt. 122 and park at the signposted visitor lot, at the corner of Hope St., a quarter-mile past the railroad and river bridge. Follow the path (originally the trackbed for the Southbridge & Blackstone Railroad; later, briefly, part of the Boston, Hartford, and Erie; and, ultimately, at the time the tracks were pulled up, in 1955, a division of the Penn Central) until you see the spur trail descending left toward the river and its adjacent canal remnants.

River Bend Farm

Although the Blackstone River includes some highly urban stretches at either end, much of its central mileage north of Woonsocket passes through rural forests and small towns founded around brick-clad mills, many now long dormant—if not demolished. Much of those woods is reclaiming agricultural land abandoned in the early 1800s during the great westward drift of the American frontier. Once one of the region's largest dairy farms, River Bend is now part of the free **Blackstone River and Canal Heritage State Park,** tel. (508) 278-7604, on Oak St. off E. Hartford Ave. in North Uxbridge. Open daily, its big red 1913 barn also doubles as the National Heritage Corridor visitor center for this section of the valley; it's the gateway to some of the best short- and medium-distance hikes in the Corridor (two to eight miles roundtrip), largely along one of the most well-preserved lengths of towpath. Other park highlights include one of the nearly 50 granite locks that stair-step down the length of the Canal; valley-wide panoramas from an overlook known as King Philip's Rock; and a particularly navigable pair of canal remnants both upstream (a scenic four miles to the Riverdale grist mill ruins in Northbridge) and downstream (through two miles of rural, wooded wetlands to the 1853 Stanley Woolen Mill). This photogenic old factory happens to still have a few looms in operation— which surely makes it one of the oldest continuously operating textile plants in the country.

In addition to its visitor displays and ranger programs, River Bend Farm hosts a summer series, **"Concerts on the Canal,"** on Sundays, and the annual **Canal Fest,** on a weekend in early June. Pick up information about other historical sights in the vicinity, too, including self-guided walking tour brochures for Whitinsville (WHITE-nsville) and Hopedale, a pair of company towns (one built by a paternalistic family, the other by Christian socialists intent on creating a utopian community), within a couple of miles to the east and west.

Douglas

About five miles west of River Bend Farm along Hartford Ave. (the old Hartford Turnpike) is the tiny commercial heart of rural Douglas (pop. 5,500), one of the region's most desirable new addresses for homeowners fleeing high suburban real-estate prices. Though books and bagels have made a beachhead in the town, it only takes a stroll through the restored **E. N. Jenckes Store,** on Main St., tel. (508) 476-7403, to be transported back in time to an era predating video stores and espresso machines. This 1833 general merchandiser, its shelves

still holding some of the stock they carried when the place was donated to the Douglas Historical Society, is maintained as a museum to 19th-century retailing. Open weekend afternoons June-Aug., or by appointment.

Bestride Rt. 16 west of Douglas Center is **Douglas State Forest,** tel. (508) 476-7872, a huge chunk of prime deer and black bear habitat abutting both the Connecticut and Rhode Island lines ($2 entrance fee per car). Some 40 miles of trails and old roads lace the forest's 4,500 acres, attracting mountain bikers, horseback riders, and hikers. (Given the big population of bucks and does, non-hunters may want to stay out of the woods during shotgun season— the week after Thanksgiving, except Sunday.) When the snow cover is thick enough, cross-country skiers and snowmobilers abound, too. Riders curious to check out the so-called Southern New England Trunkline Trail can access a good 10-mile portion of this former Southbridge & Blackstone railbed from just north of the forest's main entrance, signposted south of Rt. 16. (This particular section runs from Connecticut to Rt. 146.) Long-distance hikers can choose to embark on the yellow-blazed Midstate Trail, which commences here in Douglas at the Rhode Island line and ends some 80 trail miles north, joining the Wapack Trail at Mt. Watatic before crossing into New Hampshire.

Visitors seeking a more casual walk should try the boardwalk stroll into one of the forest's white cedar swamps, starting from the one-room Interpretive Center between the main parking area and the swimming beach at Wallum Lake. New England's 17th-century settlers so valued the rot-resistant wood of the Atlantic white cedar that they logged all they could of the three- and four-foot-diameter giants. Surviving stands of this water-tolerant coastal native are usually found in wetlands, where, when mature, they can create the most impenetrable forests in North America. (Native Americans trying to escape armor- and weapon-burdened colonial soldiers took advantage of this, favoring cedar thickets as hiding places.) The 70-year-old stand through which this boardwalk passes is more open than most cedar swamps, and most of the existing specimens are little more than half a foot in diameter, but imagine them with trunks six or eight times as large and you'll begin to appreciate their resistance to trespass. Be sure to pick up one of the interpretive trail guides at the start of the half-mile loop walk to decipher the numbered posts along the way. Or check the summer program postings for the next scheduled ranger-led tour.

Purgatory Chasm and Vicinity

Sandwiched between state forest land in Sutton is free **Purgatory Chasm State Reservation,** on Purgatory Rd. off Rt. 146, tel. (508) 234-3733. Hidden in the wooded slopes above Purgatory Brook, this abrupt ravine is easily descended from above by way of a great leg-stretching, boulder-hopping, half-mile loop trail past descriptively-named features like "Fat Man's Misery," "The Pulpit," and "Lover's Leap." On most Sundays and holiday afternoons summer through fall, park staff conduct nature programs and lead tours through the chasm. Any time of year, the reservation's bathrooms will be gratefully appreciated by area visitors. A note for cyclists: Purgatory Road is as steep as a ski jump and best approached from Sutton's Central Turnpike—unless you want a serious cardiopulmonary workout.

About two miles west of Purgatory Chasm, along the Central Turnpike, is a beautiful time capsule into the Corridor's agrarian beginnings: **Waters Farm,** off Douglas Rd. in West Sutton. The 120 hilltop acres' terrific vista over Manchaug Pond seems as unspoiled today as when the farmhouse was built, in 1757. During the 19th century, the farm became New England's—and possible the nation's—first commercial apple orchard, producing such now-antique varieties as the Sutton Beauty for shipment to markets opened up by the Blackstone Canal and, later, the valley's railroads. Now owned by the town and operated as a living history museum, Waters Farm offers a series of seasonal interpretive events utilizing the house, barn, blacksmith shop, and shingle mill: a sleigh rally in mid-January (weather permitting) or February, a draft horse "Hitch and Harness" clinic in mid-July, Apple Crisp Day in late August, "Christmas in Historic Sutton" in early December, and other special programs as volunteer labor and time allows. Call (508) 865-0101 for info on whatever's forthcoming. The biggest event of the year is the annual **Waters Farm Days,** on

the first weekend of October, including hay rides, crafts and antique displays, house tours, period children's games, farm animals, and refreshments, plus lots of people in colonial costume. Any time of year, visitors are also welcome to enjoy the five miles of trails crisscrossing the property, although during mud season (spring thaw, late March and April), your footwear will thank you for staying away.

If you have a hankering for a snack outside of the first weekend of October, you may wish to drop in on Waters Farm's neighbors on Douglas Road. The first is **Whittier Farms,** tel. (508) 865-6569, whose year-round store carries everything from fresh fruit and vegetables to baked goods, whole pies, homemade jams and relishes, and fresh milk (including that Rhode Island favorite, coffee flavor) from their herd of Holsteins. Open daily. The second is **Hillside Farm,** tel. (508) 865-2880, south of the Whittiers, with pick-your-own blueberries mid-July through mid-August. Trust me, it's easy to inhale a ripe quart of these lovely fruit while driving, so pick two.

Unless you're neighbors of the Waters descendants out in California (where scions from the old family tree have fruited beautifully), you've probably never seen or tasted a Sutton Beauty apple. If it's October or later, you're in luck: this hardy winter variety is available from Sutton's **Keown Orchards Farm Stand,** tel. (508) 865-6706, on McClellan Rd., off the Central Turnpike on the east side of Purgatory Chasm and Rt. 146. The Keowns grow 50 other apple varieties, too, from old standards like McIntosh, Cortland, Rome, and Baldwin, to the more obscure Northern Spy, Rhode Island Greening, and Milton. Artie himself, the fourth generation to work the place, is happy to tell you that nearly all of them are better than that Sutton Beauty, which was clearly intended to travel by buckboard over bad roads to distant markets without bruising (sort of a 19th-century equivalent to today's supermarket variety of Red Delicious). The farmstand opens in mid-July with the first crop of Lodi apples, an excellent summer choice for pies and sauces; by Labor Day, the pick-your-own season goes into full swing, complemented by periodic special events like the end-of-summer corn picking, shortcake-and-peaches party, or anniversary celebration with fresh apple crisp and cider. Outside of these high-profile weekends, Sutton is still far enough off the beaten track that you may have the picking (and the Keowns' warm welcome) to yourself. And until the stand closes, at Christmas, you can always drop by for a taste of the family's other products, including cherries, plums, berries, vegetables, honey, cider, jams, jellies, fruit butters, breads, and pies. Of course, apple gift packs are also available; e-mail ADKIII@aol.com for details if you can't manage to drop by in person.

Grafton

In contrast to residents of the mill towns along much of the Blackstone, Grafton's suburbanites are more likely to watch *Seinfeld* than the Daytona 500. Grafton Common, studded with statues, monuments, and a bandstand and ringed with white clapboard and red brick, three steepled churches, obligatory tchotchke-filled country general store, an antiques dealer, and an old inn—whose ground-floor pub is the local watering hole—is like an absolutely comprehensive concept of a New England village. Grafton also happens to be where the Hassanamisco band of the Nipmuck nation has its four-acre **Hassanamissitt Reservation**—all that remains of their former 5,000 square miles of territory—at 80 Brigham Hill Road. Unique in Massachusetts for having never been owned by whites, the property (whose name means "place of many small stones") was reserved for its residents in the early 17th century, when the missionary John Eliot organized one of his score of "Praying Indian" villages here. The Hassanamiscos' annual fair and powwow, begun in 1954 as a family picnic, now attracts thousands—including Indians from all over the New England, New York, and the Canadian Atlantic provinces. It's held on the last Sunday of July (nominal admission).

Though not nearly as old as the Hassanamiscos' longhouse—portions of which are believed to predate the arrival of European colonists—nearby North Grafton offers visitors an attractively rural 18th-century homestead built around the original 1718 one-room house of Joseph Willard. The **Willard House and Clock Museum**, tel. (508) 839-3500, evokes Joseph's stature as a moderately successful farmer in its simple period furnishings, but the most distinctive contents are the dozens of timepieces made by Joseph's four grandsons during their 70-year dominance of the New England clockmaking trade. The engraved faces of the tall pendulum grandfather pieces are enough to make clockwatchers out of anyone. Do take your time visiting—and don't miss the symphony of chimes at the top of each hour. Located on Willard St. a short ways south of Tufts Veterinary College's pastoral campus on Rt. 30, the museum is open Tues.-Sun. year-round; admission is $3.

BLACKSTONE VALLEY PRACTICALITIES

Accommodations

For seasonal budget accommodations, see the "Sturbridge" section, below, for information on the area's nearest camping and home hostel. If price is your most important criterion, try the turn-of-the-century **Grafton Inn,** tel. (508) 839-5931, beside Grafton's Town Common (it's the big building at the corner of southbound Rt. 140, diagonally across from the Cumberland Farm gas station). The rate for all seven third-floor rooms (all with private bath) is a no-nonsense $38.50 d year-round. Aside from bunkbeds or tents, this is the cheapest place to sleep in the state.

Anyone intending to make forays into Boston should consider staying at the Blackstone Valley's eastern edge, within a few minutes of a Commuter Rail line straight into the Hub. One place that fits the bill nicely is the **Tage Inn-Milford,** tel. (800) 322-TAGE or (508) 478-8243, beside I-495 Exit 19. Its rates make it one of the best values in all of Eastern Massachusetts—a comfortable, contemporary motel room with one queen bed is only $58 d; double beds run $62; prices include a simple morning buffet of donuts, muffins, bagels, and beverages.

An even more affordable jumping-off point for Blackstone Valley exploration is the **Quaker Motor Lodge,** tel. (508) 278-2445, on Rt. 146A, a couple miles south of downtown Uxbridge (take the Uxbridge/Chockalog Rd. exit off Rt. 146, follow signs for Rt. 146A south, and you'll end up almost at their doorstep). From outside it looks like a single-story throwback to the days of Sunday drives in big-finned Buicks, but the fully remodeled interiors are as bright and comfortable as Worcester hotels charging twice as much. The location is quiet, the owners friendly and informative, and the rates are low—only up to $55 d in summer-fall high season, as low as $42 d in winter.

You might also check out the **Uxbridge Inn,** tel. (508) 278-0330, a large 1882 structure right in the center of Uxbridge, at the junction of Rts. 122 and 16. Decor in the five modest-sized rooms available to overnight guests varies from discreet Victorian to Western sportsman (trimmed with such masculine touches as hunting trophies), all for $60 d.

The most attractive (and appetizing) accommodations are offered by the valley's B&Bs. **The Fieldstone Victorian,** tel. (508) 883-4647, is an excellent choice in Blackstone, in a pondside residential neighborhood close enough to Rhode Island to watch Woonsocket's Fourth of July fireworks, yet less than 15 minutes' drive away from Forge Park station, with Commuter Rail service to Boston. The house exudes a bygone era of luxurious craftsmanship, complemented by warm hospitality and truly gourmet breakfasts. Ask for the downstairs room and you can awake to a big picture-window view out over the neighborhood pond. The year-round rates are an eminently reasonable $75 d with private bath, $65 shared (credit cards accepted).

For a sample of colonial New England, consider a stay at Sutton's **Putnam House B&B,** tel. (508) 865-9094, a 1730s hilltop farmhouse with connecting 19th-century cupola-topped barn. Advantageously located between Waters Farm and Purgatory Chasm, the meticulously restored house has but one guest room (sleeps three), with fireplace and hand-stitched quilts, available year-round and including full breakfast and as much historical commentary on Sutton as you require.

For more accommodations suggestions, request a free copy of the *Bkackstone Valley Visitors' Guide* from the Blackstone Valley Visitors Bureau, tel. (800) 841-0919 or (508) 234-9090.

Food

With one notable exception, the communities closest to the Rhode Island line offer little beyond the ubiquitous formica-table pizza and sub joints or bar-restaurants like **Grumpy's,** on Rt. 126 in Bellingham, near the Ames shopping plaza,

dishing up everything from baked stuffed scrod and charbroiled sirloin steaks to "California stir-fry"; the **Union House Pub,** on Bridge St., in Blackstone, off Rt. 122, with basic tavern fare (and a nice patio overlooking the river); or **Sanchione's,** serving basic, inexpensive Italian fare in the basement of the Uxbridge Inn. If you love hot dogs or taco shells filled with mild all-beef chili, you might also want to look into Bellingham's **T&R Taco Wagon,** opposite the Honeydew Donut shop on the road between I-495 Exit 16 and Woonsocket.

Anyone prefering a finer dining experience should make a beeline for **The Oyster Cabin,** tel. (508) 278-4440, in Uxbridge on Rt. 146A, a mile south of the Quaker Motor Lodge, and next to the last Massachusetts exit on Rt. 146. The varnished, knotty wood tables, fieldstone fireplaces, TV over the bar, and log-cabin exterior all suggest a slightly rustic family restaurant, or a conservative surf-and-turf supper club for the kinds of folks who order Rob Roys straight up (an impression reinforced by the baskets of crackers that mark the advent of the table service). But don't be fooled—the bistro fare coming out of the kitchen (and the from-scratch clam dip that comes with those saltines) reproves you if you've judged this book by its cover. Seafood is, of course, the specialty of the house: rich bouillabaisse, perhaps a salmon fillet with lemongrass crust, or maybe fresh grouper paired with the season's best vegetables. Even haddock—that tofu of the sea—is transformed into a pleasure for the palate when complemented with a zesty diced-vegetable *basquaise.* The chef's experience—at Memphis' redoubtable Peabody Hotel—is manifest in the steaks and barbecue, too (unusually for these parts, there's even a good vegetarian entree). Exceptional desserts *and* a nice selection of wines by the glass. Entree prices ($11-20) are high for the area, but, given the quality, presentation, perfect portions, and lack of pretense, this place more than holds its own against higher-priced cosmopolitan eateries in Greater Boston or the Berkshires. Open for dinner only, Tues.-Sat. till 9 p.m., Sunday till 8 p.m., closed Monday.

A hidden gem of a far different sort is **Peg's Diner,** 87 Church St., under the big coffee cup sign in the center of Whitinsville, up the block from the Subway sandwich parlor and the big modern UniBank (whose local branches offer some of the valley's only ATMs). Behind this diner's vinyl siding is the heart and soul of a genuine 1940s Worcester Lunch Car—and the original enameled panels beneath that uncharacteristic facade would offer further proof, if they ever see the light of day again. Listen to the regulars banter with Peg as you chow down on the daily lunch special, or wake up your appetite with the aroma of hash browns and bacon sizzling on the grill.

For those who prefer the familiarity and convenience of fast food chains, you'll find both McDonald's and Burger King along Rt. 122, including a pair opposite one another on the fringes of the big Wal-Mart plaza in Northbridge.

WORCESTER AND VICINITY

It's New England's second largest city (pop. 170,000). It's home to several universities, a good business climate, a number of major attractions, and a rich history. Yet Worcester (rhymes with "rooster," or, if you want to sound like a native, pronounce it WUSS-tah), like younger sibs and second cities everywhere, suffers by its proximity to Boston. A couple of reasons are immediately obvious: though its economy is in decent shape—Worcester is home to a number of high-flying biotech companies, as well as plenty of traditional but highly skilled blue-collar industry—it neither looks nor feels like a place people get excited about. The ugly sweepstakes in Massachusetts had lots of contenders even before the state's suburbs started racing to join in, but sheer size sets Worcester apart from the rest. The city also continues to encourage downtown "renewal" built around megasized convention centers and hospital complexes, utterly disregarding opportunities to establish urban spaces on a more human scale, conducive to pedestrian street life. It'll take more than convention halls, business hotels, and hospital lobbies to entice Worcesterites themselves back into the city. And as long as local residents prefer the suburbs and Boston over their own downtown, the place will forever feel vaguely contrived and forlorn.

Is there any silver lining? Yes. There are some aspects of Worcester that one can't help but admire. The city's art and armor collections—and the palaces that house them—are well worth a detour down the interstate offramps. As the diner capital of New England, Worcester's genuine old lunch cars shouldn't be missed, either. And Worcester's bargain-priced meals and moderate-priced accommodations may be just the tonic your travel budget needs after enduring the high cost of vacationing in Eastern Massachusetts. However, if you don't appreciate fine museums, classic diners, or saving a buck, skip this burg and don't look back.

HISTORY

Worcester's growth was propelled by the Industrial Revolution, but, unlike most other New England manufacturing centers, Worcester was never a one-company or even a one-industry town. Scores of distinct industries bolstered Worcester's prewar reputation as a manufacturing powerhouse, and its history is liberally studded with companies that, in their heyday, dominated the nation or the world in producing such varied items as carpets, grinding wheels, power-plant ignition systems, and specialized textile equipment. The absence of a single ascendant star also effected a more deliberate pace of urban growth: unlike planned or highly specialized industrial cities such as Lowell or Fall River, Worcester was never a boomtown. Its ethnic composition, however, changed dramatically as factories drew a variety of immigrants from throughout Europe and the Middle East. At the start of WW I, for example, the city was 20% Swedish—enough to make such foreign-language newspapers as the *Worcester Veckoblad* about as widely read as their English-language counterparts. These days, the Swedish are well dispersed among surrounding towns, but the city's Albanian and Lithuanian communities are still among the largest of their kind in the United States.

One legacy of Worcester's broad-based research and manufacturing is a litany of influential patents and products, from the first American dictionaries, bicycles, and envelope-folding machines

Sigmund Freud (front left) and Carl Jung (front right), flank G. Stanley Hall, president of Clark University, in September 1909, on Freud's only visit to the United States; in back stand A. A. Brill, Ernest Jones, and Sandor Ferenczi

COURTESY, CLARK UNIVERSITY, WORCESTER, MASS.

to Shredded Wheat, liquid-fuel rockets, and even the original "smiley face" (conceived as part of an in-house, morale-boosting campaign for a local insurance company). Some of the city's goods have helped transform the nation: the Washburn & Moen Manufacturing Co., for example, contributed to the taming of the American frontier with their barbed wire (produced under a patent monopoly shared with an Illinois firm). But it's the little things that can really make a difference: in the late 1950s, the Worcester Foundation for Experimental Biology pioneered the first oral contraceptive. Commercially available by 1960, "the Pill" met with almost instantaneous world-wide success; not since Adam and Eve shared an apple in their garden has anything sparked such a revolution in attitudes toward sex.

SIGHTS

Worcester Art Museum
This grand 19th-century building houses a collection that rivals any in New England. Besides antiquities (including the nation's largest set of Roman mosaics), its strengths include frescoes and icons of the Middle Ages; still lifes, landscapes, and portraiture ranging in period from the European Renaissance to the American Realists; Japanese prints; portrait miniatures; and photography. The parking is even free, in front of the imposing marble facade at 55 Salisbury St., or opposite the side entrance by the museum

cafe. Open Wed.-Sun. year-round, except for selected holidays. Admission is a very reasonable $6 (free before noon on Saturday). For hours or directions, tel. (508) 799-4406.

Tested Metal
From exquisite Renaissance suits of steel to the decorative ironwork of the building itself, the **Higgins Armory Museum,** 100 Barber Ave., tel. (508) 853-6015, is dedicated to the art of metal. (Its founder was in the steel business.) The Great Hall, a Hollywood ringer for a medieval castle interior, holds the museum's namesake collection of armorers' handiwork, an exemplary set of warrior workduds from all over Europe and feudal Japan. The excellent staff demonstrations are always hits with kids (unfortunately, adults are too big to be selected as fitting models). Other attractions include a try-on costume collection, displays on heraldry and famous knights, and a modern metallic sculpture gallery. Open daily July-Aug. and Tues.-Sun. the rest of the year, the Higgins' crenelated facade is easily visible beside the I-290/I-190 junction. Admission is only $4.75.

Historical Museums
The **Worcester Historical Museum,** tel. (508) 753-8278, is the most accessible of the city's several caretakers of the past. In addition to a modest display of portraits, photographs, costumes, and assorted other artifacts on the first floor of their main building, on the corner of Elm

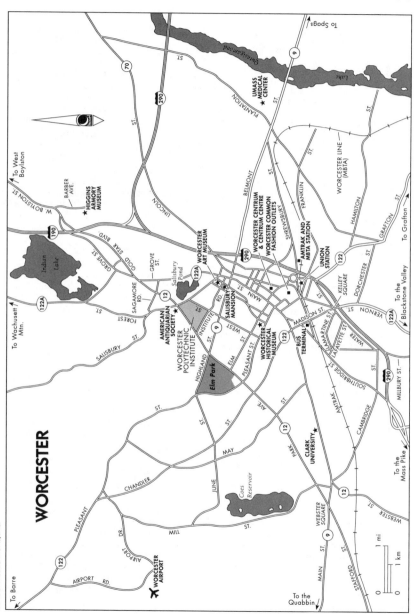

© MOON PUBLICATIONS, INC.

WORCESTER

MAJOR TAYLOR ~ WORCESTER'S CHAMPION

Worcester has long fallen in Boston's shadow when it comes to major-league sports. But, back before the Boston Red Sox even existed (let alone before they won the first World Series)—back, in other words, in the 1890s, Worcester was the proud home of the champion in the number-one spectator sport in America: bicycle racing (one of the top sports around the world, in fact).

Marshall "Major" Taylor, king of the velodrome both here and abroad, performed his feats of endurance and speed in front of paying crowds of up to 20,000. For nearly a decade, he rode high with the sport. But as an aging black athlete in a field that soon lost its luster, Taylor faced increasing financial hardship, job loss, discrimination, and, eventually, homelessness. He died in the charity ward of a Chicago-area hospital, in 1932, at the age of 54.

If you're interested in learning more about this remarkable athlete, look for Andrew Ritchie's exceedingly thorough biography, *Major Taylor: the Extraordinary Career of a Champion Bicycle Racer.*

and Chestnut (Tues.-Sun.; parking in small lot at the rear, accessible off Chestnut St.), the museum maintains the stately 1772 **Salisbury Mansion,** on Highland St., immediately behind the Worcester Art Museum. This showcase of the decorative arts, built by a leading local philanthropist and restored to its late-Federal-period 1830s glory, is open for daily tours Thurs.-Sun. 1-4 p.m. Admission to either mansion or museum is $2.

On a sloping hill at the corner of Salisbury St. and Park Ave., diagonally across from pond-filled Institute Park and at the edge of Worcester's most attractive residential district, sits the red-brick eminence of the **American Antiquarian Society,** tel. (508) 755-5221. Now primarily a research library—its museum was closed in the early 1900s, when its dabblings in science were overtaken by, among others, the Smithsonian Institution—the Society, founded by printer and diehard Revolutionary patriot Isaiah Thomas, is an unparalleled custodian of the primary documents of American history through 1877. Among its collections are an estimated two-thirds of everything ever printed in the U.S. prior to 1821, including almanacs, broadsides, political caricatures, cookbooks, sheet music,

maps, currency, Bibles, genealogies, and periodicals. It also holds the nation's finest collection of early American newspapers, comprising more than two million 18th- and 19th-century issues. Anyone with a pertinent research interest or scholarly need may apply for access as a "reader" (you must pass a brief interview with a library staffer); bring two forms of identification. (Membership is by election only, and limited to 600.) The general public may join the 2 p.m. tours held every Wednesday throughout the year. At all other times, only the small Orientation Room, with its introductory video and displays about the Society's fascinating history, is open to visitors.

Perhaps the most unusual of the city's historical collections belongs to the free **American Sanitary Plumbing Museum,** 39 Piedmont St., tel. (508) 754-9453. The unique assemblage definitively satisfies any curiosity that may have accrued in your most intimate idleness regarding the history of plumbing fixtures. Gathered with professional interest by a local manufacturer of such domestic necessities, the collection also extends to tools of the trade. Open Tuesday and Thursday 10 a.m.-2 p.m., or by appointment.

SIGHTS OUTSIDE THE CITY

St. Joseph's Abbey

Following in the tradition of European monasteries well known for making fine cognac and other aperitifs, the Trappist monks of St. Joseph's Abbey, on Rt. 31 at the north end of Spencer, produce a flavorful line of high-quality jams, jellies, and chutneys. The fruits of their labors are all to be found in their roadside gift shop, tel. (508) 885-8700, which also carries plenty of contemplative recorded music for your travels, and other religious-themed books and artifacts. Some of the Abbey's vespers are public; check out the schedule up the hill at the contemporary field-stone chapel for more information.

Moore State Park

On Rt. 31 in rural Paxton, not far from the Abbey, lies small Moore State Park, tel. (508) 792-3969. Within its wooded borders flow the waters of Turkey Hill Brook, a scenic little waterway whose 90-foot descent in less than a quarter-mile was harnessed in the early 1700s to power saws and grindstones that became, in time, the nuclei of a thriving 19th-century mill village. By the 1900s, industrialization and excessive logging snuffed the place out, leaving only stone foundations, cellar holes, bits of broken mill machinery, and a reconstructed wooden millhouse beside a small dam—abundant fuel for speculation about the village's history. Open daily year-round (free), the park also hosts various seasonal events; call for details.

Tower Hill Botanic Gardens

Capturing one of the region's best views in its splendid westward vista over Wachusett Reservoir to Wachusett Mountain, Tower Hill Botanic Gardens, tel. (508) 869-6111, is the beautiful handiwork of the Worcester County Horticultural Society. Located on French Dr. in the increasingly suburban town of Boylston, Tower Hill is three miles north of I-290 Exit 24N (Church St.). Besides formal gardens around its expansive hilltop lawn, the property also features woodland paths and an orchard of antique apple varieties. Lectures, workshops, flower shows, and guided walks complement the site's extensive plantings (on Wednesdays, a horticulturalist is available to answer your gardening questions). Outside of the winter months, pleasant little Twigs Cafe can offset your hunger pangs—a good thing, too, since you'd have to drive to the next town to find more than convenience-store snacks. Tower Hill is open Tues.-Sun. April-Dec., Tues.-Fri. in winter; admission is $5.

ACCOMMODATIONS

With one exception, all of Worcester's hotels and motels are affiliates of major national or regional chains. The most affordable actually isn't in Worcester at all: **Budgetel Inn,** tel. (800) 428-3438 or (508) 832-7000, on Southbridge St. (Rt. 12), just over the city line in neighboring Auburn, between I-290 Exit 9 and MassPike Exit 10, is a rare New England outpost of the Wisconsin-based chain and offers economy-class motel rooms for $63-75 d. A short way farther south on Rt. 12 is a **Ramada Inn,** tel. (800) 2-RAMADA or (508) 832-3221, adjacent to MassPike Exit 10 and I-395 Exit 8. Rack rates here are $110 year-round, but if you request a corporate or discounted rate, the price of a double is actually about $80.

A couple of miles up the interstate, standard business-class accommodations are the norm among downtown's three available hotels. Right beside I-290 Exit 16 is the **Hampton Inn,** tel. (800) HAMPTON or (508) 757-0400, on Summer St., opposite Treat-Me Donuts, the central post office, and one corner of the five-block Medical City complex. Doubles run $81-91. Less than three blocks away, at the foot of Main St., is Holiday Inn's up-market **Crowne Plaza,** tel. (800) 628-4240 or (508) 791-1600, opposite the historic county courthouse and classic, needle-spired Congregational church. Doubles are $119-139, though corporate customers enjoy steep discounts. This 243-room full-service hotel—Worcester's largest—is the most central of the downtown trio, within blocks of the Art Museum, Salisbury Mansion, acoustically stunning Mechanics Hall, the Worcester Centrum, and the Centrum Centre. Finally, there's the **Clarion Suites Hotel,** tel. (800) CLARION or (508) 753-3512, on Southbridge St. at Madison, opposite the bus station on the south side of downtown. Given the size of the rooms, the rates of $87-132 d are not all that out of line, despite the fortress air at the lobby level (buzzer-activated front doors posted with large security warnings), which doesn't inspire confidence about the neighborhood. (In fact, however, by day, the Clarion is within a short and quite safe stroll of both the Centrum and Worcester Common Fashion Outlets.)

A peripheral pair of chain accommodations is found on Rt. 70 north of I-290, between exits 20 and 21, including a **Days Inn & Lodge,** tel. (508) 852-2800 or (800) DAYS INN, $63-90 d; and a **Holiday Inn,** across the street, tel. (508) 852-4000 or (800) HOLIDAY, $99-119 d.

One of the exceptions to the chains, though expensive, is the best in town: **The Beechwood Hotel,** tel. (800) 344-2589 or (508) 754-5789, at the intersection of Rt. 9 and Plantation St., on the edge of the UMass Medical School campus east of I-290 Exit 15 or south of I-290 Exit 21. Defying the cookie-cutter boxes of most executive hotels, the Beechwood's distinctive circular tower has spacious contemporary rooms, some with working fireplaces. Shrewsbury Street's Italian restaurant row is also a short drive away, although Sunday brunch aficionados won't want to miss the hotel's own lavish buffet. Rates fluctuate by season and day of the week, and it's always worth inquiring about corporate or other discounts; otherwise, prices basically range $89-139 d.

FOOD

While a few good eateries exist within reasonable walking distance of all the downtown hotels, the bulk of Worcester's dining choices are spread all over the map. As a general rule, though, the city's east-west social dichotomy is reflected in its dining: east of I-290, you'll find a down-home, carbohydrate-rich cuisine and relatively conservative presentation (white Italian bread for table service, rather than jalapeño cornbread or foccaccia), while the tonier West Side yields more artful dishes, more vegetarian choices, and some of the only yuppie prices outside of hotel restaurants. These stereotypes are admittedly broad, but the locals do tend to avoid crossing the interstate simply to eat. Unfortunately, neither side is conducive to postprandial strolling—unless you're lodging and dining downtown, you'll be into your car and back out on the road no matter where you go.

In terms of the actual food, you'll find a preponderance of Italian, excellent seafood, some cozy vegetarian places, a real New York-style Jewish neighborhood deli, and a reasonable array of ethnic cuisines, most leaning toward the Middle or Far East. A dozen diners also cater to aficionados of square meals and the practiced drill of short-order cooks, though several have been so thoroughly robbed of their true identities that it would take a highly trained diner sleuth to discern their pedigree.

One particular idiosyncrasy of many of Worcester's neighborhood restaurants is a tendency not to adhere to their posted hours, so consider calling ahead before driving out of your way to a place that might be closing early or taking an unscheduled day off.

By day, downtown is awash in office workers who stream through its lunch spots and plazas. By night, on the other hand, nearly the whole center rolls down its metal shutters and does a good impression of an abandoned city (unless some big show is at the Centrum). Come summer, Main Street by night is largely ceded to young, restless, posturing cruisers, particularly in the blocks between the county courthouse and the discount, second-run Showcase Cinemas, somewhat resembling a Sam Fuller remake of *American Grafitti*. You might feel a little out of place wandering this stretch in search of spinach tortellini or iced cappuccino. Whether the colorful street life is the cause or the effect of downtown's nighttime blight, it needn't be cause for alarm. Well-lit parking lots (either free or validated after 5 p.m.) adjoin nearly every restaurant open for dinner, police visibility is on the high side (particularly during major Centrum rock concerts), and most of the racially diverse crowd—a fair-weather phenomenon anyway—is simply a city version of suburban mall-roaming teen tribes: more interested in their social, mating, and status rituals than in hassling anyone.

Downtown and Vicinity

Aside from the city's various diners, a top choice for anyone seeking a fine breakfast or lunch should be **Lucky's Cafe,** tel. (508) 756-5014, a cozy little joint at the back of a basement corridor in the center of the Northworks on Grove Street. One of several eateries inhabiting the rehabbed brick hulk of the once-thriving Washburn & Moen Manufacturing Co., Lucky's offers hefty portions of everything from French toast to roast-beef sandwiches, plus a commendable number of vegetarian selections and made-from-scratch soups so good that they make up for the apathetic service (cash only). Open weekdays 7:30 a.m.-3:30 p.m.

Another lunch spot, about five blocks north of the Northworks, is **Ciao Bella,** at 402 Grove St. (which is only southbound at that point—if headed north on Grove or Park Ave., follow the signs for Rt. 122A to Holden to get back on Grove headed south), tel. (508) 756-2426. This tiny shop does a tremendous take-out business for both lunch and dinner (they're open daily till 10 p.m.), but if you don't mind the donut-shop atmosphere, sit at one of the handful of tables and feast on terrific brick-oven pizza and calzones, giant rolled pita-style or regular sub sandwiches, or pasta (and not just any pasta, either: linguine with chopped clams and a garlicky, creamy white wine sauce—"an old bootleggers recipe"—or shellfish with tomatoes and leeks over angel hair vermicelli—"Uncle Bruno's famous recipe from the penitentiary"—or perhaps their signature sautéed spinach, sundried tomatoes, Greek olives, and a mustard-laced garlic sauce over your choice of pasta—"famous in Italian insane asylums"). Nearly everything's well under $10, and the baklava is one of the best in town.

Inexpensive, slightly jazzed-up pub fare—salads, stir-fry, and croissant club sandwiches in addition to burgers, steak tips, and barbecued ribs—is the order of the day at the family-friendly **Firehouse Café,** on Commercial St. directly

behind the Centrum (lunch and dinner daily), tel. (508) 753-7899. On the south side of downtown, just above Kelley Square (a big, confusing, five-way intersection next to I-290 Exit 13), is **Weintraub's Deli,** 126 Water St., probably the only decent deli (at least as far as visiting New Yorkers are concerned) east of Brooklyn. Besides coming their own beef and using fresh breads and bagels from the Widoff's Bakery, across the street, Weintraub's makes a mean matzoh ball soup. Good knishes and kosher dill pickles, too, plus Dr. Brown's sodas (including the often elusive celery flavor). For a sweet chaser, step up the block to **Ledermann's Coffee Bar** for some old-fashioned white-icing pastries, super-rich ruggalah, or just a cup of coffee at the counter.

If you're on the prowl for pizza right smack downtown, consider **Cafe Milano,** on Austin at

---

DINER HEAVEN

O f all of Worcester's diner manufacturers, the undisputed king was the Worcester Lunch Car Company. Between 1906 and 1961, the company turned out more than 650 diners at their Quinsigamond Avenue factory. Some of the production models that never made it out of town are still going strong, dishing up meat loaves, burgers, and omelettes that only seem to get better as those old grills age. Here's a small sample of some that please both the eye and the palate:

Ralph's Chadwick Square Diner, tel. (508) 753-9543, tucked into a veritable alley at the north end of the Northworks building, between Grove St. and Prescott. This pre-Depression lunch car is built into the side of one of the city's liveliest and grittiest nightclubs, so don't come expecting to hobnob with the suit-and-tie crowd. But if it's after dark, drop in and grab a burger and a bite of the five-alarm chili.

On the corner of Quinsigamond and Southbridge Sts., beside the towering railroad overpass, is the **Miss Worcester,** tel. (508) 752-1310, across the street from the old Worcester factory, where this very model was built back in the 1930s. Open weekdays till 3 p.m., weekends till noon, and Fri.-Sat. for a few hours starting at midnight, the "Miss Woo" is an unwavering practitioner of basic diner cookery.

A long block away, at Quinsigamond and Lamartine, is the **Corner Lunch,** tel. (508) 755-5576. Originally built in the 1950s, it was remodeled in 1968 by the Musi Dining Car Company of

New Jersey, earning it the distinction of being the only Musi in all of New England. While the fine stainless facade and snappy neon signage make it one of Worcester's most photogenic eateries, the cook proves that quality is more than skin deep. Anyone seeking a tasty, affordable square meal—hefty lasagna, two-fisted flame-broiled burgers, large fluffy pancakes and omelettes—should be sure to seek out Paul and his good-humored gang here in this semi-industrial locale. Open daily for breakfast and lunch, Thurs.-Fri. for dinner (cash only).

At 155 Shrewsbury, on the East Side, is the **Boulevard Diner,** tel. (508) 791-4535, another exceptionally well-preserved Worcester model from the 1930s, with distinctive neon, enameled porcelain exterior panels, and dark wood interior (open daily). Across the street stands the **Parkway Diner,** tel. (508) 753-9968. Though its exterior has been completely covered, its interior—and attitude—have resisted the ages. Open from breakfast through dinner, the Parkway's robust Italian food is quite capable of holding its own in a neighborhood chock-full of stiff competition.

Also on the East Side, within a few hundred yards of the Beechwood Hotel, is **Charlie's Diner,** 344 Plantation St., just south of Rt. 9, tel. (508) 752-9318. Another Worcester, this one was built in 1941. Open for breakfast and lunch, the diner's small scale belies the size of its servings.

the corner of Main about a block from the Clarion Suites Hotel, tel. (508) 753-2994. Gourmet toppings, thick or thin style, ample portions, and cheap prices (most items are under $10) are the highlights, although pasta, sandwiches, salads, and even a veggie stir-fry round out the mostly-Italian menu. Milano also has Guinness on tap. Open for lunch and dinner daily, until 11 p.m. or later. For fancier Italian, try **Shorah's Ristorante,** tel. (508) 797-0007, in the casual storefront at the corner of Foster and Commercial Sts. diagonally across from the Centrum. Yes, it serves pizzas and calzones, but come for the more interesting dishes, such as chardonnay-steamed mussels; chicken with sundried tomatoes, shiitake mushrooms, and spinach in a parmesan-garlic sauce; or veal with lobster. Giant portions and reasonable prices ($8-16) ensure a strong local following.

West of downtown, the stretch of Highland St. below the Worcester Polytechnic Institute campus offers a couple of excellent alternatives to the city's myriad Italian places, including **The Sole Proprietor,** opposite The Boynton tavern, tel. (508) 798-3474. The seafood here is as fresh and varied as anything on the coast, and, given both the portions and complementary side dishes, the $15-25 entree prices are actually more than competitive with anything in Boston, Cape Cod, or the Islands. Though the place specializes in mesquite grilling, dishes run the gamut from fried clams to baked herb-rubbed salmon over spinach with saffron risotto, tomato chardonnay sauce, and dijon remoulade. Open for dinner nightly till at least 9:30 p.m. (Fri.-Sat. until 11 p.m.) and for lunch Mon.-Saturday. A buffet of "kettle" dishes is also available for late-night patrons until 1:30 a.m. About a block farther west, behind the big picture windows at 143 Highland, is **Sahara Restaurant,**

tel. (508) 798-2181, a casual place with an above-average, inexpensive Middle Eastern menu that includes such atypical items as *mughrebeeye,* a fragrant chicken sautéed in a nutmeg-flavored sauce, and *Sheikh el Mihshi*—a spicy, richly sauced dish of baked eggplant and ground beef—in addition to all the usual kebabs, shawarma, falafel, and kibbe. Open daily from breakfast (pastries and latte) till 10 p.m., 11:30 p.m. Fri.-Saturday.

West Side

On upper Main St., in the low-income neighborhood that divides downtown from Clark University, is **The Gentle Lentil,** 800 Main St. at the corner of Castle, opposite the Rodriguez Market, tel. (508) 753-8663. Despite the name, the emphasis in this pocket-sized, four-table place is on natural rather than strictly vegetarian foods, so fish and chicken are as much a feature of the chalkboard menu as tofu and whole-wheat pasta. Fruit smoothies, almost bagel-sized cookies, and desserts that tend to feature granola-like crusts or toppings round out the selections. Farther up the street, at 912 Main, well past the big guys on little bikes hanging out doing business via pagers and payphones, is the artsy and eclectic **Kamanitza's Bistro,** tel. (508) 753-7101, next to Clark's bookstore. From seafood lasagna to jambalaya, the menu is full of satisfying choices at reasonable prices (many $10 or less).

Beyond Clark—whose urban campus is almost indistinguishable from its surroundings—Main St. intersects Rt. 12 (Webster St.) and, after a block lined on both sides with bicycle shops, merges with Rt. 9 (Park St.) at Webster Square. On the corner of Main and Rt. 12 is one of Worcester's best Chinese restaurants, **Chopsticks,** tel. (508) 755-1045. Next to O'Neill's Bike Shop is one of the city's best Mexican eateries, **Rosamaria's Cafe,** tel. (508) 767-1994, a hole-in-the-wall featuring delicious tamales, enchiladas con mole, and other heartfelt, home-style dishes.

Busy Park St., the West Side's major north-south axis, is home to several of the neighborhood's most affordable choices (as well as a lot of fast food, auto parts, and hardware stores). The **House of India,** 439 Park Ave., tel. (508) 752-1330, is one of a cluster south of the intersection with May St., a few blocks from the back of Clark University. A host of rich curries, birya-nis (rice dishes), and tandoor-baked kebabs tempt the senses, along with more than a dozen vegetarian selections ($8-13). **Da-Lat Restaurant,** virtually next door, at 425 Park Ave., tel. (508) 753-6036, is a small Vietnamese place, whose inexpensive and tasty menu has well over 100 items from which to choose. For cheap eats on the run, try tiny **Tortilla Sam's,** tel. (800) 9-FAJITA, next to Mahoney's pub, at the corner of May St. The prices reflect the modest proportions of the freshly made tortillas used for most dishes, so if whatever you want is too cheap to be true, order two. Open daily to 10 p.m., Fri.-Sat. till midnight.

In keeping with the West Side's unwritten kitchen rules, fresh ingredients, more than passing attention to vegetables, and sinful devotion to chocolate are hallmarks of casual **Restaurant at Tatnuck Bookseller Marketplace,** 335 Chandler St. (Rt. 122) west of Park Avenue, tel. (508) 756-7644. The setting—the city's largest bookstore, in a high-ceilinged former industrial building—establishes the casual tone, with a handful of books for each table's centerpiece, and another half-million volumes all around. Besides serving breakfast, lunch, and dinner daily (except Sunday, when it serves brunch), the Tatnuck Bookseller is one of the city's better dessert destinations. Anyone put off by the heavy hand with rich dressings and creamy sauces can request a low-fat or low-cholesterol substitute; vegetarians slighted by the majority of Worcester's chefs will also find a handful of items beyond the standard meatless pasta.

Northern Italian is the specialty at **Arturo's Ristorante,** up the street at 411 Chandler, tel. (508) 755-5640, along with the now-obligatory wood-fired brick-oven pizzas, all with papery thin crusts and thick toppings. The à la carte house salads are quite big, too, and despite the under-$10 prices for everything, you won't be compromising your palate in the least. If you prefer white linen and soft light or are convinced that quality dining has to cost a bundle, head next door to the **Struck Café,** the West Side's upscale anchor at 415 Chandler St. on the corner of June, tel. (508) 757-1670. Meat, fowl, or fresh fish—accompanied by a broad palette of seasonal vegetables, light sauces and reductions, a delightful array of house breads, and

very European pastries for dessert, will easily run $30 per person even without anything from the well-chosen wine list (or a tip for the attentive service). For a slightly less fancy but more affordable version, try the Struck's lunches.

East Side

Shrewsbury St., traditionally the heart of Worcester's Italian neighborhood, is the major food corridor east of I-290. **East Park Grille,** at number 172, next to the big ballfield, is one of the most popular. A small casual place with an open kitchen, a dozen tables, and some counter seats, it claims to offer "Nantucket cuisine at Worcester prices," which simply means that they offer seafood, pasta, and seafood *with* pasta, all for under $10. Even at those prices, the portions are substantial. The atmosphere is friendly but brisk; sit, stuff yourself, then roll out the door (there are no desserts to linger over here). Bring your own beer or wine, and bring cash—credit cards aren't accepted (neither are reservations, as there's no phone.[º]

Neither is there a phone at tiny **Mac's Diner,** across the street, which, like the East Park, serves heaping plates of gourmet pasta for under $10, although here the quarters are close enough that you can almost lend a hand to the chef without leaving your seat. **Porto Bello,** just down the block, at 156 Shrewsbury, tel. (508) 753-9865, provides a slightly more typical take on Italian, with all the industrial-strength red sauces you would expect. But it, too, offers some imaginative specials—a nut-crusted chicken in a spicy mascarpone sauce, for example. Closed Sunday.

GETTING THERE AND AROUND

Worcester enjoys frequent daily MBTA Commuter Rail service to Boston's South Station, tel. (800) 392-6100 or (617) 722-3200. Amtrak's Lake Shore Ltd. runs from Worcester to Chicago via Springfield, Pittsfield, Albany, and points west (tickets and schedules, 800-USA RAIL). The train station is currently at 45 Shrewsbury, on the east side of I-290, but grand old Union Station, on Washington Square, just west of the interstate, is scheduled to be fully restored and back in operation sometime before the turn of the next century.

The intercity bus terminal is on Summer St. at the southern side of downtown, between the tall Clarion Suites Hotel and the unmistakable Coney Island Lunch (whose landmark dripping-mustard hot dog sign towers over Southbridge St. around the corner from the terminal). Major service is provided by Peter Pan Bus Lines, tel. (800) 343-9999, with a dozen daily buses (both express and local) from downtown Boston (South Station) and other points in the Boston area, including a few runs directly from Logan Airport. Greyhound, tel. (800) 231-2222, also serves Worcester, also departing from South Station.

Local and suburban buses are operated by the Worcester Regional Transit Authority; for information about routes and schedules, call (508) 791-WRTA.

Information

Besides the very suburban-oriented daily newspaper, the *Worcester Telegram-Gazette,* there are two free weeklies. *Worcester Magazine* ("Womag" to insiders) is the meatier of the pair, with strong community news coverage in addition to its comprehensive club and movie listings, restaurant reviews, and lifestyle features. The *Worcester Phoenix,* like its Boston parent, is best for club listings and phone-sex ads (or for a cheaper taste of editorial content very similar to what Bostonians have to pay $1.50 for).

For some wonderful local historical anecdotes, look for Albert B. Southwick's *Once-Told Tales* and *More Once-Told Tales of Worcester County,* published by the Tatnuck Bookseller and available locally.

STURBRIDGE AND VICINITY

The town of Sturbridge may be a small place (pop. 8,000), but it's a big destination for the tour buses of New England. This is thanks to Old Sturbridge Village, a time machine that takes visitors back to a model early-19th-century New England community. Given the well-deserved press earned by the exceptional historic preservation on display within Old Sturbridge's gates, it may come as a surprise to see the degree to which the surrounding town bears more resemblance to suburban strip malls than to postcard-perfect Yankeedom. Away from US 20's commercial clutter, you'll find a more archetypal rural New England landscape, replete with clapboard frame houses, distinctive old weathervanes, granite curbstones, and classic tall-steepled meetinghouses. For recreation beyond shopping for gifts, crafts, country furnishings and accessories, candles, and antiques, there's decent flatwater paddling along the Quinebaug River— a tributary of Connecticut's Thames whose headwaters rise in Sturbridge. If you aren't preequipped with a canoe or kayak, the nearest rentals are about 20 miles east on Rt. 146 in Sutton, at the Great Canadian Canoe Company, tel. (800) 98-CANOE, where you'll also find books that can inform you specifically how and where to access the river.

Old Sturbridge Village

With 40-plus museum-quality replicas and authentic period buildings gathered from around New England—all placed in an appropriately pastoral 200-acre landscape of woods, fields, and meadows—Old Sturbridge Village conjures up a vision of rural 1830s New England as tangible as this book. Costumed guides demonstrate crafts and trades of the early 19th century, from sheep shearing to country law—and even, on occasion, some of the more unusual occupations of the era, such as entertainers and phrenologists. Celebrations throughout the year highlight the life of the community as a whole as villagers gather for holidays, harvests, contests, and other significant seasonal events. A visitor center offers introductory exhibits to set the stage, a terrific clock collection, changing displays, and an extensive book and gift shop. In addition to its modern food service, the village offers a historic tavern that serves dishes prepared from period recipes.

Located off US 20 just west of I-84 Exit 2, the village is open daily April-Dec., weekends only in January and early February, and then Tues.-Sun. until the end of March. The $15 adult admission (half that for ages 6-15) is valid for two consecutive days. Call (508) 347-3362 for further information, including recorded announcements

John "Grizzly" Adams' headstone, Bay Path Cemetery, Charlton

of forthcoming special events, or check out their Web site: www.osv.org.

NEARBY SIGHTS

The **Clara Barton Birthplace Museum,** 68 Clara Barton Rd., signposted off Rt. 12., tel. (508) 987-5375, stands in North Oxford. While most widely remembered as the founder of the American Red Cross, Barton was equally noteworthy as an early human rights advocate, suffragette, and proponent of free education. This simple frame house, in which she was born on Christmas Day in 1821, has been operated as a museum since 1928, with personal effects and descriptions of her accomplishments (Tues.-Sun. April-Oct.; $2.50).

"The Brimfield Fleas"

Three weekends each summer—the end of the second full week of May, the weekend a full week after July 4th, and the first weekend following

Labor Day in September—Sturbridge's western neighbor, sleepy little Brimfield, transforms itself into what may be the nation's most renowned flea market. During what's formally known as the **Brimfield Collectibles and Antiques Show** and less formally as "the Brimfield fleas," every pasture in town is filled with parked cars or haggling dealers—thousands of them, their wares running the gamut from exceptional to kitschy, shockingly expensive to quite reasonable. Grouped along US 20 under a variety of winsome names, some congregations of dealers are open to all, but others weed out idle browsers by charging entrance fees. The by-admission-only assemblage at Auction Acres, tel. (413) 245-3436 or (508) 597-8155, is not only the most exclusive, but also the one that launched this phenomenon back in 1959. Credit card acceptance depends on the individual dealer.

PRACTICALITIES

Camping

Off Rt. 49 in the northern end of Sturbridge—separated by the MassPike from the US 20 corridor—is **Wells State Park,** tel. (508) 347-9257, which has the enviable distinction of being one of the state's most attractive campgrounds. Shaded by a canopy of mature trees, lent a measure of privacy by being spread out on two widely separated levels of a hill that slopes down to a beautiful swimming pond, most of the park's 59 sites are also set well away from the road. The waterfront sites (numbers 17-25) are among the most popular, but for sheer serenity it would be hard to top some of the sites up the hill—especially number 32, a huge spot surrounded by some of the old drystone walls that run all through the woods. Half the sites are reservable; given the park's enormous popularity throughout the summer months, it is extremely advisable to take advantage of this fact. A dumping station is available—along with full bathrooms, including showers—but RV hookups are not. Open May 1-mid-Oct.; fees are $7 for the waterfront sites, $6 for all others.

Accommodations

April-Nov. the **Dudley Home Hostel,** tel. (508) 943-6520, a working farm about 15 miles east of Sturbridge throws open its doors to Hostelling International members for a mere $10 pp. Owner/hosts Chet and Ann Kulisa are as knowledgable as you could ask for, and their bunk accommodations, though basic, are perfectly appropriate to life in an 1834 farmhouse. Call for reservations (required) and directions. If you didn't pack any breakfast provisions, ask the Kulisas to point you toward Carl's Oxford Diner, on neighboring Oxford's Main St., next to Subway, at the one stoplight in town (the junction of Rt. 12 and I-395 Exit 4). Behind the undistinguished exterior is a nearly unchanged 1930s Worcester Lunch Car. The breakfasts aren't for dainty or discriminating palates—a typical omelette is about the size of a deflated football, with a texture more scrambled than fluffy, and most contain meat suspiciously resembling Spam—but if you're hungry enough to eat a horse and too poor to spend more than a couple dollars, it can't be beat.

A slew of chain motels line US 20 and adjacent Sturbridge roads, catering not only to the bus tours that ply the town but also to tired drivers on both the MassPike and I-84, which converge just to the north. Most are moderate to expensive; several are very expensive (particularly May-Oct., the standard high season for this area). Among the choices, in order of ascending price: **Rodeway Inn,** on Main St. (Rt. 131) east of I-84, tel. (800) 228-2000 or (508) 347-9673, $48-85 d; **Econo Lodge,** on US 20 two miles west of the Old Sturbridge Village entrance, tel. (800) 55 ECONO or (508) 347-2324, $55-90 d; **Quality Inn Colonial,** on US 20 east of I-84 Exit 2, tel. (800) 228-5151 or (508) 347-3306, $62-90 d; **Best Western American Motor Lodge,** on US 20 a block from the OSV entrance, tel. (800) 528-1234 or (508) 347-9121, $69-87 d; **Super 8 Motel,** on US 20 west of OSV, tel. (800) 800-8000 or (508) 347-9000, $59-115 d; and **Holiday Inn Express,** on US 20 west of the Super 8, tel. (800) HOLIDAY or (508) 347-5141, $89-145 d.

The only structure in Old Sturbridge Village still standing on its original site happens to be the 18th-century Federal-style **Oliver Wight House,** located on US 20 a half mile west of the Village entrance, tel. (508) 347-3327, now the centerpiece of OSV's public lodgings. Carefully restored in the mid-1980s, the dwelling combines the simplicity of Colonial decor with modern creature comforts, juxtaposing stone hearths and exposed hand-hewn beams with gleaming bathroom fixtures and touch-tone phones. The 10 rooms in the Wight run $90-110 d ($130 on flea-market days). Behind the Wight House are standard-issue motel blocks with basic economy rooms for $75-95 d ($110 during the Brimfield fleas).

A short drive away, on the original town common, beside Rt. 131, is the sprawling **Publick House Resort,** tel. (800) PUBLICK. From modern motel units up on a hill behind the trees to the main building, which predates the American Revolution, to a B&B-styled house further off Main St., this place does its best to accommodate a range of tastes and budgets—although in response to overwhelming popular demand, the Publick House's four properties command some of the highest prices in town (particularly on weekends), even in winter. The 1771 **Historic Inn** is the oldest portion—and also houses the main restaurant. Its rooms combine modern conveniences (excluding TV) with antique furnishings, high-quality reproductions, and such other characterful attributes as original, uneven wide-board flooring. Because of the building's idiosyncratic additions over time, standard rooms vary in all but price. Expect minimum-stay requirements on many holiday and fall foliage weekends and during the Brimfield fleas. Rates are $75-135 d. By contrast, the motel units up the hill in the misleadingly named "Country Lodge" are $55-119 d.

A pair of final notes: If you aren't attending the Brimfield fleas, avoid searching locally for a room on those weekends. Also, if you're arriving via the MassPike, be sure to stop by one of the Pike's information centers and scan through the rack cards for the Sturbridge area to see whether any discount coupons are offered.

Food

While the fanciest of Sturbridge's restaurants is probably the **Whistling Swan,** tel. (508) 347-2321, in a clapboard house on US 20 west of Old Sturbridge Village, the same attention to quality ingredients can be sampled in a less elaborate—and more affordable—menu in the converted barn on the side, home to the **Ugly Duckling Loft.** It's gourmet pub fare, starring all your burger, salad, and fish-and-chip favorites. A convivial atmosphere and occasional live music add to the Duckling's deserved local popularity (closed Monday).

A casual, comfortable spot for either eye-openers or midday meals is the **Sunburst,** tel. (508) 347-3097, on US 20 next to the Holiday Inn Express. Billing itself as "country style," it's actually more than just a down-home hash-slinging joint—it features such un-dinerlike fare as granola, quiche, and fruit smoothies. They don't slight the standards, either: you can order omelettes, soups, sandwiches, or just your favorite style of eggs and bacon all day, every day, year-round (except Thanksgiving, Christmas, and New Year's).

The **Casual Cafe,** tel. (508) 347-2281, a short distance west of the Sunburst, is equally relaxed, resembling a cross between a corner neighborhood cafe and your best friend's kitchen, with a one-page menu of simple Italian and Japanese dishes (guess the nationalities of the two partners) prepared on one side of the room and served on the other. Everything's well below $10, too (cash only). Open Tues.-Sat. 11:30 a.m.-9 p.m.

POCUMTUCK VALLEY MEMORIAL ASSOCIATION, MEMORIAL HALL MUSEUM, DEERFIELD, MASS.

PIONEER VALLEY

Christened by tourism promoters back in the late 1930s, the Pioneer Valley (also called Happy Valley, and known as simply the Valley to its residents) is a place that often defies Massachusetts stereotypes. Bisected by the Connecticut River, it's essentially Massachusetts' left coast, with an outsized proportion of artists, New Age retreats, laid-back attitudes, alternative lifestyles, and concern for American foreign policy. Instead of lighthouses, beaches, small harbors dotted with sails and a plethora of lobster, the Valley offers summit vistas, scenic bike trails, small town arts festivals, and native corn on the cob. It is in fact the major agricultural belt of a state more often associated with fishing than farming. Some of the most productive arable land on the planet is right here on the banks of the Connecticut. Ironically for a state that's been a trendsetter in restricting public smoking, the most lucrative Valley crop is tobacco.

The region's physical and metaphorical centerpiece is its cluster of college towns, and here, as in Boston, the concentration of academia helps support performing arts, excellent bookstores, fine food, great nightclubs, and overpriced accommodations around Commencement weekend. On the margins are the in-

evitable old industrial neighbors—none entirely devoid of tourist attractions—whose fall from economic grace remains one of the state's thorniest problems. And enveloping everything are rural one-horse towns with church steeples firmly planted in the wilderness, distinctive B&Bs tucked into the woods, and the occasional historic home or museum.

GETTING THERE

Although strong competition among airlines serving Boston tends to keep fares lower than service to any of the smaller regional airports, for proximity to the Valley you can't beat Connecticut's **Bradley Airport,** outside Hartford, with connecting Peter Pan Bus Line service almost every two hours straight up I-91 to Springfield and the Five College area (there are also car rentals at the airport).

Amtrak has daily trains to the Valley along both east-west and north-south routes. The Lake Shore Limited stops in Springfield on its daily run between Chicago and Boston (arriving before 2 p.m. from Albany and the Great Lakes, or around 6 p.m. from Boston), while two trains a day travel the Connecticut Valley from New

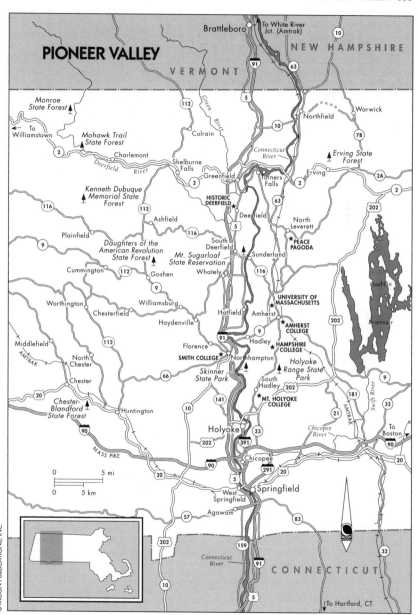

PIONEER VALLEY

© MOON PUBLICATIONS, INC.

PIONEER VALLEY FESTIVALS AND EVENTS

APRIL

Over about four weeks beginning in late April, the **Massachusetts International Festival of the Arts** hits stages in Northampton, Amherst, Holyoke, and Springfield with fully staged operas (drop any preconceptions; these productions are not your usual classical fare), theater, concerts, and films. Call (800) 224-MIFA or (413) 584-4425 for details.

JUNE

The Taste of Amherst, tel. (413) 253-0700, takes hold of downtown the first weekend of the month.

To the accompaniment of live music and the acclaim of hungry crowds for five midmonth days, local restaurants fill Court Square and adjoining streets with displays of mouth-watering fare during **The Taste of Springfield,** tel. (413) 733-3800.

The last weekend of the month, the annual **Great New England Brewers' Festival** attempts to slake the thirsts of beer aficionados with several score of ales and lagers—all from regional microbreweries and brewpubs. Tickets to the kickoff party (featuring a big-name band) are available at the Northampton Box Office in Thorne's Market; call (800) THE-TICK or (413) 586-8686. Nominal admission (beer is sold separately) is charged to the rest of the festival, held at the Tri County Fairgrounds, on Rt. 9 (Bridge St.), between downtown and I-91.

JULY

For **Independence Day,** Springfield puts on one of the larger pyrotechnic displays, down on the Connecticut River—but small towns add their own twist to celebrations of the Fourth. Monson, east of Springfield, holds an ice cream social, complete with watermelon-seed spitting contests, lawn games, and encouragements to turn out in turn-of-the-century garb and bring a picnic (see *Meet Me In St. Louis* if you need fashion advice). Call (413) 774-7476 for directions and particulars. Up the Valley, in Shutesbury, the meditative retreat center Sirius hosts an **INTERdependence Day Celebration,** tel. (413) 259-1251,

with potluck lunch, dancing, entertainment, and games for all ages.

AUGUST

The first Saturday of the month the **Teddy bear Rally** takes over the Town Common with the nation's largest assemblage of antique teddy bear dealers displaying their wares, attracting some 20,000 collectors from around the world. Sponsored by the Amherst Rotary club; call (413) 549-6602 for information.

Around the second weekend of the month, **The Taste of Northampton** turns the Armory St. parking lot behind Thorne's Market into a giant picnic area as local chefs strut their stuff. Anyone trying to hew to a strict diet should stay out of town. Call (413) 585-5058 for details.

SEPTEMBER

The weekend after Labor Day, the **Glendi Festival** brings a cavalcade of all things Greek to Springfield's Greek Cultural Center, 8 Plainfield St. (I-91 Exit 10). Music, food, art, pastries, merchandise, and more food give you a chance to practice your Zorba impressions. For more information, call (413) 737-1496. That same weekend, Greater Springfield's Polish community mounts one of the state's largest ethnic festivals: the **Kielbasa Festival,** at the Fairfield Mall, 591 Memorial Dr. (Rt. 33N) in Chicopee (MassPike Exit 5). Polka bands, rides, food. Call (413) 549-2101 for specifics.

The last half of the month is filled with **The Big E,** a huge six-state fair celebrating all things New England, at the Eastern States Exposition grounds, on Memorial Ave., in West Springfield. Agricultural events and contests, arts and crafts, local foodways, big-top circus, car races, daily parades, and big-name entertainers keep the crowds coming back each year. Tether yourself to your kids. Admission is charged. Call (413) 737-BIG E, or (413) 787-0271 for recorded info.

On the third weekend, rain or shine, the Memorial Hall Museum in Deerfield hosts its annual **Old Deerfield Fall Craft Fair,** with hundreds of exhibitors chosen from all over the United States. Call (413) 774-7476 x6 for details.

York City (Penn Station) to Springfield, with one continuing through Amherst to Vermont and Montréal, Canada. Call (800) USA-RAIL for schedules, fares, and reservations, or visit their homepage on the Web: www.amtrak.com.

Long-distance bus service to the area is provided almost exclusively by **Peter Pan Bus Lines,** tel. (800) 343-9999 or (413) 781-3320, although if you're trying to reach Springfield from Rhode Island call **Bonanza Bus Lines,** tel. (800) 556-3815 or (401) 751-8800. From either Boston's South Station or Manhattan's Port Authority, Peter Pan has a slew of daily buses to Springfield and the Five Colleges, with additional "college express" service tailored to students leaving campus for a weekend in Boston (i.e., Friday afternoon departures and Sunday or holiday returns). Peter Pan's half dozen buses from Albany and upstate New York connect to the Valley through their Springfield terminal, as do their twice-daily buses from White River Junction and eastern Vermont.

GETTING AROUND

A number of **car rental** companies are represented in both Springfield and the Five College area. Those in **Springfield** include Thrifty, tel. (800) 367-2277 or (413) 783-9181; Bud-

get, tel. (413) 732-5191; Enterprise, tel. (800) 736-8222 or (413) 783-8900; Rent-A-Wreck, tel. (413) 732-3100, and U-Save, tel. (413) 731-6900. In **Northampton** choose among Thrifty, tel. (413) 586-7500; Enterprise, tel. (413) 586-5177; and National, tel. (800) 227-7368 or (413) 586-1201. Around **Amherst** are Rent-A-Wreck, tel. (413) 549-7368. All offer free local pick-up and drop-off for customers.

If you have no intention of driving all over the countryside you may find Pioneer Valley Transit Authority (PVTA) **public buses** to be perfectly adequate for hitting the Valley's highlights, saving you enough on car rental to splurge on in-town accommodations. Just keep in mind that while a majority of the museums, parks, and historic sights mentioned in this chapter are accessible by PVTA buses, service is only Mon.-Sat. on most routes, is most frequent (and sometimes limited to) commuter hours, and doesn't run at all in summer on selected college-related routes. Call (413) 781-7882 for route and schedule information, or to request a system map be mailed to you.

For Pioneer Valley weather forecasts 24 hours a day, call (413) 731-9442.

SPRINGFIELD AND VICINITY

Springfield (pop. 157,000) occupies an area that once lay between two important cataracts along the Connecticut River, falls that were focal points for Native American commerce and settlement since possibly the dawn of Paleo-Indian occupation of the valley some 9,000-12,000 years ago. While the river is also what drew the white man—as transportation corridor, trade route, food source, and, by the Industrial Age, power supply—Springfield today has turned its back to the water with a welter of financial service office towers. Those banking and insurance outfits are the principal heirs to what was once a diverse industrial economy, one that included cars, guns, bicycles, high-performance airplanes, Breck shampoo, and Milton Bradley board games. Evidence of that former manu-

facturing might is found in the city's large surviving Victorian-era neighborhoods, mostly in the Stick and Queen Anne style.

But don't come expecting block after block of attractively maintained gingerbread carpentry and scroll-sawn detailing. Native son Theodor Geisel, better known as Dr. Seuss, successfully lifted details of the cityscape for his many books, but without the aid of such a fertile and whimsical imagination modern Springfield is no beauty. An unhealthy percentage of its historic housing stock is tattered or boarded up, and the last generation of buildings huddle defensively around the downtown convention center, doing their best to insulate any remaining white-collar employees from the city's streets. Like Cleveland before rock 'n' roll or Memphis before Graceland, Springfield is a city in need of a golden opportunity. Despite clearly lagging behind Eastern Massachusetts's economic revival, the stagnation isn't wholly systemic: a young yuppie demographic free of the reflexive pull-up-the-drawbridge mentality of suburbanite baby boomers has brought some new vitality back to downtown nightlife, and the immigrant communities definitely add flavor and culture. Tourist attractions are limited, but the nearby junction between I-91 and the MassPike has produced a sizable concentration of moderately priced motel rooms, making the city a potentially more affordable base for exploration of the Valley and neighboring regions than might otherwise be available.

SIGHTS

The Quadrangle

Forget two-for-one sales, how about four-for-one? One low price—$4—gets you into a quartet of art and history museums lining the quadrangle behind the city library on State Street.

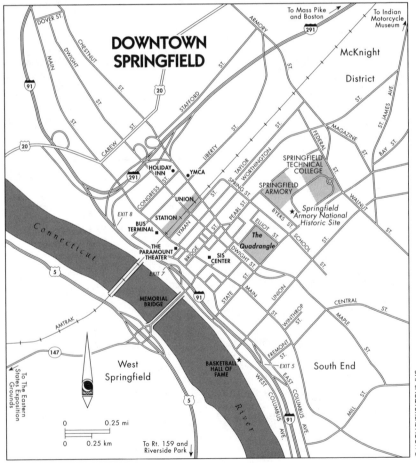

TITANICA!

The spectacular success of the 1997 movie, the "love theme," and the Broadway musical put the tragic story of the *Titanic* back in the news with almost as much clamor as greeted the tragedy itself. On its maiden voyage, the *Titanic*, "unsinkable" pride of the White Star Line, struck an iceberg in the North Atlantic on April 14, 1912, and sank, taking the lives of some 1,500 of its 2,200 passengers. If the movie and the hit songs sharpened—or at least didn't kill—your interest in the "old canoe," you won't want to miss a visit to the *Titanic* **Museum,** in Springfield's northeast suburb of Indian Orchards. (In the immediate wake of the movie, the number of visitors jumped from two or three families each weekend to 20 or 30.)

Maintained by the Titanic Historical Society (THS), the diminutive museum is packed to the ceiling with art and artifacts related to the ship and her passengers and crew. Artists' dramatic renderings of the disaster, model ships, original blueprints, carpet scraps, a *Titanic* menu, correspondence and telegrams from the vessel, crew logbooks, survivors' mementos, and much more is on display in a jumble not unsuited to the unusual locale: the rear of Henry's Jewelry Store, 208 Main St., tel. (413) 543-1891. This is exemplary of those beloved collections accumulated and catalogued without context or interpretation. A visit is akin to sifting through old shoeboxes of mixed-up family photos.

Besides enshrining the memory of all things *Titanic,* the THS publishes a glossy magazine for the faithful, organizes an annual trip to a site of the 1912 disaster, and sells an astonishing variety of videos, books, postcards, refrigerator magnets, posters, limited-edition lithographs, and even CDs of *Titanic*-inspired music.

If you could use a small detour on your visit to Springfield or your trip across the state—or are a prospective member of the Society—get off the MassPike at Exit 7, make a left on Rt. 21, after the tollbooth, and proceed south about a mile, staying on Rt. 21. After crossing the Chicopee River, turn right again on Rt. 141 (Main St.). Henry's is about half a mile ahead on the right, opposite the Grand Theater. From downtown Springfield, take I-291 east to Exit 5A (US 20/Indian Orchard) and turn east at the bottom of the ramp. In less than two miles, at the third set of lights (Berkshire Ave.), turn left, then left again on Oak, then right on Main, at the bottom of the hill. Henry's is about an eighth of a mile ahead on the left. You can also reach the place via the PVTA #106 Ludlow bus from downtown Springfield. Those who bypass this opportunity haven't entirely missed the boat: all the gift shop items are available by mail order. (Also, if you're in the vicinity of Fall River, you can catch the remainder of the THS collection—including some of its largest items—on permanent loan to that city's Marine Museum.)

The **George Walter Vincent Smith Art Museum,** tel. (413) 733-4214, is architecturally the most striking of the four, founded by a 19th-century business tycoon believed to have made his fortune in fabric manufactured for carriages (he burned all his papers to retain his privacy, so the details of his life are hazy). Though limited in breadth, the holdings include a goodly quantity of fine Japanese armor and lacquerware, and a huge collection of Chinese cloisonné. Display labels, unfortunately, aren't very informative.

Across the small Quad is the **Museum of Fine Arts,** with its one-of-this, one-of-that collection of European and modern art, while next door is the modest **Science Museum,** with its small planetarium and big dinosaur. This institution's Victorian origins are abundantly clear in the emphasis on artifact over interpretation, and

the age of some of the displays render them effectively obsolete in the face of more current knowledge (particularly the Indian Hall, which serves up an uninformed 50-year-old stereotype of native dress and gender roles), but exhibits on Springfield inventions and industry are rather fascinating. Also worthy of a peek is the **Connecticut Valley Historical Museum,** whose varied displays hint at the city's achievements, from Springfield founder William Pynchon's heretical 17th-century religious treatise (burned in Boston!) to the making of the Breck Girl. All four museums are open Thurs.-Sun. only.

Springfield Armory National Historic Site

General George Washington built the first U.S. arsenal on a Springfield hillside during the American Revolution; after he became President, he made it one of the nation's two Federal armories. Samples of its prodigious output —from hand-crafted 18th-century flintlock muskets to mass-produced semi-automatic weapons used in Vietnam—are exhibited as part of the world's largest collection of small arms, accompanied by extensive videos on the mechanics of weapons technology through the years. Open daily in summer and Tues.-Sun. Sept.-May; admission is free. The Armory collection is located in the 19th-century Main Arsenal, Bldg. 13, tel. (413) 734-8551, at the very back of Springfield Technical Community College's iron-fenced campus. The Quadrangle museums are only two blocks away.

Basketball Hall of Fame

A local YMCA instructor, Dr. James Naismith, is credited for inventing the game of basketball in 1891 with a two-page set of rules. His legacy is commemorated at the large Basketball Hall of Fame, 1150 West Columbus Ave. between I-91 and the river, tel. (413) 781-6500. There's plenty of memorabilia, including size 22 shoes, basketball postage stamps, coaching diagrams, and lots of videos of past game highlights. You can work up a sweat, too, with exhibits like the basket-shooting gallery, or the interactive video with 6-foot-11-inch Bill Walton.

Indian Motocycle Museum

When George Hendee, a national champion bicyclist during the 1880s, put a motor on a bicycle, the "motocycle" was born in America. His Indian Motocycle Company, started under a different name in 1901, begat a legendary series of 'cycles, a number of which may be seen crammed into the company's former engineering building at 33 Hendee St. a short drive east of downtown, tel. (413) 737-2624. These display machines—all in working order—are surrounded by a cherished assortment of mementos, logo items, photos, and other characterful bric-a-brac. Open daily, the museum is found off I-291 at the St. James Ave. exit; follow the small signs to the trackside industrial area backing up to the north side of the interstate. Admission $3. The Museum is also accessible via the PVTA #109 St. James Ave. bus, which runs along Main St. downtown and up State St. past both the Quadrangle museums and the Springfield Armory.

Riverside Park

Riverside Park, tel. (413) 786-9300, a summer amusement park and racetrack across the river in nearby Agawam next to the Connecticut line, has the requisite variety of rides that do their best to separate you from your equilibrium, from a neck-straining 360-degree loop-de-loop to octupus spinners, plus an ample supply simple kiddie rides. It also has a couple of wooden roller coasters, one of which—the Cyclone—is good enough to warrant a pilgrimage by coaster cognoscenti. The initial seven-story, 60-mph drop is second only to Coney Island's for steep-

---

MASSACHUSETTS' MOTHER OF ALL FARM STORES

In a world homogenized by perfect pyramidal supermarket displays of blushing, supersweet, oh-so-perfect Washington State apples, places like **Bluebird Acres** should be heralded as national treasures. On this East Longmeadow farm south of Springfield grow some 80 varieties—a poetic index of flavors ranging from contemporary favorites such as McIntosh, Royal Gala, and Northern Spy, to antique varieties including Winter Banana and Westfield-Seek-No-Further. You'll also find here the oldest variety of cultivated apple known, the Caville de Blanc (raised by 15th-century European monks), the Newtown Pippin (precursor to the Granny Smith—and Ben Franklin's favorite); and the Esopus Spitzenberg (Thomas Jefferson's favorite). Early autumn brings the widest selection, but there are summer and late fall varieties, too.

Mail-order apple gift packs are available; call (413) 525-6012 or 525-4147. The Weizbicki family's market also features other fruits, vegetables, and berries raised on their acreage; healthful fruit-sweetened desserts and whole-grain breads baked on the premises; and specialty farm products from elsewhere in the state. To put it mildly, if you have only one chance to stop for a taste of Massachusetts, stop at Bluebird Acres. From downtown Springfield, follow Main St. (Rt. 83) south to Sumner St. (Rt. 57) east. Sumner becomes Allen and soon splits; take the south fork (still Allen) across the Springfield-East Longmeadow line and turn right at the light at Parker Street. The farm is on the left.

ness, and if you don't get an adrenaline rush from the hair-raising whips, dips, and plunges that follow, have your pulse checked. A ride at the back is as close to bungy-jumping as you can get without jumping off a bridge. Open daily to 10 p.m. or later June-Labor Day, and Fri.-Sun. to end of October; adult admission $25, or $13 after 5 p.m. Parking is extra. Peter Pan Bus Lines run a Riverside shuttle from their Springfield terminal downtown on Main Street.

PRACTICALITIES

Accommodations
The city's least expensive lodgings are at **City Space/YMCA,** 275 Chestnut St. downtown next to the Amtrak station, tel. (413) 739-6951. Spartan rooms for singles or couples, all with private baths, $36 s, $41 d. If you have a car the next best is **Motel 6,** tel. (800) 4-MOTEL6 or (413) 592-5141, in Chicopee, at the junction of I-291 and the MassPike, where doubles are $44-47. Midweek off season, many of the chain motels on the unattractive mall-lined strip of US 5 in West Springfield also court the $50 mark. While many of these places nudge their prices up during the Five College area's busy mid- to late-May graduation weeks, they still handily beat the going rates in the college towns themselves. Travelers to the Berkshires who want affordable alternatives to the high prices and minimum stay requirements that grip *that* whole region on summer and fall weekends should also consider this US 5 cluster, if driving 45 minutes each way is worth double-digit savings. Just try to avoid September's post-Labor Day Big "E," held in West Springfield, which makes both vacancies and low-end rates disappear.

Aside from the national brands, the strip also sports several cheap-looking old motel courts, some of which are so heavily perfumed with disinfectant that it should come as no surprise guests can only bear the comforts of their shag carpet and waterbeds for no more than a few hours at a time. Appearances do not deceive: if it doesn't look good from the outside, believe me, it doesn't get any better inside.

If you're interested in one of the city's handful of bed and breakfast places, your only bet is to call a reservation service such as **Berkshire**

B&B Homes, tel. (413) 268-7244, which represents houses throughout the Valley. A nominal fee is charged.

Food
Springfield is acquiring a modish edge to its dining, with at least one pair of restaurants easily competitive with anything dished out by Boston's hottest spots. But its mainstay is its family-oriented dining, with hefty portions at reasonable prices. The major ethnicity represented on city menus is still traditional Italian, although a few new flavors are cropping up around the edges, including Latino, Southeast Asian, and Indian. If it's before 5 p.m., the part of Springfield that's synonymous with Italian deli lunches is the South End, in the 800-900 blocks of Main Street south of downtown. It only takes a short stroll to hit all the top spots, all family-run markets with a brisk take-out trade at the deli and sometimes a few formica tables on the side. A prime example of the breed is **Mom & Rico's,** 899 Main, tel. (413) 732-8941, featuring a broad range of made-to-order sandwiches using their top-quality meats and cheeses, along with "Mom's buffet," a smorgasbord of hearty home-style Italian standards like lasagna, eggplant parmesan, prosciutto-stuffed peppers, and cutlets, all for a pittance. For true local flavor there isn't much in the city that can top this. Closed Sunday. For dessert, step next door to **La Fiorentina Caffé & Pastry Shoppe,** tel. (413) 732-3151, for a high-calibre dose of filled-to-order cannoli, demitasse European sugar cookies, and enough white-icing multi-tiered cakes to serve a busload of wedding guests.

Another first-class choice is **Frigo's,** 90 Williams St., tel. (413) 732-5428, or, for really great Italian sausages, **Zonin,** tel. (413) 734-5123, on Winthrop St. around the corner from Mom & Rico's. After 5 p.m. choose from either the inexpensive, tried-and-true **Spaghetti Warehouse** on Congress St. opposite the Holiday Inn, tel. (413) 737-5454, or **A Touch of Garlic,** 427 White St. at Sumner (Rt. 57), opposite the Sunoco station, tel. (413) 739-0236. This informal storefront in the Forest Park neighborhood south of downtown has a deceptively simple menu of pastas and entrees—lasagna, meat, fish—made special by the quality of the ingredients and obviously heartfelt talent in the kitchen. Closed Monday.

SPRINGFIELD AREA ACCOMMODATIONS

DOWNTOWN SPRINGFIELD

Holiday Inn Springfield, 711 Dwight St., about three blocks from Amtrak and interstate bus stations, tel. (800) HOLIDAY or (413) 781-0900.; $119 d (discounts available).

Sheraton Springfield Hotel, Monarch Place, tel. (800) 426-9004 or (413) 781-1010; restaurants, indoor pool, complete health club including racquetball courts, fireplace-equipped suites, discount airport shuttle from Bradley Airport; $109-159.

Springfield Marriott Hotel, Boland Way at Columbus Ave., tel. (800) 228-9290 or (413) 781-7111; $129-154.

WEST SPRINGFIELD

All but the last of the following are found on Riverdale St. (US 5) across the river from Springfield, between MassPike Exit 4 and US 20. From north to south:

Knights Inn, midway between the MassPike Exit 4 and I-91 Exit 13A, tel. (800) 843-5644 or (413) 737-9047; pool; $38-75 d.

Super 8 Motel, opposite Knights Inn, tel. (800) 800-8000 or (413) 736-8080; $50-76 d.

Red Roof Inn, immediately north of I-91 Exit 13A, tel. (800) THE-ROOF or (413) 731-1010; $43-70 d.

Quality Inn, immediately south of I-91 Exit 13B, tel. (800) 228-5151 or (413) 739-7261; restaurant, swimming pool, in-room modem ports; $55-119 d.

Ramada Inn & Conference Center, next to Quality Inn, tel. (800) 228-2828 or (413) 781-8750; restaurant, indoor swimming pool; $49-89 d.

Hampton Inn, opposite the Ramada, tel. (800) HAMPTON or (413) 732-1300; swimming pool; $80 d.

EconoLodge, at Elm St. traffic signal next to Showcase Cinemas, half a mile south of I-91 Exit 13B, tel. (800) 55-ECONO or (413) 734-8278; $40-80 d.

Ramada Limited & Suites, 21 Baldwin St., opposite the Big E's exposition grounds, tel. (800) 228-2828 or (413) 781-2300; $64 d.

I-91 NORTH (HOLYOKE)

Holiday Inn Holidome, at I-91 Exit 15, near the huge Ingleside Mall, tel. (800) HOLIDAY or (413) 534-3311; enclosed pool, recreation facilities, kids 18 and under stay free; $89-99 d.

Super 8 Motel, at I-91 Exit 17/17A, on Northampton and Hampden Sts. (US 5 and Rt. 141), tel. (800) 800-8000 or (413) 536-1980; $40-81 d.

MASSPIKE EAST (CHICOPEE)

Comfort Inn, Memorial Dr. (Rt. 33) north of interstate Exit 5, tel. (800) 221-2222 or (413) 739-7311; restaurant, free continental breakfast; $56-95 d.

Best Western Chicopee Motor Lodge, Memorial Dr. (Rt. 33), north of interstate Exit 5, tel. (800) 528-1234 or (413) 592-6171; swimming pool, rsetaurant next door; small pets welcome; $44-64 d.

Ramada Inn, north of interstate Exit 6 (junction with I-291), tel. (800) 228-2828 or (413) 592-9101; restaurant, swimming pool; $55-75 d.

Motel 6, north of interstate Exit 6, tel. (800) 4-MOTEL6 or (413) 592-5141; pool; $44-64 d.

Plantation Inn, north of interstate Exit 6, tel. (413) 592-8200; $50 d.

Italian also makes a nominal appearance on one half of the menu of downtown's **Mexitalia,** toward the rear of the SIS Center shopping arcade on the corner of Main and Harrison, tel. (413) 781-6101, but stick to the Mexican side for the best dishes. Emphasizing solid, fresh flavors in such entrees as spinach *entomatadas,* mole poblano, shrimp *en escabeche,* and of course the familiar fajitas and burritos. This is one of a very, very few restaurants in Massachusetts that practices real Mexican regional cookery, rather than something filtered through Texas. Fine velvety flan, too. With Viva Mexico pennants along the canopy over the bar and festive colors throughout, the place has a warmth that overcomes what otherwise would be a rather fast-foodish location. Closed Sunday.

Much of the city's Spanish-speaking population actually comes from the Caribbean; transport your tastebuds to the islands via the Dominican menu at **Restaurant Latino,** tel. (413) 733-6599, 1696 Main St. by the Paramount

Theater. Or for something completely different, try **Sitar,** an inexpensive little Indian place on the other side of the theater entrance, tel. (413) 732-8011.

The blocks around the old Paramount are actually the nucleus of Springfield's nightlife. Taylor Street, opposite, is abuzz after dark with the local demi-monde supping on smoked oysters or pork medallions with leek strudel and sipping the latest seasonal lambic, stout, or ale at the **Pioneer Valley Brew Pub,** tel. (413) 732-BREW. Parallel Worthington St. has a couple of smokey bars featuring occasional live music, and a yuppie cigar bar with scores of expensive stogies lining the walk-in humidor and almost as many single malt Scotches to go with 'em. The **Zone Art Center,** tel. (413) 732-1995, sponsors a jazz concert series in their second-floor space overlooking small Stearns Square; and there is a hip-hop dance joint next door. Worthington is also home to **Caffienes,** tel. (413) 788-6646, the kind of place whose every dish could be featured on the cover of *Bon Appétit,* and whose interior belongs in *Art Today.* With entrees averaging just under $15, it's definitely at the high end of local dining, but given the caliber of the food, these are truly small-town prices. Leave room for the excellent—and ample—desserts. Open for lunch weekdays, dinner Mon.-Sat. till 10 p.m. or later.

If wild mushrooms, fruit-flavored vinegars, and herb-infused oils are all ingredients to your private Purgatory, head straight for **The Fort,** on block-long Fort St., tel. (413) 734-7475, around the corner from the Paramount. Also known as The Student Prince, this is *the* schnitzel and sauerbraten palace of the Bay State. Next to choosing one of the German house specialties the most important decision of the meal is whether to have your potatoes boiled, hashed, fried, or mashed. The decor includes stained glass depictions of city landmarks in the dining room, and a mammoth Bierstein collection in the bar. Open daily for both lunch and dinner.

The **Blue Eagle** sits "on top of the hill" at 932 Worthington by the corner of Armory St., tel. (413) 737-6135. A few blocks north of the Springfield Armory, surrounded by buildings that have a generous share of plywood instead of glass, this is a throwback to the days when veneer was spiffy, smoking was sexy, and a Delmonico steak with salad and baked potato was as fine a meal as you could ever ask for. A favorite of local police—whose headquarters are a few blocks down the hill, hence the name—this place hasn't tried to change its formula to suit '90s tastes, so don't worry about any froufrou condiments being substituted for your blue cheese or mayonnaise here.

THE FIVE COLLEGE AREA

Named after the mostly private institutions of higher education in its midst, the Five College area is balanced between the city of Northampton on the west side of the Connecticut River and a trio of smaller towns on the east: Hadley, Amherst, and South Hadley. Enrollments at the five—Smith College, the University of Massachusetts (UMass), Amherst College, Hampshire College, and Mount Holyoke College—seem, at times, to rival the area's nonstudent population, and consequently all the amenities expected of college towns are in abundant supply, from cheap pizza joints and late-night copy shops to used book, music, and clothing stores. Summers are relatively quiet as faculty recuperate and a few students stick around working summer jobs or making up incompletes, but

come fall the telephone poles and bulletin boards regain their paper livery of lecture flyers, housing wanted, and car-for-sale ads; young musicians and poets again hone their craft before attentive coffeeshop audiences; and book-laden backpacks become as ubiquitous as sneakers and blue jeans.

Besides book browsing and cappuccino sipping, this central part of the Valley is rich in artisans whose functional and decorative wares are for sale in shops, galleries, and at various annual arts festivals and street fairs. The outdoors should also rank high on any visitor's agenda, as the area boasts several fine state parks, an extensive trail network linking town conservation lands, a wildly popular bike path along a former railbed, and boating on the Con-

FIVE-COLLEGE-AREA CYCLING

The apex of leisure bicycle touring around the Five Colleges is the fully paved **Norwottuck Rail Trail,** running along more than 10 miles of the defunct Central Massachusetts Railroad's east-west route between Northampton, Amherst, and Belchertown. From King St. near downtown Northampton, the western section of this trail (also known simply as the city bike path) runs essentially parallel to Rt. 9 due west to Look Memorial Park, in the village of Florence—a popular spot for picnics, tennis, softball, and swimming (in a municipal outdoor pool). From Elwell Recreation Area, on Damon Rd., beside the Rt. 9/I-91 interchange, the eastern section crosses the Connecticut River on an impressive 1,500-foot open-truss iron bridge built in 1887, passes through fields and woods and under Rt. 9 behind Hadley's malls, runs along the forested edge of Amherst College, and finally terminates east of Lawrence Swamp—a chunk of densely wooded conservation land to the southeast of the College. (The connection under I-91 that will link the two sections should be finished by early 1999.)

With the gentle grades and smooth turns characteristic of old railroad beds, the Norwottuck makes a tempting race track for bikes or skates, but speedsters should practice restraint—the path attracts dawdlers and learners, too, not to mention pedestrians and people in wheelchairs. Additional trail access and parking is available at Bread & Circus Market, in Rt. 9's Mountain Farms Mall, in Hadley, on Station Rd. in Amherst, and, at the east end, on Wright Rd. off Rt. 9, in Belchertown.

Rental bikes are available at the Golden Harvest greenhouse and nursury on Damon Rd. opposite the Elwell lot, tel. (413) 586-6246, and from Valley Bicycles Trailside, next to the Ice Cream Peddler on Railroad St. in Hadley, parallel to Rt. 9 between West St. and Rt. 47, tel. (413) 586-4466. Valley Bicycles' main store, at 319 Main St., in Amherst, tel. (413) 256-0880, also keeps a few rentals on hand. (If you want to try a tandem, or you're a wheelchair user interested in a high-tech lightweight hand-cycle, go to the Hadley location.)

Currently in the works are the Manhan Trail (another paved rail trail, running south from the Norwottuck to neighboring Easthampton) and an extension of the Norwottuck running west-northwest along the Mill River to Williamsburg; inquire about the latest status when you rent a bike, or look for them if you're riding the trail sometime after the beginning of 1999.

Nancy Jane's *Bicycle Touring in the Pioneer Valley* (University of Massachusetts Press) contains suggestions for more wide-ranging road-touring loops around the Five College area and beyond. The book is available at most local bookstores and cycle shops. To plot your own route, pick up a copy of Rubel BikeMaps' *Western Massachusetts Bicycle and Road Map,* also available locally (or by mail from P.O. Box 1035, Cambridge MA 02140). Serious mountain bikers who think pavement is for wimps may want to consider renting a high-end, full suspension bike from Axler's Bicycle Corner, on Armory St., in Northampton (facing the parking lot behind Thorne's), tel. (413) 585-1188. Prices vary depending on exactly how loaded the bikes are, but all come with the staff's expert advice on where to go to get your money's worth of real trail riding.

necticut River. Only camping is in short supply, but at least the Five College area *does* have several outfitters to supply all your camping and hiking needs. Try **Gleason's Campers Supply,** 9 Pearl St. in Northampton, or supermarket-sized **EMS** (Eastern Mountain Sports) on Rt. 9 in Hadley.

Getting Around

Visitors who arrive by rail or interstate bus will find themselves within easy walking distance of nearly all the restaurants and most of the accommodations listed for Northampton and Amherst. PVTA public buses are only mentioned if they directly serve listed outlying sights, but, if you desire to explore the area more widely via public transit, look for their route maps at the tourist information stands on the S. Pleasant St. side of Amherst's town common or in Northampton at the Peter Pan bus terminal in Roundhouse Plaza a block behind City Hall. During the Sept.-May academic year the PVTA **Five College Bus** operates daily inter-campus shuttles free to both students and the general public; call (413) 586-5806 for schedule information. The Amherst-Smith route is the one most likely to be of use, as the end points are each within a couple of blocks of the Amherst and Northampton downtowns.

NORTHAMPTON

Jenny Lind, the 19th-century "Swedish Nightingale" whose blockbuster concert tour of the U.S. was one of showman P.T. Barnum's biggest triumphs, is alleged to have called Northampton the "Paradise of America" while honeymooning here in 1852. With a good brewpub, a couple of arthouse cinemas, three classic diners, good bookstores, a plethora of inexpensive ethnic restaurants, a busy local visual and performing arts scene, one of the nation's leading women's colleges, proximity to lots of outdoor recreation, and a liberal political climate—all in a city of under 30,000—Miss Lind, if alive today, would surely not have had to qualify her comparison. Its cultural resources also give Northampton the kind of cheerful self-esteem that rubs off on the very bricks of its buildings, as if civic pride was used in place of mortar; spend some time here and you'll notice how contagious it can be.

Northampton's past is peppered with figures who have captured the national limelight, from Rev. Jonathan Edwards, one of the fire-and-brimstone leaders of the early 18th-century religious "Great Awakening," and Calvin Coolidge, the Northampton lawyer and mayor who became President in 1923, to Kevin Eastman and Peter Laird, the creators of the Teenage Mutant Ninja Turtles. Historically the city also has had a reputation for endorsing social reform, with its staunch support for the 19th-century anti-slavery and temperance movements, active commitment to public education for all (including building a school for the deaf in 1865), and, more recently, attempts at extending legal recognition to married lesbian and gay couples.

For a sampling of the city's forgotten anecdotes, memorabilia, artifacts, and documentary photographs, visit **Historic Northampton,** 46 Bridge St., tel. (413) 584-6011. Open Thurs.-Sun. noon-4 p.m., March-December. For a thoroughly contemporary view of all that the city has to offer, peruse the racks and racks of brochures, maps, and advertising flyers at the **Greater Northampton Chamber of Commerce,** 99 Pleasant St., tel. (413) 584-1900, open weekdays till 5 p.m.

Words & Pictures Museum

Founded by Kevin Eastman, co-creator of those pizza-loving Ninja Turtles, the Words & Pictures Museum of Fine Sequential Art, 140 Main St., tel. (413) 586-8545, celebrates the art of comics with four stories of galleries. Comics from the '70s to the '90s are the heart of the permanent collection, but vintage selections trace the evolution of such different forms as the serial newspaper strip, editorial cartoon, and comic book. Changing exhibits feature plenty of the new artists pushing the boundaries of the form with today's graphic novels. Needless to say this is one

---

"THE POET OF BRAN BREAD AND PUMPKINS"

Decades before Emily Dickinson became known to the world, Ralph Waldo Emerson declared an older contemporary from across the valley a poet—not for any verse but rather for preaching the virtues of vegetarianism. Dr. Sylvester Graham's attempts to reform the nation's diet may have sounded sweet to Emerson's ears, but other observers saw the man as an annoyance, a crackpot, or worse. He earned a national following with his exhortations to eat less meat, more fruits and vegetables, and whole wheat; to avoid alcohol; and to embrace rigorous exercise. But the following was modest—in the 19th century, many of these ideas were viewed with disdain. Local newspaper editorials regularly excoriated Graham for impugning meat and potatoes and for such eccentricities as walking down Main Street in his bathrobe on the way to and from his regular skinny-dip in the Mill River.

Besides having his general tenets largely vindicated by medical and nutritional science, Dr. Graham's legacy has actually become a familiar staple of supermarket and pantry shelves in the form of the crackers made from (and named for) his patented whole-grain flour. Whether the good doctor would have approved of his crackers' indispensability for cheesecake crusts and chocolate-marshmallow s'mores, we can only wonder.

museum where kids' attention spans may exceed their parents'—though probably not by much. The downtown building can't be missed—just look for the huge gargoyle hulking atop the roof. Open Tues.-Sun. noon-5 p.m.; admission $3 adult, $1 anyone under 18.

Smith College

Bounded by West, Green, and lower Elm Streets at the edge of downtown is Smith College, one of the largest and most prestigous women's colleges in the country. The campus is rich in textbook architecture, particularly from the Victorian era through WW I. An outstanding cluster from this period is found opposite the stout Romanesque public library on West Street: Hubbard, Washburn, Pierce, and Seelye Halls, the first three by the noted Boston firm of Peabody and Stearns, and all built between 1878 and 1898. This side of campus has enough of a characteristically collegiate look to it that Tyler Annex, at the end of Green Street was used for the establishing exterior shots at the start of the movie version of *Who's Afraid of Virginia Woolf?*

Complementing the collection of buildings are the contents of the **Smith College Museum of Art** , on Elm St. opposite Bedford Terrace, tel. (413) 585-2760. The permanent holdings include numerous famous names in western art history from late 19th-century French impressionism and American romantic landscape painters through postwar New York's abstract expressionism. A few Egyptian and classical antiquities, some 18th-century portraiture, select prints and photographs, and contemporary changing exhibitions round out the collection. One very nice touch: children's activity guides and puzzles based on the paintings are provided. Open Tues.-Sun. during the academic year and August; Wednesday and weekends only in January, June, and July.

The other highlight is the college botanic garden, housed in the **Lyman Plant House** on College Lane overlooking Paradise Pond, tel. (413) 585-2748. Besides March bulbs, November chrysanthemums, and everything in between, the free greenhouses hold a number of exotic tropical and desert species. Adjoining outdoor gardens are tagged to aid your study of plant taxonomy.

River Road to Mt. Sugarloaf

Following commercial King St. (US 5) north from downtown, take the turn on Elm St. for **Hatfield,** crossing I-91 at Exit 21. Once over the interstate this two-lane road veers north through the state's only town whose Main Street has as many barns and tractors as most other small communities have garages and cars. The neatly partitioned farmlands on either side of the road sit atop sandy loam up to 20 feet deep, a fertile patrimony that helps local farmers set record crop yields year after year. Though onions, cucumbers, and potatoes are its chief products now, Hatfield has in its time raised a bumper crop of American educators, too: Sophia Smith, founder of Smith College; Ephraim Williams, founder of Williams College; the first president of what became Princeton University; and Elisha Williams, an early president of Yale were all born here. If the town had had its way, it would have also become the Harvard of western Massachusetts, but the colonial legislature turned down Hatfield's 1762 petition to found a Queen's College.

Also in Hatfield is **"the Bashan,"** a 1,000-foot stretch of sandy beach for swimming, something not widely found along the Connecticut River, whose shorelines are more sedimentary silt and mud than anything else. Accessible via unpaved Bashan Rd., which loops like a "D" toward the river, the Bashan's roadside parking area will be obvious about seven-tenths of a mile from the southern turn-off from Main.

In summer and fall, wagons are often left along Main Street with piles of fresh produce, handwritten cardboard signs with the prices, and coffee cans in which to leave your money. Picnickers bound for the summit of Mt. Sugarloaf, visible dead ahead, should stock up on whatever suits your fancy, as up ahead in South Deerfield lies an excellent bakery waiting to accompany your garden tomatoes and other sandwich stuffers with fine fresh bread. In summer it would almost be criminal to take this excursion

The farm-lined Connecticut River rolls toward the distant Holyoke Range.

and not stop for fresh berry picking at Hatfield's **Tee-Zee Farm** on Main St. (June strawberries) or **Nourse Farms** in adjacent Whately (June strawberries, late July-early Sept. raspberries). On weekends after mid-August, a slight detour will bring you to Whately's **Quonquont Farm,** for pick-your-own peaches and apples. To get there turn on Christian Lane north of Nourse Farms, away from the river for about two miles. At the lane's end in the center of Whately turn right and follow the signs north just under two miles to the farm. To check picking conditions in advance, call (413) 665-3081.

Rising over Whately's farms and the Rt. 116 bridge over the Connecticut is a wooded sandstone promontory, **Mt. Sugarloaf.** From below it may not seem all that lofty, but once on top you'll discover outstanding panoramic views over the central Pioneer Valley. Bookending a low ridge running parallel to the Connecticut River, the peak is open till sunset daily year-round, although the road to the top is passable to traffic

April-Nov. only. Winter or summer, a hike or bike ride to the top makes an excellent workout. If you lack a car, the PVTA #390 South Deerfield bus stops at Sugarloaf's base year-round until late evening, but you must catch it on N. Pleasant St. in Amherst, at the UMass campus.

Beside the mountain is **South Deerfield,** a small community known chiefly in these parts for being the headquarters of the **Yankee Candle Company,** on US 5 between I-91 exits 24 and 25, tel. (413) 665-8306. Watch the candle production through the windows of the factory floor, or dip your own. Of course you can buy fresh from the source, so to speak: over 100 tempting scents are available, including amaretto, bridal bouquet, fresh-cut grass, lemon sherbet, Oreo, root beer, sophisticated romance, and strawberry jam. Stroll the medieval castle, Santa toy factory, and year-round Bavarian Christmas village with its 14 themed shops to meet all your shopping needs. All are conveniently located indoors, and are open daily. They also feature local specialty foods, such herb- and fruit-flavored vinegars from Bittersweet Herb Farm, on the nearby Mohawk Trail. Road warriors take note: this place is also equipped with the largest, most immaculate bathrooms you'll find outside of a hotel presidential suite, complete with diaper-changing tables in both women's *and* men's rooms.

Also don't miss the **Yankee Candle Car Museum** across US 5 at the corner of Elm St., tel. (413) 665-2020. Over 50 European cars, from antique touring models to contemporary high performance vehicles, illustrate the breadth of automotive designers' ingenuity. Vintage Jaguars, an early VW Beetle, antique BMWs, and an unusual Messerschmidt "micro-car" are among the vehicles on display. Open daily, admission $3.

If getting a whiff of all those candied candles hasn't dimmed your appetite, know that one of the Pioneer Valley's most cosmopolitan tables is set at **Sienna,** an elegant chef-owned restaurant on South Deerfield's Elm St., tel. (413) 665-0215. The short, seasonally adjusted menu puts New England staples—local cheeses, game, fish, greens, squash, apples, cranberries—in a very imaginative new light, often with Southwestern touches. Knowledgeable staff, a good wine list, and understated elegance in the decor all add grace notes to the evening. Dinner only

Wed.-Sun.; reservations strongly advised. Next door is a little bit of picnic heaven: **Elm Farm Bakery,** whose take-out menu runs the gamut from great breads and scones to cookies and pastries, plus a daily round of sandwiches. Open Mon.-Sat. till 6 p.m., Sunday till noon.

Accommodations

If you can help it you should at all costs avoid that local phenomenon known as Commencement Week. Actually there are two: the western half of Massachusetts simply doesn't have enough rooms to accommodate all five colleges' holding graduation simultaneously, so the ceremonies are staggered over two weekends in mid-to-late May. Parents and others determined to stay in the area during these times had better kiss their vacation budgets goodbye, as with very few exceptions $150 doubles and two-night minimums are the rule around Commencement time.

NORTHAMPTON LODGING FOR WOMEN ONLY

Northampton's large lesbian community has given rise to the appearance in the surrounding area of a handful of bed and breakfast establishments catering specifically to women—lesbian or straight. The nearest is over the river in Hadley: the **Tin Roof B&B,** tel. (413) 586-8665, has three rooms with shared bath and resident cats; convenient to local dining and the Norwottuck Rail Trail; $60. A half hour's drive west, in the hilltown of Worthington, the **Little River Farm,** tel. (413) 238-4261, offers a true rural retreat on 41 streamside acres, with a small menagerie of farm animals for company; decent-sized rooms all have private baths, plus that rarity of rarities—comfortable reading chairs with good lighting. Open Feb.-Oct.; $70 s, $75 d, including a full homemade breakfast that puts those fresh eggs to good use. Twenty minutes' drive northwest, in Goshen, is the equally private **Innamorata,** tel. (413) 268-0300, a rambling saltbox-style colonial farmhouse with an accent on floral elegance (Innamorata also welcomes gay men). Open year-round; $50-85 with shared bath and home-baked continental breakfast.

Centrally located a stone's throw from the heart of downtown, the **Hotel Northampton,** 36 King St., tel. (413) 584-3100, is a true grande dame, built to cater to the merchant princes of the Roaring Twenties. Age has not lessened the devotion to comfort, as demonstrated by well-appointed rooms blending modern amenities with the plush elegance one would associate with such a historic place. Standard doubles run $99-125, and at least $150 during Commencment. Whether or not you stay the night, visit the 1786 Wiggins Tavern incorporated into the hotel's ground floor for a civilized retreat from collegiate youth and attitudes. For a few shekels less, try the Colonial-themed **Autumn Inn,** 259 Elm St., tel. (413) 584-7660, one of whose virtues is its location in the residential neighborhood west of the Smith College campus: peaceful, yet proximate to all local restaurants and attractions. A favorite among business travelers looking for motel amenities (good-sized rooms, restaurant serving breakfast, outdoor swimming pool) without the numbing sameness of the national chains, this 28-room inn is popular enough to be able to require a two night minimum on all weekends between April and Thanksgiving. Doubles start at $96 May-Dec., and are nominally lower off-season unless occupancy is high.

Similar prices—$99 plus—also pertain at **The Inn at Northampton,** behind the Mobil station at the Pleasant St. (US 5)/I-91 interchange (Exit 18 on the interstate) south of downtown, tel. (800) 582-2929 or (413) 586-1211. At least they do for Commencement and fall foliage season; otherwise, doubles at this 124-room property—the town's largest—can drop to as low as $59 Sun.-Thurs. in winter. The French Provincial decor is distinctly a cut above standard motels, but insufficient soundproofing and an overly powerful smell of chlorine wafting through rooms overlooking the tiny indoor pool hold it back from the league of truly classy joints.

The only moderate-priced accommodations in town are off Pleasant St. between downtown and I-91 Exit 18 at the **Days Inn,** 117 Conz Ave., tel. (800) DAYS INN or (413) 586-1500. Doubles run up to $85 under normal circumstances, higher for Commencement. The cheapest motel in the area—in fact, one of the cheapest chain motels in the state—is north of Northampton on US 5 in South Deerfield: **Motel**

6, between I-91 northbound Exit 24 and southbound Exit 25, tel. (413) 665-7161. Doubles are under $50 even in high season. Given the Olympic-sized indoor swimming pool and the good eating to be had nearby (i.e., Sienna on Elm St.), it's even tolerable that the interior is the chain's standard spartan motif, accented with their usual steelplate security.

If the premium most bed and breakfast places charge over standard room rates has kept you from considering them except for special occasions, you'll be pleased to note that several Pioneer Valley B&Bs are actually a relative bargain compared to in-town lodgings. One that also captures the essence of rural New England is **Twin Maples,** tel. (413) 268-7925, off Rt. 9 in neighboring Williamsburg, at the threshold of the Hilltowns. After being warmly made welcome, retire to your antique bed in this restored 200-year-old farmhouse, then wake up to a hearty and delicious breakfast typically including eggs fresh from the henhouse and maple syrup made on the premises. Shared bath. Doubles $60-70.

Food

Diner fans have an embarassment of riches in Northampton: not just one, but three classic diners, all of which are known as much for evening or late-night hours as their traditional breakfasts. Right smack downtown on Strong Ave. is **Kathy's Diner,** tel. (413) 586-2225. Out on the mostly tacky, commercial, auto-oriented strip at 324 King St. (US 5) is the dependable **Bluebonnet Diner,** tel. (413) 584-3333, a 1950 Worcester Lunch Car diner (remodelled inside) with large adjoining dining room. And in the adjacent village of Florence, three miles west along Rt. 9, is the diner collector's dream: the **Miss Florence Diner,** 99 Main St., tel. (413) 584-3137, a Worcester Lunch Car model from the 1930s, well-preserved inside and out. They don't come any more photogenic than the Miss Flo, especially at dusk; fortunately the food is as good as that neon is handsome.

As with any college town, fast food for student budgets is a staple; but being Northampton, a hungry sophomore could eat out nightly and never touch a fried hamburger from a multinational chain. Pizza is the mainstay of town menus, but there are numerous other options: a plateful of piping hot fresh tortellini or linguine from the **Fresh Pasta Co.,** for example, at 249 Main St., almost opposite the Academy of Music (open daily until 9 p.m.); burritos and grilled items from ¡Cha Cha Cha! down the street next to the Words & Pictures Museum; great peasant Mexican food from **La Veracruzana,** another block down at 31 Main St.; or Mediterranean favorites at the **Grecian Corner,** 16 Main St. at Strong Ave., open daily for lunch and dinner, tel. (413) 584-3899. All of these are just a step up from self-serve, but that hardly detracts from the fact that you'll get good fresh meals at great prices. All have meatless options, but for real vegetarian comfort food in cozy surroundings try **Bela,** 68 Masonic St., open Tues.-Sat. until 9 p.m., tel. (413) 586-8011.

Unquestionably a local institution, **Joe's Cafe,** 33 Market St., tel. (413) 586-JOES, feature a sign out fronts showing a man in poncho and sombrero; inside, murals of happy campesinos are discernable in the dim light of Chianti bottle lamps. Maybe Joe was born José, but his eponymous cafe is actually a very cozy full-menu Italian restaurant with the well-worn look of a place that runs tabs for regulars. Generous portions, quality food, and fair prices keep everyone—students, suits, seniors—coming back for seconds. People in search of serious local color should belly up to the bar in the next room. Microbrew fans note: Sturdy Catamount Amber Ale from Vermont is on tap. Open daily from lunchtime till midnight.

Ask almost anyone for the best pizzeria in town and you'll be directed to **Paradiso,** tel. (413) 586-1468, under the can't-miss "pizza" sign on steep Crafts Avenue between Main Street and the bus station. Wood-fired brick oven pizza fans, vegetarians (including those who eschew dairy products—soy cheeses available), and pesto enthusiasts will feel pampered in the lively, comfortably cavernous streetside rooms; people wanting a quick slice will have to go elsewhere (122 Main Street's **Pinocchio Rosticceria,** for example) or settle for lots of leftovers. Under the same ownership and equally popular is **Spoleto,** a few blocks away at 50 Main St., tel. (413) 586-6313. Very hip atmosphere and moderately priced Italian pastas, seafood, meat and more; open daily for dinner and Mon.-Sat. for lunch. To sample all the fun without having to raise a fork, simply visit the bar. Both places serve nightly until at least 10 p.m.

For even better Italian, try **Mulino's,** 21 Center St. opposite the Iron Horse Music Hall, tel. (413) 586-8900. Focaccia sandwiches, pastas, seafood, pizzas, and calzones fill out a menu liberally laced with vegetarian selections. Most entrees are around $10, which helps explain the regular crowds. Another local favorite is the **Eastside Grill,** a Cajun-influenced restaurant at 19 Strong St., tel. (413) 586-3347. Locally regarded as one of the town's best, the extensive menu is certainly as rich and filling as anything south of the Mason-Dixon, but quality suffers from the enormous popularity of the place, and despite the stab at Louisiana idioms they neglect to teach anyone at the bar about Sazeracs. On weekends expect a long wait; bring a book.

If you want to try something more indigenous than Yankee etouffée, consider comfy **Paul and Elizabeth's,** tel. (413) 584-4832, in the Thorne's Market complex on Main St., the sort of natural foods restaurant that has become a Valley trademark. Of course, nearly everyone's menu in the area is now vegetarian-friendly, but why settle for less than the real McCoy? Everything is prepared from scratch, free of additives but full of flavor. Delicious soups, pastas, fish, breads, hummus, and tempura are among the standard menu items, along with desserts that demonstrate that spiking your blood sugar isn't a prerequisite to luscious taste. Open weekdays until 9:30 p.m., 10 p.m. weekends. Nearby **La Cazuela,** 7 Old South St., tel. (413) 586-0400, is a vividly designed restaurant where good portions of tasty, occasionally outstanding Mexican and Southwestern food at moderate prices will please the appetite as much as the decor will please the eye. Chilies of every stripe—Anaheims, smoky chipotles, large poblanos, fresh jalapeños, mild Hatches—are a recurring motif. Extensive choices for vegetarians here, too. Try that chocolate mousse if your blood sugar level *does* need a whallop. Open for dinner seven days a week and for brunch (starting at 11 a.m.) on weekends. If it's spice that you crave, you could also try the **India House,** 45 State St., tel. (413) 586-6344. A meal here may be a bit pricier than at the competition, but the premium is handily justified by the food, presentation, and service.

There are pubs in this town. There are purveyors of pub grub. And then there's the **Northampton Brewery,** 11 Brewster Court (entrance on Hampton Rd.), tel. (413) 584-9903. Not only is it Noho's only brewpub, it's a brewpub with an excellent kitchen. From the blackened keilbasa with horseradish to the veggie fajitas, it all scores high marks for quality, quantity, and cost. They're no slouch with those beers, either. Of course, if all you really want is a good burger in a collegial setting, without the yuppie trimmings, then skip around the corner to **The Blue Flame,** on Old South St. just below La Cazuela. There's a great jukebox to go along with those burgers, too.

Finally, an out-of-towner deserves special note: **The Squire's Smoke & Game Club,** in the Brassworks complex on Rt. 9 in Haydenville about 10 minutes' drive west of downtown Northampton, tel. (413) 268-7222. Located in the handsomely renovated welding shop of a former 1876 brass faucet factory, this is essentially a barbecue joint that went to culinary school and then hitchhiked around the world. The multicultural menu of open-fire grilled and smoked dishes is bold, flavorful, and proportioned for big appetites: paté comes in slabs, the salad is big enough for two people, and entrees come with plenty of side dishes. In short, there's no chance of leaving hungry—or disappointed. Open for dinner Wed.-Sunday.

For elaborate confections, simple sweets, and crusty country bread, look no farther than 192 Main Street. **Bakery Normand,** a Konditorei your Bavarian grandmother would have approved of, has all these and more at reasonable prices. Open Tues.-Sat. until 5:30 p.m., Sundays until half past noon. For desserts and coffee in a cafe setting, head across the street to the most characterful hangout in town, the **Haymarket Bookstore Café,** tel. (413) 586-9969, with an obscure entrance down Crackerbarrel Alley (in addition to the one on Main St., next to Beyond Words). In this delightful rabbit warren of mostly book-lined, mostly basement rooms, trippy rock plays perpetually on the stereo, the baked goods and caffeine drinks are tasty, and the prices are rock bottom (triple-layer mocha chocolate mousse cake for about $2 a slice is no hallucination). During school vacations the place is moderately relaxed, but the vibe pervades even when it's a zoo of students and student-wannabes. A semi-quiet room (the smokers' annex before butts were banned) offers solitary ruminants and knots of intent philosophizers, a respite from the rocking scene in the main rooms. Even the book selection contributes: alongside typical categories like literature, poetry, and anthropology are sections for Canadian history and CIA criticism. Open Tues.-Sun. 8 a.m.-midnight, Fri.-Sat. until 2 a.m.

Equally high in the funky cafe/hangout rankings is **Sylvester's,** 111 Pleasant St. in the house where Sylvester Graham used to practice curbing his appetites for all flesh, hooved or human. Weekend brunches are packed, but other times of the week it's a great spot to spread out and read the paper or chat with friends as you savor charbroiled burgers, veggie sandwiches, slabs of French toast, deluxe homefries smothered in vegetables, bacon, and cheese (with eggs on the side), or simply some of their own banana bread or baked goods and a cup of java.

After Midnight: So you're hungry, and it's late. *Really* late; everything seems closed. What to do? Fortunately for you, in Northampton you actually have some choices: the previously mentioned Kathy's Diner is open until 2 a.m. on Fri.-Sat. nights; so is the Haymarket Bookstore Cafe. **Jake's,** 17 King St. next to the old Calvin Theater, is open until 3 a.m. Fri.-Sat., and **Grampy's,** farther north along King St., is open 24 hours. As long as you're driving, you could go to the **Fillin' Station,** just off I-91 Exit 24 on US 5 in Whately, an all-night truckstop and diner rolled into one (look for the big Diner sign on the roof). They have showers, too, if you crave cleanliness as much as meal. Across the river in Hadley, in Campus Plaza on Rt. 9, is the **McManus Eating Place,** open Sun.-Thurs. until 3 a.m. and Fri.-Sat. all night. If all else fails, remember the policeman's home away from home, **Dunkin Donuts.** It's on King Street and it never closes.

Entertainment

The benefits of a college town are self-evident with a glance at the marquee of **The Pleasant Street Theater** a few steps off Main St., featuring classic revival cinema in a setting that properly fits going out to the movies. On the other end of Main near the Smith campus, the city-owned **Academy of Music** also offers better-than-your-average-mall movie programming, leavened by live concerts in a beautifully ornate old theater.

When it comes to live music, a pillar of the folk, folk-rock, groove-rock, jazz, country, blues, roots, and acoustic music scene in New England is **The Iron Horse Cafe,** 20 Center St., tel. (413) 584-0610, ext. 2 (recorded schedule). To those who recall the time when the founder scrambled to fill his single small storefront, the Horse may seem to have become *too* successful, with a larger space and lines often running out the door waiting to snap up the handful of standing-room-only tickets released for otherwise often sold-out nightly shows. It's well-deserved success, though: if you can get a seat, you're in for a treat. Fortunately, the beer list has grown to match the caliber of the music. The club draws crowds for weekend brunches in its full-service café, too. Advance tickets are available in person or by phone (with additional service charge), tel. (800) THE TICK or (413) 586-8686, from the Northampton Box Office on the second floor of Thorne's Market, on Main St. in downtown Northampton.

For live rock with a harder edge from both local and touring headliners, plus lots of energetic DJ-spun dance mixes, check out **Pearl Street Nightclub,** 10 Pearl, tel. (413) 584-7771. As with the Iron Horse, tickets for all shows are available at the Northampton Box Office. Ambient, techno, metal, blues, and other danceable beats are also found at **The Grotto,** 25 West St. in the cluster of shops at the edge of the Smith College campus, tel. (413) 586-6900. Open nightly, often without a cover charge early in the week. Both clubs have gay nights: Friday at the Grotto, Wednesday at Pearl Street.

Additional live local music is featured in scattered venues around the area, from jazz and acoustic in restaurants and cafes to outdoor rock festivals in summer; pick up a copy of either *The Valley Advocate* or the *Valley Optimist Magazine,* the free weekly papers available from newsboxes all around the Five College area, for further entertainment suggestions.

AMHERST AND VICINITY

The quintessential college town, Amherst (AM-erst) enjoys an abundance of cheap eats, high-quality new and used bookstores, graceful academic architecture, and earnest political activism. Before granting degrees became such big business, the town was almost strictly a farming community. Even its major 19th-century industry—straw hats—was agricultural. The rural character isn't all gone, either: there's a pick-your-own berry farm on Sunset Avenue within a few blocks of downtown. Now the academic center of the Five College area, by virtue of having three of the namesake institutions (UMass, Amherst, and Hampshire) within its borders, Amherst's population fluctuates by some 12,000 between summer and the rest of the year.

The town is named after a British general who earned recognition in the seige of Quebec City during the French and Indian Wars; though local students, primed with anti-establishment cynicism, know of Lord Jeffrey Amherst as the man who practiced germ warfare against the Indians. The New York-based general, charged with defending the western colonial frontier in the Ohio Valley in 1763, proposed to his minions on the battlefront that infected blankets from smallpox-suffering soldiers be somehow traded to the local Indian tribes. There's no proof the deed was done, and historian Francis Parkman for one assumes Gen. Amherst was too honorable to stoop so low. But coincidentally, Mingo, Delaware, and Shawano Indians in the Ohio territory were stricken some months later by a deadly outbreak of the disease. In a display, perhaps, of its everlasting disapproval, the town persists in subtly spelling Lord Amherst's first name differently than any history books—a vexing thing for any Jeff, dead or alive.

Emily Dickinson

Between her birth, in 1830, and her death, 56 years later, poet extraordinaire Emily Dickinson led much of her famously reclusive life within the brick house built by her grandfather at 280 Main St., in later years barely even straying as far as her brother's place next door. Tours of the **Emily Dickinson Homestead** are limited, so reservations are advised—call (413) 542-8161. Admission is $3. Open Wed.-Sun., May-Oct.; otherwise open only on Wednesday and Saturday until it closes in mid-December, and again in spring after reopening in March. Dickinson's well-visited grave is in West Cemetery, just off N. Pleasant St.; look for the small plot in the middle

of the perimeter drive, enclosed with an iron fence. Modern compilations of Dickinson's work are easy to come by locally (the Jeffery Amherst Bookstore at 55 S. Pleasant has a whole wall of books by and about her), but to get back to the originals check out Amherst's public **Jones Library** on Amity Street. This handsome 1926 Colonial Revival fieldstone structure, opposite downtown's Amherst Cinema, has a special Dickinson collection of manuscripts, personal artifacts, and even a model of her bedroom, available whenever the library is open (lunch hour excepted).

The library also has a special collection of Robert Frost's works, including a first draft of his most famous poem, "Stopping by Woods on a Snowy Evening," that shows how he nearly wrote himself into a corner at the end. Already in his 40's and only just beginning to gain national acclaim, Frost came to Amherst College around WW I, returning on and off over the next 30-odd years of "barding around" various colleges as a lecturer and poet in residence. Whether or not you peruse its poetry collections, the Jones is definitely worth a visit if only to be transported briefly back to an age when public literacy was held in such high regard that towns fell over themselves building castles to its advancement. Its warm, walnut- and mahogany-paneled, Oriental-carpeted, antique-filled interior, more private mansion than public institution, is a wonderful place to wait out passing rainshowers, heat waves, or travel ennui. Closed Sunday, and Monday too July-Aug., if the town council so votes.

Amherst College

Founded in 1821 by Noah Webster (who wrote A-P of his famous dictionary while a resident of the area), among others, Amherst College was originally intended for promising young men aspiring to the ministry but lacking the means. Since then it's evolved into a selective coeducational liberal arts institution with tuition high enough to most assuredly take the means out of anyone who has them. The hilltop campus beside S. Pleasant St. (Rt. 116) and College St. (Rt. 9) is rich in classical architecture, including an exemplary Greek Revival chapel by Isaac Damon, one of the young American republic's earliest trained builders.

In comparison to the post-impressionist emphasis to some of the area's other college art collections, Amherst's free **Mead Art Museum,** tel. (413) 542-2335, is strong in pre-20th-century art, particularly of early America and the European Renaissance. A richly panelled 1611 English Jacobean banquet hall originally imported for the New York mansion of a college benefactor, devotional sculptures dating back to the age of Columbus, and samplings of various non-Western traditions, from West Africa to 9th-century Assyria, are among the Mead's other highlights. Located east of the college quadrangle next to the free-standing, bell-chiming Stearns Steeple, the museum is open daily Sept.-May, and Tues.-Sun. afternoons June-August.

At the southeast corner of the quadrangle is the free **Pratt Museum of Natural History,** tel. (413) 542-2165, providing a general introduction to the evolution of broad classes of animals—amphibians, reptiles, camels, fish, and yes, humans—in a setting reminiscent of Victorian science museums, hushed as a crypt and filled with elegant wooden display cases. Utah may have cornered the market on dinosaur bones, but the big lizards' shoe size is best calculated here along the Connecticut River, where ancient perambulations in Mesozoic mud left a motherlode of over 30,000 documented footprints. A full third of these are in the museum's collection, gathered over the course of several decades of pioneering ichnology (stone print study) by Amherst professor (and later college president and state geologist) Edward Hitchcock. Rock hounds will find plenty of minerals, crystals, and meteorites to pour over, and a topographical diorama for that broad overview of Valley geology. Open daily during the academic year, Sept.-May, and weekends in summer.

South of Amherst: The Holyoke Range

Unsurpassed views over the Connecticut River Valley from numerous open ledges are the highlight of the **Holyoke Range State Reservation** and adjoining **Skinner State Park,** stretching over eight miles between Mt. Holyoke by the banks of the Connecticut River and Long Mountain to the east. Holyoke and its sister peaks are part of an east-west basalt ridge formed by cooling lava from early Mesozoic Era volcanic eruptions, some 170-200 million years ago. (The ridge continues across the river at Mt. Tom State Reservation, south of Northampton on US 5.) Outcroppings yield such features as the distinctive rock formations at "Titan's Piazza" on Mt. Holyoke's southwestern side, or the vertiginous cliffside trail openings in the east end of the range. Views over the Connecticut River and its large oxbow lake, a former river meander bypassed by the main channel after an 1840 ice jam, are best from the western end. Tourists have been enjoying this panorama at least since 1821, when the first Mountain House was built atop Mt. Holyoke. The present **Summit House,** tel. (413) 586-0350, was originally built in the 1850s, complete with its own horse-drawn cog tramway and a paddlewheel steamer to ferry prospective guests to the foot of the mountain. After a near-fatal brush with the hurricane of 1938, the building was restored in the late 1980s, and is now open weekends mid-May-mid-October. The porch is a favorite of Valley hawkwatchers, as it puts you right up with the thermal-riding red-tailed and broad-winged raptors during their spring and fall migrations. From mid-April through mid-November, it's possible to drive to the summit from Rt. 47 in Hadley; parking, when available, is $2. Outside of summer the daily PVTA #303 Smith/Mt. Holyoke bus stops at the foot of the summit access road on its run between downtown Northampton and South Hadley.

One could easily spend days trying to exhaust the variety of loops and long ridge hikes made possible by the number of trails within these parks, which is why they're deservedly the most popular hiking and cross-country skiing spots in the area (i.e., parking is scarce in summer and on weekends with lovely weather). Connections are also possible to the 36-mile orange-blazed Robert Frost Trail north through Amherst to Mt. Toby, in Sunderland, and to the white-blazed Metacomet-Monadnock Trail, which overlaps the range's ridgeline trail en route between New Hampshire and Connecticut. Orient yourself to the various possibilities with a free trail map and advice from rangers at the year-round visitor center on Rt. 116 at "the Notch," roughly in the middle of the mountain range. More detailed is New England Cartographics' full-color *Holyoke Range* topographic trail map, on sale at most area bookstores and outfitters. A variety of seasonal ranger-led programs are also offered, almost exclusively beginning at the Notch; call (413) 253-2883 for a recorded summary of what's happening and when. During the academic year the daily PVTA #301 Mt. Holyoke College bus stops at the visitor center; catch it in downtown Amherst at bus stops along North or South Pleasant St. (Rt. 116).

Route 47: North Tobacco Road

One of the more scenic roads for drivers and cyclists alike is farm-lined Rt. 47 (River Dr.), between Rt. 9 in Hadley and Rt. 116 in Sunderland. Following the banks of today's dam-controlled river, the road traverses farmland studded with the barns used for drying locally grown high-grade shade-leaf tobacco, prized for fine cigar wrappers. The Valley's rich mantle of topsoil, tens of thousands of years in the making, is the prime reason why tobacco—a very demanding crop—does so well here. Roadside stands offer summer's more edible bounty, from asparagus to zucchini, and **Lakeside Strawberries** beckons fruit-pickers during June's sweet, brief, berry

Signs advertise fresh produce for sale along Rt. 47.

season. The passing farmhouses themselves may reward careful observers with a glimpse of original Connecticut Valley doors, an early colonial ornamental style peculiar to the region. They're easy to spot: the double leafs of the oversized entrance are surmounted by a deeply scroll pediment, like an antique highboy or grandfather clock.

It's appropriate to start this route at the free **Hadley Farm Museum**, tel. (413) 584-8279, on Rt. 9 (Russell St.) a few steps from the stoplight junction with Rt. 47. Call it a high-tech museum from two centuries ago: within the restored rafters of a 1782 barn are preserved a hodgepodge of early American household and farm implements, from a 17th-century mortar and pestle to a spoke-wheeled Concord coach, which illustrate the mechanical advantages applied to agrarian life in the fertile Connecticut River Valley. Open Tues.-Sun. mid-May-October.

Also nearby is the **Porter-Phelps-Huntington Museum,** 130 River Rd., tel. (413) 584-4699, the early colonial period house whose barn, sold off in 1930, is what now holds all those Hadley farm tools. While it may be short a building, the museum is fortunate in having 10 generations' worth of household effects, including the diaries of the women who lived here. Unlike the many historic sites described solely in terms relevant to a male owner or builder, the history of this 1752 house is interpreted through the voices of other occupants—servants and slaves among them—whose quotidian lives were faithfully observed by a long line of diarists. Open Sat.-Wed., May 15-Oct. 15. Admission is $4.

Art and Spirit: Leverett Backroads

The hills above the river are home to a number of gifted artists and artisans whose work—functional, decorative, and everything in between—is on display in the Barnes Gallery of **Leverett Crafts & Arts,** 13 Montague Rd., tel. (413) 548-9070. The LC&A's resident Mudpot Potters also open their studios to the public on the first Saturday of each June. Hewing more to the academic than tourist calendar, LC&A is closed July-August. Artists aren't the only ones who appreciate the soul-soothing serenity of Amherst's backroads neighbors to the north. But even if you knew beforehand that Cambodian Buddhists inhabit these hills, it's still a surprise to find the white dome of their **Nipponzan Myohoji Peace Pagoda,** tel. (413) 367-2202, atop a hill in North Leverett, with plastic bunting strung from the top and golden images of Buddha serenely seated within niches around the building's perimeter. If contemplation has been elusive in your travels, refresh yourself with a quiet moment by the carp-filled goldfish pond in the small garden. To reach the pagoda, continue north on Montague Rd. from LC&A, turn onto Cave Hill Rd., and keep an eye out for the discreet sign at the top of the hill. Park in the gravel lot by the Wat Phnom Welcomes You Khmer Buddhist Society sign, and stroll up the path the quarter mile to the top.

If you've chosen to cycle rather than drive this route, you may wish to refresh yourself at the **Village Coop,** tel. (413) 367-9794, by the crossroads of North Leverett Rd. and Rattlesnake Gutter Road. Besides stocking all the produce and packaged goods you'd expect of any decent natural foods grocery, they have such fresh bakery items as bread, bagels, and—on Friday from lunchtime until 9 p.m. closing—freshly baked pizzas whole or by the slice, laden with vegetables and reasonably priced to boot. (Since slices are only kept warm by a heat lamp, quality diminishes with time out of the oven.) Dramatic Rattlesnake Gutter Rd., signposted off Cave Hill Rd. south of the Peace Pagoda, is the route of choice to reach this little gem in the woods; when you see the road you'll know why you wouldn't want to drive it after sundown, or in anything larger than a pickup.

Another special treat in the vicinity is the **Book Mill Cafe,** at the Montague Center end of the Greenfield Rd., near the junction of Rts. 63 and 47. The restored grist mill high on the banks of the Sawmill River is a combination used bookstore, gallery, eatery, and folk music coffeehouse. The book selection betrays the proximity of the Five Colleges: you're as liable to find Romanian cultural history, experimental American fiction, and lavish art texts as anything off the bestseller lists of a few months ago. Large picture windows overlooking the collapsed mill dam provide the ideal backdrop for browsing potential purchases while noshing from a short menu of soups, salads, sandwiches, and baked or frozen desserts. Organic locally roasted coffee beans

are ground into every variety of caffiene fix you'd ever want, and if you sit out on the decks over the river sipping your java (or herbal tea), you might believe you'd found a woodland Shangri-La. Open 10 a.m.-6 p.m. daily, Thurs.-Sat. in summers until 8 p.m. The downstairs room features live music most weekend eves, too; call (413) 367-9206 for schedule and ticket information.

Accommodations

Given the town's reliance on academic business more than summer tourism, high season motel rates are generally limited to Commencement, fall foliage weekends, and, in some instances, fall alumni reunion or homecoming weekends. Otherwise midweek prices throughout the year are rather constant. (Bed and breakfasts, being so much smaller, follow their own idiosyncratic rules based on popularity.) Outside of Commencement week, the least expensive lodgings are motels amid Hadley's busy commercial strip along Rt. 9 (Russell St.); all of the lodgings sport modest outdoor swimming pools. While Rt. 9 is as amenable to strolling out for a good breakfast or dinner as it is to watching sandhill cranes, at least the Norwottuck Rail Trail runs quite close by. National brands in this bunch include **Econo Lodge,** 237 Russell, tel. (800) 55-ECONO or (413) 584-9816, and **Howard Johnson Inn,** 401 Russell, tel. (800) I-GO-HOJO or (413) 586-0114. Econo's doubles run $48-78 except during Commencement (when you can expect up to $150).

Within walking distance of downtown restaurants, shops, rail and bus depots, and tourist sights are several choices, from plain to fancy. The **University Motor Lodge,** at the intersection of Triangle St. and N. Pleasant, tel. (413) 256-8111, has standard motel rooms for $49-89. More centrally located on the town common at the foot of the Amherst College campus is **The Lord Jeffery Inn,** tel. (413) 253-2576. The venerable Lord Jeff has been providing comfortable lodging to parents, alumni, and visitors for over 70 years, the staid charm of its public rooms suggesting the cozy society of an old alumni club, particularly when the huge parlor fireplace has a nice blaze going. Ever since surging insurance premiums turned guestroom fireplaces into mere ornaments, the preferred quarters within these rambling Colonial-style walls are those upstairs, with the views over the common, although the more readily available, ground-level rooms facing the back gardens are also quite nice. Depending on size, doubles range from a low of $68-98 to a high of $88-118.

For a comfortable home-style bed and breakfast on a quiet residential street between the UMass campus and downtown, try the **Lincoln Avenue B&B,** tel. (413) 549-0517, a turn-of-the-century home with five guest rooms (most with shared baths, all with a/c), protected bicycle parking, large yard (good for weddings), friendly dalmation, and full breakfasts—all for only $80-90 d April-Dec., $65-80 off-season. Happily, there's *no* price hike for Commencement here. Or consider the opulent **Allen House Victorian Inn,** 599 Main St., tel. (413) 253-5000, an 1886 Queen Anne-style home so meticulously restored, from the William Morris wallpapers and ornately carved Eastlake mantles to the original exterior house colors, that guests are essentially privileged time travelers. Part of that privilege is private baths for even the smallest of the five bedrooms, afternoon high tea, and full breakfasts that draw rave reviews from guests. Rates range $45-95 d during the year, $125-135 on Commencement.

The busy decor, doilies, and dark woods of high Victoriana aren't to everyone's taste, of course. Simple, airy elegance combining modern amenities and antique or reproduction furnishings may be found a short drive up N. Pleasant St. in North Amherst at the attractive **Black Walnut Inn,** tel. (413) 549-5649. The symmetrical Federal-era facade of brick made on the premises, backed by a beautiful old 1876 coach barn, conceals seven very different guest rooms, several with private outside entrances, all with private baths, a/c, cable, and phones. Given the house specialty that almost invariably accompanies the generous full breakfasts, this friendly place could easily change its name to the Apple Pie Inn. Double rooms are $95-110; the family-sized suite is $125.

Additional lodging suggestions are available from the **Amherst Chamber of Commerce,** tel. (413) 253-0700.

Food

Like its collegiate sisters around the state, Amherst has an abundance of cheap eats in fast-food settings, cafes ringing to the sounds of musicians and espresso machines, a smattering of ethnic alternatives, and those no-surprises prime-rib-and-shrimp-scampi places favored by visiting alumni. Vegetarian, whole-grain, non-dairy, and soy-based options also abound, prompting an occasional barrage of abbreviated questions such as, "Fish or soy [sauce]?" or "white or brown [rice]?" when you place an order. Nearly all the prime dining choices are within a short walk of one another.

Looking for a good breakfast? If you're staying in one of the motels along Rt. 9 in Hadley, consider a jaunt three miles up Rt. 116 to North Amherst and **Daisy's,** N. Pleasant St. at Pine (take a right at Rt. 116's first traffic light, the restaurant will be at the next light), tel. (413) 549-6643, where you'll find a full menu of omelettes, pancakes, and other favorites. Or start off on a really healthful note at **The Raw Carrot** cafe and juice bar, in the Carriage Shops on E. Pleasant behind the Café Mediterranean, tel. (413) 549-4240. When a bagel and coffee is the only eye-opener you need, there's always the local **Bruegger's,** at 170 N. Pleasant diagonally across from the post office, tel. (413) 253-5713. All three are open daily.

Time for a snack? Sweet things both baked and frozen are the specialty of **Bart's Homemade,** 103 N. Pleasant, tel. (413) 253-9371. Their premium ice cream and yogurt are available in various markets around the Valley, but here you can sample from the source. Fine desserts are also found at the **Black Sheep Deli,** 79 Main, tel. (413) 253-3442, along with coffee, sandwiches, salads, and other gourmet deli items. As if the newspapers and those Grand Marnier chocolate chip cookies weren't incentive enough to hang out discussing love and politics, there's live acoustic music on many evenings, too. Open Mon-Sat. 7 a.m.-11 p.m., Sunday 8 a.m.-9 p.m.

The standout in the pizza category—despite the McDonald's drive-through ambiance—is **Antonio's,** tel. (413) 253-0808, 31 N. Pleasant Street. Black beans, potatoes, tortellini, green salad—if it fits on a pizza, you'll find it here. Open daily until 1 a.m. Nearby, the **Cafe DiCarlo,** 71 N. Pleasant St., tel. (413) 253-9300, offers Italian bistro fare with a gourmet touch, priced just high enough to keep the casual patio and dining room undergraduate-free.

Duck down the shoulder-width alley next to Antonio's to find Boltwood Walk, the restaurant-filled fringe of the public parking lot behind the downtown commercial block. Choices include a little Tex-Mex cafe, a budget-priced burrito shop, and expensive, upscale Northern Italian from **La Cucina di Pinocchio,** tel. (413) 256-4110. All are open daily for lunch and dinner, stay open until at least 10 p.m., and offer outdoor seating in warm weather.

Ask Valley locals about Chinese food and many will send you straight to **Amherst Chinese,** 62 Main St., tel. (413) 253-7835, especially if they think you'll appreciate large quantity at low cost (out of over 120, only three items cost more than $10). In late summer, many of those tasty vegetables come straight from the owners' farm. Open daily from lunch until 10 p.m. or later. For something a bit more dashing and artful, head to **Panda East** at 103 N. Pleasant St., tel. (413) 256-8923. Or consider sampling the Malaysian cuisine at **Rasa Sayang,** on N. Pleasant at the corner of Main, or try the

multinational Far East menu around the corner at **Amber Waves,** 63 Main St. next to Atticus Books, tel. (413) 253-9200. This storefront counter-service place dishes up Thai noodles, Japanese soups, Vietnamese curries, and South Indian *dosa* (a savory crepe) at surprisingly low prices considering the huge serving. Open daily from lunch till 10:30 p.m. (9:30 p.m. Sunday). Cuisines from the East are also locally represented by a pair of Indian restaurants—one being the inexpensive **Paradise of India,** at 87 Main, tel. (413) 256-1067—but if you have time and transportation, go to Northampton for the real spicy stuff served in more elegant surroundings.

Next to the Black Sheep Deli mentioned above, the best place to just hang around over espresso, dessert, and conversation—or soup and a good book—is **Bonducci's,** tel. (413) 256-1390, on S. Pleasant St. across from the little tourist information kiosk/Peter Pan Bus stop at the edge of the common. It's open daily at least until 10 p.m.

GREENFIELD AND VICINITY

Since its establishment on the heels of the French and Indian Wars in the late 1700s, Greenfield has been the commercial center of the upper Pioneer Valley—a modest role it has managed to uphold as economics has shifted from rivers to railroads to interstates. Located at the confluence of the Green, Deerfield, and Connecticut Rivers just below Turners Falls, the town secured a future as a shipping center for local agricultural goods when the 1795 South Hadley Canal extended the navigable length of the Connecticut from Springfield to Greenfield's doorstep. Transportation improvements soon allowed more productive midwestern farms to undercut local ones, forcing Valley farmers to turn to dairy products and meat, market goods too perishable to be shipped from out of state. Greenfield kept pace: with its direct rail link to Boston's growing urban population, Greenfield became the state's largest beef producer. Refrigeration and the Chicago stockyards eventually took away this business, but by then it had diversified into manufacturing.

The 1875 opening of the Hoosac Tunnel through the Berkshires to upstate New York allowed Greenfield to continue thriving as a rail center on the Boston-Albany route, and opened up markets for its industrial products. While other Valley industrial towns went into decline after WW I, Greenfield became a national leader in producing machine tools, although as the gateway of the scenic Mohawk Trail west to the Berkshires, the town continued to benefit from evolving transportation infrastructure. Though major manufacturing has left town, services such as insurance and education have helped fill the void, leaving Greenfield almost where it began: a market town to surrounding smaller communities and waypoint for people and things headed elsewhere, this time on interstates rather than rivers or rails.

Attractions of the upper Valley include the great fly-fishing along the remote Green River gorge, historic Old Deerfield, and Turners Falls, springboard to the Connecticut River Greenway State Park. As for Greenfield itself, no major museums, concert halls, pro sports teams, or natural landmarks beckon travelers to steer through town, and given the lay of the roads, it's entirely possible to pass around or at least skirt the edges without stopping. But that would be a mistake. The downtown is recommendable simply for being a traditional American small town—one of that dwindling number of places that hasn't yet succumbed to homogenized malls, themed gentrification, or blight. Maybe you don't need any clothes, office supplies, housewares, or sundry other items from downtown's businesses, but savor the fact that storefronts here aren't identical to those in towns across the country. There's even a classic old 1920s moviehouse right there on Main—split up into a multiplex inside, to be sure, but still keeping its doors open and continuing to draw an audience despite inexpensive videos, satellite movie channels, and cable TV. In short, mom 'n' pop and their kids are still in business here, and for that, if nothing else, Greenfield deserves at least your passing attention.

A well-researched walking tour brochure to the downtown historic district is available from the **Franklin County Chamber of Commerce** visitor center, at 395 Main next to the moviehouse, tel. (413) 773-5463. Open weekdays until 5 p.m., the Chamber also stocks plenty of additional information on regional attractions, bed and breakfast lodging, and shopping.

TURNERS FALLS

At least as far back as the Early Woodland Period, 5,000-6,000 years ago, Turners Falls was a vital crossing point and fishing spot for the indigenous people of the Connecticut Valley. To early colonists the falls were a navigational impediment to be overcome by a lock and canal, but in the 1860s a speculative industrialist from Fitchburg recognized the "Lowell system" of canal-fed hydropowered turbines could take advantage of the site for manufacturing. The planned town quickly grew into a large paper producer, bolstered in the early 1900s by hydroelectric power generation. Then the Depression so thoroughly wiped out Turners Falls' livelihood that it has essentially remained as a hollowed-out shell of its former self ever since. But what a shell! Nowhere else in the state has a Victorian commercial streetscape been left so untouched.

Actually, Turners Falls is no ghost town. Such gems as the **Shea Community Theater,** 71 Avenue A, tel. (413) 863-2281, ext. 3338, draw people to the village for a taste of professional theater and varied concerts, from pop to jazz. Businesses still exist here, too, such as **Thomas & Thomas Rod Makers,** 2 Avenue A at the foot of the bridge over the Connecticut, tel. (413) 863-9727. This small outfit founded by Thomas Dorsey and Thomas Maxwell over a quarter of a century ago has become famous among fly-fishing connoisseurs for their premium quality split-cane, bamboo, and graphite fly rods. Scheduled tours of the facility are available Mon.-Fri., and if you like what you see you can buy it. In May of odd-numbered years the company hosts Fly Fair USA, a domestic counterpart to Holland's renowned biennial fly-fishing festival. The landscaped grounds of Thomas & Thomas overlook the canal whose rushing waters gave birth to the town back in 1867. On the canal's banks, the **Franklin County Bikeway,** is being constructed—a 40-mile recreational and commuter on- and off-road bike route from Northfield to Deerfield via Turners Falls and Greenfield.

Updates on the bikeway's progress are available at the **Great Falls Discovery Center,** tel. (413) 863-3221, adjacent to Thomas & Thomas. This year-round visitor center for the **Connecticut River Greenway State Park,** a string of public open land through the belly of Massachusetts, is also the place to pick up information on river recreation, such as canoe rentals from Rt. 2's Barton Cove Nature Area on the other side of the Turners Falls Dam, the daily summer riverboat cruises aboard the *Quinnetucket II* through the French King Gorge upstream, or access points for swimming and boating (and primitive island camping) downstream. Or simply visit the center to study their displays on riparian ecology, Native American history in the Valley, and the ongoing efforts to restore Atlantic salmon to the Connecticut River. Speaking of anadromous fish—the kind that live in salt water but reproduce in fresh—if the little salmon smolts released in the river in years past have survived to maturity in the open ocean, you can watch them return to their upstream spawning grounds, along with shad and herring, via the **Turners Falls Fishway** behind the center, Wed.-Sun. mid-May-mid-June. Unlike their Pacific cousins, the Atlantic salmon are capable of

A summer squall passes an old tobacco barn on McClellan Farm Road, East Deerfield.

spawning and returning to the sea several times—*if* they can make the journey back downstream without being sucked into hydropower turbines.

DEERFIELD

Though US 5 hurries along its edge with the typical highway's contempt for the impediments of the past, Deerfield village is so steeped in timeless repose that rushing through it feels as alien as doing cartwheels in a library. A frontier settlement all but wiped off the map not once but twice, Old Deerfield, as it is known (as compared to the town's adminstrative seat, South Deerfield) is clearly not of the present. Despite the modern music broadcast by Deerfield Academy's student-run radio or the predominance of late-model minivans and sport-utility vehicles, the village's single main avenue, "The Street," distinctly evokes the 18th and early 19th centuries. It's not a false front worn like an actor in frock coat, but a solid, foundation-square history as deep as the laid hearthstones, handwrought iron hardware, and surrounding fields farmed for 200 years. It's a legacy carefully preserved, but still lived in. And it's quite accessible, as a fair fraction of the village is one big museum.

Historic Deerfield

With over 50 historic structures on 93 acres and over 20,000 antiques, Historic Deerfield is rightly considered one of the foremost jewels of colo-

nial Americana. The postcard-perfection of The Street provides a seamless backdrop for the museum's 13 houses, which are open to the public and staffed by well-versed guides who warmly describe the lives of the original residents. Though tour subjects span the 17th, 18th, and 19th centuries, they will all sound like dear old friends by the time the docent biographers are done. Several of the houses and a converted barn are also filled with specific antique collections, including clocks, Chippendale furniture, colonial silverware, embroidery, scenic painted wallpaper, and enough English ceramics and porcelain china to keep the proverbial bull busy for weeks. Year-round programs range from open-hearth cooking demonstrations to a mid-July antique car show. Open daily except Thanksgiving, December 24, and Christmas, admission to Historic Deerfield's houses and museums is $12 for a two-day pass; call (413) 774-5581. Tickets are sold in the building opposite the Deerfield Inn; parking is just behind. Individual house tours last about half an hour, and are given on demand.

On a side street in the village, independent of Historic Deerfield but sharing research libraries, is the **Memorial Hall Museum,** 8 Memorial St., tel. (413) 774-7476. Begun in 1870 by the Pocumtuck Valley Memorial Association, the museum was originally dedicated to the double martyrdom of the village at the hand of Indian raiders during the 1675 King Philip's War and, decades later, during the Anglo-French conflicts that spilled over to the New World. The true cross of that mission, a door gashed by hatchets during the 1704 Deerfield Massacre, is still prominently displayed, but now the museum also explores the Indian side to those events. Its displays of Native American artifacts serve a dual purpose, too—illustrating the history of the Pocumtuck tribe that occupied the Valley prior to the English settlers, and exposing the fallacies of 19th-century artifact collectors to the light of modern anthropology. The rest of the museum is a country decorator's dream, preserving local history through an extensive collection of furnishings, tools, kitchen wares, costumes, quilts, and toys—including Bangwell Putt, oldest rag doll in America. Open daily May-Oct., admission is free with a Historic Deerfield ticket, or $6 alone.

PRACTICALITIES

Camping

Three miles east of Greenfield beside Rt. 2 in Gill is **Barton Cove,** a small tents-only campground on a little peninsula jutting out into the Connecticut River above the Turners Falls dam and marina. Owned and operated by Northeast Utilities as a condition of their license to operate the power station embedded in nearby Northfield Mountain, Barton Cove provides full bathrooms, showers, firewood and ice, even canoe rentals and weekend sunset riverboat cruises. Sites are $12 (rentals, rides, and supplies are all extra). A nature trail explores the glacially formed features of the peninsula and the quarry which yielded thousands of dinosaur tracks for museums and classrooms of the 19th century. Throughout the camping season, late May through early September, it's also possible to observe the bald eagles nesting on the tiny island in Barton Cove itself. Sites are reservable: call (413) 863-9300 after the campground is open or (413) 659-3714 before.

The nearest state campground is in the **Erving State Forest** almost 20 miles east of Greenfield, tel. (978) 544-3939. Signposted from Rt 2 and 2A, the 30-odd tree-shaded sites are dispersed along an unpaved woods road near fishstocked Laurel Lake. With only pit toilets and no showers, the fee is $4 a night. Open May 1-mid-October.

Accommodations

The Pioneer Valley's only hostel—indeed, the only Massachusetts hostel west of Worcester—is about 20 miles northeast of Greenfield, near the Vermont border. The **Monroe and Isabel Smith Hostel,** named after (and a successor to) the couple who founded the first American Youth Hostel in 1934, occupies a Victorian house at the corner of Highland Ave. and Pine St. in Northfield, tel. (413) 498-3505. Unfortunately this Hostelling International affiliate is only open mid-June through the end of August. Otherwise it is as pleasant a hostel as can be, with just over a dozen beds spread out throughout well-maintained albeit institutionally furnished rooms adjacent to the college-like campus of the Northfield-Mt. Hermon prep school. Private quarters are available for couples and families. Rates are $14 pp for hostel members, $17 pp for everyone else.

Most of Greenfield's limited lodging options are found at I-91 Exit 26, around the large rotary junction with Rt. 2 west and Rt. 2A through town. The cluster includes a **Super 8 Motel** on Colrain Rd., off the northwest side of the rotary, tel. (800) 800-8000 or (413) 774-5578, doubles $38-69; **Candlelight Inn** on the southwest side, tel. (413) 772-0101, doubles $48-84; and **Howard Johnson Inn** on the east side, tel. (800) I GO HOJO or (413) 774-2211, doubles $64-89. (Built in the '50s, this HoJo's is possibly the last remaining Bauhaus-style property in their chain; until the mid-'90s it was complemented by the last remaining Georgian-style Howard Johnson—their original design—at the other end of the Mohawk Trail, in Williamstown.)

For a splendidly isolated couples' retreat, a tad rustic but quite comfortable, head northwest of Greenfield to **The Warwick Inn,** tel. (978) 544-7802. Opened to the stagecoach trade in late 1827, the inn is easily found in the center of Warwick, a hamlet on Rt. 78 north of Rt. 2 that's been truly forgotten by time. Two guest suites share the premises with an artists' gift shop and cozy little tavern open two nights a week. Friday night, folk musicians from the surrounding hills come down to jam and eat pizza, which somebody fetches from some nearby town for everyone who's ponied up for it. The surrounding state forest has trails for blueberry-picking, hiking, and cross-country skiing (rentals available nearby), and understandably the autumn foliage is breathtaking. Open year-round; $70 d. Similar retreats are available to the west.

You spare-no-expense types needn't feel left out in the cold, either, so long as there's a room at **The Deerfield Inn,** on The Street in Old Deerfield, tel. (800) 926-3865 or (413) 774-5587. Owned by Historic Deerfield, the 23-room inn is richly endowed with American decorative arts, in this case a mix of genuine priceless antiques and museum-quality reproductions with wallpaper and fabric to match. "Gracious" is a descriptor that can never be overused here: the setting, atmosphere, and service are the very definition of the word. High season doubles begin at $185, including breakfast.

Food

Like a score of other towns around the state, Greenfield has been bitten by the brewpub bug. Unlike some of the trendy contenders who care more about making big bucks than good beers, **The People's Pint,** 24 Federal St., tel. (413) 773-0333, is a real down-home tavern dedicated to crafting enjoyable food and drink. Sample their ale, stout, porter, and seasonal brews with a menu of hearty from-scratch soups, salads, and sandwiches.

If ethnic food is your desire, then consider either the **China Gourmet,** on Rt. 2A just east of the I-91 rotary, tel. (413) 774-2299, or **Royal Panda,** just off Main St. in a set of shops on the corner of Fiske Avenue. Of the two, China Gourmet displays more craft in preparation and art in presentation, and offers more elegance in the surroundings, with high-backed booths providing intimacy. Better fortunes in the cookies, too. Royal Panda has the monopoly on funny-colored cocktails, though, complete with paper parasols and names that sound like the cast of a James Bond movie. Both places are reasonably priced, serve lunch and dinner, and are open Sun.-Thurs. until 10 p.m., Fri.-Sat. to 11 p.m.

To stock up on groceries for a picnic, camping, or road trip, try **Green Fields Market,** 144 Main St., a natural foods cooperative with fine breads (challah, sourdough, rye, wheatberry), cheeses, condiments, and all the bulk gorp fixings you could want. Their deli has healthful sandwiches, from-scratch soups, a salad bar, and sinful desserts to counterbalance it all. Open till 8 p.m. weekdays, 5-6 p.m. weekends. Alternatively, the huge chain supermarkets located across from one another on Rt. 2 just west of the I-91 rotary stay open 24 hours.

THE HILLTOWNS

Nestled among the narrow, wild rivers carving their way through the high, rolling uplands on the Pioneer Valley's west side are a series of tiny communities known collectively known as the Hilltowns. Look at a map and the Hilltowns seem convenient to any number of access points, from the MassPike and I-91 to Rt. 2. But measuring miles from the nearest interstate exit doesn't take into account the rugged terrain—which turns any trip through the region into a long, graceful roller-coaster ride. In places, the land is so rugged that Hollywood used it to stand in for Africa in the Tarzan movies of the 1930s.

The Hilltowns prospered in the 1700s, after the English had finally defeated the French and their Indian allies (forcing a majority of the surviving Native Americans into the most isolated corners of New England), with agriculture, sheep-raising, lumbering, and cottage industries powered by those fast-tumbling streams.

But the vast tracts of boulder-free Ohio Valley land drew away the farmers, sheep stations in Australia undercut local wool prices, and sawmills couldn't wait around for the logged-off forests to grow back. Subsequently bypassed by railroads and most highways, much of the region seems to have fallen into a slumber that may outlast the 20th century.

Pine, birch, and spruce have reclaimed much of their ancestral territory, overcoming stone walls and old family burying grounds. Terrific fall foliage is one result, along with great tracts of sugarbush, stands of sugar maple whose spring sap is transformed into liquid gold in rustic backyard evaporators throughout the region. The extensive reforestation has also benefited the state's population of black bear and other wildlife.

Though often hidden from the main roads by trees, farming does continue in the region, and

HILLTOWNS FESTIVALS AND EVENTS

MARCH

The third Saturday of the month, the **Chester Hill Maple Fest,** in the Old Chester Center, is an old-fashioned community event (think country block party), whose highlight is the $6 all-you-can-eat pancake breakfast.

APRIL

Late April brings scores of paddlers to Huntington for the annual **Westfield River Wildwater Canoe Races.** Spectators line the banks of the snowmelt-swollen river below Knightville Dam or lean over the railing of Norwich Bridge, on Rt. 112 by the Huntington General Store, to catch the action. Race day is preceded by numerous workshops for experts and novices alike. (Don't let lack of a boat keep you from participating; if you're genuinely interested in spending a few hours in near-freezing water learning canoe handing tips, coordinators will try to pair you up with somebody for the practicums.)

MAY

Railroad buffs will appreciate **Chester On Track,** a one-day celebration of all things related to trains, held toward the end of the month. Call (413) 667-8711 for details.

JUNE

Huntington's needle-spired Stanton Hall hosts an annual **invitational art show** the first weekend in June, showcasing the talents of local artists.

JULY

Celebrate one of the nation's first scenic highways—inaugurated in 1910—at **Jacob's Ladder Days,** in Chester the first weekend of the month. A bike ride up the steep, thoroughly beautiful route is one of several activities.

The Hilltowns leave fireworks displays to their bigger neighbors down in the Pioneer Valley, but for a small-town American **Independence Day** *sans* rockets' red glare, it would be hard to trump Chesterfield's little parade of floats and antique cars.

The **Blandford Mountain Bluegrass Festival** usually takes place the second weekend of the month at the Blandford Ski Area (follow signs from Rt. 20 in Russell) with a whole passle of great bands providing a finger-pickin' good time for no more than you'd pay for a single indoor concert by any one of the headliners. Call (413) 562-3111 for the latest concert information and ticket prices.

Midmonth, the **Bryant Homestead Country Craft Fair,** tel. (413) 634-2244, graces the William Cullen Bryant Homestead's expansive lawns in Cummington with art, music, and food. The weekend event is highly regarded for the caliber of the jury-selected artisans, many of whom live in the vicinity. Displays of Victorian costumes, craft demonstrations in the barn, and special children's activities are regular features, along with tea served on that gracious verandah. Nominal admission.

On the third or fourth Saturday of the month, the Blandford Fair Grounds host the **Glasgow Lands Scottish Festival,** with Highland games, dancing, the ever-popular Tea Room (serving scones, watercress sandwiches, and the like), farm animals, and lots of people practicing their burrs.

OCTOBER

The triathlon season in New England has been stretched in recent years by the new **October Runover,** a canoe/mountain bike/running event held on Columbus Day weekend around Littleville Lake in Huntington. The Jacob's Ladder Business Association, sponsors of the event, can provide details for prospective racers or spectators.

the few large dairy herds Massachusetts has left are usually found ruminating on Hilltown pastures. Every August, hometown agricultural fairs fill the calendar, celebrating harvests and seasons—and sheer survival in the face of pressure to sell out to developers.

Though there are plenty of deer crossings, there's only one stop light, and if you doubt the leisurely quality implied by such insouciant traffic control, just see if you can hurry through without being seduced—by signs for pick-your-own berries, by a sudden ridgeline view across a valley, by small old-fashioned general stores, or by the sheer beauty of late afternoon light imparting an amber glow to a roadside meadow full of wildflowers.

Campers, hikers, skiers, fly-casters, and whitewater paddlers all have good reason to linger in these parts, and road cyclists looking for some genuine thigh-burning challenge will find plenty of routes that do just that. About the only drawback for the Hilltown visitor is the minimal number of eateries—but, fortunately, Northampton isn't too long a drive from where the lack is most severe.

Although urban planners, highway department signmakers and state tourism blurb writers consider the region part of the Pioneer Valley, the Hilltowns have been increasingly vocal about drawing clear boundaries between their own little slice of rural nirvana and the far more populous and commercial valley below. Until the tourism machinery comes to recognize this demarcation, though, information about the region will continue to be buried within brochures from the Greater Springfield Convention & Visitors Bureau.

This is a region that isn't simply conducive to long, meandering, even aimless-seeming drives between towns—it mandates them. And each little one-horse town, in its turn, offers *some* reason for stopping. What follows is a selection of ideas and teasers as to what you'll find here. But one of the great joys of exploring the Hilltowns is discovering some unanticipated little pleasure.

CLIMBING JACOB'S LADDER ~ US 20

Today, the route of US 20 roughly corresponds to the Jacob's Ladder Trail, an early scenic auto road named for farmer Jacob Carter of Becket.

The original Jacob's Ladder Trail was so precipitous that Carter often had to help cars up the last stretch with his team of oxen. The modern federal highway has straightened most of the old route's curves. But some vestiges remain in the form of the many pull-outs you'll see along the way (back in the early days of the trail, such resting spots were called "thank you, ma'ams"). Another surviving remnant is the Summit House, built in 1926 at the top of Morey Hill (the high point of the Ladder). Adjacent is a deer statue that once advertised a live deer exhibit that constituted but one of many highway attractions for tourists. Note the stone cairn, begun in 1910 by tourists and auto clubs from around

the nation who left token rocks to commemorate the road's dedication (on September 10, 1910—earlier than the Mohawk Trail) and their victorious ascents.

Jacob's Well, a spring used to refill overheated radiators, is also still visible, about a half mile east of the Summit House. As for the original roadbed, look for its ravine around the Rising Sun golf course, 0.9 miles west of the Summit House.

Huntington

Huntington is a town built around water. Every year since 1954, the city has played host to the annual **Westfield River Wildwater Canoe Races** (these days to the delight of a few thousand spectators along the boulder-strewn banks). Spring runoff in the hills usually creates conditions as challenging as any professional could want, but if Mother Nature proves stingy, the US Army Corps of Engineers helps out with releases from their Knightsville Reservoir upstream. The first boats launch at 11 a.m. the third Sunday in April; awards ceremonies take place by 5 p.m. Parking on highway shoulders isn't permitted, so park in available turnouts and lots along the course (which roughly follows Rt. 112). Norwich Bridge, next to the Huntington General Store, is always a good vantage point, while **The Bantam Rooster,** on US 20, in downtown Huntington, is a fine little cafe in which to grab a bite before, during, or after the race.

If you want to sample the Westfield yourself, **C.M. Gardner State Park** ($2 day-use fee), on Rt. 112 north of Norwich Bridge, is a good spot for canoeing and home to a fine swimming hole in low water (summer), when pools form. Just for river access, try the small parking area opposite Moltenbray's Market, north of the town center.

Knightville Dam, near the Huntington-Worthington line, has a reservoir that has been host to wading birds of all sorts—mergansers and blue herons among them—as well as the occasional bald eagle. Trails from here run up an old logging road beside the river into Bliss State Forest and end at Chesterfield Gorge. Hunting is popular around here, so if you head out in the week after Thanksgiving, wear bright colors and don't do any bushwhacking.

If you're interested in camping, try one of the 15 sites in **Chester-Blandford State Forest.**

HILLTOWNS BED & BREAKFASTS

For romantic getaways at small, very individual bed and breakfast homes, the Hilltowns can't be beat, and in sharp contrast to many coastal and island resort areas, full country breakfasts and moderate prices are the rule rather than the exception. Your B&B hosts can also point you toward the recreation of your choice, from hiking, cross-country skiiing, flycasting, and whitewater paddling to shopping for antiques and crafts or even theater-going. Sound intriguing? Book a stay at one of the accommodations listed below and discover the rejuvenating Hilltown magic for yourself.

Unless otherwise noted, none of the following accepts credit cards. Moreover, ATMs are next to nonexistent in these parts, so if you owe a balance on your reservation, stock up in advance on greenbacks in one of the bigger Pioneer Valley towns, such as Northampton or Greenfield.

Vicinity of US 20 West of MassPike Exit 3
The General Knox House, on General Knox Rd. in Woronoco, a village of the town of Russell, tel. (413) 562-6439. This rather pastoral setting—with ponds, animals, and plenty of solitude—is only a couple of miles from Westfield State College, and close to the MassPike for easy access to the Berkshires or the Five College area. Rates are $60 d with shared bath and big breakfast.

Carmelwood, on Montgomery Rd. in Huntington, tel. (413) 667-5786. Overlooking the Westfield River from on high, this late-19th-century house demonstrates that Victorian charm isn't all ribbons and overstuffed upholstery—it can be casual and comfortable enough that you don't feel too anxious about spoiling the furniture. Diversions abound, on the premises and off, and fine breakfasts give a taste of local products such as fresh berries and organic vegetables grown in the house garden. Rates are $70 d with shared bath.

Baird Tavern, on Old Chester Rd. in Blandford, tel. (413) 848-2096. As the name suggests, this sturdy 1768 Colonial was originally a tavern along the Old Post Road between Springfield and Albany. Now that modern highways prefer straight lines and easy grades, the tavern has been pleasantly marooned at the threshhold of Hampden County's deep woods—close to several state parks, ski areas, and plenty of thoroughly scenic back roads. This seat of repose has been beautifully re-

stored, down to the wide floorboards and wrought-iron door latches (knobs were a postcolonial innovation), and elegantly furnished throughout. The owners also lay on a great gourmet breakfast. Rates are $70 d with shared bath.

Strawberry Banke Farm B&B, on the Skyline Trail in Middlefield, tel. (413) 623-6481. Though the house is a 1780 Colonial with a dining-room fireplace and beautiful views, don't come expecting discreet stenciling or neo-colonial frills. A stay here, in fact, is nothing short of sleeping in a three-dimensional work of folk art: owner Judy Artioli, a painter and sculptor, has let her imagination run rampant over the whole house—to vivid, eye-catching, sometimes whimsical effect. There's a small gallery of her work in a refinished shed, too. Rooms are $65 d with shared bath, $70 d with private—including full homemade breakfast.

Vicinity of Rt. 9 West of Northampton
Twin Maples, 106 South St., Williamsburg, tel. (413) 268-7925. Eleanor and Martin Hebert offer three rooms (shared bath) and serve a full breakfast utilizing homemade jams, maple syrup, muffins, and eggs straight from the hen house (I'd return just for Eleanor's walnut French toast). Rooms run $60-65 (plus a $5 surcharge for one-night visits; two-night minimum on holiday weekends—a category that includes Commencement, usually at the end of May).

The Whale Inn, on Rt. 9 in Goshen, just 20 minutes from downtown Northampton, tel. (413) 268-7246. Providing travelers with quiet hilltop nights and starry skies since 1923, the Whale Inn's half-dozen Early American-style rooms are still free of televisions and telephones, but simple hospitality at these rates is a *welcome* throwback to a bygone era: $35 s, $55 d, $75 for the two-room suite—all with modern private baths and continental breakfast. Built in 1799 as a parsonage, the place has been very comfortably converted, with a nice combination of old and new. A solid meat-and-potatoes restaurant occupies the first floor, along with a bar that's no stranger to smoking, swearing, laughing out loud, and large cocktails. It's a good place to meet the locals (and not the second-home-in-the-country crowd, either).

The Seven Hearths B&B, on Rt. 143 in Chesterfield, tel. (413) 296-4312. The generous country charm at this large 1891 Dutch gambrel-roofed house is complemented by a surfeit of fireplaces—not only does each guest room have one, but one room even has two. Hikers, cyclists, and cross-country skiers will particularly appreciate the soothing hot tub. A continental buffet is offered weekday mornings, and weekends feature a belt-stretching country breakfast. Rooms with shared baths are $65 d, those with private baths $75 d (discounts for stays of longer than three nights).

The Worthington Inn, on Rt. 143 in Worthington Center, tel. (413) 238-4441. The white Saratoga fencing along the pastures adds a touch of Kentucky's horse country, but this historic 1780 attached farmhouse is quintessential New England. Three fireplaces in the common rooms and down comforters in the bright, uncluttered guest rooms keep the elements at bay—and the full breakfasts will sustain you in any season. Nearby activities include hiking, horseback riding (stable space is available), cross-country skiing, or catnapping on the porch. Each of the three rooms runs $70-90, including private bath and gourmet breakfast.

Cumworth Farm, Rt. 112, Cummington, tel. (413) 634-5529. A 25-acre working farm with sheep, cattle, sugarbush for maple syrup, and pick-your-own blueberries and raspberries provides the backdrop for this informal B&B, whose six guest rooms are in the 200-year-old farmhouse. The hot tub (nominal extra charge for use) occupies a little shed of its own—perfect for stargazing or soothing tired skiing muscles. Rates are $75 d with shared bath and full breakfast.

The Hill Gallery, on Cole St. in Cummington, tel. (413) 238-5914. This contemporary home, designed by its owner, artist Walter Korzec (note the a terrific southern exposure), features a swimming pool and two ponds in addition to a variety of collectibles and original art. Each of the two available guest rooms is $70 d, including private bath and full breakfast. A self-contained cottage is available seasonally, too.

Windfields Farm, Windsor Bush Rd., Windsor, tel. (413) 684-3786. Though technically located in the Berkshires, this place is so close to the Hilltowns that the US Postal Service gave it a Cummington address. To those in the know, this constitutes the best of two worlds—a good pedigree and no attitude. The early-19th-century farm has a spring-fed (i.e., cold!) swimming pond down by the woods, fresh blueberries for summer breakfasts,

acres of potential birdwatching territory, and the kind of hospitality that makes you feel as if you're coming home. The two bedrooms share a bath (and a separate entrance), but there's no lack of privacy if you want it—if you can resist the easy fellowship kindled among guests by your affable hosts, Arnold and Carolyn. (If you like family heirlooms—including a real horsehair mattress handed down through a couple of generations—ask for the Blue Room.) Come prepared to hike or, in winter, cross-country ski—trails for both start virtually at the farmhouse door, including one to Windsor Jambs, a sheer-walled little gorge to the west with a cascading brook. Rates of $70 d include a hearty farm breakfast featuring their own eggs, maple syrup, and organic garden produce. Closed in mud season, March-April.

Vicinity of Rt. 2,
the Mohawk Trail, West of Greenfield
Penfrydd Farm B&B, in Colrain, tel. (413) 624-5516. Outside, it's a 160-acre working farm, com-

stock and scenery on Penfrydd Farm

HILLTOWNS BED & BREAKFASTS
(continued)

plete with coquettish llamas, long-wool sheep grazing on the sloping pastures, and a miniature donkey that draws kids like a pocket draws lint. Inside, it's a handsomely restored farmhouse, with hefty exposed beams, gleaming plaster walls, and artful, eclectic decor. All in all, this slice of Vermont's pastoral beauty and liberal hospitality is one of the state's best-kept secrets. The price is a great value, too: $55 with shared bath, $65 private, including a hearty breakfast. Credit cards accepted.

The Maple House, tel. (413) 339-0107. At $55 year-round, it's another of the least-expensive B&Bs in the state, and quite a good value in it's casual, family-friendly way. Anyone with visions of Massachusetts as a largely urban state will be pleasantly surprised to find places like this, high in the rugged foothills of the Green Mountains. Make this cheerful B&B your base for whitewater rafting, top-notch trout fishing, cross-country skiing, snowshoeing, stargazing, foliage viewing, swimming in the pri-

vate lake, or doing some serious biking along surprisingly well-paved mountain roads. Or, just snooze on the porch after polishing off a wholesome and filling country breakfast.

Stump Sprouts Guest Lodge, West Hill Rd. in West Hawley, off Rt. 8A south of Rt. 2, tel. (413) 339-4265. Known primarily for its cross-country skiing, Stump Sprouts commands 450 mountainside acres with breathtaking views, plenty of wildlife (including resident pileated woodpeckers), and a trail network that provides exceptional skiing or hiking, as the seasons dictate. Like an immaculate and slightly funky alpine hostel, the lodge offers six rooms with bunkbeds, shared baths, and shared meals. There's also a sauna and a fireplace-warmed common space where guests can gather and swap tales. Catering to groups and individuals who appreciate the great vibes, rates are $42-58 d including full breakfast; home-style dinners are also available.

Since there are no showers and only outhouse toilets, the nightly rate is just $4.

Chester

Chester has the distinction of being able to boast that it is the site of both the highest and the lowest recorded temperatures in the state. On August 2, 1975, the mercury here hit 107° F. Five and a half years later, the temperature dipped to -35° F on January 12, 1981.

But what Chester really wants to talk about is trains. Since restoration of its 1840 railroad depot and acquisition of an old saddletank steam locomotive and Calvin Coolidge-era caboose, Chester has become serious about preserving railroad history. For its part, the town was once home to a short-line railroad servicing a local granite quarry. The roundhouse and coal tower of "the Chester & Becket" line still remain, and so do some keystone arch bridges (the earliest such spans built for any US railroad). To add homage to honor, the town further celebrates the iron horse every May in the railroad-themed event Chester On Track.

Fans of live professional theatre should be sure to make a date with **The Miniature Theatre**

of Chester, tel. (413) 354-7771, whose summer season can always be counted on for a handful of fine productions staged in the intimacy of Chester's Town Hall auditorium, on Middlefield Rd. by the corner of US 20. Eminently affordable, the performances typically run Thurs.-Sat. evenings and Wednesday, Saturday, and Sunday matinees all through July and August. Do like the cast and director do—have lunch or dinner around the corner in the village center at the Classic Pizza shop, the **Blue Note Cafe.** If you collect license plates, you may want to stop in simply to admire the decor.

For most of the 19th century, North Chester (about five miles as the crow flies from Town Hall, or over a dozen miles by car) was a thriving mill village, with grist mills, saw mills, and textile mills, along with factories producing wooden bowls, whip butts, and bedsteads. Today, it's a couple of buildings on a quiet country road. You can still spot stone foundations along the banks of the river right around Smith Bridge (which happens to be an 1887 truss bridge—one of three such structures in the state). One remaining building, the Cushman Tavern, dates back to 1770. George Washington may have slept here, since the road along this, the Middle Branch of the Westfield River, was part of the stagecoach route from Boston to Albany. (Amtrak now favors the West Branch valley.)

The first weekend each August, North Chester (well, *Greater* North Chester) hosts the **Littleville Fair**, tel. (413) 296-4354, an annual tradition since 1922. The fair combines a mini-modified tractor pull, a pony draw, a garden tractor pull, a magic show, a music revue, exhibits, food, and music.

Middlefield

The town of Middlefield lies on the Skyline Trail, which splits off US 20 in Chester and runs northwest along a high ridge above Factory Brook. Where the trees thin out or give way to meadows, this route affords absolutely amazing views across the western face of the hills.

The town center constitutes a little survey of postcolonial architecture, including a 1901 Queen Anne town hall, a Greek Revival general store, and, opposite the store and next to the church, an 1868 Italianate house built for a woolen manufacturer. In 1902, the church itself was created when enterprising parishioners joined a Baptist meeting house to a Methodist chapel, added a new bell tower, and turned the whole thing Congregational.

If you follow signs from Huntington for the Littleville Dam boat ramp, you'll end up on East River Road in North Chester, which hugs the banks of the Westfield River's Middle Branch. Stay on the road for about five miles past the turn for the boating area and you'll hit signs for Middlefield's hidden gem, lovely **Glendale Falls**, a series of cascades over a steeply sloping, 150-foot rock ledge.

Since 1856, the **Middlefield Fair**, on the second weekend of August, has been entertaining the community. These days, the attractions include a truck pull, a sheep show, horse and oxen draws, helicopter rides, crafts, rides, games, food, country bands, and other music.

ROUTE 112:
THE HEART OF THE HILLS

Census takers up here must feel like the Maytag repairman. The populations in most of these towns peaked around 1830, then drained away down the Erie Canal (which had opened the way to the midwest only five years earlier). Now, Rt. 112 zigzags broadly through a quiet upland oasis of farms and foliage—which is exactly what draws most of the residents who commute to jobs down in the Pioneer Valley. Tucked among these undulating heights between the South River, the Mill River, and the Middle Branch of the Westfield River are historic sights, summer performing arts, detour-quality natural features, and springtime sugar shacks—not to mention a number of deteriorating but still bike-able back roads gratifyingly free of traffic. Most of the Hilltowns' best dining options are also in this area.

Maple Paradise

In most respects, spring thaw—better known as Mud Season—is the least favorable time to be traveling around the rural parts of Massachusetts. But even the transformation of February's terra firma into March's boot-sucking quagmires has a silver lining of sorts: spring also heralds the start of Sugaring Season.

The forests of upland Massachusetts are filled with sugar maples, whose foliage, in autumn, produces the spectacular blaze-orange vistas for which New England is famous. In spring, these maples produce a thin, clear sap that gets boiled down—into maple syrup, sugar, cream, and candy—and baked or mixed into maple doughnuts, milk shakes, and ice cream at dozens of rustic little backwoods "sugar shacks" throughout the towns in the hills above the Pioneer Valley. While they're in syrup production, many of these offer simple pancake and waffle breakfasts—a truly incomparable experience when the fragrant steam from the evaporators wafts through the dining area.

The following selection will get you started with your maple syrup appreciation. Just keep in mind that the exact length of the Feb.-April season is strictly dependent on the weather. For a recorded update on the season's progress—or to receive a brochure of all the shacks in the vicinity—call the **Sugar Season Hotline**, tel. (413) 628-3912.

Best tableside view: Red Bucket Sugar Shack, on Kinne Brook Rd., in Worthington, tel. (413) 238-7710. Follow the signs from Rt. 112 south of Worthington Center. The evaporator is adjacent to the dining area, so when the sap is boiling, meals are fragrant as well as tasty. Open Saturday until 2 p.m., Sunday until 4, early March through early April.

Best atmosphere: Gray's Sugar House, off Baptist Corner Rd., Ashfield, tel. (413) 625-6559. Gray's cheese-grater lighting and old farm implements hanging over the rows of checkered-cloth-covered picnic tables gives it a distinct edge in ambiance over most other sugar shacks in the region. Pull up a red-upholstered tree stump and enjoy some fine pancakes and waffles (oatmeal and whole-wheat variations available, of course—after all, the Five Colleges are only 30 minutes away) with fresh maple syrup from the evaporator in the next room. Open weekends 8:30 a.m.-5:30 p.m., from late February or early March to the second Sunday in April, weather permitting. Follow the signs from Rt. 116 immediately east of the Ashfield Historical Society museum.

Best food: South Face Farm, on Watson-Spruce Corner Rd., Ashfield, tel. (413) 628-3268. The breakfasts that accompany this farm's maple elixir are impressive, with thick-cut homemade French bread for their French toast and good from-scratch batter for their pancakes and waffles. South Face also makes a point of featuring local products from neighboring farms (bacon, blueberries, cider, and the freshest eggs you've ever tasted unless you raise your own brood hens). Open weekends 8:30 a.m.-3:30 p.m., from early March to the second Sunday in April. In season, look for the farm's signs from the junction of Rt. 112 and Rt. 116W.

Worthington

Besides having the only stop light in the area, Worthington is home to the **Hickory Hill Ski Touring Center,** a great place to practice your cross-country technique on miles of groomed trails through the sugarbush. In any season, the Worthington Country Store can replenish the snack pack in your car or bike panniers (for some local baked goods, try Penny Molyneux's Penny Loafers).

Cummington and Vicinity

William Cullen Bryant derived most of his wealth and prestige from owning and editing the *New York Evening Post* for 50 years. But Bryant gained his first and perhaps most lasting fame with the publication of his poem "Thanatopsis," now an American literary standard, which he composed, while still only 17, largely at his family's Cummington farm. The rambling farmhouse is now a National Historic Landmark, preserved as the **William Cullen Bryant Homestead** and maintained by TTOR.

At birth, in 1794, Bryant's head was so large that his alarmed parents, in the hopes of reducing its proportions, commenced a regimen of dunking it in cold water every day until he was 12. This regimen doesn't seem to have dampened his precocious energy—besides maintaining multiple careers in journalism and literature, Bryant also translated ancient Greek classics, traveled widely, brokered the political fortunes of Abraham Lincoln and others, and attended to his extensive orchards. Even into his 80s, he preferred vaulting over his garden gates to going through them.

In later life, Bryant made the house his summer retreat—and it has been restored to reflect that period. Bryant's modifications to the property, and the furnishings the writer gathered for the house on his numerous trips abroad, are among the subjects touched upon by guides who lead tours Fri.-Sun. (and Monday holidays) 1-5 p.m. from the last week of June through Labor Day, then Sat.-Sun. through mid-October. Admission $5. The homestead is also open for special fall and winter events, including a juried fall arts and crafts show and the annual "Christmas at the Homestead," tel. (413) 634-2244, held the first full weekend of December.

Since 1870, the last weekend in August has been marked with the **Cummington Fair,** a genuine agricultural family fair featuring polka, vaudeville, crafts, oxen and horse draws, sheep obstacle courses, tractor pulls, a parade, youth dairy judging, food, and bands.

The Sunday of Labor Day weekend, the town of **Plainfield,** next door to Cummington, combines an annual arts and crafts show with an annual firemen's fund-raising barbecue dinner, behind Town Hall.

For an exceptional yet inexpensive deli lunch, stop at the **Old Creamery Grocery,** on Rt. 9 at the Rt. 112 split. From the outside (notwithstanding the fiberglass cow on the roof), this market looks like a fairly nondescript country

HOWES BROTHERS PHOTOGRAPHIC COLLECTION, ASHFIELD HISTORICAL SOCIETY

Ashfield

One of the more attractive of the Hilltowns, Ashfield boasts a main street (Rt. 116) graced by some fine old clapboard commercial buildings, such as the former Merrill Tavern, Ernie's General Store, and combination florist, hardware, and antique store. Visit the Ashfield Historical Society museum for a more intimate sampling of the town's past—and for a look at its collection of historic glass-plate photographs by the hometown Howes brothers.

Two TTOR sites, one on each side of town, merit visits in the area. Chapelbrook Reservation, a little over two miles down Williamsburg Rd. from Rt. 116 in South Ashfield, includes a wooded and sometimes precipitous half-mile ascent up Pony Ledge, a rocky cliff just west of the road-shoulder parking area. On the opposite side of the road, Chapel Brook hurries east in a chattering series of cascades. Longer hikes are possible in wildflower-rich Bear Swamp Reservation, on Hawley Rd. west of the Rt. 112/116 junction.

In terms of comestibles, the hills around Ashfield are home to two of the better sugar shacks in the region (see "Maple Paradise," above). But if you're in the mood for something that won't make your fillings ache, try the **Countrypie Pizza Company,** 343 Main Street, tel. (413) 628-4488, across from the sturdy Belding Library (and next to the shop whose wares hang invitingly from the porch railings in summer). If you're a thin-crust pizza fan, you'll like this well-made version—particularly given the inexpensive price for the gourmet toppings. You can also call to place your order in advance.

general store. Walk inside, however, and the question becomes, What country? The place rents videos of François Truffaut and Tod Browning films up front and sells import beers from Ukraine and England in the back—it's no wonder that the muddy pickup trucks in the lot have their radios tuned to NPR, or that the big bear-like guy in clod-hopper boots buying night crawlers is also wearing an earring.

Chesterfield and Vicinity

Anyone hungry to get out of the car and sample the natural beauty of the Hilltowns region will find Chesterfield a modest but lovely buffet of less-strenuous options. Chesterfield Gorge, maintained by TTOR, invites outdoor enjoyment, from catch-and-release fishing to simple strolling (starting at the Gorge, you can make a 10-mile riverside walk via a restricted-access fire road through neighboring Gilbert A. Bliss State Forest all the way to the Knightville Dam).

For a little more time in the Hilltowns outdoors, **D.A.R. State Forest,** off Rt. 112 in Goshen, east of Chesterfield, tel. (413) 268-7098, is home to 50 campsites available May through Columbus Day for only $6 each (half of the sites are reservable in advance). The campground (which boasts a recycling collection area, flush toilets, and a shower) is in a wooded area; most sites have bases of gravel and dirt, no big setbacks from the road, but reasonable spacing from one another. The forest offers opportunities for canoeing, swimming, hiking, and cross-country skiing (it's also a great place to see bears banging around in dumpsters).

THE MOHAWK TRAIL

Named for the precolonial mountain passage that gained infamy as a warpath for New York Mohawks (whose swift raids against both Indians and later settlers in the Connecticut River valley made them the most feared of the region's tribes), the modern Mohawk Trail (Rt. 2) was conceived as one of the nation's first scenic highways—and was the first built specifically to promote tourism. Paved in 1914 to encourage visitation to what was then one of the state's most economically depressed regions, the road essentially follows the Deerfield River upstream from Greenfield. It parts company with the river near the former whistle-stop village named Zoar, climbs steeply up the Cold River valley and over the glacier-flattened Hoosac Range to the incongruously named town of Florida, and then finally drops down through sharp hairpin curves into the Berkshire city of North Adams. Vintage motel courts and souvenir stands selling plastic tomahawks continue to ply their business along its length, while the surrounding communities display evidence of the new telecommuting class of entrepreneurial residents with cosmopolitan tastes in food, art, and recreation. Though the road is still narrow and winding in enough places to keep a driver's attention firmly affixed to the road, anticipate heavy traffic, from brake-burning big trucks to pokey old "leaf-peepers" during the height of fall foliage season.

The "Mohawk Trail" moniker, by the way, is retained merely to orient folks from outside the area; to the people who live out here, this is generally considered simply "West County." By either name, it's a region of solitude and reflection—and not only at the Vipassana Meditation Center or Japanese Buddhist zen-do nestled off the back roads. Sample this contemplative spirit at one of the local B&Bs, and reacquaint yourself with night skies filled with stars rather than streetlights.

These hills are also, though, alive with an array of cottage industries—and numbers of self-employed people working in them. Naturally, this gives rise to abundant representation of crafts and arts—some of which have become surprisingly refined in such isolated concentration. The area, for instance, is a center for artistic glassmaking. But bookbinding in particular has become exceptionally well developed here—evident in the presence of craft printers including Thistle Bindery, Pennyroyal Press, Wild Carrot Press, and Cheloniidae Press.

Catching Some Whitewater (or a Picnic)

From lovely picnic areas along Rt. 2, the Deerfield River is conveniently accessible to swimmers, waders, kayakers, and inner-tube floaters—though you should use caution during rafting season, as releases from the dams upstream can cause the river level to rise quite rapidly. For a bigger thrill, take advantage of the whitewater rafting opportunities that have sprouted upstream of the town of Charlemont.

There, in a pair of ten-mile stretches of the river between small hydroelectric dams, the Deerfield offers two distinct experiences. The lower section offers great introductory whitewater on a four- to five-hour trip that climaxes in the running of Zoar Gap—a fairly serious Class III challenge that requires rafters to pay more attention than earlier Class II rapids do. It isn't hard to end up swimming on this one, although nasty bruises can result if you do go in the drink. (Custom dictates that *guides* who get dumped owe a beer to each of their colleagues.) But it isn't life-threatening water unless you forget all the instructions of the previous three hours (guides deliberately dump people in easy rapids, get stuck on rocks, describe all the horrifying accidents that have occurred, and otherwise attempt to turn the early portions of the trip into a tutorial on respecting the power of the river and the relative helplessness of the rafters, so *most* people appreciate the Gap when it comes, and give it the respect it deserves). Though the most exciting portion is short-lived, cascades of adrenaline are still guaranteed.

Upper Deerfield trips (advertised as "Dryway" or "Monroe Bridge" runs) feature enough Class III-IV rapids that the thrill-a-minute adrenaline rushes are broken only by anticipatory lulls in which everyone in the boat tries to find a more secure foothold. Minimum age on this portion is 14 (minimum age on the lower river is seven), and previous experience (on whitewater) is advised, although outfitters take anyone who sounds competent.

Outfitters based in Charlemont begin running trips in early April, when snowmelt naturally keeps the river raging, and continue well into the fall as long as the local power company has enough water behind its dams to make big releases on behalf of recreational paddlers. The two largest and most experienced companies are **Crab Apple Whitewater,** tel. (800) 553-7238, www.crabappleinc.com, and locally owned **Zoar Outdoor,** tel. (800) 532-7483 or (413)

339-4010, e-mail zoarout@aol.com. Trips include either a picnic lunch along the riverbank or a cookout upon return to base camp. Weekend trips are more expensive than weekday runs, and the more difficult Dryway excursions are priced higher than those on the Lower Deerfield. Wet suit rentals are usually extra-or, of course, you can bring your own (they're generally unnecessary in summer, when air temperatures are high enough to offset the frigidity of the mountain-fed waters). For maximum savings, sign up for one of the first trips of spring (not only are prices slashed, but wet suits are thrown in for free).

Anyone fit can make the trip; people with disabilities are accommodated with special trips on boats fitted with oar rigs for the guide. Otherwise, it's the passengers who do all the paddling—your river guide just issues commands and encouragement, and steers the boat. Trips have become so popular that the companies have no problem reaching their permitted limit of 130 people daily, particularly on weekends at the height of summer. Reservations must always be made at least a day or two in advance (to allow for adequate equipment and guide preparation), but you should try to reserve a month or more in advance for weekend trips. Midweek even in summer isn't so problematic, but a week or two would still be prudent advance notice.

April through October, Zoar Outdoor also offers individual and group kayaking lessons and skills clinics; call for details and prices.

Staying on Terra Firma

The area is rich with hiking opportunities, too, of course—although finding either trail maps or trailheads takes more effort than you may be accustomed to. Even when you do find them, the trails up here are often so little used as practically to require bushwhacking, anyway.

There are plenty of great unpaved forest roads for mountain bikers who appreciate scenery and are up for some strenuous hills. Even the paved roads pose formidable challenges for slick-tire cyclists willing to burn their thighs on steep grades in exchange for lots of crisp, pine-scented air. At press time, bicycling was still relatively obscure up here—the state's urban bikers, if they bother hopping into a car at all, find it more convenient to take the interstates to the growing mountain-bike meccas of northern New England's ski resorts. But bike rentals are becoming available locally (look for rows of shiny new bikes lined up next to relaxed-looking folks in lawn chairs by the side of the road). And, with proper route planning and car racks, if your Mohawk Trail wanderings are based out of accommodations closer to the urban heart of the Pioneer Valley, there's no reason not to consider renting gear slightly farther afield—in the Five College area around Northampton or Amherst.

Shelburne Falls

Actually comprising the principal villages of two adjoining towns—Shelburne and Buckland—Shelburne Falls is a picturesque little paradise of crafts, gifts, artisans, and galleries—with some unusual sights and a handful of "travelers' necessaries" thrown in.

The Deerfield River runs through the center of this Victorian town, a fact that brought about what is today one of Shelburne Falls' prettiest features—the **Bridge of Flowers,** an old trolley bridge now liberally festooned with flowers and used exclusively for pedestrian traffic. For a bit of *natural* spectacle, check out the glacially-sculpted **"potholes"** just east of Bridge St., below Salmon Falls. Now incorporated into the diminutive Deerfield Dam and Powerhouse #3, the falls and their potholed riverbed are a favorite venue for picnics, after-school hanging out, boulder-hopping, and peoplewatching. Just don't doze off—the dam makes frequent releases of water, especially during the whitewater rafting season. (The potholes aren't just a natural attraction but also a point of local pride. In the restored 450-seat Memorial Hall Theater, 51 Bridge St., for example, an outfit calling itself Pothole Pictures presents last-run movies, generally on Friday at 8 p.m.)

For travelers, Shelburne Falls can be an oasis not just for shopping and sightseeing. Restaurants like the red-meat-free Copper Angel (overlooking the Bridge of Flowers from the Buckland side), the vegetarian-friendly deli at the back of McCuskers Market (across the street), and the Shelburne Falls Coffee Roasters (on Bridge St., over the river) cater to the cosmopolitan tastes of locals and visitors alike, all at quite reasonable

Mohawk Trail "trading post," East Charlemont

prices. An ATM, and the public restrooms in the tourist information center—both on Bridge St.—may make you happier than the sight of the flower-covered bridge. **Note** that west of Shelburne Falls, dining and accommodations options drop off dramatically until you enter the Berkshires, on the other side of the Hoosac Range. Neither will you find any ATMs between Shelburne Falls and North Adams. And gas, in the few places it's to be found, isn't cheap.

Charlemont and Vicinity

Originally auctioned off to settlers as Township Number Two, Charlemont derives its name from the appellation "Charles's Mount," so it's called CHARL-MONT (not SHARLAMONT). Besides having become the nominal center for whitewater rafting in the state, it's a remarkably well-situated jumping-off point for exploring *three* state forests. **Mohawk Trail State Forest** boasts miles of hiking trails, a swimming hole, and a campground with more than 50 sites spread out in clusters among the conifers alongside the well-named Cold River. Open May through mid-October, the property features full toilet and shower facilities but no RV hookups of any kind. Reservations for its $6 sites may be made by calling (413) 339-5504. (There are also five rustic year-round cabins for $8 and $10 per night, depending on size; these must be reserved for a minimum of two days in winter, by the week in summer, and generally book up six months in advance.) At **Monroe State Forest,** one highlight for hikers is the trip up to Raycroft Lookout, a panoramic old viewing spot built by the CCC near the top of the valley, above Zoar Road. Monroe also has a handful of free wilderness campsites. On Rt. 8A south of the Mohawk Trail, **Kenneth Dubuque Memorial State Forest** contains a historic charcoal kiln (rebuilt by a Tibetan mason from Greenfield—a man who possesses a tooth of the Dalai Lama), Moody Springs (a mineral flow prized for its alleged curative powers), and 15 free wilderness campsites.

LIBRARY OF CONGRESS/LC-D418-68524 DLC

THE BERKSHIRES

Berkshire County, the westernmost part of Massachusetts, is home to some of the state's most varied topography. Here, the valleys of the south-flowing Housatonic and the north-flowing Hoosic are flanked by the state's highest peaks. Here, the Appalachian Trail—that 2,000-mile footpath from Maine to Georgia—traverses large undeveloped tracts of state forest. Here, too, are small towns as quaint as any in New England.

Drawn by the clemency of the area's summer weather, the great mansion-building industrialists of last century's Gilded Age turned this region into one of the nation's premier resorts. Today, the Berkshires (as these hills and valleys are colloquially known) are home to a good dozen or more major performing arts festivals each summer, the weekenders filling up the romantic Victorian bed and breakfast inns are as likely to come for the fine arts as for the fresh air.

Historically, the Berkshires have been a place apart. Prior to European contact, the region was a cultural and linguistic intervale between Algonquian-speaking Pocumtucks to the east and Mohawks from the powerful Iroquois league to the west. Whether because of Mohawk attacks or diseases brought by Dutch traders venturing up the Hudson River, the area was all but uninhabited by the onset of English colonization. Mountainous topography hindered travel and farming, although by the early 1700s a few hardy settlers had ventured up river valleys from the north and south. The tug-o'-war between European colonial powers also inhibited early settlement—the English farmsteads on such a remote frontier were too easily harassed by Indian proxies armed by the French. Only after the French and Indian War ended, in the 1760s, could Massachusetts persuade real-estate speculators to cast a favorable eye on the territory—although until the end of the American Revolution, the region was also claimed by New York (and, given, the number of Manhattanites who flock to the region every summer, it often seems as if New York is still trying). Since the region falls into the blind spot that Bostonians—and state government—have for anything west of the interstate beltway, Berkshirites have had plenty of second thoughts about the outcome of those old boundary disputes.

In practical, spoken, and ideological terms, the county is divided between north and south, with Pittsfield and Lenox in between. North

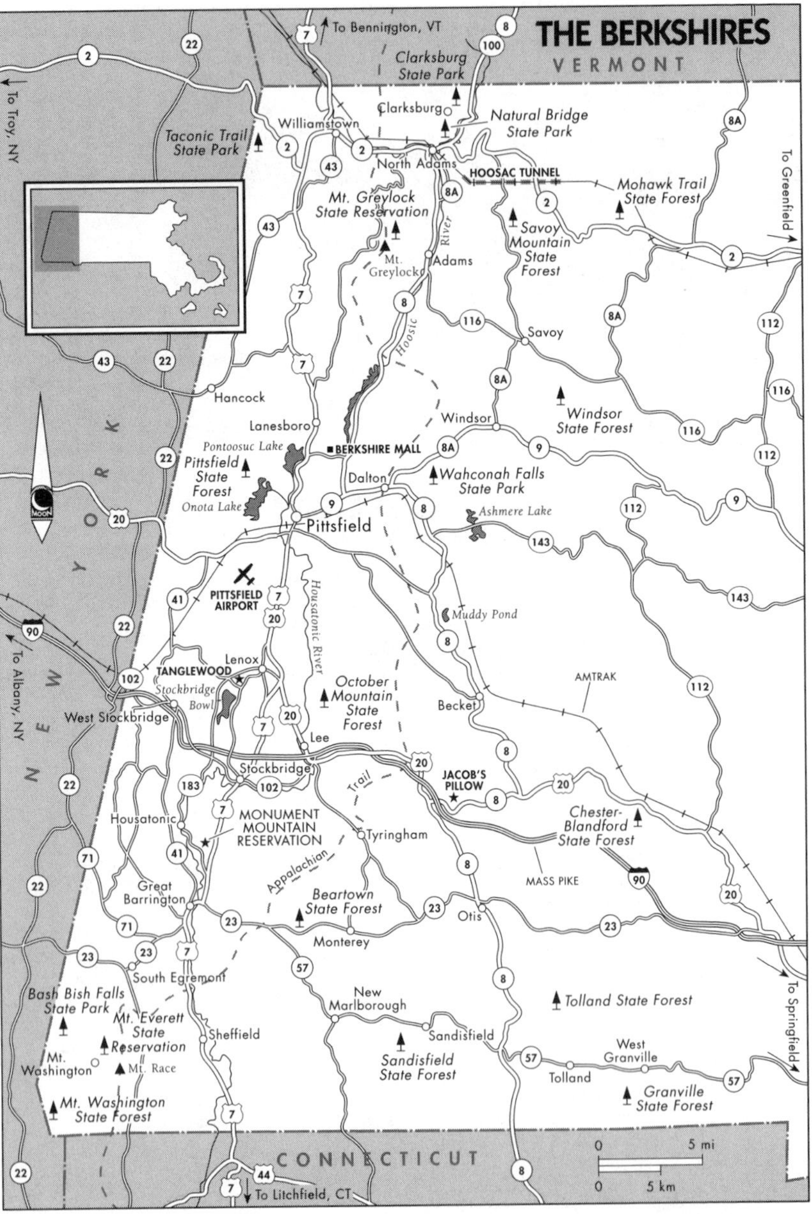

THE BERKSHIRES
VERMONT
CONNECTICUT
NEW YORK
To Bennington, VT
To Troy, NY
To Greenfield
To Albany, NY
To Springfield
To Litchfield, CT
Clarksburg State Park
Clarksburg
Natural Bridge State Park
Williamstown
North Adams
HOOSAC TUNNEL
Taconic Trail State Park
Mohawk Trail State Forest
Mt. Greylock State Reservation
Mt. Greylock
Adams
Savoy Mountain State Forest
Hoosic River
Savoy
Hancock
Lanesboro
Windsor
Windsor State Forest
Pontoosuc Lake
BERKSHIRE MALL
Pittsfield State Forest
Dalton
Wahconah Falls State Park
Onota Lake
Pittsfield
Ashmere Lake
PITTSFIELD AIRPORT
Housatonic River
Muddy Pond
AMTRAK
Lenox
TANGLEWOOD
Stockbridge Bowl
West Stockbridge
October Mountain State Forest
Becket
Lee
Stockbridge
JACOB'S PILLOW
Housatonic
MONUMENT MOUNTAIN RESERVATION
Tyringham
Chester-Blandford State Forest
Appalachian Trail
MASS PIKE
Great Barrington
Beartown State Forest
Otis
Monterey
South Egremont
New Marlborough
Tolland State Forest
Bash Bish Falls State Park
Mt. Everett State Reservation
Sheffield
Sandisfield
Mt. Washington
Mt. Race
Sandisfield State Forest
West Granville
Tolland
Granville State Forest
Mt. Washington State Forest
0 5 mi
0 5 km
© MOON PUBLICATIONS, INC.

THE APPALACHIAN TRAIL

The Appalachian Mountains stretch more than 2,000 miles, from Springer Mountain, Georgia, to Katahdin, Maine. The foot trail that runs along this rugged spine—familiarly known as the AT—is a National Scenic Trail, administered and maintained by an alliance of hiking and nonprofit outdoor groups. One of these is the Appalachian Mountain Club (AMC), which oversees the 88 miles of the trail that fall within Massachusetts. Between Sage's Ravine, near the Connecticut border, and the Clarksburg State Forest, near Vermont, the AT hits the highs and lows of the Berkshires, from the floodplains of the Housatonic to the top of Mt. Greylock. Several state forests contain portions of the AT, allowing day-hikers to sample this famous route. Three-sided shelters spaced a day's hike apart make overnight stays possible—and, if you set up a car shuttle, you can save yourself from having to retrace your footsteps.

Berkshire Regional Transit Authority bus routes cross the AT near the trail campsite in Clarksburg and again about 30 miles south, near the Kay Wood shelter, in Dalton; they also come within a two-hour hike of the Tom Leonard shelter, 40 miles farther south, in Great Barrington. So public transit can also aid in completing a loop within all but the AT's southern portion. Call BRTA, (413) 499-BRTA, to request a free system map and schedule.

To best plan an overnight on the AT in Massachusetts, get hold of a copy of the detailed *Guide to the Appalachian Trail in Massachusetts & Connecticut,* published by the Appalachian Trail Conference, overseers of the entire trail. Find the guide at Bascom Lodge, on Mt. Greylock or local bookstores or outfitters; or order by phone from the AMC, tel. (800) 262-4455.

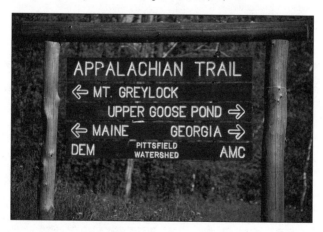

County is less traveled and has smaller towns and fewer tourist amenities, although its attractions are certainly nothing to sneeze at. South County, physically separated from the rest by the MassPike, is by turns stereotypical and conventional (Norman Rockwell Country), honest and artistic (Great Barrington), and unpaved and out-of-the-way (High Roads and Low Roads). In the middle are a pair of polar opposites: Pittsfield, the manufacturing town wounded by the 1980s recession, and Lenox, the attractive epicenter of all the cozy inns and high culture Western Massachusetts has to offer.

The common thread is the great outdoors, which is never more than a few turns away. Whether discovered deliberately or accidentally, the Berkshires back roads reward curiosity with sculpture gardens and antique stores, farmstands and waterfalls, "u-pick" orchards, multistate vistas, and ever-abundant foliage.

BERKSHIRE FOLIAGE REPORTS

State foresters' recorded foliage reports are available beginning in mid-September by calling the Massachusetts Office of Travel & Tourism hotline, (800) 227-MASS, and selecting the appropriate menu option, or by visiting the Web site www.mass-vacation.com.

THE LAND

Berkshire County owes its geological characteristics and plant communities to a pair of ancient mountain-building epochs, or orogenies, and to the equatorial location of the Laurentia continental plate, the portion of the earth's crust that now underlies much of North America. Sediments from the bottom of the early ocean Iapetus were uplifted by Laurentia's collision with a smaller plate of primordial volcanic islands ringed by lime-secreting coral reefs. This scrunching together (more than 400 million years ago, during the first Appalachian orogen) produced mountains here as tall as the Rockies, but millions of years of erosion wore those great peaks down and spread their soils all the way to Michigan. What's left is today's Taconic Range.

Tectonic convergence of Laurentia—the island precursor to England and Northern Europe—and Gondwana (whose leading edge back then is now northwest Africa) resumed about 350 million years ago, launching the second major phase of Appalachian orogeny. Over a few hundred million years, this dynamic geological event buckled the worn-down nubbins of the ancient Taconics—in effect turning them on their side, with the oldest foundation layers exposed to the west and younger layers to the east. (The spindling also produced anomalies in which younger rock seems to lie beneath older.) The heat and pressure of the affected continents metamorphosed the calcerous (lime-bearing) layers of tropical coral into marble and those Iapetus sediments into schists and gneiss. As the soft marble eroded faster than hard neighboring schistose layers, the Berkshire valley was hollowed out. The soil composition at higher elevations is thus more acidic than the lime-buffered valley below, and the community of small shrubs

and wildflowers differs accordingly, with such unusual alkali-loving plants as the delicate hooded ladies' tresses and fen cuckoo flower inhabiting the Housatonic and Hoosac floodplains.

GETTING THERE AND AROUND

Boston is by no means the only choice for Berkshire-bound travelers arriving by a scheduled airline. **Albany,** New York, is the county's nearest major airport—and Connecticut's **Bradley Airport,** outside Hartford, is a close second. The only direct train to the area is Amtrak's Lake Shore Limited, which stops in Pittsfield on its daily run between Chicago and Boston. The eastbound train arrives shortly after noon, the westbound near sundown. Given that Pittsfield's "station" is no more than a broken-plexiglass bus shelter beside a small parking lot in a large vacant area near to (but out of sight of) the town square, you won't want to arrive late unless you plan to stay at the Pittsfield Crowne Plaza, two blocks away. (It's about six blocks to the nearest car rental agency, but it closes about an hour or two before the train arrives from Boston.) For passengers from the south, connecting service is available through Albany-Rensselaer from New York City (Penn Station). Call (800) USA-RAIL for schedules and fares, or visit Amtrak's homepage: www.amtrak.com.

Long-distance bus service to the area is provided by **Peter Pan Bus Lines,** tel. (800) 343-9999 or (413) 781-3320, and **Bonanza Bus Lines,** tel. (800) 556-3815 or (401) 751-8800. From Boston, Peter Pan has a single evening bus to Williamstown and North Adams via Springfield and the Five Colleges (plus a morning bus on Fridays), arriving late enough to require special arrangements or guaranteed reservations at any in-town accommodations. The three daily departures from Boston to the central Berkshires (Lee, Lenox, and Pittsfield) are much more conveniently timed to catch Pittsfield's car rental agencies or regional public transit during normal operating hours. From Manhattan's Port

---

For Berkshire County weather forecasts 24 hours a day, call (413) 499-2627.

Authority, Bonanza offers several daily buses up the Housatonic River valley through Connecticut and the Berkshires, stopping at every town on US 7 from Sheffield to Williamstown. Additional May-Sept. service substitutes South Egremont for Sheffield. As for riders coming from upstate New York or Toronto, the US 20 route from Albany to Pittsfield, Lenox, and Lee is shared by both bus companies.

Getting Around

If you intend to rent a car locally, about your only practicable options are **Enterprise Rent-A-Car,** 558 East St. in Pittsfield, tel. (800) 325-8007 or (413) 443-6600, or **Larkin's Car Store,** on South Main in Great Barrington, tel. (413) 528-2156. (Don't worry about schlepping out to South Main from Bonanza's downtown bus stop—Larkin's has free local pickup and delivery.) Bicycle rentals—predominantly hybrids and mountain bikes—are available from **The Spoke Bicycles,** 620 Main in Williamstown, tel. (413) 458-3456; **Plaine's,** 55 W. Housatonic in Pittsfield, tel. (413) 499-0294 (includes helmets and locks free; also rents road bikes); **Main Street Sports & Leisure,** 102 Main in Lenox, tel. (413) 637-4407; and **Gaffer's Outdoors,** on Main St. in Sheffield, tel. (413) 229-0063. Generally, car racks are on hand at all these stores, but if you're certain to need one, call ahead to ensure that it has your name on it.

The Berkshire Regional Transit Authority operates eight interurban bus routes, known as "the B," through all but the county's southern quarter, Mon.-Sat. until 6 p.m. year-round. Pittsfield is the system's hub, and most routes serve its neighborhoods and shopping centers, but there's hourly service south—via the downtowns of Lenox, Lee, Stockbridge, and Housatonic—to Great Barrington, and also north along Rt. 8 to Adams, North Adams, and (via a transfer) Williamstown. Fares vary by distance, from 60 cents within Pittsfield to $6 between Williamstown and Great Barrington. Inquire at any local tourist information booth to obtain a system map and schedule, or call (800) 292-BRTA or (413) 499-BRTA.

NORTH COUNTY

The county's separation from the rest of Massachusetts is most keenly felt in the northern Berkshires, whose formidable, mountain-imposed isolation was finally pierced by the late 19th-century Hoosac Tunnel. This rail link spurred local manufacturing and finally gave the state a grip on its northwestern corner. Don't be fooled by the map: though within only 40 miles from interstates on each of three sides, this deeply scenic area is still well insulated from the speed-driven world outside. Count on at least an hour of traversing curvy ups and downs with long, slow grades and only the occasional passing lane, with an intermittent corridor of small towns and villages along the river valleys. It's well worth the effort—whether you like culture, nature, history, gastronomy, or simply great views out the window. Unless you're camping (or staying at North Adams' Holiday Inn), collegiate Williamstown has the widest array of accommodations, and almost (but not quite) monopolizes the region's good eating, too.

WILLIAMSTOWN

Secreted away in its own far corner, Williamstown is the home of Williams College, a prestigious liberal-arts institution whose idyllic campus is nearly inseparable from the town itself. A generous sampling of sturdy Georgian architecture lends the tiny community (pop. 8,400) such a classic look of colonial New England that one half-expects to see townsfolk striding around in frock coats and black buckle shoes. But the annual influx of some 2,000 students helps keep "Billsville" from getting too stuffy. Wooded mountains rise gently on nearly all sides, creating a beautiful setting for the town's lofty church towers and chapel spires.

Town and college have a common origin, in the will of a colonial land surveyor and commander of Fort Massachusetts—the last of a string of frontier garrisons built in the 1740s to counter French influence among the Mohawks and to repel Dutch advances east of the Hud-

Miss Linley and Her Brother *(1768)*, by Thomas Gainsborough, hangs in the Sterling and Francine Clark Art Institute.

STERLING AND FRANCINE CLARK ART INSTITUTE

son. (A fieldstone chimney from a long-demolished Mohawk Trail tourist restaurant built on the fort site is all that marks the spot today, at the back of a supermarket parking lot on Rt. 2 in North Adams.) One of the area's earliest English settlers, Ephraim Williams, Jr., acquired a very comfortable chunk of property in the town west of the fort, which is where his will stipulated that a school be founded. Nearly 40 years passed before his wishes could be fulfilled, not because the bequest was contingent upon renaming the town in his memory (a condition that was easily and happily met), but because it required resolution of territorial boundary claims on the town to be settled in favor of Massachusetts.

Free Art
Fans of French Impressionism may simply swoon upon wandering through the **Sterling and Francine Clark Art Institute,** on South St., tel. (413) 458-9545, whose collection includes over 30 Renoir paintings and a generous sampling of Degas, Monet, and others. Built by an heir to the Singer sewing machine fortune, the museum was located here in part out of a

Cold War concern that New York City was too likely a target for Khruschev's missiles. This gem also has noteworthy exhibits of silver, sculpture, 19th-century American paintings, and works of the Italian Renaissance. Completely free, the Clark is open Tues.-Sun. year-round, plus Monday holidays between Memorial Day and Columbus Day.

A pleasant stroll away toward the middle of campus is the **Williams College Museum of Art** (also free), tucked behind the octagonal brick facade of the former college library on Main St, tel. (413) 597-2429. Although there are hundreds of works spanning the broad chronology of visual arts, the exceptional collection is particularly strong in contemporary and non-Western art. Temporary installations are frequently featured, including a regular series of site-specific work. Open Tues-Sun. year-round, and Monday holidays in summer.

Founding Notions
Although difficult to find, the free **Chapin Library of Rare Books,** tel. (413) 597-2462, is worth tracking down for the glimpse it gives of the nation's founding documents. Displayed here in one room are historic handwritten copies of the Declaration of Independence and Articles of Confederation, a draft of the U.S. Constitution, two early versions of The Bill of Rights, and George Washington's copy of *The Federalist Papers.* Examples of the library's many other treasures are also occasionally displayed. Prized possessions include a copy of Dante's *Divine Comedy* illustrated with woodblock prints, the first four folios of William Shakespeare, an illuminated 9th-century vellum copy of the four Gospels commissioned by Charlemagne, and other incunabula—especially in the sciences. One artifact which rarely leaves storage is the complete bound edition of Audubon's *Birds of America,* as its double elephant folio size is prohibitively large for any display case (imagine doubling your average open newspaper and you'll get the idea). The library, open weekdays only and closed between noon and 1 p.m. for lunch, is located on the second floor of Stetson Hall, the ivy-covered building farthest back behind the gothic cathedral-like hulk of Memorial Hall, across Main St. from the college art museum.

ADDITIONAL WILLIAMSTOWN ACCOMMODATIONS

Best Western Springs Motor Inn, on rural stretch of US 7 beneath Mt. Greylock in New Ashford, tel. (800) 528-1234 or (413) 458-5945; $60-95 d, $98-120 on Tanglewood weekends.

Chimney Mirror Motel, 295 Main St. (Rt. 2), tel. (413) 458-5202; $48-88 d.

Four Acres Motel, 213 Main St. (Rt. 2), tel. (413) 458-8158, www.fouracresmotel.com; $55-105 d.

Maple Terrace Motel, 555 Main St. (Rt. 2), tel. (413) 458-9677, www.mapleterrace.com; $49-83 d.

Northside Motel, 45 North St. (US 7 North), tel. (413) 458-8107; $50-77 d.

The 1896 Motels: Brookside and Pondside, Cold Spring Rd. (US 7 South), tel. (413) 458-8125, www.1896house.com; $41-108 d.

The Willows, 480 Main St. (Rt. 2), tel. (413) 458-5768; $55-75 d.

Villager Motel, 953 Simonds Rd. (US 7 North), tel. (413) 458-4046; $50-85 d.

Performing Arts

Now in its fifth decade, the **Williamstown Theatre Festival** is a highly respected showcase for the nation's leading stage actors (many of whom are familiar to TV and movie audiences, too). Productions range from old chestnuts and classics (with a conspicuous fondness for Tennessee Williams) to more recent plays and, in the cozy but air-conditioned confines of "The Other Stage," works-in-progress by newer playwrights. An outdoor event known simply as "the Free Theatre" has a short run each season, usually on the college's Buxton Field—but otherwise, all main stage performances are held in the Adams Memorial Theatre, a Greek Revival structure on Main St. between North and Park. The two-month Festival runs from late June through late August, with evening performances Tuesday or Wednesday through Saturday, plus Thursday and weekend matinees. Call (413) 597-3399 for a pre-recorded schedule, or contact the box office, tel. (413) 597-3400, to charge tickets by phone.

Camping and Accommodations

Excellent tent camping awaits about eight miles northeast of Williamstown at **Clarksburg State Park,** off Rt. 8 north of North Adams, tel. (413) 663-8469. Nearly 50 sites are well spaced amid a varied, wooded area, often shielded from each other by shrubs and topography. Some overlook an adjacent swimming pond. Since amenities are limited to drinking water and pit toilets, campsites are just $4 a night, available on a first-come, first-served basis mid-May through mid-Sept. Given the spectacular fall foliage, it seems almost criminal that Clarksburg's season is so short, but that's what happens when the state park system is chronically underfunded.

Lodging options range from moderately priced family-run motels and bed and breakfast homes to a pair of luxury inns. Arriving in town without reservations isn't wise throughout much of the year: besides graduation, Williams gives dedicated older alumni frequent excuses to return for gatherings of one sort or another, and occupancy levels rise in response to everything from Saratoga Springs horse racing (90 minutes west) to the cultural summer smorgasbord throughout the central and southern Berkshires. One side effect is the two-night minimums at most B&Bs and several of the motels and inns during summer and fall foliage weekends.

Representative of the town's B&Bs are **The Williamstown B&B,** on US 7 a few steps south of Main St. and the town green, tel. (413) 458-9202; and **Goldberry's** across the street, tel. (413) 458-3935. Both serve full breakfasts and are moderate in price, and neither accepts credit cards. Comparable rates are found among the string of small, plainly furnished motels lining the commercial strip on Main St. (Rt. 2) east of campus or US 7 north—throwbacks to a pre-Interstate era of motor touring. The Main St. strip also comprises **The Orchards,** tel. (800) 225-1517 or (413) 458-9611, whose English antiques, Oriental carpets, and living-room grand piano epitomize the upper stratum of the town's available accommodations. Luxury.

For a truly rural experience, consider TTOR's **Field Farm,** 554 Sloan Rd. in South Williamstown, tel. (413) 458-3135. More country estate than working farm, the 254-acre former home of Pacific Northwest lumber heir (and Williams alumnus) Lawrence Bloedel encompasses some of the most scenic views in all Berkshire County. Guests may enjoy the views over continental breakfast, while playing tennis, snowshoeing the property's trails, or lounging by the shallow outdoor pool. Giant picture windows on the 1948 contemporary's facade hint at its exemplary American Modern design, carried through to the interior decor in textbook style, from authentic Charles Eames and Arne Jacobsen furniture right down to the Lucite drawer pulls. The Bloedels' substantial collection of modern art was donated to the Williams College Museum of Art, but many pieces are on permanent loan to the farm and dot the house and grounds. Expensive (cash or checks only).

Food

Do students live on pizza alone? Williamstown's eateries certainly lend credence to this conclusion. Do students care if what they eat is any good? The quality of the pizza served here suggests that on this subject, at least, Williams College could use some curricular review. Why so many smart people are willing to settle for bad food is as mysterious as the popularity of bad beer. The point of this small lesson is simply that if you've graduated to something better than a slice of pallid dough with a slather of red sauce and canned mushrooms, you'll want to make a beeline for **Hot Tomatoes,** 100 Water St., tel. (413) 458-2722, strictly take-out (but there are picnic tables out back on the banks of the Green River). Open daily 7 a.m.-2 p.m. and 4:30-11:30 p.m. in summer, till 1 a.m. during the school year. **Michael's Pizza,** at 460 Main St. (Rt. 2), on the commercial strip east of the town center, tel. (413) 458-2114, has a runner-up with its top-heavy vegetarian pizza, but otherwise stick to eggplant parmesan or spanakopita to appreciate why this no-frills leatherette-and-veneer place is so popular. Closed Monday but otherwise open for lunch and dinner.

If you prefer burgers or fajitas to pizzas, consider checking out **The Water Street Grill,** diagonally across the street from Hot Tomatoes and a tad south, in the neocolonial house at number 123, tel. (413) 458-2175. The Grill's wood planks, beams, and fireplace are appropriate to its all-American surf-and-turf menu, supplemented by barbecue ribs and fajitas.

These last are also available in the tavern up front, which is otherwise the province of the burger-and-nachos crowd and, on Friday and Saturday nights, live acoustic music. Tavern and grill are both open daily for lunch and dinner (to 11 p.m.), with the bar open to 1 a.m. For something with more panache than buffalo wings, try **Mezze,** 84 Water, tel. (413) 458-0123, an attractive little Mediterranean-style bistro complete with a balcony overlooking the quick little Green River. Appetizers here are sized for sharing or for combining to constitute a full meal; prices are reasonable, too. Take advantage of the late-serving kitchen for a postprandial dessert at the very least—they're definitely worth staying up for. Open daily for dinner and weekends for lunch.

Equally laid back yet more upscale in price and preparation is **Robin's Restaurant,** under the blue awning at the end of nearby Spring St., tel. (413) 458-4489. You can lunch on a sandwich laden with leeks and Black Forest ham, or platters of rich creamy patés with country breads and fresh mixed green salads; dine on prime rib with sour cream horseradish, fresh ravioli with seasonal vegetables, a mixed grill of gourmet sausages and tender duck leg, or perhaps roasted native trout with a citrus sauce. Good portions and relaxed atmosphere take the edge off the prices. The view from the deck in summer is like something out of a Colorado ski town, with the old-fashioned commercial brick buildings stretching up the street and, in the distance, over the college art museum, the forested slope of East Mountain. A weekend brunch is also served.

If all these highfalutin options sound too rich, head up to **Pappa Charlie's Deli,** 28 Spring St., tel. (413) 458-5969, a proper inexpensive sandwich counter the names of whose offerings almost constitute a cultural literacy trivia quiz (remember Bebe Rebozo?). Most of the names have some connection to the college or town (if you know what Bo Derek and Billsville have in common, you've suffered exposure to some very obscure media indeed). Across the street, at the **Cobble Cafe,** tel. (413) 458-5930, twins Sandy and Ned Smith create fresh, inspired, and regularly changing dishes that will have you glancing outside just to be sure you're not in San Francisco. The decor, ambiance, and wine list will certainly reinforce the California impression (until a cluster of smokers lights up in the one-room dining area), but the tab will be mercifully more modest. Lots of good desserts change with the seasons and the chef's whims. If pecan pie is on the menu, be assured that it's the best east of Texas—not at all gooey or too sweet. Serving breakfast daily, lunch Mon.-Sat. to 3 p.m., and dinner. The Cobble's owners also have a larger, dinner-only restaurant, the **Wild Amber Grill,** a few blocks away at 101 North St. (US 7), tel. (413) 458-4000. Some very exciting ethnic notes grace the menu, although more conservative, classic preparations also appeal to alumni and parents who stay at the adjacent Williamstown Inn. Entree prices in the $15-22 range certainly keep students at bay. Any filet mignon aficionados feeling snubbed by most of my restaurant recommendations should definitely consider a pilgrimmage, as should dessert lovers: all the sweet endings are made in house with excellent results. Open nightly except Tuesdays. Reservations accepted and, on summer weekends, strongly advised.

Just next door to the Cobble, at 37 Spring, is the **Clarksburg Bread Co.,** tel. (413) 458-2251, a strong contender in the Berkshires' Best Bread Sweepstakes. Owners Dale and Jamie Ott also offer a tempting array of other sweet and savory goods, from cookies, muffins, and cakes to soups and sandwiches. Open Tues.-Sat. 7 a.m.-4 p.m. If arriving late in town, you can still pick up their bread, at least, at the local natural foods co-op, **Wild Oats Community Market,** in the Colonial Shopping Center on Rt. 2, east of town. Campers and hikers in particular may appreciate the big selection of bulk items. The Appalachian Trail crosses Rt. 2 about 1.5 miles east of Wild Oats' door.

Information

During the summer months, the **Williamstown Board of Trade,** tel. (413) 458-9077, staffs an information booth on the corner of Main and North Sts., next to the Williams Inn. Accommodations brochures, advertisers' guides to both ends of the Berkshires, and the weekly *What's On*—an arts-oriented events calendar covering everything from movies and theatre to current exhibitions and gallery talks—are all dispensed free, along with directions, if needed.

NORTH ADAMS

Straddling both the Hoosic River and the rail link between eastern Massachusetts and upstate New York, North Adams for most of its life throve on manufacturing. The huge brick mills lining the river banks downtown were built to answer the demand for printed cotton. After textiles started moving south, where "union" was still a dirty word, electronics took a turn on the huge shop floors. Besides building the circuitry that helped detonate the first atomic bombs, Sprague Electric Company rode the coattails of America's postwar love affair with quiz shows and sitcoms, churning out capacitors for TV sets. When this industry, too, found cheaper labor, North Adams lost its last major assembly line. It took a long time for the city to wake up to the fact that manufacturing wasn't coming back, and in the meantime, a significant number of the city's empty 19th-century commercial buildings were turned into parking lots or replaced by generic modern storefronts. Now that historic preservation is more widely appreciated, the huge old mills and remaining downtown blocks are being renovated rather than demolished. And, hard though it may be for some of the old guard to accept, the leading light in the city's revival is, of all things, modern art.

MASS MoCA

When the Massachusetts Museum of Contemporary Art, or MASS MoCA, (413) 664-4481, opens its first 200,000 square feet of exhibition space, in early 1999, it will instantly rank as one of the largest art museums in the nation. If the ultimate grand design for the 13-acre, 28-building old Sprague mill complex is ever acheived, it will be the largest art museum in the world. Regardless of whether it ever gets to fulfill the civic dream of displaying a site-specific, half-mile-long work by Claes Oldenburg, the museum is already achieving its vision of becoming a true multidisciplinary cultural center. Collaborators in this mission range from New York's Guggenheim Museum and the Japanese American Cultural & Community Center of Los Angeles (each of which will loan works or sponsor live arts performances) to Internet content and film special effects producers (which are leasing research and development space). Don't assume that this museum keeps regular daylight hours, either: a nightclub, Mort Cooperman's **Night Shift Cafe,** is one of the tenants, and, since 1995, this founder of New York's storied Lone Star Cafe has featured regular weekend performances covering a spectrum wide enough to include both Ani de Franco and Willie Nelson. All of which complements MASS MoCA's visual arts exhibits, which include hundreds of sculptures and oversized installations from the 1960s and '70s drawn from the famous collection of Count Giuseppe Panza di Biumo. Parts of the complex are opening to the public as they are completed, and weekend hard-hat tours show visitors the sections still under renovation. By all means, drop by Marshall St. just north of the Rt. 2 overpass and see what's cooking.

Western Heritage State Park

Completion in 1875 of the Hoosac Tunnel transformed North Adams into a vital waypoint on the rail line between Boston, Albany, and the Great Lakes. Boring a 4.75-mile tunnel—the world's longest at the time—beneath Whitcomb Summit was no cakewalk: fortunes were spent, nearly 200 lives were lost, and a quarter-century of labor was expended. If an assistant engineer hadn't had a wintertime accident while transporting some new-fangled nitroglycerin (thus discovering that the stuff could be handled safely while frozen), the whole project might have ended in failure. (Which would have deprived Boston of Asian accents for who knows how long—it was Chinese workers from San Francisco, after all, escorted by Pinkerton guards to North Adams to break a strike at the Sampson shoe factory, who founded Boston's Chinatown. Without the Hoosac Tunnel, they'd have all ended up in New York City.) The

NO SASSING YOUR WAITRESS.

story of this engineering feat and the changes it wrought is the centerpiece of this historical museum, appropriately installed in old freight buildings and boxcars beside the Furnace St. Bypass on the edge of downtown. There's also plenty of railroad paraphernalia, and a large working model railroad layout. Donations are appreciated, but admission is free. Open daily year-round, except for the first two weeks of January; tel. (413) 663-6312.

Natural Bridge State Park

Compared to the great freestanding sandstone arches out west, Natural Bridge State Park's modest 30-foot span over impatient little Hudson Brook is a junior achiever. It's unique nonetheless, being the only *marble* natural bridge in all of North America. Nathaniel Hawthorne was but one of many 19th-century visitors to the site, and historic graffiti of some who followed him still remain, along with the considerable remains of the marble quarrying that lasted here until shortly after WW II. Picnic tables give you the opportunity to let the place grow on you a little—which it will if you set aside visions of a metamorphic Golden Gate. Parents can rest easy knowing there's plenty of safety fencing to keep little ones from going overboard. Open late May through mid-October, the park is signposted off Rt. 8 north of North Adams; admission $2 per car.

North Adams Food

For a cup of coffee, light sandwich fare, or baked goods, visit the **Appalachian Bean Cafe,** 67 Main St., tel. (413) 663-7543, in the historic commercial block opposite the all-too-modern Brooks Drugs. In the Holiday Inn down the street **Due Baci,** tel. (413) 664-6581, provides the city's only reason to eat in town, with hearty Italian food in a relaxed atmosphere. Diner fans, pie lovers, breakfast-at-noon devotees, or anyone headed south with an unsated appetite should otherwise make a beeline down Rt. 8 to attractive and modestly prosperous Adams, home of the delightful **Miss Adams Diner.** Sitting on Park St., across from the Congregational Church in the Capra-esque downtown—lined with what may be the state's last penny-operated parking meters—this 1949 original serves up classic Blue Plate meat-and-gravy dishes and con-

MISS ADAMS DINER

temporary ethnic and vegetarian specials with equal skill, Tues.-Sat. 6 a.m.-3 p.m. and Sunday till 1 p.m. Don't miss the homemade pies, either, even if you have to feed another penny to your meter.

MOUNT GREYLOCK

At 3,491 feet, Mt. Greylock's cool, windswept summit is Massachusetts' highest, and, despite the number of structures at the top, whenever the clouds part it offers visitors a superlative, three-state, 100-mile panorama. Though short and stubby by western U.S. standards, Greylock's steep, rugged slopes will challenge even jaded hikers. Given the varied terrain, number of intersecting trails, and potential for suddenly diminished visibility, a map is as important as good footwear. Before tackling the slopes, forearm youself with the appropriate topographics or trail guide; try The Mountain Goat, on Water St., in Williamstown; the Arcadian Shop, on US 7 nearly opposite the Quality Inn in Lenox; the Greylock visitor center, midway up from the southwest entrance; or the small book shop at the summit's Bascom Lodge. Perhaps the most informative of the available topo trail maps is also available by mail: send $4 to New England Cartographics, P.O. Box 9369, North Amherst MA 01059, tel. (413) 549-4124.

Until snows close the access roads, cars may ascend the summit via narrow, twisty, frostheaved old Notch Rd., off Rt. 2 between Williamstown and North Adams, or the long steady grind up the southwest flank from US 7 in Lanesboro. Respect the speed limits: around the next blind curve may be some local cyclists concentrating on their workout, or white-tailed deer sauntering across the road.

Sleeping at the Summit

It's hard to beat the sunset view from the enclosed porch of the Appalachian Mountain Club's **Bascom Lodge,** a rustic stone and timber affair a stone's throw from Greylock's summit. "Rustic" is no idle poeticism: the single-sex shared bunkrooms (only four rooms are private) are as plain as pine planks, and showers are strictly cold water. Up here, nights, even in the height of summer, can be quite brisk if not downright near freezing, so pack accordingly. The experience of staying at this historic lodge can't be topped, even though there's nothing rustic about the price: nonmember rates start at $30 pp, $35 pp on Saturday nights and all of August. For $5-15 more, you can include breakfast, dinner, or both. The AMC members' discount is high enough ($7 per night) to warrant serious consideration of joining (individual membership is $40), especially if you think you might want to stay in any of the other AMC-operated alpine huts scattered along the Appalachian Trail through New Hampshire. Bascom Lodge, like all the AMC properties, is wildly popular, so make reservations a month or more in advance, if possible, by calling (413) 443-0011. If you're hoping to find a space tonight, you may have a chance if you arrive on a midweek day outside of August, but call (413) 743-1591 to check on current week availability. The lodge is open midMay through late October.

The mountain's only **campground** is on Sperry Rd., below the summit's western side, with 35 campsites—some with very good setbacks from each other and the road—spread along an unpaved spur. No showers are available, toilets are outhouses, and there's *no potable water* unless you've got high-tech purifying gear to deal with the nearby streams (for the closest drinking water, it's more than a mile to Bascom, three to four miles to the Visitor Center). Camping costs but $4 a night, Memorial Day through mid-October. Sperry Road dead-ends at Stony Ledge, a beautiful picnic spot with a spectacular view down into the Hopper, a distinctive, troughlike feature on the western flank, into which flow a pair of small brooks. The ledge looks out over one of the few old-growth forests in Massachusetts, with stands of red spruce more than 150 years old—in addition to those streambeds 1,400 feet below and Greylock's summit, the highest of the four peaks across the valley, 1,000 feet above.

The campground usually gets busy on holidays, but visitation fluctuates year to year much more than at the lodge. Even Fourth of July weekends have been known to boast available space. Reservations aren't accepted, but if you haven't made reservations, call (413) 499-4262 to find out whether it's already full for the night you're there.

LONG HIKES AND HIGH VISTAS

Because of its height and the Appalachian Trail traversing its peak, Mt. Greylock gets the lion's share of attention from overnight and day hikers, but even greater wilderness can be found across the narrow Hoosic River valley atop the flattened summits of the Hoosac Range, southern foothills to Vermont's Green Mountains. The townships making up this pay-phone- and stoplight-free area were auctioned off by the Massachusetts provincial authorities in 1762 to defray the expenses of the French and Indian War. At least one buyer found his purchase unacceptable, returning it with the demand for a refund; in this and other instances, settlers came only after being granted the land for free. The remote and rocky soil eventually caused the first farmers and shepherds to throw in the towel and move to the Midwest, but today, such qualities are rare gifts in the highly urbanized east, especially when found in such abundance as up here. Fat-tire cyclists can roam miles of rough fire roads and dirt-bike trails through state forests convincingly like the primeval landscape encountered by the earliest settlers, with only telltale stone walls or abandoned backwoods cemeteries to indicate otherwise. Dedicated hiking trails are nearly as widespread, and aficionados of bushwacking and orienteering—armed with the proper topo maps, of course—will be in their natural element.

Savoy

Mountainous Savoy, pop. 634, is a little slice of northern New England, with thick conifer forests, few maintained roads (and even fewer paved ones), and little more than a few houses and the volunteer fire department garage for a town. Vermont native and Mormon founder Joseph Smith lived and preached here in the early 1800s—which was about Savoy's heyday. The population peaked in 1850, and the town has mostly occupied that long twilight of rural communities everywhere. Savoy's largest landowner is the state, whose **Savoy Mountain State Forest** comprises thousands of wooded acres crisscrossed with mountain-bike-able old fire and logging roads, which give access to the many scattered historic burial grounds predating the American Revolution. The property's north-western quarter also has a network of hiking trails, some of which originate from the campground off Central Shaft Road. Access roads into the forest are signposted from both Rt. 2, on the north side, and Rt. 116, on the south.

The most popular hikers' destination is **Spruce Hill**, a 2,566-foot outcropping of gneiss and schist slabs that crowns the high point of the Hoosac Range, over whose nearby western summit the famous Mohawk Trail (Rt. 2) passes. Three exposed ledges offer fine views in all directions (most dramatic is from the last, which opens westward over the Hoosic River valley to Mt. Greylock). Adams and North Adams spread out in miniature below, along with the invisible West Portal of the Hoosac Tunnel, which passes nearly 2,000 feet beneath the hill and slightly to the north. Forest visitors who enter from Rt. 2 via Central Shaft Rd. will pass the huge and rather eerie vent structure for which the road is named, which caps the mineshaft sunk mid-tunnel to speed up its construction. If the weather warrants, cool off after a hike with a dip in refreshingly brisk North Pond, about half a mile south of the Spruce Hill trailhead ($2). Since the trailhead isn't marked, the pond is also a good first stop, a place to pick up a map of the state forest trails and roads. These are available from the ranger station at the campground, another half-mile south, too.

You'll certainly need a map to find **Tannery Falls**, actually a series of cascades along Ross and Parker Brooks. The largest, 100-foot drop comes just above their confluence—whence flows Tannery Brook. Ross's stream bed constitutes a living encyclopedia of how water finds its way over, around, and through rock. Come during spring runoff and you'll never again doubt that water can move mountains. The falls are off unmarked Tannery Rd., impassable from the west to all but hikers, bikers, and Humvees; if driving as close as possible is important, approach from Black Brook Rd., a signposted turn off Rt. 2 uphill (west) of the Mohawk Trail State Forest entrance.

A state **campground** offers 45 sites, flush toilets, and showers amid woods and on a large meadow with a few old apple trees, whose blossoms add color and fragrance to the evergreen surroundings each June. Three rustic log cabins built by the Civilian Conservation Corps are tucked away on the densely wooded slope above South Pond, each with wood stove, table, two double bunks, and sneaky chipmunks who stomp around in search of carelessly exposed or poorly wrapped midnight snacks. Unlike sister North Pond, a short distance by trail through the woods, South has no lifeguard or changing rooms. Campsites, $6, are available late May through mid-October and may be reserved, tel. (413) 663-8469. *Very* popular cabins, $8, are available year-round for two to 14 days at a time; reservations are accepted up to six months in advance. One cabin is wheelchair accessible; so is one campsite.

Windsor

South of Rt. 116, Windsor is Savoy's more affluent twin. A far smaller portion of its deeply wooded landscape is accessible to the public, but what it lacks in quantity it makes up in quality. Straddling a ridge between two watersheds, **Notchview Reservation** encompasses open hayfields and shrub-filled swamp, chatty mountain streams and boreal forest fragrant with pine resin and balsam fir. Such variety, abetted by the small township of bluebird houses by the entrance, makes for good birdwatching. Hikers are enticed by more than a dozen miles of trails (leave the mountain bikes behind on this one— they're forbidden), while cross-country skiers flock here in winter. With a higher elevation and longer season than most other Berkshire or Hilltown cross-country ski areas, and a network of groomed and natural trails expansive enough to make everyone feel as if they have the place to themselves, Notchview is understandably popular among the nordic crowd. The visitor center by the parking lot is heated and has both an indoor waxing area and changing rooms; for 24-hour recorded info on ski conditions, call (413) 684-0148. A TTOR property, Notchview has a $2 admission, $7 in winter for skiers. The entrance is signposted from Rt. 9 east of Rt. 8A.

Along Notchview's eastern edge lies Windsor State Forest, best known for picturesque **Windsor Jambs,** a boulder-filled cleft through which a small brook spills south toward the Westfield

River in a series of boulder rapids and one big 50-foot drop. It's possible to park within a few skips of the cable-guarded edge—follow the signs for the forest from Rt. 9, and then for the Jambs—but the 1.5-mile pine forest walk from the campground opposite the forest headquarters adds a note of real discovery. (For a longer and more strenuous hike, of about eight miles roundtrip, connect to the Jambs Trail via Notchview's accurately named Steep Bank Brook Trail.) Pick up a state forest map from the headquarters to find out about the other available hiking trails and mountain-bike-able gravel roads.

The campground is small, with outhouses, water, and fire grills but no showers or hookups of any sort. Clustered under the tall pine canopy, the 24 available sites are slotted together as if in a parking lot—close enough eliminate all privacy, so you can see and hear every camper in the place. Fortunately, it's hardly ever full. Open Memorial Day through Columbus Day; $4. Swimming in the dammed stream across the road is free to campers; others pay a day-use fee of $2 per car.

Resources for Hikers and Campers

Any camping necessities you need can be replaced or replenished at the Mountain Goat, in Williamstown, or the Arcadian Shop, on US 7 in Lenox. Neither Savoy nor Windsor has any stores of any kind, so buy your provisions beforehand—or make a grocery run down East Hoosac St. to Adams (from Savoy) or down Rt. 9 to Dalton (from Windsor). Besides its Big Y Foods supermarket, on Myrtle St., Adams has an atmospheric Polish deli right at the base of East Hoosac. If nasty weather forces a change in plans, some of the closest moderately priced indoor accommodations include such Hilltown bed and breakfasts as Windfields Farm, the Hill Gallery, or Cumworth Farm, all in Cummington.

For more thorough reading on the ecology of these and other outdoor highlights of the Berkshires, pick up René Laubach's locally published *A Guide to Natural Places in the Berkshire Hills,* at almost any of the region's bookstores, giftshops, and sporting goods stores.

PITTSFIELD AND VICINITY

It wasn't too long ago that Pittsfield was a major General Electric company town—home initially to the company's electronic transformer manufacturing operation (which succeeded inventor William Stanley's pioneering electric generator business) and later to GE's plastics division. Although Pittsfield is still the largest, most industrial, and most visibly commercial city in the region, major corporate restructuring and massive layoffs have derailed the community's gravy train. Though the number of empty storefronts downtown may make it seem unlikely, if you look hard enough you'll probably find something among the city's diverse attractions that'll pique your interest.

SIGHTS

Literary Pittsfield
One of the nation's most unloved high-school reading assignments was written in Pittsfield, on Holmes Road, at the city's rural southern edge. But don't worry—you won't be tested to see whether you ever actually finished reading *Moby-Dick* if you visit Herman Melville's **Arrowhead,** tel. (413) 442-1793. Between 1850 and 1863, Melville and his family occupied this farmhouse below Mt. Greylock, whose broad southern profile is sometimes said to resemble the titular great white whale from Melville's epic. While primarily a literary shrine to the 19th-century author, the propery is also home to the Berkshire County Historical Society, whose interesting and inspired series of changing exhibits depicting Berkshire County history are presented out in the capacious old barn. Open late May through October, daily until early September and then Fri.-Mon. through season's end; admission $4.50. Serious pilgrims will also want to visit the **Melville Memorial Room,** on the upper level of the Berkshire Athenaeum (a fancy name for Pittsfield's public library), in a modern building just off the town square. Open Mon.-Fri. till 9 p.m. during the school year and Mon.-Sat. till at least 6 p.m. in summer.

The Berkshire Museum
This graceful turn-of-the-century institution, at 39 South St. (US 7), opposite the Crowne Plaza, tel. (413) 443-7171, has a nice diversity in its collections, from decorative arts to natural history. American paintings by members of the Hudson River School and romanticists of the American West are particular strengths, along with a huge costume collection and artifacts from Berkshire history. Kids love interacting with creatures in the vivarium and aquarium exhibits. Open Tues.-Sun. year-round; admission is $3 (free Wednesday and Saturday mornings).

Plastics
Simply as home to the world headquarters of General Electric's plastics division, Pittsfield would qualify as a national leader in everything to do with the stuff—from basic research to manufacture—but there are also another 40 plastics-related companies in town. Their location here in the Berkshires isn't as unusual as you might think: the region has been associated with plastics since 1881, when the American Zylonite Company opened in Adams as a licensed producer of the English-patented Xylonite, one of the first synthetic plastics. (It was similar to celluloid, which was invented in nearby Albany.) GE brought plastics to the banks of the Housatonic with research into insulators for their electrical components. Use, in both industrial and commercial applications, blossomed after the end of WW II: among the myriad products with roots here in Pittsfield are your car's tail lights, the water bottle you take hiking, your polycarbonate eyeglasses, perhaps the biodegradable grocery bags you use.

One way to see what the plastics wizards are up to now is a visit to the **Living Environments Concept House,** a large contemporary home on New York Avenue. Across the street from GE's mammoth factory, "the Plastics House" was originally designed to test new materials and technologies. Once word of the futuristic house spread, the company opened it to tours; the $6 admission benefits the local chapter of the United Way. Open only by reserved tour, on Thursday afternoon and occasionally on Saturday morning. Call (800) 696-6948 or (413) 442-6948 for reservations.

Play Ball

Whenever the Pittsfield Mets are defending their home turf, fans of the Great American Pastime mustn't miss a visit to **Wahconah Park,** on Wahconah St., behind pink Adrienne's Diner. The Mets may be near the bottom of the professional minors (a player here in the short-season Class A league is three promotions away from the majors), but this grand old ballpark is still one of the most widely acclaimed venues for professional baseball. With pigeon-scaring plastic owls dangling from the rafters, a "lounge" right along the first-base line, delays when the setting sun gets in the umpire's and catcher's eyes, and occasionally inspired play, it is everything baseball is supposed to be. Don't miss it.

The Mets play nearly 40 games at home each season, mid-June through early September. Ticket prices are $2.75 general admission, slightly higher for box seats and the upper grandstand. For schedule or game times, call (413) 499-METS x1.

Pittsfield State Forest

Berry Pond, at 2,150 feet elevation the highest natural body of water in the state, provides Pittsfield State Forest visitors with a beautiful, contemplative backdrop for summer's pink azaleas in bloom on adjacent Berry Mountain, or for the early fall broadwing hawk migration from grassy Berry Hill, with its wide open views to the Catskills in neighboring New York. Canoeing and fishing are allowed (the pond is stocked with trout), but no swimming. (The only swimming available is at Lulu Pond, a tiny puddle most suited to small children; $2 per car for day

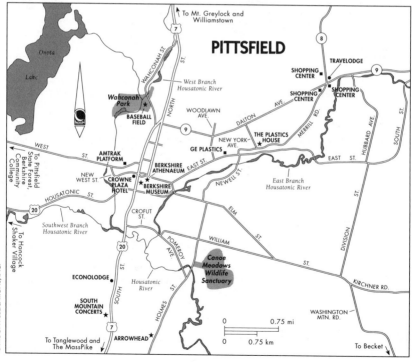

© MOON PUBLICATIONS, INC.

use.) The forest is open year-round for hiking, mountain-biking, and skiing. A wooden lodge with fireplaces may be reserved in four- or eight-hour blocks for cross-country skiers (for day use, not overnight); tel. (413) 442-8992.

Numerous trails exist, some following various brooks along small stony ravines and beside cascades, others ascending the peaks that belong to the westernmost range of mountains in Massachusetts, the Taconics. The north-south Taconic Crest Trail, in fact, passes through the property. Hike all the way to the Hancock Shaker Village, passing old homesites of the Shakers in the regrown forest, or roll your wheelchair along the interpretive trail designed for visitors with physical disabilities. To deter vandals, **Balance Rock,** in the northern end of the park unit, is closed to vehicles all year, but you can park by the gate on Churchill St. and walk a mere quarter-mile, or hike from the Lulu Pond picnic grounds (though, given the amount of grafitti defacing it, the rock may instill more sadness than awe). Complete trail maps are availible at the entrance, west of town, at the end of Cascade St.; follow signs from US 20 (West St.) or Churchill St., off US 7.

PERFORMING ARTS

The region's only professional resident dance company, the **Albany Berkshire Ballet,** tel. (413) 445-5382, is also one of the few arts groups of any kind that performs in the Berkshires year-round. Their annual *Nutcracker* holiday production travels to several different venues between Albany and Eastern Massachusetts, but their summer repertory is staged at Berkshire Community College's Robert Bolland Theatre near the end of West St., nestled at the edge of the Pittsfield State Forest. The Bolland is also home to the **Berkshire Opera Company,** which stages two full-scale productions, sung in English, for brief runs (less than a week) in July and August; tel. (413) 528-4420 for details.

Since 1918, **South Mountain Concerts** have included performances by the finest chamber artists and ensembles in an attractive little concert hall on a wooded mountainside two miles south of downtown Pittsfield on US 7. As a gift to those residents who have endured the summer crush—or latecomers who have missed out on other regional performing arts events, the South Mountain series begins the weekend after Labor Day and runs every Sunday afternoon until mid-October. Call (413) 442-2106 for further information.

AROUND PITTSFIELD

Hancock Shaker Village
"The City of Peace," on US 20 west of Pittsfield, was one of the earliest settlements begun by the United Society of Believers in Christ's Second Appearing, a religious order founded by Ann Lee, member of a reform-minded Quaker sect in the English Midlands. A year before the outbreak of the American Revolution, Mother Ann emigrated to New England with her brother and seven other Shakers (so-called for their style of worship), in search of potential converts and the sacred place she had seen in her visions. Her unorthodox teachings promoted the worship of God through handiwork, the conviction that she was the personification (the Second Appearing) of a feminine side of God, a rejection of private property ownership, and celibacy. (Under the grim conditions prevailing in rural 19th-century America—when women typically endured multiple successive pegnancies until spared by premature death, often in childbirth, or menopause, whichever came first—celibacy could be a blessing indeed.) The practical corollaries to such beliefs—equality between the sexes, rejection of slavery, and communal living, among others—aroused the ire of many contemporaries, who persecuted Shakers wherever they went. Mother Ann and her brother both died in 1784, before any Shaker villages were established. But the sect flourished in the 1800s, in the rising tide of America's enthusiasm for utopian communities, and founded 24 self-sustaining settlements between Maine and Kentucky. Only two remain, but the Shaker talent for elegantly simple design and unparalleled craftsmanship continues to inspire appreciative collectors, decorators, and imitators.

After surviving for 170 years, the Hancock settlement became a big museum to the Shakers' agrarian life. Historical exhibits, working artisans, and the many buildings themselves attest

HANCOCK SHAKER VILLAGE

Shaker children pose for a winter photo, 1929

to the evolution of Shaker aesthetics. Seasonal special programs and an excellent series of Saturday-night Shaker dinners interpret the group's customs and crafts; call (413) 443-0188 for event schedules and reservations, where necessary. A shop sells books, small gifts, and many Shaker-style items produced by the village's professional artisans, while a pleasant little cafe offers a delicious and modestly priced taste of Shaker cookery. Admission, good for two consecutive days, is $10 adults, $5 children; open daily April 1 through late November. Yyou can't miss the place, on US 20 west of Pittsfield. A cafe in the the village is also open for a Shaker Christmas, the first weekend of December, and for mid-February's Winter Week, which coincides with school vacations.

The Crane Museum

The history of American papermaking is the subject of this modest museum, on Rt. 8 (Housatonic St.) in the center of town, tel. (413) 684-2600, housed in a beautiful ivy-covered old stone mill beside the Housatonic River. Crane & Co., the owner, is the sole supplier of all the paper used in making our national currency, and there are extensive displays of paper money from around the world, as well. Open weekday afternoons only, 2-5 p.m., June-Sept.

Wahconah Falls

Fed by the Windsor town reservoir upstream, Wahconah Falls Brook descends through a narrow defile of broken metamorphic rock in a series of cascades, each with its own plunge pool. Protected by **Wahconah Falls State Park,** hemlocks—a shade-tolerant tree typical of rock ravines—grow in profusion, along with trees like beech and yellow birch, species that enjoy the cool microclimate of the falls. This entrance to this free park is signposted from Rt. 9 east of Dalton., heading for the Hilltowns.

PRACTICALITIES

Camping

Berry Pond is arguably the most scenic of the three camping areas in **Pittsfield State Forest,** tel. (413) 442-8992. It offers 13 primitive tent sites for $4 a night. Lower-elevation Parker Brook campground has 18 less-private sites (a dozen in the woods and six in a field), all for $5 a night. As at all state-owned campgrounds, that one-dollar gap reflects the difference between pit and flush toilets. There are no hookups and no dumping station for RVs (which, because of size, are restricted to the field sites). Pond sites vary considerably in comfort—if you want one with enough grassy, level earth to avoid either sleeping on the gravelly area next to your car or on a 30-degree slope, keep in mind that the campgrounds see heaviest use on weekends in July and August (yes, the Tanglewood crowd sleeps in tents, too) and again during foliage season—the last three weeks the place is open. Typically, late spring weekends or midweek anytime yield plenty of splendid isolation. Open mid-May through mid-October, the campground has the added benefit of being alcohol-free, so you needn't ever worry about being stuck next to a keg party. From US 7 or US 20 in Pittsfield, follow signs to the entrance on Cascade Street.

Accommodations

Pittsfield can't pretend to compete with all the country inns and luxurious spas of Lenox and South County, but it is home to a couple of national chains, as well as a pair of vintage motels which, despite their simplicity, match prices with the best of them during summer high season. The **Crowne Plaza** is the most central of the familiar brands, sitting smack downtown on US 7 by the Berkshire Museum, tel. (800) 445-8667 or (413) 499-2000. Very expensive. Alternatively, head to the mall-lined east end of town at the junction of Rts. 8 and 9 to find the **Travelodge,** tel. (800) 578-7878 or (413) 443-5661; or south on US 7 to the **Econo Lodge,** 1055 South St., tel. (800) 55-ECONO or (413) 443-4714, $58-120 d.

Food

When it comes to eating, Pittsfield boasts some real gems. One is **Elizabeth's Café & Pizzeria,** 1264 East St., tel. (413) 448-8244. The drive out past the gray leviathan of the former GE Polymer Plastics plant will have you wondering whether you're going the wrong way, but keep going—look for the trim two-story house with the shocking pink porch. Sit downstairs for a ringside view of the open kitchen and you'll get the added bonus of counsel from co-owner Tom, who's genuinely concerned that you like what you order and get enough to eat ("How hungry are you? You like meat? Get the special—you won't be disappointed"). The food is as delicious as the atmosphere is casual—deep-dish pizzas top-heavy with fresh veggies and real cheese, piping-hot pastas accompanied by hunks of crusty fresh bread, and huge house salads garnished with fresh mozzarella and fruit. The polenta shouldn't be missed—and anchovy lovers will definitely want to try the *bagna caoda.* Open Tues.-Sun. (and, in summer, also Monday), for dinner only. An entirely different kind of Italian—equally good in its own right—can be found literally around the corner, at the **East Side Cafe,** on Newell Street. A neighborhood bar with a big family clientele clamoring for the booths that occupy half of the narrow premises, the East Side serves pure comfort food. Wednesday is pasta night (5-8 p.m.), Thurs.-Sun. are pizza nights (to 10 p.m. Thursday and Sunday, to midnight Fri.-Sat.), when the brick oven is stoked to dish out some excellent Neopolitan pies with the choicest pepperoni, sausage, and the like—at great small-town prices.

Other Than Italian

The Allendale Center strip mall, at the junctions of Rts. 8 and 9, on the east edge of town, is dominated by a large fishing trawler either rising from the pavement of the parking lot or sinking stern-first down into it (perhaps a metaphor for Pittsfield's own fortunes). Tucked away on the north end of the plaza is **Truffles & Such,** tel. (413) 442-0151, one of the area's best restaurants for over a dozen years. Everything about it is a pleasure: great food, desserts, microbrew menu, decent wine prices, summer greens fresh from the owners' garden, and pleasant ambiance (although sometimes the background music gets a little too elevator-like). Last-minute arrivals are not only made welcome but are also accorded as much time as they need to enjoy their meals; rather than being rushed out the door, you'll be sincerely encouraged to linger over dessert and coffee—even if it's an hour and a half past closing time and you have the place to yourself.

Half a block from the main downtown square, **The Brewery at 34 Depot Street,** tel. (413) 442-2072, stands just uphill of the forlorn little Amtrak platform. The burritos, burgers, sandwiches, and pub appetizers here are all big and delicious enough—and surprisingly inexpensive—to warrant a visit on their own, but they can also be accompanied by some very decent fresh-brewed beer from Old Saddleback Brewing, which shares the premises there behind the glass windows by the front. A large no-smoking section and a good kids' menu (accompanied by root beer or cream soda—also brewed on the premises) make this a better-than-average pub all around.

West of downtown, **Kim's Dragon Restaurant,** 1231 West Housatonic St. (US 20), tel. (413) 442-5594, isn't the only Vietnamese restaurant in the region, but it is by far the best value (despite an ambiance on par with your average McDonald's). Heaping portions of Viet favorites, from soup to crispy noodles, curry to fresh spring rolls, are dished up at some of the most affordable prices in the Berkshires. Open daily for lunch and dinner.

Eye-Openers and Ice Cream

The postcard towns to the south may have a near monopoly on Victorian charm and $5 desserts, but industrial old Pittsfield has the best coffee house in the county outside of Great Barrington: aptly named **Sip of Seattle,** at 216 Elm St., near the intersection with Holmes Road. Flanked by such funky neighbors as Dead Ahead (where Jerry Garcia still lives in spirit) and a used record store, the Sip is open daily (to 9 p.m. Mon.-Thurs., to 11:30 p.m. Fri.-Sat., and to 3 p.m. Sunday), serving all the caffeinated concoctions you'd expect from a place named for Jet City. The Sip's sandwiches, desserts, bagels, and muffins will satisfy carbo and sugar cravings, too.

Ice cream fans will find the local outpost of **Ben & Jerry's,** on US 7 just south of downtown, where it stays open until 11 p.m. in summer. Less expensive local alternatives to this Vermont-based chain do exist, but they're best avoided unless you're fond of frozen Cool Whip.

LENOX

During the closing decades of the 1800s, a veritable Who's Who of American industry—Carnegie, Westinghouse, Procter, Vanderbilt, and dozens of others—came to prefer the Berkshire Hills over Narragansett Bay for their summer dalliances. It was this shift that turned the region into a fashionable inland counterpoint to such famous seaside summer retreats as Newport or Boston's North Shore. Fortunes made in manufacturing and finance poured into scores of palatial homes designed and landscaped by the best architects of the day. Families summering in these mansions during the Gilded Age filled their days with dinners and fancy dress balls, costume parties and in-house theatricals, tennis and croquet, endless rounds of visits to neighbors and social peers, and intrigues, romances, gossip, and afternoon tea. The Federal income tax, the First World War, and the Great Depression all curbed the excesses of this era, but some of the grand "cottages" (more like châteaux) remain as testimony to those years, when "society" was a full-time occupation. Some have been converted into plush inns, spare-no-expense spas, or private institutions, but they all continue to lend Lenox a certain perpetual grace—as attractive as the summer air was to those old millionaires. Neither have the cosmopolitan influences faded: proximity to Tanglewood (the summer home of the Boston Symphony Orchestra) ensures that village shops and restaurants continue to reflect the tastes of affluent urbanites, particularly from Manhattan.

Of the 70 or so cottages built around the region, only about half have avoided demolition or conflagrations—such as the fire that leveled Andrew Carnegie's Stockbridge estate, Shadow Brook, in 1956. (Jesuits built a 300-room seminary on the property, which is now occupied by the Kripalu fitness and yoga retreat.) Most of the survivors have been taken over by private schools, religious orders, condominiums, or luxury resorts. Anyone interested in an illustrated peek at the gilded past should look for *The Berkshire Cottages,* by Carole Owens, in local bookstores or libraries.

The Lenox Library Association, on Main St., also has some historic cottage photos on display. Even without any burning desire to delve into local history, this public library is a nice place to stop—especially on a rainy day. There's a little gallery at back, artifacts displayed in cases, and a cozy magazine reading room at the rear of the building where you can comfortably catch up on the world beyond your holiday. Closed Sunday year-round, and, in winter, Monday, too.

Pleasant Valley Wildlife Sanctuary

Managed by the Massachusetts Audubon Society, the Pleasant Valley Wildlife Sanctuary, tel. (413) 637-0320, encompasses a tributary of the Housatonic and the flanks of Lenox Mountain, whose summit fire tower affords good panoramic views. Catch a glimpse of beavers at work in one of the several ponds along Yokun Brook, look for ferns along Pike's Pond Trail, or watch for hummingbirds feeding from the red-blossomed plants in the hummingbird garden. The sanctuary is on an unpaved road off US 7/20 opposite the Quality Inn, about 6.6 miles north of the MassPike; follow the sign of the Society's blue tern logo. Open Tues.-Sun. year-round; admission $3 adults, $2 children.

PERFORMING ARTS

Tanglewood

For well over half a century, Tanglewood has been the summer home of the Boston Symphony Orchestra. For many years now, it has also been the lifeblood of the Berkshires, drawing upwards of 300,000 visitors between late June and Labor Day. With the addition of a second concert hall, in 1994, and a schedule that intersperses jazz and popular music with the classical and operatic performances, there are more opportunities than ever to sup from this outstanding musical banquet. Koussevitzky Music Shed concerts are held Fri.-Sun., while Seiji Ozawa Concert Hall events take place most Wednesdays and Thursdays. Ticket prices vary widely ($13.50-61 for fixed seating), but al fresco lawn seating is a relative bargain ($10-14, free for children under 12). Bring a blanket or lawn chair, and consider a light dose of mosquito repellent. Lawn tickets are only available in person at the gate. Call (800) 274-8499 for a recorded schedule; to charge tickets by phone, call Ticketmaster, (800) 347-0808 (service fee charged).

Shakespeare at the Mount

Each year, the grounds and converted stables of author Edith Wharton's former mansion, the Mount, ring with the sounds of a solid summer of the Bard. In addition to five or six major Shakespeare plays, each season of **Shakespeare & Company** features new adaptations of Wharton short stories or novels and selected works by modern playwrights—all performed by an energetic group of seasoned professionals and aspiring young actors. Well signposted off Plunkett St. at US 20, the Mount boasts four separate spaces—both indoors and out—that are put to use, from the main stage, under the trees of the sloping back lawn, to the occasionally sultry barebones stage inside the old stables. Late May through late October, performances are scheduled throughout the day and week, often with different productions overlapping on different stages. For schedule information or to get on the mailing list, call (413) 637-1197, or visit the homepage www.shakespeare.org; to charge tickets by phone, call the box office, at (413) 637-3353.

Edith Wharton, the first woman to receive a Pulitzer Prize (for her 1920 novel, *The Age of Innocence*), built **the Mount** in 1902 for use as a summer residence. She took an active hand in the design and landscaping, putting into practice ideas propounded in her books on these subjects. Hour-long house tours combine history and architecture with literary biography throughout the day Tues.-Sun. from Memorial Day through Labor Day, then weekends only through the end of October. Admission is $4.50; for information, call (413) 637-1899.

common wood sorrel (Oxalis acetosella)

YVONNE DUNTON

Other Music Series

Chamber music is one of the bedrocks of the Berkshire scene—and not only by its ubiquity throughout the region but also by virtue of being one of the only musical styles available off season. The **Armstrong Chamber Concerts** are an example; you can catch performing a couple of times each in fall and spring, at the Lenox Town Hall Theater on Walker Street. Call (413) 637-3646 for details on upcoming appearances.

For those who prefer Kenny Rogers or Bela Fleck to Mozart and Brahms, the **National**

Music Foundation, 70 Kemble St., tel. (413) 637-4718, hosts a summer series of popular music covering a spectrum so wide it includes aging Top 40 stars, gospel, jazz, big bands, country, and Motown. Catch the performances at the Foundation's 1,200-seat auditorium July-Aug. evenings.

As you've undoubtedly gathered by now, the Berkshires is musically quite conservative—reflecting the fact that the region has yet to become much of a playground for people under 30. MASS MoCA's Night Shift Cafe is the only place you'll hear anything close to alternapop. But then, North Adams is the only place in Western Massachusetts that let WalMart in, too. Since the rest of the county would sooner host a monster truck rally than a Pearl Jam concert, enjoy the clean air and out-of-doors while you can, and save your nightclub dollars for the Pioneer Valley or Boston.

ACCOMMODATIONS

It's a simple fact of Berkshire life that Tanglewood is the cash cow of the summer tourist season. It's quite a phenomenon: stick a bunch of musicians in a big old shed out in the boondocks, then watch the demand for food and lodging leap about 1,000% whenever they sit down on stage and strike up a tune. And so, every weekend of July and August, the restaurants, traffic, and lodging around Lenox all go haywire. Between concert-free midweek nights and Tanglewood weekends, room prices—especially among the low-end accommodations—vault up $60-100. (Note, too, that because more and more concerts are scheduled during the week, many Berkshire innkeepers consider "weekends" to run Thurs.-Sunday.) The droves of leaf-peepers who flock to the Berkshires on weekends in October also cause spikes in the room rates—although not as dramatic.

To avoid being deluged by a full house of new guests each night, nearly every B&B and small inn requires a two- or three-day minimum stay on weekends throughout the Tanglewood and foliage seasons—and, unfortunately, most motels have followed suit. The only antidote is distance: if you intend to stay in the region on a summer weekend without spending a small for-

---

ADDITIONAL LENOX ACCOMMODATIONS

Several East Coast and national chains are represented locally along US 7 and US 20 a short drive from the Lenox village center. Listed in order from north to south:

Susse Chalet, 194 Pittsfield-Lenox Rd. (US 7), tel. (800) 5-CHALET or (413) 637-3560. Expensive during Tanglewood season, inexpensive otherwise.

Quality Inn, 130 Pittsfield-Lenox Rd. (US 7), near the Arcadian Shop, tel. (800) 442-4201 or (413) 637-4244; largest of the lot, and also the one showing its age most clearly, with crumbling exterior concrete, drapes and fixtures showing wear, and an inadequate hot water system; $89-159 d during Tanglewood season, $45-79 otherwise.

Howard Johnson, on the Pittsfield-Lenox Rd. (US 7) opposite the Yankee Motor Lodge, tel. (800) I-GO-HOJO or (413) 442-4000. Luxury during Tanglewood season, expensive otherwise.

Black Swan Inn Best Western, US 20 on Laurel Lake, just south of the Lenox-Lee town line, tel. (800) 876-SWAN or (413) 243-2700; restaurant, swimming and fishing on the property; $65-130 d, $105-150 on foliage weekends, $140-195 Tanglewood weekends.

---

tune, try a B&B in the Hilltowns, many of which are within a very scenic 30- to 45-minute drive from Lenox. Most importantly, if you *do* want to stay in some charming Lenox B&B on a summer weekend, reserve it *before* the early April release of the Symphony's performance schedule. Autumn is rather predictable, too, so there's no excuse for delaying your foliage-viewing reservations, either.

For a near-complete list of local lodgings (*sans* prices), drop by the Lenox Chamber of Commerce visitor center, in the Academy Building, on Main St., and pick up a brochure. You can also request a copy by phone (tel. 413-637-3646) or e-mail (info@lenox.org). The Chamber can help refer you to available lodgings that meet your budget, too. Their Web site—www.lenox.org—also has links to all the available homepages for accommodations operators who are Chamber members. Bookings at additional B&Bs are also available through reservations services such as **Berkshire Bed & Breakfast Homes,** tel. (413) 268-7244.

Camping

Covering the east side of the Housatonic valley between Pittsfield and the MassPike is **October Mountain State Forest.** Largest in Massachusetts' park system, October Mountain covers parts of three towns and half of a fourth. The Appalachian Trail runs across its ridges, and a web of mountain-bike-able old dirt roads and paths run through the thick forest. A pleasant, spacious campground occupies a set of grassy terraces off Willow Hill Road, across the town line from the village of Lenoxdale. A dozen of the 50 sites are nicely tucked into the woods behind the terraces, and RV sites are concentrated near the entrance, almost out of earshot from the rest. Amenities include flush toilets, water, and a dumping station, but no showers. Open mid-May through mid-October; $6. For some reason, this property tends to get overlooked—perhaps because its lakes are rather difficult to approach with a vehicle and its trails are generally better suited to bikers than hikers. At any rate, in summer, the campground has been known to be totally deserted at midweek. The gravel quarry across the road is the only drawback—on weekdays, the beepbeepbeepbeep of frontloaders in reverse is as audible as an alarm clock. Willow Hill Rd. is a turn off East St. in Lee; follow signs from US 7/20 in Lenox or from US 20 just east of MassPike Exit 2.

Inexpensive: $35-60

Without benefit of a hostel in the region, about the only recourse for Berkshire-bound budget travelers is the **Wagon Wheel Motel,** tel. (413) 445-4532, one of a cluster along US 7 between Lenox and Pittsfield dating back to before Elvis movies and Eisenhower's presidency. Not greatly changed in the decades since then, the Wagon Wheel greets the visitor with a set of the namesake wheels and a fiberglass twin of Roy Rogers' Trigger. The dark-paneled rooms are showing their age—TVs, phones, and a/c are the only concessions to modernity—but with midweek prices beginning at less than $50

d—even in July and August—it's a relative bargain for Massachusetts, no matter what the condition. Nov.-April, rates may even dip below $35 d—if the parking lot is empty or you're a AAA member. Conversely, on Tanglewood weekends, the rates top $115 d (more for queen or king rooms!), and a two-night minimum goes into effect. On foliage weekends, rates peak around $85. Needless to say, these are prices that prey on the desperate, and you can do better—even if it means hopping on the MassPike and driving 40 minutes east to West Springfield for the night.

Moderate: $60-85

The Wagon Wheel's neighbor is the plain but well-maintained **Mayflower Motor Inn,** tel. (413) 443-4468. Except on Tanglewood weekends (when prices almost double and two-night stays are required), all but king-bed rooms fall within the moderate range. Even the peak rates won't produce any little shampoo bottles, but there is a small, heated in-ground pool and a volleyball and badminton court to distract kids from the cable TV. Off season, rates dip below $60 d. Year-round, the staff is as helpful as any gold-key concierge. If you're looking for a longer stay with abundant elbow room, inquire about the cottage suites.

Across the highway, **Yankee Motor Lodge,** tel. (413) 499-3700, offers immaculate, comfortable rooms in a sturdy ranch motif, with such fringe benefits as personal coffee makers and, in many rooms, mini-fridges. A modest outdoor swimming pool also sits in the center of the front lawn. Tanglewood rates start at more than $130 d (three-night minimum), dropping to $78-111 Sun.-Thurs., depending on room size. Except for a premium on prime foliage weeks of early October, off-season rates are generally $65 d weekdays, $100 d weekends.

Expensive: $85-110

Lenox is chock-full of attractive B&B inns. Many have spacious green lawns and well-tended flowerbeds. And most have at least some rooms within this range in summer. Expect minimum stays at least on high-season weekends. Quite often, these establishments also offer various two- or three-day packages, which can included complimentary dinners, museum passes, lift tickets, biking guidebooks, and other special treats. From pools to tennis courts, evening hors d'oeuvres to bedtime aperitifs, nearly all have charms and amenities that inspire loyalty among guests.

One such place that never fails to win repeat business is the **Birchwood Inn,** 7 Hubbard St., opposite The Church On The Hill, tel. (800) 524-1646 or (413) 637-2600, www.bbonline.com/ma/birchwood. The oldest house still standing in Lenox, this B&B has 12 well-appointed rooms and two suites—all but two with private baths; rates vary between weekdays, weekends, and Tanglewood season (three-night minimum on weekends), but range $60-150 d Nov.-June and $70-210 in summer and fall. For bargain hunters, there's a three-night Mon.-Wed. summer package that's a real steal given the Toner family's hospitality, the quality of their full breakfast, and a great front porch. The Birchwood is also noteworthy for adopting sensible measures to cut down energy and packaging waste—still a rather novel idea for far too many folks in the hospitality business.

Novelty is also a word that springs to mind for the **Brook Farm Inn,** on Hawthorne St., tel. (800) 285-POET or (413) 637-3013, www.brookfarm.com, a lovely Victorian steeped to the chimneytops in verse. The present owners, Anne and Joe Miller, inherited a huge library of poetry upon buying the place, and, more by accident than design, encouraged guests to join them in exploring this great treasury. Now Joe leads informal readings by and for guests; a poem du jour is posted by the door to the breakfast room; and the hundreds of volumes of poetry and poets on tape are available at any hour for any guest to enjoy. The euphonious undercurrent is upheld by the fine full breakfasts, afternoon teas, decanters of welcoming sherry, and summer Sunday recitals by students from Tanglewood's music camp up the street. There's also a small outdoor pool beyond the hammock out back. Off season, be sure to inquire about the fireplace rooms. Rates are $80-200 d.

FOOD

Whether or not you hear a single note of symphonic music or word of drama, you can't help but feel the impact of the local art scene—in the wait times for tables at local restaurants in the summer. Suffice to say, if you're dining out prior to a scheduled event, allow yourself *plenty* of time. (If you're going to Tanglewood or Shakespeare & Co., consider following the local custom of buying a ready-made picnic from one of the local gourmet provisioners and dining al fresco on either institution's lovely grounds prior to the performance.)

A top breakfast contender in the village is **Carol's,** 4 Franklin St. next to the gas station, whose casual attitude is summed up in its sunflower-themed decor. Good bagels, home-made challah French toast, and omelettes are among the regular options. Like many of the clientele, the service is straight out of New York: fast enough to give you whiplash, familiar enough to call out across a few tables to see if you need anything. Not bad for lunch, either.

Adjacent **Salerno's Gourmet Pizza,** 8 Franklin St., tel. (413) 637-8940, clearly emphasizes take-out business (its fixed-seat fast-food-style booths don't inspire lingering), but the food more than makes up for the absence of crystal stemware and white linen. Vegetarians, calamari fans, and people who like tomato-free pizza will all find selections among Salerno's offerings, which also include strombolis, calzones, lasagna, and more. For fancier fare, head around the block to the **Church Street Cafe,** tel. (413) 637-2745. During the busy summer season—to judge from the accents at neighboring tables, the art on the walls, and the creative culinary talent at work in the kitchen—it's like a little far-flung corner of Greenwich Village. The New Yorkers return south in the fall, but the innovative cuisine remains year-round, and ,while the extraordinarily popular patio seating isn't available in winter, the food and wine can more than hold its own indoors.

The rest of the village's dining options line up along the two blocks of Church Street. Other Lenox restaurants are located north of the village on the US 7 commercial strip extending up to the Pittsfield line. At the start of this stretch, **Sweet Basil Grille,** at the Brushwood Farms shops on US 7, tel. (413) 637-1270, serves robust Italian fare, from the tried-and-true pasta with a sauce of fresh tomatoes and basil to more unusual combinations such as sautéed shrimp with ripened brie. Be sure to bring an appetite—portion control is out the window. For a more family-friendly atmosphere, head up the highway a short distance to **Zampano's,** tel. (413) 448-8600, whose reasonably-priced Italian fare is complemented by rotisserie chicken, richly sauced seafood dishes, and an all-you-can-eat salad bar. The heavy-textured dressings make one wonder if someone has a private stake in a mayonnaise company, but the menu makes strong assurances that sauces and dressings are all formulated for low calorie yields, so ladle them on.

During the day, anyone yearning for somethings sweet will find fulfillment on Housatonic St. in the center of the village. **Bev's Homemade Ice Cream** has a well-deserved monopoly on super-premium frozen dairy desserts, while **Suchèle Bakery,** across the street, makes and sells fine pastries, tarts, sticky buns, and other assorted baked goods. Hardcore dessert mavens may want to go around the corner to **Cheesecake Charlie's,** on Main St., which offers rich New York-style confections in 50 flavors. Penitent calorie-counters should note that Charlie's shares premises with with **Wholesome Harold's,** a delicatessen that almost serves as the confectioner's alter ego. If you can't find a pleasing morsel at either Charlie's or Harold's, try stepping into the grocery next door and loading up on celery and carrots.

NORMAN ROCKWELL COUNTRY

The area between the MassPike's two westernmost exits is a rather remarkable slice of small-town America—places that could almost have been lifted straight off Norman Rockwell's easel. Since Rockwell's death, in 1978, this attempt at mimicking his art may be half-deliberate; but while he was still alive, the mirror was turned the other way: in 1953, America's most famous illustrator moved to Stockbridge from southern Vermont, and inevitably both town and townsfolk found their way into his work and, ultimately, our nation's self-image. Despite the seasonal flood of visitors pouring off the MassPike—and the typical cluster of fast food and motels that's sprouted around Exit 2 in neighboring Lee to cater to this traffic—this area has retained its character to a charming degree. It isn't all gentrified, either—outside of Stockbridge, there's plenty of evidence that posing for tourists isn't the only way residents make their living.

STOCKBRIDGE

Tiny Stockbridge, whose small downtown is dominated by the great clapboard girth of the historic 1897 Red Lion Inn, may look vaguely familiar. Perhaps you've seen it in the calendars Norman Rockwell painted for Brown & Bigelow, or on some of his famous covers for the *Saturday Evening Post*. Stockbridge was the model for Rockwell's almost mythic view of small-town America at Christmas (first published by *McCall's* magazine in 1967), so it would be fair to say this place has become an archetype for what old-fashioned America *ought* to look like. Here's the Red Lion's wide verandah, filled with rocking chairs. Next door, the tidy little shops share Main Street with large, handsome houses set behind big lawns and trim fences. Down the street, the bells in the Children's Chime Tower, at the western end of Main, are diligently rung, at the request of their 19th-century donor, on evenings from "apple blossom time until frost." As proof of the disregard for the so-called improvements of the latter 20th century, there's not a single stop light in the entire village.

Norman Rockwell Museum

In an attractive contemporary museum (designed by Robert A.M. Stern), tel. (413) 298-4100, on the landscaped estate of an old Berkshire cottage at the edge of Rockwell's adopted home town, you'll find more than 500 paintings and drawings by America's most renowned illustrator (Rockwell himself was always careful to call himself a commercial artist). It's the world's largest collection, and only the most flint-hearted skeptic of human nature won't be moved by the well-curated display of the painter's humor, wit, keen eye for detail, and, yes, sophistication. The Stockbridge studio in which Rockwell worked for the last 25 years of his life has also been relocated to the grounds of the museum,

NORMAN ROCKWELL MUSEUM

No Swimmin', *by Norman Rockwell*

tastefully signposted off Rt. 183.Open daily except Thanksgiving, Christmas, and New Year's; $9 adults, $2 children.

Chesterwood

Daniel Chester French, one of the most recognized sculptors of the early 20th century, lived and worked in the Berkshires each summer from 1896 until his death, in 1931. His lovely wooded property, Chesterwood, tel. (413) 298-3579, is now maintained for the public by the National Trust. A huge collection of the artist's study models, finished works, and works by contemporaries are preserved in the house, studio, and barn amid views and gardens as inspiring as when French labored on such famous commissions as the Lincoln Memorial. Don't ignore the paths through the woods—the bench at the Hemlock Grove overlook, in particular, is one of the most contemplative seats in the county. A contemporary sculpture show also adorns the grounds each summer. The house is open daily May-Oct., and in November for "Christmas at Chesterwood," during Veteran's Day. Admission is $5.50 just to the grounds and gardens, $7.50 including house tour ($2-4 for kids, depending on age), $17 for a family of four. Located on Williamsville Rd.; the way to the property is well marked off Rt. 183 in the Glendale section of Stockbridge.

Naumkeag

Atop 50 sloping acres on Prospect Hill, a little over half a mile north of Main St., stands Naumkeag, tel. (413) 298-3239, one of the area's surviving Gilded Age "cottages." Under the stewardship of The Trustee of Reservations, Naumkeag is today one of the few cottages open to the public. Designed by noted Shingle Style architect Stanford White (of the prominent firm McKim, Mead, and White), with gorgeous landscaping added a generation later by Fletcher Steele, the 1885 house has a dark-paneled opulence appropriate to the high-powered legal work of its first owner, Joseph H. Choate. The Choates chose the estate's Native American name because they thought it meant "haven of peace" (actually, it's Algonquian for "fishing place" or "eel fishing place").

Naumkeag is open daily late May through mid-October; admission is $5 for the gardens only, $7 including house tour. (From Main St. in Stockbridge, turn on Pine, opposite the Red Lion Inn and US 7 south, and take the left fork—Prospect Hill Rd.—about half a mile.)

Other Historic Sights

Stockbridge's Main Street still has a couple of grand contemporaries of Naumkeag, now converted to institutional use and effectively closed to the curious public. The pair of historic homes that *are* open reflect very different circumstances—both historic and economic. Built by the Reverend John Sergeant in 1739, after he had become a missionary to the local Native Americans, simple **Mission House** (which was relocated to its present address from a nearby hilltop), tel. (413) 298-3239, was also briefly home to Calvinist preacher Jonathan Edwards, whose fire-and-brimstone sermons inspired a national "Great Awakening" during the 1740s. Visitors with dour preconceptions of early colonial living conditions and lifestyles may be somewhat surprised at how cheery the meticulously restored interior of this place really is. The fine collection of 17th- and 18th-century household artifacts is complemented by displays devoted to the Stockbridge Indians—the indigenous subjects of these men's missionary work. Owned by TTOR, the Mission House is open daily late May through mid-October; admission is $5.

Across the street is SPNEA's **Merwin House,** tel. (413) 298-4703, a graceful, 1820s Federal-era structure whose interior evokes its use as a summer home around the nation's centennial. That's when the southern Berkshires began to catch the fancies of wealthy New Yorkers such as the Doane family, who christened their then-rural retreat "Tranquility." The home's furnishings reflect both the Doanes' eclectic good taste and the life of ease that typified fin-de-siècle Stockbridge, a life still flickering in Victorian lawn games, afternoon high tea, and other special events. Open for tours on the hour Sat.-Sun. 11-4, late May through mid-October; admission $4.

Farther down Main Street, across from the distinctive Chime Tower, is the **Stockbridge Cemetery,** an old burying ground locally noted for a feature known as "the Sedgwick Pie": Revolutionary War officer and early settler John Sedgwick and his descendants have been buried in a circle so that upon their resurrection they shall be face to face with the rest of their family. (Edie Sedgwick, the Andy Warhol groupie and heiress who died from a highly publicized drug overdose in the 1970s, is *not* among the family members in this little Judgment Day circle.)

Berkshire Botanical Garden

At the junction of Rts. 102 and 183 are 15 acres of display gardens whose regiments of color provide a beautiful frame for almost any sort of day. Wander through wildflowers and spring bulbs in April and May, a formal rose garden a month or two later, a particularly fine array of daylilies in summer, and large swaths of perennials all year long. There's a loop through the woods, an herb garden, a children's garden, and a gift shop, too. Workshops and guided strolls are also offered. Open 10-5 daily May-mid-Oct.; admission $5. Tel. (413) 298-3926.

Ice Glen

Not far from the Stockbridge sidewalks packed with summer tourists lies this little hemlock gorge, owned by the town and named for the cool microclimate that pervades well into summer. A couple of miles of trails take in the glen, with its impressive stand of both erect and fallen trees, and adjacent Sedgwick Reservation, with

its observation tower. Parking is available in a small lot at the end of Park Street, or at the small turnout in Ice Glen Road, near a small sign for walkers.

The Play's the Thing

Since 1928, the Berkshire Playhouse, tel. (413) 298-5576—originally an 1889 social club called the Stockbridge Casino—has hosted one of the nation's top summer theaters, home to many notable directors and famous actors alike. This intimate stage, on the corner of Yale Hill Rd. and Rt. 102 in Stockbridge doesn't resort to retreads of popular Broadway or traditional hits, either: the productions constituting the **Berkshire Theatre Festival** are all new or rarely performed plays and musicals. Performances during the late June-through-Labor Day season are Mon-Sat. evenings and Thursday and Saturday afternoons. Call for schedule and box office information.

Food

A few strides down an alley from the bustle of the street sits **Naji's,** 40 Main, tel. (413) 298-5465, a tiny cafe offering a menu split between Middle Eastern fare—falafel, tabouli, and gyros, for example—and more generic cafe items like soups, sandwiches, calzones, and burgers. Lebanese desserts are available, too. This place has roots deep in pop-cultural history: its prior incarnation was as the restaurant run by Alice Brock, made famous by the Arlo Guthrie song "Alice's Restaurant Massacree." Across Main St. sits **Daily Bread,** a bright storefront bakery with plenty to soothe a nagging sweet tooth. Coffee drinkers in search of a good caffeine fix won't be disappointed by the espresso drinks, either. If you're dining al fresco at Tanglewood or lunching upon some stony ledge overlooking the Housatonic valley, fill your picnic basket with breads or baguettes here. (If you're headed south, you'll find the parent store on Railroad St. in Great Barrington.)

One of the landmarks of the Berkshires is the **Red Lion Inn,** tel. (413) 298-5545, whose wide verandah fills the corner of Main where US 7 turns south. You can't miss it—although you probably *should* if you don't feel like joining the busloads of tourists disgorged into the joint, and you definitely *will* miss it if you're wearing blue jeans, as there's a dress code. But the dining room may appeal greatly to meat and potato eaters tired of yuppie restaurant suggestions. You won't be confronted with unpronounceable salad greens or fruit-infused vinegars and oils on the menus of this grand country inn, nor chipotle sauces, cilantro marinades, or mango relishes—nothing, in fact, but solid New England cookery. The Baron of Beef presides over these century-old rooms, and if his tender pink roasts, ribs, and steaks aren't enough, there's plenty of fish and fowl to choose from. The region's harvest bounty stars in soups and side dishes—and, of course, there's apple pie for dessert.

LEE

Like the town of Adams in the northern half of the county, Lee is the sort of place where you half expect to come across Jimmy Stewart serenading Donna Reed. A trim little factory town whose hard, white marble has been used in buildings from the US Capitol to St. Patrick's Cathedral, Lee has an admirably staid downtown, anchored at one end by its soaring church steeple and drug store soda fountain, and at the other by a true-blue diner and paper mill. As one of the Berkshires' two junctions with the MassPike, Lee is also the major gateway to the county, with a small strip of national-brand motels north and southwest of the exit ramps and more (if not cheaper) gas stations than you'll find in adjacent towns. For an introduction to the Berkshires' social geography, US 20 from Lee to Lenox, next door, is a good short summation, running the gamut from *It's A Wonderful Life* to *The Great Gatsby*.

New England abounds with beautiful ecclesiastic architecture, but even among stellar peers the **First Congregational Church** in downtown Lee is a standout. The present building, dating to 1857, has the distinction of being the tallest timber structure in the nation, thanks to the needle-sharp 105-foot spire atop the 90-foot clock tower. The interior is equally remarkable: the trompe l'oeil paintings surrounding the sanctuary are among the finest you'll ever see. Take a peek when the church secretary is present, Mon-Thurs. mornings, or visit during Sunday services.

Food
You might as well accept the fact that when it comes to eating out in the Berkshires, big-city prices are the rule. Sure, all the major fast-food empires have local outposts, but for good fare, be prepared to drop more dollars than dimes. Happily, however, Lee possesses several exceptions. Topping the list is **Joe's Diner,** on the bend in Center St., tel. (413) 243-9756. This is the home of the square meal; tuck into a sandwich, soda, and maybe even pie for less than $5—amazing, but true. It's a favorite of what seems like half the county, from New York celebrities to local quarry workers—which is why Lee's selectmen eat here before their Monday meetings, to chat up constituents, and every politician campaigning for state office considers it a mandatory stop. Fortunately, Joe keeps sufficiently long hours to give you every opportunity to become a regular, too. If you need directions, just ask anyone in the Berkshires.

Another reasonable bet is the **Cactus Cafe,** 54 Main St., tel. (413) 243-4300, serving Mexican food daily for lunch, dinner, and weekend breakfast. We're not talking plain tacos, here: quinoa salad, smoked mushroom quesadillas, molé sauce, fresh seafood, and vegetarian entrees are standard fare. If you skip the homemade desserts and then develop a yen for something sweet after stepping outside, just cross the street to 43 Main and take a seat at the genuine soda fountain inside **McClelland's Drug Store,** tel. (413) 243-0135, which, while lacking the patina and old fittings of the type that Andy Hardy used to frequent, still captures the essence of summertime or after-school leisure, no matter what the season or time of day. Floats, frappes, sundaes, or just plain scoops of Ben & Jerry's ice cream are available at old-fashioned prices.

TYRINGHAM

The only Massachusetts town named after a woman (Jane Tyringham Beresford, cousin of a colonial governor), Tyringham is not so much a town as it is a view. The narrow, frost-heaved country road that cuts between Rt. 102 in Lee and Rt. 23 in Monterey and Otis—the town's main street, and nearly it's only paved one—is lined with 19th-century farms, presenting as pure a picture of back-road Berkshires as you could ask for. Even the rare craftsman-style post office at the town center seems rather fitting in its residential, midwestern way. Which makes Santarella—also called the **Gingerbread House,** tel. (413) 243-3260—that much more of a head-turner, standing out amid the traditional farmhouses along Main Road. Formerly the residence and studio of Henry Hudson Kitson, a prolific sculptor best known for his minuteman statue on Lexington's Battle Green, this whimsical imitation of a thatch-roofed English cottage now houses an art gallery and gift shop. Open May-Oct., admission $1. This area was popular with Kitson and his 19th-century contemporaries because of the Four Brooks Farm, owned by Richard Watson Gilder, the editor of *Scribner's* and *Century,* major illustrated turn-of-the-century newsweeklies. Gilder invited many famous acquaintances—Augustus Saint-Gaudens, Mark Twain, Henry Adams, and John Burroughs, among others—to summer here. Besides artists and writers, Tyringham was appealing to the Shakers, who built one of their handful of Massachusetts communes on the west side of the valley. A few of their buildings remain, but all are privately owned.

Tyringham Cobble

Cobbles begin with intrusions of hard, metamorphic rock within softer geological material. When the soft stuff erodes, it leaves a pile of rock stranded within a valley or plain. The spindling of the Berkshire region during the Appalachian orogen forced pressure-softened quartzite into the ancient coral deposits that, when flipped on their sides and eroded, produced the present valleys through the county. The hardened quartzite left behind has given the county a wealth of cobbles, ranging from broken and jumbled rock piles to abrupt ledges.

Tyringham Cobble is a stony ridge of gneiss rising 400 feet from pastoral Tyringham Valley, giving hikers broad, bird's-eye views over surrounding farm pastures and meandering Hop Brook. The Appalachian Trail crosses the property, and a two-mile loop trail encompasses both the summit and valley floor. The birdwatching is excellent here, with the mix of wooded and open land yielding a wide variety of both resident and migratory species. Parking and trailhead are marked with the TTOR logo on Jerusalem Rd., a turn off Tyringham Road.

BECKET

Becket has a huge summer population, following in a tradtion begun back in the early decades of this century, when auto touring over the Jacob's Ladder Trail made these hills accessible. Summer camps for city kids were also popular around here: Camp Greylock and Camp Wah-titoh were boys' and girls' camps, respectively, begun in 1916. Artists, too, have gravitated to Becket's hilltop serenity and wooded solitude, among them Ted Shawn, who founded a summer-study colony of dancers in the early 1930s. Over the decades, what is now known as **Jacob's Pillow Dance Festival,** tel. (413) 243-0745, has become the nation's premier celebration of dance. For 12 weeks each summer, the rustic stage hosts a diverse collection of dance groups from around the nation and the world, performing in a range of styles from classic ballet to contemporary movement as yet unnamed. Most performances take place Tues.-Sat, mid-June through Labor Day; call for schedule and box office information. The Pillow is found tucked into the Beckett woods off George Carter Rd., well signposted from US 20 a short distance east of the MassPike overpass and junction with Rt. 8.

ACCOMMODATIONS

Outside of winter, there are no budget accommodations per se in the Rockwell Country area, but the economy-class chain motels in and around MassPike Exit 2 in Lee provide an ample supply of inexpensive or moderate rooms—even during weekdays in summer and fall (Tanglewood weekends, of course, send rates at even the most lowly motel into triple digits). During high season, the fastest way to save a bundle is to share a bathroom; in the inns that offer them, the price for such shared-bath accommodations can often be half what someone down the hall is paying for a private bath. Off season, the difference between private and shared can be big enough to pay for dinner.

Depending on the season, remember to expect two- to three-night minimums at nearly every bed and breakfast or B&B-style inn.

For information about a score of additional B&Bs and fine inns from West Stockbridge to Tyringham, call the Stockbridge Chamber of Commerce's lodging hotline, (413) 298-5327, or drop in on their small kiosk on Main St., opposite the library.

Moderate: $60-85

Lee's motel cluster at the interchange monopolizes this category. On US 20 north of the turnpike, the **Super 8 Motel**, tel. (800) 800-8000 or (413) 243-3271, stands next to Burger King. During summer, its standard double is $60-70 (as opposed to at least $110 on Tanglewood weekends), but during winter it drops back to $45. Nearly across the street is the **Ramada Limited** (formerly the Pilgrim Motel), tel. (800) 2-RAMADA or (413) 243-1328, whose rates hit $85 d on summer weekdays ($145 for Tanglewood), but drop as low as $45-55 in winter. South of the interstate, on a quiet stretch of Rt. 102 toward Stockbridge, is a **Days Inn**, tel. (800) DAYS INN or (413) 243-0501, with a high-season rate of $69 d outside of Tanglewood (when it springs to $129-155) and fall foliage weekends ($85-95). From November through April or early May, it matches the $45-55 d rates of its competitors.

For something less generic, look to **The Morgan House Inn**, tel. (413) 243-0181, at 33 Main St., in downtown Lee, whose 11 rooms are among the more affordable in the area until the Boston Symphony rolls into Tanglewood. Between November and early June, rooms with private baths are $65-80 midweek, $75-100 weekends; until the end of October, these rise to $95-130, with Tanglewood and foliage weekends see it up to $125-160. For those willing to share a bath, rates are $55-65 off season, and $80-90 at their peak. All these rates include a full breakfast.

Expensive: $85-110

The **Arbor Rose B&B**, in Stockbridge, beside the Berkshire Theatre Festival's home on Rt. 102, tel. (413) 298-4744, www.arborrose.com, is one of those increasingly rare bed and breakfast places that feel less like a calculated investment in the hospitality business and more like someone's actual home. Comfortable rather than extravagant, graced (as opposed to cluttered) with antiques, blessed with a fine porch and a picturesque backyard millpond (belonging to the old sawmill now used as a stable), this place will easily put you right at home. Peak-season rates are $95-175 d; off season (November through mid-June), they're $85-125.

After waking up at **Conroy's B&B**, off US-7 in Stockbridge, tel. (413) 298-4990, and sitting down to your button-popping breakfast buffet of homebaked goodies, survey the broad lawn with its maple trees—most colorful in autumn—you, too, may think of becoming a country squire. That was the fate of the Californian owners of this handsome Federal-style farmhouse, who so fell in love with the place that they never left. Tasteful period wallpaper and furnishings complement your hosts' good cheer; in winter, their warm welcome is abetted in two of their four rooms by working fireplaces (see for yourself at www.conroysinn.com). Rates are $95-120 d in summer and fall ($75 with shared bath), $75-95 in winter ($55 shared). If you're searching for an apartment-sized suite with full kitchen, stop here: available in summer, it runs $225 a night (inquire about weekly rates).

Luxury: $150+

For thousands of visitors who have come through the region aboard tour buses, a night in the Berkshires means one thing: a night in **The Red Lion Inn**, tel. (413) 298-5545, www.RedLionInn.com, the cornerstone of Stockbridge's Main Street. With over 100 rooms and nearly a score of suites, the elegance of its front rooms and reception area is softened by the relaxed hubbub of guests coming and going or hanging out in one of many inviting spaces, from the courtyard gardens to the front-porch rockers. Befitting such a grand old place, antiques abound, along with careful reproductions, custom fabrics, fireplaces, and modern marble baths. As in luxury hotels worldwide, common descriptives don't serve here: regular double rooms are all "deluxe" (and priced accordingly, of course). April-Oct., rates run from $165 d with private bath to $355 for the Firehouse Suite. Off season, doubles are $97-130. Bargain hunters should consider the rooms with shared baths, which run only $87 in summer and $72 in winter, including breakfast in the formal main diningroom.

GREAT BARRINGTON

Not every Berkshire County town is a postcard-perfect specimen of small-town New England gentility or a historic center serving the recreational yearnings of society's elite. Great Barrington certainly has its share of graceful and historic architecture—and plenty of wealthy New Yorkers crowd its fancy bistros and summer chamber concerts. But the town firmly resists wholesale gentrification. Hardware stores and blue-collar lunch counters share downtown with sushi restaurants and chic boutiques, body-pierced kids mix with well-coifed Manhattanites at the ice-cream shop, and auto dealerships sit next to creative cafes.

Great Barrington also merits a couple of lines in the pages of history. In 1868, the eventual founder of the NAACP, William E.B. Du Bois, was born on the banks of the Housatonic River in downtown Great Barrington. He was raised in a home that once stood in a tree-filled meadow southwest of town, "with unbelievably delicious strawberries in the rear." Both sites are marked—the latter by a small, easy-to-miss plaque off Rt. 23 just west of the junction with Rt. 71. A few months after the Berkshires' Gilded Age rolled into town on the blue dolomite parapets and pink marble columns of Searles Castle (the construction of which provided the young college-bound Du Bois with his last summer job), Great Barrington became the nation's pioneer in electrification—Main Street was wired to an alternating current (AC) system designed by William Stanley. Thomas Edison may have invented the light bulb, but his support for the direct current (DC) that illuminated it stifled early attempts at delivering electric light to small businesses and homes unable to afford their own generators. In contrast, Stanley's AC inaugurated electric utilities as we know them today.

If you're headed south out of town on Rt. 23, you may notice the **Newsboy Monument,** beside the road shortly west of the railroad tracks. You can almost hear the bronze likeness shouting "Extra! Extra! Read all about it!" from atop his pedestal, which is decorated with the heads of a dog, cat, lion, and faun. Given to the town in 1895 by one of the owners of the original *New York Daily News*—a local resident—the statue honors "hardworking newspaper carriers" everywhere.

Housatonic

As artists breathe life into the old textile mills along the eponymous river, the village of Housatonic, on Rt. 183 in Great Barrington's northwest corner, has become a miniature SoHo of art galleries and studios. Annual open-studio weekends in the fall allow visitors to peek at the inner worlds of the local creative community. Most of the galleries are open weekends and by chance or appointment on weekdays. Perhaps none captures the essence of Housatonic's gleeful role as David versus the Manhattan Goliaths better than **Le Petit Musée,** 137 Front St., tel. (413) 274-1200, a tiny little room facing the railroad tracks. Although it's almost doubled in size since first opening, it may still live up to its original claim to being the smallest art gallery in the world. Needless to say, not an inch of wall space goes unoccupied. Given the scale of the items for sale, this is a good first stop for would-be arts patrons on artist-sized budgets themselves. Adjacent **Front St. Gallery,** tel. (413) 274-6607, is a more conventional-sized space run by and for a cooperative of local artists.

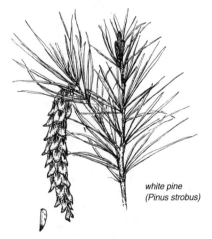

YVONNE DUNTON

*white pine
(Pinus strobus)*

Take a short walk under the railroad tracks and over the river to check out three additional exhibition spaces: **Tokonoma,** at the bend in Rt. 183; **Spazi Contemporary Art,** tel. (413) 274-3805, on the top floor of the lumber mill next door (open Wed.-Sun. except in winter); and **RiCA,** or River Contemporary Art, tel. (413) 274-0200, in the long brick trolley shed past the bend (also Wed.-Sun. until cold weather takes hold).

When you've developed an appetite, cozy little **Christina's Just Desserts & Country Cafe,** on Pleasant St. across from the schoolyard, will satisfy it. Walk past the large cases of tempting pastries and baked goods (if you can) and you'll find the cafe proper, with a lunch menu of soups made from scratch, unusual sandwiches, and quiche. Or, if you prefer, you can fashion a picnic on your way south on Rt. 183, first with a stop at **Berkshire Mountain Bread,** a short distance past RiCA, whose tasty sourdough rolls and loaves are available straight from the kitchen door Sun.-Thurs. till 10 p.m.—and then with a stop at **Taft Farms,** a couple of miles farther, at the corner of Division Street. With the fixings of a great repast in hand, the next stop should be the peak of Monument Mountain, rising to the north.

Monument Mountain

At 1,735 feet, Monument Mountain affords a striking westward vista over the Housatonic River valley (the view east is marred by a gravel pit). From the exposed rock ledges called Squaw Peak, you can survey the motley quilt of open farmland and forest stretching to the north-south ridge of the Taconic Range that marks the border with New York. The place has a significant place in literary history, too; it was here in 1850 that Herman Melville first met his successful contemporary, Nathaniel Hawthorne, on a hike with their editor and with newspaper mogul William Cullen Bryant. Melville's eventual dedication of *Moby-Dick* to Hawthorne is one of several strong signs of an affection which, unfortunately for Melville, seemed to be somewhat unrequited; when Hawthorne finally left the Berkshires, he did so without a word of warning or farewell, an act which Melville found quite hurtful.

After the steep ascent to its lookout, the single trail makes a loop around the wooded base of the small mountain, returning to the parking lot beside US 7. From the north, the trailhead parking comes soon after you pass Great Barrington Regional High School; from the south, it comes abruptly on the left after US 7 crests a rather long steep hill. In either case, succumbing to the pressures of speeding traffic will result in overshooting the lot, which is marked by the TTOR's standard diminutive sign.

PERFORMING ARTS

Music of the 17th and 18th centuries is the specialty of the **Aston Magna Festival,** tel. (413) 528-3595, held July through early August. The acoustically bright interior of the great stone St. James Church on Main St., next door to Town Hall, makes an appropriate setting for the Saturday concerts—all of which are performed on authentic period instruments. Call for program details and ticket prices. Classical music is also featured at the **Stockbridge Chamber Concerts,** which, its name notwithstanding, are performed July-Aug. at Great Barrington's John Dewey Academy for boys, located behind the stone wall and curtain of trees at 389 Main St., on the south end of downtown. Yellow House Books, at 252 Main St., functions as the chamber series' box office; drop by or call (413) 528-8227 for schedule or ticket information. A bonus of the series are the pre-concert tours of the school's home, the former 45-room **Searles Castle.** Modeled after the French Chenonceaux chateau from the Loire Valley, this imposing mansion was designed in the 1880s by Stanford White, a former apprentice to the renowned Boston architect H.H. Richardson. Built for Mary Hopkins, widow of San Francisco railroad tycoon Mark Hopkins, its name comes from the interior decorator who became her second husband. In general, the academy is not open to the public.

ACCOMMODATIONS

Though no national chain motels have settled in Great Barrington, the north side of town features a handful of local variants. But only one of these—the friendly **Mountain View Motel,** tel. (413) 528-0250, next to the Panda West restaurant on Rt. 23, a mile east of US 7—is competitive with the cluster around the MassPike interchange in Lee. The **Southern Berkshire Chamber of Commerce,** tel. (413) 528-4006, lists over a score of motels, inns, and B&Bs in their free *Lodging Guide to the Southern Berkshires,* available by phone or in person from their small information center in front of Bill's Pharmacy on the south end of Main Street. That phone number will also yield tips on last-minute weekend availability among Chamber members.

Some fine campgrounds are to be found in several state forests surrounding Great Barrington. As market town to the south county, this is the best place south of US 7's Pittsfield-Lenox strip to take care of backpacking needs or replenish back seat coolers. Fuel for your camp stove and other supplies are readily available at **Appalachian Mountain Gear,** open daily at 777 South Main St., tel. (413) 528-8811. The market across the street, **Guido's,** can enliven your camp menu with its high-quality produce and terrific selections of cheeses, breads, fresh and smoked fish and meats, and gourmet condiments, including many items of local origin.

FOOD

The center of Great Barrington has a lot to offer, from the plain to the fancy. Fussy early risers in pursuit of cappuccino and muffins, or picnickers seeking the makings of a great spread will both want to check out **Daily Bread,** 17 Railroad St., with its wholesome and delicious baked goods. There's a small counter along the big front window, where you can sit, hot coffee in hand, and savor not having to dash to the office. **The Berkshire Coffee Roasting Company,** nearby on Main St., also serves espresso drinks, teas, and bakery items. **Bev's Homemade,** adjacent to Daily Bread on Railroad St., is another source of caffeine—and sugar, too, by the creamy, super-premium bucketful. If two scoops of Bananas Foster or Raspberry Chocolate Chip ice cream isn't your idea of the perfect lunch, then consider the hearty soups or filled Jamaican patties (a Caribbean calzone). **Martin's,** at the end of Railroad St., is a basic sandwich, burger, and all-day-breakfast sort of place, but granola, tofu, and brie are on the menu, too. Skip the pies, though; brought in from Pittsfield, they're a dis-

appointment. Open for breakfast and lunch (till 3 p.m.). If deli take-out is all you want, consider **The Deli,** 343 Main St., opposite Town Hall, or, for more upscale offerings, **The Market Place,** 2 State Rd., next to the bridge at the top of Main Street. Featuring all sorts of prepared salads, soups, quiches, entrees, and desserts, in addition to sandwiches, muffins, and breads, the Market Place is open Tues.-Sat. to 7 p.m., Sunday to 3 p.m.

Open for lunch and dinner, **20 Railroad Street,** whose name betrays its location, is *the* place for burgers, sandwiches, and soups, in an always-crowded roadhouse rich with dark wood and upbeat background music. The sheer variety of toppings, fillings, and seasonings—plus nightly dinner specials—will prove tantalizing to all but vegetarians (for whom choices are limited). Originally a speakeasy, the bar has only gotten livelier with age. Reasonably priced and unpretentious.

Not too far away, across the tracks behind Town Hall, is **Kintaro,** 48 Castle Hill St., tel. (413) 528-5678, a lofty, sparely decorated Japanese restaurant and sushi bar located in the former railroad depot. Fine, fresh sashimi, maki, and nigiri sushi varieties are naturally the specialties of the house, but anyone who shies away from raw or marinated fish will find plenty of palate-pleasing noodles, tempura, and teriyaki, too. An especially nice touch is the several different types of sake. The restaurant's former life is pleasantly evoked by the deep rumble of occasional passing trains. Open for dinners only, nightly from 5:30 p.m.; takeout available. **Castle Street Cafe,** tel. (413) 528-5244, next to the charming Mahaiwe (m-HEY-wee) Theater, another dinner-only place boasts an upscale menu emphasizing freshness, seasonal variations, and sensory appeal. A small spot that attracts quite the cosmopolitan crowd, it's pricey, but some find the food worth it. Also open for Sunday brunch, but closed Tuesdays. Reservations are accepted for groups of five or more only.

While commercial Stockbridge Road (US 7), on the north side of town, isn't conducive to after-dinner strolls—unless you enjoy car dealers' lots and supermarket plazas—the ambiance hasn't scared off such fine places to strap on the feed bag as **Hickory Bill's Barbeque,** tel. (413) 528-1444, at the rear of the parking lot next to the upscale **Boiler Room Café.** Yankees aren't particularly known for good barbecue, but even Texans tip their hats to Hickory Bill, whose ribs and brisket could be served west of the Red River without any apologies. Don't skimp on the side dishes—they're all quite good—and leave room, if you can, for the superb sweet-potato pie.

HIGH ROADS AND LOW ROADS: THE RURAL SOUTH COUNTY

These are all routes radiating out of Great Barrington—east and southeast onto the Berkshire Plateau, south along the Housatonic River valley to Connecticut, west into the Taconic Range along the New York state line. The towns and villages along these routes are often so small that you would miss them in the dark, and even in daylight you can pass them in the proverbial blink of an eye. Venture along these roads, though, and you'll come across old-fashioned general stores, great camping and hiking opportunities, a few spots to get your feet wet, and the occasional historic sight. You'll also find hidden art studios, country restaurants, antique shops, and get-away-from-it-all inns out here—along with plenty of scenic back roads ideal for cycling. Nearly all the attractions, no matter how remote, are enumerated on quaint directional signs found at the appropriate intersections with main roads; if you're traveling over 35 mph, they pass in illegible white blurs. Be sure to stock up on fuel and cash, too—no ATMs or reasonably priced gas stations exist out here.

ROUTE 23 EAST: THE GENERAL KNOX TRAIL

At the start of the American Revolution in April, 1775, Boston was firmly occupied by the British. Capturing the city required artillery, which the colonial militia didn't have. Benedict Arnold—who would eventually betray the American cause—persuaded Massachusetts to grant him a colonel's commission in order to attack the British Fort Ticonderoga, in New York, and capture their cannon and mortars for use in the rebel lines at Cambridge. Before Arnold finished raising a raiding party of 400 men, Connecticut commissioned the unorthodox Ethan Allen and his Green Mountain Boys to do the same thing. Arnold caught up to

Allen just 20 miles from the fort, and together they stormed the unsuspecting outpost in the middle of the night on May 10, in such competition that the British commander couldn't even figure out to whom he should surrender. Unfortunately for the two bickering colonels, they had to leave Ticonderoga empty-handed, as they had no way of transporting the fort's heavy guns back to Cambridge. Fortunately for the fledgling Continental Army, which initiated the siege of Boston two months later, an enterprising book dealer-turned-soldier, Henry Knox, determined that Ticonderoga's artillery could be dragged over frozen roads with teams of oxen—an arduous 300-mile feat he managed to accomplish in early 1776. When, finally, the British Navy found itself facing 55 of its own guns from the Dorchester Heights above Boston Harbor, it could not stay. And, without naval assistance, the garrison of troops in Boston couldn't stay, either. The intrepid Knox was promoted to general for his invaluable aid in winning the city (without firing a shot), ably commanded George Washington's artillery for the remainder of the Revolution, and went on to become America's first Secretary of War.

On its way east from Great Barrington to US 20, at the village of Woronoco, Rt. 23 roughly follows the Berkshire portion of the route taken by Knox and his unwieldy gun sleds. These days, most of the route passes through state forests, giving the towns along the way a substantially more rural quality than their sister communities in the Housatonic valley. Residents of these wooded hills often succumb to "otisitis" (for the tiny town of Otis), a pleasingly relaxed state of well-being that Type A personalities may mistake for narcolepsy.

Beartown State Forest
Along this route through the Berkshires, swimming opportunities are limited by residency requirements for use of local lakefront beaches,

but **Benedict Pond** ($2), in the Beartown State Forest, off Rt. 23 east of Great Barrington, is a pleasant exception. For a panoramic prelude to your dip, walk around to the pond's eastern tip and its junction with the Appalachian Trail. Turn north for the short scramble up to the Ledges, a rocky precipice affording a fine view all the way to the Catskills in neighboring New York. During fall foliage season, the state forest's oaks, maples, and birches present a carpet of color. The AT is the forest's principal hiking trail; others are shared with horses, mountain bikes, and sometimes even motorized dirt bikes.

Monterey

Shortly after passing the turnoff for Beartown State Forest, eastbound travelers will come upon the gas pumps of the **Roadside Store,** a veritable shack in the woods. The tiny cafe within this nondescript spot is a local institution, dishing up simple breakfasts and lunches at bargain prices (the hubcap-sized buckwheat pancakes cost less than $3, and so do the lean burgers—made from their own beef, raised nearby) in an atmosphere that blends diner with commune. If you're looking for a satisfying whole-grain bread for your picnic basket, the Roadside sells a hearty loaf.

No visitor to the little town of Monterey should resist the impulse to drop in on the **Monterey General Store,** in the village center, right on Rt. 23, just opposite the Tyringham Road. A true one-stop shop, it carries groceries (including exceptionally good locally produced goat cheese), local and out-of-town newspapers, videos, some housewares, and fishing supplies, and also features a couple of small tables back by the deli counter. Naturally, it's the town's social center.

Out in the back woods on unpaved Art School Rd., north of Rt. 23 off Tyringham Rd., is **Joyous Spring Pottery,** tel. (413) 528-4115. Between May and October, you can visit the gallery/studio/home of ceramic artist Michael Marcus, who produces and sells pottery inspired by the traditional unglazed wares of Bizen, one of the oldest and most famous Japanese pottery centers. The great 43-foot *noborigama*—multichambered kiln—on the hillside beneath the trees is also traditional; when fired, it becomes like a living dragon. At the very end of Art School Rd. is the **Bidwell House,** tel. (413) 528-6888,

a historic farmstead built in the middle of the 18th century for the first minister of the vicinity. Though exhibiting the symmetrical design so characteristic of the Georgian style, it's still a country home at heart, making up in period furnishings what it lacks in exterior ornament common to more cosmopolitan mansions of the same era. Woods now grow in what used to be the surrounding fields, where old drystone walls remind visitors of the annual crop of rocks harvested after each spring thaw. Open Tues.-Sun. and Monday holidays, late May through mid-October (admission is charged).

Route 23 Camping

The dozen campsites in Beartown State Forest are unattractively plain and crowded close together around a semicircular driveway a short walk from Benedict Pond, with primitive outhouses, water, picnic tables, fireplaces, and no showers. They're open mid-May through Columbus Day; $4.

More scenic camping—some of the state's best, in fact—is found farther east, at **Tolland State Forest,** on the banks of huge Otis Reservoir in adjacent Hamden County. All 90 campsites here are located on a wooded peninsula jutting out into the lake. While varying considerably in size, proximity to one another, and terrain, the setbacks from road and neighbors are uniformly decent, and the woods are generally thick enough to provide a measure of privacy. A dozen or more sites are prime—right on the water, totally out of view of the road, and, because of the curve in the shoreline, not even in view of too many other sites on either side. Amenities include showers, flush toilets, and water; open Mid-May through mid-October; $6. To reserve, call (413) 269-6002. Since state camping fees were cut in half in the early 1990s, the park has become more of a magnet for rowdies, but avoid holiday weekends (when beer kegs in pickup beds are as common as kerosene lanterns) and you shouldn't be too bothered. (If you are, there's a private lakeshore campground just outside the gates of the public one, where after-dark quiet rules are respected and enforced: **Camp Overflow,** tel. 413-269-4036.) Located off Tolland Rd. in the far east corner of Otis, between Rts. 23 and 8, signposted from both.

ROUTE 57:
INTO THE HIGH COUNTRY

Southeast of Great Barrington, the population thins out, and general stores boasting such Berkshire touches as gourmet provisions and the *New York Times* give way to ones carrying shelves of ammo. The roadside cafe serving buckwheat pancakes gives way to the roadhouse bar featuring keno machines, Pabst Blue Ribbon on tap, and a parking lot full of pickups. As Berkshire cultural resources fade into the rearview mirror as Rt. 57 heads through rural New Marlborough and Sandisfield, over the Clam and Farmington Rivers, and into the high hills of Tolland and Granville, you don't need a sociology or marketing degree to detect the demographic changes. Neither do you need to be a naturalist to notice the dramatic changes in the landscape, with the oak forest and fields of the Housatonic floodplain being replaced by the characteristic northern forests running down from Vermont along the higher elevations of the Berkshire Plateau, and the pale ribbons of white birch growing increasingly common.

One of the more obscure regions of the state, this part of Berkshire and neighboring Hamden County is better known to folks from Connecticut than from Massachusetts. Cyclists and rambling motorists will find a web of scenic back roads flanked by hardwood forests that conceal mountain laurel groves, a couple of waterfalls, potters' and other artists' studios, a few antique stores, a fish hatchery, and, off Rt. 57 in West Granville, **The Berry Patch,** tel. (413) 357-6679, offering pick-your-own blueberries daily in late summer. State forests host a slew of trout-stocked lakes for fishing and canoeing, and miles of off-road trails favored by mountain and dirt bikers or snowmobiles, depending on the season. Cross-country skiers looking for dedicated trails should head to Granville's **Maple Corner Farm Cross-Country Ski Center,** signposted from Rt. 57, tel. (413) 357-6697.

Pedalers should prepare for a variety of terrain—gentle when following riverbeds, quite hilly in between—and road conditions, from good pavement to rutted gravel. For suggested routes, pick up a copy of Lewis Cuyler's *Bike Rides in the Berkshire Hills.*

New Marlborough

Like railroad towns of a later century, New Marlborough was one of several numbered townships established to promote colonial English use of the former Indian path west from Springfield. Laid out in 1735, the town prospered as the path eventually became a stagecoach route and as small industries producing gunpowder, newsprint, and buggy whips utilized local streams and timber. Bypassed by the railroad, New Marlborough's present population of 1,200 is barely two-thirds what it was at its peak in the 1870s.

About a half mile off Rt. 57 on New Marlborough Hill Rd. is the parking area and trailhead for **Questing,** a TTOR property. Old pastures outlined by numerous drystone walls have reverted to thick oak forest, but cellar holes from the old Wishing Well Hill settlement—one of the earliest by whites in the county—are still evident, their depressions and stonework discernible among the ferns and leaf litter. Logging roads and woodland trails offer plenty of serenity and, depending on the season, fleeting glimpses of local wildlife (although it's more often heard than seen). In late spring and early summer, be sure to take in past the large upland meadow to see what's in bloom. As with all other Berkshire TTOR properties, no bikes are allowed on the trails.

If you are trying to impress a special someone (or yourself) with a meal to remember for months to come, **The Old Inn On The Green,** tel. (413) 229-3131, should top your short list. Located right on Rt. 57 at the intersection of Southfield Rd., this beautifully restored 18th-century stagecoach inn offers the sort of exceptional prix fixe dining that, like travel abroad, should be experienced at least once. Each Saturday night throughout the year (except for two weeks in January), here reigns the sort of confident creativity that pairs parsnip flan and dried cherry sauce with roast duck, cilantro and jicama with Maine crab, or dandelion greens and vermouth-poached orange pulp with caramelized scallops. Classic French techniques prevail—fish en papillote or Forestière, quail "en Boule," wilted greens in a soufflé, veal breast roulade—but they're tempered by lighter stocks and sauces typical of New American cuisine. Jaded skeptics may rightly ask—since several other Berkshire restaurants are capable of composing equally sensuous meals—why drive all the way out here and pay these prices? Because, dear Watson, no other restaurant has a setting like this one. The exclusively candle-lit small dining rooms, each with its own hearth, are like an old oil painting come to life, and leave you vaguely anticipating the sound of horse hooves and shouting stage drivers as the coach from Albany stops en route to Boston. You will not find a more romantic meal. In addition to these weekly extravaganzas (under $50 for three courses), a shortened à la carte menu (entrees $18-23) is presented on Thursday, Friday, and Sunday evenings year-round (and seasonally on Monday and Wednesday, as well).

Accommodations are also available, either in the old inn or next door, on its companion property, **Gedney Farm,** tel. (800) 286-3139, www.oldinn.com, whose big Normandy-style dairy barn features a renovated interior that belongs in the pages of *Architectural Digest.* Simple yet refined decor boldly accented by warm Southwestern colors and Turkish kilim upholstery characterizes the guest rooms, many of which have two levels or lofts with fireplaces and whirlpool baths. The morning's fresh fruit and baked goods set a standard for continental breakfasts (included), and the staff provides impeccable service (10% extra, added automatically). Rates are $175-205 d, $225-285 for the suites, but inquire about midweek specials and package deals. For those who prefer antiquity, rooms at the Old Inn are $120 with shared bath, $160-175 with private. There's a two-night minimum on weekends July through October, and on holidays year-round.

Even if you don't sleep or dine here, you may still want to drop in to see the art gallery in the farm's Grand Percheron horse barn, wander the sculptures exhibited on the grounds, or attend one of the gallery's special events—such as the annual decorative arts sale during the post-Thanksgiving holiday season. In sum, there's always something cooking around here, and it rarely fails to please.

Route 57 Camping

Ten free year-round wilderness tent sites are available on a first-come, first-served basis in **Sandisfield State Forest,** a short hike in from the parking area at West Lake. The forest has

two parts, both signposted from Rt. 57 east of the Old Inn on the Green. The first two State Forest signs—at the bend immediately beyond the Inn and at a dirt road 2.5 miles farther east—are both for the York Lake day-use area on the south side of the highway, with family beach and bathhouse ($2). West Lake is north of the highway; turn at the *third* sign.

A couple of towns east, in dense woods along the Connecticut border, lies **Granville State Forest,** a true hidden gem of a spot about two miles south of Rt. 57 in Granville. Forty campsites catering to tenters are strung along the banks of a babbling brook, with plenty of elbow room and an atmosphere of northern New England serenity; drinking water, outhouses, no showers; open May 1 through mid-October; $4. The forest also has a swimming pond and hiking trails. Campers in need of provisions for a stay at Granville—from flashlight batteries to fresh-baked bread, boot laces to Ben & Jerry's—may rely on the friendly **High Country General Store** on Rt. 57 in Tolland Center, a couple of miles west of the state forest turn-off. For fresh peaches, plums, nectarines, apples and pears, check out **Nestrovich Fruit,** a few miles east on Rt. 57, near Rt. 189, open late July through May 1 (thanks to the miracles of cold storage, Ray Nestrovich's apples and pears are as succulent in April as in November).

ROUTE 7: ANTIQUE ALLEY

There are more than two dozen antique dealers between Great Barrington and the Connecticut line—most in the town of **Sheffield,** along US 7, or its side roads, a concentration that has won the town and its main street the appellation "Antique Alley." Appearances aside, don't come expecting to find garage sales: with half of Manhattan picking over their wares on the way through town, undiscovered—and undervalued—treasures are rarer than four-leaf clovers.

Sheffield's preoccupation with the past extends—albeit quietly—to a genuine historic site, the last battleground of Shays' Rebellion. A simple little obelisk in a field beside the Sheffield-South Egremont Road marks the spot where reform-minded farmers who took up arms against debtors' courts finally lost their cause, in

February 1787. Here, too, the Appalachian Trail, which comes down from East Mountain, crosses the Housatonic floodplain and passes along this all-but-forgotten battlefield before climbing back up the ridge on the west side of the valley.

Even here—far from the patrician trappings of Lenox cottages now serving as theaters and concert halls—the performing arts have taken modest root—the **Barrington Stage Company** performs at the Mt. Everett High School's Consolati Performing Arts Center, on Berkshire School Rd., late June through early October. Call (413) 528-8888 for box office info.

Bartholomew's Cobble

Designated a National Natural Landmark for its botanical variety, Bartholomew's Cobble is home to well over 700 plant species, thanks to an unusual combination of both "soft," limey soil and "hard," acidic soil. The wooded tumble of soft marble and hard quartzite whose properties have created this unique environment on the banks of the Housatonic is ringed by a self-guiding interpretive trail that begins at a small visitor center and parking lot on Weatogue Rd., near the Ashley Falls village, in southern Sheffield. Other trails take in meadows and the nearby hill with fine views of September's migrating hawks. Open daily; $3 adults, $1 children.

On the Cooper Hill Road side of the property stands the 1735 **Colonel John Ashley House,** one of Berkshire County's oldest. The builder of this well-crafted farmhouse was a young lawyer, surveyor, and eventual slave owner. Mum Bett, the colonel's slave, set a legal precedent in 1781 by successfully suing for freedom under the newly ratified Massachusetts Constitution. House tours are offered Wed.-Sun. 1-5 p.m. in peak season (between the last week of June and early September), on weekends and holidays in the shoulder seasons (late May through mid-October). Admission is $5. Owned by TTOR, both the cobble and its historic house are signposted (with TTOR's usual discretion) from Rannapo Rd., which loops off of US-7A; for information on either, call (413) 229-8600.

River Trips

The Housatonic—the "golden river" mentioned by W.E.B. Du Bois in his childhood recollections—provides plenty of good flatwater canoe-ing on its meandering course through the Berkshires' southern half. TTOR sponsors a variety of small-scale, naturalist-led canoe outings— by day, at sunrise, even by moonlight—that usually end at TTOR's Bartholomew's Cobble; tel. (413) 229-8600. The Massachusetts Audubon Society does the same; its regional headquarters, at the Pleasant Valley Wildlife Sanctuary, tel. (413) 637-0320, can provide a schedule and take reservations once you know which trip you wish to join. Do-it-yourselfers can rent canoes in Sheffield at **Gaffer's Outdoors,** on Main St., tel. (413) 229-0063, or opt for a no-hassles river shuttle, with Gaffer's providing both the boat and the transportation.

ROUTE 23 WEST: OVER THE TACONICS INTO NEW YORK

West from Great Barrington, Rt. 23 passes through the southerly, more shopping-oriented of the two Egremont villages before crossing the state line into New York and intersecting the Taconic Parkway. South Egremont's antique dealers and cafes are all worthy diversions, but a prime attraction is the state forest land in the state's most remote mainland town, Mt. Washington. For population size and remoteness, the Elizabeth Islands may have a smaller year-round population than this region (fewer than 30, compared to 101) and equally difficult access (boat only, of course). But when it comes to real Massachusetts boondocks, tall mountains and miles of rough, frost-heaved roads help this corner trump the rest.

Bash Bish Falls

Given the splendid isolation of this corner of the commonwealth, most visitors to beautiful, 200-foot **Bash Bish Falls** arrive via New York's easily accessible Rt. 22. Bash Bish Brook tumbles noisily through a deep, irregular granite gorge before splitting picturesquely around a huge boulder and falling a final 50 feet to a large pool filled with submerged rocks. Bash Bish Falls is located on Falls Road at the Massachusetts-New York state line; look for the signposted turnoff on Rt. 41 in South Egremont. A trail to the top of the falls leaves from the first of two unmarked but fairly obvious upper parking lots, with paving for a half-dozen or more cars; west of this is a second lot, the New York state line, and the well-marked lower parking lot (with a short, level path to the pool at the base of the falls).

Surrounding the falls—on the Massachusetts side—is **Mt. Washington State Forest,** tel. (413) 528-0330, one of the few places in the state where timber rattlesnakes can still be found (a testament to the landscape's ruggedness, which has proven resistant to habitat-threatening human occupation). Besides a few long trail loops—only one of which is open to mountain biking—the forest has 15 backcountry campsites. A good half-mile hike in from the parking area, they're free and open year-round, but pre-registration is required at the forest headquarters at the end of the paved portion of East Street.

Food

The tiny community of South Egremont seems to have passed a law prohibiting bad food from being served within the town limits. Whether you're after cheap omelettes or expensive profiteroles, you're more than likely to get your money's worth wherever you go here.

If you're headed into or out of the woods, or in need of something to get you going, **Mom's Country Cafe,** tel. (413) 528-2414, is just for you (never mind Damon Runyon's caveat about places called "Mom's"). From 6:30 a.m. until after 9 p.m., sit down to full country breakfasts, burgers, pizzas, pasta, salads, and soups in a friendly cabin-like setting for not much money at all. The place even delivers locally. You might also try **The Gaslight Cafe,** tel. (413) 528-0870, a few hundred yards farther east, on the same side of Rt. 23. This little cafe has several virtues (not immediately apparent from a glance at the Woolworth's lunch-counter-style menu). The back patio is one, and the smoking section's sun-soaked view down to Karner Brook is another. The food's good, the proprietor friendly to a fault, and in blueberry or apple season you'd do well to stop here for the pies alone. In September, when the apples are Macouns (a truly underappreciated variety) and the weather justifies a little hot-buttered-rum topping, skip dessert at your peril.

If you'd rather see a side dish of wild rice than a side order of french fries, consider a visit to **The Old Mill,** tel. (413) 528-1421, on Main St. (Rt. 23) inside a restored 18th-century blacksmith shop and grist mill. Fish, meat, and poultry are paired with interesting sauces, accompaniments, and garnishes for meals that will delight all the senses (if you don't want to eat a full meal, you can visit the bar). Call for reservations in July and August. In a similar vein—if perhaps not quite as exciting or setting as high a standard—there's the restaurant of **The 1780 Egremont Inn,** on Old Sheffield Rd., tel. (413) 528-2111. The Inn also features a tavern with its own menu featuring "casual fare" (meaning you can always get a burger if that's what you want).

Rounding out the high-priced end in a class by itself, **John Andrew's,** tel. (413) 528-3469, serving dinner and weekend brunch at the corner of Blunt Rd. and Rt. 23, almost at the New York line. It feels like somebody's home, and, indeed, it is—the chef-owner lives upstairs. His wife is likely the one to greet you at the door. Local artists have done a striking job with the interior, but take it in before the food comes—after that, your attention will be on your plate. The small, frequently changing menu features local produce, meats, and fish, in signature dishes such as white corn-meal pizza with smoked salmon and mascarpone. A couple of vegetarian entrees are always available, and the kitchen is very accommodating on requests for making others meatless (a vegetable stock is even kept in reserve for substitution where desired). Only dieters or teetotalers will end up paying less than $30 a head, but even at full price it's an excellent value. Reservations advised.

Accommodations

No guest has ever minded being talked into spending an extra night at the **Baldwin Hill Farm B&B,** tel. (413) 528-4092, a fine Egremont farmhouse surrounded by the sort of pastoral beauty that makes urban dwellers dream of permanently going back to the land. Hayfields, pastures, woodlots, barns, and gardens fill the foreground around the outdoor swimming pool, and the Taconic Range and Berkshire Hills provide a scenic backdrop. As for the hospitality—well, suffice it to say that Dick and Priscilla Burdsall could have invented the whole concept. Located at the top of Baldwin Hill Road North/South; rates are $70-94 d, depending on whether baths are shared or private. The price includes a full country breakfast, the particulars of which are chosen by guests the night before.

Farther south on Rt. 41, near Sheffield's border with Connecticut, lie several B&Bs. They charge a pretty penny for the sweet solitude that abounds under the ridge of Mt. Everett and Mt. Race. For an alternative under $100, the **Race Brook Lodge,** tel. (413) 229-2916, is carved out of a 19th-century barn. Old hand-hewn beams and plain white plaster lend rustic touches, there's a remarkable absence of chintz and frills, but fully modern private baths and big, comfortable beds mean you'll be anything but roughing it. After helping yourself to a continental breakfast, consider hiking up to the Appalachian Trail, accessible from the back door. Once a month, an informal—and very popular—jazz brunch takes over the common rooms on the main floor.

BOOKLIST

OTHER TRAVEL GUIDES

Berger, Josef (Jeremiah Digges). *Cape Cod Pilot, a WPA Guide.* Boston: Northeastern University Press, 1985 (originally published in 1937). Full of anecdotes that capture the flavor of yesteryear's Cape, mixed with a good brace of factual history, told in a pleasing yarn-spinner's fashion.

Chesler, Bernice. *In & Out of Boston with & without Children.* Chester, CT: Globe Pequot Press, 1992. If you've got kids, you may feel I've slighted your young ones. You won't feel that way with Chesler's volume (which covers eastern Massachusetts).

Federal Writers' Project. *The WPA Guide to Massachusetts.* Boston: Northeastern University Press, 1987. This reprint of the 1937 original is a great snapshot of the state in a totally different era and economic situation—just before the complete decline of its industrial manufacturing base. Although historical fact isn't always strictly adhered to by the writers, the book serves well in a general way.

Sweetser, M. F. *King's Handbook of Boston Harbor.* Boston: Friends of Boston Harbor, Inc. Like the rest of the Moses King Corp.'s series of 19th-century guidebooks, this title is copiously illustrated; thoroughly descriptive; and rich in history, anecdote, and verse (including many sailors' shanties). The final 1888 edition has become a collector's item, but this modern paperback reissue by the Friends of Boston Harbor—a community advocacy group whose volunteers contribute mightily to visitor programs on the Boston Harbor Islands—is readily available in Boston bookstores or directly from the Friends themselves (Box 9025, Boston MA 02114; 617-740-4290; ISBN 1557091080).

Waldstein, Mark. *Mr. Cheap's Boston.* Cheshire, CT: Bob Adam's Inc., 1995. Good, extensive listings of everything that can be had for a fair price (or less) around the metro area. Every consumer category you could ask for, plus cheap eats. Not recommended so much for tourists (unless you want to know where to get cheap furniture or auto parts), but for anyone seeking to cut the costs of even temporary residency, this book will pay for itself.

Wilson, Susan. *Boston Sites and Insights.* Boston: Beacon Press, 1994. Thorough, informative, and well written, this guide (by a *Boston Globe* reporter) lists about 100 Boston-area attractions, from familiar must-see sights to the lesser known, and provides the essential background to each. Recommended.

RECREATION GUIDES

Hiking

Appalachian Mountain Club. *AMC Massachusetts and Rhode Island Trail Guide.* Boston: Appalachian Mountain Club Books, 1995. Long considered the definitive resource for serious hikers. The density of information is sometimes difficult to navigate, but there's no arguing with its thoroughness. Includes a pocket of topo maps to such popular hiking areas as Mt. Greylock and the Blue Hills.

Brady, John, and Brian White. *Fifty Hikes in Massachusetts* Woodstock, VT: Backcountry Press, 1992. Handy for day-trips, ranging from cakewalks to strenuous hikes.

Laubach, René. *A Guide to Natural Places in the Berkshire Hills.* Lee, MA: Berkshire House, 1992. The director of the Massachusetts Audubon Society's Western Region, Laubach is an unequivocal authority in all matters winged, quadruped, geologic, and mytologic.

Merrimack River Watershed Council. *A Guide to Trails from Canada to the Atlantic Ocean.* Lawrence, MA: MRWC, 1995. New Hampshire's Heritage Trail and Massachusetts' Merrimack River Trail are currently a work-in-progress network of both rural and urban trails running the length of the Merrimack River. This thick pocket guide describes access points, trail segments, and featured scenic and historic highlights for each riverfront town's contribution to the network—and provides local contact names and addresses for further or updated information. Seventeen Massachusetts towns are included, with five site-specific maps. Charge it by calling (978) 681-5777 ($14) or pick it up in person from the Merrimack River Watershed Council, 56 Island St., Lawrence MA 01840-1803. A comparable canoeist's guide to the river is also available.

Stevens, Lauren R. *Hikes & Walks in the Berkshire Hills.* Lee: Berkshire House, 1990. Warmly recommended for anyone planning to spend lots of time in the Berkshires out of doors.

Biking

Angiolillo, Paul. *Mountain Biking Southern New England.* Birmingham, AL: Menasha Ridge Press, 1993. A Falcon Guide, one of Dennis Coello's "America by Mountain Bike" series. Thorough, well-organized, informative. Describes 33 rides throughout Massachusetts.

Cuyler, Lewis C. *Bike Rides in the Berkshire Hills.* Lee: Berkshire House, 1995. Detailed, descriptive, well-mapped.

Jane, Nancy. *Bicycle Touring in the Pioneer Valley.* Amherst, MA: University of Massachusetts Press, 1995. When the first edition was penned, back in the late 1970s, it quickly became a Valley classic.

Lyons, Steve. *The Bicyclist's Guide to the Southern Berkshires.* Lenox, MA: Freewheel Publications (PO Box 2322, Lenox, MA 01240), 1993. Very thorough.

Morse, Robert. *25 Mountain Bike Tours in Massachusetts.* Woodstock, VT: Backcountry Press, 1991.

Pioneer Valley Planning Commission. *Touring Jacob's Ladder by Bicycle or Car.* Self-published (distributed to bookstores around the Pioneer Valley). An exceptionally good little volume, with maps, detailed descriptions, and even graphic depictions of the elevation changes for each of the dozen routes—most of which are loops. There are shorter and longer options for everyone, no matter what your stamina level.

Stone, Howard. *Short Bike Rides/Eastern Massachusetts,* and *Short Bike Rides/Western Massachusetts.* Chester, CT: Globe Pequot Press, 1997. Though not as descriptive (or digressive) as some of the other suggestions above, these books are sufficiently informative and well-mapped to guide you around a number of scenic and not-too-tiring loop rides throughout the state.

Paddling

Appalachian Mountain Club. *AMC River Guide: Massachusetts/Connecticut/Rhode Island.* Boston: Appalachian Mountain Club Books, 1991. The AMC's standard diligence is applied to Southern New England's navigable rivers. Access, difficulty ratings, distances, and full descriptions are supplied for a handful of major watersheds, including about a dozen rivers in Massachusetts. Paddlers who favor lakes and ponds should look for Alex Wilson's *AMC Quiet Water Canoe Guide,* AMC Books, 1993, covering the same three states.

Housatonic Valley Association and Berkshire County Regional Planning Commission. *A Canoeing Guide for the Housatonic River in Berkshire County.* Lenox, MA: HVA (tel. 413-637-3188), third edition. A concise guide to the three navigable branches of the Housatonic and its main stem, from Pittsfield south to the Connecticut state line, with unambiguous maps, clear directions, good introductory and historical notes, and simple ratings for each stretch of open water. Available from Berkshire County outdoor equipment stores, or directly from the Housatonic Valley Association.

Lessels, Bruce, and Norman Sims. *The Deerfield River Guidebook: Whitewater, Fishing, Recreation*. N. Amherst, MA: New England Cartographics, 1993. A complete guide to some of the best whitewater in the state—and some of the most technical water in the country. A must for the serious kayak, C-1, canoe, or rafting enthusiast. Available from New England Cartographics, PO Box 9369, N. Amherst, MA 01059.

Nashua River Watershed Association. *The Nashua River Canoe Guide*. Groton, MA: NRWA, 1994. Though this guide is not much larger than a packet of snapshots, the descriptions of each navigable stretch of the Nashua and its tributaries contain all the essentials for a safe, successful canoe trip: maps showing access points, summaries of water conditions and potential hazards, and distances (although no elapsed time cues). Order by phone ($8) or mail: Nashua River, (978) 448-0299 Watershed Association, 592 Main St., Groton MA 01450.

Tougias, Michael. *Exploring the Hidden Charles: a Guide to Outdoor Activities on Boston's Celebrated River*. Boston: AMC Books, 1997.

FOR THE ARMCHAIR OR PASSENGER SEAT READER

Borchert, John. *Megalopolis: Washington, D.C., to Boston*. New Brunswick: Rutgers University Press, 1991. A narrative lesson, derived from surveys done for a geographer's conference, on the geology of the Eastern Seaboard virtually from the inside of a car. A handy introduction, brief and pointed.

O'Brien, Greg, ed. *A Guide to Nature on Cape Cod and the Islands*. Hyannis, MA: Parnassus Imprints, 1995. Excellent set of essays on Cape and Island geology; marsh ecology; bird, plant, and sea life; and weather—all followed by useful question-and-answer sections.

Oldale, Robert N. *Cape Cod and the Islands : the Geologic Story*. Hyannis, MA: Parnassus Imprints, 1992. The definitive text on this subject.

Skehan, James William. *Puddingstone, Drumlins, & Ancient Volcanos: a Geologic Field Guide along Historic Trails of Greater Boston*. WesStone Press, 1979.

FIELD GUIDES TO ALL THAT BREATHES—AND SOME THINGS THAT DON'T: PLANTS, BIRDS, ANIMALS, ROCKS, ART, AND ARCHITECTURE

Carlock, Marty. *A Guide to Public Art in Greater Boston, from Newburyport to Plymouth*. Boston: The Harvard Common Press, 1993. A detailed, well-organized, and well-written guide to exactly what the title says: public art around Boston and much of eastern Massachusetts. Artists' careers, numerous photos of the works themselves, and precise addresses so that you can find everything. Highly recommended.

Clark, Admont G. *Lighthouses of Cape Cod, Martha's Vineyard, Nantucket: Their History and Lore*. Hyannis: Parnassus Imprints, 1992. Everything you ever wanted to know about the 28 lighthouses in this part of Massachusetts. Hardback only.

Corbett, William. *Literary New England, A History and Guide*. Winchester, MA: Faber and Faber, 1993. Excellent companion for anyone who wants to find out more about the state's (and the region's) connection to the printed word, written by a poet who puts them together quite eloquently himself. Addresses and occasional directions for hard-to-find places are provided for historic sites, graves, and museums accessible to the public and pertinent to the subject. Highly recommended.

George, Diana Hume, and Malcolm A. Nelson. *Epitaph and Icon : a field guide to the old burying grounds of Cape Cod, Martha's Vineyard, and Nantucket*. Hyannis, MA: Parnassus Imprints, 1983.

Rezendes, Paul. *Tracking & the Art of Seeing—How to Read Animal Tracks & Sign.* Charlotte, VT: Camden House Publishing, 1992. Amply illustrated, so descriptive you can almost smell the clean scent of pine trees as you turn the pages, and so passionately persuasive that you'll positively itch to go out snowshoeing through a forest in the dead of winter, and you may never again step over a pile of scat on a wooded trail without taking a closer look.

Southworth, Susan, and Michael Southworth. *AIA Guide to Boston.* Chester, CT: Globe Pequot Press, 1992. Very detailed and authoritative. A worthy companion for architecture aficionados.

Sutton, Ann, and Myron Sutton. *Eastern Forests—an Audubon Society Nature Guide.* New York: Alfred Knopf, 1985. Trees, shrubs, flowers, mammals, birds, insects—if it's organic, it's in here (humans excepted, of course). Not encyclopedic, but comprehensive enough to satisfy any amateur naturalist eager to start identifying everything that crawls, hops, and blooms in the backwoods of the East Coast states. Easily more than half of the entries can be found in Massachusetts.

Jorgensen, Neil. *A Sierra Club Naturalist's Guide to Southern New England.* San Francisco: Sierra Club Books, 1978. The best introduction to Massachusetts ecology.

FOOD AND LODGING GUIDES

American Association of International Hostels. *American Association of International Hostels Directory.* Issued by the AAIH, P.O. Box 28038, Washington, D.C. 20038. The national directory of "alternative" hostels in the U.S.—that is, hostels that are closer to those Aussie and Kiwi places generically known as "backpackers" than to the more traditional Hostelling International places. Genuinely pocket-sized.

Benson, John. *Transformative Adventures, Vacations & Retreats.* Portland, OR: New Millennium Publishing (tel. 503-297-7321), 1994. A national compendium of places that offer special opportunities to rejuvenate your mind, body, and spirit. Over a dozen Massachusetts centers are included, offering everything from macrobiotic clinics to mud baths, ayurvedic healing to Zen meditation.

Campus Travel Service. *US and World Wide Travel Accommodations Guide.* Available by mail order, tel. (714) 525-6625, for $12.95 plus shipping. You don't have to doctor the date on your old student ID to take advantage of these college and university lodgings. Since most are dorm rooms, availability is highly seasonal, but this guide lists all the dates, prices, and contact information you need.

Davis, Mary Dymond. *Going Off The Beaten Path: An Untraditional Travel Guide to the U.S.* Chicago: Noble Press, Inc., 1991. This book takes a scattershot approach—listing all sorts of resources by subject or theme—to a broad array of subjects: cities with heavy rail mass transit, vegetarian restaurants (a partial national list), and organizations from the North East Workers on Organic Farms to contemporary local equivalents of the New Deal's CCC. By turns encyclopedic and incomplete, orderly and messy, it undeniably covers ground you'll find nowhere else. Sections relevant to Massachusetts-bound travelers include the lists of retreats, places to trade your labor for lodging (long-term), and groups in need of volunteers. (Maybe you'll spot a cause you would like to support.)

Halliday, Fred. *Halliday's New England Food Explorer: Tours For Food Lovers.* New York: Fodor's Travel Publications, Inc., 1993. Prose doesn't get any warmer or more satisfying than in this moveable feast, a personal tour of selected New England restaurants, bakeries, diners, and markets. Chapters are organized as one- or two-day trips by car, with stops for each meal and lodging recommendations where necessary; treat the itineraries as menus from which to choose rather than as meals of many courses. If you aren't hungry within five pages, you have more self-control than most monks. Highly recommended.

Hyman, Mildred. *Elderhostels: The Students' Choice*. Santa Fe, NM: John Muir Publications, 1991. (Publisher's address: PO Box 613, Santa Fe NM 87504; tel. 505-982-4078.) State-by-state list of Elderhostel programs, including about a half-dozen in Massachusetts. The author surveyed program participants about everything from dorm conditions and food quality to teacher preparedness and overall atmosphere. Provides all essential names and numbers.

Jensen, John, and Mary Jensen. *Worldwide Guide to Retreats*. Newport Beach, CA: CTS Publications (PO Box 8355, Newport Beach CA 92660; tel. 714-720-3729). International guide (with many listings for Massachusetts) to priories, abbeys, missions, and sanctuaries that offer accommodations (typically for $30-40 a night), including full details on prerequuisits or expectations that visitors partake in chores, spiritual life, or other activities.

Williams, Jim. *Hostel Handbook*. Self-published; write to the author (gregarious owner of New York's Sugarhill Hostel) at 722 St. Nicholas St., New York, New York 10031. Every hostel in the US, regardless of affiliation, is listed in this handy pocket reference, which is updated each winter. Good transportation tips add icing to the cake.

YMCA. *The Y's Way*. Available from the YMCA in Chicago, tel. (800) USA-YMCA. A free directory of about 40 YMCA properties in North America and overseas that offer accommodations, although only properties that have paid for it are listed. Other "residence" Ys exist, but identifying them is trickier. To try, you need the latest annual YMCA Directory, available from the YMCA Program Store, tel. (800) 747-0089. Bear in mind, though, that some residence Ys cater to runaways or other people at society's margins rather than travelers. The Ys that cater to Massachusetts travelers are all indentified in the book you're holding now. Note: the YWCA of the USA (726 Broadway, New York New York 10003), tel. (212) 614-2700, publishes a list of YWCAs that offer rooms for female travelers. Massachusetts' only entry is in Boston.

HISTORY

Primary Documents

Apess, William (Barry O'Connell, ed.). *On Our Own Ground: The Complete Writings of William Apess, a Pequot*. Amherst, MA: University of Massachusetts Press, 1992. Apess' was the first Native American autobiography published, in 1829. His writings cover history, politics, and his own life as an Indian who had assimilated well among the English colonists.

Arber, Edward, ed. *Travels and Works of Captain John Smith*. Birmingham, England: English Scholar's Library, 1884. The writings of the man who named New England, and whose map, used by the Mayflower Pilgrims, already contained the name of their settlement—Plimoth—thanks to the arbitrary choice of 10-year-old heir-apparent Prince Charles, with whom Smith wished to gain favor.

Biggar, H.P., ed. *The Works of Samuel de Champlain*. Six-volume work includes the observant French captain's detailed log of his anchorages along the Massachusetts coast during his 1605-1608 voyage, with descriptions and harbor chart for the Indian village at Patuxet (which, of course, became the site of the Pilgrims' Plimoth Plantation).

Bradford, William (Samuel Eliot Morison, ed.). *Of Plymouth Plantation, 1620-1647*. New York: Alfred A.Knopf, 1952. The leader and sometime governor of the Pilgrim settlement in Plymouth tells the story in his own inimitable style (helpfully edited, annotated, and indexed by one of the foremost scholars of colonial and maritime history). Unless you have a special interest in Bradford's orthography, no other edition can compare—which is why this one has never gone out of print.

Burrage, Henry S., ed. *Early English and French Voyages, Chiefly From Hakluyt, 1534-1608*. New York: Barnes & Noble, 1959, c. 1906. There were two 16th-century Richard Hakluyts—an uncle and his nephew. Each supported English colonial ventures in the New

World. Burrage draws on the younger Hakluyt's 1589 *Principall navigations, voiages, and discoveries of the English nation,* compiled from interviews and first-person accounts. Precolonial Massachusetts and its inhabitants are described by several of the explorers featured.

Heath, Dwight B. *Mourt's Relation.* Bedford, MA: Applewood Books, 1963. First published in 1622 as *A Relation or Journall of the beginning and proceedings of the English Plantation setled at Plimoth in New England, by certaine English Adventurers both Merchants and others* (shortened in 1736 to a title taken from "G. Mourt," unknown signer of the introduction), this volume is believed to have been taken in large part from the letters and journals of Edward Winslow, one of the Pilgrim leaders. Although clearly conceived as a bit of PR on behalf of the widely condemned "Separatists" (it omits, for example, any mention of the settlers' high mortality over their first winter), it is unique in its day-to-day detail, most of which can only have been written on the spot—unlike Bradford's history of the colony's early days, written several decades after the fact.

Higginson, Rev. Francis. *New England Plantation.* Boston : The Massachusetts Historical Society, *Proceedings of the Massachusetts Historical Society* 62 (1929), pp. 305-321. A description penned in 1630.

Maverick, Samuel. *A Briefe Description of New England.* Boston : The Massachusetts Historical Society, *Proceedings of the Massachusetts Historical Society* 2nd Series, vol. I (1884-5), pp. 231-249. A rather detailed description, dated 1660, by a trader who settled in what's now East Boston several years before John Winthrop and his Puritan flock.

Morton, Thomas (annotated by Charles Francis Adams). *The New English Canaan.* Boston: Massachusetts Historical Society, 1883. Although roundly excoriated by the Puritans for his moral laxity, Morton is illuminating in his description of the Massachusetts Bay Colony—this is an account written by an unsympathetic eyewitness. Its accuracy in many

details was endorsed by Samuel Maverick (above).

Rowlandson, Mary White. *The Captive: The True Story of the Captivity of Mrs. Mary Rowlandson Among the Indians and God's Faithfulness to Her in Her Time of Trial.* American Eagle Publications, 1990. (ISBN 0929408039) This thrilling first-person account of a colonial minister's wife's 11-week abduction during King Philip's War launched a genre—but nobody could touch the success of this, the bestselling secular book of the 17th and 18th centuries.

St. John de Crévecoeur, J. Hector. *Letters from Nantucket and Martha's Vineyard.* Bedford, MA: Applewood Books, 1986. Excerpted from this 18th-century French immigrant's well-observed correspondence about his life as an American farmer in both New York and Massachusetts. A classic.

Williams, John. *The Redeemed Captive Returning to Zion.* Bedford, MA: Applewood Books, 1989. One of a number of popular captivity narratives published in the 18th century, Rev. Williams' 1707 best-seller told of his family's capture three years earlier from Deerfield by Native Americans during territorial warring between English and French proxies along the Massachusetts frontier. His wife and two of his children were slain, but one daughter actually ended up not only staying with their captors, but also marrying one. (*Her* story is told by John Demos—see below.)

Winthrop, John (Richard S. Dunn, ed.). *The Journal of John Winthrop, 1630-1649.* Cambridge: Belknap Press of Harvard University Press, 1996. The first governor of the Massachusetts Bay Colony, whose painted portrait has become the archetype of Puritan severity, tells his version of the founding of the theocracy whose legacy, some say, endures well unto this day.

Wood, William (Alden T. Vaughan, ed.). *New England's Prospect.* Amherst, MA: University of Massachusetts Press, 1993. The 1634 description of what had only recently been christened "New England," by one of its early English settlers. This was one of the most persuasive accounts—widely consulted by prospective colonists.

Wroth, L.C., ed. *The Voyages of Giovanni de Verrazzano, 1524-1528.* New Haven, CT: Yale University Press, 1970. Includes the Florentine navigator's descriptions of the Massachusetts coast, particularly Martha's Vineyard and Cape Cod (before either island or the commonwealth had those names), written during his attempt to find a sea lane to the Far East.

Native Americans and Indian-Colonial Interaction

Bourne, Russell. *The Red King's Rebellion: Racial Politics in New England, 1675-1678.* New York: Oxford University Press, 1990. An exceptional work on King Philip's War, this book is less concerned with a definitive interpretation of motives (a controversial arena) than with describing the social fabric rent by that conflict—a topic frequently slighted.

Cronon, William. *Changes in the Land: Indians, Colonists and the Ecology of New England.* New York: Hill and Wang, 1983. Articulate and meticulously researched. The curious reader will easily amass a vast additional reading list on its interdiscinplinary content—colonial history, Indian history, ecology, anthropology—from the exceptional bibliographic essay that ends this highly recommended, prize-winning book.

Demos, John. *The Unredeemed Captive: A Family Story from Early America.* New York: Vintage, 1994. Counterpoint to the famous autobiographical sketch of minister John Williams' capture by the French and Mohawks in the 1704 Deerfield Raid (see above) is this National Book Award nominee about Williams' daughter, Eunice, who stayed with the Indians, converting to Catholicsm and marrying a Mohawk.

Foreman, Carolyn T. *Indians Abroad, 1493-1938.* 1943. Samoset and Squanto, two vital figures in colonial American history, are among the Indians whose experiences as slaves, curiosities, and ambassadors to the Old World are described in this volume.

Jennings, Francis. *The Invasion of America: Indians, Colonialism, and the Cant of Conquest.* New York: W.W. Norton, 1975. One of the major so-called revisionist histories, scrutinizing the motives of the Pilgrim/Puritan migration to these shores. Was war a deliberate strategy to abet land-grabbing (itself a policy stemming from a strict interpretation of Scripture)? Read the evidence in this impressive work. (Some of Jennings' conclusions inform the brief account of Indian-settler interaction found in the "History" section of "The Islands" chapter.)

Russell, Howard S. *Indian New England Before the Mayflower.* Hanover, NH: University Press of New England, 1980. Although it's been criticized for being uninformed about anthropological theory, little else can match this volume's detailed explication of the quotidian life among Native Americans, their farming practices, building styles, social organization, and the like. Contains a well-reasoned rebuff to those who cast doubt on Squanto's teaching the Pilgrims to use fish as fertilizer.

Salisbury, Neal. *Manitow and Providence: Indians, Europeans, and the Making of New England, 1500-1643.* New York: Oxford University Press, 1982. Argues against crediting manifest superiority of Europeans for their success in displacing New England's Native Americans, and gives credit instead to the spread of Western Europe's social and economic revolution to America. Well researched and full of fascinating details culled from primary sources, this book is highly recommended despite at least one minor but highly conjectural interpretation of the historical record.

Simmons, William. *Spirit of the New England Tribes: Indian History and Folklore, 1620-1984.* Hanover, NH: University Press of New England, 1986. Though academic in its rigor (presenting multiple versions of stories to illustrate comparative points), this is possibly the best source of the region's Native American myths and legends in print.

The Revolution

Bailyn, Bernard. *The Ideological Origins of the American Revolution.* Cambridge: Belknap Press of Harvard University Press, 1967. This Pulitzer Prize-winning work has become one of the standard texts on the American Revolution. A generation after publication, it still holds up admirably well, although readers who have grown up with the recent novelistic trends in literary social studies will find the style less lively than what they're accustomed to.

Bobrick, Benson. *Angel in the Whirlwind: the Triumph of the American Revolution.* New York: Simon & Schuster, 1997. Eminently readable, thorough, and detailed—even without the weight of academic footnotes. George Washington and Benedict Arnold are the contrapuntal figures central to the story, but a large cast of supporting characters puts in memorable appearances as well.

Commager, Henry Steele, and Richard B. Morris, ed. *The Spirit of 'Seventy-Six: The Story of the American Revolution as Told by Participants.* Indianapolis, IN: Bobbs-Merrill, 1958. The authors, distinguished historians, produced a benchmark document in this two-volume anthology, deftly weaving together diaries, letters, affidavits, military reports, and other written miscellany, with just enough introductory notes to give it all a narrative frame. Reprinted by New York's Da Capo Press in 1995.

Cook, Don. *The Long Fuse: How England Lost the American Colonies, 1760-1785.* New York: Atlantic Monthly Press, 1996. In contrast to the usual arguments in favor of wily patriots and their Yankee strategems on and off the battlefield, this volume makes a plausible case for what might be called the predecessor of the Vietnam syndrome. In other words, England's rotten political establishment and inconsistent military will may have been just as critical to American victory as anything done on this side of the Atlantic.

Fischer, David Hackett. *Paul Revere's Ride.* New York: Oxford University Press, 1994. A can't-put-it-down story of that famous silversmith and patriot, brimming with historical anecdote about the American Revolution. Some scholars take issue with Fischer's reliance on certain 20th-century sources—for the name of Revere's horse, for example—and question, in general, the degree of importance imputed to Revere, but critiques notwithstanding, this book will provocatively enlighten anyone raised with the standard glossy high-school review of American history.

Maier, Pauline. *From Resistance to Revolution: Colonial Radicals and the Development of American Opposition to Britain, 1765-1776.* New York: Knopf, 1973.

Middlekauff, Robert. *The Glorious Cause: The American Revolution, 1763-1789.* New York: Oxford University Press, 1986. The second volume in the Oxford History of the United States series, this is a good starting point for would-be students of the Revolution.

Tuchman, Barbara W. *The First Salute.* New York: Knopf, 1988. The Revolution as told by one of history's best narrators, with emphasis on the American patriots' European predecessors, the repercussions throughout the Old World after the Americans' success, and the critical military skills of particular generals and admirals—among them George Washington.

Tyler, John. *Smugglers and Patriots: Boston Merchants and the Advent of the American Revolution.* Boston: Northeastern University Press, 1986.

Zobel, Hiller. B. *The Boston Massacre.* New York: W.W. Norton, 1970.

Other Historical Works

Allport, Susan. *Sermons in Stone, the Stone Walls of New England and New York.* New York: W.W. Norton, 1990. An exceptional miscellany full of history, geology, and local lore. Demonstrates how much about the historical landscape one can learn from careful observation of a few piled stones.

Brown, Dona. *Inventing New England—Regional Tourism in the Nineteenth Century.* Washington, D.C.: Smithsonian Institute Press, 1995. An excellent treatise on the artifices of "colonial" townscapes and quaint fishing villages designed purely to appeal to urban dwellers who wanted to see Real, Natural New England.

Druett, Joan. *Petticoat Whalers: Whaling Wives at Sea, 1820-1920.* New York: HarperCollins, 1991. Contrary to its popular image, the whaling industry was *not* an all-male preserve, as this finely researched volume makes plain.

Kittredge, Henry Crocker. *Cape Cod: Its People and Their History.* Boston: Houghton Mifflin Co., 1930 (post-epilogue © John Hay 1968); Parnassus Imprint edition (Hyannis, MA), 1987 and 1995. A classic account, nicely written.

McManis, Douglas. *Colonial New England, a Historical Geography.* New York: Oxford University Press, 1975. An excellent introduction to all aspects of the region's colonial history, from exploration to demographics and commerce.

Morison, Samuel Eliot. *Builders of the Bay Colony.* Boston: Northeastern University Press, 1981. One of the most engaging historical writers in American literature, in my opinion. Written in anticipation of the state Tercentennary, these essays are the best distillation of the record on early Puritan and Pilgrim leaders (all men—alas, women are not considered).

Morison, Samuel Eliot. *The Maritime History of Massachusetts 1783-1860.* Boston: Northeastern University Press, 1979. A classic, written with a clear love of the sea and sailing.

Porter, Katherine Anne. *The Never-Ending Wrong.* Boston: Little, Brown, 1977. A passionate examination of the Sacco and Vanzetti case.

Russell, Francis. *A City in Terror: 1919, The Boston Police Strike.* New York: Viking Press, 1975. A detailed recapitulation of a restive era in the history of organized labor, focusing upon the strike that gave conservative Governor Calvin Coolidge the national recognition that took him to the White House. A good, sometimes quite colorful narrative.

Stilgoe, John R. *Common Landscape of America, 1580-1845.* New York: Oxford University Press, 1985. The Harvard professor famous for his undergraduate course on cultural geography (commonly known as "Gas Stations") has a number of sublimely entertaining and seriously informative books to his credit, most of which are recommended. This is one of several that use Massachusetts examples and experiences to illustrate Americans' changing attitudes toward "the traditional arrangement of space and structure," here focusing particularly on the conflict between rural and urban visions.

Willison, George S. *Saints and Strangers.* 1945. The *Mayflower* carried two very different groups of passengers on its 1620 voyage— those whom we now call Pilgrims (and who called themselves "Saints"), and the profit-minded colonists chosen by the "Merchant Adventurers" who financed the whole endeavor to accompany them. The motives, interests, and objectives of these factions are not as uniform as our high-school social studies texts would have had us believe, as this very thorough analysis reveals.

BIOGRAPHY AND RECOLLECTION

This is an entirely arbitrary sampling of books whose characterizations of the state, in sum or in part, constitute tiny fragments in what could be considered the mosaic of contemporary Massachusetts.

Beatty, Jack. *The Rascal King: The Life and Times of James Michael Curley, 1874-1958.* Reading, MA: Addison-Wesley, 1992. Massachusetts' most colorful politician, James M. Curley was immortalized in Edwin O'Connor's bestselling 1956 novel, *The Last Hurrah,* and its equally successful movie version starring Spencer Tracy. Though virtually adopted as his official biography, both book and film are romanticized views of a life that was in fact *not* his. For the real scoop on the populist mayor, congressman, and governor, check out this thorough biography.

Cohen, Cynthia, ed. *From Hearing My Mother Talk: Stories of Cambridge Women.* Cambridge: The Cambridge Arts Council, 1979. A small treasure, out of print for lack of funding, in which elderly Cantabrigians reminisce about everything from the profound to the profoundly ordinary. The Oral History Center, 403 Richards Hall, Northeastern University, Boston, MA 02115, tel. (617) 373-4814, grew out of this work.

French, Mary Adams. *Memories of a Sculptor's Wife.* Boston: Houghton Mifflin, 1928. Life during the Berkshires' cultural renaissance, by the wife of Stockbridge summer resident Daniel Chester French.

Hentoff, Nathaniel. *Boston Boy.* New York: Knopf, 1986. Notable in large part because of its rare glimpse into Boston's jazz scene.

Morgan, Judith. *Dr. Seuss & Mr. Geisel: a Biography.* New York: Random House, 1995. Springfield's most famous native son.

Sewall, Richard. *The Life of Emily Dickinson.* New York: Farrar Straus Giroux. Not only one of the better biographies of the Amherst poet, but a good historical glimpse of 19th-century Pioneer Valley.

Shand-Tucci, Douglass. *The Art of Scandal: the Life and Times of Isabella Stewart Gardner.* New York: HarperCollins, 1997. Fine, thoroughly researched bio of "Mrs. Jack" Gardner, wife of a Boston Brahmin; mentor and patron of writers, painters, and such other social untouchables as Jews and blacks; loyal Red Sox fan; and an underappreciated influence on the birth of American good taste. The home she designed herself, containing the art she amassed—considered the nation's first great art collection—is now one of Massachusetts' finest museums.

Shand-Tucci, Douglass. *Boston Bohemia, 1881-1900, Ralph Adams Cram: Life and Architecture.* Amherst, MA: University of Massachusetts Press, 1994. Mixing biography (of arguably the nation's finest church architect) with architectural history, this multilayered book also probes the Boston society of Cram's contemporaries, including John Singleton Copley, John Singer Sargent, and Isabella Stewart Gardner. Noteworthy in part for identifying the significant contributions of gays to Boston's cultural Belle Epoque (Cram, the author suggests, was probably a homosexual).

Von Mehren, Joan. *Minerva and the Muse.* Amherst, MA: University of Massachusetts Press, 1995. An acclaimed biography of Margaret Fuller, literary critic and first editor of *The Dial,* the Transcendentalist literary magazine published between 1840 and 1844.

Von Schmidt, Eric and Jim Rooney. *Baby, Let Me Follow You Down: The Illustrated Story of the Cambridge Folk Years.* Amherst, MA: University of Massachusetts Press, 1994. A comprehensive oral history of one of the most celebrated music scenes in the country.

X, Malcolm, and Alex Haley. *The Autobiography of Malcolm X.* New York: Ballantine Books, 1973.

MISCELLANEOUS

Amory, Cleveland. *The Proper Bostonians.* New York: E.P. Dutton, 1947. You won't find a more engaging portrait of the titular ruling elite of Boston's Brahmin past, told with mostly affectionate wit and humor. The anecdotal descriptions of the city's First Families and their milieu are recommended even now for their ability to illuminate the roots of contemporary Boston folkways, although some of the tales—regarding the colorful Isabella Stewart Gardner, for example—have been proven to be more fable than fact.

Beston, Henry. *The Outermost House.* New York: Holt, Rinehart and Winston, 1928. A classic account of a year spent on the dunes of Outer Cape Cod.

Davison, Peter. *The Fading Smile: Poetry in Boston, 1955-1960.* New York: Knopf, 1994. Davison, himself a poet and local editor, reminisces about the poets he knew in the local heyday of that art: Frost, Richard Willbur, L.E. Sissman, Sylvia Plath, Philip Booth, and others.

Hoerr, John P. *We Can't Eat Prestige: The Women Who Organized Harvard.* Philadelphia: Temple University Press, 1997. A timely tale of labor history in modern, anti-union America.

Kidder, Tracy. *Soul of a New Machine.* Boston: Little, Brown, 1981. Possibly the finest example of a business case study given the narrative edge of a thriller. The subject is Data General and the invention of the first minicomputer—ostensibly a Massachusetts story about the beginnings of the modern industrial revolution—but readers are invariably drawn in by the intimate, objective sense of people and their lives that Kidder has made his trademark. Pioneer Valley subjects are examined in all of Kidder's subsequent works, on custom home building (*House,* 1985), primary education (*Among Schoolchildren,* 1989), and nursing homes (*Old Friends,* 1993), among other topics.

Kurlansky, Mark. *Cod : A Biography of the Fish that Changed the World.* New York: Walker & Co., 1997. A highly readable exploration of one of the economic mainstays of the Bay State.

Lukas, J. Anthony. *Common Ground: A Turbulent Decade in the Lives of Three American Families.* New York: Vintage Books, 1986. A Pulitzer Prize-winning account of three Boston families during the city's school busing crisis of the early 1970s, when the Federal District Court ordered an end to racial segregation in the city's public schools (served as the basis of a four-hour PBS documentary in 1990). Dramatic events, dramatically told—highly recommended.

McCord, David T.W. *About Boston: Sight, Sound, Flavor and Inflection.* Boston: Little, Brown and Company, 1973. First published in 1948, but still one of the most lyrical introductions to Boston.

Saxenian, AnnaLee. *Regional Advantage: Culture and Competition in Silicon Valley and Route 128.* Cambridge: Harvard University Press, 1994. A careful dissection of the corporate failures of Rt. 128, "America's Technology Highway," and how it lost its hegemony of the high-tech industry to California's Silicon Valley.

Thoreau, Henry David. *Cape Cod.* New York: Penguin Books, 1987 (first published 1865). Thoreau the travel writer is as engaging and piquantly observant as Thoreau the pondside philosopher.

Thoreau, Henry David. *Walden.* New York: Bantam Books 1962 (first published 1854). What, you're visiting Concord and haven't read this? Shame! Get thee to a bookstore or library now!

Whitehill, Walter Muir. *Boston: A Topographical History.* Cambridge: Harvard University Press, 1959. One of the definitive texts on the evolution of Boston's cityscape. Well illustrated, dense with facts, and possibly a little disorientingly specific for the reader unfamiliar with Boston. Still, after a visit, this volume will surely help elucidate the methods to the city's apparent madness.

Whynott, Douglas. *Giant Bluefin.* New York: Farrar Strauss Giroux, 1995. A look at the lives of Cape Cod bluefin fishermen, in the tradition of Tracy Kidder and John McPhee.

PUBLISHERS

The following publishers are all highly recommended for consistently offering good nonfiction books on Massachusetts-related topics (a small sampling of which appear among the entries below). Contact the publishers directly for complete catalogues of their currently available titles and new releases.

Applewood Books, 128 The Great Road, Bedford MA 01730; tel. (800) 277-5312 or (781) 271-0055, fax (781) 271-0056, online www.awb.com. Reprints works from the 17th and 18th centuries.

Arcadia, 1 Washington Center, Dover NH 03820; tel. (603) 743-4266, fax (603) 743-4267. Arcadia's "Images of America" series, of town- and neighborhood-specific collections of annotated historical photos, includes many from Massachusetts.

Berkshire House Publishers, 480 Pleasant St., Lee MA 01238; tel. (413) 243-0303. Specializes in books about the Berkshire Hills.

Mill Hill Press, 134 Orange St., Nantucket MA 02554; tel. (508) 325-7055. Good source for books about Nantucket and the sea.

Parnassus Imprints, 30 Perseverance Way, Suite 7, Hyannis MA 02601; tel. (508) 790-1175. Specializes in books about Cape Cod.

The University of Massachusetts Press, Box 429, Amherst MA 01004; tel. (413) 545-2217, fax (413) 545-1226, online www.vyne.com/umass press/. Although UMass Press titles cover many disciplines of both academic and general interest, and are international in subject, a significant proportion have some connection with Massachusetts.

INDEX

CEMETERIES AND BURYING GROUNDS

THE PILGRIMS

REFUGES AND SANCTUARIES

SPNEA
(SOCIETY FOR THE PRESERVATION OF NEW ENGLAND ANTIQUITIES)
AND TTOR
(THE TRUSTEES OF RESERVATIONS)
PROPERTIES

ABOUT THE AUTHOR

Author and photographer Jeff Perk has fished for trout in Lake Taupo, climbed Mt. Roraima, catalogued Cuzco's desserts, baked Sacher tortes in Bora Bora, and, as a result, has never gotten around to owning a TV. The liberal-arts major and former dues-paying member of Boston's silicon fraternity spent a few years backpacking across South America, yacht-hitching around the South Pacific, and squeezing through slot canyons in the American Southwest before hoodwinking the normally vigilant Moon crew into letting him write this guide to his adopted home state. When not searching for a lemon meringue pie at least as good as Shari Hoelker's (in Millard, Nebraska), Jeff feigns authorial self-discipline in Jamaica Plain, Massachusetts.

www.moon.com

Enjoy our travel information center on the World Wide Web (WWW), loaded with interactive exhibits designed especially for the Internet.

ATTRACTIONS ON MOON'S WEB SITE INCLUDE:

ATLAS
Our award-winning, comprehensive travel guides cover destinations throughout North America and Hawaii, Latin America and the Caribbean, and Asia and the Pacific.

PRACTICAL NOMAD
Extensive excerpts, a unique set of travel links coordinated with the book, and a regular Q & A column by author and Internet travel consultant Edward Hasbrouck.

TRAVEL MATTERS
Our on-line travel zine, featuring articles; author correspondence; a travel library including health information, reading lists, and cultural cues; and our new contest, **Destination X,** offering a chance to win a trip to the mystery destination of your choice.

ROAD TRIP USA
Our best-selling book, ever; don't miss this award-winning Web guide to off-the-interstate itineraries.

Come visit us at: **www.moon.com**

MOON
TRAVEL
HANDBOOKS

LOSE YOURSELF IN THE EXPERIENCE, NOT THE CROWD

For 25 years, Moon Travel Handbooks have been the guidebooks of choice for adventurous travelers. Our award-winning Handbook series provides focused, comprehensive coverage of distinct destinations all over the world. Each Handbook is like an entire bookcase of cultural insight and introductory information in one portable volume. Our goal at Moon is to give travelers all the background and practical information they'll need for an extraordinary travel experience.

The following pages include a complete list of Handbooks, covering North America and Hawaii, Mexico, Latin America and the Caribbean, and Asia and the Pacific. To purchase Moon Travel Handbooks, check your local bookstore or order by phone: (800) 345-5473 M-F 8 am.-5 p.m. PST or outside the U.S. phone: (530) 345-5473.

"An in-depth dunk into the land, the people and their history, arts, and politics."
—*Student Travels*

"I consider these books to be superior to Lonely Planet. When Moon produces a book it is more humorous, incisive, and off-beat."
—*Toronto Sun*

"Outdoor enthusiasts gravitate to the well-written Moon Travel Handbooks. In addition to politically correct historic and cultural features, the series focuses on flora, fauna and outdoor recreation. Maps and meticulous directions also are a trademark of Moon guides."
—*Houston Chronicle*

"Moon [Travel Handbooks] . . . bring a healthy respect to the places they investigate. Best of all, they provide a host of odd nuggets that give a place texture and prod the wary traveler from the beaten path. The finest are written with such care and insight they deserve listing as literature."
—*American Geographical Society*

"Moon Travel Handbooks offer in-depth historical essays and useful maps, enhanced by a sense of humor and a neat, compact format."
—*Swing*

"Perfect for the more adventurous, these are long on history, sightseeing and nitty-gritty information and very price-specific."
—*Columbus Dispatch*

"Moon guides manage to be comprehensive and countercultural at the same time . . . Handbooks are packed with maps, photographs, drawings, and sidebars that constitute a college-level introduction to each country's history, culture, people, and crafts."
—*National Geographic Traveler*

"Few travel guides do a better job helping travelers create their own itineraries than the Moon Travel Handbook series. The authors have a knack for homing in on the essentials."
—**Colorado Springs** *Gazette Telegraph*

MEXICO

"These books will delight the armchair traveler, aid the un-decided person in selecting a destination, and guide the seasoned road warrior looking for lesser-known hideaways."

—Mexican Meanderings **Newsletter**

"From tourist traps to off-the-beaten track hideaways, these guides offer consistent, accurate details without pretension."

—Foreign Service Journal

Archaeological Mexico	**$19.95**
Andrew Coe	450 pages, 25 maps
Baja Handbook	**$15.95**
Joe Cummings	380 pages, 44 maps
Cabo Handbook	**$14.95**
Joe Cummings	265 pages, 18 maps
Cancun Handbook	**$13.95**
Chicki Mallan	270 pages, 25 maps
Colonial Mexico	**$16.95**
Chicki Mallan	300 pages, 38 maps
Mexico Handbook	**$21.95**
Joe Cummings and Chicki Mallan	1,200 pages, 232 maps
Northern Mexico Handbook	**$16.95**
Joe Cummings	590 pages, 68 maps
Pacific Mexico Handbook	**$17.95**
Bruce Whipperman	580 pages, 69 maps
Puerto Vallarta Handbook	**$14.95**
Bruce Whipperman	330 pages, 36 maps
Yucatan Handbook	**$15.95**
Chicki Mallan	470 pages, 62 maps

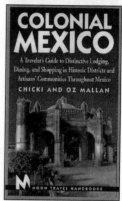

LATIN AMERICA AND THE CARIBBEAN

"Solidly packed with practical information and full of significant cultural asides that will enlighten you on the whys and wherefores of things you might easily see but not easily grasp."

—*Boston Globe*

Belize Handbook	**$15.95**
Chicki Mallan	390 pages, 45 maps
Caribbean Handbook	**$16.95**
Karl Luntta	400 pages, 56 maps
Costa Rica Handbook	**$19.95**
Christopher P. Baker	780 pages, 74 maps
Cuba Handbook	**$19.95**
Christopher P. Baker	740 pages, 70 maps
Dominican Republic Handbook	**$15.95**
Gaylord Dold	420 pages, 24 maps
Ecuador Handbook	**$16.95**
Julian Smith	450 pages, 43 maps
Honduras Handbook	**$15.95**
Chris Humphrey	330 pages, 40 maps
Jamaica Handbook	**$15.95**
Karl Luntta	330 pages, 17 maps
Virgin Islands Handbook	**$13.95**
Karl Luntta	220 pages, 19 maps

NORTH AMERICA AND HAWAII

"These domestic guides convey the same sense of exoticism that their foreign counterparts do, making home-country travel seem like far-flung adventure."

—*Sierra Magazine*

Alaska-Yukon Handbook	**$17.95**
Deke Castleman and Don Pitcher	530 pages, 92 maps
Alberta and the Northwest Territories Handbook	**$17.95**
Andrew Hempstead and Nadina Purdon	530 pages, 72 maps,
Arizona Traveler's Handbook	**$17.95**
Bill Weir and Robert Blake	512 pages,54 maps
Atlantic Canada Handbook	**$17.95**
Nan Drosdick and Mark Morris	460 pages, 61 maps
Big Island of Hawaii Handbook	**$15.95**
J.D. Bisignani	370 pages, 23 maps
British Columbia Handbook	**$16.95**
Jane King and Andrew Hempstead	430 pages, 69 maps

Colorado Handbook	**$18.95**
Stephen Metzger	480 pages, 59 maps
Georgia Handbook	**$17.95**
Kap Stann	370 pages, 50 maps
Hawaii Handbook	**$19.95**
J.D. Bisignani	1,030 pages, 90 maps
Honolulu-Waikiki Handbook	**$14.95**
J.D. Bisignani	380 pages, 20 maps
Idaho Handbook	**$18.95**
Don Root	610 pages, 42 maps
Kauai Handbook	**$15.95**
J.D. Bisignani	320 pages, 23 maps
Maine Handbook	**$18.95**
Kathleen M. Brandes	660 pages, 27 maps
Massachusetts Handbook	**$18.95**
Jeff Perk	600 pages, 23 maps
Maui Handbook	**$14.95**
J.D. Bisignani	410 pages, 35 maps
Montana Handbook	**$17.95**
Judy Jewell and W.C. McRae	480 pages, 52 maps
Nevada Handbook	**$18.95**
Deke Castleman	530 pages, 40 maps
New Hampshire Handbook	**$18.95**
Steve Lantos	500 pages, 18 maps
New Mexico Handbook	**$15.95**
Stephen Metzger	360 pages, 47 maps
New York City Handbook	**$13.95**
Christiane Bird	300 pages, 20 maps
New York Handbook	**$19.95**
Christiane Bird	780 pages, 95 maps
Northern California Handbook	**$19.95**
Kim Weir	800 pages, 50 maps
Oregon Handbook	**$17.95**
Stuart Warren and Ted Long Ishikawa	588 pages, 34 maps
Pennsylvania Handbook	**$18.95**
Joanne Miller	448 pages, 40 maps
Road Trip USA	**$22.50**
Jamie Jensen	800 pages, 165 maps
Southern California Handbook	**$19.95**
Kim Weir	750 pages, 30 maps
Tennessee Handbook	**$17.95**
Jeff Bradley	530 pages, 44 maps
Texas Handbook	**$18.95**
Joe Cummings	692 pages, 70 maps
Utah Handbook	**$17.95**
Bill Weir and W.C. McRae	490 pages, 40 maps

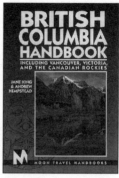

Washington Handbook	**$19.95**
Don Pitcher	870 pages, 113 maps
Wisconsin Handbook	**$18.95**
Thomas Huhti	590 pages, 69 maps
Wyoming Handbook	**$17.95**
Don Pitcher	610 pages, 80 maps

ASIA AND THE PACIFIC

"Scores of maps, detailed practical info down to business hours of small-town libraries. You can't beat the Asian titles for sheer heft. (The) series is sort of an American Lonely Planet, with better writing but fewer titles. (The) individual voice of researchers comes through."

—Travel & Leisure

Australia Handbook	**$21.95**
Marael Johnson, Andrew Hempstead, and Nadina Purdon	940 pages, 141 maps
Bali Handbook	**$19.95**
Bill Dalton	750 pages, 54 maps
Bangkok Handbook	**$13.95**
Michael Buckley	244 pages, 30 maps
Fiji Islands Handbook	**$13.95**
David Stanley	280 pages, 38 maps
Hong Kong Handbook	**$16.95**
Kerry Moran	378 pages, 49 maps
Indonesia Handbook	**$25.00**
Bill Dalton	1,380 pages, 249 maps
Japan Handbook	**$22.50**
J.D. Bisignani	970 pages, 213 maps
Micronesia Handbook	**$14.95**
Neil M. Levy	340 pages, 70 maps
Nepal Handbook	**$18.95**
Kerry Moran	490 pages, 51 maps
New Zealand Handbook	**$19.95**
Jane King	620 pages, 81 maps
Outback Australia Handbook	**$18.95**
Marael Johnson	450 pages, 57 maps
Philippines Handbook	**$17.95**
Peter Harper and Laurie Fullerton	670 pages, 116 maps
Singapore Handbook	**$15.95**
Carl Parkes	350 pages, 29 maps
Southeast Asia Handbook	**$21.95**
Carl Parkes	1,000 pages, 196 maps

South Korea Handbook	$19.95
Robert Nilsen	820 pages, 141 maps
South Pacific Handbook	**$22.95**
David Stanley	920 pages, 147 maps
Tahiti-Polynesia Handbook	**$13.95**
David Stanley	270 pages, 35 maps
Thailand Handbook	**$19.95**
Carl Parkes	860 pages, 142 maps
Vietnam, Cambodia & Laos Handbook	**$18.95**
Michael Buckley	720 pages, 112 maps

OTHER GREAT TITLES FROM MOON

"For hardy wanderers, few guides come more highly recommended than the Handbooks. They include good maps, steer clear of fluff and flackery, and offer plenty of money-saving tips. They also give you the kind of information that visitors to strange lands—on any budget—need to survive."

—US News & World Report

Moon Handbook	**$10.00**
Carl Koppeschaar	141 pages, 8 maps
Moscow-St. Petersburg Handbook	**$13.95**
Masha Nordbye	259 pages, 16 maps
The Practical Nomad: How to Travel Around the World	**$17.95**
Edward Hasbrouck	575 pages
Staying Healthy in Asia, Africa, and Latin America	**$11.95**
Dirk Schroeder	197 pages, 4 maps

MOONBELT

A new concept in moneybelts. Made of heavy-duty Cordura nylon, the Moonbelt offers maximum protection for your money and important papers. This pouch,

designed for all-weather comfort, slips under your shirt or waistband, rendering it virtually undetectable and inaccessible to pickpockets. It features a one-inch high-test quick-release buckle so there's no more fumbling around for the strap or repeated adjustments. This handy plastic buckle opens and closes with a touch but won't come undone until you want it to. Moonbelts accommodate traveler's checks, passports, cash, photos, etc. Size 5 x 9 inches. Available in black only. **$8.95**

ROAD TRIP USA

Cross-Country Adventures on America's Two-Lane Highways

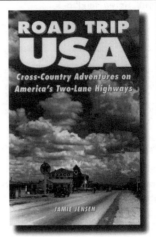

ROAD TRIP USA
Cross-Country Adventures on America's Two-Lane Highways

JAMIE JENSEN

$22.50   800 pages

"For those who feel an adrenaline rush everytime they hear the words 'road trip,' and who understand that getting there is at least half the fun, this is quite simply the best book of its type ever published."
—*Conde Nast Traveler* web site

"Just might be the perfect book about hitting the summoning highway . . . It's impossible not to find something enticing in *Road Trip USA* to add to your next cycling expedition. An encyclopedia of roadside wonders."   **—Harley Davidson *Enthusiast***

"For budding myth collectors, I can't think of a better textbook."
—*Los Angeles Times*

"A terrific guide for those who'd rather swat mosquitoes than take the interstate."
—Colorado Springs *Gazette Telegraph*

"Jensen is well-versed in travel, has an enjoyable yet informative style and will guide you along each mile. Don't leave home without it!"   *—Mobilia*

"Zany inspiration for a road Gypsie in search of off-the-beaten-path adventure."
—*The Toronto Globe and Mail*

"A historic journey into the heart and soul of America."
—*Route 66 Magazine*

"Jamie Jensen and the 12 intrepid contributors to *Road Trip USA* have been everywhere and seen everything compiling this exhaustive, delightful, destination-anywhere guide to American road-tripping."

—*Citybooks,* **Washington D.C.**

"Not only a fantastic guide . . . a great companion!"

—*The Herald,* **Columbia S.C.**

THE PRACTICAL NOMAD

✈ TAKE THE PLUNGE

"The greatest barriers to long-term travel by Americans are the disempowered feelings that leave them afraid to ask for the time off. Just do it."

✈ TAKE NOTHING FOR GRANTED

"Even 'What time is it?' is a highly politicized question in some areas, and the answer may depend on your informant's ethnicity and political allegiance as well as the proximity of the secret police."

✈ TAKE THIS BOOK

$17.95   576 pages

With experience helping thousands of his globetrotting clients plan their trips around the world, travel industry insider Edward Hasbrouck provides the secrets that can save readers money and valuable travel time. An indispensable complement to destination-specific travel guides, *The Practical Nomad* includes:

airfare strategies

ticket discounts

long-term travel considerations

travel documents

border crossings

entry requirements

government offices

travel publications

Internet information resources

WHERE TO BUY MOON TRAVEL HANDBOOKS

BOOKSTORES AND LIBRARIES: Moon Travel Handbooks are distributed worldwide. Please contact our sales manager for a list of wholesalers and distributors in your area.

TRAVELERS: We would like to have Moon Travel Handbooks available throughout the world. Please ask your bookstore to write or call us for ordering information. If your bookstore will not order our guides for you, please contact us for a free catalog.

> **Moon Travel Handbooks**
> **P.O. Box 3040**
> **Chico, CA 95927-3040 U.S.A.**
> **tel.: (800) 345-5473, outside the U.S. (530) 345-5473**
> **fax: (530) 345-6751**
> **e-mail: travel@moon.com**

IMPORTANT ORDERING INFORMATION

PRICES: All prices are subject to change. We always ship the most current edition. We will let you know if there is a price increase on the book you order.

SHIPPING AND HANDLING OPTIONS: Domestic UPS or USPS first class (allow 10 working days for delivery): $4.50 for the first item, $1.00 for each additional item.

Moonbelt shipping is $1.50 for one, 50 cents for each additional belt.

UPS 2nd Day Air or Printed Airmail requires a special quote.

International Surface Bookrate 8-12 weeks delivery: $3.00 for the first item, $1.00 for each additional item. Note: We cannot guarantee international surface bookrate shipping. We recommends sending international orders via air mail, which requires a special quote.

FOREIGN ORDERS: Orders that originate outside the U.S.A. must be paid for with an international money order, a check in U.S. currency drawn on a major U.S. bank based in the U.S.A., or Visa, MasterCard, or Discover.

TELEPHONE ORDERS: We accept Visa, MasterCard, or Discover payments. Call in your order: (800) 345-5473, 8 a.m.-5 p.m. Pacific standard time. Outside the U.S. the number is (530) 345-5473.

INTERNET ORDERS: Visit our site at: www.moon.com

ORDER FORM

Prices are subject to change without notice. Be sure to call (800) 345-5473,
or (530) 345-5473 from outside the U.S. 8 a.m.–5 p.m. PST for current prices and editions,
or for the name of the bookstore nearest you that carries Moon Travel Handbooks.
(See important ordering information on preceding page.)

Name: _____ Date: _____

Street: _____

City: _____ Daytime Phone: _____

State or Country: _____ Zip Code: _____

QUANTITY	TITLE	PRICE

Taxable Total_____

Sales Tax (7.25%) for California Residents_____

Shipping & Handling_____

TOTAL_____

Ship: ☐ UPS (no P.O. Boxes) ☐ 1st class   ☐ International surface mail

Ship to: ☐ address above ☐ other _____

_____

Make checks payable to: **MOON TRAVEL HANDBOOKS**, P.O. Box 3040, Chico, CA 95927-3040
U.S.A. We accept Visa, MasterCard, or Discover. **To Order**: Call in your Visa, MasterCard, or Discover number,
or send a written order with your Visa, MasterCard, or Discover number and expiration date clearly written.

Card Number: ☐ **Visa** ☐ **MasterCard** ☐ **Discover**

☐ ☐ ☐ ☐ ☐ ☐ ☐ ☐ ☐ ☐ ☐ ☐ ☐ ☐ ☐ ☐

Exact Name on Card: _____

Expiration date:_____

Signature: _____

U.S.~METRIC CONVERSION

1 inch = 2.54 centimeters (cm)
1 foot = .304 meters (m)
1 mile = 1.6093 kilometers (km)
1 km = .6214 miles
1 fathom = 1.8288 m
1 chain = 20.1168 m
1 furlong = 201.168 m
1 acre = .4047 hectares
1 sq km = 100 hectares
1 sq mile = 2.59 square km
1 ounce = 28.35 grams
1 pound = .4536 kilograms
1 short ton = .90718 metric ton
1 short ton = 2000 pounds
1 long ton = 1.016 metric tons
1 long ton = 2240 pounds
1 metric ton = 1000 kilograms
1 quart = .94635 liters
1 US gallon = 3.7854 liters
1 Imperial gallon = 4.5459 liters
1 nautical mile = 1.852 km

To compute celsius temperatures, subtract 32 from Fahrenheit and divide by 1.8. To go the other way, multiply celsius by 1.8 and add 32.

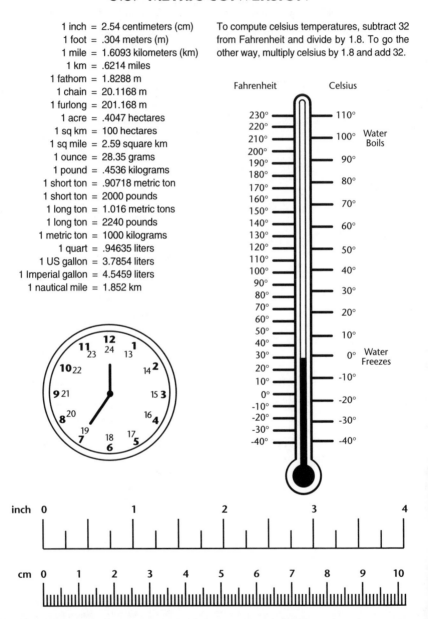